Interpersonal Skills in Organizations

SUZANNE C. DE JANASZ, Ph.D.
James Madison University

KAREN O. DOWD, Ph.D.
James Madison University and The Empower Group

BETH Z. SCHNEIDER, MBA
James Madison University

McGraw Hill

Boston   Burr Ridge, IL   Dubuque, IA   Madison, WI   New York
San Francisco   St. Louis   Bangkok   Bogotá   Caracas   Kuala Lumpur
Lisbon   London   Madrid   Mexico City   Milan   Montreal   New Delhi
Santiago   Seoul   Singapore   Sydney   Taipei   Toronto

McGraw-Hill Higher Education ⚛

A Division of The McGraw-Hill Companies

INTERPERSONAL SKILLS IN ORGANIZATIONS

Published by McGraw-Hill, an imprint of The McGraw-Hill Companies, Inc. 1221 Avenue of the Americas, New York, NY, 10020. Copyright © 2002 by The McGraw-Hill Companies, Inc. All rights reserved. No part of this publication may be reproduced or distributed in any form or by any means, or stored in a data base or retrieval system, without the prior written consent of The McGraw-Hill Companies, Inc., including, but not limited to, in any network or other electronic storage or transmission, or broadcast for distance learning.

Some ancillaries, including electronic and print components, may not be available to customers outside the United States.

This book is printed on acid-free paper.

4 5 6 7 8 9 0 QPD/ QPD 0 9 8 7 6 5 4

ISBN 0-07-244122-4

Publisher: *John E. Biernat*
Sponsoring editor: *Andy Winston*
Senior developmental editor: *Laura Hurst-Spell*
Senior marketing manager: *Ellen Cleary*
Project manager: *Jean R. Starr*
Manager, new book production: *Melonie Salvati*
Media producer: *Jennifer Becka*
Designer: *Matthew Baldwin*
Cover design: *Joanne Schopler*
Cover image: *© David Ridley/SIS*
Supplement coordinator: *Elizabeth Hadala*
Printer: *Quebecor World Dubuque Inc.*
Typeface: *10/12 Times Roman*
Compositor: *Interactive Composition Corporation*

Library of Congress Cataloging-in-Publication Data

De Janasz, Suzanne C.
    Interpersonal skills in organizations / Suzanne C. de Janasz, Karen O. Dowd, Beth Z. Schneider.
      p. cm.
    Includes index.
    ISBN 0-07-244122-4 (alk. paper)
    1. Organizational behavior. 2. Psychology, Industrial. 3. Interpersonal relations. I.
Dowd, Karen O. II. Schneider, Beth Z. III. Title.
    HD58.7 .D415 2002
    158.7—dc21

                2001030784

www.mhhe.com

Dedication

From Suzanne:

To my children, Gaby and Alex, for proving you are never too young to learn interpersonal skills; to my husband, Chris, for being my most devoted fan; to my parents, Stan and Mary, for always believing in me.

From Karen:

To my parents, who knew I wanted to be a writer before I did, and my husband Tom, who made it possible.

From Beth:

To my husband, Jeff, and my mother, Dorothy Zuech, who support me through all my endeavors.

Contents in Brief

Contents

Unit 2   Interpersonal Effectiveness: Understanding and Working with Others

Chapter 5   Conveying Verbal Messages   85

Chapter 6   The Importance and Skill of Listening   103

Chapter 7   Feedback   121

Chapter 8   Understanding and Working with Diverse Others   145

Unit 3 Advanced Interpersonal Skills

Chapter 9 Persuading Individuals and Audiences 171

Chapter 10 Networking and Politicking 191

Chapter 11 Negotiation 217

Preface

Birth of an Idea

Recently a group of executives who serve as the College of Business dean's board of advisors at our university identified a critical ingredient currently missing in most business school graduates. While they were technically competent—they could read a balance sheet, do a market analysis, and develop cash flow projections—many graduates lacked interpersonal skills, or the ability to work effectively with others. The executives created a wish list of "soft skills," faculty were hired, and the Interpersonal Skills course was born. Since that time, nearly 3,000 students have taken part in this required undergraduate course, and over 1,000 new students take the course each year.

In the beginning, the cadre of faculty dedicated to this course selected two books and additional readings to support the course objectives. In response to student and recruiter feedback, we have improved continuously both the content and delivery of the course. One such improvement stemmed from students' concerns that the books were inadequate for a variety of reasons. We agreed and continued to search for a book that met our needs. Frustrated with our inability to find the interpersonal skills text for our particular audience, we decided to write it.

"I Want to Buy This Book for My Boss"

As our colleagues and students have heard about this book, a common response is not simply "Where can I buy this book," but "My boss could use this—can you send him (or her) a copy?" The truth is this book is very relevant to a variety of readers. While it was written primarily with an undergraduate student audience in mind, each of the authors is experienced working with graduate students, adult learners, and working managers. In addition to our current teaching and research responsibilities, one or more of us has been a management consultant, a corporate trainer, an internal organization development consultant, a director of a career services center at a top-tier graduate business school, or a small business owner. Because of the depth of experience we offer, we are convinced that the material, with slight modification, is very appropriate for graduate students, adult learners, and managers as well as for undergraduate students. In short, this book is appropriate for anyone who wants to improve his or her ability to interact with others in the workplace.

A Unique Focus on Developing Managerial and Interpersonal Skills

In researching textbook options for our course, we found:

- Many useful resources but not any one resource that met all of our instructional needs.
- A dearth of coverage of areas we deemed important to our students, including diversity, project management, facilitation, and personal goal setting.
- A majority of books written for the graduate student or midlevel manager level rather than the primarily undergraduate audience served by our course.

Emphasis on Both Personal and Professional

Some texts focus solely on managerial skills but provide little if any assistance in helping the reader understand how understanding him or herself (intrapersonal effectiveness) relates to interpersonal and managerial effectiveness. The premise and sequencing of our book is that for students to be successful as managers in business, they must first have a solid understanding of self and how the self interacts with others to facilitate organizational success. Accordingly, we incorporate information on personal qualities needed for success in business and provide personal examples throughout the book focusing on family and other relationships alongside professional examples focusing on the workplace.

Balance between Theory and Practice

Our book offers a balance between theory and application. In our experience students and managers benefit by having some conceptual background on the topic of interpersonal skills but relate best to practical information that can be applied immediately to school, job, or team settings. Providing tips and techniques as well as conceptual grounding motivates the reader to learn a particular skill. Some popular interpersonal skills texts provide substantial theoretical and conceptual grounding of each skill area covered and are written primarily for a graduate audience rather than for undergraduates or working managers. In each chapter, we strike a balance by providing both sufficient conceptual material and applied material appropriate for use in real-life personal, academic, and professional situations, using conversational, user-friendly language.

Coverage of New Topics or More Thorough Coverage of Existing Topics

We have included a number of topics that are covered minimally if at all by other textbooks. Reviewers who have read our manuscript report that our treatment of topics such as self-disclosure and trust, stress and time management, conveying verbal messages, listening, diversity, ethical decision making, and negotiation are more thorough than what exists now. Other topics such as project management, facilitation, and problem solving are new and not addressed substantively in other books.

Focus on Experiential Learning

In addition to the latest thinking about each of the topics covered, we provide exercises at the end of each chapter that have been tested in the workplace or classroom and evaluated positively by both undergraduate and graduate students as well as working managers. A number of exercises are offered at the end of each chapter. The variety of exercises accomplishes several objectives. First, the instructor can accommodate multiple learning styles by fashioning a subset of exercises appropriate for a particular audience. "One size does not fit all." Second, the combination of experiential and reflective exercises help give students concrete experience, feedback, and an opportunity to reflect on ways to improve their current skill level. Finally, in an age where we see increasing levels of virtual and distance education delivered, the numerous observational and reflective exercises can facilitate learning even in settings that lack face-to-face interaction.

Why Focus on Interpersonal Skills?

The need to focus on improving interpersonal skills is recognized by more than business school faculty, deans, and executive advisory groups. In a recent survey by the American Society for Training and Development, more than one-third of people identified communication or interpersonal relationship skills as the most important quality in a good boss, and 42 percent said poor interpersonal skills makes bosses less effective.[1] Another recent article notes that the lack of interpersonal skills may be the major reason highly qualified professionals are not promoted.[2] The rise of teamwork in contemporary organizations has increased the need for every employee to work effectively with and through others. Individuals on work teams need to be able to communicate and collaborate effectively with others whose personalities, approaches, and work styles may differ greatly. In addition, as power to make decisions and implement solutions is transferred down the condensed hierarchy to nonsupervisory employees, the ability to marshal needed resources in the absence of power or authority makes interpersonal and managerial skills more critical than ever. Even those in leadership positions need to be skilled on the softer side of management along with the right knowledge and experience. Recent studies report communication skills, interpersonal skills, and initiative are what corporations seek when hiring MBAs.[3]

Organizations are looking for employees with outstanding interpersonal skills to help organizations remain flexible and viable in today's competitive workforce. Organizations are profoundly affected by interpersonal interactions within and between employees, customers, suppliers, and other stakeholders. The more effective the relationships and interpersonal communications are, the more productive for the organization and the individuals.[4]

According to Harvard professor Robert Katz, there are three types of necessary managerial skills: conceptual, technical, and interpersonal. As one moves through the managerial layers, the need for technological and conceptual skills changes, whereas the need for interpersonal skills remains proportionate for all managerial levels: lower, middle, and top.[5] Improving interpersonal skills goes beyond the classroom and the boardroom; the lessons learned can have broad applications in helping individuals to better deal with problems and conflicts with family and friends.[6] Interpersonal skills help individuals initiate, build, and maintain relationships—in both personal and professional life.

"For things we have to learn before we can do them, we learn by doing them."

Aristotle

A Pedagogical Approach That Works

In today's service-oriented, knowledge- and information-focused, global marketplace, interpersonal skills are essential. However, these skills seldom occur naturally; for most of us they must and can be learned.[7] If these skills are neither learned nor practiced, the good news is that it is never too late to start. Recognizing the need for these skills and acquiring and enhancing them can help workers be continuous learners and remain marketable.[8]

We have designed the text and the supplementary materials to aid students and practicing managers in assessing their level of effectiveness and enhancing their capability in each of 20 skill areas. Each chapter begins with a set of questions that relate to the learning objectives of the chapter. Next, we include a case study that helps the reader understand how the skill (or lack thereof) applies in real world situations. Then, we lay out the background about the skill—what it is and why it's important. Then we offer strategies and techniques for learning and using the skill. The chapters are written in an easy-to-read style with numerous practical examples in both professional and personal settings. After the chapter summary and list of key terms and concepts, the reader can test his or her understanding of the written material and ability to apply the skills through the many exercises in each chapter. Some exercises are reflective while others are experiential. Some exercises are designed to be performed in a class environment while others can be performed outside the classroom. Some exercises allow for receiving feedback from others; others encourage self-feedback.

How the Book Is Organized

The book is organized in a practical, experiential learning format that facilitates learning. Each of the 20 chapters can be used as a stand-alone, modular chapter independent of the rest of the book or used in conjunction with other chapters. The chapters are grouped into four units: understanding self (intrapersonal skills), working with others (interpersonal skills), advanced interpersonal skills, and working in teams.

In the first unit, intrapersonal skills, we begin the process of looking within ourselves to analyze our strengths and weaknesses and gain a better understanding of our personal perceptions, views, beliefs and work style. Unit 1 topics include self-awareness, self-disclosure and trust, personal values and goal setting, and time and stress management. In the second unit we move to interpersonal skills, or interacting with others, through verbal communication, listening, feedback, and working with diverse others. The third unit focuses on more advanced interpersonal skills such as persuasion, politicking, negotiation, networking, coaching, mentoring, and empowerment. In the final unit, we focus on working with and leading groups of others by discussing teaming, running meetings, managing projects, making effective and ethical decisions, solving problems, and facilitating teams.

In each chapter, we discuss how a skill or concept can be incorporated into one's self-development, how a skill or concept is used in interactions with others, especially in team settings, and how the skill or concept is applied in the context of managerial roles in organizations.

Note to Instructors

Teaching interpersonal skills using an experiential, learner-centered approach differs greatly from those classes in which a more controlled, lecture-oriented approach may be appropriate. In order to help instructors transition from professor to facilitator, lecturer to experiential exercise leader, we took pains to carefully construct an Instructor's Manual and supporting materials that support this goal.

The IM contains sample syllabi and assignments, chapter-by-chapter explanatory notes, teaching plans, ideas for implementing the material in the classroom, ways to motivate the discussion on a topic, detailed instructions for using the activities and exercises, discussion questions, additional resources, and sample test questions. To enhance the overall learning experience, a companion video (with about 20 illustrative clips and suggestions for using them) and website (**www.mhhe.com/iso**) are available. To help instructors manage the learning process, PowerPoint slides and an electronic test bank are also available.

Endnotes

1. American Society for Training and Development, Inc., "More than one-third of people surveyed identified communication skills or interpersonal relationship skills as the most important quality in a good boss," *Training and Development,* Feb. 2000, p. 16.

2. David Satave, Jim Weber, "The ABCs of Supervision: Technical Skills Are Only Half the Story," *Journal of Accountancy,* Feb. 1998, p. 72.

3. Shari Caudron, "The Hard Case for Soft Skills," *Workforce,* July 1999, p. 60; also Karen O. Dowd and Jeanne Liedtka, "What Corporations Seek in MBA Hires: A Survey." *Selections,* Graduate Management Admission Council, Winter 1994, Fairfax, VA; and annual employer survey, National Association of Colleges and Employers, Bethlehem, PA.

4. Michael B. Coyle, "Quality Interpersonal Communication—an Overview," *Manage,* April 1993, p. 4.

5. Robert L. Katz, "Skills of an Effective Administrator," *Harvard Business Review,* September–October 1974, p. 91.

6. City Business/USA Inc., "Acuson's Interpersonal Skill Training Goes to School," *The Business Journal,* Oct. 2, 1995, p. S6.

7. Coyle, 1993.

8. Patricia Buhler, "Managing in the '90s," *Supervision,* Nov. 1997, p. 23.

Acknowledgments

As is true of any substantive effort such as writing a book, there are many people to thank—more than can be listed here individually. Many thanks to all of our teachers, colleagues, friends, and family members, from whom we learned what interpersonal skills are (and aren't!). Special note needs to be made of several individuals and groups. Our editors and production staff, ably headed by Andy Winston and Laura Spell. The staff at Primis who encouraged us to use a preproduction version to "test out" our materials. Our colleague Dr. Charles Pringle for providing feedback and guidance at many points in the process. Our colleagues at the College of Business, James Madison University, especially the Dean's Office, the Core Curriculum Committee, and our Management Program faculty and staff, for their support and ideas. Our fellow Interpersonal Skills instructors who truly know the definition of "team." Our associates at Brecker & Merryman, Inc. (An Empower Group Company) in New York who kept us current with today's workplace realities.

Special mention needs to be made of our reviewers, who gave us substantive, honest feedback that strengthened the final product. They include:

Uzoamaka P. Anakwe, Pace University

Thomas D. Clark, Xavier University

Roger A. Dean, Washington and Lee University

Barry Gold, Pace University

James C. Hall, Pace University

Robert A. Herring III, Winston-Salem State University

Ronald Snell, University of Wisconsin–River Falls

Raymond T. Sparrowe, Cleveland State University

Susan Stites-Doe, SUNY College at Brockport

Our many academic friends, especially those in the Organizational Behavior Teaching Society, the Academy of Management Careers division, and the National Association of Colleges and Employers, who provided a sounding board for our ideas about the book. Our families and friends, especially Chris, Alex, and Gabby de Janasz; Tom Dowd; and Jeff, Andrew, and Nicholas Schneider, for supporting our work (and for bringing home pizza during late-night writing marathons!). Most importantly we wish to acknowledge our terrific students, who keep us honest and are a joy to work with.

1

Journey into Self-awareness

How do I:

✓ Determine my strengths and understand how they might guide me in personal and professional choices?

✓ Figure out what motivates me in order to find personal and professional success?

✓ Assess my limitations and develop a plan for improving in these areas?

✓ Gain understanding and insight into my personality, attitudes, and behaviors?

✓ Identify the biases I have that preclude my understanding and appreciating others?

✓ Evaluate my emotional intelligence and identify areas for personal improvement?

Marjorie Morgan, age 22, was excited about her first job out of college. She had worked summer jobs and one internship, but never in an environment as professional as the bank for which she'd work upon graduation. After taking some time off in the summer, she began work in August. Eager to show she was worthy of having been hired, she worked hard the first six months on the job. She enjoyed her co-workers, got along well with her manager, and was even involved in a technology project through which she was able to meet people from other departments of the bank.

The project objective was to develop a new system through which customer complaints could be handled. The present system barely met the needs of the bank's customers and was inefficient and costly to run. Over a period of several weeks, Marjorie and her project team members worked diligently to study the problem and develop a solution.

The team consisted of Marjorie plus five co-workers: two people were about her age and the other three were considerably older. Four of the five were college educated and all but one team member had greater tenure than she had. Of the six-person team, four were Caucasian and two were African-American. The team did not have an official leader. Things ran smoothly for several weeks, until the time came for decisions to be made. As soon as a deadline was imposed on the group Marjorie became aware of some significant personality differences within the project team. Two members, who had always arrived late to meetings, were procrastinating on their assignments for the project. Two others who had attended the meetings began to spend more time socializing than working. One person who had been reluctant to state his opinion about the data that had been collected now said he thought the group needed more time before it would be ready to make a decision. Marjorie had been very task-oriented all along and was eager to finish the project and move on to other projects within the bank. She was very frustrated with the lack of progress being made by the group and was concerned about being part of a team that wasn't going to meet its assigned deadline. Yet she was reluctant to speak up. She felt she was too young and hadn't been at the bank long enough to be credible with her teammates and take charge of the project. She didn't think she could approach her boss about the situation. She was perplexed about why the group was experiencing so many problems. Marjorie thought to herself, "Why can't they get along? Why can't everyone on the team be more like me? I work hard and have pride in how this project is going to turn out. Why don't the others?" She began to wonder if this was the right place for her.

1. Why is Marjorie upset?

2. In what ways are the work styles of Marjorie's teammates different from hers? What causes those differences?

3. Can these differences be resolved? Why or why not?

4. How would you handle the situation if you were Marjorie?

"Know thyself"

Socrates

As early as the time of Socrates, we have known about the importance of self-awareness. Understanding oneself is key not only to our ability to succeed, but also to our ability to work effectively with others. Studies show that the best managers are those who are keenly aware of their own strengths—*and* their weaknesses.[1] They are able to capitalize on their strengths and either improve their weaknesses or work with others whose qualities complement theirs. They are able to understand others—their motivation, needs, style, capabilities, and limitations—and use this information to motivate and get results from them. They also understand the importance of keeping current with self-knowledge and regularly engage in self-assessment exercises and experiences that allow them to continually learn about and improve themselves. This chapter describes self-awareness: what it is, why it's important, and how to improve your level of self-awareness. It also addresses how strong self-knowledge can enhance your ability to manage and work with others and provides a number of exercises that enable you to assess yourself and develop improvement plans.

What Is Self-awareness?

Self-awareness is knowing your motivations, preferences, and personality and understanding how these factors influence your judgment, decisions, and interactions with other people.[2] Self-awareness includes many things. Your internal feelings and thoughts, interests, strengths and limitations, values, skills, goals, abilities, leadership orientation, and preferred communication style are just a few of the elements that self-awareness comprises.

Benefits of Self-awareness

Self-awareness or self-knowledge is the starting point for effectiveness at work. As Machiavelli, the cunning author and statesman, wrote, "To lead or attempt to lead without first having a knowledge of self is foolhardy and sure to bring disaster and defeat." Self-awareness has many benefits, among them:

- understanding yourself in relation to others.
- developing and implementing a sound self-improvement program.
- setting appropriate life and career goals.

- developing relationships with others.
- understanding the value of diversity.
- managing others effectively.
- increasing productivity.
- increasing your ability to contribute to organizations, your community, and family.

For example, knowing what you are good at and what you enjoy doing may help in selecting a career or job that is professionally satisfying and therefore financially and personally satisfying. Relying solely on others' thoughts or beliefs about what is best for you can lead to personal and professional unhappiness. It makes no sense to spend one-third (or more) of your precious time doing what you abhor! By knowing yourself—your strengths, weaknesses, likes, and dislikes—you'll know where you belong.[3]

> *"There are three things extremely hard: steel, a diamond, and to know one's self."*
>
> Benjamin Franklin

How to Gain Self-awareness

The first step to becoming aware of ourselves is to recognize our weaknesses, strengths, biases, attitudes, values, and perceptions. There are many ways to enhance our self-awareness. Some of these include analyzing our own experiences, looking at ourselves through the eyes of others, self-disclosure, acquiring diverse experiences, and increasing our emotional intelligence.

Self-analysis

One means to gain insight into ourselves is through reflecting on, examining, and analyzing our behavior, personality, attitudes, and perceptions.

Behavior

Behavior is the way in which we conduct ourselves—the way in which we act. Our behavior is influenced by our feelings, judgments, beliefs, motivations, needs, experience, and the opinions of others. Patterns of behavior develop through our reactions to events and actions over a period of time. Behavior consists of four components:[4]

Motivation—the drive to pursue one action over another. What underlying factors move you to make a particular decision or choice? For example, what drives you to do a good

Figure 1–1
Means for Obtaining
Self-awareness

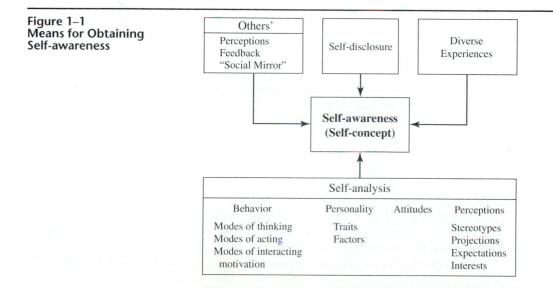

job? The answer might be a competitive nature, strong achievement orientation, or a difficult childhood experience. Being aware of your core drivers, those things that motivate you—positively and negatively—can help you understand the roots of your behavior and make adjustments as necessary to modify your behavior.

Modes of thinking—the way you process the various inputs received by the brain. How do you analyze information and make judgments about how to use and apply that information? For example, do you process information quietly by reflecting on your own, or do you process information out loud by talking with others? Being aware of how you take in and make sense of information can help you understand how you make judgments and decisions that lead to choosing one behavior or course of action over another.

Modes of acting—the course of action you apply in a given situation. What approach do you choose to apply in response to stimuli, events, people, thoughts, and feelings? For example, when someone does something that offends you, do you react in anger? Or do you react quietly, assessing your options before acting? Being aware of how you express your reaction to the things that happen to and around you can help you understand the alternatives available to you when certain events arise.

Modes of interacting—the way in which you communicate and share ideas, opinions, and feelings with others. Whom do you feel comfortable relating to? How do you typically share your thoughts, feelings, and ideas with others? For example, are you comfortable in large groups of people? In team situations? Or do you prefer to work on your own? Being aware of how you talk to and work with others can help you understand how your preferred style meshes with those with whom you work and live.

Personality

Personality describes the relatively stable set of characteristics, tendencies, and temperaments that have been formed by inheritance and by social, cultural, and environmental factors.[5] These traits determine how we interact with and react to various people and situations. Some aspects of our personality are believed to be a result of nature—those traits with which we are born and that we possess through heredity. Other characteristics of our personality are thought to be a result of our environment—those factors that we acquire through exposure to people and events in our lives.

Personality traits are enduring characteristics that describe an individual's attitude and behavior.[6] Examples are agreeableness, aggression, dominance, and shyness. Most of these traits have been found to be quite stable over time.[7] This means a person who is cold and uncaring in one situation is likely to behave similarly in other situations. Through a significant amount of research over time, psychologists believe the basic structure of human personality consists of five broad factors referred to as "The Big Five Model."[8] Even though some of these factors are inherited, some factors can be modified through training, experience, and a conscious attempt to change.

1. **Extroversion** represents the degree to which an individual is social or antisocial, outgoing or shy, assertive or passive, active or inactive, and talkative or quiet. A person rating high on these dimensions is extroverted, while the opposite end of the scale is introverted.

2. **Agreeableness** measures the degree to which a person is friendly or reserved, cooperative or guarded, flexible or inflexible, trusting or cautious, good-natured or moody, soft-hearted or tough, and tolerant or judgmental. Those scoring high on these dimensions are viewed as agreeable and easy to work with, while those rating low are viewed as more disagreeable and difficult to work with.

3. **Emotional stability** characterizes the degree to which a person is consistent or inconsistent in how they react to certain events, reacts impulsively or weighs options before acting, and takes things personally or looks at a situation objectively. Those who rate high on emotional stability are viewed as generally calm, stable, having a positive attitude, able to manage their anger, secure, happy, and objective. Those who rate low are more likely to be anxious, depressed, angry, insecure, worried, and emotional.

4. **Conscientiousness** represents the degree to which an individual is dependable or inconsistent, can be counted on or is unreliable, follows through on commitments or reneges, and keeps promises or breaks them. Those who rate high on conscientiousness

are generally perceived to be careful, thorough, organized, persistent, achievement-oriented, hardworking, and persevering. Those who score lower on this dimension are more likely to be viewed as inattentive to detail, uncaring, disrespectful, not interested or motivated, unorganized, apt to give up easily, and lazy.

5. Openness to experience characterizes the degree to which one is interested in broadening their horizons or limiting them, learning new things or sticking with what they already know, meeting new people or associating with current friends and co-workers, going to new places or restricting oneself to known places. Individuals who score high on this factor tend to be highly intellectual, broad-minded, curious, imaginative, and cultured. Those who rate lower tend to be more narrow-minded, less interested in the outside world, and uncomfortable in unfamiliar surroundings and situations.

What are the characteristics of your personality? How do you know this? (See Exercise 1–B.) Which aspects of your personality do you like, and which would you like to modify? While it's true that some of these factors are very ingrained, few of these factors are fixed in stone. It's up to you to identify those qualities that are working well for you and worth keeping, as well as those qualities that aren't working well for you that you should change or abandon.

Self-monitoring

Self-monitoring is the tendency to adjust our behavior relative to the changing demands of social situations.[9] It is many times studied in conjunction with the five broad factors of personality to examine how varying situations will affect a person's desire or ability to control aspects of their personality. The concept of monitoring our own personality can help us come to grips with both those qualities we view as positive and those we would like to change. By being aware of the role of self-monitoring, we can assess our own behaviors and attitudes, diagnose which elements we are satisfied with, and identify and develop plans for addressing those aspects we want to change. When self-monitoring, it is important to want to set personal standards in accordance with certain accepted norms. High self-monitors are very sensitive to external cues and constantly adapt (and often hide) their true selves to conform to a situation or set of expectations. Low self-monitors are more consistent, displaying their feelings, attitudes, and behaviors in every situation. In an organizational setting, it is probably best to avoid the extremes. You don't want to be a high self-monitor (solely concerned with what others think) or a low self-monitor (not at all interested in what others think). Always trying to please everyone or conforming to gain everyone's approval—while it might facilitate getting what you want in the short-term—can be harmful to you in the long-term. Conversely, never adjusting your behavior relative to the audience or situation can be disastrous. (See Exercise 1–C.)

All of the personality dimensions can have a significant impact on job performance and interpersonal relationships.[10] By understanding the meaning of these factors, you can pinpoint areas for personal and professional development and growth. Knowledge of our ratings on each of these dimensions can also help us in selecting a career. Much research in the area of person/job fit demonstrates that individuals who select professions that suit their personality are more likely to be satisfied and productive.[11] Finding work that matches our personal preferences may require a fair amount of investigation; this invest-ment in time and resources pays big dividends—success and happiness. For example, a person who is low on the extroversion and agreeableness factors would probably not be happy (or successful) as a traveling sales representative. The sheer nature of the job requires an outgoing, friendly individual in order to contact and build a rapport with clients. A poor fit between one's personality and job can be a recipe for disaster.

Attitudes

Attitudes are evaluative statements or "learned predispositions to respond in a consistently favorable or unfavorable manner with respect to a given object."[12] As human beings, we can choose how we think and feel about a situation or event. Imagine you are on an airplane that has been diverted to another airport due to bad weather. You can choose to become irritated and show your anger to the flight attendant, or you can be patient, acknowledge that nothing can be done to change the situation, and take out a good book to read while waiting for your flight to land. The emotions we choose to act on determine our attitude. This in turn is reflected in our behavior.[13]

Attitudes are narrow in scope. They can vary from situation to situation. For example, we might have a positive outlook when we are with our friends, feel negatively about our work, and have a neutral attitude toward our academic experience. Attitudes are derived from parents, teachers, peers, society, and our own experiences. Attitudes are one of the less stable facets of our personality, which means they are easier to influence and change than our behaviors or values.[14] Some can change at will depending on the situation, the people involved, other events that occurred to us in a particular day, how we're feeling as a situation unfolds, and how we respond as events evolve over time.

Strong attitudes can have an impact on our professional and personal relationships.[15] As students and managers, it is helpful to remember how much of a role our attitude can play in our success. Our demeanor, whether we're with others or grappling with an issue on our own, can make a significant difference in what behaviors we choose to exercise and in the outcomes of our efforts. Have you heard the saying "she takes lemons and turns them into lemonade"? This is an example of the power of one's attitude. Our attitude can determine whether we think positively and take control of a situation or think negatively and feel helpless about our ability to change or respond to a situation. Our attitude is an important component of our ability to be productive at work or in school. Our attitude can influence those around us. Being aware of our own attitudes, and making choices about which attitude to display to others, is very important for us as individuals and as managers. Our attitude can affect our job behavior as well as our interactions with others. Our friends, significant others, family members, co-workers, and others are definitely influenced by our thoughts and feelings toward situations. As managers, it is also important to recognize that our employees are affected by the attitude we display toward them and toward the work that needs to get done.[16] A manager's attitude is a large factor in how people feel about their jobs. If a manager is upbeat most of the time and supportive of his/her colleagues, employees will generally respond well and work hard to produce the desired results. On the other hand if a manager is pessimistic and belittling toward his/her employees, staff morale will suffer and, ultimately, so will the expected outcomes.

Perceptions

Perception describes the process by which individuals gather sensory information and assign meaning to it.[17] When we encounter a person or situation, we use our senses to absorb various inputs. Next, our brains select aspects from stored information in order to process and organize these inputs. Finally, our brains interpret and evaluate the person or situation. Perception is person-specific—no two people will take in, organize, and evaluate inputs the same way. Your perspective on a situation can be entirely different from the way another looks at the exact same situation. Two friends walking by the window of a crowded restaurant spot a couple engaged in conversation. One friend,

Figure 1–2

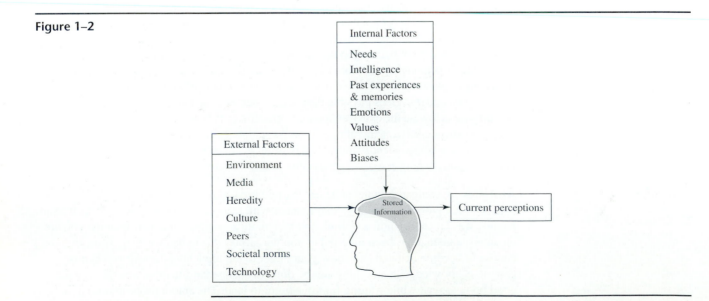

taking notice of their mannerisms and gestures, concludes that it "looks like they're breaking off their relationship." The other friend vehemently disagrees. "No, they're probably discussing a plan to spend more time together." Which friend is right?

Individual perception may not always be consistent with reality; it is only the perceiver's interpretation of reality. For example, when you go to a movie with a group, your opinion and those of your friends might differ. You each perceived the same event through a different set of lenses. One might have seen the movie as an action film, another as a romance. There's probably some element of truth in both perspectives. What's reality for you is based on your interpretation of the event. Your reality can be shaped and impacted by learning about others' perceptions of the same incident. For example, checking your perception with others, and sharing yours with them, might change your opinion of the movie or increase your understanding of it. At work, the best managers are those who augment their own perspective with the views of others. Our perceptions can—and should—change based on new inputs.

It is important to be in touch with our perceptions—what they are and how they're being formed. Equally important is being aware of the perceptions of others. Others' behavior toward you is heavily influenced by their understanding of the situation, and your behavior toward others is equally dependent on your assumptions about them and the situation. It is crucial to understand and disclose your own perspective as well as to solicit information from others about their understanding of the same situation.

Our perceptions are influenced by many factors, such as our culture, environment, heredity, the media, peers, past experiences, intelligence, needs, emotions, attitudes, and values. Perception can be a result of multiple causality: many factors from a variety of sources may simultaneously impact individual perception. This makes it even more important to be fully aware of the factors that influence our perception. This way we can check ourselves to ensure our own experience and perspective are not distorting our perceptions of reality.

As human beings, we tend to form perceptions based on our biases. If we are not aware of our biases and don't check our understanding with others, we may miss out on important information and situations by relying on distorted perceptions. Some of the more common filters that influence our perceptions are stereotyping, selective perception, projection, expectations, and interest.

■ **Stereotyping:** making assumptions about an individual or a group based on generalized judgments rather than on facts, or a means to make assumptions when there is little or no information. Many who stereotype others do so on the basis of observable demographic characteristics, such as race or ethnicity, gender, age, disability, religion, and sexual orientation. For example, some companies are reluctant to hire older workers for certain job roles for fear that they lack the energy and stamina to perform at a desired level. Stereotyping is a convenient but faulty way to make assumptions about a person's behavior and abilities. Rather than relying on a stereotype that is probably largely false, it is best to check your own perceptions and come to an event or meet a new person with an open mind. This will allow you to form your own perspective rather than rely on biases that have been shaped by judging and attributing certain behaviors to all members of a group.

■ **Selective Perception:** interpreting information for meaning and accuracy, and discarding information that is threatening or not relevant. We are constantly bombarded with stimuli. This has always been true but even more so today thanks to the availability of the Internet, downloadable newspapers, 24-hour news channels, cell phones, e-mail, and fax machines. In an effort to reduce the breadth and impact of continuous stimuli, our brains attend to information according to our own experiences, interests, attitudes, and background. This means we are constantly "filtering"—absorbing and processing only those inputs we think we can handle, or want to handle, at any given time. For example, people tend to dislike thinking about their own mortality so they avoid the subject of wills and funeral planning. A college student whose main concern is graduating is probably not likely to be thinking of retirement plans. A manager with a project deadline is probably not going to read information for a meeting that's scheduled for next month.

Selective perception provides a useful purpose, but it hinders communication with others. Rather than automatically "tuning out" information with which you disagree, it is best to keep an open mind, being open to all new views about a situation before prematurely developing your own perception.

■ **Projection:** the attribution of one's own attitudes, characteristics, or shortcomings to others. For example, someone who cheats and lies might make the assumption that everyone cheats and lies. This validates our own perceptions of the way things are, or at least the way we think things should be. However, projecting our beliefs onto others denies them the opportunity to provide us with a unique and fresh perspective. Rather than transferring your own experience and feelings to another, it is best to consider each new situation and person in your life as unique, paying attention to *their* features and characteristics rather than yours.

■ **Expectations:** forming an opinion about how we would like an event to unfold, a situation to develop, or a person to act, think, or feel. We tend to perceive, select, and interpret information according to how we expect it to appear. For example, when proofreading a paper you have written, you may pass over mistakes because you know what you intended to say, so you perceive it to be correct. Actually, the best way to proofread your own copy is to read it backwards! That way you're not preconditioned to see a word as you perceive or expect it; you see a word as it really is (try it!).
By understanding what our expectations are and viewing a situation with a clear slate—minus preconceived notions about what to expect—we are better able to approach situations and people and form our own opinions based on actual experience rather than on assumptions.

■ **Interest:** basing our activities and inputs on things that are likeable or appealing to us. We tend to focus our time and attention—consciously or subconsciously—on those things that are enjoyable and meaningful to us. For example, if we are in the market to buy a new home we will notice "for sale" signs in front of houses that previously would have gone unnoticed. If you have an interest in people, you might focus on a career in teaching or counseling, while ignoring other subjects such as computer science. The tendency to be drawn to things that interest us can be positive, in that it helps conserve our energy for the things that matter to us. However, as you increase your own self-understanding, it is important to reach out to things that go beyond what interests you at the time. By doing this we can broaden ourselves and our understanding of the things that are important and meaningful to others.

By understanding ourselves, we can begin to change our perceptions that are often affected by the biases described above. It is imperative for us to understand and confront our biases. By doing so, we will increase our level of self-understanding and will be more understanding of others and their perspectives. The workplace is increasingly global and diverse. Companies are now involved in developing new business models. We will be better able to compete in this world and better equipped to formulate and embrace these new models—by expanding our self- and other-awareness. This will help us to be better managers and, just as important, better people.

Others' Perceptions

Another means for gaining self-awareness is through understanding how others view us, and also understanding how we are shaped by others' opinions of us. Stephen Covey refers to this concept as the "**social mirror**."[18] Covey explains that we gain perceptions of ourselves as a result of what other people say about us or how they react to us. We adopt a view of ourselves based on other people's views. How do others view us? How do we change our actions as a result of what we think others are thinking about us? These are the questions to ask to get a handle on how we are shaped by others' perceptions. By seeing ourselves through others' eyes, we can learn about our strengths and also about areas in which we can improve.

Learning to read accurately how others see us enhances our "self-maps," our images, and judgments of ourselves. For example, you might say to yourself, I'm not a creative person or I'm an athletic person after hearing comments from others about our artistic or athletic ability. The social mirror is based on our memory of how others have reacted towards us or treated us. Through feedback from others we can gain more insight or perspective into aspects of ourselves and our behaviors.[19] However, our potential may not be based accurately on this information. The social mirror can be wrong or only partially correct. For example, an overbearing parent might say something negative such as "You'll never amount to anything." In this case, be very careful to first assess the statement—is it true? If not, to what degree and what can be done to change? If the statement is not a reflection of reality, then work hard to dispel this image of you in your own mind, if not the person who said it to you. Negative self-statements can be very damaging to one's esteem. The social mirror is designed to help you learn about yourself, but not everything that's said to you by others should be accepted by you as reality.

Self-disclosure

Another means of gaining self-awareness is through **self-disclosure**—sharing your thoughts, feelings, and ideas with others. Talking with others allows us to share our feelings and responses. Self-disclosing is a key factor in improving our self-awareness; we must disclose information and interact with others to further clarify our perceptions.[20] Through verbalizing our perceptions, we verify our own beliefs, affirm our self-concept, and validate data received from an objective source. For example, if you've received a low grade on an exam, it's helpful to discuss this with someone else. They can listen to your concerns and give you feedback. They might empathize with the fact you've received a low grade, then offer to problem-solve, for instance, identify a future test-taking strategy you can use. They might also remind you that in general you do well in school. This helps you to maintain perspective even while going through a hard time about the exam.

Diverse Experience

Another way of increasing self-awareness is through acquiring multiple experiences in diverse situations and with diverse others. For example, living or studying in a country other than your home country, learning a new language, traveling, reading books on new subjects, and acquiring broad work experience are ways to broaden our experience base. Even negative situations such as having to face a life-threatening illness, going through your own or your parents' divorce, and overcoming a personal problem such as dyslexia can provide enormous learning and enhance your experience base.

As we encounter new situations, we use skills and acquire new ones, meet people and develop friendships, see new places, and learn first-hand about things we might have only read about. Being open to new experiences broadens our horizons. It helps us to see ourselves in a new light while giving us new information about ourselves and our ability to interact with the world. This boosts our confidence level and encourages us to reach out to further our experiences even more. It makes us more open to new ideas and diverse people with varying ways of living, working, and thinking. Expanding our experience base puts us into situations that test our abilities, values, and goals. This greatly aids in increasing our level of self-awareness.

Emotional Intelligence

Many of the elements of self-awareness are embodied in a new concept known as **emotional intelligence** or **EQ.** EQ is "a type of social intelligence that involves the ability to monitor one's own and others' emotions, to discriminate among them, and to use the information to guide one's thinking and actions."[21] As the ancient philosopher Aristotle said,

> "Anyone can become angry—that is easy. But to be angry with the right person, to the right degree, at the right time, for the right purpose, and in the right way—this is not easy."

Aristotle was a wise man. He recognized that as human beings we are able to experience a full range of feelings. Learning when, how, where, why, and with whom to share them is more complex than we might think at first glance. Emotional intelligence enables us to do this.

Emotional intelligence is a concept used to describe the levels we possess of key emotional responses. These include self-control, zeal and persistence, and the ability to motivate oneself to use our emotions, feelings, and moods and those of others to adapt and navigate in society. A guiding principle of emotional intelligence is that having and expressing emotions is a good thing. But expressing emotions, especially in the business world, requires an innate sense of what's appropriate to say, when, where, and with whom. EQ is developing an awareness of your feelings and emotions and using them in appropriate ways. Your level of emotional intelligence—the degree to which you are savvy about the use of emotions when communicating with others—is a huge factor in one's ability to be successful. EQ is considered to be just as important or even more important than IQ, one's "intelligence quotient." IQ and EQ involve different parts of the brain. IQ affects our ability to reason, to process information, to think analytically. EQ affects our ability to use emotions in relating to others at work and in our personal lives. Important criteria for professional success in any field are the "people" skills that are derived from understanding our emotions and responses to working with others. This type of self-knowledge is critical to our ability to relate to others and make decisions about our lives and work. The good news is that unlike one's IQ, which is determined primarily at birth, EQ is a quality we can actually learn about and improve.

There are six fundamentals for achieving emotional competency—a learned capability based on our EQ:[22]

- Self Awareness—emotional awareness, accurate self-assessment, self-confidence, ability to recognize emotions and their effects on you and others.
- Self-regulation—self-control, trustworthiness, conscientiousness, adaptability, innovation, ability to manage disruptive emotions and impulses.
- Motivation—zeal, achievement drive, commitment, initiative, optimism, and the ability to remain persistent in the face of adversity.
- Empathy—understanding others, service orientation, developing others, leveraging diversity, political awareness, the ability to read and respond to others' feelings.
- Social Skills—interacting smoothly, managing interpersonal relationships, handling emotional responses to others, influence, communication, the ability to build bonds with others.
- Group Work Skills—collaboration and cooperation, team capabilities, conflict management, the willingness to work towards shared goals.

Understanding our levels of emotional intelligence is essential for our self-awareness. By knowing how we presently function when dealing with our emotions in situations with others, we can develop new goals, behaviors, and attitudes toward ourselves as well as others. The best managers have discovered it is essential for them to work on and demonstrate top-quality people skills.[23] Working to increase your emotional intelligence can help you do this. In the process, you can become a better manager as well as a better person.

Summary

Self-awareness is an essential skill for developing personally and professionally. If you have a high degree of self-awareness, you'll be able to capitalize on your strengths and develop plans for improving or compensating for your limitations. Part of being self-aware is being able to monitor and change our behavior. By concentrating on self-improvement, we demonstrate to others our willingness to learn and grow, increasing the likelihood of being able to develop close relationships and success in a profession.

Key Terms and Concepts

Agreeableness

Attitudes

Behavior

Conscientiousness

Emotional intelligence (EQ)

Emotional stability

Expectations

Extroversion

Interest

Modes of acting

Modes of interacting

Modes of thinking

Motivation

Openness to experience

Perception

Personality

Projection

Selective perception

Self-awareness

Self-disclosure

Self-monitoring

Social mirror

Stereotyping

Endnotes

1. Daniel Goleman, "What Makes a Leader?" *Harvard Business Review,* Nov.–Dec. 1998, p. 93.

2. Robert Cooper, *Executive EQ: Emotional Intelligence in Leadership and Organizations* (New York: Berkley Publishing Group, 1998).

3. Peter F. Drucker, "Managing Oneself," *Harvard Business Review,* March/April 1999, pp. 65–74.

4. Patricia A. Hoffman and Gene Powell, "The Aura of a Winner: A Guide to Behavioral Hiring," *Journal of Property Management* 61, no. 5 (September–October 1996), pp. 16–20.

5. This definition is adapted from S. F. Maddi, *Personality Theories: A Comparative Analysis* (Homewood: Ill.: Richard D. Irwin, 1980), p. 10.

6. A. H. Buss, "Personality As Traits," *American Psychologist,* November 1989, pp. 1378–88.

7. Barry M. Staw, Nancy E. Bell, and James A. Clausen, "The Dispositional Approach to Job Attitudes: A Lifetime Longitudinal Test," *Administrative Science Quarterly* 31, pp. 56–77.

8. Murray Barrick and Michael Mount, "The Big Five Personality Dimensions and Job Performance: A Meta-analysis," *Personnel Psychology,* Spring 1991, p. 11.

9. M. Snyder, *Public Appearances/Private Realities: The Psychology of Self-Monitoring* (New York: Freeman, 1987).

10. Barrick et al., 1991.

11. Charles A. O'Reilly III, Jennifer Chatman, and David F. Caldwell, "People and Organizational Culture: A Profile Comparison Approach to Assess Person Organization Fit," *Academy of Management Journal* 34, pp. 487–516.

12. M. Fishbein and I. Ajzen, *Belief, Attitude, Intention and Behavior: An Introduction to Theory and Research* (Reading, Massachusetts: Addison-Wesley, 1975), p. 6.

13. Barry G. Smale, "The Power of Positive Attitude," *Fund Raising Management* 25, no. 8 (Oct. 1994), p. 24.

14. Gregory R. Maio, David W. Bell, and Victoria M. Esses, "Examining Conflict between Components of Attitudes: Ambivalence and Inconsistency Are Distinct Constructs," *Canadian Journal of Behavioural Science* 32 (April 2000), pp. 71–83.

15. Andrew E. Schwart, "How to Handle Conflict," *The CPA Journal* 67, no. 4 (April 1997), p. 72.

16. Adrian Furnham, "Managing Demotivated People Is a Tough Task," *Business Day,* August 22, 2000, p. 19.

17. David W. Johnson, *Reaching out: Interpersonal Effectiveness and Self-actualization* (Boston: Allyn & Bacon, 1997), p. 4.

18. Stephen R. Covey, *Seven Habits of Highly Effective People: Powerful Lessons in Personal Change* (New York: Simon and Schuster, 1989).

19. Don L. Bohl, "360-Degree Appraisals Yield Superior Results," *American Management Association Compensation and Benefits Review* 26, no. 5 (Sept. 1996), pp. 16–19.

20. S. Harris, *Know Yourself? It's a Paradox,* Associated Press, 1981.

21. Peter Salovey and David J. Sluyter, eds., *Emotional Development and Emotional Intelligence: Educational Implications* (New York: Basic Books, 1997).

22. Daniel Goleman, "Emotional Competence," *Executive Excellence,* April 1, 1999, p. 19.

23. Goleman, 1998.

Exercise 1–A
Assessing Yourself

Circle the response that most closely correlates with each item below.

	Agree	Neither	Disagree

1. I am aware of my strengths and weaknesses.   1 (2) 3 4 5
2. I have a plan for developing new skills and improving in other areas.   1 (2 (3) 4 5
3. I regularly engage in self-assessment exercises.   1 2 3 (4 (5)
4. I understand what motivates my behavior and choices in life.   (1) (2) 3 4 5
5. I know what my core values are and how they affect the choices I make.   (1) (2) 3 4 5
6. I am satisfied with the quality of my interactions with others.   1 (2 (3 4 5
7. I am able to control my emotions in difficult situations.   1 2 (3) (4) 5
8. I have realistically appraised my core abilities as well as my limitations.   1 2 (3) 4 5
9. I am satisfied with the way in which I communicate with others.   1 (2) 3 4 5
10. I understand how I best process information.   1 (2) 3 4 5
11. I weigh alternatives before selecting a course of action.   (1) 2 3 4 5
12. I work well in team situations.   1 (2 (3 4 5
13. I am comfortable in large groups.   (1) 2 3 (4) 5
14. I understand the strong points and the disadvantages of my personality.   (1) (2) 3 4 5
15. I understand whether I am extroverted or introverted and know how this impacts my ability to work with others.   (1) 2 3 4 5
16. I am an agreeable person at work or in school.   (1) 2 3 4 5
17. Others would describe me as conscientious.   (1) 2 3 4 5
18. I am open to and seek new experiences.   (1) 2 3 4 5
19. I am skilled at monitoring my own behavior, reading others' views of me accurately, and taking in but not relying exclusively on the opinions others have about me.   1 (2) (3 4 5
20. I consciously work at developing and displaying a positive attitude.   1 (2) 3 4 5
21. I check my perceptions with others.   1 (2 (3) 4 5
22. I move beyond stereotypes when getting to know others.   1 (2) 3 4 5
23. I am open to things that don't immediately interest me.   (1) 2 (3) 4 5
24. I limit the degree to which I project my beliefs and values onto others.   (1) 2 3 4 5
25. I come to new situations and people without preconceived expectations.   1 (2 (3) 4 5
26. I have a realistic view of how I am perceived by others.   1 (2 (3) 4 5
27. I am comfortable sharing my thoughts and feelings with others.   1 (2) 3 4 5
28. I am open to being with and learning from people who are different from me.   (1) 2 3 4 5

	Agree	Neither	Disagree

29. I am able to use my emotions appropriately in business settings as well as in personal life.

① ② 3 4 5

30. I am able to relate to others' problems and be a source of help and support to others.

① ② 3 4 5

If you scored more than 90, you may want to consider creating a plan for improving your self-awareness. *53*   *66*

**Exercise 1–B
The Big Five Locator
Questionnaire**

1. Participants are to complete the Big Five Locator Questionnaire. On each numerical scale indicate which point is generally more descriptive of you. If the two terms are equally descriptive, mark the midpoint.

2. Complete the scoring sheet, following the instructions.

3. Place the scores on the Big Five Locator Interpretation Sheet.

Source: The Big Five Locator is a quick assessment tool to be used with an instructor and willing learners. Care should be taken to follow up this profile with a more reliable personality assessment instrument. This instrument was developed by P. J. Howard, P. L. Medina, and J. M. Howard "The Big Five Locator: A Quick Assessment Tool for Consultants and Trainers," from *The Annual, Developing Human Resources,* by J. William Pfeiffer and David Leonard Goodstein, Vol. 1, "Training," 1996, pp. 119–122. Reprinted by permission of John Wiley & Sons, Inc.

The Big Five Locator Questionnaire

Instructions: On each numerical scale that follows, indicate which point is generally more descriptive of you. If the two terms are equally descriptive, mark the midpoint.

1.	Eager	5	4	3	2	1	Calm
2.	Prefer Being with Other People	5	4	3	2	1	Prefer Being Alone
3.	A Dreamer	5	4	3	2	1	No Nonsense
4.	Courteous	5	4	3	2	1	Abrupt
5.	Neat	5	4	3	2	1	Messy
6.	Cautious	5	4	3	2	1	Confident
7.	Optimistic	5	4	3	2	1	Pessimistic
8.	Theoretical	5	4	3	2	1	Practical
9.	Generous	5	4	3	2	1	Selfish
10.	Decisive	5	4	3	2	1	Open Ended
11.	Discouraged	5	4	3	2	1	Upbeat
12.	Exhibitionist	5	4	3	2	1	Private
13.	Follow Imagination	5	4	3	2	1	Follow Authority
14.	Warm	5	4	3	2	1	Cold
15.	Stay Focused	5	4	3	2	1	Easily Distracted
16.	Easily Embarrassed	5	4	3	2	1	Don't Give a Darn
17.	Outgoing	5	4	3	2	1	Cool
18.	Seek Novelty	5	4	3	2	1	Seek Routine
19.	Team Player	5	4	3	2	1	Independent
20.	A Preference for Order	5	4	3	2	1	Comfortable with Chaos
21.	Distractible	5	4	3	2	1	Unflappable
22.	Conversational	5	4	3	2	1	Thoughtful
23.	Comfortable with Ambiguity	5	4	3	2	1	Prefer Things Clear-Cut
24.	Trusting	5	4	3	2	1	Skeptical
25.	On Time	5	4	3	2	1	Procrastinate

Scoring The Big Five Questionnaire

Instructions:

1. Find the sum of the circled numbers on the *first* row of each of the five-line groupings (Row 1 + Row 6 + Row 11 + Row 16 + Row 21 = _____). This is your raw score for "adjustment." Circle the number in the ADJUSTMENT: column of the Score Conversion Sheet that corresponds to this raw score.

2. Find the sum of the circled numbers on the *second* row of each of the five-line groupings (Row 2 + Row 7 + Row 12 + Row 17 + Row 22 = _____). This is your raw score for "sociability." Circle the number in the SOCIABILITY: column of the Score Conversion Sheet that corresponds to this raw score.

3. Find the sum of the circled numbers on the *third* row of each of the five-line groupings (Row 3 + Row 8 + Row 13 + Row 18 + Row 23 = _____). This is your raw score for "openness." Circle the number in the OPENNESS: column of the Score Conversion Sheet that corresponds to this raw score.

4. Find the sum of the circled numbers on the *fourth* row of each of the five-line groupings (Row 4 + Row 9 + Row 14 + Row 19 + Row 24 = _____). This is your raw score for "agreeableness." Circle the number in the AGREEABLENESS: column of the Score Conversion Sheet that corresponds to this raw score.

5. Find the sum of the circled numbers on the *fifth* row of each of the five-line groupings (Row 5 + Row 10 + Row 15 + Row 20 + Row 25 = _____). This is your raw score for "conscientious." Circle the number in the CONSCIENTIOUSNESS: column of the Score Conversion Sheet that corresponds to this raw score.

6. Find the number in the far right or far left column that is parallel to your circled raw score. Enter this norm score in the box at the bottom of the appropriate column.

7. Transfer your norm score to the appropriate scale on the Big Five Locator Interpretation Sheet.

Big Five Locator Score Conversion Sheet

Norm Score	Adjustment	Sociability	Openness	Agreeableness	Conscientiousness	Norm Score
80						80
79			25			79
78						78
77	22					77
76			24			76
75						75
74						74
73	21		23			73
72		25				72
71				25		71
70	20	24	22			70
69					25	69
68				24		68
67		23	21		24	67
66	19					66
65		22		23	23	65
64			20			64
63					22	63
62	18	21	19	22		62
61					21	61
60		20				60
59	17		18	21	20	59
58						58
57		19				57
56			17			56
55	16	18		20	19	55
54			16	19		54
53						53
52		17			18	52
51	15					51
50		16	15	18	17	50
49						49
48	14	15			16	48
47			14	17		47
46		14			15	46
45			13			45
44	13			16	14	44
43		13				43
42			12			42
41				15	13	41
40	12	12	11			40
39						39
38				14	12	38
37		11	10			37
36	11					36
35		10		13	11	35
34			9			34
33	10	9			10	33
32				12		32
31			8			31
30		8			9	30
29	9			11		29
28		7	7		8	28
27				10		27
26		6			7	26
25	8		6			25
24				9	6	24
23						23
22			5		22	22
21	7	5				21
20				8		20

Enter Norm
Scores Here:　　　Adj =　　　S =　　　O =　　　A =　　　C =

(Norms based on a sample of 161 forms completed in 1993–94.)

Name _____ Date _____

Big Five Locator Interpretation Sheet

Scores:

Adjustment   _____

Sociability   _____

Openness   _____

Agreeableness   _____

Conscientiousness   _____

Strong Adjustment: secure, unflappable, rational, unresponsive, guilt free	Resilient	Responsive	Reactive		Weak Adjustment: excitable, worrying, reactive, high strung, alert
	35	45	55	65	
Low Sociability: private, independent, works alone, reserved, hard to read	Introvert	Ambivert	Extrovert		High Sociability: assertive, sociable, warm, optimistic, talkative
	35	45	55	65	
Low Openness: practical, conservative, depth of knowledge, efficient, expert	Preserver	Moderate	Explorer		High Openness: broad interests, curious, liberal, impractical, likes novelty
	35	45	55	65	
Low Agreeableness: skeptical, questioning, tough, aggressive, self-interest	Challenger	Negotiator	Adapter		High Agreeableness: trusting, humble, altruistic, team player, conflict averse, frank
	35	45	55	65	
Low Conscientiousness: spontaneous, unconcerned with deadlines, adaptable, fickle, impulsive	Flexible	Balanced	Focused		High Conscientiousness: dependable, organized, disciplined, cautious, stubborn
	35	45	55	65	

Note: The Big Five Locator is intended for use only as a quick assessment for teaching purposes.

Source: The Big Five Locator is a quick assessment tool to be used with an instructor and willing learners. Care should be taken to follow up this profile with a more reliable personality assessment instrument. This instrument was developed by P. J. Howard, P. L. Medina, and J. M. Howard "The Big Five Locator: A Quick Assessment Tool for Consultants and Trainers," from *The Annual, Developing Human Resources,* by J. William Pfeiffer and David Leonard Goodstein, Vol. 1, "Training," 1996, pp. 119–122. Reprinted by permission of John Wiley & Sons, Inc.

**Exercise 1–C
Self-monitoring
Questionnaire**

For the following statements, indicate the degree to which you think the following statements are true or false by circling the appropriate number. Use the following key as a guideline for scoring:

5 = Certainly, always true

4 = Generally true

3 = Somewhat true, but with exceptions

2 = Somewhat false, but with exceptions

1 = Generally false

0 = Certainly, always false

1. In social situations, I have the ability to alter my behavior if I feel that something else is called for.　　5 **4** 3 2 1 0

2. I am often able to read people's true emotions correctly through their eyes.　　5 4 **3** 2 1 0

3. I have the ability to control the way I come across to people, depending on the impression I wish to give them.　　5 **4** 3 2 1 0

4. In conversations, I am sensitive to even the slightest change in the facial expression of the person I'm conversing with.　　5 4 **3** **2** 1 0

5. My powers of intuition are quite good when it comes to understanding others' emotions and motives.　　5 4 **3** 2 1 0

6. I can usually tell when others consider a joke in bad taste, even though they may laugh convincingly.　　5 4 3 **2** 1 0

7. When I feel that the image I am portraying isn't working, I can readily change it to something that does.　　5 **4** 3 2 1 0

8. I can usually tell when I've said something inappropriate by reading the listener's eyes.　　**5** 4 3 2 1 0

9. I have trouble changing my behavior to suit different people and different situations.　　5 4 3 **2** **1** 0　3

10. I have found that I can adjust my behavior to meet the requirements of any situation I find myself in.　　5 **4** 3 2 1 0

11. If someone is lying to me, I usually know it at once from that person's manner of expression.　　5 4 3 **2** 1 0

12. Even when it might be to my advantage, I have difficulty putting up a good front.　　5 4 **3** 2 **1** 0　2

13. Once I know what the situation calls for, it's easy for me to regulate my actions accordingly.　　5 4 **3** 2 1 0

Scoring Key:

Add up the circled numbers, except reverse the scores for questions 9 and 12. On those, a circled 5 becomes a 0, 4 becomes a 1, and so forth. High self-monitors are defined as those with scores of 53 or higher.　45　　30

Source: Reproduced with permission, based on R. D. Lennox and R. N. Wolfe, "Revision of the Self-monitoring Scale," *Journal of Personality and Social Psychology,* June 1984, p. 1361.

Exercise 1–D
The Social Mirror

(thought)

To recognize the potential inaccuracy or incompleteness of the "social mirror," or others' opinions about you as a person, take a moment to reflect on how the social mirror has affected you. Use the questions as a guide. Reflect back on all aspects of your life: personal (dealing with family and friends, roommates, neighbors, significant others), academic (teachers, coaches, classmates), and professional (bosses, co-workers, subordinates, mentors) to examine what influences others have had on your self-image and other areas of importance to you (community, religion, sports, etc.).

1. What would others say about you that is generally positive?

_____

_____

_____

_____

2. What "constructive suggestions" would others offer to help you improve or change?

_____

_____

_____

_____

3. What do you most like about yourself?

_____

_____

_____

_____

4. What do you most dislike in yourself and would like to change?

_____

_____

_____

_____

5. What beliefs do you have about yourself that limit you?

_____

_____

_____

_____

6. How might these beliefs have been created or influenced by your social mirror?

_____

_____

_____

_____

7. Since it is possible—perhaps even likely—that these weaknesses or limitations are more apparent than real, what could you do to turn them into strengths?

_____

_____

_____

_____

Source: This exercise is adapted from Stephen Covey's *Seven Habits of Highly Effective People*. Leadership Training Manual.

Exercise 1–E
Selective Perception

How does selective perception affect the interpretation of what we see and hear?

_____

_____

_____

Your instructor will read two scenarios. Following the reading of each situation, write in the appropriate column what you see and hear from the description (what picture comes to mind?), what judgments you make or conclusions you draw about the situation, and what (if any) actions you would take.

Scenario One:

_____

_____

_____

Scenario Two:

_____

_____

What I see/hear:	My judgment:	What actions I would take:
1.		
2.		

Questions to be considered individually and discussed in small groups

1. Why do we interpret the same scenario differently from others?
2. What impact does this have on developing relationships?
3. What if in scenario one the person you "met" was a woman? How would your interpretation of the situation change?
4. What if in scenario two, the person with the daughter was her mother instead of her father? Or perhaps the discussion was between a father and his son? How would your interpretation of these situations change?
5. Why is it important to know what our biases are?
6. Let's say it's three years in the future. You've been working for a *Fortune* 500 firm as a member of a product development team. The meeting is about to start when a man matching the description in scenario one walks in. What's your judgment? Why?
7. As the meeting proceeds, he's about to open his mouth. Before he speaks, do you assume that he is credible or not credible until proven otherwise?
8. How do our biases help/hinder us in the workplace?

Exercise 1–F
Emotional
Intelligence Test

Answer the following questions by placing a check in the appropriate column; determine your results using the scoring instructions.

	Always	Usually	Sometimes	Rarely	Never
1. I'm aware of even subtle feelings as I have them.		✓			
2. I find myself using my feelings to help make big decisions in life.		✓			
3. Bad moods overwhelm me.		✓			
4. When I'm angry, I blow my top or fume in silence.		✓			
5. I can delay gratification in pursuit of my goals instead of getting carried away by impulse.		✓			
6. When I'm anxious about a challenge, such as a test or public talk, I find it difficult to prepare well.				✓	
7. Instead of giving up in the face of setbacks or disappointments, I stay hopeful and optimistic.				✓	
8. People don't have to tell me what they feel—I can sense it.			✓		
9. My keen sense of others' feelings makes me compassionate about their plight.			✓		
10. I have trouble handling conflict and emotional upsets in relationships.		✓			
11. I can sense the pulse of a group or a relationship and state unspoken feelings.			✓		
12. I can soothe or contain distressing feelings so they don't keep me from doing things I need to do.			✓		

Source: Reproduced with permission, Daniel Goleman, *Emotional Intelligence*, Bantam Books, Oct. 1995.

Figure Your Score

For numbers 1, 2, 5, 7, 8, 9, 11, and 12:

> Always = 4
> Usually = 3
> Sometimes = 2
> Rarely = 1
> Never = 0

For numbers 3, 4, 6, and 10

> Always = 0
> Usually = 1
> Sometimes = 2
> Rarely = 3
> Never = 4

Results

36 or above: You probably have superior emotional intelligence

25–35: Good level of emotional intelligence

24 or under: Room for improvement

Questions

1. What is your EQ? How accurate do you feel this score portrays you?
2. What if anything about your score surprised you?
3. What, if anything, about your score is most in sync with your view of yourself?
4. Evaluating the six fundamental components of EQ, in which area are you the strongest? Explain, citing a brief example.
5. In which area are you the weakest? Explain, citing a brief example.
6. What implications does your score have for your personal life? Professional life?
7. What steps can you take to increase your EQ?

**Exercise 1–G
Journal Writing**

In a separate notebook, keep an ongoing journal to record your thoughts, perceptions, insights, and goals for future interpersonal development. An entry should follow each class session or topic area. Your instructor will select the entry format and inform you of the collection dates.

The length of the entry is up to you. You should not be writing to impress; this is for your own personal learning and development. Write whatever you want, your ideas, feelings, and reactions relevant to the interpersonal skill being discussed. Your entry may be either negative or positive, as long as you try to be genuine and authentic. What you write should represent what you felt, thought, or learned that seemed important to your development. Entries might include such areas as:

- insights gained or concepts being explored.
- reactions to the instructor, course, or other participants.
- feelings/thoughts about yourself related to the course content, participants, and so on.
- questions raised, resolutions made, things tried, risks taken.

Begin your first entry by doing a personal analysis based on your current perceptions of your interpersonal skills. Answer the following questions to give yourself a basis to compare your future development.

1. How would you describe your overall interpersonal effectiveness?
2. How would you describe your interpersonal relationships? Write about your best and worst relationship.
3. What are your personal strengths regarding interpersonal skills usage?
4. What are your weaknesses regarding interpersonal skills usage?
5. What are your goals for interpersonal development?

Every subsequent journal entry should include:

- The date.
- The interpersonal area being covered.
- A re-evaluation of your strengths and weaknesses.
- What you have learned regarding the skill area or yourself or personal improvements obtained.
- Goals and action steps for future growth and development.

**Exercise 1–H
Try This . . .**

1. Identify a behavior of yours that you would like to change. Practice a different form of that behavior for one week. For example, if you constantly interrupt others, try to go a week without interrupting others. Keep a record of every time you change this behavior. Reward yourself at the end of the week for being conscious of the need to change. Attempt a different behavior in week two. And so on.
2. Observe a person you admire at work or in school off and on for several days. How would you describe their attitude? What evidence do you have of this? What can you do to emulate their positive qualities?
3. Write on a sheet of paper adjectives that you wish could describe your personality. Identify some ways in which you could make changes to incorporate these qualities into your interactions with others.
4. Ask a few close friends for feedback about you as a person, your strong qualities, and areas you could change.
5. The next time you find yourself under a lot of pressure, think clearly about a way in which you could react that is very different from your normal, more emotional reaction. For example, if you usually get physical when you're angry with someone, think of an alternative way to handle your anger.

**Exercise 1–I
Reflection/Action Plan**

This chapter focused on self-awareness—what it is, why it's important, and how to acquire and increase the degree to which you possess it. Other elements which comprise the self, including personality, attitude, and emotional intelligence, were also discussed. Complete the worksheet below upon completing all reading and experiential activities for this chapter.

1. The one or two areas in which I am most strong are:

_____

_____

_____

_____

2. The one or two areas in which I need more improvement are:

_____

_____

_____

_____

3. If I did only one thing to improve in this area, it would be to:

_____

_____

_____

_____

4. Making this change would probably result in:

_____

_____

_____

_____

5. If I did not change or improve in this area, it would probably affect my personal and professional life in the following ways:

_____

_____

_____

_____

2

Self-disclosure and Trust

How do I:

✓ Improve my relationships by sharing my thoughts and feelings?

✓ Learn to trust others, especially when trust has been broken?

✓ Determine the appropriate amount to disclose to others?

✓ Use situational cues to guide self-disclose and trust?

✓ Share my feelings about and reactions to people and situations, in addition to facts?

✓ Demonstrate that I am worthy of others' trust?

Mary Townsend has been on the fast track at the investment firm for which she has worked for five years. She entered graduate school shortly after graduating with honors from an elite university in the northeast. While in graduate school she interned with an investment firm in New York City that was at the time coheaded by John White, a close friend of the family. During her tenure at the firm, she exceeded all performance expectations and rose to the rank of vice president within three years. Now in line for another promotion, her performance has slacked off. Her record is inconsistent. One minute she appears to be at the top of her game, the next she is preoccupied and unreliable.

Her immediate supervisor, Jane Montgomery, has tried to talk with Mary about her inconsistent performance, to no avail. Jane, a director in the firm, placed a call to John White. John no longer heads the firm but often serves as a sounding board to senior management on important personnel and client issues in his role as senior partner. Jane has requested that John meet with Mary.

After an initial greeting, John praises Mary for her past performance with the firm and then expresses concern over her current performance. Mary responds by revealing that she feels she is in over her head. "Promise not to tell anyone," she pleads, and begins to discuss numerous personal incidents that are affecting her performance such as the breakup of a long-standing romance, financial problems brought on by overextending her credit, and a falling out with her family over their concerns about her lack of interest in getting married, having children, and settling down.

While sympathetic, John is dismayed at what he learns from Mary about her troubles. He concludes Mary's personal problems are detracting from her ability to focus on her job. John recommends to Mary's supervisor that she be let go as soon as a "legitimate" opportunity presents itself. One such opportunity is the upcoming announcement that due to the growth of on-line investment companies, the firm will be less reliant on the individuals at Mary's level.

1. What could Mary have done to minimize the degree to which her personal problems spilled over into work?

2. Did Mary disclose too much about herself, setting herself up for a negative recommendation from John? How would you have handled this situation?

3. Did John overstep his bounds in his conversation with Mary about her performance? What about the promise he made to her?

"Trust no one. Not your closest advisors, your spouse, your brother, your God. Trust only yourself, or you will face pain every day of your life."

These harsh words were spoken by the Egyptian king portrayed by Yul Brynner in the epic Cecil B. de Mille movie, *The Ten Commandments*. Fortunately, times have changed and we now know better! While it is good advice to not be too trusting early on in a relationship, the best relationships—in life and in business—are those that are built on mutual trust. Trust is built through a combination of shared experiences over time and willingness to talk with others about aspects of yourself that are relevant to your relationships. This chapter discusses self-disclosure and trust, their meaning and importance in life and in business.

What Is Self-disclosure?

Self-disclosure is the process of letting others know what you think, feel, and want. It is revealing to another how you are reacting to the situation and sharing experiences that are relevant to that situation.[1] By revealing information about yourself, others with whom you associate are better able to understand what makes you tick—your motivations, fears, work style, strengths, and weaknesses. This knowledge helps others to determine strategies for working effectively with you. In addition, as you self-disclose, others reciprocate, enabling you to better develop strategies for understanding and working effectively with them. To be effective, self-disclosure includes:[2]

■ Feelings more than facts—When you share your feelings about or reactions to others, let them get to know the real you. Saying you have three sisters is interesting information, but revealing the kind of relationship you have with them helps others get to know you better.

■ Greater breadth and depth over time—Have you ever cared about someone but felt uncomfortable sharing your feelings? In order for self-disclosure to facilitate the building of a relationship, it has to grow gradually in depth (becoming more revealing about your feelings toward a particular issue or set of issues) and breadth (discussion to cover more issues, such as work, family, leisure, and religious beliefs).

■ A focus on the present rather than the past—While sharing about your past might help explain why you behave the way you do, it is not advisable to share all your past skeletons. Doing so might feel cathartic, but it might leave you feeling vulnerable, especially if this disclosure is not reciprocated. Stay in the present.

■ Reciprocity—To the degree possible, try to match the level of self-disclosure offered by people with whom you become acquainted. Be careful not to overdisclose prematurely, before the relationship has had time to build familiarity and trust. At the same time, if others are not forthcoming, it is not necessary to hold out until they self-disclose. Don't be afraid to take the first important step to building a relationship. Lead by example, and others will follow suit. If they don't, pull back.

Self-disclosure is different from self-description. **Self-description** is the disclosure of nonthreatening information such as age, address, major, or organization for which you work. Self-disclosure is revealing selected information about yourself that is not easily transparent to others, such as how you feel about issues that are important to you. Not surprisingly, self-disclosure has an element of risk. At times, information is shared that might affect others' perceptions and acceptance of you as a person. For every action, there is a reaction, and in the case of self-disclosure, the benefits far outweigh the risks. People who engage in healthy, give-and-take dialogue with others are good managers of other people and of their relationships with others. Nothing ventured, nothing gained.

Benefits of Self-disclosure

The many benefits to self-disclosure accrue to both individuals and the relationships between individuals. Individuals who self-disclose reap psychological and physiological benefits. By self-disclosing and reciprocating others' self-disclosure, we can improve our communication and relationships with others.

■ Sharing with others about ourselves or problems we are facing often brings an enormous sense of psychological relief. Think about a time you did poorly on an exam or ended a relationship with a significant other. How did you handle the situation? Some go for a long walk, cry, sleep, or exercise; most will eventually talk to a friend or loved one. Through disclosing to others, we gain an added perspective that helps us to see our disappointment or frustration in a different light.

■ Disclosing to an appropriate person (one who is sympathetic, supportive, trustworthy, and a good listener) can help us validate our perceptions of reality. By hearing ourselves talk, we process thoughts that are in our heads that help us to better understand the current situation in which we are involved. Often this brings with it a self-validation that tells us either our thoughts are on the right track or our thoughts and perceptions need some tweaking. Imagine you are distraught over a strained customer interaction and fear that the customer will cease to do business with your firm. Being new to the firm, you are unsure how management will respond to this "error" and decide to get a co-worker's opinion on the situation. You disclose the situation and your concerns with her; she responds by not only agreeing with how you handled the situation but also by providing information that this customer has a reputation for "being difficult." You can see how self-disclosure can open us up to new information about ourselves that improves our ability to look at the world through realistic—rather than idealistic—lenses.

■ Self-disclosure can also help reduce stress and tension. By "getting things off your chest," you feel as if a burden has been lifted. If a customer was verbally abusive toward you or a co-worker took credit for your contributions, you are likely to bottle up your feelings in the interest of appearing professional. However, should these feelings remain unexpressed, you might explode! By sharing your problems or concerns with others, you might find ways to resolve them. Even if you find no resolution, you might feel relieved that you are not alone in your feelings—misery loves company. This intimacy brings us closer to others and increases our comfort in knowing that stress reduction through self-disclosure is available now and in the future in our relationships.

■ Self-disclosure also improves us physiologically. By sharing ourselves with others, our stress levels go down, lowering anxiety and altering vital signs such as heart rate and blood pressure. By positively affecting the mind–body connection, the case can be made that self-disclosure actually can lead to better physical—and emotional—health. This concept is one of the core tenets of counseling and hot-line/crisis-prevention programs.

■ Self-disclosure can result in clearer lines of communication with others. By showing our willingness to self-disclose, and encouraging others to share self-information with us, we improve our ability to understand diverse perspectives and viewpoints. We become more confident in our ability to clarify others' intentions and meanings, and in giving feedback and having open discussions that minimize uncertainty and confusion.

■ Self-disclosure can lead to strengthened, enhanced relationships. As co-workers get to know each other, disclosure leads to liking which leads to more disclosure which leads to more liking—a cyclical effect. Without self-disclosure, the level of intimacy and trust will be lower than in a group that discloses freely and appropriately. With disclosure comes trust, and with trust comes collaboration among co-workers.[3] Such collaboration and trust is essential to innovation, which is critical for organizations to compete and survive.[4]

■ Research shows that the more co-workers enjoy working together, the more productive they can be on projects and in team situations. For example, when working as a team under a tight deadline, knowledge of each other's work styles can help a team pull together and produce a top-quality project even when operating under time pressure. Conversely, a team that has not gotten to know each other will have difficulty pulling together on a tough assignment. This explains why team-building—processes and activities undertaken to help team members identify with each other and the team as a whole—is strongly endorsed by many organizations.[5]

We are accustomed to sharing information with people in our lives with whom we are intimate: our parents, loved ones, and close friends. The lesson here is that even in work situations, it is important for project team members and co-workers to get to know each other personally. Naturally there are limits to what is expected and to what is appropriate. There is no need to disclose information of such a personal nature that it becomes awkward or embarrassing for you or your co-worker. And given the prevalence of sexual harassment incidents, we are all well-advised to restrict our disclosing to "safe" subjects. A rule of thumb to use is this: If the information would help a co-worker or colleague better understand how to work with you in the present, then the information is probably relevant and should be disclosed. If the information has little or nothing to do with the project you are working on, your ability to do the job, or your work style, it is probably less relevant and does not need to be shared.

Fears Associated with Self-disclosure

Only recently has self-disclosure been encouraged in business. As organizations become less hierarchical and more team-based, employees have less structure and fewer authority figures to rely on, increasing their need to work collaboratively in making decisions and getting things done. In other words, we can't rely on bosses to issue directives and achieve results based on sheer possession of authority. Collaboration depends to a certain extent on trust. And trust is fostered through self-disclosure.

What does this mean for those who are shy or reserved? Or come from families in which self-disclosing was frowned upon? Or are afraid to disclose themselves to others? Or for people who have been hurt by disclosing information to others who have used it against them?

There are several reasons why individuals are uncomfortable or hesitate to disclose information about themselves to co-workers. First there is uncertainty about how the information is going to be received and utilized. Will it be used against them in a performance appraisal? Will it be revealed to others outside the immediate work situation? Some are afraid of being judged harshly by others, concerned that things that are said in one context might be repeated in an unrelated context. Others have had previous negative experiences with self-disclosure in personal situations, affecting their willingness to be open in work situations. It is quite common early in an intimate relationship to reveal much about oneself before the other person is willing to open up. One says "I love you" and the other, now feeling threatened by the implied commitment, says nothing, causing the original discloser to withhold any further disclosure. Or, perhaps you revealed something personal to someone only to have that person violate your trust by disclosing the information to someone else.

Sometimes managers fear self-disclosure because they are concerned that others, especially subordinates, will perceive their willingness to share as a weakness or a shortcoming, leaving them vulnerable. Paradoxically, those managers who are willing to self-disclose are usually viewed very favorably by their co-workers. This happens because subordinates are able to see the manager as more human—complete with strengths and vulnerabilities—than before, allowing subordinates to feel closer to and interested in their manager.[6]

The benefits of self-disclosure far outweigh the concerns. If you are not used to talking about yourself to others, you will want to start slowly and with people you can trust. As you get to know a person or members of a group, gradually reveal information that helps others understand how to work effectively with you. As they disclose to you, you can increase your level of disclosure accordingly. By following your instincts about what is appropriate and relevant you will eventually find that it feels quite natural to talk about yourself with others. Soon you will find your project team members and co-workers will appreciate getting to know you, and that together you will be able to produce results beyond what was possible when you—and they—were more reserved.

Some Guidelines for Self-disclosure

- Discuss situations as they happen; don't wait until they are old news. The impact of your disclosure will be greater and more understandable within the context of your relationship when you share your thoughts and reactions to situations at the time instead of days, weeks, or months later. For example, if you are a member of a team evaluating a new computer system for potential adoption, withholding your concerns about the viability of this new system might prove problematic. On the one hand, you are concerned that others may look at you as too rigid or unable to accept change. However, you may have information or concerns that, if shared, would completely alter the decision-making process—in a way that would benefit your organization.

- Choose the appropriate time and place. Just as you may not choose to propose marriage in a crowded bar or noisy restaurant, you wouldn't want to tell your boss of your need for personal time right after he shares news that the department is being downsized.

- Choose the appropriate level of disclosure. Similar to the time and place, you need to match the depth and breadth of your disclosure to the situation. You would be ill-advised to reveal your innermost dreams and fears to your boss on the first day of your new job.

- Share feelings and thoughts rather than facts—move from self-description to self-disclosure as appropriate.

The Role of Self-disclosure in Increasing Self-awareness

We have discussed the many benefits of self-disclosure in the business world. While it is important to disclose to others, it is equally important to be honest with ourselves about our strengths and weaknesses. Sometimes this is difficult because we see ourselves differently than others see us. Or because we're not completely in touch with our inner selves—who we really are, what we believe, and how we come across to others. A concept that explains why this is true is the Johari Window.[7] Created by Joseph Luft and Harry Ingram, the **Johari Window** helps us understand how well we know ourselves and how much of ourselves we let others know. The Johari Window is depicted below in a grid that is divided into four regions, which represent the intersection of two axes:

1. Degree to which information about you (values, attitudes, beliefs) is known to or understood by you, and

2. Degree to which information about you is known to others

The basic premise of the Johari Window is that our personal and professional relationships can be greatly improved through understanding ourselves in depth and then selecting those aspects of self that are appropriate to share with others. The authors believe that the more we share of ourselves with others, the more we can develop high-quality relationships. In order to complete this exchange, we must be fully aware of those aspects of ourselves that are "hidden" from view and those that are neither seen nor known by ourselves.

The **open area** consists of information about us that is known to us and to others, such as our name, job title or role, level in the organization, and possibly something about our

Figure 2–1
The Johari Window

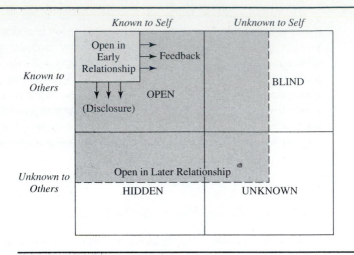

personal life such as our marital status or college from which we graduated. When we first begin a relationship, the open window is relatively small. We begin with safe information, such as the weather, school, and sports. As we build a relationship, we disclose more facts and feelings about ourselves and our beliefs, and the window enlarges vertically, reducing the hidden area. The larger the open area, the more productive and mutually beneficial the interpersonal relationship is likely to be.

The **hidden area** comprises information that we know about ourselves but is hidden from others. This information can range from our concerns about a boss or job to financial, family, or health problems. Not sharing hidden information can create a barrier that protects a person in the short-term. Over time, this lack of sharing can lead to distrust and miscommunication. In business this can have negative consequences such as reduced trust and morale. As we increase our comfort with and practice disclosing more and more information about ourselves through shared experiences with others, the hidden area shrinks. If we are more reserved, this area will remain rather large, resulting in relationships that aren't likely to develop beyond the acquaintance level.

The **blind area** denotes information that others are aware of but we are not. For example, we might have an unknown nervous habit of tapping a pencil or wiggling a foot during meetings when we are feeling stressed or bored. We might see ourselves as patient and helpful, yet our subordinates see us as micromanagers. As we receive feedback from others on their observations of our personalities and behaviors, the blind area will decrease and the open area will become more complete. The more we understand our strengths and weaknesses, and are open to others' views of us, the better managers we can be of our personal and work lives.

The **unknown area** contains information that is unknown by us and by others. This window is unknown due to our lack of experience or exposure to various situations, or due to our inability to process difficult events that occurred earlier in our lives. Until we have experienced certain things in life, we will not fully know how we will react or feel. Until others have seen us in certain situations or we have disclosed to them how we behaved or felt, this information will remain unknown to them. For example, the first time you felt you loved someone (other than a family member), you may have found those feelings hard to express. How you express "love" may be unknown to you and to your significant other. This unknown window can also contain information that is forgotten or purposely suppressed. This window can become smaller over time as we grow, develop, and learn. Personal growth is a process. Self-awareness allows us to assimilate our experiences and move beyond them, rather than being unaware of, or worse, paralyzed by them. It also allows us to move forward in a positive way as we experience life and learn from both our successes and our mistakes.

What Is Trust?

By adding trust to self-disclosure, we are able to complete the relationship equation. The two elements form a cycle: the more you trust the more you disclose, and the more you disclose the more you trust. How do we define trust? **Trust** is a multifaceted concept which captures one's faith or belief in the integrity or reliability of another person or thing. In business, as in life, trust is an essential building block in developing relationships with customers, colleagues, and business associates. Think of a relationship you've had where trust has been broken. Perhaps a promised raise didn't materialize, a client misrepresented his or her financial situation, or a friend informs you that your significant other—who attends school in another state—was seen kissing someone else. Isn't it difficult to relate to that person now? To believe that person's promises? Does the lack of trust make you less inclined to make plans or have anything to do with this person?

Trust is essential for mature relationships. According to Schindler and Thomas, trust is composed of five elements.[8] (See Figure 2–2.) You are more likely to be seen as trustworthy if you demonstrate:

- **Integrity**—honesty and sincerity. In short, you say what you mean and mean what you say. Integrity also relates to your ability to honestly disclose and share your thoughts, beliefs, and feelings.

- **Competence**—knowledge and ability. You are aware of your strengths and limitations, offering help where you can and seeking resources and assistance when needed.

- **Consistency**—conformity with previous practice; good judgment in handling situations. When you are consistent, for example, you do what you say you will do; friends and associates believe in your ability to follow through and do the right thing in a given situation.

- **Loyalty**—faithfulness to one's friends and ideals. A trustworthy person supports friends and associates both within and outside their presence. One who sings your praises in front of you but then spreads rumors behind your back is not only duplicitous but also untrustworthy.

- **Openness**—not closed to new ideas; willing to share ideas with others. This component of trust suggests that you are aware of yourself and comfortable sharing and disclosing with others. In addition, when someone shares with you, you encourage them and offer acceptance and support, as opposed to judgment and ridicule.

While an essential component of good relationships, trust does not come without some element of risk. The riskiness of trust is evident in the following definition: Trust is the "willingness of a party to be vulnerable to the actions (whether words, conduct, or decisions) of another party based on the expectation that the other will perform a particular action important to the trustor."[9] Trusting is a two-way street. The person who places confidence in an individual must rely on that person to treat the information that was given in confidence. The element of risk is compounded by the inability of the

Figure 2–2
Five Elements of Trust

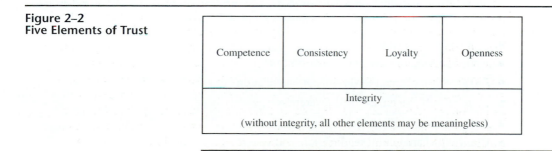

Competence	Consistency	Loyalty	Openness
Integrity			
(without integrity, all other elements may be meaningless)			

Personal Trust-Builders   There are some tangible things we can do to build up others' trust in us. Some of these include:

- Follow through on promises and commitments made; and its converse—don't promise what you can't produce.
- Don't reveal confidences told you in private.
- Avoid participating in unnecessary gossip about specific individuals.
- Don't make self-flattering or boasting statements about your capabilities.
- Develop a reputation for loyalty—a willingness to stand by, protect, and save face for others.
- Be consistent: reliability and predictability helps others to build faith in your ability to deliver on promises made.
- Be realistic: don't overcommit to the extent you are breaking promises.
- Develop personal competence; by improving your knowledge and skills people can count on you to hold up your end of the bargain.
- Gain a reputation for honesty and truthfulness: "say what you mean and mean what you say."
- Make sure your actions are consistent with your spoken words: "walk the talk."

truster to monitor or control the other party. For this reason trust is best when built up over time. As we gain experience with the judgments and behaviors of others, we can gradually build confidence in their ability to follow through on commitments and keep their word.

Organizational Trust-Builders

Trust is essential in the work environment. Clients and customers need to be able to rely on information obtained from a company and its employees. Subordinates need to be able to trust their managers, managers need to be able to trust senior management, and everyone needs to be able to expect consistent reactions from their co-workers and associates. Trust is—and trustworthy behaviors such as those listed above are—a necessary foundation for a healthy work environment. Without trust, employees become overly protective of themselves and their immediate work environment, choosing to withhold information and avoid taking risks.[10] Organizations with low or no trust are susceptible to high turnover, rumor-mongering, low productivity, and increased absenteeism.

These behaviors often exist in organizations going through a merger or acquisition. As the products, services, employees, and cultures of two or more companies are joined together, clashes inevitably result. The more openly and effectively each company can communicate with its employees about the changes as they occur, the better the employees will be able to adjust and move forward in their work on behalf of the newly merged organization. Research shows that those companies that make information available to their employees are more successful at achieving their business goals than are those companies that keep their employees in the dark or misrepresent information to them.[11] Organizational cultures associated with trust emphasize:[12]

- Depth of relationships
- Understanding of roles and responsibilities
- Frequent, timely, and forthright communication
- Member self-esteem and self-awareness
- High levels of skill competence
- Clarity of shared purpose, direction, and vision
- Honoring promises and commitments

Ten Managerial Tips for Developing Trust[13]

Practice what you preach—narrow the gap between your intentions and your behavior.

Open lines of communication—declare your intentions to others and invite feedback on your performance.

Accept disagreements, differences of opinion, and conflict—when things go wrong and problems arise, seek out solutions.

Keep confidential information confidential.

Let others know what you stand for and what you value.

Create an open environment—make it safe for others to be with you and to share with you.

Maintain a high level of integrity and honesty.

Know yourself and how others perceive you and your actions—build on your competencies and accept your limitations.

Build credibility with others by being consistent and reliable.

Avoid micromanaging—this sends the message that "I don't trust you."

A Note of Caution

Trust is not a right; it is earned. Trust is person-dependent. That is, we do not automatically trust every individual in every situation. Perhaps we might trust certain but not all aspects of a person. If your co-worker supports you, is loyal to you, and holds sensitive issues in confidence, you will trust her. However, if your co-worker reveals that she has been unfaithful in her relationship with her spouse, suddenly her trustworthiness becomes suspect. Perhaps you have faith in your boss's wisdom and leadership, but the idea of him watching your pet while you're out of town makes you uneasy.[14] Our ability to trust is also situation-dependent. Trust depends on our having the information and experience needed to make good judgments in a given situation or situations.[15]

Trust is earned. It evolves over time, based on past successful experiences that build on each other to eventually build a climate of trust. Trust is fragile. It is easier to destroy than it is to build. Consider the couple who have been married for 10, 20, or more years. One untrustworthy act could destroy decades of trusting behaviors, with trust likely never to fully return. By valuing and fostering trust and trustworthiness in your personal and professional relationships, you will be able to build mutually satisfying, long-term relationships in both your work and life.

Summary

Self-disclosure and trust are two mutually reinforcing skills that, when practiced with the appropriate persons at the right time and place, can serve to deepen and improve personal and professional relationships. By letting another person know your values and your beliefs about and reactions to a situation, you not only improve your own understanding and concerns about a situation, but also improve the quality of communication, collaboration, and performance with that person. There are fears and risks associated with disclosure, however; knowing what, when, and how to disclose can serve to mitigate the fears and risks.

By letting others know you, you pave the way for them to develop trust in you. When others trust you, they are more likely to disclose to you. The mutually reinforcing nature of disclosure and trust forms the basis of healthy personal and professional relationships. Organizations that are characterized by a lack of trust, such as the case during times of change (i.e., downsizing and mergers), become hotbeds for employee gossip, absenteeism, and turnover. By practicing the tips and techniques we shared, you can improve your comfort level and skills in self-disclosure and trust.

Key Terms and Concepts

Blind area

Competence

Consistency

Hidden area

Integrity

Johari Window

Loyalty

Open area

Openness

Self-description

Self-disclosure

Trust

Unknown area

Endnotes

1. David W. Johnson, *Reaching out: Interpersonal Effectiveness and Self-actualization* (Boston, MA: Allyn & Bacon, 2000), p. 46.

2. David W. Johnson, 2000, pp. 46–47.

3. B. H. Sheppard, "Negotiating in Long-Term Mutually Interdependent Relationships among Relative Equals," in R. J. Bies, R. J. Lewicki, and B. H. Sheppard (Eds.), *Research on Negotiation in Organizations* 5 (Greenwich, CT: JAI Press, 1995), pp. 3–44.

4. Deborah G. Ancona and David F. Caldwell, "Demography and Design: Predictors of New Product Team Performance," *Organization Science* 3 (1992), pp. 321–341.

5. Jon R. Katzenbach and Douglas K. Smith, "The Wisdom of Teams," *Small Business Reports* 18, no. 7 (July 1993), pp. 68–71.

6. Irvin D. Yalom, "It's Lonely at the Top—Isolation as a Problem for CEOs," *Inc.* 20, no. 5 (April 1, 1998), pp. 39–40.

7. Joseph Luft, *Of Human Interaction* (Palo Alto, CA: National Press, 1969).

8. P. L. Schindler and C. C. Thomas, "The Structure of Interpersonal Trust in the Workplace," *Psychological Reports,* Oct. 1993, pp. 563–73.

9. R. C. Mayer, J. H. Davis, and F. D. Schoorman, "An Integrative Model of Organizational Trust," *Academy of Management Review* 20 (1995), pp. 709–734.

10. Robert D. Costigan, Salem S. Ilter, and J. Jason Brown, "A Multidimensional Study of Trust in Organizations," *Journal of Managerial Issues* 10, no. 3 (Fall 1998), pp. 303–318.

11. Costigan, Ilter, and Brown, 1998.

12. Jeffrey Cufaude, "Creating Organizational Trust," *Association Management* 51, no. 7 (July 1999), pp. 26–35.

13. Robert Glaser, "Paving the Road to TRUST," *HR Focus* 74, no. 1 (Jan. 1997), p. 5.

14. The complexity of trust explains why U.S. public opinion was divided during the 1999 Clinton impeachment hearings. Many believed in Clinton's competence as a leader but questioned his morals and integrity.

15. Keith J. Blois, "Trust in Business to Business Relationships: An Evaluation of Its Status," *Journal of Management Studies* 36, no. 2 (March 1999), p. 197.

Exercise 2–A
Assessing Yourself

Circle the response that most closely correlates with each item below.

		Agree	Neither	Disagree

1. I am comfortable revealing myself to others.
   1 ②3 4 5

2. I don't overdisclose and only disclose to those who reciprocate.
   1 2 ③4 5

3. When I disclose, I focus on information about me that is relevant in the present.
   ①2 3 4 5

4. I gradually increase my level of disclosure with a person over time.
   1 ②3 4 5

5. I encourage others to disclose safely and appropriately.
   1 2 3 4 ⑤

6. I restrict my disclosure to people I know I can trust.
   1 2 ③4 5

7. I use self-disclosure as a way to build trust with others.
   1 2 ③4 5

8. I reveal aspects of my hidden window to trusted colleagues.
   1 ②3 4 5

9. I feel comfortable disclosing to both close friends and to people with whom I work.
   ①2 3 4 5

10. I choose appropriate subjects about which to self-disclose.
    1 ②3 4 5

11. I refrain from offering information that is too personal at work.
    1 ②3 4 5

12. I am not fearful of people getting too close to me.
    ①2 3 4 5

13. When self-disclosing I focus on my thoughts and feelings rather than on facts.
    1 ②3 4 5

14. I am open to receiving feedback about myself from others.
    ①2 3 4 5

15. I consciously try to learn about those aspects of myself that are typically "hidden" from myself and/or others.
    1 ②3 4 5

16. I am able to trust others easily.
    1 2 ③4 5

17. I am constantly improving my knowledge base, capabilities, and skills.
    1 2 ③4 5

18. I am making a conscious effort to be a trustworthy person.
    1 2 ③4 5

19. My friends consider me loyal.
    1 ②3 4 5

20. I follow through on promises and commitments I make.
    1 2 ③4 5

21. I try to avoid being overextended.
    1 ②3 4 5

22. I avoid gossip about others.
    1 2 3 ④5

23. I am realistic about my capabilities.
    1 ②3 4 5

24. My actions are consistent with my words.
    1 ②3 4 5

25. I am consistent and reliable.
    1 2 ③4 5

26. I consciously avoid micromanaging others.
    1 2 ③4 5

If your total exceeds 78, you might want to create a plan for increasing your comfort with and skills in self-disclosure and trust.

Exercise 2–B
Interviewing

Find someone at work or in your class whom you do not know very well. Using the list below, select five questions to ask that person as a way of getting to know him or her better. Your instructor may select certain questions to be used by all participants.

1. What is an interesting book you have read recently and why did you like it?
2. What is your favorite movie and why?
3. What do you like to do most with a free hour?
4. If you could be anywhere in the world right now where would you be and why?
5. What makes you feel most humble?
6. What one day in your life would you like to live over and why?
7. What is the worst problem facing (your home country/the United States)?
8. What would you change about the school you are attending or your present employer?
9. If you could choose to be any animal, what would it be and why?
10. What is the most honest thing you have ever done?
11. Choose a word that best describes your personality.
12. What television show do you like the most and why?
13. If you could tape the ugliest thing you know, what would it be?

Questions

1. Why did we do this exercise?
2. What did you learn about others from the questions you asked?
3. How did you feel asking some of the questions?
4. Were any of the questions more difficult to ask? Why?

Exercise 2–C
People Hunt

Mill around the classroom and identify people who can help you complete the following chart.[1] Write the names of the people you identify in the "match" columns. Try not to use the same person more than three times in your chart. Challenge yourself to meet and talk with as many people as possible.

Information	Match 1	Match 2	Match 3
Same height as you within two inches: _____			
Uses the same toothpaste as you. Toothpaste brand: _____			
Uses the same shampoo as you. Shampoo brand: _____			
Has the same color eyes as you: _____			
Same favorite fast food: _____			
Same favorite color: _____			
Same number of siblings: _____			
Same hometown or country: _____			
Same favorite TV show: _____			

After completing the chart, answer the following questions:

1. In what ways did this exercise help you get to know others better?
2. What did you learn about yourself from this exercise?
3. What things do you and don't you have in common with others?
4. What additional items can be asked to uncover other similarities between you and others?
5. How can you apply this exercise to improving your relationships with others?

[1]If this is a distance learning class, students should use whatever means to identify people who match the following criteria.

**Exercise 2–D
Icebreakers**

Name, Face, and Fact

Participants sit in a circle and the first person states his or her name and a fact related to him or her. Facts can include items from the following categories: favorite food, hometown street name, college major, favorite color, favorite book, favorite travel destination, and so on.

Name Repetition

Participants stand in a circle and, taking turns, each person says her or his name. Participants then throw a ball to another member in the circle, each stating her or his name first followed by the name of the person to whom she or he is throwing the ball. Each time a person receives the ball, his or her name is stated as well as that of the person to whom the ball is thrown.

Name Tags

Participants write their name in the center of a piece of paper. In each corner of the paper participants write personal information such as where they are from, their college major, their ideal job, their favorite travel destination, their favorite movie/TV show/book, and so on. Participants mill about the room and introduce themselves to as many others as possible in the time allowed, being sure to listen intently to what each person is disclosing to others.

Show and Share

Participants bring in a personal item—an item that reveals something significant about their personal "essence" or identity. The item can be something the participant enjoys, carries at all times, is of sentimental value, or that holds some personal meaning. Participants show and discuss the meaning behind the object. Others give feedback on what they think the item says about the participant as well as share how they can personally relate to the other's show-and-share item.

Multiple Introductions

Participants stand and mill about the room, introducing themselves to one new person every two minutes. The instructor asks the class to concentrate on one question at a time per person met. After two minutes, the instructor calls time and the participants introduce themselves to a new partner and engage in a two-minute discussion about the next topic on the list. Suggested topics, which can be written in advance on a board, include:

1. Your college major and why you chose it.
2. What you did last summer (and what you wished you had done instead!).
3. Why you chose the college you're attending or attended.
4. Your first job and what you liked, disliked, and learned about it.
5. A favorite hobby or nonschool, nonwork activity.
6. What you would do (and in what priority order) if you won the lottery.
7. Your favorite book, TV show, Broadway play, or movie and why.
8. Your favorite travel destination.
9. What you would do if you didn't have to work for a living.
10. What you liked about this exercise—and what you didn't—and why.

Exercise 2–E
Fishbowl

A fishbowl is a clear glass container we can see through and into from every angle. The fishbowl exercise is designed to help participants identify personal things that can be seen by others that they feel comfortable disclosing to others. This activity may be done in small groups or in front of the class.

Inside the fishbowl is an assortment of small cards, each containing a topic. Participants select a card and present a short (1–2 minute) impromptu talk regarding an experience they have had relating to the topic. Participants use as many descriptors as possible to allow everyone to be able to understand and relate to the situation. Participants should be as expressive as they can be, telling a story, emphasizing their feelings and those of the other people involved in the story, as well as their and others' reactions to what was occurring. Participants should include:

- A description of the players—all those involved in the situation.
- Information about the setting, atmosphere, surroundings, and so on.
- Details about the situation as it occurred.
- Thoughts and feelings they had about the experience as it unfolded.
- Outcomes, including lessons learned, awareness gained, and others.

Note: If this exercise is being done outside of a classroom, participants should pair up with a friend at school or work and take turns sharing stories as explained above.

Sample fishbowl questions (your instructor has more)

- Your happiest/saddest holiday memory.
- Your most/least enjoyable travel experience.
- An accomplishment you worked hard to attain.
- A lesson you learned in childhood that remains with you to this day.
- A time when you felt angry/happy/embarrassed/lucky.
- A memorable experience from grade school.
- A time you realized you were more like your mother/father than you care to admit.

Exercise 2–F
Johari Window
Questionnaire

Friendship Relations Survey

This questionnaire was written to help you assess your understanding of your behavior in interpersonal relationships. There are no right or wrong answers. The best answer is the one that comes closest to representing your quest for good interpersonal relationships. In each statement, the first sentence gives a situation and the second sentence gives a reaction. For each statement indicate the number that is closest to the way you would handle the situation.

5 = You *always* would act this way.
4 = You *frequently* would act this way.
3 = You *sometimes* would act this way.
2 = You *seldom* would act this way.
1 = You *never* would act this way.

Try to relate each question to your own personal experience. Take as much time as you need to give a true and accurate answer for yourself. *There is no right or wrong answer.* Trying to give the "correct" answer will make your answer meaningless to you. *Be honest with yourself.*

		Never				Always
1. You work with a friend, but some of her mannerisms and habits are getting on your nerves and irritating you. More and more you avoid interacting with or even seeing your friend.		1	2	3	(4)	5
2. In a moment of weakness, you give away a friend's secret. Your friend finds out and calls you to ask about it. You admit to it and talk with your friend about how to handle secrets better in the future.		1	(2)	3	(4)	5
3. You have a friend who never seems to have time for you. You ask him about it, telling him how you feel.		1	2	(3)	4	5

4. Your friend is upset at you because you have inconvenienced him. He tells you how he feels. You tell him he is too sensitive and is overreacting.   1 2 ③ 4 5

5. You had a disagreement with a friend and how she ignores you whenever she's around you. You decide to ignore her back.   1 2 ③ 4 ⑤

6. A friend has pointed out that you never seem to have time for him. You explain why you have been busy and try for a mutual understanding.   1 2 3 ④ 5

7. At great inconvenience, you arrange to take your friend to the doctor's office. When you arrive to pick her up, you find she has decided not to go. You explain to her how you feel and try to reach an understanding about future favors.   1 2 ③ 4 5

8. You have argued with a friend and are angry with her, ignoring her when you meet. She tells you how she feels and asks about restoring the friendship. You ignore her and walk away.   ① 2 3 4 5

9. You have a secret that you have told only to your best friend. The next day, an acquaintance asks you about the secret. You deny the secret and decide to break off the relationship with your best friend.   1 ② 3 4 5

10. A friend who works with you tells you about some of your mannerisms and habits that get on his nerves. You discuss these with your friend and look for some possible ways of dealing with the problem.   1 2 3 ④ 5

11. Your best friend gets involved in something illegal that you believe will lead to serious trouble. You decide to tell your friend how you disapprove of his involvement in the situation.   1 ② 3 4 5

12. In a moment of weakness, you give away a friend's secret. Your friend finds out and calls you to ask about it. You deny it firmly.   ① 2 3 4 ⑤

13. You have a friend who never seems to have time for you. You decide to forget her and to start looking for new friends.   1 2 ③ 4 5

14. You are involved in something illegal, and your friend tells you of her disapproval and fear that you will get in serious trouble. You discuss it with your friend.   1 2 ③ 4 5

15. You work with a friend, but some of her mannerisms and habits are getting on your nerves and irritating you. You explain your feelings to your friend, looking for a mutual solution to the problem.   ① ② 3 4 5

16. A friend has pointed out that you never seem to have time for him. You walk away.   ① 2 3 4 5

17. Your best friend gets involved in something illegal that you believe will lead to serious trouble. You decide to mind your own business.   1 2 ③ 4 5

18. Your friend is upset because you have inconvenienced him. He tells you how he feels. You try to understand and agree on a way to keep it from happening again.   1 2 3 4 ⑤

19. You had a disagreement with a friend, and how she ignores you whenever she's around you. You tell her how her actions make you feel and ask about restoring your friendship.   1 2 ③ 4 5

20. A friend who works with you tells you about some of your mannerisms and habits that get on his nerves. You listen and walk away.   ① 2 3 4 ⑤

21. At great inconvenience, you arrange to take your friend to the doctor's office. When you arrive to pick her up, you find she had decided not to go. You say nothing but resolve never to do any favors for that person again.   1 2 ③ 4 5

22. You have argued with a friend and are angry with her, ignoring her when you meet. She tells you how she feels and asks about restoring the friendship. You discuss ways of maintaining your friendship, even when you disagree.   1 ② 3 4 5

23. You have a secret that you have told only to your best friend. The next day, an acquaintance asks you about the secret. You   1 2 3 ④ 5

call your friend and ask her about it, trying to come to an understanding of how to handle secrets better in the future.

24. You are involved in something illegal, and your friend tells you of her disapproval and fear that you will get in serious trouble. You tell your friend to mind her own business.

1 (2) 3 4 5

Friendship Relations Survey Answer Key

In the Friendship Relations Survey there are twelve questions that deal with your willingness to self-disclose and twelve questions that are concerned with your receptivity to feedback. Transfer your scores to this answer key. Reverse the scoring for all questions that are starred; that is, if you answered 5, record the score of 1; if you answered 4, record the score of 2; if you answered 3, record the score of 3; if you answered 2, record the score of 4; and if you answered 1, record the score of 5. Then add the scores in each column.

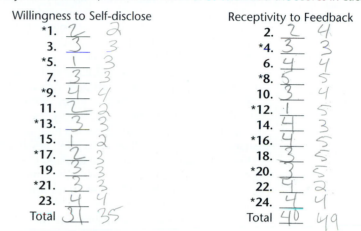

Willingness to Self-disclose		Receptivity to Feedback	
*1.	2 2	2.	2 4
3.	3 3	*4.	3 3
*5.	1 3	6.	4 4
7.	3 3	*8.	5 5
*9.	4 4	10.	3 4
11.	2 2	*12.	1 5
*13.	3 3	14.	4 3
15.	1 2	*16.	4 5
*17.	2 3	18.	3 5
19.	3 3	*20.	3 5
*21.	3 3	22.	4 2
23.	4 4	*24.	4 4
Total	31 35	Total	40 49

On the Friendship Relations Survey Summary Sheet, add the totals for receptivity to feedback and willingness to self-disclose to arrive at an index of interpersonal risk taking which you will use in Chapter 3.

Friendship Relations Survey Summary Sheet

Draw horizontal and vertical lines through your scores (Part *a*) and the group's receptivity to feedback and willingness to self-disclose (Part *b*). The results should look like the Johari Window.

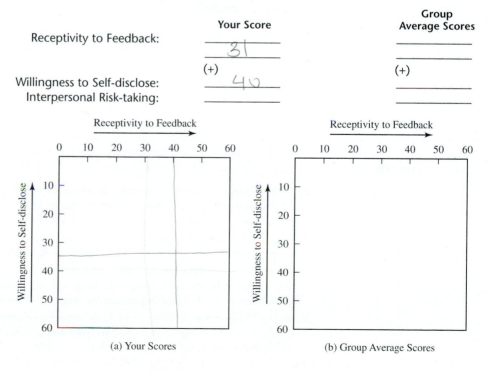

	Your Score	Group Average Scores
Receptivity to Feedback:	31	
(+)		(+)
Willingness to Self-disclose:	40	
Interpersonal Risk-taking:		

(a) Your Scores

(b) Group Average Scores

Exercise 2–G
It's in the Bag

This exercise builds on the Johari Window by helping participants to think through some things that are commonly shared with others (the open area) and some things that are not commonly shared with others (the hidden area). It also allows other group members to provide feedback on how they see the participant.

1. Participants will need a brown paper bag (as small as a lunch bag, as large as a grocery bag), scissors, glue, several recent magazines that can be cut up, and possibly construction paper, string, small toys or objects, crayons, paint or pencils, tape, and/or paste.

2. On the outside of the bag, participants attach pictures or small objects that represent personal aspects that are commonly shared with other people. Examples are a picture of an athlete to represent an interest in sports, a favorite CD cover that depicts talent in music, a small trinket won at an amusement park concession that portrays a hobby. On the inside of the bag, participants place pictures or items that depict aspects that are not commonly shared with others (such as an article about depression, a religious memento, or a political button). Participants may use words, symbols, phrases, pictures, objects, or anything else that seems relevant to self-portrayal.

3. Participants take turns discussing their bags with their partners or group. Participants may choose to talk only about the outside of their bags, or they may want to talk about both the outside and inside of their bags. Everyone should feel comfortable sharing as much or little as they would like.

4. Team members should comment and give feedback on what the team member has shared. Does it match their perception or what they have seen or heard of this person? They may want to comment on qualities that this person has left out that they see clearly or admire in this person. Whatever their impressions of this person or feelings about their bag, participants should feel free to comment on it, being careful to use good feedback and listening skills.

Upon completion of the activity, discuss (or complete on your own) the following questions:

1. How did you feel discussing the outside of your bag?

2. How did you feel listening to others discussing the outsides of their bags?

3. What impact did this experience have on your willingness and comfort to disclose to others in the future?

4. Did you share any information from the inside of the bag? If so, what enabled you to feel comfortable enough to do this? If not, why do you think you want this information to remain hidden?

Source: This exercise is adapted from the "Bag Exercise" in David W. Johnson, *Reaching out: Interpersonal Effectiveness and Self-actualization,* 7/e. Reprinted by permission of John Wiley and Sons, Inc., 2000, pp. 77–78.

Exercise 2–H
Circle of Friends

It is important to examine our interpersonal relationships to determine whether the levels of disclosure and trust we have enhance the relationships we value.

1. In the first column, list the people closest to you in different categories: family, friends, co-workers (include classmates, teammates, or professors), and others (anyone with whom you have a valued relationship and are in frequent contact).

2. In the second column, rate your level of trust with each individual on a scale of 1–5, with 1 having very little trust and 5 having a high degree of trust.

3. In the third column, rate your level of disclosure with the individual on a scale of 1–5 with 1 being very low, dealing with trivial and nonthreatening information, and 5 being a high level of highly personable and sensitive information.

4. In the fourth column, write comments as to the quality of the relationship, such as a comparison on congruency between trust and self-disclosure and notes as to what you want and need to do to improve the relationship.

Name of Individual	Level of Trust (1–5)	Level of Self-disclosure (1–5)	Comments on the Relationship
(Family Members)			
(Friends)			
(Co-workers)			
(Others)			

Look over your completed chart and answer the following questions:

1. Is there a correlation between the level of self-disclosure and the level of trust? Why or why not?
2. How satisfied are you with the level of trust and disclosure in your relationships?
3. In what ways are the relationships progressing the way you want them to?
4. How can you improve the level of disclosure or trust in each of the most important relationships?

Exercise 2–I
Trust-Building Activities

The following two activities are designed to expose participants to—and build their comfort level with—trusting others.

Blind Walk

Working in pairs, participants will take turns leading each other around. One member closes his or her eyes, with his or her eyes remaining closed for the entire turn. The other member leads him or her around by the arm. The member should take the participant to as many different places as possible, incorporating other sensory experiences such as touch, smell, and hearing. Participants should then alternate and allow the other member to experience being "blind."

Trust Meal

In pairs, participants share a meal while one member is blindfolded. The sighted member leads the blindfolded partner through the meal, explaining and/or answering any questions or concerns. The blindfolded person may choose to request assistance or attempt to eat without help.

Questions

1. What was comfortable/uncomfortable about each of the above exercises?
2. What were your feelings as you were going through each role in each exercise?
3. What did you learn about yourself and others through each exercise?

Exercise 2–J
Ideal Cards: A Self-disclosure Activity

1. Students get into groups of five to seven members.
2. The instructor distributes play money and two Ideal Cards to each participant.
3. The instructor explains the following ground rules for buying, selling, or trading Ideal Cards before the exchange phase is begun:
   a. Each individual *must* sell or trade at least one of his/her Ideal Cards sometime during the entire experience.
   b. Each individual *may* buy, sell, or trade Ideal Cards within his/her group. Cards may be bought or sold for any mutually agreed-upon price or traded outright.
4. Participants trade cards within their subgroups.
5. When the trading within subgroups is completed, the instructor announces that participants may exchange cards (in accordance with the rules) with any other person in the room.
6. Following the activity, reflect silently on the following questions:
   a. What were the original Ideal Cards you received? Why did you want to keep/trade them?
   b. How much money did you have at the end of the experience?

    c. Were you more interested in obtaining meaningful Ideal Cards or in accumulating the most money possible?

    d. Which Ideal Cards did you most wish to obtain? Why?

    e. Are you satisfied with the Ideal Cards you now have? Why or why not?

7. Now discuss your reactions to these questions in your original group.

8. The instructor leads a discussion of the entire experience.

Examples of Ideal Cards

1. To persevere in what I am doing.
2. To be honest.
3. Never to be worried about having enough food.
4. To be a member of the opposite sex.
5. To be needed and to be important to others.
6. To have better feelings about myself.
7. To have a better relationship with God.
8. To be a good conversationalist.
9. To have my opinions respected.
10. To develop my potential.

Your instructor has more.

Source: J. Pfeiffer & J. E. Jones, *The 1975 Annual Handbook for Group Facilitators,* University Associates, 1975. Reprinted by permission of John Wiley and Sons, Inc.

Exercise 2–K
Try This . . .

1. Watch a television show or movie (or read a book) in which trust plays a large part—perhaps trust is broken (e.g., *The Little Mermaid, Working Girl*) or is built over time (e.g., *You've Got Mail,* the Helen Keller story). Describe the role that self-disclosure and trustworthiness played in either the building or destroying of trust. What are some lessons that could be learned and applied in your own life from these depictions? What are behaviors to be avoided?

2. Take someone with whom you would like to enhance your interpersonal relationship to your "special place" (somewhere you feel special, peaceful, content, or comfortable). Discuss with that person what is going on in your life and your feelings and reactions to the situations. Encourage the other person to take you to a special place to discuss what is going on with him or her.

3. Practice "trust-building." Be aware of trust behaviors you are trying to incorporate into your daily interactions with others. Once a week for a month, record the times you have consciously or unconsciously done things that build others' trust in you. Examples can include returning money you've found in a public place to the appropriate office, planning your time so as to be able to follow through on commitments, and keeping a secret told you by a good friend from a mutual acquaintance.

**Exercise 2–L
Reflection/Action Plan**

1. When do you think it is appropriate to receive feedback from and self-disclose to others?

   _____

   _____

   _____

2. How comfortable are you with self-disclosure? What aspects are most difficult for you?

   _____

   _____

   _____

3. How does trust affect your receptivity to feedback and willingness to give feedback?

   _____

   _____

   _____

4. In what ways is your current use of trust and self-disclosure effective in your relationships with friends and loved ones?

   _____

   _____

   _____

5. What specific changes about your self-disclosure and trusting behaviors would you make that would enhance relationships with your friends?

   _____

   _____

   _____

6. If you made the changes listed above, what impact would this have on your relationships? Explain.

   _____

   _____

   _____

3 Establishing Goals and Identifying Values

How do I:

✓ Implement goal setting to achieve personal and professional goals?

✓ Clarify what is important to me: my values and needs?

✓ Develop a personal mission statement?

✓ Write effective goals?

✓ Make progress toward my goals, especially when I hit a roadblock?

Marsha Smith was enjoying her work as an associate at a leading investment bank in New York. The hours didn't bother her. As the first person from her family to attend college, she was used to working hard for what she wanted in life. She had worked part-time all the way through high school and college to pay for tuition, room, board, and other immediate expenses. Now in her third year, she was contemplating her next career step. Most of her friends had moved on to graduate business school, but her boss had convinced her to stay on. With all the excitement over "new economy" growth clients, there was plenty of interesting work to go around. She was traveling overseas frequently, had a great set of friends, had a terrific boyfriend, and was enjoying her current situation. So what was troubling her? In the back of her mind Marsha realized she wasn't sure what she should do next. For possibly the first time in her life she didn't have to focus single-mindedly on one goal, such as paying for college. She now had multiple priorities in which she was interested. But she didn't have a clue as to how to start making plans to attain any one of them. Besides, she thought, "I'm always working anyway. How would I have time to even think of anything else? So it doesn't really matter that I'm not sure where I'm headed." Or does it?

1. What are the issues that Marsha is facing?

2. Should Marsha follow the rest of her friends to graduate business school?

3. Why is it difficult for her to set new priorities for herself?

4. What steps does Marsha need to take?

5. What advice would you offer Marsha?

6. How can Marsha set new goals and work toward them while fulfilling her obligations to her present position?

"If you don't know where you are going, you'll probably end up someplace else."

Yogi Berra

These words provide the premise for and reasoning behind setting goals. If we don't have a plan to direct our lives, where will we end up? Effective goal setting gives us direction and purpose while providing a standard against which to measure our performance. It also allows both individuals and organizations to have a clear understanding of what they are trying to accomplish. This chapter describes personal goal setting and values clarification: what goals and values are, the benefits of being aware of your goals and values, and how to improve your ability to set meaningful goals that are aligned with your core values. We also address how effective goal setting can help you set objectives and make plans for achieving these objectives in both your personal and your work life. At the end of the chapter are a number of exercises that enable you to assess your goal-setting skills and develop improvement plans.

What Is Goal Setting?

Goal setting is a means of identifying our work/life priorities and developing strategies for attaining personal and professional objectives. Consider the lives of successful people. Do they seem to have a strong commitment to their plans? Are they organized, efficient, confident, or well prepared? Most likely you answered yes to most if not all of these words. Successful individuals and organizations have learned that the key to achieving meaningful results is through effective goal setting.

For example, Jack Welch decided, shortly after graduating from college, that one day he wanted to be the CEO of General Electric (he achieved this goal twenty years after setting it!). Bernie Carlson, who anchored CNN's news desk for twenty years, decided at the age of 13 he wanted to be a network news anchor. Jerry Garcia, the infamous lead of the rock group The Grateful Dead, said he knew as a youngster he wanted to head a rock band. And Scott Adams, the successful "Dilbert" cartoonist, claims to have envisioned himself as the world's greatest cartoonist.

Contrast these goal setters with those who are unable or unwilling to set goals and achieve them. Consider people you know who seem to set goals frequently but never attain them. Are they realistic about what they can achieve? Do they have the required resources to attain their goals (e.g., time, money, or support from others)? Do they have the necessary capabilities, training, and education? Chances are they may not have one or more of these resources that are so important to success.

Why Is Goal Setting Important?

The goal-setting process has several benefits:

- Morale/Esteem—Achieving goals gives you an internal reinforcement of your personal abilities. Successful goal completion broadens your belief in what you can accomplish.

- Purpose/Direction—Establishing written goals formalizes our dreams and wishes. Through the process of careful examination and self-analysis, we begin to understand what we want to achieve. Goal setting defines the destination point while providing the map to lead us there. Writing goal statements and developing an action plan gives our life purpose and direction. These statements provide us with short-term motivation and long-term vision. Whether or not you are aware of your goals or strategies, they are affecting your life's direction. Once you bring them into consciousness and formalize them, you can guide your life more strategically.[1]

■ Motivation—Goal setting helps us to build internal momentum. Through goal setting, we direct our actions toward fulfilling our dreams and ambitions. Usually this process starts by setting incremental steps to achieving a goal. If you want to run a marathon, you start your training by running in small amounts that increase over time. Momentum begins to build as soon as you set your goal, and continues as you take steps toward achieving it. To borrow from a physics principle, a person who sets goals becomes "an object in motion [that] remains in motion." Directing your life toward fulfilling dreams motivates you to achieve continual success.

■ Productivity—Goal setting gives us a way to measure our success. Systematically setting goals provides balance and perspective to our decisions about how to allocate our time and resources. Having a clear plan of action greatly focuses the expenditure of time, money, and energy. Goal setting boosts performance to a higher level and helps in overcoming challenges. Up to a point, performance also increases with the level of goal difficulty, provided the individual working to attain the goal is committed to achieving it.[2]

Key Behaviors for Effective Goal Setting

The approach you choose to set goals greatly affects your ability to be successful in attaining your goals. A few fundamental behaviors underpin most successful goal-setting efforts:

■ Being Realistic—be honest with yourself about your skills and abilities and in evaluating all related conditions needed to attain your goals. You can only influence or change things over which you have control. Understand that there will be setbacks. Continually search for means to overcome obstacles and secure all necessary resources.

■ Being Positive—we face obstacles and challenges in everything we do. The ability to maintain in the face of adversity is a key success factor in goal setting. Adopting an optimistic "can-do" attitude can give you the boost to continue the uphill climb. It is also helpful to describe goals in a positive tone; focus on achieving a positive rather than trying to eliminate a negative. For example, say, "I want to master this new version of a software program" rather than saying, "I need to improve my miserable computer skills."

■ Starting Small—begin with smaller, simpler, more manageable goals. Successfully completing small goals will build confidence and create momentum towards future goal-setting behavior. Setting incremental benchmarks for marking your progress will make broader, long-term goals seem attainable.

■ Taking Full Responsibility—even though you may need to solicit the help and support of others, you are in control of your actions. Set your goals with the understanding that you have the power to direct your energy towards personal productivity.

■ Persevering—effective goal completion requires the ability to maintain strong forward motion. Perseverance is essential for successfully reaching every goal you want to achieve.

"Success is not measured by those who fought and never fell, but by those who fought, fell and rose again."

(Anonymous)

Clarifying Values

To determine what goals you want to achieve, start by clarifying your own **values,** those things in life that are the most meaningful to you right now. Identifying your values will help you answer the question "What do I want to achieve with my life?" Once you determine your values and why they are important to you, you can then work on a plan for achieving your goals. For example, Marsha, in our case study, might write down some of the things that are important to her. These might include continued learning, spending time with family and friends, and being secure financially. This might explain why going to graduate school has not been her uppermost priority. She might be concerned about having to borrow money to pay the tuition, or about the time it would cause her to spend away from friends and family.

According to Milton Rokeach, a *value* is "an enduring belief that a specific mode of conduct or end-state of existence is personally or socially preferable to an opposite or converse mode of conduct or end-state of existence."[3] In other words, we work toward what we value—and our values guide our behavior. Rokeach identifies two general types of values contained in an individual's belief system: instrumental values and terminal values.[4]

- **Instrumental values** are the how's of goal setting—the standards of behavior by which we achieve desired ends. Courage, honesty, compassion, and loving are examples of instrumental values.
- **Terminal values** are the what's—the end states or goals that we would like to achieve during our lifetime. Such values include wisdom, salvation, prosperity, or sense of accomplishment.

Personal values are also tangible and intangible.

- **Tangible values** are things that you can see, feel, or hold, including the kind of car you want to drive, the level of income you want to have, the size of the house you want to own. Tangible values consist of the material things you want to possess.
- **Intangible values** deal with concepts rather than things. Freedom, independence, happiness, friendship, and love are intangible values and can be defined differently for each person. Intangible values consist of ideals you wish to strive toward or pursue.

Take a minute and write your definition of personal satisfaction. What are the behaviors you'll use to achieve this satisfaction? What will bring you enjoyment or fulfillment? Is this short term or long term? Which values are terminal, the things you must have accomplished? Which aspects of satisfaction are derived from your instrumental values? What aspects are tangible or intangible?

Now write your definition of success. What will you need to accomplish or attain in order to say you are a success in your life? Set these definitions aside for later reflection.

Writing Effective Goals

Developing personal goals begins with creating written goal statements. Written goal statements are the aims or the targets you want to achieve. These goal statements deal with various aspects of your life such as career, personal, financial, and so on. Objectives or an action plan should accompany every goal statement. The plan should specify the strategies needed or means for reaching your ends. For instance, our case example Marsha could have as a goal "To achieve the level of vice-president within the next two years." Her action plan could include talking with her boss about potential career options within the firm, taking extra courses at night to develop the technical skills needed to advance, and networking with several alumni from her college who work at the firm who are in senior positions to gain their support and advice.

One system used successfully by managers and others who wish to incorporate goal-setting principles into their lives is the "SMART" system.[5] *SMART* refers to a goal that is specific, measurable, attainable, realistic, and time-bound. By ensuring your goal statements are SMART, you create a system for managing action steps and increase the likelihood that these goals are attained. Use this approach as a checklist for writing your goal statements and action plan.

- **Specific**—write your goals, including as many details as possible, leaving no room for misinterpretation. Rather than writing, "I would like to be in better shape," define what "in better shape" means to you. Say "I want to lose 10 pounds," or "lower my cholesterol by 20 points," or "lower my blood pressure by 15 points." Specific goals are focused and incremental, giving clarity to your direction and purpose.

- **Measurable**—provide a means to measure your progress, a way to measure actual performance against desired performance standards. Set up checkpoints to evaluate your progress from the time you start to the time you expect to attain your goal. Write your goals in quantifiable terms, to determine to what extent you completed each goal and fulfilled each objective. For example, "I will write one essay per week to improve my writing skills."

- **Attainable/Believable**—set an actionable, believable goal. In addition to being fully dedicated, you also need the resources and capabilities required for attaining a goal. Goals that are believable have a much higher probability of success. Make sure you have secured all necessary resources and that you anticipate and develop a strategy for dealing with any obstacles that could bar your success. For example, say "I will raise my G.P.A. from a 2.5 to a 3.0. To do this I will get tested at the Learning Center to see if I have a learning disability."

- **Realistic/Achievable**—write your goals with consideration for your capabilities and limitations. A goal should be challenging enough that you stretch your abilities to gain attainment, but not so difficult that it is impossible to fulfill. Studies show "that given an adequate level of ability and commitment, harder goals will lead to greater effort and performance than easier goals."[6] Goals should also have realistic deadlines. Closely tied to the notion of realistic goals is the aspect of control. Only set goals that are within your means to achieve. Say "I will contact 10 percent more potential clients this week than usual," rather than "I will sell 10 percent more than usual this week." The former statement reflects things that are within your control as well as realistic. The latter reflects a desire about something that may not be totally within your control.

- **Time Bound**—develop a specific deadline for meeting each of your goals; otherwise they will remain dreams and never become reality. Setting a deadline creates a commitment to begin and pursue a goal until it is attained. Saying "I'd like to lose 10 pounds" is specific, measurable, and realistic, but without a target date for completion, you might find yourself continuously repeating "I'll start my diet to-morrow." Time bound also relates to attainable, as some goals may be unattainable within a compressed time frame, yet possible within a longer time frame. In fact, when setting goals that span a longer time horizon, it is best to establish incremental time frames to make long-term timeliness more manageable and acceptable. Plan a schedule or time frame for goal completion that is sufficient to allow you to achieve the goal, at the same time not allowing for so much slack time that you lose interest or focus.

Another important criterion that can be added to **SMART goals** is to make sure the goal is yours. Personal goals are just that, personal. You will be less likely to accept and complete goals that someone else gives you.[7] Goals should be a direct reflection of your values, aspirations, and life mission, not someone else's like your friends', parents' or roommates'. If you are pursuing an accounting degree because a parent believes it's a good solid career, yet you just don't see yourself as an accountant, you may want to reevaluate this goal. You are more likely to stick with and attain goals you desire than goals set for you by others. Likewise, when you are in a position to influence others such as subordinates or children, encourage them but let them set their own goals.

Goal-Setting Strategies   There are several strategic steps you can take to overcome potential pitfalls while ensuring progress towards achieving your goals.

1. *Visualize the outcome*—imagine being at the completion point of your goal. State your goals as if you have already accomplished them. Say things like "I am the owner of a

Cadillac" or "I am the executive vice president of my advertising firm." Positive self-talk will reinforce your belief in your ability to live your dreams.

2. *Strive for performance, not outcomes*—throughout the process, you should strive to give 100 percent effort and to perform to the best of your ability. This will allow you to feel confident and proud of your smaller accomplishments. Barry Goldberg, the prominent TV producer (*Spin City, Family Ties*), says he has always focused on creating the best television program possible, seeking first and foremost to produce high-quality entertainment; money and success resulted as a by-product.

3. *Develop a support network*—determine the resources that will be necessary for you to achieve your goals. Obtain support and commitment from individuals who will be essential in ensuring your success. Associate with people who will support you in attaining your goals. If someone in your network is hindering your ability to accomplish your goals, reevaluate whether continued association with this person is desirable.

4. *Limit the number*—focus on a limited number of goals at a time. Having too many goals will only drain your resources and reduce the potency of your efforts. One way to do this is to focus on those goals that relate to your key roles at a point in time. Another way to do this is to create a master plan—a 10- or 20-year plan—in which you map out the pursuit of specific goals according to your personal and professional mission.

5. *Allow for setbacks*—we are all human. If you get sidetracked or make a mistake while trying to accomplish your goal, forgive yourself and get back to your plan. If you do not move on, you will never accomplish your goals. When experiencing a setback, it may be an appropriate time to tap into your support network. Let's say you are mid-way in achieving your goal to quit smoking over a three-month period when your favorite uncle is diagnosed with a terminal illness. You might find it difficult to cope with this tragedy without returning to your pack-a-day habit. At this point, you might choose to reevaluate and adjust your goal; you might also seek out friends or relatives who can help you get through this crisis.

6. *Be honest with yourself*—evaluate objectively how well you accomplish your goals and objectives. The only way you can improve is to understand what you did wrong and focus on how you can change. Ask yourself, "Why did my last semester go so badly?" or "Why were my grades so low?" You might answer yourself, "Poor study habits, lack of time or discipline, and lack of priorities."

7. *Reward small accomplishments*—once you have reached an incremental, objective step or milestone, provide yourself with a reward.[8] Celebrating your continual accomplishments will help to maintain your optimism and belief in your abilities while refueling your commitment and motivation to goal achievement.

8. *Don't lose sight of the big picture*—make a habit of reviewing your goals on a daily basis. Use positive self-talk to reinforce your beliefs and reiterate the purpose behind your actions. Remain flexible yet diligent. Allow for necessary changes and restructure as needed while still working toward the ultimate end. Understand how everything you do facilitates your ability to complete your goal.

9. *Revisit the process*—goal setting is not a one-time action; it is an ongoing process. Your values, roles, and dreams may change. Your resources may need to be reevaluated or you may need to make adjustments to overcome unforeseen obstacles. Goals should remain fluid, enabling you to plan, react, and adapt to changing circumstances as needed.

Summary

This chapter focused on goal setting: why it's important, how to set goals, and how to achieve goals.

Refer back to your definitions of success and satisfaction. Through the process of writing your goals and action plans, are you now on the right road to securing these values? If not, what changes should you make to get there?

Use your goal-setting skills to enhance and guide your life. Consider incorporating goal setting as a fundamental part of your daily life. Challenge yourself to move to the next dimension. As Walt Disney said, "If you can dream it, you can be it."

Recall the individuals mentioned earlier in the chapter who set goals early in their lives and worked toward them. By using the goal-setting process, you can create a precise map to direct you to any potential destination.

Key Terms and Concepts

Goal setting	Tangible values
Instrumental values	Terminal values
Intangible values	Values
SMART goals	

Endnotes

1. Edwin E. Bobrow, "Goal Oriented Selling," *American Salesman* 41, no. 1 (Jan. 1996), p. 22.

2. Shawn K. Yearta, Sally Maitlis, and Rob B. Briner, "An Exploratory Study of Goal Setting in Theory and Practice," *Journal of Occupational and Organizational Psychology* 68, no. 3 (Sept. 1995), p. 237.

3. Milton Rokeach, *The Nature of Human Values* (New York: Free Press, 1973).

4. Rokeach, 1973.

5. Robyn D. Clarke, "Going for the Goal," *Black Enterprise* 29, issue 6 (Jan. 1999), p. 83.

6. Yearta, 1995.

7. Wendy Warren, "First Step in Finding Success Is Deciding What Route You Want to Take," *Knight-Ridder/Tribune Business News,* Jan. 2, 1996.

8. Susan B. Wilson, "How Good Are You at Setting Goals?" *Executive Female,* July–August, 1994, p. 73.

**Exercise 3–A
Assessing Yourself**

Circle the response that most closely correlates with each item below.

		Agree	Neither	Disagree

1. I have developed a written list of short- and long-term goals I would like to accomplish.   1 2 3 (4) 5

2. When setting goals for myself, I give consideration to what my capabilities and limits are.   1 (2) 3 4 5

3. I set goals that are realistic and attainable.   (1) 2 3 4 5

4. My goals are based on my hopes and beliefs, not on those of my parents, friends, or significant other.   (1) 2 3 4 5

5. When I fail to achieve a goal, I get back on track.   1 2 (3) (4) 5

6. My goals are based on my personal values.   (1) 2 3 4 5

7. I have a current mission statement and have involved those closest to me in formulating it.   1 (2) 3 (4) 5

8. I regularly check my progress toward achieving the goals I have set.   1 (2) (3) 4 5

9. When setting goals I strive for performance, not outcomes.   1 2 (3) (4) 5

10. I have a support system in place—friends, family members, and/or colleagues who believe in me and support my goals.   (1) 2 3 4 5

11. I apply SMART characteristics to my goals.   (1) 2 3 4 5

12. I prioritize my goals, focusing only on the most important or valuable ones at a particular point in time.   1 (2) 3 4 5

13. I reward myself when I achieve a goal, or even when I reach a particular milestone.   (1) 2 (3) 4 5

14. I revisit my goals periodically, and add and modify goals as appropriate.   1 (2) 3 4 5

Sum your circled responses. If your total is 42 or higher, you might want to explore ways to improve your skill in the area of goal setting.   28

**Exercise 3–B
Values Inventory**

1. From the list below, choose five items that are most important to you. Rank the top five items according to your current values. This is only a partial list; fill in the (other) blanks with items that are of personal value to you. Give the most important item a 1, the next most important a 2, and so on.

Values	Current	5 years	10 years	20 years	30 years
Security					
Financial independence		1			
Having children			2		
Owning a home					
Free time			3		
Rec...					
Frien...					
Help... fort...					
Fam...					
Trav...					
Hav...					
Play...					
Hav... job...					
Hav...					
Bei... informed person					
Having a sense of accomplishment	3	4	4		
Spiritual fulfillment					
Doing well in school	2				
(other)					
(other)					

(handwritten note, partially covering table)
3) They fit quite well
4) Death in family ⇒ how important family is

UNIVERSITY OF
DENVER
1864
Residence Hall Association
Take the plunge!

http://dor.du.edu/rha • rha@dor.du.edu • (303) 871-7455

2. From the same list, indicate in the columns which values would comprise your top five ranking in 5 years, 10 years, 20 years, 30 years. Look back over your rankings. Does anything surprise you? Were there any drastic changes from the present through 30 years?

3. In examining your current values, how do these fit in with the way in which you currently allocate your time? Do these values fit in with your dreams, goals, ambitions, and life principles?

4. What major, unanticipated event could cause you to modify your rankings (serious illness, business failure, marriage, etc.)? Discuss how this event would impact your rankings.

**Exercise 3–C
"This Is Your Life"—A
Personal Goal-Setting
Exercise**

(thought)

Fast-forward your life video and contemplate a celebration dinner (roast) to honor you. Imagine it is years into the future and we are celebrating your accomplishments at a retirement dinner. Assume that each of the following will deliver a speech: family member, close friend, business or professional associate, community or religious representative.

How would you prefer to have these people think about, see, and perceive you and your actions? Identify the main points each would make in your honor. What would you ideally like to have said concerning your accomplishments, relationships with others, contributions to society, and so on?

Family Member's Speech

- Always there (family first)
- Would give up anything
- Very giving

Close Friend's Speech

- Dependable
- Fun
- Giving

Business or Professional Associate's Speech

- Hard worker
- Tenacious + determined
- Successful

Community or Religious Representative's Speech

- Role model
- Gives back
- Great values

From reviewing the speeches, is there a common thread or theme? Write a phrase or caption that would summarize your life principle.

- Very giving + selfless
- Successful in all aspects of life
- Always there to help.

Source: Adapted from Stephen Covey, *Seven Habits of Highly Successful People.*

Exercise 3–D
Your Personal Mission
Statement

1. Use the space below to write your personal mission. Your mission statement reflects your personal constitution, set of beliefs, and value system. In it, you should address such questions as:

   1. What is my purpose? What do I believe?
   2. What do I value?
   3. What do I treasure?
   4. What is really important to me?
   5. How do I want to approach living my life?
   6. How do I want to approach life on a daily basis?

2. Answer these questions by first reviewing the speeches from Exercise 3–C to ensure a multifaceted mission statement. You might also organize your mission statement using the roles from Exercise 3–E. Use the space below to record insights and understandings that you have about yourself and your life plan.

My purpose in life is to be successful in all aspects of life, including family, friends, career, and community. The most important thing to me is family, so family always comes first. A successful career is also very important. I want to be financially stable to support a wife and kids and not have money be an issue.

Clarifying your mission is an ongoing process. Revisit and update you mission periodically.

Exercise 3–E
Your Key Roles and Goals

1. Identify the key roles you play in your life. Examples are friend, son or daughter, student, significant other, spouse or partner, employee, athlete, student, resident assistant, or community leader. Think of them in terms of your mission statement. As you identify your key roles, ask yourself the following questions:

1) Are my roles in harmony with my mission statement? Why or why not?

2) What can I do to make my roles and mission more congruent?

2. Be specific. Describing roles as work, personal, or community is too general. List several roles. Your roles help you to determine the goals you want to achieve.

3. Brainstorm specific goals related to each role. Using the grid below, write out your goal statements, ensuring they are SMART.

Key Role:	Goal/s to Be Achieved:	By When:	Resources Needed (from Whom, Where):	Potential Barriers Likely to Face:	Plan to Overcome or Adjust to Barriers:
(example:) Student	-Line up summer internship	-By Jan. 15	-Contact names from Career Center	-Lack of time due to school activities	-Set aside two hours each week to contact employers

**Exercise 3–F
Personal Goal Setting**

1. In the space below, brainstorm your goals in the following categories. Write down as many as you wish, including goals that are short-, mid-, and long-term.

Academic, intellectual

Health, fitness

Social: family, friends, significant other, community

Career, job

Financial

Other

2. Of the goals you have listed, select from each of the six categories the two most important goals that you would like to pursue in the short term (next 6–12 months). Write these below.

1. _____

2. _____

3. _____

4. _____

5. _____

6. _____

7. _____

8. _____

9. _____

10. _____

11. _____

12. _____

3. From the twelve goals listed above, choose the three that are the most important to you at this time, the three you commit to work on in the next few months. Write a goal statement for each one, using the following guidelines:

- Begin each with the word "To . . ."
- Be specific.
- Quantify the goal if possible.
- Each goal statement should be realistic, attainable, and within your control.
- Each goal statement should reflect your aspirations—not those of others such as parents, roommates, significant others, and the like.

1. _____

_____

2. _____

_____

3. _____

_____

4. On a separate sheet of paper, develop an action plan for each goal statement. For each action plan:

- List the steps you will take to accomplish the goal.
- Include dates (by when) and initials (who's responsible) for each step.
- Visualize completing the goal and, working backwards, specify each step necessary between now and then to reach the goal.
- Identify any potential barriers you might experience in attaining the goal. Problem-solve around these obstacles and convert them into steps in your action plan.
- Identify the resources you will need to accomplish these goals, and build in steps to acquire the necessary information into your action plan.

5. Transfer the dates of each step for each goal in your action plan to a daily calendar.

6. Keep an ongoing daily or weekly record of the positive steps you take toward meeting each goal.

Exercise 3–G
Try This . . .

1. Watch a current TV show and answer the following questions:
   - What are some of the positive goal-setting behaviors exhibited by a primary character in the show? Describe these behaviors and the outcome achieved in the show.
   - Is there a character who offers a negative role model with respect to goal setting? Describe this person's behaviors related to goal setting (or lack thereof) and the outcomes.

2. View a movie in which achievement or goal setting is a theme, such as *Tucker, Braveheart, Don Quixote, Moby Dick, The Bridge on the River Kwai, October Sky, Mr. Holland's Opus, For the Love of the Game, Hoosiers, Remember the Titans, Top Gun, Armageddon, Saving Private Ryan, E.T., Casablanca*, and answer the following questions:
   - Describe the main character's mission, its impact on that person's behaviors, and how he or she dealt with setbacks.
   - Identify elements of the character's behavior that you would like to apply to your own life. What would this look like?

**Exercise 3–H
Reflection/Action Plan**

This chapter focused on goal setting—what it is, why it's important, and how to acquire and increase the degree to which you possess it. We also discussed the importance of values and tying goals in with your key priorities. Complete the worksheet below upon reading and finishing the experiential activities for this chapter.

1. The one or two areas in which I am most strong are:

_____

_____

_____

_____

2. The one or two areas in which I need more improvement are:

_____

_____

_____

_____

3. If I did only one thing to improve in this area, it would be to:

_____

_____

_____

_____

4. Making this change would probably result in:

_____

_____

_____

_____

5. If I did not change or improve in this area, it would probably affect my personal and professional life in the following ways:

_____

_____

_____

_____

4

Time and Stress Management

How do I:

✓ Manage myself so that I can achieve more and feel better?

✓ Make better use of my time, that is, work smarter and not harder?

✓ Identify stressors in my life and find ways to reduce or change my response to them?

✓ Recognize and overcome barriers to self-improvement?

Janet Smythe is a sophomore in college. She is a good student, has made several close friends, and enjoys being in school. Janet has been called in to the office by one of her instructors. "Janet," the instructor began, "I am concerned about your performance in class. When you're in class you seem interested and alert, yet you've turned in every assignment late. Is there a problem I should be aware of?"

Yes, Janet wanted to say, but didn't. She thought to herself . . . the real story is I'm having serious personal problems and they are affecting my concentration. I've just learned my mother is very ill. She will need a lot of support from the family as she pursues cancer treatment in the coming months. I'm the youngest child in my family. With all my siblings away from home, I'm trying to fill in by going home on weekends to help. I'm exhausted from the weekly trips back and forth and too preoccupied during the week to concentrate on my assignments.

That's what she should have said. Instead, Janet said, "No, not really. I'm just having a little difficulty remembering my assignments. I'll try to do better."

1. Do you agree with the approach Janet chose to use with her instructor?

2. Why do you think Janet didn't share what was on her mind?

3. What are some strategies Janet could use to better manage the serious situation in which she finds herself?

4. If you were Janet how would you handle the situation?

"You must be in your own corner!"

Zig Ziglar (Motivator/Author)

As many of us have heard before, if you don't take care of yourself, who will? In this chapter we explore the concepts of stress and time management, what they are, why they're important, how time and stress can be managed. We also discuss how to overcome barriers to interpersonal effectiveness so that you can devote your full energies to doing what it takes to succeed and to be happy in life as well as in business.

What Are Time and Stress Management and Why Are They Important?

What distinguishes top performers from those who are just moderately successful? Naturally our genetic history, family background, education, and work history affect the opportunities that are available to us and our ability to seek and choose among these opportunities. And to be honest, plain luck, "being in the right place at the right time," is a factor in one's success. More and more, however, we are realizing that our ability to manage and allocate time and to handle our response to stress, have a lot to do with the extent to which we ultimately succeed, in life as well as in business.

Time Management

Time management is the ability to allocate our time and resources to accomplishing our objectives. Skill in managing how we spend our time allows us to prioritize and accomplish more goals in life, resulting in a sense of well-being because we are able to see the fruits of our labors. It gives us a chance to achieve a balance between work and personal life that can be more satisfying, as opposed to restricting our activities to one arena at the expense of the other. Effective managers find that time management increases productivity. The popular saying, "work smarter, not harder" applies here. By focusing our energy on well-chosen activities, we can actually see our results. This in itself can be motivating, which can then increase our drive to achieve even more.

Managing our time also reduces stress levels. Taking control of our time means taking of our life. This results in a feeling that we are in charge. "I exercised today, and now I can go back and study for the exam with a clear head" is an example of this, which is better than thinking subconsciously "I have no time, I have no life. I didn't exercise and now I don't even have the energy to study for this exam." Time management gives us more time to enjoy the activities that are important to us, such as spending time with family, socializing, reading, and favorite hobbies. This means we are better able to enjoy a varied, textured life. As human beings, we have many dimensions. We are not meant to simply work. Most of us have the need to be many things—a friend, a partner, a family member, part of a community. As we incorporate many elements of life into one, each of those elements is enhanced by our involvement in the others.[1]

Stress Management

Stress management is the ability to manage our response to situations that occur in our lives. Stress is a fact of personal and organizational life. Stress, when not understood or managed, can result in a variety of responses, including physiological, psychological, and organizational. A **physiological** response is one in which physical problems develop as a result of mental anguish.[2] Heart disease, high blood pressure, bulimia, anorexia nervosa, migraine headaches, cancer, gastrointestinal disorders, asthma, diabetes, allergies, skin disorders, cholesterol, and weakened body defenses are some examples of physical conditions that are often brought on by mental stress.[3] According to Crampton et al., physiological disorders have been recognized as one of the 10 leading work-related diseases in the country today by the National Institute of Occupational Safety and Health (NIOSH). **Psychological** effects are not always as readily identifiable as physiological responses.[4] Depression, sudden bursts of violence or anger, anxiety, chemical dependency, alcohol abuse, and phobias are examples of psychological reactions to stressful situations.

Organizational stress effects include job dissatisfaction, absenteeism, turnover, accidents, low morale, poor interpersonal relations, low productivity, and poor customer service. Stress caused by organizational problems is often difficult to manage, as the factors causing the stress are rarely under our control. Some jobs are highly stressful by design—air traffic controllers, dentists, and coal miners are extreme examples. Even businesses that are not commonly viewed as stressful are now prone to high stress levels, especially after so many businesses experienced drastic downsizing of staff in the early 1990s. In addition, employees are working more hours now than they were in the 1960s. The average worker now sends and receives about 190 messages per day (voice mail, e-mail, fax, etc.) and is interrupted an average of six times per hour, according to a study sponsored by Pitney Bowes.[5] These trends, coupled with the desire of many employees, male and female, to lead more balanced lives and spend time with their families and friends, are resulting in an increase in organizational-induced stress.[6]

These sources of stress can be problematic in personal life and in business. Stress is inevitable, but we can manage how we respond to stress. Managing stress is an important skill for both managers and their employees. Those managers who are able to understand their stressors and manage them—and who can help their employees do the same—will be more productive and successful than those who aren't.

Why Is Management of Our Time and Our Response to Stress Important?

Radical and lightning-quick changes are a permanent feature in today's contemporary business environment. Those managers who are able to stay current with these changes and adopt appropriate response strategies to these changes are more likely to succeed—and to help their employees succeed as well. Some of these response strategies—and the reasons why they are important—are described below.

Strategies for Time and Stress Management

Time Management Strategies

There are times in our lives when time doesn't seem to exist, or when it feels like we have no time to think or breathe. This is fine if it happens only periodically. But if you're constantly running from one high-priority task to another, it's likely you'll soon be either suffering from burnout (where you're too fatigued to have an interest in the things on which you're spending time) or doing everything only marginally. It's time to cut back. It's better to do fewer things with quality than many things poorly.

Time management is an important personal and managerial skill. It is a process of setting or taking on objectives, estimating the time and resources needed to accomplish each objective, and disciplining yourself to stay focused on the objective while completing it. It doesn't mean filling every minute. It means allowing for some "slack" time for the unexpected: those unforeseen circumstances that are inevitable.

It is an irony that we can't actually "manage" time. We can't change the amount of time we have. There are only 24 hours in a day, 168 in a week. We manage ourselves in order to be more efficient with our time. We can concentrate on the choices we make and be aware of what's motivating us to make the choices we make. We can focus on getting things done by being productive—getting the right things done . . . on time, on budget, and through the use of all your resources.

How to Manage Your Time   Use the chart below to evaluate your current usage of time, identifying your patterns of behavior and your current time wasters.

Figure 4–1

Typical Time Wasters	Degree to Which I Do These:				
	High		Medium		Low
Procrastination	1	2	3	4	5
Disorganization	1	2	3	4	5
Perfectionism	1	2	3	4	5
Visitors and interruptions	1	2	3	4	5
Telephone, voice-mail, e-mail, Internet	1	2	3	4	5
Daydreaming and distractions	1	2	3	4	5
Lack of focus or interest	1	2	3	4	5
Doing too many tasks at once	1	2	3	4	5
Accepting too much work	1	2	3	4	5
Paperwork and administrative tasks	1	2	3	4	5
Poorly planned meetings	1	2	3	4	5
Lack of necessary resources	1	2	3	4	5
Failure to use technology	1	2	3	4	5

If you scored less than 40, you may want to consider ways to reduce your wasted time. To do this, identify what is of value to you by determining what you consider to be important ways to spend your time. By referring to the personal and professional goals you established, you should be able to decide how to spend your time.

Other tips for time management include the need to:

■ Plan and prioritize.

"Failing to plan is planning to fail"

Benjamin Franklin

Planning is essential to effective time management.[7] The 10 or 15 minutes you spend organizing your schedule can save you hours of time during your week.[8]

■ Get in the habit of preparing "to do" lists. Make a list of everything you need to do for that day and prioritize the list according to the importance of completing each task. Bear in mind that most people will not complete every item on "to-do" lists; however you will accomplish more with a list than without one.

■ Follow the "80/20" rule. It is speculated that 80 percent of results are achieved from 20 percent of focused time. This includes spending more time doing useful activities, tracking what makes that 20 percent so productive, and making the transition of devoting more time to productive work.[9]

■ Plan for your time-specific activities and non–time-specific activities. For "time-specific" activities, determine in advance how close to completing the task you want to be by a certain time. This requires self-discipline and allows you to budget your time and accomplish more than you would in a non–time-bound scenario. Also plan your down time. Everyone needs a break to rest and recharge. Oddly enough, you can actually get more work done if you take several short breaks than if you don't.

■ Find your optimal working time. This is referred to as your biological "prime time"—and plan to maximize use of this time by scheduling and doing demanding jobs during these peak periods and less demanding tasks at other times.

■ Prioritize tasks by level of importance: vital, important, should be done today, or can be done tomorrow. For complex tasks or projects, break them down into manageable steps and set up a time line for completing each step.

■ Organize. Choose or set up the right environment for the task. This may require you to clear away unnecessary materials, reduce distractions (turn off phone or close door), and eliminate environmental interference (heavy traffic or neighbor's music). If all else fails, go to a place, such as a library, where you can work without distractions.

■ Delegate. Determine what tasks and activities would be possible to allocate to others. Clearly specify the task and the expected outcomes to ensure they will complete the task without requiring periodic coaching or redoing.

■ Differentiate between what's urgent and what's important. Most of us *expend* time on what's urgent—those unplanned events that are often thrust on us by others and beg for your immediate attention. Yet not enough of us *invest* time on what's important—those priorities that are meaningful and to which you are committed to spending time. The figure below illustrates the intersection between task and event importance and urgency. Be careful in deciding here. The interruption from one of your children or a roommate—a quadrant two activity—might be an investment if you are committed to spending time with your family and friends. The frequent interruption by a co-worker who likes to chat—also a quadrant two activity—is probably an expenditure. Responding to that person every time they come in unannounced takes time from the priority on which you're working and sends the message that it's okay for them to continue doing so. Often when something comes up that was unplanned it takes away from what is important.[10] The more time spent on important but not urgent activities (quadrant three), the better you will be able to manage your time. If you devote time to the important, the urgent will often take care for itself. Learn to focus on the important and manage your ability to keep to the deadlines you have set; this will prevent the important from becoming urgent.

■ Avoid postponing. Procrastination is one of the biggest time wasters. Unfortunately many times we "put off until tomorrow what we could be doing today." While some people enjoy the adrenaline rush this produces (e.g., waiting until the last minute to write a paper and having to stay up all night to get it done), rarely will you produce

**Figure 4–2
Time Management Matrix[11]**

Quadrant 1	Quadrant 2
IMPORTANT AND URGENT	NOT IMPORTANT BUT URGENT
• Most problem-solving activities • Meeting immediate deadlines • Writing a report due in one hour • Exercise	• Answering the telephone • Checking e-mail • Dealing with interruptions, such as requests for info or help
Quadrant 3	**Quadrant 4**
IMPORTANT BUT NOT URGENT	NOT IMPORTANT AND NOT URGENT
• Reading a book related to your current priorities • Preparing for an upcoming event • Spending quality time with friends and family	• Worrying or being angry • Watching TV beyond time needed to unwind • Surfing the Internet for no reason

your best work operating this way. By waiting until the last minute, many procrastinators find they have been unrealistic about the time required to do the job right. For example, when writing a paper at the last minute, you're likely to have difficulty finding resource materials that are necessary to do a quality job.

Waiting until the last minute also leaves little or no time to review your work, polish it, and ensure it's accurate and of sufficient quality. It's far better to plan ahead, leaving yourself some time toward the end of a project to take care of details that couldn't have been anticipated. Another negative consequence of procrastination is alienation of co-workers. For example, you might be known by your co-workers as one who always waits until the last minute. This not only causes stress for you but also for your co-workers, many of whom might wish they would not have to work with you again. Avoid this by planning and being realistic about what you can and want to achieve.

Commit to evaluating periodically how you use your time. Do time audits—reexamine your goals and whether you allocate time appropriately to achieve them. To keep your schedule organized, reasonable, and attainable, incorporate tasks that are important to you. A balance between discipline and flexibility is key. Stay focused on your overall priorities (remember the 80/20 rule), while continually monitoring your progress and revising your plans as necessary.

Stress Management Strategies

Stress is an upset in the body's balance, in reaction to an adverse or disturbing event. Hans Selye, a pioneer in stress research, defines stress as "the non-specific response of the body to any demand made upon it."[12] Stress comes about not from an event, such as failing an exam or winning the lottery, but from how we respond to it. Stress is found everywhere, in all aspects of life. It is inevitable and unavoidable. The sources of stress vary from person to person. Stress can be derived from external factors such as traffic jams or an ineffective or inefficient work environment. Stress also stems from internal factors such as our emotional state, our perspective on life, or the way we choose to respond to various situations or demands.

Types of Stress

There are two types of stress: "good" and "bad." Good stress, or **eustress,** is positive and presents opportunity for personal growth or satisfaction and pushes people to higher performance. Bad stress, or **distress,** is negative and results in debilitating effects.[13] Surprisingly, too little stress can be as detrimental as too much stress. As the figure below demonstrates, when we lack any stress or pressure to perform, we may utilize minimal effort and achieve suboptimal performance. Conversely, too much stress might make it difficult to concentrate or perform effectively or efficiently. Whether a particular stress factor we are experiencing is "good" or "bad" depends largely on how we perceive the stressor and respond to it. In other words a situation can be termed "stressful" or not—depending on how we choose to look at and handle it.

Figure 4–3
Performance/Stress Graph

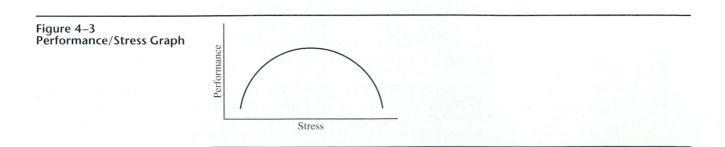

Responses to Stress

Not all individuals respond in the same way to the same stressor.[14] Everyone has a unique level of tolerance. One person might be elated upon being promoted, while another might be traumatized at the prospect of being promoted. We might find it impossible to work while children play noisily in the street, while our neighbor finds his concentration is actually improved by this external noise.

A variety of remedies or techniques is available for different types of stress. Psychological problems are much better understood today than in the recent past. Various drugs and other therapies are available for treating a wide variety of problems. Psychological problems are best dealt with by consulting a professional such as a counselor or therapist. These professionals can help individuals suffering psychological effects of stress by helping them to understand these situations and manage their response to them more effectively.

Because of the likely connection between emotional or mental concerns and physical ailments, physiological problems are best dealt with through consultation with both a health professional and a mental health professional or wellness counselor. Typically an individual experiencing physiological stress will be given a test battery to diagnose the sources of the stress and potential solutions to the problems being experienced. A treatment program will be varied and might include regular exercise, better nutrition, relaxation techniques and, in some cases, prescription drugs as appropriate.

Organizational problems are complex. If you are suffering from job-related stress it is important to evaluate your work style, your level of job satisfaction, the fit between you, your boss, your co-workers and your organization. Those who feel the least (bad) stress are those who are in a work environment in which they can thrive, rather than one in which they are drained. Talking with your boss or co-workers about your concerns can help. But if change is not forthcoming, leaving the organization for one better suited to your personality is a good option.

How to Manage Stress

There are a number of coping strategies that can be used to cope with stress. We'll never eradicate stress, but we can make choices about how we handle it.[15] Several suggestions follow; you'll be able to provide others from your own experience.

- Identify your stressors and stress levels. A **stressor** is a situation, activity, or person that causes you to feel stressed, out of control, or frazzled. **Stress levels** refer to the degree to which you let the source of the stress affect you. It is crucial to understand exactly what your stressors are, in other words, what your "hot buttons" are. What causes you to tense up, feel aggravated, be angry or resentful? What causes you to get a headache or your blood pressure to rise? What causes you to think no one understands you or that there's no way out of a problem you're facing? It's also important to understand your own unique stress levels. How stressed do you get? What causes a severe versus just a regular headache? We cannot manage stress unless we know what causes stress, and how those causes are impacting us psychologically, physiologically, and organizationally. Look at the chart (Figure 4–4) and see if any of these signs of stress look familiar to you. Understanding your stressors—and being able to recognize them *before* they occur—is an essential skill in stress management. Understanding your stress levels—the degree to which you react to certain stressors—can help you to manage your response to stress effectively.

- Implement time management skills. For some, feeling a lack of control over a situation causes stress. When this occurs, try to exert some influence over those aspects of a situation that are within your control. Making a change in your environment that reduces the impact of the offending stressor can often do this. For example, if you are feeling overwhelmed by a term paper assignment, you could find a quieter place in which to work, organize your work space by using files or piles for the various sections of the paper, or play soft music. These changes can be helpful in reducing stress levels.

**Figure 4–4
Signs of Stress**

Physical Signs	Emotional Signs	Mental Signs	Relational Signs	Spiritual Signs	Behavioral Signs
Appetite changes	Bad temper	Lacking humor	Isolation	A feeling of emptiness	Pacing
Headaches	Anxiety	Dull senses	Defensive	Apathy	Swearing
Fatigue	Nightmares	Lethargy	Intolerance	Inability to forgive	Substance abuse
Insomnia	Irritability	Boredom	Resentment	Cynicism	Nail biting
Indigestion	Depression	Indecisiveness	Loneliness	Loss of direction	Slumped posture
Colds	Frustration	Forgetfulness	Nagging	Doubt	Restlessness
Weight change	Oversensitivity	Poor concentration	Lower sex drive	Need to prove self	Risk aversion
Teeth grinding	Mood swings	Personality changes	Aggression	Negative outlook	Eating disorders
Tension	Fearfulness	Stuck in past	Abuse	Gloom	Headaches

■ Sharing and disclosure. Being open about your thoughts and feelings—with yourself and with others—is a surprisingly effective technique for reducing stress levels. Sometimes just being able to talk out loud about a situation and how it's affecting you can help you to process aspects of the situation in such a way that you develop a new attitude about or outlook on it. This changed understanding can result in a more positive perspective on the situation. For example, receiving a bad grade on a paper can be viewed negatively—as a disappointment, or positively—as a chance to get some useful feedback from the instructor that could improve your writing in the future.

■ Keep a journal. Journal writing involves setting aside some time on a regular basis to reflect on what's happening in your life. By writing your thoughts and feelings about and reactions to certain events and people, you can air your emotions about something of significance to you, enabling you to acquire a new perspective on the situation.

■ Talking to a trusted friend, relative, co-worker, or professional helper such as a resident advisor, counselor, physician, or minister can be enormously helpful in reducing stress levels. We all get extremely upset at times, making it difficult for us to see things objectively. An empathetic set of ears can help us to view things differently and adopt a perspective we might not have imagined on our own.

■ Visualization and mental imagery are becoming increasingly popular techniques for reducing stress. "See yourself making the perfect putt on the green." "Picture where you want to be in five years." "See yourself finishing school and driving a new car." These are all examples of visualization and mental imagery—imagining yourself in a situation, playing out how you ideally see yourself behaving and looking, creating a mental picture of yourself and how you'll feel by achieving a goal you've set. The theory behind visualization is "success breeds success." By thinking positively we can at times will ourselves to act and behave in a way that gets us where we want to be.

■ Many people who are committed to reducing stress in their lives find that relaxation techniques can have a marked effect on stress levels. Some of these include:

■ Taking one or more slow, deep breaths. Often when we're becoming stressed we begin to take shallower breaths without even being aware of this. This causes us to be short of breath and to have difficulty concentrating. By taking a "time-out" and taking a few deep breaths, we automatically calm the body and the mind and are able to concentrate on the matter at hand. Try this technique before a presentation or during an emotional conversation.

(continued)

- Practicing yoga or meditation. Yoga is a form of gentle exercise that positively influences the mind–body connection through the use of deep breathing, stretching, and slow but firm movements in a calm atmosphere. Meditation involves setting aside time on a regular basis to clear the mind of details and focus on being alert and calm. Usually meditation involves learning to concentrate on one image or sound, subduing other images and sounds. Practicing meditation for a few minutes each day can help reduce psychological and physical stress levels.[16] Health professionals and even some insurance companies have endorsed both yoga and meditation as proven methods for reducing stress.

- Progressive muscle relaxation (PMR) and guided imagery. In PMR, you isolate various parts or muscle groups in your body, and then tense and relax these muscles several times before moving to the next muscle group. Typically, the pattern begins at one end of the body and concludes at the other. Guided imagery involves engaging our ability to recall a special place or memory (or imagining a fantasy place, such as floating in a cloud) and invite the same positive feelings or sensations to return. Both of these techniques can be done alone or with the use of an in-person or recorded facilitator or guide who can help you focus your thoughts on your body or your imagination in a powerful, stress-reducing way.

- Another important means for reducing stress is to eat healthily and exercise regularly.[17] Most scientists and nutritionists agree that proper nutrition and eating habits play a big role in keeping our systems fit. Two tips to consider include:

  - Try to avoid or restrict consumption of alcohol and caffeine, both of which deplete the system rather than replenish it. Most nutritionists who treat clients for a variety of stress-related ailments share this advice. One wonders why we care enough about our unborn children to instruct pregnant women to avoid alcohol and caffeine, yet once we are old enough to know better, we ignore this advice!

  - Eat for energy throughout the day, rather than simply eating for the sake of eating; this can also help you cope with stress. Comfort eating involves eating foods that bring immediate pleasant sensations yet yield little value long term. Comfort eating is hard to avoid since many of us find the process so, well, comforting! Unfortunately, comfort eating usually results in indulging in unhealthy foods and in undesirable quantities. Eating for energy is an entirely different mindset. It involves asking yourself throughout the day—how am I doing right now (physically, mentally, and emotionally), and what foods would be helpful? Which foods will help sustain me, and even help me thrive, versus which ones will drain me or fatigue me? An example is the midafternoon slump many of us face. Our first choice might be to eat a candy bar, although it would be better to eat a piece of fruit. Not only does fruit supply more energy over a longer period of time, it also adds valuable nutrients and fiber to the system.

  - Create time for relaxation. This might seem impossible to the overworked student, the multitasking investment banker, the harried new parent, or the care giver of an aging parent or ill significant other. Taking at least some time out for you each day, away from the demands of others and the environment, can be rejuvenating and stimulating.

Overcoming Fear of Failure

No discussion of time and stress management is complete without mentioning a common obstacle to our being effective: fear of failure. Knowing the right course of action to take isn't always enough. Sometimes we run into obstacles. These obstacles shouldn't stop us. They can be addressed and, in most cases, overcome.

Figure 4–5

Hints for Overcoming Fear of Failure[18]

Look at failure as an event, not a reflection on you personally.

Remind yourself that everyone experiences failure.

Look for the "why" and find a solution.

Ask yourself what you learned.

Associate with positive people and abolish fear and failure statements.

Create a new environment.

Access new information; let adversity become advantage.

Create a new perspective or mindset—develop new "self-talk"—for instance, background thoughts.

Take one step at a time; keep moving forward.

One of the most common barriers to interpersonal effectiveness is fear of failure. **Fear** is an "emotion that occurs either as a response to external stimuli or as a result of an internal process that incorporates memory or introspections."[19] Fear can be good or bad. It can have negative or positive effects on people. **Good fear** maintains our alertness and vigilance. Based on knowledge, reason, and instincts, good fear keeps you from danger or harmful situations. Sometimes good fear can actually "adrenalize" you. For example, in public speaking, a little nervousness is actually good—it can enhance your vitality and enthusiasm. **Bad fear** holds you back instead of propelling you forward. It keeps you from applying your full energies to a situation. Some of the reasons for this are concern about rejection, making mistakes, taking risks, and failure. Negative fear stifles learning and interferes with decision making; it also prevents you from being yourself and discovering new talents and interests.

Don't let bad fear stifle creativity or self-expression. Giving in to fear can paralyze you, rendering you passive or unable to act. This can keep you from growing, developing, and ultimately succeeding. At its worst, bad fear can hinder your ability to take chances and be open to new experiences, threaten your existing relationships, and prevent new ones from developing. At its best, good fear can bring out new dimensions of your abilities and personality.

Summary

Management consultant and author Roy Zenger tells us that the only person who likes change is a wet baby. We can accept and even embrace change. By learning to adapt we can remain vibrant. With practice, managing our time and stress can become as much of a habit as brushing teeth or stopping at a red light. By doing so we are more likely to achieve success and satisfaction—in life as well as in business.

Key Terms and Concepts

Bad fear

Distress

Eustress

Fear

Good fear

Organizational stress

Physiological stress

Psychological stress

Stress

Stress levels

Stress management

Stressor

Time management

Endnotes

1. Grace K. Baruch and Rosalind C. Barnett, "Role Quality, Multiple Role Involvement and Psychological Well Being in Mid-life Women," *Journal of Personality and Social Psychology* 3 (1986), pp. 578–585.

2. Suzanne M. Crampton, John W. Hodge, Jitendra M. Mishra, and Steve Price, "Stress and Stress Management," *SAM Advanced Management Journal* 60, no. 3 (Summer 1995), p. 10.

3. Christine K. Nowroozi, "How Stress May Make You Sick," *Nation's Business* 82, no. 12 (Dec. 1994).

4. Crampton et al., 1995.

5. Kim Bachman, "Feeling Stressed?" *CMA Management* 73, no. 9 (Nov. 1999), p. 14.

6. Ann Wilson Schaef and Diane Fassel, *The Addictive Organization: Why We Overwork, Cover Up, Pick Up the Pieces, Please the Boss and Perpetuate Sick Organizations* (San Francisco, CA: Harper and Row, 1988).

7. Patricia Buhler, "Time Management Is Really Self-management," *Supervision* 57, no. 3 (March 1996), p. 24.

8. Gary Izumo, Joyce Bishop, and Kathleen Cole, *Keys to Workplace Skills: How to Get from Your Senior Year to Your First Promotion* (Upper Saddle River, NJ: Prentice Hall, 1999).

9. Harry Plack, "Managing Time Can Be Crucial," *Baltimore Business Journal* 17, no. 40 (Feb. 18, 2000), p. 27.

10. Jeffrey Gitomer, "Difference between Urgency and Importance," *LI Business News* 46, no. 53 (Dec. 31, 1999), p. 21A.

11. Stephen R. Covey, *The Seven Habits of Highly Effective People* (New York: Simon and Schuster, 1989).

12. R. Kreitner and A. Kinicki, *Organizational Behavior* (Homewood, IL: Irwin, 1992).

13. Patricia M. Buhler, "Managing in the 90's," *Supervision* 60, no. 12 (Dec. 1999), p. 14.

14. Crampton et al., 1995.

15. Buhler, 1999.

16. Herbert Benson, M.D. and Miriam Z. Klipper, *The Relaxation Response* (Wholecare Books, ISBN 0380815958, Feb. 2000).

17. S. Arbetter, "Handling Stress," *Current Health* (Oct. 1992).

18. Jeffrey Gitomer, "Tips to Getting over Biggest Fear: Failure," *The Business Journal* 17, no. 19 (March 24, 2000), p. 41; Victor Parachin, "Eliminating the Fear of Failure . . . How to Fear Less and Hope More," *Supervision* 55, no. 2 (Feb. 1994), p. 7.

19. Mark Rodgers, "No Fear?" *Dealer News* 33, no. 2 (Feb. 1997), p. 74.

Exercise 4–A
Assessing Yourself

Circle the response that most closely correlates with each item below.

Agree Neither Disagree

1. I allocate my time and resources to those objectives that are the most important to me. ① 2 3 4 5

2. I am realistic and open-minded when setting time objectives for myself. ① 2 3 4 5

3. I say "no" to requests that might throw my life out of balance or make it more difficult for me to manage my time. ① 2 3 4 5

4. I do fewer things with quality instead of taking on so much that quality suffers. ① 2 3 4 5

5. I manage my time wisely. 1 ② 3 4 5

6. I allow for "slack"—unscheduled time—in order to have on reserve time that can be used to deal with the unexpected. 1 ② 3 4 5

7. I focus my energy on well-chosen activities. ① 2 3 4 5

8. I leave time in my schedule for regular exercise. ① 2 ③ 4 5

9. I live a balanced life, with time for myself, family, friends, work, helping others, and personal interests. 1 2 ③ 4 5

10. I have identified my "time wasters" and developed plans for reducing or eliminating them. 1 2 3 ④ 5

11. I keep a regular "day planner" and/or daily "to-do" lists. 1 ② 3 4 5

12. When planning projects I budget my time and plan accordingly. 1 2 ③ 4 5

13. I have a quiet, organized place to which I can go to get work done. ① 2 3 4 5

14. I focus 80% of my energies on "important" tasks—those that are meaningful to me, not merely those "urgent" tasks that are thrust on me by others. 1 ② 3 4 5

15. I avoid procrastination, setting goals and determining incremental steps needed to attain them. 1 2 ③ 4 5

16. I limit interruptions when working on a project deadline. 1 ② 3 4 5

17. I am aware of the major stressors in my life and have a plan for reducing or eliminating them or for managing my response to them. 1 2 3 ④ 5

18. I would consult a professional if I had a serious psychological problem such as difficulty controlling anger. 1 2 3 4 ⑤

19. I would consult a professional if I had a serious physiological problem such as bulimia or alcoholism. 1 2 3 4 ⑤

20. I understand my work style and needs and choose to work in organizations with which I am compatible. 1 ② 3 4 5

21. I keep a journal or engage in self-reflection as a way of managing stress. 1 2 3 4 ⑤

22. I regularly disclose my thoughts and feelings to others as a way of managing stress. ① 2 3 4 5

23. I have adapted a specific stress reduction activity such as relaxation, yoga, meditation, visualization, etc. 1 2 3 4 ⑤

24. I consciously choose foods that will add energy to my day rather than deplete my energy. 1 ② 3 4 5

25. I understand my fears and don't let them stop me from pursuing my goals. 1 ② 3 4 5

Sum your circled responses. If your total is 75 or more you might want to explore ways to improve your skill in the area of goal setting.

74 ⑳

**Exercise 4–B
Personal Time
Management**

I. "Where Does the Time Go" Survey

The following survey shows how much time you spend in current activities. When taking the survey, estimate the amount of time spent on each item. Once you have this amount for daily items you will need to multiply them by seven or five. After each item's weekly time has been calculated, add all these for a grand total. Subtract this amount from 168, the total possible hours per week.

1. Number of hours of sleep each night   ____ × 7 = ____
2. Number of hours grooming per day   ____ × 7 = ____
3. Number of hours for meals/snacks (including
   shopping and preparation)   ____ × 7 = ____
4. Number of hours travel each workday   ____ × 5 = ____
5. Number of hours travel time each weekend   = ____
6. Number of hours per week for regularly scheduled
   activities (clubs, church, socializing, etc.)   = ____
7. Number of hours per day for chores, errands, extra
   grooming, and so on.   ____ × 7 = ____
8. Number of hours of work per week   = ____
9. Number of hours in class per week   = ____
10. Number of hours per week socializing, dating.   = ____
11. Add the totals for items 1–10   = ____

Subtract the number from line 11 from 168: 168 − ____ = ____

These are the remaining hours you have each week for extra activities—studying, family, sports, hobbies, TV, relaxation. Surprised? Where does the time go!

Questions

1. How do you believe you spend your remaining hours?
2. How effectively do you believe you spend these hours?
3. What do you believe are your biggest time wasters?
4. In what areas of your life can you "gain" hours?
5. How can you redistribute your hours to have more time available for the things you want to do?

II. Weekly Tracker

Break down your weekly "extra" activities to identify where you actually spend your extra hours. Use the following time chart to track your activity for one week. Fill in all the hours with the activities you perform. Be honest with yourself to get an accurate picture and pattern of where your time is spent.

	Monday	Tuesday	Wednesday	Thursday	Friday	Saturday	Sunday
5 AM							
6 AM							
7 AM							
8 AM							
9 AM							
10 AM							
11 AM							
12 PM							
1 PM							
2 PM							
3 PM							
4 PM							
5 PM							
6 PM							
7 PM							
8 PM							
9 PM							
10 PM							
11 PM							
12 PM							
1 AM							
2 AM							
3 AM							
4 AM							

Questions

1. Is your actual weekly time consistent with the figures you put in your survey?
2. What are your extra time periods and your time wasters?
3. How can you manage your time more effectively?

Adapted from: **http://www.gmu.edu/departments/csdc/time.html**

Exercise 4–C
Daily Action Sheet

Make a list of the things you have to do tomorrow. Use the following priority code to assign a level of importance to each item. Then list the resources needed to accomplish these tasks.

Priority code

A = vital, must do today

B = important, must be done today

C = should be done today

D = can be done tomorrow

E = trivial, not necessary to do

Date: Task:	Priority Ranking
1. Dinner–Dad	B
2. Class	C
3. Hmwk	C
4. Swim	C
5. AKPsi Table	C
6. Service Learning Fair	C
7. Homework	
8. Service	
9. TV	
10.	
11.	
12.	

Questions

1. Were you able to accomplish all that you wanted to on this particular day? *No*

2. Were most of the items you completed in your "most important" category? If not, why not? *Yes*

3. Were you able to move some items from the "must do" list to another day, or even drop them altogether? *Yes*

4. What can you do to maximize the way you spend your time? *Yes*

Exercise 4–D
Life Stress Test

The Holmes and Rahe Schedule of Recent Experiences Survey (with some author modifications)

Instructions:
Place a check mark next to each event you experienced within the past year. Then add the life change units associated with the various events to derive your total life stress score.

Life Event	Life Change Unit
_____ Death of partner	100
_____ Divorce	73
_____ Separation from mate	65
_____ Detention in jail or other institution	63
_____ Death of a close family member	63
_____ Major personal injury or illness	53
_____ Marriage	50
_____ Being fired at work	47
_____ Reconciliation with mate	45
_____ Retirement from work	45
_____ Major change in the health or behavior of a family member	44
_____ Pregnancy	40
_____ Sexual difficulties	39
_____ Gaining a new family member (e.g., through birth, adoption, oldster moving in)	39
_____ Major business readjustment (e.g., merger, reorganization, bankruptcy)	39
_____ Major change in financial state (e.g., a lot worse off or a lot better off than usual)	38
_____ Death of a close friend	37
_____ Change to a different line of work	36
_____ Major change in the number of arguments with partner (e.g., either a lot more or a lot less than usual)	35
_____ Taking out a mortgage or loan for a major purchase (e.g., for a home, business)	31
_____ Foreclosure on a mortgage or loan	30
_____ Major change in responsibilities at work (e.g., promotion, demotion, lateral transfer)	29
_____ Son or daughter leaving home (e.g., marriage, attending college)	29
_____ Trouble with in-laws	29
_____ Outstanding personal achievement	28
_____ Partner beginning or ceasing work outside the home	26
_____ Beginning or ceasing formal schooling	26
_____ Major change in living conditions (e.g., building a new home, remodeling, deterioration of home or neighborhood)	25
_____ Revision of personal habits (dress, manners, association)	24
_____ Troubles with the boss	23
_____ Major change in working hours or conditions	20
_____ Change in residence	20
_____ Changing to a new school	20
_____ Major change in usual type and/or amount of recreation	19
_____ Major change in church, synagogue, or mosque activities (e.g., a lot more or a lot less than usual)	19

Life Event	Life Change Unit
_____ Major change in social activities (e.g., clubs, dancing, movies, visiting)	18
_____ Taking out a mortgage or loan for a lesser purchase (e.g., for a car, TV, freezer)	17
_____ Major change in sleeping habits (a lot more or a lot less sleep, or change in part of day when asleep)	16
_____ Major change in number of family get-togethers (e.g., a lot more or a lot less than usual)	15
_____ Major change in eating habits (a lot more or a lot less food intake, or very different meal hours or surroundings)	15
_____ Vacation	13
_____ Christmas	12
_____ Minor violations of the law (e.g., traffic tickets, jaywalking, disturbing the peace)	11

Total score =

Source: Adapted from T. H. Holmes and R. H. Rahe, *"The Social Readjustment Rating Scale," Journal of Psychosomatic Research,* August 1967, p. 216. Used with permission. Copyright 1967, Pergamon Press.

Exercise 4–E
Relaxation Exercises

I. Progressive Muscle Relaxation

1. Close eyes tightly.
2. Squeeze nose and mouth together so that whole face is scrunched up.
3. Pull your chin into your chest and pull shoulders together.
4. Tighten your arms to your body and clench your hands together.
5. Pull in your stomach.
6. Squeeze your thighs and buttocks together and tighten your calves.
7. Stretch your feet, then curl your toes.
8. At this point, every muscle should be tightened. Now relax your body, one part at a time in reverse order starting with your toes. Focus on how you feel as you relax, releasing tensions that might have built up in various parts of your body.

This exercise can also be done by tightening one area at a time for 5–10 seconds and then releasing that area for relaxation, then moving on to another area. If you get distracted, you don't need to begin again. Do this over a few times to feel the true benefit of total relaxation.

II. Deep Breathing

1. Sit back or lie down, placing your hand over your stomach.
2. Close your eyes and breathe slowly, deeply so that your stomach rises, not your chest.
3. Hold in and count to 10, slowly breathing out through your mouth, counting to 10, relaxing your body as you exhale.

III. Visualizing or Mental Imagery

1. Close your eyes
2. Create a quite peaceful scene in your mind (an ocean beach, a mountain view, or special place for you). Use music or pictures if it helps. Block out all thought except for your single vision.
3. Focus on your scene for 2–3 minutes. Do not allow yourself to be distracted.
4. Breathe deeply and let your mind take you to this peaceful place.

**Exercise 4–F
College Time
Management Tracking**

Complete the following checklist and develop a plan of action for your remaining time in college.

Freshman Year

Strategic Step	**Action Plan and Time Frame**
Identify career resources	
Seek information regarding your field of study	
Map out plan of action for classes and extracurricular activities	

Sophomore Year

Strategic Step	**Action Plan and Time Frame**
Declare major/minor(s)	
Develop resumé	
Research and identify internships	

Junior Year

Strategic Step	**Action Plan and Time Frame**
Finalize resumé	
Attend job and internship fairs	
Apply for internships and prepare for interviewing	
Research job opportunities	

Senior Year

Strategic Step	**Action Plan and Time Frame**
Send resumés and cover letters	
Begin interviews and narrow down focus	
Graduate and start career path	

Exercise 4–G
Try This . . .

1. Identify someone you know whom you admire. Observe that person's routine over a period of time. What time or stress management behaviors do you see this person using?

2. Watch a TV show or see a movie. Some suggestions include *Office Space, Falling Down,* and *9 to 5*. Make a list of the time and stress management behaviors you see (and don't see) in the major characters.

3. Consider a friend of yours who's going through a particularly difficult time right now. List some relaxation or stress reduction techniques you think might work for your friend. Think of ways you can be helpful (not meddling) in suggesting them to your friend.

4. Organize your work area so you can be more efficient.

5. Make a list of all foods you eat for a week. At the end of the week, identify the items that either give you energy or detract from your energy. Make a list of three high-energy foods you can substitute for low-energy foods in the coming week. Examples: fruit juice instead of soda; water instead of coffee; fruit or granola bar instead of candy bar.

6. Keep a journal for a week. At the end of the week look it over and assess whether it was helpful to you in sorting things out.

**Exercise 4–H
Reflection/Action Plan**

This chapter focused on time and stress management—what they are, why they're important, and how to acquire and increase the degree to which you possess them. Complete the worksheet below to reflect on what you have learned on these topics and to develop plans for incorporating that learning into your work and life.

1. The one or two areas in which I am most strong are:

_____

_____

_____

_____

2. The one or two areas in which I need more improvement are:

_____

_____

_____

_____

3. If I did only one thing to improve in this area, it would be to:

_____

_____

_____

_____

4. Making this change would probably result in:

_____

_____

_____

_____

5. If I did not change or improve in this area, it would probably affect my personal and professional life in the following ways:

_____

_____

_____

_____

5 Conveying Verbal Messages

How do I:

✓ Improve my ability to send clear messages?

✓ Reduce barriers associated with ineffective communication?

✓ Determine which communication medium will best serve my needs in varying situations?

✓ Send messages that directly express and address my wants, needs, and opinions?

✓ Get my message across in a way that doesn't cause defensiveness on the part of the receiver?

David Jameson was in a bind. After years working as a technical specialist he was promoted to supervisor in his department. This required him to be responsible for people who had at one time been his co-workers, which created a good deal of resentment on the part of his co-workers. Yet he had business objectives to meet. Much was expected of him, and senior management was eyeing Dave for another promotion soon if all went well. After several weeks Dave discovered an unsettling communication pattern. Whenever he would ask that something be done, his co-workers would nod in agreement. But when the time for the deadline came, the expected outcome hadn't happened. Just last Monday he met with Ann and Frank, telling them they needed to complete the computer drafts for the Winston project by the end of the business day on Thursday. However, the reports were still not on his desk on Friday morning. When he had finished talking to them on Monday, they gave him no response or inclination that the project would not be complete on time. Dave thought he was communicating clearly. He had informed them of the deadline and simply left it at that when neither of them gave him a response. What was their problem? Dave didn't want to condescend to his subordinates by looking over their shoulders and checking on their progress, but he was afraid he might have to do this if things didn't change soon.

1. What issues are involved here? What's going on?

2. If you were one of Dave's co-workers, what would you think and how would you feel about the situation?

3. What ideas or suggestions do you have for Dave?

"The medium is the message."

Marshall McLuhan

Master communicator Marshall McLuhan said it best when he inferred that the medium used to send a message is just as important as the actual message, if not more so. Another way to say the same thing is "It's not just the message, it's the messenger." Both form and substance are important in the communication process. Everything we do or don't do, say or don't say, communicates something, and so does the way in which we send messages. Communicating effectively consists of both sending and receiving messages in ways that are both verbal and nonverbal. It's almost impossible not to communicate, unless, of course, we're sleeping! Studies show that we may spend as much as 80 percent of our time communicating.[1] In this chapter we look at verbal communication—what it is, why it's important, and how to both send and receive messages effectively.

What Is Communication?

Communication is a process in which information flows from a source to a receiver and back.[2] We communicate because we want something to happen or we want to satisfy a need. In fact, the majority of our work and life is devoted to communicating with others. For example, in business, the average supervisor spends about 80 percent of his/her time communicating, of which approximately 10 percent is spent writing, 15 percent reading, 30 percent speaking, and 45 percent listening.[3]

Because we communicate constantly, we need to communicate effectively—to do it right. It's not easy to be an effective communicator all the time. To do this takes work, effort, and practice.

The Communication Channel

When a message needs to be sent, a communicator (the *sender*) **encodes** a message according to her or his own perceptions, experiences, and abilities. The sender then determines which **communication channel**[4]—the method or medium—is most appropriate to use to convey the message. The message travels across the communication channel and is then decoded by the *receiver*(s) who interpret (**decode**) the message according to their own perceptions, abilities, and experiences.

The sending of a message from source to receiver constitutes one-way communication. Adding the final stage, known as **feedback,** creates two-way communication. Feedback is the process by which the receiver puts the message back into a channel to seek clarification, confirm what the receiver thought the sender said, or check for understanding and possible misinterpretation. Feedback can be verbal or nonverbal through the use of paraphrasing, questioning, nodding, gesturing, or even eye movement.

Feedback is an essential component of two-way communication. It allows the receiver to show the sender they are paying attention and clearly understand the messages being sent. By listening, repeating, reaffirming, and asking questions, it is more likely that the sender and receiver can understand fully what each is saying. This process doesn't guarantee there will be agreement, but it does ensure understanding. Two-way

Figure 5–1[5]
The Communication Channel

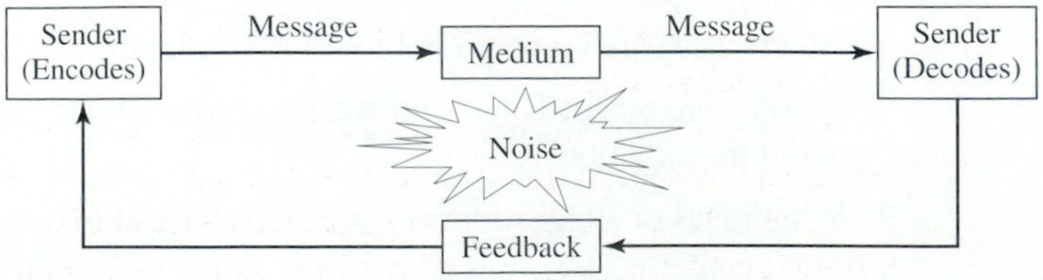

communication is so essential that you should consider all of your business communications to be two-way unless you are simply making an announcement or issuing an important directive that can't be challenged.[6]

Effective Media Selection

As the quote at the beginning of this chapter implies, the medium you choose through which you convey your message is just as important as the content of the message itself. The advertising world has long understood this principle. In the business world it is just as true that "it's not just what you say but how you say it that counts." This saying has survived because it is so practical, so true. The medium (or media, if more than one medium is needed) selected to transmit a message can enhance or reduce the effectiveness of the message being sent. We have several choices available for communicating directly with others; they include oral, written, and electronic forms. Choosing among these forms of communication requires you to assess the message you need to send, your intended audience (from one to a hundred or more), and the response you hope to receive from the audience.[7] Each method has its advantages and disadvantages.

■ *Oral communication* or spoken communication tends to be the most preferred form of communication for managers. Oral communication should be used when it is important to engage in discussion and come to a consensus with one or more persons. One prominent benefit of oral communication (in person, via telephone or video-conference) is that it provides an automatic two-way exchange—both the sender(s) and receiver(s) can share information and obtain immediate feedback. This helps the sender shape the message as soon as a response is received on numerous points. Face-to-face contact is typically more effective than other types of oral communication, as both verbal and nonverbal signals are readily and simultaneously available.

On the other hand, oral communication does have its drawbacks. Communicating orally via a phone call, video conference, or meeting often results in people arriving at the exchange less prepared than if they were communicating in writing. In oral communication it is easy for the participants to forget the major points that were made soon after the meeting concludes. Without a common written record it is likely some of the promises made won't be followed up. Oral communication activities also tend to cause the participants to experience "information overload." Communicating orally is not the best choice when a large amount of complex information needs to be delivered. One way to improve oral communication as a medium is to add a written component. Taking minutes during a meeting, entering personal notes about follow-up actions in a day planner, and issuing a short e-mail summarizing agreed-upon action steps and deadlines are some of the ways oral contact can be strengthened as a medium of communication.

■ *Written communication* is the most effective method for sending precise or complex information. It is also appropriate when making an announcement that does not require two-way dialogue. Written communication should not be used when the subject is controversial and requires further input from others and decisions to be made. The written document, such as a letter, contract, memo, report, or presentation, has several benefits. Written communication is an effective way to get a message to a large number of individuals in a time- and cost-efficient manner. A written document or set of documents also ensures a "paper trail"—a record of exchanges made between individuals and groups. Written communication provides a formal or official document. Most of us prefer a legal, binding contract to be in written rather than in oral form. Written evidence is far more binding than is oral recall of events. Written information can also provide a reference for later use. For example, a work team that regularly records minutes for meetings will save time at each meeting by not having to recall what was said and agreed upon in previous meetings.

Written communication also has its drawbacks. It is too easy for us to write a long letter when a short memo would be sufficient. Written communication prevents a two-way dialogue, or results in a lengthier exchange if two-way communication is desired. In written communication it is nearly impossible to decode the nonverbals—those nuances, movements, and gestures that serve to reinforce and clarify a sender's message and intent.[8] Written communication is also prone to misinterpretation and inaccuracy. Just because something is written doesn't mean it's necessarily true or will be correctly interpreted! To improve the effectiveness of written communication, carefully evaluate messages sent or received to determine bias, misinterpreted connotations, and hidden agendas along with seeking verbal or written clarification to accurately encode or decode messages.

■ *Electronic communication* is effective for sending brief messages quickly to one or more persons. It is useful for clarifying agreements that have already been reached, when fast turn-around time is needed, and when members of a team are working "virtually" (meaning they're not all in the same location). Electronic communication should not be the primary medium when the message that needs to be sent is negative, controversial, or requires additional dialogue.

Much electronic communication in the workplace now takes place via e-mail, faxing, teleconferencing, cell phones, voice mail, and other means such as websites and Internet technology. While some of these means can be extremely fast, accurate, and efficient, they still require judgment, discretion, and "people skills" to be used correctly. New technology presents unique challenges in communication not only in speed and distance, but in evaluating the audience, which can comprise one or hundreds of individuals, with virtually little knowledge or understanding of the receiver(s).[9] Due to the relative ease of sending a message, many senders neglect the need for careful execution of their communication. How many of us have read about the guy who jilted his girlfriend in favor of another via e-mail—only to find he had sent the "jilt" e-mail to the new girlfriend, and the "amorous" e-mail to his old girlfriend! Or the CEO of a prominent entertainment company who confessed in a commencement speech that he had unintentionally sent the company's disappointing quarterly earnings report to representatives of the media rather than to his board.[10] Thoughtful use of electronic forms of communication requires that we develop effective human communication skills in conjunction with new technology and equipment. Electronic communication has the potential downside of reducing the quality and amount of human interaction. Figure 5–2 provides some tips for using—and not using—electronic communication.

Figure 5–2
E-mail Communication:
DOs and DON'Ts

■ DO keep your address list up to date. DON'T set aside until "later" letters and messages you receive from colleagues giving you their new contact information.

■ DO send business-related messages during work hours. DON'T send or receive personal e-mail during work hours.

■ DO remember that anything you "say" in an e-mail can potentially be "seen" by many others besides those to whom you send the e-mail. DON'T send any e-mail that is personally negative about or potentially damaging to another person.

■ DO have a personal e-mail account separate from your account at work or school. DON'T use your work account for both business and personal purposes.

■ DO send brief messages to announce noncontroversial information or to confirm something that's already been agreed to. DON'T send lengthy announcements or messages about something that is best handled through face-to-face discussion or debate.

■ DO send appreciative notes to people with copies to their supervisors. DON'T give negative feedback via e-mail.

■ DO copy your boss on important messages that are relevant to them. DON'T leave your boss and significant members of your team out of the loop. DON'T go over your boss's head, even though you have access to the personal e-mail address of her or his boss.

■ DO keep hard copy of important documents for the record.

■ DO clarify important details verbally. DON'T rely on e-mail communication on important matters (the person you're writing to might be out of town).

■ DO batch your messages. DON'T send multiple messages throughout the day to the same people concerning the same project.

■ DO send personalized e-mails. DON'T send mass e-mails, or if you do, don't include everyone's address at the top—that's giving away sensitive information. Send your message to yourself and blind copy it to the others.

Barriers to Communication

As anyone who has ever been in an argument or had difficulty getting a message across knows, communicating is a complex skill. There are many obstacles to getting communication right. One of the reasons for this is that in communication, many potential areas for interference or "noise" exist. **Noise** is any distortion factor that blocks or disrupts the flow of information between sender and receiver, hindering the communication process. These distortion factors can range from emotional states or language differences to telephone static or a downed e-mail system. Using American slang (such as "cool," "bad," or "hot") when discussing the results of a new product design to a foreign counterpart could lead to a distortion of the interpreter's meaning, which would constitute noise.

Even good communication processes contain noise factors; it is inherent in all forms of communication. One way to improve our communication skills is to become aware of these barriers to communication and learn how to minimize or reduce their adverse effects.

Information Overload

As human beings, most of us have the ability to process only so much information. Some of the behaviors that can cause information overload for the receiver of your messages are listed below.

■ **Presenting too much material:** Keep the information to an amount that is easily absorbed by the person or persons with whom you are speaking. Check for understanding and pause frequently, giving the person time to formulate clarifying questions and indicate to you that they understand what you are saying.

■ **Presenting information that is overly complex:** When feasible, practice your main message or messages ahead of time, ensuring you deliver the message succinctly and coherently. If necessary, back up your words with visuals, or send data or a summary report ahead of time.

■ **Presenting information too quickly:** Deliver your message slowly, in an organized fashion, focusing on just a couple of points at a time.

■ **Presenting at a level of difficulty that goes beyond the person's understanding:** Always know your audience. If you don't, begin your message with a few overview comments and perhaps some questions to determine how much information the receiver already has on the subject.

■ **Not giving the person sufficient time to process the information:** Give your listeners an opportunity to ask questions and to provide their perspective before asking for a decision. When possible, try to hold off on a decision until all the necessary information is available, perhaps at another time.

Trust and Credibility

Lack of trust is a huge barrier to effective communication. For example, if a company begins to lay off workers after having told them layoffs would not occur, those employees will be less likely to believe anything else told them by their managers. If you need to communicate with someone with whom trust has been broken, take the time to talk with the person, listening to his or her concerns, emphasizing the importance of the long-term relationship. If possible, wait until trust has been rebuilt before asking for a decision or insisting on their cooperation.

Lack of credibility prevents the listener from fully receiving your message. The receiver can hear your words but won't believe you or acknowledge your perspective, because they question your knowledge base. New entrants into the workforce often experience this problem with more senior workers sometimes questioning their expertise. The best way to build credibility is to prepare, prepare, prepare. The more thoroughly you have done your homework before approaching someone with an issue or solution, the more likely you are to be well received.

Time

Lack of time is a major concern for practically all of us, whether we're a student, home-maker, parent, or manager (or all of the above!). Poor communication often results from lack of time. Being in a hurry does not lend itself to studied, thorough responses or decision making. Rushing to communicate often leads to errors, leaving out important details, or saying things that you later regret having said. The best way to approach this problem is to develop a habit of focusing on just one communication at a time. This flies in the face of the "multitasking" environment so favored in many industries today wherein employees are encouraged and expected to perform multiple tasks simultaneously. While not everyone can or prefers to multitask, studies suggest that multitasking causes a good deal of stress. When dealing with an important issue, person, or customer, focus your attention on one communication at a time. This will reduce errors and improve the quality of your communication. For example, when sending an e-mail message, take time to proofread it before sending it. When on the telephone, devote full attention to your listener and resist putting him or her on hold or call waiting (except in an emergency). When conducting a meeting, close the door to the meeting room to reduce distractions. You can't always adhere to these principles. But when what's being said or who's saying it is very important to you, it's worth doing it right.

Another communication problem that arises over the concept of time is today's increased expectation of speedy response. The use of e-mail, voice mail, and fax machines has resulted in a "just in time" mentality in the workplace. It used to take first-class mail three to four days to arrive at a destination. It wasn't uncommon for a manager to answer a letter within the next week or even two. Today that's hardly practical. Generally an e-mail message, phone message, or drop-by conversation in the office hallway carries with it the expectation of an almost immediate response. This can pose problems for you as the number of messages that need handling simultaneously mounts. Many successful managers are finding that it helps to batch their communications or group their responses by category. For example, you can attempt to set aside time each day for responding to and sending e-mail messages, a different time for responding to and making phone calls, and yet a different time of day for quick hallway conversations with co-workers. Of course this won't always be possible, but by setting some limits over the way in which you respond to these inquiries, you'll have a better chance of responding to each contact appropriately, accurately, and within a reasonable period of time.

Filtering

Filtering is the intentional manipulation of information to make it more favorable to the receiver. The way information is sent, the tone and the framing of the material can greatly distort a message to serve an individual's or a group's needs. Filtering can make objective decision making difficult because the true message is never accurately sent or received. For example, a manager afraid of offending his subordinates may sugarcoat a message about the need to work overtime by leaving out information that clarifies why the work can't wait. Or an employee might inform a manager of errors, but leave out details on the extensive amount of damage that occurred. To resist filtering when you speak, present information based on the relevant facts. Deliver information sensitively but firmly and honestly. To prevent receiving filtered information, ask probing questions about a situation that's being presented to you. Ask follow-up questions about each detail that is of interest to you, focusing on results and outcomes, not just the facts that have been presented.

Emotions

Another factor that can hinder effective communication is **emotions** or emotional states. Emotions are strong feelings such as fear, love, hate, happiness, and anger. Because emotion is the opposite of reason, it is difficult to anticipate, predict, control, or read emotion in yourself and in others. Emotions are neither right nor wrong, but rather an expression of human reactions. However, communicating emotionally can prevent us from being objective about a situation. To reduce the potential for miscommunication, consider the emotional state of both the sender and the receiver in all interactions with others. In most business situations, it's best if both parties can remain as open and objective as possible. This is not to say that emotions will be nonexistent. However, it is wise to understand the potential effects emotional states can have on the communication process. A good rule of thumb is to stop and think. This might seem simple, but it requires an amount of self-discipline. Assess the impact of what you are about to say on the other person. Say things that won't offend others, to avoid diverting their attention, which interferes with your ability to make a point. It is a good idea to leave a discussion and return to it later if you find yourself so emotional about the subject that your feelings are getting in the way of your being able to communicate. Similarly, if a person with whom you are speaking is reacting emotionally, it's a good idea to part and regroup later.

Message Congruency   The communication process is much more than just the spoken word. Studies have found that 55 percent of communication is transmitted through physiology (body language) while 38 percent of communication comes through the tone of voice and only 7 percent through words.[11] These statistics reinforce the need for sending verbal and nonverbal messages congruently. Communicators must carefully consider the potential message being sent nonverbally, through gestures and body language. The nonverbals must reinforce the message, not contradict it. You may be misunderstood if you are rolling your eyes when you are confirming your acceptance of a suggestion. Are you trying to be sarcastic in your affirmative answer? If so, then confirm your opinion with congruent verbal and nonverbal statements. The goal is to make things clear for the receivers of your messages; don't send mixed signals. Practicing these techniques should improve your ability to have both you *and* your message taken seriously.

Assertive Communication

Assertive communication is a form of communication in which you speak up for your rights and take into account the rights and feelings of others.[12] Elements of assertive communication include:

- Fairness
- Directness
- Tact and sensitivity
- Honesty

The purpose of assertive communication is to keep contact lines open and show respect for others while affirming your beliefs and preferences. Unfortunately, many of us feel uncomfortable being assertive; some falsely equate assertiveness with aggressiveness and instead use passive styles of communication.[13]

Passive communication includes indirectness, avoiding conflict, being easily persuaded/bullied, being overly concerned about pleasing others, and screening or withholding your thoughts and feelings to the extent that the person with whom you're communicating has no idea of your real opinion on the matter being addressed. We use passive communication when we are fearful of losing someone's affection or have low self-esteem, or when we have decided the issue isn't worth taking a stand. Frowning, crying, whispering under our breath, or simply saying nothing are all ways we demonstrate passive communication. Usually the primary purpose of responding passively to a person or situation is to avoid confrontation at all costs. Passive communication is usually not recommended, as it results in you seldom getting what you really want. It can be useful, however, if avoidance is truly desirable, such as when you're in an organization where you have chosen not to speak up about everything with which you disagree.

Aggressive communication includes exerting control over others, humiliating others, dominating, being pushy, always needing to be right, using absolute terms, and blaming others.[14] We respond aggressively when we want to be in control, are insecure, are afraid, don't value the opinions of others, or have unresolved anger. The purpose of aggressive behavior is to win or dominate—to prove one is right and others are wrong. Aggressive communication is usually not recommended, as it results in a win–lose situation where you get your way at the expense of someone else's. It can be appropriate, however, if you are in an extreme situation that dictates the need for an aggressive response, such as directions in crisis management or a physical attack.

Assertive communication is usually the most appropriate communication style.[15] There are times when we all feel somewhat passive or even aggressive. But for the most part, it's a good idea to learn to be firm about your needs and to insist on those needs getting met. Have you ever had a roommate who ate your food or wore your clothes without asking? A boss who wouldn't give you a much-deserved raise? How did you handle this? Assertive communication will provide you with the ability to pass on information accurately and intelligently to accomplish objectives while still having respect for others and not having them feel "put down."[16]

How to Communicate Assertively

Nearly all of us have been involved in group projects, whether in school, business, or both. Many of us have also been in groups where one (or more) member contributes little or nothing to the task. What do you do? Do you ignore the situation, hoping that (1) it will improve, or (2) someone else will deal with the nonperformer? Using assertive communication may help you to remedy these and similar situations.

There are three parts to developing an assertive statement:[17]

- Your *perspective/perception* of the situation: In your own words, what is the issue or situation as you see it? For example, "I've noticed that the common areas are frequently messy and dirty."

- Your *feelings* about the situation: Describe how the situation makes you feel without placing blame on others. For example, "I feel frustrated since I am holding up my end of the deal yet others don't seem to do theirs."

- Your *wants* regarding the situation or outcome: Own your request for a resolution by using "I" instead of "you." "I would like to revisit our roommate agreement and come up with a plan that we all can live with regarding the cleanliness of our apartment."

Taking Responsibility and "I" Messages

An element of assertive communicating involves "taking responsibility." It is human nature to try to assess or make sense of our and others' behavior. However, the assumptions we make about the behavior of others are not necessarily consistent with reality; instead, our assumptions reflect our own values and beliefs. When conversing with another person, it is important to remember this fact, to clarify assumptions, and to be willing to accept at least some of the responsibility for any ambiguity in the communication. Some ways to take responsibility and clarify assumptions include:[18]

- Specify the behavior(s) on which the assumption is based: "Your facial expression suggests to me that I may not have made my point very clearly," rather than "Are you following what I'm saying?"

- If your assumption is based on your own expectation of the listener's behavior, state that expectation specifically; do not assume that the listener knows the details of your expectation: "I'm expecting that report next Monday at 4:00. Can we agree on that?" rather than "Is that report going to be done on time?"

- If your assumption compares the listener's behavior with that of other members of a reference group, clarify that group and exactly how the behavior compares: "The other members of the department always submit their weekly production reports on Monday, and each of your last four reports weren't submitted until Thursday," rather than "You didn't submit you weekly production reports promptly."

- Elicit feedback about your assumptions. Ask the listener to tell you whether the assumption is accurate: "Am I correct in assuming that you've already begun writing the report that's due next Monday?"

Another element of assertive communication is in the use of "I statements."[19] Most of the messages we send to people about their behavior are "you" messages—messages that are directed at the other person and have a high probability of putting them down, making them feel guilty, making them feel their needs are not important, making them defensive, and generally making them resist change. Examples of "you" messages are usually orders or commands ("Stop doing that! Get in the car!"), blaming or name-calling statements ("You are acting like a baby! You are driving me crazy!"), or statements that give solutions ("You should forget that idea. You better reconsider your plan"). Statements like these tend to remove the responsibility for behavior change from the other person. Morris Massey, a popular self-help author and coach, calls this being "should on."[20] Perhaps the worst example of a "you" message is the "if . . . then" threat: for example, "If you don't . . . then I will . . . "

Conversely, an "I" message allows a person who is affected by the behavior of another to express the impact it has on him or her and leave the responsibility for modifying the behavior with the person who demonstrated that particular behavior. An "I" message consists of three parts:

- the specific behavior
- the resulting feeling you experienced because of the behavior
- the tangible effect on you

Thus a teacher might say to a student: "When you tap on your desk with your pencil, I feel upset because I get distracted and have difficulty teaching," rather than "You had better stop tapping your pencil!" Or a wife might say to her husband: "When I try to talk and you don't say anything, I feel confused because I don't know how you feel about helping me," rather than "You never talk to me!" In effect, the "I" message removes the possibility of defensiveness and allows the sender to project, "I trust you to decide what change in behavior is necessary." "I" messages build relationships and don't place the sender in the position of enforcing a new behavior, as is frequently the case with the "you" message.

Sending Messages Effectively

We have all been talking and listening for so long that we tend to think we're experts. We have survived up to this point and gotten some results, so we must be doing something right. Despite the fact that most of the time we're probably somewhat or very effective, there's always room for improvement; the better your communication, the better your performance, interactions with co-workers, and relationships with others in your personal life. Studies show that up to 70 percent of business communication is ineffective in achieving its intended purpose.[21] Figure 5–3 provides some suggestions for increasing your skills in communicating effectively.

Figure 5–3
Twelve Tips for Sending Effective Verbal Messages

- Be direct: others may not pick up on your hints or may misinterpret them.
- Consider your audience: communicate with them in terms of their interests, values, and backgrounds.
- Be clear: don't ask questions when you need to make a statement. Focus on one thing at a time; know your purpose and have an objective; think and organize your thoughts before speaking.
- Watch the nonverbal aspects of communicating: make your facial expression and gestures congruent with your verbal statements.
- Pay attention to the receivers: watch for their nonverbal clues, not just what they're saying.
- As necessary, be redundant: repeat when needed or restate something to make it clearer to the receiver.
- Communicate bit by bit: make the pieces sufficiently understandable individually and as a whole.
- Use varying techniques to send your message; we all process information differently and have varying learning styles.[22]
  - Some are *auditory*—they have to hear it to learn it.
  - Some are *visual*—they need to read it or see it on paper.
  - Some are *kinesthetic*—they need to have hands-on use or personal practice to learn.
  - Some are *didactic*—they ask questions and get full background info before processing what others are saying.
- Cover your bases: write it, review it, demonstrate it, and defend it.
- Build in feedback and check for understanding. Encourage and incorporate means that allow others to know you want feedback. They are unlikely to do it automatically. Ask for feedback and clarification.
- Be straightforward with no hidden agenda or lies; deal with issues straight-on and in a timely manner, often, and openly.
- Be supportive: avoid labels, sarcasm, dragging up the past, negative comparisons, and "you" messages and threats.

Summary

What and how we communicate affects our behavior as well as that of others. Effective communication is the means for developing better human relations and ultimately better organizational performance.

Verbal communication is not as easy as it might seem. Developing skills in communicating verbally with others is important for managerial success as well as success in our personal relationships. If you have a high degree of proficiency in communicating, people will be able to interpret your messages clearly. Part of communicating verbally is being able to communicate assertively. By sending messages clearly, seeking and giving feedback fairly, and working to overcome obstacles to effective communication, we increase the likelihood of personal and professional success.

Key Terms and Concepts

Aggressive communication	Encode
Assertive communication	Feedback
Communication	Filtering
Communication channel	Information overload
Decode	Noise
Emotions	Passive communication

Endnotes

1. John R. Ward, "Now Hear This," *IABC Communication World,* July 1990, p. 20.

2. D. K. Berlo, *The Process of Communication* (New York: Holt, Rinehart and Winston, 1960), pp. 30–32.

3. G. R. Bell, "Listen and You Shall Hear," *The Secretary* 47 (1984), pp. 8–9.

4. Berlo, 1960.

5. Berlo, 1960.

6. Duane Bazzett, "Communicating Effectively," *Supervision* 60, no. 12 (Dec. 1999), p. 3.

7. Bazzett, 1999.

8. One notable exception to this would be tone—usually referred to in a verbal context (e.g., she spoke to me in an obnoxious tone), but could be part of a written message through the choice of sarcasm and other nonverbal message amplifiers.

9. "Talking to the World," *The Economist* (US), (Dec. 25, 1999), p. 83.

10. In case you were wondering . . . this was Disney's Michael Eisner!

11. Albert Mehrabian and M. Weiner, "Decoding of Inconsistent Communication," *Journal of Personality and Social Psychology,* June 1967, p. 109.

12. Matthew McKay, Martha Davis, and Patrick Fanning, *Messages: The Communication Skills Book,* Second Ed. (Harbinger Publications, Inc., 1995).

13. R. E. Albert and M. L. Emmons, *Your Perfect Right: A Guide to Assertive Behavior* (San Luis Obispo, CA: Impact Publishers, Inc., 1974).

14. Stephen Robbins and Phil Hunsaker, *Training in Interpersonal Skills* (Upper Saddle River, NJ: Prentice Hall, 1996).

15. E. Raudsepp, "Are You Properly Assertive?" *Supervision,* June 1992, p. 17.

16. Alfred Fleishman, "Going Back a Little Bit," *St. Louis Business Journal,* Jan 3, 2000, p. 29.

17. McKay et al., 1995, p. 128.

18. This is adapted from an exercise in J. William Pfeiffer and John E. Jones, *Structured Experiences Kit,* entitled Taking Responsibility, C-CAE/0-15 (San Francisco, CA: Jossey-Bass Pfeiffer, 1980).

19. Ibid.

20. Morris E. Massey, *The People Puzzle: Understanding Yourself and Others* (Reston, VA: Reston Publishing Co., Inc./Prentice Hall, 1979).

21. Robert N. Lussier, *Human Relations in Organizations*, Fourth Ed. (Boston, MA: Irwin McGraw-Hill, 1999), p. 104.

22. Sharon Kay, "How Employees Process Information," *Supervision* (Dec. 1998), p. 6.

Exercise 5–A
Assessing Yourself

Circle the response that most closely correlates with each item below.

	Agree	Neither			Disagree
1. I ask for and give feedback as a way of clarifying meaning.	1	(2)	3	4	5
2. I pay attention to others by listening, reaffirming what I think I've heard, and by asking questions.	1	(2)	3	4	5
3. I strive for two-way communication.	(1)	2	3	4	5
4. I communicate orally when the subject matter is important and requires others' input.	(1)	2	3	4	5
5. I communicate in writing when the subject matter is complex or when I need documentation.	1	2	3	(4)	5
6. I communicate electronically when the message is brief, is not negative, and doesn't require face-to-face communication.	(1)	2	3	4	5
7. I keep information I'm relaying on to an easily absorbable amount and speed.	(1)	2	3	4	5
8. I rebuild trust (if broken) before attempting to communicate.	1	2	3	(4)	5
9. I prepare thoroughly before communicating.	1	(2)	3	4	5
10. I focus my attention on one important communication at a time.	(1)	2	3	4	5
11. I proofread my written and electronic messages before sending.	(1)	2	3	4	5
12. I batch my responses to e-mail messages and phone calls.	1	2	(3)	4	5
13. I consciously communicate in a way that men and women can understand and respond favorably to.	1	(2)	3	4	5
14. I speak in a straightforward manner without filtering my messages.	(1)	2	3	4	5
15. I consider the emotional state of both the sender and receiver, and adapt my behavior accordingly.	1	2	(3)	4	5
16. I speak directly and firmly, addressing my concerns without ignoring the needs of others.	(1)	2	3	4	5
17. I take responsibility for my statements rather than putting others on the defensive.	1	2	(3)	4	5
18. I send "I" messages when I communicate.	1	(2)	3	4	5
19. I clarify my assumptions about others while speaking with them.	1	(2)	3	4	5
20. I consider the needs and background of my audiences.	1	(2)	3	4	5
21. I don't phrase statements in the form of a question.	1	(2)	3	4	5
22. I match my nonverbal gestures and expressions with my verbal comments.	(1)	2	3	4	5
23. I take into account others' different learning styles when I speak.	1	2	3	(4)	5
24. I am straightforward and deal with issues head-on.	1	2	(3)	4	5
25. I am supportive of others.	1	(2)	3	4	5

If your score is 75 or greater, it may be helpful to create a plan to improve your verbal communication skills.

60   51

Exercise 5–B
Completing the
Channel—Two-Way
Communication

The sender will sit or stand facing away from the group. (If the sender can be hidden from sight this would be helpful.) The sender will then proceed to describe a series of objects to the class. The participants are to draw what they believe is being described to them as accurately as possible. Participants are not allowed to ask questions or have any discussion with the sender. They are to work on their own and make no audible responses. (The instructor will record how long the first activity took, and participants are to write down how many objects they think they have drawn correctly.)

The sender will now face the group and proceed to describe another series of objects. The participants are to draw the objects the best they can from the description. This time participants are allowed to ask questions and discuss the objects with the sender. The instructor will write down the length of time the second activity took.

Questions

1. What happened during the drawing of the first object? How did you respond? How did you feel doing the task? How many of the objects did you actually get right?

2. What happened during the drawing of the second object? How did you respond? Did you ask for any clarifications? How did you feel doing the task? How many did you actually get right?

3. From the class results, what assumptions can be made in comparing one-way versus two-way communication? Does it take more time to communicate effectively?

Source: Exercise is adapted from *Managerial Psychology,* by Harold J. Leavitt, University of Chicago Press, 1958, pp. 118–28.

Exercise 5–C
The Assertion
Inventory

Many people experience difficulty in handling interpersonal situations requiring them to assert themselves in some way, for example, turning down a request, asking a favor, giving someone a compliment, expressing disapproval or approval, etc. Please indicate your degree of discomfort or anxiety in the space provided *before* each situation listed below. Utilize the following scale to indicate degree of discomfort:

1 = none
2 = a little
3 = a fair amount
4 = much
5 = very much

Then, go over the list a second time and indicate *after* each item the probability or likelihood of your displaying the behavior if actually presented with the situation.* For example, if you rarely apologize when you are at fault, you would mark a "4" after that item. Utilize the following scale to indicate response probability:

1 = always do it
2 = usually do it
3 = do it about half the time
4 = rarely do it
5 = never do it

*Note: It is important to cover your discomfort ratings (located in front of the items) while indicating response probability. Otherwise, one rating may contaminate the other and a realistic assessment of your behavior is unlikely. To correct for this, place a piece of paper over your discomfort ratings while responding to the situations a second time for response probability.

Degree of Discomfort	SITUATION	Response Probability
3	1. Turn down a request to borrow your car	1
1	2. Compliment a friend	1
2	3. Ask a favor of someone	3
3	4. Resist sales pressure	2
3	5. Apologize when you are at fault	2
2	6. Turn down a request for a meeting or date	4

Degree of Discomfort	SITUATION	Response Probability
2	7. Admit fear and request consideration	2
4	8. Tell a person you are intimately involved with when he/she says or does something that bothers you	4
4	9. Ask for a raise	4
3	10. Admit ignorance in some areas	2
2	11. Turn down a request to borrow money	3
2	12. Ask personal questions	3
4	13. Turn off a talkative friend	5
2	14. Ask for constructive criticism	3
3	15. Initiate a conversation with a stranger	4
1	16. Compliment a person you are romantically involved with or interested in	3
4	17. Request a meeting or a date with a person	4
5	18. Your initial request for a meeting is turned down and you ask the person again at a later time	5
2	19. Admit confusion about a point under discussion and ask for clarification	2
3	20. Apply for a job	2
2	21. Ask whether you have offended someone	2
4	22. Tell someone that you like them	5
3	23. Request expected service when such is not forthcoming, e.g., in a restaurant	3
5	24. Discuss openly with the person his/her criticism of your behavior	5
2	25. Return defective items, e.g., store or restaurant	1
3	26. Express an opinion that differs from that of the person you are talking to	3
3	27. Resist sexual overtures when you are not interested	2
4	28. Tell the person when you feel he/she has done something that is unfair to you	4
2	29. Accept a date	2
2	30. Tell someone good news about yourself	2
2	31. Resist pressure to drink	2
4	32. Resist a significant person's unfair demands	4
4	33. Quit a job	1
2	34. Resist pressure to do drugs	2
3	35. Discuss openly with the person his/her criticism of your work	3
3	36. Request the return of borrowed item	4
2	37. Receive compliments	1
2	38. Continue to converse with someone who disagrees with your	5
4	39. Tell a friend or someone with whom you work when he/she says or does something that bothers you	5
4	40. Ask a person who is annoying you in a public situation to stop	5

Lastly, please indicate the situations you would like to handle more assertively by placing a circle around the item number.

Add the total scores for each column.

Degree of Discomfort ___131___   112   120 Response Probability _____

Assertiveness
Inventory Scoring Grid

Response Probability

	√ Low (105+)	High (40–104)
√ High (96+)	UNASSERTIVE ⌄	ANXIOUS PERFORMER
Low (40–95)	??? DON'T CARE	ASSERTIVE

Degree of Discomfort

Exercise 5–D
Communication Styles

For the following situations describe a passive, aggressive, and assertive statement or response. Discuss the potential consequences for each.

I. You've been standing in line at the bookstore for over an hour and someone cuts in front of you.

Passive response ✓

Do nothing

Aggressive response

Reclaime spot

Assertive response

Remind person you were there first

II. You live in an apartment with three other people. One person is very messy and sloppy, leaving dishes on the table and in the sink, eating your food, leaving garbage in all rooms of the apartment.

Passive response

Do nothing

Aggressive response

Ask for them to clean up / remind how all live in the apartment

Assertive response ✓

Break dirty dishes

III. A telemarketer calls you on the phone when you are in the middle of completing work for a deadline. They are going through their sales pitch for buying magazines.

Passive response

listen to pitch

Aggressive response

tell them you have work to do

Assertive response

hang up

IV. You go to an expensive steakhouse and you order your steak medium rare and it is served to you well done.

Passive response

Eat it

Aggressive response

request for it to be re-done

Assertive response

demand a free meal

Questions

1. From the above situations, which responses would you most likely give? What is your rationale?

2. Is there a pattern for your behavior? Describe.

3. If your approach to these situations is primarily passive, why is this so? Are you getting your needs met?

4. If your approach to these situations is primarily aggressive, why is this so? What impact might this have on others?

5. Which responses are the most effective and why?

6. What are some alternate responses that would work effectively in these situations?

**Exercise 5–E
Practicing Assertive
Communication**

1. You have been working with your project group for the last few weeks. During this time you have had three meetings and at each meeting Dan has either come late or left early. Even when he is at the meeting, it seems that his mind is elsewhere. Everyone's input on the project is needed and you're concerned that his lack of participation and preparation will affect the outcome.

   Apply principles of assertive communication in formulating a script for how you would approach Dan to resolve the situation.

   _____

   _____

   _____

   _____

   _____

2. You have been working for the same retailer for three summers and on your holiday vacations from school. You were hired in at $6.25 per hour the first summer and were told that you would have an evaluation and get a raise after 60 days. The summer went by and you never received a raise or evaluation. You worked the holiday and returned the following summer. You were given a 25-cent raise when you began the summer but again had no evaluations or raise. You worked the second holiday season at the same rate and they seemed very happy to have you back for a third summer. You have always been on time, are dependable, and take on additional tasks. You need to have more income this summer and believe you deserve a raise.

   Apply principles of assertive communication in formulating a script to ask your boss for a raise.

   _____

   _____

   _____

   _____

   _____

   _____

**Exercise 5–F
Taking Responsibility**

For each of the following comments:

1. Write the underlying assumption(s) about the speaker's intent in making the statement.

2. Rewrite the comment to reflect efforts to take responsibility and to communicate assumptions clearly. Utilize the strategies discussed in the chapter.

1. "Can't you work under pressure?"

   Assumption: _Trying to get the worker to work better under pressure_

   Rewritten statement: _What can I do to help you work better under pressure?_

2. "You're not listening to me."

   Assumption: _____

   Rewritten statement: _I feel like I am not being heard_

3. "Will you work overtime Friday?"

Assumption: _Assume person will work_

Rewritten statement: _Could you work overtime F.?_

4. "Joyce, what have you done with the production figures?"

Assumption: _____

Rewritten statement: _J where can I find the product figures?_

5. "Are you getting all this down in writing?"

Assumption: _____

Rewritten statement: _Am I talking too fast to write it all down?_

6. "Why are you mad at me?"

Assumption: _____

Rewritten statement: _What did I do wrong?_

7. "You've never appreciated my work."

Assumption: _____

Rewritten statement: _I feel like my work is not being appreciated_

Source: Exercise adapted from an exercise in J. William Pfeiffer and John E. Jones, *Structured Experiences Kit,* entitled Taking Responsibility, C-CAE/0-15 (San Francisco, CA: Jossey-Bass Pfeiffer, 1980).

**Exercise 5–G
Try This . . .**

1. Watch a favorite TV show. Identify the characters who are utilizing effective verbal communication, and those who aren't. Describe the behaviors and attitudes of each, as well as the results they're getting (or not getting).

2. Identify a character in a book or a movie (e.g., *Patton, Wall Street, Moby Dick*) who exemplifies either assertiveness or aggressiveness. What about this character would you like to emulate? Why? What are the results or consequences of their assertive or aggressive style?

3. Go through some recent e-mails you've sent or received. Are there errors? Are any of them negative? Are any of them about subjects that would be better discussed in person?

4. Evaluate your most recent conversation with a significant other, spouse, close relative, co-worker, or friend. Did it go well? Why or why not? What could you do to improve your communication with this person?

Exercise 5–H
Reflection/Action Plan

This chapter focused on the skill of verbal communication—what it is, why it is important, and how to improve your skills in this area. Complete the worksheet below upon completing all readings and experiential activities for this chapter.

1. The one or two communication areas in which I am most strong are:

_____

_____

_____

_____

2. The one or two communication areas in which I need more improvement are:

_____

_____

_____

_____

3. If I did only one thing to improve in this area, it would be to:

_____

_____

_____

_____

4. Making this change would probably result in:

_____

_____

_____

_____

5. If I did not change or improve in this area, it would probably affect my personal and professional life in the following ways:

_____

_____

_____

_____

6

The Importance and Skill of Listening

How do I:

✓ Ask a friend to be a good listener or sounding board for me when I have something important to discuss with him or her?

✓ Use behaviors that demonstrate that I am a good listener or sounding board?

✓ Differentiate between positive and negative listening behaviors?

✓ Accurately send nonverbal messages?

✓ Accurately interpret others' nonverbal messages?

It all started out so well. I had been working 12-hour days for three months at the investment firm where I work as an analyst. I was getting ready to propose to my girlfriend, a fellow analyst. I had the flowers bought and the limo reserved. We were going to one of the best restaurants in the city. She knew I had something special planned but she wasn't sure exactly what. I had high hopes for the evening.

My girlfriend Amy's parents had been having serious marital problems. Up until now, we all thought they'd be able to resolve the situation and hopefully stay together. But on the day of my planned proposal, I received a frantic phone call from Amy. Through her tears I could make out what had happened. Her parents had announced to their kids that they were getting divorced. All of a sudden I panicked. I was trying to listen to Amy, absorb what she was saying, while at the same time I admit I was worrying about the evening that lay ahead, just hours away. I was angry with her parents. They were in on my secret—I had arranged to pick Amy up at her parents' house in the suburbs for what could be the most important date of my life. Why couldn't they have waited until after I proposed to tell their kids? They knew how much this night would mean to their daughter, not to mention me. Oops, I thought. You're getting a little ahead of yourself here. Calm down. Don't think about yourself right now. Think about Amy. Maybe if I just listen quietly it will all blow over. She'll have a good cry and then we can talk about tonight and how much we'll enjoy it.

All seemed to be going well. She was talking and I was saying the right things, waiting for an opportune time to raise the question about the evening ahead. After listening to her for what I thought was an acceptable length of time (to me it seemed interminable!), I finally said, "Well, at least we have our special night out tonight. That will be a nice distraction." Uh-oh. That response was greeted with complete silence. Gotta be careful here, I said to myself. I started to backtrack. "I mean—isn't it better to try to have some fun right now? We'll have plenty of time to talk about this later." That did it. Had I read her wrong! Amy started lambasting me. How could I be so selfish? So unsupportive? She had no intention of going out with me tonight, the worst night of her life. And wouldn't I be a better boyfriend by offering to stay home with her? This was definitely not my plan. I was thinking about the flowers, the limo, the dinner reservation, the ring. All of a sudden I realized I hadn't heard a thing she had been saying. Not really heard, anyway.

1. Where did Justin go wrong?

2. Why wasn't Amy interested in going out with him?

3. What are some of the reasons why Justin had a difficult time reading Amy?

4. What should Justin do?

"If you think you know it all, then you haven't been listening"

La Rochefoucauld

Communication is a two-way street. When done correctly, **communication** is a fluid, evolving process involving the sending and receiving of messages between two or more people. Communication is enhanced when all parties have the opportunity to both speak as well as listen, when all have a chance to check their perceptions of what they're hearing, and when principles of both verbal and nonverbal communication are followed. This chapter reviews the basic concepts of effective listening and how these principles can be applied in personal and professional life.

What Is Listening?

Listening, the process of taking in what we hear and mentally organizing it to make sense of it,[1] is an invaluable component of the communication process. No matter how accomplished a speaker is, if no one is listening the speaker is not reaching his or her audience. Listening is an essential skill for those who want to be successful in work and in life. Yet truly effective listeners are hard to find. When was the last time you truly felt listened to? When did you feel someone really made an effort to get to know you—to understand where you were coming from and why or to help you solve a problem without meddling and without shifting attention to *their* problems and away from yours? The challenge of listening is exemplified by Mark Twain's famous words:

"There's a reason why God gave us two ears and only one mouth."

How many of us were fortunate enough to be taught the skill of listening in school or on the job? Listening is critical for effective communication, yet few people have actually acquired training in this essential skill. Most of us have had exposure to the art of talking and presenting, but listening is a skill that is simply overlooked, perhaps because it is assumed that everyone can or will do this. Talking is one of the first skills we practice. Parents can hardly wait for their child to speak for the first time. Yet the most training we receive in listening is when someone says those infamous words "You're not listening to me" or "You had better listen to what I say!"

Many confuse the ability to hear or simply recognize sound with the skill of listening or the ability to comprehend what is heard. The act of simply "hearing" is a passive activity. The act of listening—truly listening—demands attention, concentration, and effort.

There are several different types of listening:[2]

Passive listening occurs when one is trying to absorb as much of the information presented as possible. The listener acts as a sponge, taking in the information with no or little attempt to process or enhance the messages being sent by the speaker.

Attentive listening occurs when one is genuinely interested in the speaker's point of view. The listener is aware something can be learned from the interaction. In attentive listening, the listener will make assumptions about the messages being relayed by the speaker and fill in gaps with assumptions based on what the listener wants to hear rather than on what the speaker is actually saying. At this level of listening, the listener doesn't check to see whether what they have heard is what the speaker intended to say. Many barriers and biases can hinder this form of interaction.

Active or **empathetic listening** is the most powerful level of listening and requires the largest amount of work on the part of the listener. In active listening, communication is a vibrant, two-way process that involves high levels of attentiveness, clarification, and processing of messages. In active listening, the listener not only hears and reacts to the words being spoken but also paraphrases, clarifies, and gives feedback to the speaker about the messages being received.

Active listening follows the "70/30" principle: when in the role of listener, true active listeners spend almost 70 percent of their time listening and less than 30 percent of their time talking.

The Importance of Active Listening

Active listening shows the listener that you are concerned. By paying full attention to the speaker, the listener is able to focus on the key elements of the message being sent, ask questions to clarify meanings, and offer statements that enhance both the speaker's and the listener's understanding of what is being said. Active listening leads to getting better information. By asking clarifying questions, the listener motivates the speaker to be more precise when explaining the nuances of a situation, enabling the listener to obtain details that otherwise might not have surfaced. Imagine the mother asking her teenage son how his day went. If she accepts his one-word answer ("fine"), she limits her understanding of his situation and might communicate that she really doesn't care to know more.

Active listening encourages further communication. In passive listening, a one-way form of communication, the listener simply takes at face value what is said by the speaker without processing or inquiring about the information. In active listening, it is common for the listener to be an active participant in the conversation, asking questions and probing for details in such a way that the speaker feels both supported and encouraged to share more information about a situation, enhancing both the speaker's and the listener's understanding of what is taking place.

Active listening also has the potential to enhance relationships. It takes more time to listen actively to someone else. Just taking this time to focus on a person and his or her issues can improve the relationship. Listening actively also involves offering mutual support and developing common understanding, both of which serve to strengthen trust and enhance interactions between the people involved. Returning to the mother and son example, if she took the time to listen and ask a few thoughtful follow-on questions, her son might begin to open up about his day. For example he might talk about the fact he failed his geometry exam, won a wrestling match, or that his best friend was arrested for drug possession. When we take the time to truly listen—using our ears and eyes to take in a more complete story—others feel cared for. These feelings are usually reciprocated, resulting in an enhanced relationship.

Another benefit of active listening is it can sometimes calm down another person who is feeling very upset about a situation. Think for a moment about airline ticket agents and how calm most of them are when confronted by an aggressive or just tired passenger. Most airline ticket agents have received customer service training that emphasizes the importance of listening to the customer. While an agent can seldom do anything that would directly respond to the passenger's needs, such as change the weather or get the flight to leave on time, the best agents are skilled at focusing their attention on passengers in distress, hearing them out, and quietly helping the passengers problem-solve about the situation in which they find themselves. These agents use their training to make the passenger feel heard and understood. They listen, ask clarifying questions, empathize, and offer potential solutions for consideration by the passenger—all in a way that is intended to calm passengers.

Active listening invites others to listen to you. By listening actively you set a good example for others and remind them that listening is a valuable skill that they can also use. Once a person has been listened to actively they are more likely to reciprocate. This benefit of active listening is echoed in one of Stephen Covey's best selling "Seven Habits"—seek first to understand and then to be understood.[3] Typically, when two people disagree, one is likely to say something like "Okay, we don't agree. Let me tell you why you're wrong and how my way is superior." Perhaps that statement is a bit exaggerated, but it demonstrates the need of many of us to be right and have our say—first and foremost. Imagine how this exchange would differ if it sounded like this: "Okay, we don't agree. Why don't you tell me your idea and why you think it will work." When we actively listen to another, chances are very high that they'll do the same in return.

Active listening leads to better cooperation and problem solving. We're all human and it's easy to make mistakes when we think we understand what someone is trying to say. By listening actively, asking questions, and probing for understanding, together the listener and speaker are generally able to develop more creative solutions than if the listener had remained passive, not offering any insight or support. Team members and employees report that when their team leaders and managers demonstrate real interest in them and their ideas by listening and paying attention to their concerns, their willingness to work collaboratively increases dramatically.

Barriers to Effective Listening   University of Minnesota studies suggest people often have difficulty truly listening:[4]

- The average person remembers only half of what he or she has heard, even when the message came just a day or so ago.
- At all organizational levels, at least 75 percent of what we hear is heard incorrectly.
- Within two or three weeks, we remember less than 25 percent of the original content.
- An average person spends 80 percent of his or her waking hours communicating, and 45 percent of that time is spent on listening. However, adults typically practice listening at no better than 25 percent efficiency.

Barriers to Effective Listening

Despite its importance in promoting effective communication, active listening is often neglected. Many factors contribute to difficulties in listening.[5] These include:

- *Physiological limitations.* Poor listening can be partly blamed on our physiological process. Most individuals have the ability to speak at about 120 words per minute, while our brains have the ability to recognize words at the rate of 600 or more words per minute.[6] This gap creates a great deal of idle time for our brains to be wandering or processing other fragments of information from various sources. During the communication process, all our senses—sight, hearing, touch, taste, and smell—have the potential to operate, thereby stimulating our brain's simultaneous processing of both the speaker's words and everything else around us.

- *Inadequate background information.* Most listeners hate to admit when they haven't heard all of the information necessary to engage in conversation, so they stumble along hoping to catch up. They seldom do.

- *Selective memory.* Some employees treasure every accolade and never hear a single criticism. Others hear only the complaints and never the praise. We have a tendency to hear—and remember—what we want. There's a reason ad agencies run commercials over and over on TV and on the web. Without reinforcement of key messages, it's easy to forget entirely or to remember only selectively what a company has paid millions for you to remember. Interestingly, studies show that steps taken to increase viewers' recall, such as adding an attractive spokesperson or using flashy video, result in viewers remembering the attractive person and not the product or what it can do for them!

■ *Selective expectation.* If you expect dishonesty, poor work attitudes, or inattention, you'll probably get them. This is an example of the "self-fulfilling prophecy." Many employees expect not to be listened to. So many managers are preoccupied with immediate tasks and seldom have the time to devote to individual employee concerns that employees become accustomed to not being heard and understood. Often they'll just give up and resign themselves to the short, nonattentive interactions with managers to which they've become accustomed, or withhold information expecting it wouldn't be attended to anyway.

■ *Fear of being influenced or persuaded.* Some managers hold certain beliefs so dear to their hearts that they are biased—unable to entertain another's point of view about a matter. Typically managers who feel this strongly about an issue have a tendency to turn off speakers, disputing their cherished beliefs even before they are fully explained.

■ *Bias and being judgmental.* When you don't like a person, it's hard to hear what he or she says. Sometimes this bias is based on wrong or incomplete information, e.g., "She's only 17, what could she know?" or "He's a bigot, so why should I listen to him?" When we make a negative judgment about the speaker, we typically stop or severely curtail our desire to listen to the speaker.

■ *Boredom.* Thought processes are four to five times the usual speed of speech. When you can guess what an employee is going to say seconds or even minutes before he or she speaks, your thoughts wander. When you return, the speaker may have gone on an unexpected track whose beginnings you lost and whose point you never do understand.

■ *Partial listening and distractions.* You may hear the literal words, but miss the connotation, facial expressions, or tone of voice. In essence, you get only part of the message. Perhaps you were trying to remember an important point when an employee interrupts to ask if they can leave to deal with an emergency at home. Chances are you didn't give that employee your full attention—even though your empathetic response to their situation would have gone a long way.

■ *Rehearsing.* Many of us use the time during another's talking to come up with a bulletproof rebuttal. If we are doing this, we aren't really listening. Sometimes we are so intent on winning an argument that the conversation veers in a different direction during our "rehearsal," resulting in our losing the segue for and impact of our carefully crafted rebuttal.

■ *Selective perception.* Perception is the process by which individuals take in and process stimuli according to their own experiences or attitudes. As such, we create our own reality, apart from what may actually be occurring. Since communication has a great deal of room for our individual interpretation, from the meaning of words to the interpretation of nonverbal signals, individual perception can easily distort the true message or its intent. Perception can be influenced by a number of factors such as our needs, opinions, personality, education, or environment. Selective perception is a process where we select or pay attention to only that information that adheres to or reinforces our own beliefs, views, or needs, causing severe distortion of messages.

■ *Interference from emotions.* Communication is susceptible to interference by emotions. Though we use communication to express our emotions, not everyone is able to understand, control, or explain their feelings adequately or fully. Emotions are neither right or wrong but rather an expression of human reactions. By observing nonverbal cues, we are better able to interpret the true level and type of others' emotional states. We can then utilize empathy to neutralize emotional responses, paving the way to begin work on understanding the content of the communication. The emotional state of both the sender and the receiver must be considered in eliminating problems in the communication process.

Selective Perception   Most listeners hear what they want to hear. For example, many a manager has told a new employee that the organization gives "merit" pay increases. That new employee hears these words as "automatic" salary boosts, to which they feel entitled. Later, when the employee inevitably complains, the manager protests that the word "merit" means selective, and the employee will insist that to them the word "merit" means automatic. Who is right? Technically, the manager is. But in the interest of fostering good communication, it's up to the manager to be more explicit, give examples, and manage expectations by mentioning that only a small percentage of employees actually receive merit increases.

Characteristics of Active Listening

Active listening can be difficult for some people. Fortunately, listening skills can be developed and improved. Just as effective speaking is an acquired skill, so too is good listening. It requires a willingness to constantly practice, utilize various techniques, and evaluate progress.

Here are several strategies you can use to become an active listener.

- Show interest and be sincere in listening. Use both verbal and nonverbal cues to demonstrate that you truly care about the speaker and his or her message.

- Ask questions if you don't understand completely. Ask for clarification on points of contention ("Did he say that we would need to lay off employees or just cut costs?") as well as follow-up questions ("When will she have to start this process?").

- Avoid distractions. Avoid doing two (or more) things at once. Make the speaker feel like she or he is the most important person in the world.

- Use direct eye contact. Look away from the computer, the report, or your calendar while communicating with friends and associates. Also, be sensitive to cultural differences in interpreting the meaning that might be conveyed by making—or avoiding—eye contact with others.

- Do not interrupt. To quote the American etiquette expert, Letitia Baldridge, "Good listeners don't interrupt—ever—unless the building's on fire."[7] Pause and count to three to make sure the speaker has completed his or her statements.

- Read both the verbal and nonverbal messages. Good listening technique involves good detective work. Take the time and energy needed to understand the whole message and not just what is being spoken.

- Be empathetic. Recognize and acknowledge the other person's feelings and emotions. If they're distressed, cracking a joke or making light of the situation might be interpreted as the listener doesn't care about the speaker. The earlier example of the airline agent certainly applies here.

- Paraphrase to correct misinterpretations, reflect the literal message, and improve retention. Repeat statements for clarification. Say, "If I heard you correctly . . ." or "So what you are saying is . . ."

- Evaluate the message *after* hearing all the facts. A common habit of listeners is forming a response before the speaker is finished.[8] Avoid judgments by allowing the individual to complete the entire message before assessing the content and merit of the statements.

- Concentrate on the message as well as the messenger. Focus on the delivery as well as the content of the message itself, but be sure to check your potential biases about the messenger *before* you start the listening process.

(continued)

- Give feedback to check accuracy, express your perspective, and broaden the interaction. For example, you might say, "So you want me to complete this report by Friday?" or "It sounds like we disagree; are there any elements of the plan on which we can both agree?"
- Listen with your entire body. Use direct eye contact, lean forward, nod your head, and use nonverbal communication to denote understanding or to get clarification.
- Don't talk so much! If you know you have tendencies toward verbosity, be on guard. As former U.S. president Calvin Coolidge said, "No one ever listened himself out of a job!"

Nonverbal Communication

Nonverbal communication is conveying meaning or expressing feelings consciously or subconsciously through means other than words. In a direct conversation between two individuals, up to 65 percent of the social meaning is sent through nonverbal means such as hand gestures, rolling of eyes, nodding the head, or looking away while someone is speaking.[9] How often have you experienced talking with someone who says they're listening even though they're watching television? Or having someone say they agree to something while shaking their head in disagreement? Conversely, have you experienced empathy from someone as evidenced by their nodding in support rather than sharing their agreement with you verbally? We often communicate nonverbally in ways that contradict what we're saying verbally. Nonverbal messages are often sent subconsciously, leading others to believe that they hold more of the true meaning than the verbal message.[10] Nonverbal communication is powerful. It is important to understand first how *we* communicate nonverbally, and then how to interpret correctly nonverbal messages that are sent to us by others.

The communication process involves much more than the spoken word. Key is sending verbal messages congruent with our nonverbal signals: do they reinforce the message? Or do they contradict the intended message and confuse the receiver? For example, a boss who says he or she loves your ideas while rolling his or her eyes would lead you to believe that the boss might lack confidence in your suggestions.

There are several ways in which we communicate nonverbally. By increasing awareness of your own tendencies to communicate nonverbally, as well as the potential meaning of others' nonverbal communication, you can increase confidence in your ability to communicate effectively.

Kinesics involves body movement, gestures, and posture. This includes eye contact, leaning, and body positioning. For example, we tend to use eye contact to provide information, express interest or intimacy, or to facilitate accomplishing of tasks. Many gestures are passed from one generation to the next without conscious effort. The way your dad looked at you when you did something wrong may be echoed in your behavior toward others. Check yourself and ask for feedback if you think others may find your gestures offensive. In addition, there are differences—some small, some vast—in the use, acceptability, and interpretation of gestures in other cultures. As said before, it is important to know your audience.

Para-language refers to the tone of voice, volume, pitch, or speech rate. Is the sender using a strong, loud tone of voice or are they soft-spoken or timid in making an announcement? It is important to check both your message and how you deliver it to

(continued)

ensure it will be interpreted and responded to as intended. The same message can have very different meanings depending on which words are emphasized. For example,

- *Where* is your mother? Might be used when another adult is helping a child locate his or her mother.

- Where is *your* mother? Might be said by a child's classmate at the start of the annual May Day parade.

- *Where is your mother?* Might be said by a neighbor staring alternatively between her newly broken window and a child wearing a baseball glove.

Environment refers to the layout of the space or room, lighting, color scheme, noise, decorations, and so on. The way in which you arrange your office may send a message to subordinates that may denote invitation or seclusion. For example, arranging your desk with your back to the door sends a very different message than arranging your desk facing the door. Also, placing chairs on the other side of your desk, facing you, places a barrier—figuratively and literally—between you and your co-workers. If you want to send a more egalitarian message, arrange your chairs next to your desk, or sit around a table with chairs when speaking with your employees or associates.

Chronemics is the study of how human beings use and structure time. Are you always late, early, right on time? What is the message you're sending, and how is this being perceived by your superiors, peers, or subordinates? If you are always late to meetings, what do others interpret about this behavior? What if you're always early? Is what your actions are communicating the message you intended to send? Again, there are cultural differences in how chronemics plays out in communication. Be aware of these differences to ensure mutual understanding.

Proxemics is the study of what you communicate by the way you use interpersonal space. According to anthropologist Edward T. Hall, we unconsciously use different distances or zones to communicate and interact with others.[11] You may notice that when talking to a close friend, you stand very near—perhaps a foot or less away. Conversely, when you go to the beach, you are more likely to look for a spot that is 10 or more feet from the next occupied space. How closely we stand to others with whom we communicate has a powerful effect on how we regard others and how we respond to them. For example, Americans prefer a "safe zone" when interacting with others, a space of a couple of feet or more. By contrast, many people in Latin American countries stand quite close and often touch those with whom the speak—in personal and even business conversations.

Haptics (tactile communication) refers to the use of touch. Touch can provide a strong nonverbal cue. Individuals tend to touch those they like or those with whom they have a close association, such as when a friend puts her arm over her friend's shoulder to express warmth and encouragement. Other types of touch can indicate varying degrees of aggression, such as pointing a finger or smacking another's hand. Touch-based communication varies depending upon the type of relationships, including functional/professional (dental examination, haircut), social/polite (handshake), friendship/warmth (clap on the back), and love/intimacy (kisses and hugs).

The old saying, "Actions speak louder than words" holds true. Figure 6–1 illustrates some common examples of nonverbal communication. Nonverbal messages tend to be ambiguous, so they may still need verbal clarification. Silence is probably one of the most misunderstood forms of nonverbal communication. Imagine you are at a team meeting and a major decision is about to be ratified. Some members vocalize their agreement while others remain silent. Are they in agreement, still thinking, bored, angry, tired, disinterested, or daydreaming? Interpreting nonverbal messages is a complex task; there is not one universal interpretation for each gesture or response. Before you interpret a nonverbal message, ask clarifying questions or get a verbal response to ensure a correct interpretation.

**Figure 6–1
Common Nonverbal
Behavior and
Interpretations
(in Western Industrialized
Countries)[12]**

Nonverbal Behavior	Common Interpretation
Darting eyes	Lying, bored, distracted, uninterested
Crossed arms	Closed to other's opinion, defensive
Tapping fingers	Impatient, nervous
Body lean (forward)	Interest, paying attention
Rubbing hands	Anticipation
Chin rub	Disbelief
Hands on hips	Anger, frustration
Steepling fingers	Authority, superiority
Rubbing nose	Lying, doubt
Quiet voice	Uncertainty, shyness, scared
Raised eyebrow	Amazement, disbelief

Summary

Listening is an essential skill for establishing and enhancing personal and professional relationships. If you are a good listener, you'll notice that others are drawn to you. Friends and associates confide in you and relationships thrive.

Listening also involves observing and interpreting nonverbal messages—yours and those of others. By concentrating on sending and receiving the whole message, verbal and nonverbal, we increase the likelihood for professional success and personal satisfaction.

Key Terms and Concepts

Active (or empathetic) listening

Attentive listening

Chronemics

Communication

Environment

Haptics

Kinesics

Listening

Nonverbal communication

Para-language

Passive listening

Proxemics

Endnotes

1. B. Goss, "Listening as Information Processing," *Communication Quarterly* 30 (1982), pp. 304–307.

2. Stephen Robbins and Phil Hunsaker, *Training in Interpersonal Skills* (Upper Saddle River, NJ: Prentice Hall, 1997).

3. Stephen R. Covey, *Seven Habits of Highly Effective People* (New York, NY: Simon and Schuster, 1989).

4. G. R. Bell, "Listen and You Shall Hear," *The Secretary* 47, no. 9 (1984), pp. 8–9.

5. Adapted from John Morgan; revised by Beth Schneider in *Interpersonal Skills for the Manager*, Institute of Certified Professional Managers, Jan. 2000.

6. Max Messmer, "Improving Your Listening Skills," *Management Accounting (USA)*, March 1998, p. 14.

7. Winston Fletcher, "Good Listener, Better Manager," *Management Today,* Jan. 2000, p. 30.

8. Fletcher, 2000.

9. M. Knapp and A. Vangelisti, *Interpersonal Communication and Human Relationships* (Boston, MA: Allyn & Bacon, 1995).

10. Desmond Morris, *Body Talk* (New York: Crown Trade Paperbacks, 1994).

11. Edward T. Hall, *The Hidden Dimension* (New York, NY: Doubleday, 1990).

Exercise 6–A
Assessing Yourself

Circle the response that most closely correlates with each item below.

	Agree	Neither	Disagree
1. When I listen, I focus on both hearing and understanding.	1 ②3 4 5		
2. When I listen, I devote time and energy to active, rather than passive, listening.	1 ②3 4 5		
3. I concentrate on paying full attention when I listen; I listen with my entire body.	1 2 ③4 5		
4. I ask questions to clarify meaning when I listen and give feedback to check accuracy.	①2 3 4 5		
5. I paraphrase the speaker from time to time to show I'm listening and to prevent misinterpretations of what the speaker is saying.	1 ②3 4 5		
6. I spend more time listening than talking.	①2 3 4 ⑤		
7. When I listen, I check my perceptions to ensure I'm interpreting the speaker's intentions correctly.	1 2 ③4 5		
8. I am an attentive and active participant in the conversation taking place.	1 ②3 4 5		
9. When I listen, I strive to show support to the speaker.	①2 3 4 5		
10. When I listen, I don't rush to judgment.	1 2 ③4 5		
11. When I listen, I avoid interrupting or sidetracking the speaker.	1 2 ③4 5		
12. I set aside time in my key relationships for active listening.	①2 3 4 5		
13. I avoid prejudging what I think the speaker will say and making negative judgments about people; I concentrate on the message, not the messenger.	1 2 ③4 5		
14. I avoid forming my response before the speaker has made his or her point, evaluating messages only after hearing all the facts.	1 2 ③4 5		
15. When I listen, I ask the speaker to repeat when I am unsure of what the speaker has just said.	①2 3 4 5		
16. I am open to hearing views that are contrary to mine.	①2 3 4 5		
17. I use empathy to neutralize emotional statements made by the speaker.	1 ②3 4 5		
18. I actively learn and practice new listening techniques.	1 2 ③4 5		

		Agree	Neither	Disagree

19. I avoid becoming distracted, not doing two things at once while listening. — 1 ②3 4 5

20. When I listen, I use direct eye contact, as appropriate. — ①2 3 4 5

21. When I listen, I pay attention and respond to both verbal and nonverbal cues. — 1 2③4 5

22. I send verbal messages that are congruent with messages I'm sending nonverbally. — ①2 3 4 5

23. I use gestures that match the verbal message I am sending. — ①2 3 4 5

24. I use a context-appropriate tone or inflection in my message. — ①2 3 4 5

25. I arrange my room or office to indicate my openness to communication. — 1 2③4 5

26. I am aware of how I use time to communicate messages and feel they are congruent with my intent. — 1 2③4 5

27. When speaking with others, I maintain an interpersonal space that is appropriate for the situation and relationship. — 1 ②3 4 5

28. I am aware of the potential interpretations of common nonverbal behaviors as well as the need to check for meaning. — 1 ②3 4 5

Total up your points. If you scored 87 or more, you may want to consider creating a plan for improving your listening and nonverbal skills. *78 56*

**Exercise 6–B
Listening via the
Rumor Mill**

Five volunteers will be listeners. Four of the volunteers leave the room. All others in the room serve as observers, taking note of effective or ineffective listener behaviors (i.e., paraphrasing, eye contact, interrupting the speaker). The instructor tells the first listener (A) a brief story or reads a short passage. Another volunteer (B) returns to the room. The first volunteer (A) relates the story to (B). They then have a conversation. Another volunteer (C) returns and has (B) relate the story to (C). This process continues through five volunteers. The final listening volunteer (E) writes on the board what (E) recalls of the story. The volunteers compare notes—and laugh at the distortions between the first version of the story and the last!

Questions

1. How much of the original story was retained? What implications does this have for our ability to communicate effectively?

2. What types of information were easiest to remember? Why?

3. What active listening techniques were used in helping to absorb the information?

4. Which techniques that weren't used could have helped in recalling information? Give examples of how you would have used these techniques.

5. What could the senders have done to encourage active listening?

6. In what ways did the listeners change the context of the information to make it more personable or memorable according to their own needs?

Exercise 6–C
Active Listening

This exercise involves triads. Each triad counts off into threes: 1, 2, 3, 1, 2, 3, and so on. In the first round, all the 1s in their respective triads take the pro position (see topics below), all the 2s take the con position, and all the 3s act as observers. After a topic is given, two individuals representing opposing viewpoints have one minute to collect their thoughts, and then five–seven minutes to arrive at a *mutually agreeable position* on that topic.

The observer should use the form below to capture *actual examples* of what the individuals said or did that indicated active and less-than-active listening. When time is called, the pro individuals share their opinion of which listening behaviors they performed well and which ones they'd like to improve. Then the con individuals do the same. Finally, the observers share their observations and insights, using examples to reinforce their feedback.

If additional rounds are used, rotate the roles so that each person plays a speaking role, and if possible an observing role.

Round 1:
Topic selected: _____

Notes:

Round 2:
Topic selected: _____

Notes:

LISTENING FEEDBACK FORM

Indicators of Active Listening	Pro	Con
1. Asked questions for clarification		
2. Paraphrased the opposing view		
3. Responded to nonverbal cues (e.g., body posture, tone of voice)		
4. Appeared to move toward a mutually satisfying solution		
Indicators of Less-than-Active Listening		
5. Interrupted before allowing the other person to finish		
6. Was defensive about their position		
7. Appeared to dominate the conversation		
8. Ignored nonverbal cues		

Potential topics to be used:

1. Gun control
2. Capital punishment
3. Race as a criterion for college admission
4. Prison reform
5. U.S. intervention in wars outside of the U.S.
6. Legalization of marijuana
7. Mandatory armed forces draft

8. Interracial adoption
9. Premarital and extramarital sex
10. Prayer in schools
11. Diversity in the workplace
12. Pornography on the Internet

Questions

1. Did you arrive at a mutually agreeable solution? What helped you get there?
2. What were some factors that hindered this process?
3. How comfortable did you feel "arguing" the position you were given? How did this influence your ability to actively listen?
4. If the position you were given was exactly opposite your values or beliefs, did you see this topic differently now than before the exercise?
5. What steps can you take to improve your ability to listen actively to friends or associates, especially when you don't agree with their viewpoint?

**Exercise 6–D
Tools of Active
Listening**

Instructions

A. *For each of the following active listening tools, write examples in the appropriate blanks.*

1. Empathetic Responses *E*

Empathy is the ability to understand things from the other person's point of view. Empathetic responses communicate acceptance and your willingness to listen to the speaker.

Use empathetic responses when:

■ you want to convey acceptance and establish rapport.

■ you want to encourage the speaker to continue talking.

Example   Speaker: I am really tired of being told I am empowered to do my job when the truth of the matter is what and how I work is still highly controlled.

Listener: I can understand that. But what do they really mean you are empowered?

2. Restatement *H*

Restatement is a repetition of part of the speaker's own words, to show the speaker you have received the information being communicated.

Use restatement when:

■ you want to "check out" the meaning of something the speaker has said.

■ you want to encourage the speaker to explore other aspects of the matter at hand and discuss these with you.

Example   Speaker: With these changes the report will have to be redone. It's going to take at least two or three days to do it.

Listener: So we have 2 to 3 days to redo the report?

3. Paraphrasing *H*

Paraphrasing involves stating, in your own words, your interpretation of the speaker's message.

Use paraphrasing when:

- you want to confirm that you understand the speaker's feelings, and their relation to the content of the communication.
- you want to help the speaker evaluate his/her feelings about the matter at hand.
- you want to help the speaker reach a solution to a problem.

Example   Speaker: I'll be working on this project with Blackwell, and he's sharp technically, but he's not the easiest person in the world to work with.

Listener: *So you have to work w/ him even though you don't really want to*

4. Summative Statements H

Summative statements condense large portions of what has been said, highlighting the key ideas.

Use summative statements when:

- you want to focus the discussion.
- you want to confirm mutual understanding at a particular point in the discussion.
- you want to get agreement on certain points which have been raised, in order to close the conversion.

Example   Speaker: I have some problems with this team effort. Few of us have been at every meeting, fewer still complete their action items and we seem to be going nowhere.

Listener: *We need to put more effort into the project*

5. Questioning Techniques E

Questioning techniques are key tools in active listening. In particular, *open-ended* and *specifier* questions used in combination by the listener can help the speaker express feelings and thoughts about a problem. Asking questions sends the message that you are willing to work at understanding.

Example   Speaker: The other day I heard that one of my major clients dropped us for another company.

Listener: Open-ended: _____

Specifier: _____

6. Nonverbal Behavior

Use eye contact and a shift in posture to tell the speaker that you are listening. Anticipate and block interruptions/distractions. Observe speaker's nonverbal behavior and mentally note its message.

Example   Speaker: Sitting a few feet from the conference table with his body facing away from the others, the speaker gives input only when solicited and in short, one- or two-word phrases.

Listener: _____

_____

B. *Match the following examples to their respective active listening tools.*

Examples   *Active Listening Tools*

1. "As I understand it you feel . . ."   a. Restatement
   "So the key ideas you expressed are . . ."
   "What we have agreed on is . . ."

2. Face squarely, lean forward, uncross arms/legs,   b. Summative Statements
   nod head, eye contact, facial expression

3. "Two or three days?"   c. Empathetic Responses

4. "How did you feel about it?" "Which one?"   d. Paraphrasing

5. "You feel it would be difficult to get along."   e. Questioning Techniques

6. "Uh-Huh," "I see," "I understand"   f. Nonverbal Behavior

Source: Taken with permission from de Janasz et al. *Fundamentals of Facilitation*, 1992, p. 4–28.

Exercise 6–E
Are Talk Show Hosts
Good Listeners?

Watch an hour-long talk show on television and observe how the host/s and guests are communicating. Answer the following questions, supporting your answers with specific examples you noted during your observation.

1. Is the host actively listening to the guest's problems or concerns? How do you know?

   _____

   _____

   _____

2. Is the guest actively listening to the host and other guests (as appropriate)? How do you know this?

   _____

   _____

   _____

3. What active listening techniques do the hosts and guests use to clarify each other's messages?

   _____

   _____

   _____

4. If you were hosting this particular airing of the talk show, in what ways would you have communicated differently and what impact would that have had on the outcome?

   _____

   _____

   _____

**Exercise 6–F
Improving Nonverbal
Observation Skills**

1. Observe on TV or in everyday life how people use body movements to convey meaning. Make notes of their:

   ■ Facial gestures—look at their eyes, eyebrows, mouths.

   ■ Arm and hand gestures.

   ■ Feet, balance, and posture.

   ■ Breathing.

   What patterns do you pick up? Are there clusters of body movements, such as simultaneous hand, face, and posture changes?

   ■ If so, are the components of the clusters congruent with one another? If not, why not?

   ■ Are the nonverbal clusters congruent with the speaker's verbal message? Explain.

2. Stand in the middle of a room or empty space and have someone walk slowly toward you. Ask that person to stop walking as soon as you begin to feel uncomfortable. Instruct him or her to move closer and further away until you are at a comfortable distance. This is your personal buffer zone.

   ■ Does this zone change when different people walk toward you? Explain.

   ■ Compare your notes with one or two others who have done this exercise. Were there differences? To what can you attribute these differences?

   ■ Experiment with others' buffer zones. For example, stand "too close" while waiting in line, on an elevator, or in a bus. Observe that person's response to you. (Proceed carefully . . . possibly with members of your own gender.)

   Source: Adapted from Matthew McKay, Martha Davis & Patrick Fanning, *Messages: The Communication Skills Book,* 2nd ed., Oakland, CA: New Harbinger Publications, 1995, p. 58.

**Exercise 6–G
Interpreting Body
Language**

Hand Gestures

Demonstrate and describe the meaning of any hand gestures of which you are aware. Discuss how other nonverbal or verbal messages could change or influence the meaning of the gestures. Discuss how other cultures use hand gestures.

Facial Emotions

By just using your face and keeping all other body parts still, try to convey any emotion, feeling, or message to your group. Discuss how other verbal or nonverbal messages could change or influence the meaning of the gesture. Discuss how the nonverbal signals could be misinterpreted or skewed.

Source: Adapted from John Suler, Department of Psychology, Rider University, **www.rider.edu/users/suler**, 2000.

**Exercise 6–H
Nonverbal Role-Play**

In small groups, create a role-play involving only body language with no talking. Pick a scene and characters and let the rest be improvised by the members. Do not overplay the scene; allow the audience to guess and make assumptions based on use of everyday nonverbal cues.

   The group will present its role-play in front of the class. You may or may not set up the scene for the audience. Play out the scene for a few minutes.

Questions

1. Based on the body language, what was the scene depicting?
2. What was the relationship of the members to each other?
3. What were the personalities of the members?
4. What issues were affecting the group?
5. What emotions, behaviors, or feelings would you assume from the body language?

Source: Adapted from John Suler, Department of Psychology, Rider University, **www.rider.edu/users/suler**, 2000.

**Exercise 6–I
Try This . . .**

Listening

1. Try being silent for one hour.
2. Try not talking at a party.
3. The next time you eat with a group, try not talking for the first half hour.
4. Listen to your favorite TV show without looking at the screen. Listen for verbal cues that would be enhanced by nonverbal cues.

Nonverbal communication

1. From a distance observe a conversation and try to determine the emotions or content of the conversation by watching the body language.
2. Watch your favorite TV show without the volume. See if you can follow the story line and interpret feelings.

**Exercise 6–J
Reflection/Action Plan**

This chapter focused on listening and nonverbal communication—what they are, why they're important, and how to improve your skills in these areas. Complete the worksheet below upon completing all reading and experiential activities for this chapter.

1. The one or two areas in which I am most strong are:

   _____

   _____

   _____

   _____

2. The one or two areas in which I need more improvement are:

   _____

   _____

   _____

   _____

3. If I did only one thing to improve in this area, it would be to:

   _____

   _____

   _____

   _____

4. Making this change would probably result in:

   _____

   _____

   _____

   _____

5. If I did not change or improve in this area, it would probably affect my personal and professional life in the following ways:

   _____

   _____

   _____

   _____

Feedback

7

How do I:

✓ Tell someone they are not completing the job correctly without making them feel defensive?

✓ Praise someone for giving extra effort?

✓ Give constructive feedback to a member of my project team?

✓ Let my co-workers and boss know I am open to receiving constructive feedback?

✓ Give myself objective feedback and check these perceptions with others?

Susan Dougherty was a "high potential" manager at a global industrial company. She had been with the company for 10 years. During that time she had excelled as a technical specialist. A year ago, she was promoted to a managerial position. She didn't really want it, as she was very happy where she was. This new position required her to be more involved in internal politics than desired. She had solid credentials—a bachelors and masters in engineering from a top school. She had an excellent performance record and was respected by all who worked with her.

The reason Susan was promoted is that her company needed to have more women in prominent leadership roles at the company. To help her make the transition, they gave her an opportunity to participate in the company's management development program. Through the program she was learning a lot about herself, including her strengths and weaknesses as a manager. As part of the program, she was invited to sit down for about an hour with a senior member of the human resources staff to discuss her progress.

As Susan prepared for this meeting, she was full of self-doubt. She had been told by her manager that there were some concerns about her ability to do the job. Not her technical expertise—that was unquestioned—but about her ability to be a manager, to supervise and relate to others. She was a bit abrupt in her interactions with others, and typically more task oriented than those she supervised. Also she seemed to be more comfortable when she was working alone rather than as part of a team. Susan also disliked "schmoozing with the higher-ups," a "necessary condition for anyone here on their way up," as her manager explained to her.

Susan was confused. She wasn't sure how she should handle the upcoming meeting. She hadn't really wanted the job in the first place, yet she did want to do well. She was confident of her technical abilities but unsure she had what it takes to be a good manager. She wasn't sure how much to divulge to the HR representative, or if that person would be able to help her. She was really shaken. This was the first time in her professional career she had received some potentially damaging feedback. And she didn't know what to do.

1. What should Susan do?

2. What are the key issues involved here?

3. What kind of feedback and help should she elicit from her manager? From the HR representative? From her co-workers? From close friends?

4. What can Susan do on her own to prepare for the meeting—and to make a decision about how to proceed within the company?

Many receive advice, only the wise profit from it.

Syrus

Today's companies are being pressured by the marketplace to come up with the best ideas and the most innovative products. How do these companies and their employees know whether their efforts are successful? Ultimately, consumers indicate their approval of a company's products and services through their purchasing behavior and other company-initiated mechanisms, such as customer satisfaction surveys. By asking for and responding to this "advice," organizations remain viable competitors in our continuously changing environment. The old adage "no news is good news" no longer suffices. Organizations—and the employees within them—need to know how they're doing so they can continually develop and improve. Whereas customers provide this information to organizations, managers are responsible for letting employees know how they're doing and whether adjustments need to be made.

Sounds simple, right? Like most interpersonal skills, giving and receiving feedback are not as easy as they might appear. This chapter discusses the concept of feedback, its definition, functions, importance, and utility in personal and organizational settings. We also discuss the common sources and types of feedback and provide guidelines and tips for effectively giving, receiving, and asking for feedback.

What Is Feedback?

The answer to this question depends on the context in which it is asked. **Feedback** is a multifaceted concept involving the sharing of information. Why and how this feedback is shared varies with the function being performed. There are three functions of feedback:[1]

1. Feedback indicates progress made during a conversation or interaction.

When we actively listen to others by making eye contact, nodding, asking questions, or demonstrate empathy for the speaker, we are providing verbal and nonverbal responses that we understand (or not) what another is telling us. In this way, feedback helps us monitor our behavior in interactions with others. It gives us an idea about how what we (or others) say is received.

Imagine you are a host or hostess at a popular restaurant in your town. A potential female patron enters the restaurant and you inquire whether she prefers the smoking or nonsmoking section. If she replies, "How long is the wait?" she has given you a clear signal or feedback that she didn't hear your question. You reply, "It will be about twenty minutes. Do you have smoking preference?" The would-be patron replies, "That's fine. I'd like the nonsmoking section." This time her feedback to you indicates that she heard and understood your question.

The process of sending and receiving feedback is continuous in both personal and organizational settings. In most communication processes, we quickly shift from receiver to sender of information—sometimes simultaneously. What we say communicates a message, and it might also provide feedback or a response to the previous message that was sent. In this way, the ability to provide feedback is critical to the success of any communication exchange.

2. Feedback provides information concerning the effect we have on others.

In the course of interacting with personal or professional associates, words or actions may have positive or negative effects. When someone offers you a compliment, you likely smile and feel a momentary boost in your self-esteem. By saying, "thanks for noticing" or "I appreciate your saying that," you share with the complimenter how their actions make you feel. Disclosing our reactions to others—whether positive or negative—helps to develop and build effective interpersonal relationships. Imagine you are on a date with your significant other. While discussing upcoming plans, your significant other's eyes wander in the direction of an attractive patron heading toward the restroom. This bothers you. If you say nothing, your feedback in the form of a nonresponse suggests the behavior has not impacted you negatively. However, if you say, "When you look at others while we're having a conversation, it makes me feel as if what we're talking about is not important to you," you provide feedback about the negative effect on you of wandering eyes. When giving this type of feedback, you let others know how their behavior affects you and allow them to choose an appropriate response. If you say nothing, this bothersome behavior is likely to continue.

3. Feedback provides information that enables one to compare actual performance with a given standard or expectation.

Most people are eager to know how they are doing. As a student, you receive much feedback on your schoolwork. Grades on exams and assignments, written suggestions for improvement, and face-to-face meetings with faculty provide you with feedback on your performance or how well you are doing relative to others in your class or your teacher's expectations. Through feedback, you receive direct information about how you are performing and how to direct your future efforts in terms of corrective action (do more of this, stop doing that). If the feedback is constructive—it is truthful, fair, and not given as a personal attack—the information gained can be invaluable in enhancing our performance and helping us grow personally and professionally.[2]

Feedback involves offering your perceptions and describing your feelings in a nonjudgmental manner and supplying data that others can use to examine and change behaviors.[3] Knowing how to ask for feedback and being open to others' inputs about you is another important component of feedback. This function of feedback—aimed at improving performance—is the primary focus of this chapter; however, many of the suggestions can easily be applied in other contexts.

Why Giving Job Feedback Is So Important . . . in Organizations

The importance of giving, receiving, and incorporating feedback into organizational life is increasing today largely due to innovations in the use of technology and heightened diversity in the workplace. London identifies four sets of issues that provide the rationale for mastering feedback skills in today's business environment. These include:[4]

■ *Electronic performance monitoring:* Advances in technology are making it easier for companies to provide feedback individually to greater numbers of employees. Where giving structured feedback used to be a time-consuming process and was only offered on an ad hoc or as-needed basis, new software packages and employee performance databases make it possible to provide ongoing feedback to large numbers of employees. Employees can now receive information that is targeted to helping them improve their performance on an ongoing basis, increasing their chances for promotions and other professional opportunities. One disadvantage is that the use of technology-based performance feedback systems may reduce the amount of personal contact between managers and their employees. Knowing how to give and receive feedback electronically will ensure workers can adapt more positively to this new way of evaluating performance.

■ *Self-paced learning:* The availability of new technology now makes it possible for companies to provide their employees with self-learning packages. Employees can work at their own pace and obtain feedback about how well they are grasping new learning. Some employees, who are used to receiving external feedback from others, may have difficulty adjusting to a self-paced system. Knowing how to supplement electronic feedback by soliciting personal feedback from others about learning and skills will differentiate marginal employees from those who are truly committed to developing and to helping a company move forward.

■ *Cross-cultural training:* Cultural awareness is critical in today's workplace. Understanding the cultural factors affecting you and those around you will ensure that you will be able to give and receive workplace feedback intelligently, sensitively, and successfully. Training in how to incorporate cultural factors into employee feedback sessions can ensure your judgments are not biased. This practice will also safeguard you from unintentionally discriminating against or violating the civil rights of your employees.

■ *New jobs and roles:* Workplace change is now a constant. Positions and roles are continually being re-engineered, often with little or no additional training offered to employees as they start new jobs or new roles within their organization. As a result, seasoned employees are expected to give feedback to new employees or team members on company expectations and requirements. This is beneficial because it ensures that employees experience many aspects of the business and become successful at teaching, coaching, and mentoring others. On the other hand, continual adaptation to new roles can be a mentally and emotional taxing experience for new and existing employees. Knowledge of effective feedback mechanisms can reduce the strain caused by having to continually train new people.

In this new environment, feedback also travels upward from employees to managers. Feedback mechanisms are put in place for employees to share progress toward goals, relay current problems, and inform management about how they feel about their jobs, co-workers, and the organization in general.

Why Feedback Is Important . . . for Individuals

The ability to give, receive, and ask for feedback is important to us personally. Giving feedback greatly benefits those with whom you work. When information about performance is given in such a way that the person can learn and grow from the feedback, it can be an enormous boost for professional confidence and competence. Helping others to better understand the company and how to excel at their jobs can result in enhanced employee morale, improved employee relations, greater teamwork, and enhanced productivity.

By receiving feedback, we are in touch with others' perceptions of us and can change our behaviors and attitudes (if we desire to do so). Feedback informs us of what we need to do to be more efficient or effective. It adds to our understanding of our strengths and weaknesses and aids us in developing self-improvement plans through which we can learn new skills and evaluate our use of these skills. Through enhancement and improvement, we can reinforce positive actions and correct insufficient or disruptive behaviors.

Asking for feedback has many benefits. By asking for feedback, we demonstrate our commitment to improve and our dedication to do things right. This strengthens our affiliation or sense of belonging with an organization. If we see ourselves as temporary or short-term employees, we won't care what others think of us. When we ask for feedback, we signal a desire to remain involved with an organization in a longer and more meaningful capacity. Asking for feedback also builds and enhances our esteem. Through feedback we can receive reinforcement of the things we do well. This is a confidence-builder and critical for developing a positive self-identity. Receiving constructive feedback can also be beneficial. Through constructive feedback, we find out in a nonthreatening way how we can change and ways to improve. Constructive feedback, when offered appropriately, can also result in significant behavior changes. Feedback can have a strong impact on our actions and on our attitude. We all have blind spots. The better we understand our behaviors and their impact on others, the better equipped we will be to choose alternative behaviors.[5]

Sources of Feedback

Feedback typically comes from one of three primary sources:[6] (1) others—superiors, peers, customers, friends, contacts, and parents; (2) the task itself—feedback can be directly built into the task we are attempting; and (3) self—honest, realistic appraisal of how we're doing relative to others' and our own expectations.

■ *Others*—As we interact with others, we receive much input as to how we are doing. This can be an excellent source of feedback. While it is helpful to ask for and obtain feedback from others, overly positive and overly negative feedback should be treated with care. Your self-identity and self-awareness should be strong enough that you can assess your own behavior and evaluate judgments about you against your own perceptions about yourself. When you receive feedback that is overly positive (e.g., "You did a great job today") from someone who is not aware of mistakes you made in your preparation, accept the feedback gracefully but don't "believe your own press." Vow to make changes so that the next time you receive this feedback, you will feel it is richly deserved. Sometimes we receive negative feedback (e.g., "Why can't you ever do anything right?"). When this happens, use your self-awareness to evaluate this feedback. If there's a kernel of truth, accept it and make changes. If not, forget about it and focus on the positives you know you have to offer instead.

■ *The Task Itself*—When developing project plans, it is a good idea to build in mechanisms through which you evaluate the progress of the project and the people responsible for getting the work done. As a member of a project team, you might suggest building in regular checkpoints—periodic points during which the team evaluates the progress made to date, makes changes, and continually monitors the project until its end. The team can also discuss and debrief the project throughout and at the end as a means for getting feedback about which elements went well and which ones could be improved the next time around. Evaluating a project at its end provides an excellent source of feedback, as the actual project output is tangible evidence of the quality (or lack thereof) with which a project was done. For example, a quality improvement team will know whether their project is successful if the number of defective parts declines. Similarly, a customer service team can evaluate their progress by tracking the ratings given by customers in customer satisfaction surveys.

■ *Self*—Our own thoughts and perceptions can be good sources of feedback, although it is difficult for us to be completely objective when self-evaluating! While we can sometimes be our own worst critics, studies show that workers often overestimate their own performance. Few employees or even students think they are just average. Giving feedback to yourself is easy, but doing it objectively can be difficult. Generally if self-esteem is an issue, you'll be harder on yourself than others. However, this may not apply to people from cultures whose values differ from yours. It is helpful to supplement your own evaluation with comments from others. Take for example the student who asked his close friends for some feedback about himself. That showed intelligence as well as courage. It must have been a good strategy—that student is now president of a major consumer products company! When giving yourself feedback, it helps to assess yourself relative to others in similar roles, rather than making your assessment in a vacuum. Evaluate honestly those things you're doing well and those areas in which you can improve, and make plans to make the necessary changes. You can also check your self-evaluations with those of others.

To know what to do is wisdom. To know how to do it is skill. But doing it, as it should be done, tops the other two virtues.

Anonymous

Characteristics of Effective Feedback

Effective feedback provides both instruction and motivation.[7] A supervisor who demonstrates the proper sequence of steps in responding to a customer's technical questions has provided instruction to an employee. When the employee performs these steps correctly in a subsequent call, the boss responds, "Nice job! I really liked how thorough you were in asking questions to discover the best solution." This kind of feedback reinforces desired behavior and motivates the employee to continue and improve performance. To ensure that your feedback fulfills these two objectives, it should possess the following characteristics:

12 Characteristics of Effective Feedback

1. Specific	7. Timely
2. Nonpersonal	8. Frequent
3. Work related	9. Purposeful
4. Documentable	10. Constructive and balanced
5. Descriptive	11. In the appropriate setting
6. Nonprescriptive	12. Interactive

■ *Specific:* General comments like "You did a good job" or "That is all wrong" tend not to be helpful. Instead, focus your comments on a specific activity or behavior so others know exactly how they can improve their performance in the designated area. "That was a tough decision. I'm impressed with how you weighed the pros and cons and selected the best course of action." "I'd like to talk with you about your proofing of these reports."

■ *Nonpersonal:* How you deliver feedback is as important as what you say. Avoid blaming ("You're the reason we have mistakes around here") and referring to assumed personality traits ("How come you're so lazy?"). Direct your feedback at the behavior itself and not the worker. An example of this is, "I am concerned about the fact you've been late every night this week."[8]

■ *Work related:* When giving feedback to someone on the job, only refer to behaviors that are directly related to the job. "We need to talk about your absences," rather than "I understand you've been going nightclubbing every night this week."

■ *Documentable:* When giving specific work-related feedback, make sure it is based on fact rather than hearsay. "Our records show you've been using company phones for making personal calls" will be accepted more readily than, "Betty tells me you're on the phone a lot." Also keep a written record of any conversations you have when using feedback to help employees correct undesirable behaviors. This could be important if in the future you need to fire a poor-performing employee.

■ *Descriptive:* Focus your feedback on a specific behavior that can be changed or controlled by the recipient, describing behavior rather than evaluating it, for example, "I've noticed the filing system is getting a bit disorganized." Discuss what the person did and the feelings aroused by it, rather than labeling or name-calling. "You interrupted me and I get frustrated when I lose my place" rather than "You're inconsiderate."[9]

■ *Nonprescriptive:* Avoid moralizing or giving feedback that is judgmental or prescriptive. When you lecture employees about what you think they should do, they are likely to become defensive and tune out your feedback.

**Figure 7–1
Benefits of Giving,
Getting, and Asking for
Effective Feedback**

Benefits of		
Giving	Getting	Asking for Feedback
■ Ensures that individuals focus on meeting organizational goals and objectives.	■ Builds our confidence by reinforcing our strengths.	■ Demonstrates our commitment to improve.
■ Reinforces positive and effective actions and behaviors.	■ Directs us toward areas needing improvement.	■ Demonstrates our dedication to doing things right.
■ Provides corrective action of ineffective or problematic behaviors.	■ Helps us understand our blind spots—weaknesses of which we're unaware.	■ Shows our commitment to continued service in an organization.

■ *Timely:* Give feedback promptly, immediately after the event or incident, if possible. While promptness is important, it is OK to wait briefly if it means delivering feedback in a private setting and once emotions have cooled. "Let's debrief how the meeting went tomorrow, after we've both had a chance to think about it." Don't delay giving feedback, as it will reduce the likelihood that others will understand and learn from their mistakes. In addition, don't withhold the feedback. Saying nothing when performance is inadequate or when someone treats you inappropriately is equivalent to indicating your acceptance with his or her behavior.

■ *Frequent:* The best performance feedback is given frequently and on an ongoing basis. Ideally, there should be no surprises at your formal performance appraisal (typically once each year); feedback about specific incidents should have already been delivered. This allows the formal review to focus more proactively on the future, on clarifying and reinforcing personal strengths and development goals.

■ *Purposeful:* Focus feedback on only one or two specific topics. "Let's talk about what happened during the last week of the project." As they say in marriage counseling, "Don't throw in the kitchen sink." If you're discussing a team member's lack of follow-through on a project, don't take the opportunity to offer a laundry list of other unrelated concerns.

■ *Constructive and balanced:* Feedback is more likely to be accepted when it contains a balance of positive and negative comments. When giving feedback, it's helpful to start the conversation with a specific positive comment. This reinforces to the employee that she is valued by you and the organization. Initial positive feedback reduces an employee's defensiveness and increases their openness to any constructive criticism that follows. "I am really pleased with the quality of your work on the Miller project. I'm wondering if there's a way you could bring others from the team into more phases of the Genovese project."

■ *In the appropriate setting:* While there are some cultural exceptions, it is appropriate to give positive feedback to employees either in private or public. Constructive feedback should always be shared in a private setting to avoid embarrassment, resentment, and defensiveness. "I'd like to talk with you. Let's go somewhere where we're out of earshot."[10]

■ *Interactive:* Good feedback takes into account the needs of both the giver and the receiver. Feedback is best when it is a two-way interchange. One way to do this is to solicit an employee's perspective on a subject or incident before deciding how to handle it. "I've shared your teammates' view of the situation. What is your perspective on what occurred? How do you think we should approach this situation?" By asking for and integrating the employee's perspective with your own, you can reduce misunderstandings, develop better solutions, and most importantly, gain their commitment to a solution—*their* solution.

Challenges in Providing Feedback

Giving feedback, especially constructive feedback, about something in a person that has to change, is one of the most difficult things for a manager to do well. Studies show that many managers dread feedback sessions with their employees and often resist or ignore doing so. Giving feedback is one of the toughest managerial responsibilities, yet it is one of the most important. Anxiety over giving feedback exists for several reasons:

1. Managers are uncomfortable giving negative feedback and discussing performance weaknesses. While many of us can and do give out compliments and "pats on the back," few look forward to doling out criticisms and therefore ignore or delay giving feedback.

2. Employees tend to have an inflated view of their own performance; most people rate themselves above average when, statistically, about half will be below average. The perceptual differences between a manager and employee underscore the difficulty in and conflicting nature of giving feedback.

3. Managers are afraid of the reaction they might get when delivering negative feedback to some employees. They fear that employees will respond defensively, perhaps even with hostility.[11] Recent research on workplace incivility demonstrates that such behaviors have become more commonplace and of concern in the workforce.[12]

4. As organizations have downsized and increased spans of control, managers have less time available to provide effective feedback to greater numbers of employees. With other more pressing matters tugging at them, managers may feel unable to make "time for all those intimate, eyeball-to-eyeball encounters"[13] amidst all the other things for which they are accountable.

Despite how difficult giving feedback might appear to be, it is important for managers to give constructive feedback. Feedback—and the lessons derived from it—are the lifeblood of an organization. Without feedback, employees are left in the dark, frustrated over not knowing where they stand. This can lead to interpersonal conflicts, absenteeism, and turnover.[14]

Tips for Preparing and Leading a Feedback Session

By following the tips and techniques below, you'll find it easier to **give feedback** and ensure that employees accept and positively act upon it for improved performance:

■ **Prepare a script.** If possible, identify in advance the situation that will be discussed and develop a "script" for how you intend to approach the situation, using an outline such as the one in Figure 7–2. Most people fear the unknown and unexpected. By preparing a script and thinking through possible responses, you are likely to reduce the discomfort associated with providing constructive feedback. See Figure 7-3 for a sample script.

■ **Examine your motives.** Evaluate why you need to give feedback and your rationale for doing so. Assess potential barriers or obstacles, the strength of your relationship with the intended recipient, competitive pressures that might impact the situation, the perceived imbalance of power, and the credibility you both possess in the organization. This assessment can bring to the surface problems that could arise when giving (or receiving) feedback. Understanding your reasons and the factors affecting the potential feedback session aids in developing a successful strategy for giving feedback.[15]

**Figure 7–2
Outline for Feedback
Session**

Brief Description of Situation:

Opening: Overview/Purpose of Meeting: (state why you are meeting and what you hope to accomplish)

Feedback: (explain the situation objectively, using facts to back up your assertions about a specific behavior and its impact on fellow employees or team members)

Interaction/Clarification: (invite a response—as what the employee's perception of the situation is)

Suggestions: (offer a suggestion for change or brainstorm a solution with the employee)

Clarify Expectations/Close/Next Steps: (agree to meet again at a specific time to review progress)

**Figure 7–3
Sample Script**

The situation. As Director of Marketing, you have been receiving some signals that your star salesperson, Margaret, has been ruffling the feathers of some of her customers and peers. John, a buyer for Belk's (a department store), sent you a letter detailing the harsh treatment he received from Margaret when he requested to change his current order. You also heard from another of your employees that Liz, a co-worker of Margaret's, was seen crying in the employee lounge immediately following a heated discussion with Margaret. Stories like these are out of the ordinary when it comes to Margaret; however, you have also heard through the grapevine that Margaret may be experiencing some personal problems. Margaret has been an outstanding performer for the last four years; however, you are concerned about an emerging pattern of interpersonal issues involving Margaret. You plan to approach Margaret in the following way:

Opening: "Margaret, I'd like to talk with you about your performance over the last two months. My goal is to get some clarity about two specific situations and offer assistance in improving your current performance."

Feedback: "Margaret, for the last four years, you've had steadily increasing sales and have been a star performer. Lately, however, I've received some distressing information about how harshly you treated a Belk's buyer, and of a strained discussion with Liz."

Interaction/Clarification: "I'm not sure what to make of these instances; could you help shed some light on what's going on?" (Listen to her response.)

Suggestions: "Margaret, I am committed to helping assist you in removing whatever's in the way of you performing at your peak . . . is there anything I can do to help?" (Wait for her suggestions. If none are forthcoming, offer some, such as additional training, time off.)

Clarify Expectations/Close/Next Steps: "Sounds like we have a good plan. So we're both on the same page, what changes should I expect to see over the next few weeks?" (Listen to her response.) "Let's plan on meeting again in three weeks . . . how about Friday the 19th at 2:00 P.M.?"

■ **Ask for input.** Get the employee's or team member's opinion about and perspective on the situation. This enables others to examine their own perspective and allows you to determine whether a situation is completely understood. It also paves the way for getting their ideas on how to proceed, making them feel part of the process and the organization instead of isolated or victimized by it. By ensuring two-way communication, both parties confirm data and perceptions, assuring the dialogue meets expectations on both sides.[16]

■ **Offer help, support, and suggestions.** If appropriate, offer to be of assistance by meeting with the employee periodically to check progress or, if appropriate, by recommending internal or external resources that might be available (e.g., an employee assistance program). Be supportive of the employee as a person. Make clear it is only his or her behavior that is of concern to you. Explain the impact of desired results—how the requested change will benefit them as well as others. Emphasize joint problem solving. This reduces their defensiveness and resistance to your suggestions.

■ **Clarify expectations and specify next steps.** Ask the employee for feedback on your feedback. Have you made your expectations clear? Have you provided adequate resources or information? Once the situation and options for improvement are understood, it's time to discuss suitable next steps and a plan to follow up. As a manager, you demonstrate the seriousness of the situation and signal your commitment to the requested change by asking the employee to meet with you, call, or send you a progress memo on a regular basis.

Constructive feedback can have positive results if handled and presented properly. Start the session positively, discuss what needs to change, and involve the employee in developing action steps he or she can focus on and work towards for development. This ensures ending the feedback session on a positive note.[17]

Tips for Receiving Feedback

When **receiving constructive feedback,** it is important to demonstrate an openness to hearing the information and benefiting from it. Even if you feel a bit uncomfortable having the attention focused on you and your behavior, try to be objective and not take things personally. If the person giving you feedback is well trained, they'll deliver the information fairly and effectively. If the person lacks this training, there are a few steps you can take to ensure things go well.

■ *Keep an ongoing performance folder.* Keep in the folder letters or e-mails which commend your performance. If a problem surfaces, keep careful documentation of whom you talk to and what is said. Keep a running list of projects in which you've been involved, noting your contributions to each. This is a good idea to do even if you don't receive constructive feedback. But if you do, this record might provide you with information that can be useful when asked to share your perspective on the situation.

■ *Evaluate your own progress on a regular basis.* Whenever assigned to a new project, task force, or work group, make it a habit to request feedback early on and throughout the project. This makes it easier for co-workers and teammates to approach you with concerns if any surface and often prevents a formal feedback session from being necessary.

■ *Let someone know if a change in your personal circumstances is affecting your work.* We are often reluctant to bring personal problems to work or school. Yet if something serious is happening and is affecting the quality of our work, it's better to talk with someone before the problem gets out of hand. This way, co-workers can manage their expectations about and make allowances for what is hopefully a temporary downturn in your performance.

Asking for Feedback

As we have discussed, it is important for employees and team members to receive feedback. This inspires us to improve, grow, and develop both as people and as professionals.[18] However, many teammates, managers, and organizations are reluctant or fail to provide feedback. Feedback is a two-way process. If feedback is not forthcoming, it is up to you to request it. Questions such as "How am I doing?" "How can I improve?" and "Can we debrief—what worked and what didn't?" demonstrate your willingness to receive feedback, and might also provide you the opportunity to give feedback. As a manager, you must show that you value feedback and input from all affected by your performance. As renowned management author and consultant Peter Drucker said, "The leader of the past was a person who knew how to tell. The leader of the future will be the person who knows how to ask." Studies show that managers who requested feedback, analyzed it, and made action plans based on the information were perceived to be more effective.[19]

Often a manager will be relieved when you bring up the need for feedback. He or she might have been too busy, or perhaps was avoiding the situation because of the fears mentioned earlier. Whatever the reason, there are times when you might need to empower yourself by requesting a feedback session. Below are a few suggestions to ensure things go smoothly:

■ Demonstrate you're open to continual change and learning.

■ Learn why you're not getting the feedback. Do most employees in the organization not get feedback, or are you the only one? By understanding why feedback has been absent, you will be better able to devise a plan for requesting and receiving feedback more regularly.

■ Assess why you want feedback before you request it. Make sure you're not overly dependent on someone else's view of you. According to Deborah Tannen, some women tend to seek more feedback than men, on a continual basis, and see it as more important.[20] Regular feedback is useful. Requesting it too frequently is not, as it may send a message that you lack confidence in your abilities.

■ Ask for suggestions on how you can improve. End any feedback session with a question about ways in which you can improve. This assures the giver of the feedback that you are listening and taking the feedback seriously. Restate or clarify their suggestions to show the giver that you understand and are committed to making the needed changes.

Summary

Personal and organizational success is not possible without feedback. Individuals and organizations need to know how they're doing in order to determine whether to modify current strategies, actions, and behaviors. Simply put, if it's not working, then why do it! While the need for feedback is obvious, many lack the skill and confidence to give effective feedback and avoid doing so. By following the tips and techniques for effectively providing, accepting, and asking for feedback, you will improve your performance and that of your co-workers and subordinates.

Key Terms and Concepts

Asking for feedback

Descriptive

Documentable

Feedback

Giving feedback

Nonprescriptive

Receiving feedback

Endnotes

1. K. W. Watson and L. L. Barker, *Interpersonal and Relational Communication* (Scottsdale, AZ: Gorsuch Scarisbrick Publishers, 1990), p. 186.

2. C. R. Zemke Bell, "On-Target Feedback," *Training,* June 1992, p. 36.

3. A. R. Cohen, S. L. Fink, H. Gadon, and R. D. Willits, *Effective Behavior in Organizations,* Fifth Ed. (Boston, MA: Irwin, 1992), p. 295.

4. Manuel London, *Job Feedback: Giving, Seeking and Using Feedback for Performance Improvement.* (Mahwah, NJ: Lawrence Erlbaum Associates, 1997).

5. J. Luft, *Group Processes* (Palo Alto, CA: National Press Books, 1970).

6. Cohen et al., 1992, p. 295.

7. Robert Kreitner and Angelo Kinicki, *Organizational Behavior,* Third Ed. (Boston, MA: Irwin/McGraw-Hill, 1995), p. 407.

8. Harriet V. Lawrence and Albert K. Wiswell, "Feeback Is a Two-Way Street," *Training and Development,* July 1995, p. 49.

9. Cohen et al., 1992, p. 295.

10. Robert W. Lucas, "Effective Feedback Skills for Trainers and Coaches," *HR Focus,* July 1994, p. 7.

11. Stephen Robbins, *Managing Today,* Second Ed. (New Jersey: Prentice Hall, 2000), p. 219.

12. L. Andersson and C. Pearson, "Tit for Tat? The Spiraling Effect of Incivility in the Workplace," *Academy of Management Review* 24, no. 3 (1999), pp. 452–471.

13. Richard Nemec, "Getting Feedback," *Communication World,* March 1997, p. 32.

14. Bill Yeargin, "If You Criticize, Make It Constructive," *Boating Industry,* Oct. 1997, p. 24.

15. Lawrence et al., 1995.

16. Ibid.

17. Crain Communications, "Tips for Providing Feedback to Employees," *Investment News,* Nov. 23, 1999, p. 34.

18. Richard Koonce, "Are You Getting the Feedback You Deserve?" *Training and Development,* July 1998, p. 18.

19. Dick Sethi and Beverly Pinzon, "The Impact of Direct Report Feedback and Follow-Up on Leadership Effectiveness," *Human Resource Planning,* Dec. 1998, pp. 14–16.

20. Koonce, 1998.

Exercise 7–C
Practicing Giving
Performance
Feedback

1. Once you have been placed by your instructor in a small group, introduce yourselves, clarify your understanding of the task, and decide on roles.

2. Choose a timekeeper, a recorder, and a spokesperson.

3. Develop a script for conducting a face-to-face feedback session with one of your employees or teammates. Choose a situation modeled on either an actual or a hypothetical work or project situation. (Other options include an employee who has been coming in late to work, a teammate who doesn't follow through on promises made to the group, and an employee whose dealings with customers have been the source of recent written complaints.)

4. Use the outline on page 128 to draft your script.

5. Be prepared to present the script to the group as a whole. The script can be read or role-played in front of the group.

Questions

1. What was the hardest thing you faced in developing this script?

2. Can you see this script working in real life? Why or why not?

3. What about the script makes it easier to give appropriate feedback?

4. In what situations are you involved wherein you could see this approach helping you?

Exercise 7–D
Peer Feedback

1. Divide into working teams.

2. Complete a "peer feedback sheet" on each team member. Check the three to five areas in which a team member is demonstrating superior, exemplar performance, and the three to five areas in which a team member could improve. At the bottom of the sheet offer examples that back up each assertion made in the checklist. Complete a feedback sheet for each member of the team, including yourself.

3. Share the positive aspects of each team member with the group. Hand the papers out so each individual can read in private about areas in which he or she can improve.

4. Discuss the findings and determine ways you can work together to support each other in developing exemplar characteristics as a team.

Peer Feedback

To:
From:

Item	Exemplar	Improve
1. Enthusiasm/attitude	_____	_____
2. Motivation/willingness to work	_____	_____
3. Responsibility/accountability	_____	_____
4. Effort	_____	_____
5. Completion/quality of assigned tasks	_____	_____
6. Punctuality	_____	_____
7. Ability to meet deadlines	_____	_____
8. Dedication to team	_____	_____
9. Attendance/participation	_____	_____
10. Sharing of ideas and feedback	_____	_____
11. Communication with team	_____	_____
12. Creativity	_____	_____
13. Accuracy	_____	_____
14. Respect for others	_____	_____
15. Flexibility	_____	_____
16. Ability to get along with team	_____	_____
17. Organization	_____	_____
18. Ability to create group "synergy"	_____	_____
19. Leadership	_____	_____
20. Other (specify): _____	_____	_____

Peer Feedback

To:
From:

Item	Exemplar	Improve
1. Enthusiasm/attitude	_____	_____
2. Motivation/willingness to work	_____	_____
3. Responsibility/accountability	_____	_____
4. Effort	_____	_____
5. Completion/quality of assigned tasks	_____	_____
6. Punctuality	_____	_____
7. Ability to meet deadlines	_____	_____
8. Dedication to team	_____	_____
9. Attendance/participation	_____	_____
10. Sharing of ideas and feedback	_____	_____
11. Communication with team	_____	_____
12. Creativity	_____	_____
13. Accuracy	_____	_____
14. Respect for others	_____	_____
15. Flexibility	_____	_____
16. Ability to get along with team	_____	_____
17. Organization	_____	_____
18. Ability to create group "synergy"	_____	_____
19. Leadership	_____	_____
20. Other (specify): _____	_____	_____

Peer Feedback

To:
From:

Item	Exemplar	Improve
1. Enthusiasm/attitude	_____	_____
2. Motivation/willingness to work	_____	_____
3. Responsibility/accountability	_____	_____
4. Effort	_____	_____
5. Completion/quality of assigned tasks	_____	_____
6. Punctuality	_____	_____
7. Ability to meet deadlines	_____	_____
8. Dedication to team	_____	_____
9. Attendance/participation	_____	_____
10. Sharing of ideas and feedback	_____	_____
11. Communication with team	_____	_____
12. Creativity	_____	_____
13. Accuracy	_____	_____
14. Respect for others	_____	_____
15. Flexibility	_____	_____
16. Ability to get along with team	_____	_____
17. Organization	_____	_____
18. Ability to create group "synergy"	_____	_____
19. Leadership	_____	_____
20. Other (specify): _____	_____	_____

Peer Feedback

To:
From:

Item	Exemplar	Improve
1. Enthusiasm/attitude	_____	_____
2. Motivation/willingness to work	_____	_____
3. Responsibility/accountability	_____	_____
4. Effort	_____	_____
5. Completion/quality of assigned tasks	_____	_____
6. Punctuality	_____	_____
7. Ability to meet deadlines	_____	_____
8. Dedication to team	_____	_____
9. Attendance/participation	_____	_____
10. Sharing of ideas and feedback	_____	_____
11. Communication with team	_____	_____
12. Creativity	_____	_____
13. Accuracy	_____	_____
14. Respect for others	_____	_____
15. Flexibility	_____	_____
16. Ability to get along with team	_____	_____
17. Organization	_____	_____
18. Ability to create group "synergy"	_____	_____
19. Leadership	_____	_____
20. Other (specify): _____	_____	_____

Peer Feedback

To:
From:

Item	Exemplar	Improve
1. Enthusiasm/attitude	_____	_____
2. Motivation/willingness to work	_____	_____
3. Responsibility/accountability	_____	_____
4. Effort	_____	_____
5. Completion/quality of assigned tasks	_____	_____
6. Punctuality	_____	_____
7. Ability to meet deadlines	_____	_____
8. Dedication to team	_____	_____
9. Attendance/participation	_____	_____
10. Sharing of ideas and feedback	_____	_____
11. Communication with team	_____	_____
12. Creativity	_____	_____
13. Accuracy	_____	_____
14. Respect for others	_____	_____
15. Flexibility	_____	_____
16. Ability to get along with team	_____	_____
17. Organization	_____	_____
18. Ability to create group "synergy"	_____	_____
19. Leadership	_____	_____
20. Other (specify): _____	_____	_____

Peer Feedback

To:
From:

Item	Exemplar	Improve
1. Enthusiasm/attitude	_____	_____
2. Motivation/willingness to work	_____	_____
3. Responsibility/accountability	_____	_____
4. Effort	_____	_____
5. Completion/quality of assigned tasks	_____	_____
6. Punctuality	_____	_____
7. Ability to meet deadlines	_____	_____
8. Dedication to team	_____	_____
9. Attendance/participation	_____	_____
10. Sharing of ideas and feedback	_____	_____
11. Communication with team	_____	_____
12. Creativity	_____	_____
13. Accuracy	_____	_____
14. Respect for others	_____	_____
15. Flexibility	_____	_____
16. Ability to get along with team	_____	_____
17. Organization	_____	_____
18. Ability to create group "synergy"	_____	_____
19. Leadership	_____	_____
20. Other (specify): _____	_____	_____

Exercise 7–E
Feedback Role-Play

1. Divide into triads or small groups.

2. Person A is the listener—the one who's receiving the feedback. Person B is the talker—the one who's giving the feedback. Person C is the observer/recorder—the one who observes and comments on the interaction between Person A and B.

3. Using one of the example scenarios below, Person B gives feedback to Person A. Person A practices the tips for accepting feedback given in the book. Person B practices the tips for giving feedback given in the book. Person C observes the interaction and evaluates Person A using the feedback rating sheet below.

Feedback Rating Sheet

1. _____ The Listener asked the Talker to cite specific examples of the behavior being discussed.

2. _____ The Listener asked clarifying questions and paraphrased the Talker.

3. _____ The Listener actively listened—asked probing questions of the Talker.

4. _____ The Listener was not judgmental or evaluative.

5. _____ The Listener focused on specific behavior.

6. _____ The Listener offered balanced feedback (positive followed by suggestions for improvement).

7. Other examples of effective feedback behaviors of the Listener (specify):

Feedback Role-Play Scenarios

1. A roommate conflict (e.g., due to messiness, playing loud music, not paying their bills).

2. A problem with your significant other (e.g., due to always being late, not being a good listener, overspending).

3. A nonperforming employee (due to lateness, frequent absences, cursing on the job, wearing inappropriate attire).

4. A serious employee offense (concerns about possible theft, potential sexual harassment, potential discrimination).

Exercise 7–F
Giving Feedback: A
Reflection Worksheet

We often give feedback to others without thinking about it. Recall two recent occasions when you gave others feedback. Answer the following questions.

Think of a situation in which you gave feedback and the other person got upset with you or did not change his or her behavior.

1. In what way did you give feedback—what were specific things you said or did to convey your message?

   _____

   _____

   _____

2. How did this person react to your feedback? Did the reaction surprise you?

   _____

   _____

   _____

3. Evaluate your feedback, using the tips and techniques shared in the chapter. If you could relive this moment, what would you do differently, and what might you leave unchanged? Explain.

   _____

   _____

   _____

Think about a time when you gave feedback to another person and it was successful.

4. Describe how you gave the feedback (what you said, did).

   _____

   _____

   _____

5. How did this person react to your feedback?

   _____

   _____

   _____

6. What made your feedback effective? Was there anything you could have done differently to make the feedback even more successful? Explain.

   _____

   _____

   _____

Source: This exercise is adapted from William Gudykunst, Stella Ting-Toomey, Sandra Sudweeks, and Lea Stewart: *Building Bridges: Interpersonal Skills for a Changing World*, p. 236. Copyright © 1995, Harcourt Brace and Company. Reproduced by permission of the publisher.

**Exercise 7–G
Giving Self-feedback**

1. Working on your own, complete the self-feedback worksheet below. The sheet concerns your involvement in project teams.

2. At the bottom of the worksheet, describe your positive team qualities and areas you'd like to improve. Give specific details on how you intend to make changes.

3. Share the results with a partner.

4. Discuss the activity with the large group using the questions below:

   - In what areas are you stronger?
   - Weaker?
   - What can you do to improve in those areas?
   - What suggestions do you have for others who wish to improve?
   - Have you been in teams previously where these behaviors helped keep the team on track?
   - Or in situations where the lack of these qualities hindered a team from being effective?
   - What did you learn about yourself as a team member from this exercise?

Self-feedback Worksheet

In team projects:

1. _____ I participate willingly.
2. _____ I stay with the task assigned.
3. _____ I start by clarifying the assignment with the group.
4. _____ I try to encourage the group to get back "on point" when needed.
5. _____ I use the experience as a potential learning activity.
6. _____ I try consciously to be aware of my own behavior style and those of others.
7. _____ I try to engage in active listening.
8. _____ I try to provide positive feedback to group members.
9. _____ I help the group keep track of time.
10. _____ I help the group summarize results.
11. _____ I volunteer to record for the group.
12. _____ I process learning by taking notes.
13. _____ I volunteer to be a group spokesperson.
14. _____ Other (specify):

Things I do well:

Ways I can improve:

**Exercise 7–H
Try This . . .**

1. Ask a close friend or co-worker for some feedback about you as a person—your strengths and weaknesses—and suggestions they would offer you for improvement.

2. Conduct a self-evaluation of your own performance as an employee, student, or roommate. What do you do well? In what areas can you improve?

3. Watch a favorite TV show and look for examples of people who are either receiving or giving feedback. What positive feedback behaviors are they portraying? Negative behaviors?

4. Read the autobiography of a significant business leader. What does this person say about the importance of feedback in his or her personal development? In forming development programs for others?

**Exercise 7–I
Reflection/Action Plan**

This chapter focused on feedback—what it is, why it's important, and how to improve your ability to give and receive it. Complete the worksheet below upon completing all reading and experiential activities for this chapter.

1. The one or two areas in which I am most strong are:

_____

_____

_____

_____

2. The one or two areas in which I need more improvement are:

_____

_____

_____

_____

3. If I did only one thing to improve in this area, it would be to:

_____

_____

_____

_____

4. Making this change would probably result in:

_____

_____

_____

_____

5. If I did not change or improve in this area, it would probably affect my personal and professional life in the following ways:

_____

_____

_____

_____

8 Understanding and Working with Diverse Others

How do I:

✓ Understand the biases I may have toward others who are different from me?

✓ Confront those biases by challenging stereotypes perpetuated by society and the media?

✓ Come to grips with others' biased perceptions toward me?

✓ Accept others' approaches and perspectives when they are completely different from my own?

✓ Learn to work effectively with others of different races, genders, ages?

✓ Seek out opportunities to increase the diversity and the benefits it brings to me personally and as a member of an organization?

✓ Help others do the same?

It was the summer before my senior year, and I was about to take part in the internship of a lifetime. I[1] was one of about twenty U.S. college students selected by a Fortune 500 corporation to be part of a very prestigious management internship program. All of us were to be flown into the area's largest airport, picked up by the human resources manager and taken to housing owned by the corporation. As part of our upcoming orientation, we were given the names of students with whom we'd be living in adjoining suites and encouraged to contact them in advance. After all, we'd be together for twelve weeks!

I remember the first time my suitemate and I spoke. It was about two weeks before we met. I called her to find out what things she was going to bring and, basically, to see what kind of person she was. I said, "Hello my name is Reza Chamma and you and I are assigned suitemates." She then introduced herself and asked, "What are you?" Bewildered, I replied, "What do you mean?" Did she think I was an alien and she wanted me to assure her that I was a human being? Then she asked, "Are you Chinese or what?" My mouth gaped open in astonishment; I had never before been asked such an odd question. I guess she thought my last name was an Asian name, but still, what person comes out and asks such a direct question? Further, does it really matter where my last name comes from? In answer to her question, I told her that I was Middle Eastern. She replied with a curt and cold "Oh." So far, this girl struck me as stuck-up and politically incorrect.

I was one of the first interns to arrive. I was taken to my room and after unpacking for about an hour, I took a nap. I awakened to noises in the adjoining room. I walked through the bathroom and met my suitemate for the first time. As soon as I saw her, I hugged her. (In the Lebanese culture, we hug and kiss cheeks as opposed to shaking hands as in American culture.) My suitemate immediately pulled away after I hugged her; I was baffled by her reservation towards me. Was she still stuck on the whole "Oh you are a foreigner" thing? Did she already form an opinion of me? Would we ever get along? Thoughts raced through my head as I imagined the dreadful relationship we were likely to have while sharing such close quarters. The rest of the day, my suitemate did not even acknowledge my presence.

The next morning, we walked down to breakfast together. We didn't speak until we sat down with our food. Here was my chance to find out a little about her. I had to know why she treated me the way she did. Was she rude to me because I was "different" from her? Or, was she rude to everyone? After chatting about "safe" subjects like our majors and hoped-for jobs upon graduation, we talked about our earlier school experiences. I found out that she went to private schools her whole life. All her classmates, teachers, and administrators were white. She had never interacted with anyone from a race other than her own. While she didn't verbalize her feelings about me, I could clearly detect her discomfort with me— as if she wasn't sure what to make of me or whether she could trust me. I was shocked!

After breakfast, we were moved into a large conference room. We were given activities to do that helped us learn more about our fellow interns. When we reassembled to talk about our experiences, my suitemate sat on the opposite side of the room. She didn't even make eye contact with me. We took turns sharing how we reacted to the activities; when it was my turn, my suitemate stopped paying attention and began whispering to another woman next to her. It was as if she had no interest in what I had to say. Boy, was this going to be an interesting summer!

1. Why was Reza so taken aback by her suitemate's reaction to her?

2. What could she have done to improve her relationship with her roommate?

3. We see that Reza is upset by her suitemate's reaction. In what ways does she contribute to the problem?

4. While there may be some hurdles that Reza and her suitemate will have to overcome, what are some benefits of living with someone who is "different" from you?

5. At this point, what would you do if you were in Reza's shoes? Why?

"To know one's self is wisdom, but to know one's neighbor is genius."

Minna Antrim (Author)

What comes to mind when you hear the word "diversity"? Many people, especially in the United States, think of diversity in a single dimension: race or ethnicity. In this chapter we discuss diversity more broadly. We address what diversity is, why it's important in business, how to build sensitivity to diversity, and how to manage diversity both as an individual and in the context of organizations.

What Is Diversity?

What is **diversity**? According to R. Roosevelt Thomas Jr., president of the American Institute for Managing Diversity, diversity is "dealing with the collective mixture of differences and similarities along a given dimension . . . [it] extends to age, personal and corporate background, education, function, and personality. It includes lifestyle, sexual orientation, geographic origin, tenure with an organization, exempt or nonexempt status, and management or nonmanagement."[2] Others extend this definition further to include diversity of individuals' values, beliefs, and opinions. As depicted in Figure 8–1, understanding and managing diversity for superior organizational performance

**Figure 8–1
Primary and Secondary
Dimensions of Diversity[3]**

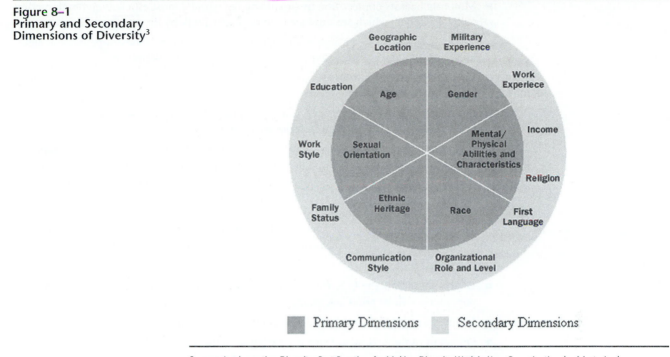

Source: *Implementing Diversity: Best Practices for Making Diversity Work in Your Organization,* by Marty Loden.
© McGraw-Hill Professional Publishing, 1995.

presupposes a broad definition, which includes both primary and secondary individual differences. In short, diversity reflects the sum total of individuals' uniqueness.

Managing diversity is a philosophy about how differences among individuals and organizations can be embraced rather than feared, encouraged rather than squelched. Empirical and anecdotal evidence tells us that organizations that are open to diversity— where people from different backgrounds and with diverse points of view are encouraged to be fully involved in the decision-making process—will "achieve a competitive advantage against organizations that are either culturally homogeneous or fail to successfully utilize their diversity."[4] As the makeup of the U.S. population changes, organizations must mirror those changes in order to reach and understand the changing needs, languages, and preferences of their clients and customers.[5]

Companies are finding that utilizing diversity in all aspects of the workforce makes not only strong moral sense, but also strong business sense as well.[6] By ensuring that diversity is built into various groups of organizational members, such as project teams, business start-up teams, customer service response teams, and top management and its sales force, businesses are able to achieve:

■ Access to a changing marketplace.

■ Large-scale business transformation.

■ Superior customer service.

■ Workforce empowerment.

■ Total quality.

■ Alliances with suppliers and customers.

■ Outsourcing partnerships.

■ Continuous learning.

There are numerous examples demonstrating the financial benefits that can accrue in companies that embrace diversity. Here are a few:

■ Xerox plants using diverse work teams are now 30 percent more productive than conventional plants.[7]

■ Procter & Gamble achieves 30–40 percent higher productivity at its 18 diverse team-based plants than at its nondiverse plants.[8]

- Motorola beat its competition by producing the world's most efficient and high-quality cellular phones, which are produced almost exclusively by diverse work teams.[9]

- Research has shown that organizations that proactively recruit, develop, and leverage multinational leaders are better positioned in the global marketplace.[10]

- KFC experienced phenomenal success when it introduced its kosher line of chicken menus in Israel.[11]

- GE Power Systems experienced 13 percent productivity gains from cross-functional and multicultural teams versus homogeneous teams.[12]

- Numerous empirical studies of work teams demonstrate that when tasks are complex and not clearly defined, heterogeneous teams outperform homogeneous teams. "Super teams," those that were diverse in numerous respects and selected because of their differences, outperformed those that were homogeneous.[13]

In addition to the examples of positive effects of diversity listed above, there are some compelling statistics that should convince all of us of the importance of being open to and managing diversity.

- By the year 2050, the U.S. Bureau of Census estimates that 50 percent of the U.S. population will be non-Caucasian.[14]

- Estimates indicate that at least 10 percent of the workforce is homosexual.[15]

- Over half of the U.S. workforce is now between the ages of 34 and 54. Only 11 percent are over 55 years of age. However, workers 55 and older are the fastest growing segment of the workforce, a phenomenon known as the "graying of America."[16]

- Seventy percent of new entrants into the U.S. workforce are now women and minorities.[17]

- The spending power of African-, Asian-, and Hispanic-Americans is now estimated to be more than $650 billion, up from $424 billion in 1994.[18]

Managing diversity is one of the primary business issues faced by global companies and organizations today. This reality means organizations are targeting their diverse customer bases in unique ways not previously seen. For example, the growth of online pharmacies can be explained by the explosive growth (and spending power) of the baby boomer generation and older relatives for whom they care. These progressive organizations have recognized the increased need for pharmaceuticals due to the aging population and growing acceptance and use of Internet technology among the U.S. population. Companies that embrace and adapt to changes in the workforce, and those whom they serve, will be better positioned to compete in the coming years.

Barriers to Accepting Diversity

Despite a general awareness in business that diversity is a positive factor, individuals still experience numerous personal barriers to accepting diversity. Those who came from homogeneous backgrounds are especially vulnerable to attitudes that prevent them from being more open to diversity—both in the workplace and in their personal lives. There are several barriers that sometimes prevent us from accepting diversity. These include:

- **Prejudice**—unjustified negative attitude toward a person based on his or her membership in a particular group, such as not wanting to consider any college students for employment at your business because you believe they are all irresponsible, carefree partiers who will not be reliable workers based on what you have read about, seen on TV reports, or one experience you had with a lazy worker who happened to be a college student.

- **Ethnocentrism**—a tendency to regard one's own group, culture, or nation as superior to others,[19] such as what sometimes occurs in a selective club, religious sect, or political organization. People who are ethnocentric see their group-related customs or beliefs as "right" and evaluate others' beliefs or practices against this yardstick.

- **Stereotypes**—set of beliefs about a group that is applied universally to all members of that group, such as "all poor people are uneducated" or "all Jews are cheap." While some stereotypes can appear to portray a group in a favorable light, such as "all Asians are good at math," stereotyping, whether positive or negative, is never a good idea because seldom does one statement hold true for all members of a group. Stereotyping is not always bad; it is a means to categorize and simplify a complex world. It is when stereotyping results in negative feelings or actions (such as discrimination or prejudice), leads to inaccurate perceptions, or results in closed-mindedness and myopic viewpoints that stereotyping can be a barrier.

- **Blaming the Victim**—making incorrect causal attributions, such as "she was asking for it" when referring to a young woman who is attacked while walking home after attending a friend's party. Sometimes we do this because of a common belief that people generally get what they deserve. However, these beliefs may prevent us from understanding and appreciating others' actions and perspectives. These beliefs may also falsely insulate us from the realities and challenges we all face.

- **Discrimination**—barring an individual from membership in an organization or from a job because of her membership in a particular group. An example of unfair discrimination is the company that only interviews men for a position that requires a lot of travel.

- **Harassment**—consciously shunning or verbally or physically abusing an individual because of membership in a particular group, such as individuals ganging up on a man because he's gay. Such harassment (and acceptance thereof) may start young, as in the case of the school bully who picks on the smaller or more studious children.

- **Sexual Harassment**—approaching a person in an unwanted, uninvited, intimate way, interfering with that person's productivity or advancement.

- **Backlash**—negative reaction to the gaining of power and influence by members of previously underrepresented groups, leading to fear, resentment, and reverse discrimination.

How to Gain Awareness

We all have some prejudices. It's part of being human. We were all brought up with a certain set of values and experiences. We cannot deny who we are; the family, community, and country we come from; or the factors that make up our personality, beliefs, and personal characteristics. We can, however, commit to improving ourselves and our ability to understand and relate to others. There are some positive steps you can take to be more open to others and their perspectives. Some of these include reducing your prejudices and stereotypes, minimizing miscommunication, and building relationships with diverse others.

Reducing Your Prejudices and Use of Stereotypes[20]

- Recognize that diversity exists and learn to value and respect fundamental differences.
- Admit to your own biases and prejudices and commit yourself to reducing them.
- Examine the stereotypes and actions that reflect your views of others, analyze your feelings based on these, and develop plans for changing your biases.
- Dispel myths about diverse others when you are in a group of friends or associates.

Minimizing Miscommunication with Diverse Others

- Educate yourself about differences by reading, listening, and broadening your experience base.
- Practice effective communication skills (e.g., listening attentively, interpreting non-verbal cues, sending and receiving messages). When conversing with others whose

first language is different from yours, pay careful attention to what they say and ask questions about what you don't understand.

■ Use words that are inclusive rather than exclusive (for example, refer to "participants" rather than to a group by its primary gender).

■ Avoid adjectives that spotlight certain groups and imply the individual is an exception (for example, the "female pilot" or the "black doctor" or the "qualified minority student").

■ Be aware of current connotations of words; what seemed acceptable yesterday may be offensive to certain groups today. For example, the state of Virginia is now calling its upcoming year 2007 founding of Jamestown event a "commemoration" rather a celebration, in deference to concerns raised by Native Americans, who feel differently about the coming of "white people" than do Caucasians.

■ Avoid forming an opinion as to the value of another's communication based on dress, mannerisms, accent, or eye contact. For example, northerners may perceive southerners to be ignorant and uneducated, while southerners may think northerners are pushy and rude. Concentrate more on the message than the messenger.

Building Relationships with Diverse Others

■ Seek opportunities to interact with a wide variety of peers and associates.

■ Form positive relationships with diverse others.

■ Seek feedback from diverse others about how well you are communicating respect for them and valuing their diversity.

■ Rather than treating diverse others as strangers, treat them as invited guests by showing interest in them. Share information about yourself and invite them to reciprocate.

■ Encourage your peers to be candid by openly discussing their personal opinions, feelings, and reactions with you.

■ Build trust by being open about yourself and being trustworthy when others share their opinions and reactions with you.

■ Make goals to work with diverse others to achieve mutual goals.

Gender Differences

The face of the world's workforce is changing. Women will account for almost 50 percent of the American workforce by 2005, and this figure is expected to continue to grow.[21] Understanding the potential gender-based differences in communication styles, related traits, and work styles can allow members of both sexes to overcome stereotypes, biases, and behaviors that can hinder individual and organizational effectiveness.

Although men and women are equal, they are different. According to the latest research, so too is the way in which men and women communicate. John Gray, Deborah Tannen, and Kathleen Reardon are among the experts who have examined the reasons for and provided supporting evidence of these differences. In general, the research demonstrates that women tend to use communication to connect with others; they express feelings, empathize, and build relationships. In contrast, men tend to use communication to assert their status and request action; in so doing they tend to use more direct, succinct language. Women, however, tend to be more indirect, vague, and even apologetic when they speak. This language pattern demonstrates not only how women pay deference to others but also why some business associates view women as inferior to men.[22] There are many theories as to why this is so, and how this tendency may evolve and change as more women assume managerial positions in the workplace.

Figure 8–2
Male/Female Communication Differences[23]

	Male	Female
Content	Sports, money, business	People, feelings, relationships
Style	To resolve problems, denote status, and view conversation as a competition	To seek understanding, use conversation to connect with another individual
Structure	Get to the point without descriptive details	More detailed and descriptive, apologetic and unclear

Some surveys have shown that women managers are rated higher than their male counterparts in workplace communication, approachability, conducting performance evaluations, being a team player, and empowering others.[24] However, women are perceived to be unclear when giving instructions and also have a tendency to deflect the spotlight, making them appear "unleaderlike." Men may experience fewer task-related problems since their orders tend to be less ambiguous and subtle than their female counterparts. However, some employees might find their male co-worker or boss to be competitive and unsympathetic.

These differences between communication purpose and style (see Figure 8–2), along with cultural views on gender roles, have led to stereotypic beliefs about gender (see Figure 8–3) which may limit our ability to work closely and effectively with members of the opposite sex. Understanding that these beliefs are generally stereotypes will allow individuals and organizations to move away from discriminating or making false assumptions while managing and working with diverse others. Hopefully, the more exposure and knowledge we gain through working with members of the opposite sex, the better able we are to evaluate individuals based on all dimensions of their being, rather than the stereotypical traits associated with one's particular gender.[25]

So how can the sexes work more effectively together? Recognize that there are strengths in both the "female" and "male" styles. Men can learn from women's managerial style by using appropriate relationship building in the workplace, while women can learn from men's style to be less subtle and more assertive and direct, especially when giving instructions. Learn more about perceived differences between women and men both socially and in the workplace. Be aware that in many situations, gender might play a role in our ability to understand others. Be familiar with cultural gender stereotypes and avoid actions, language, and behaviors that perpetuate negative or hindering views. Other suggestions for males and females are included in Figure 8–4.

Figure 8–3
Traits Associated with Gender Stereotypes[26]

Male-Associated Adjectives	Female-Associated Adjectives
Aggressive	Affectionate
Autocratic	Complaining
Capable	Cooperative
Competitive	Emotional
Coarse	Easily Influenced
Decisive	Forgiving
Humorous	Indecisive
Individualistic	Illogical
Loud	Mild
Objective	Passive
Opportunistic	Sensitive
Reckless	Subjective
Tough-minded	Tactful
Unemotional	Weak

Figure 8–4
Bridging the Gender Gap

Means to Bridge the Gender Gap: For Women

- Maintain the strong "relationship" focus that women are known for. In today's team-based environment, the ability to relate to and work effectively with others is critical.

- Be more direct and assertive, less hesitant. Don't ask, "Can you complete this by Friday," when what you mean is "I must have this report by Friday for my meeting with the client. Can I count on you?"

- Don't be afraid to speak up, especially in groups or meetings. Don't wait to be asked to speak. Come prepared with data or other information and share it confidently. If others interrupt you, politely request to finish.

- Be well read in areas sometimes thought of as the male domain, such as sports, finances, economics, science, and business. Part of being able to work effectively with diverse others requires understanding their perspective.

- Humor is fine but avoid self-deprecating humor; others may take the humor literally and reduce their faith in your abilities.

- Explain without apologizing. Men may interpret "I'm sorry" as an apology or acceptance of fault when women are communicating empathy, as in "I'm sorry that happened to you."[27]

- Avoid using vague terms and disclaimers, such as "You're welcome to disagree with me, but . . ." or "I'm not an expert, however, . . ." Express your views confidently; others will respect this quality.

- Avoid situations with co-workers that could be construed as intimate.

Means to Bridge the Gender Gap: For Men

- Maintain the direct, concise way of communicating that men are known for, especially in business situations. This increases the odds that others clearly understand your expectations and wishes.

- Add a relationship focus to your interactions with others at work. This is especially important in today's team-based, empowered environment.

- Encourage others to speak before you share your point of view. Others will listen more carefully to you if you first model this behavior.

- Be well read in areas sometimes thought of as the female domain, such as psychology, communication, interpersonal skills, relationships, group dynamics, self-improvement. The more you understand others' perspectives, the better you can understand and collaborate with them.

- Humor is fine but avoid stereotyping humor that is insensitive to members of certain groups.

- Avoid using the "fix-it" approach when others approach you about problems they are facing. Resist the urge to jump to a quick solution. Use active listening techniques to fully understand the problem and then ask if others want your advice or assistance.

- Avoid labeling. Refrain from using the words "girls," "gals," or "ladies"; these terms can be demeaning and labeling. Stick to the term "women" when talking to or about females.

- Be willing to make and admit mistakes; it helps humanize you in the eyes of subordinates and co-workers.

- Avoid situations with co-workers that could be construed as intimate.

Cross-Cultural Diversity

In this increasingly global world, it is extremely important to understand the differences among cultures and how these differences can potentially affect communication between members of diverse cultures. Many communication barriers exist even when we speak the same language. Adding cultural and language differences to the mix can compound the potential for miscommunication. By understanding and acknowledging how the following elements vary across cultures, you can improve your ability to understand, and be understood by, others.

Semantics and Connotations

It is difficult at times to perfectly translate meaning from one language or culture to another. Many companies have found they made mistakes when trying to market a product made in one country to meet the needs of another. For example, Chevrolet experienced much difficulty marketing the Nova in Spanish-speaking countries. In Spanish, the phrase "no va" means "won't go!" While a boot is a type of footwear in America, in Australia and England it refers to the trunk of a car.

Social Conventions

Each culture has acceptable social conventions and norms that affect the communication process. What is considered rude in one culture is seen as perfectly acceptable in another. For example, in some cultures it is appropriate to use a stern, direct tone in admonishing strangers or in conducting business deals: Australians tend to be curt while Middle Easterners tend to talk very loudly. Acceptable levels of assertiveness are also an area of difference. In many Asian countries, businesspeople tend to be more indirect and vague in negative situations in order to maintain harmony in their business relationships. Gender status can determine roles and denote status, as is evident in many Middle Eastern cultures where women are expected to remain submissive and not speak or disagree with male counterparts in any way.

Nonverbal Communication

Nonverbal signals and gestures can be a source of embarrassment to an uninformed stranger. Direct eye contact in America and Latin America is expected in interactions, whereas some Europeans would experience discomfort with such lengthy, direct stares. Varying cultures view and utilize time differently. For example, North Americans and Japanese expect business meetings to begin on time—promptness is a virtue—but in South America it is not only accepted, but expected that you will be one to two hours late. In Latin America and southern Europe, standing close to others and touching are appropriate and expected, whereas in the United States people like their personal space and prefer not to be touched in business situations.

There are many areas of difference between cultures. Language differences are the most pronounced, but other differences can be just as significant. According to Hofstede, there are five dimensions of cross-cultural differences: power distance, individualism versus collectivism, uncertainty avoidance, masculinity versus femininity, and long-term versus short-term orientation.[28] These differences can play a significant role in our ability to develop professional and personal relationships.

■ **Power distance** refers to the acceptance (or lack thereof) of unequal power distribution. In countries where power distance is high, citizens show deep respect for age and seniority and rarely bypass hierarchy in important decisions. Countries with high power distance are characterized by paternalistic management, where a supreme authority maintains tight control over policies and procedures. Latin America, Arab countries, and France are examples of high power distance countries.

In countries where power distance is low, competence is valued over seniority and status is less important. Countries with low power status are characterized by participative management, where decision making is shared across employee levels, and the opinions of many are considered before taking action. The United States, Australia, northern Europe, and Israel are examples of low power distance countries.

■ **Individualism vs. collectivism** refers to how loose or tightly integrated the society seems, the degree to which the people of the country prefer to act as individuals rather than as members of groups. In countries with an individualistic approach, individual achievement is emphasized and decision making is open to everyone involved. People who live in individualistic cultures are valued for their self-motivation and self-interest. Countries that can be characterized as individualistic include the United States, the United Kingdom, Canada, Australia, and the Netherlands.

In countries with a collectivist approach, the emphasis is on group harmony, total involvement in decision making, and a focus on decisions made in the best interest of the group. Countries that have a collectivist approach include Japan, many Latin American countries, and South Korea.

■ **Uncertainty avoidance** reflects the degree of threat felt when facing ambiguity and risk. In countries that are high in uncertainty avoidance, rules and procedures are preferred and followed, there is a limited display of emotion, and citizens have the expectation of lifetime employment. Examples of countries with high uncertainty avoidance are Greece, Guatemala, and Japan.

In countries with low uncertainty avoidance, risk taking is prevalent, entrepreneurship is encouraged, and citizens change jobs frequently. Countries with low uncertainty avoidance include Singapore, Hong Kong, and Ireland.

■ **Masculinity vs. femininity** refers to the degree to which emphasis is placed on assertiveness, relationships, and quality of life. In countries that are more "masculine," individuals are encouraged to be assertive. Task orientation and competitiveness are valued qualities, and money and status are valued highly. Examples of countries that are more "masculine" in their approach include Japan and Italy.

In countries that are more "feminine," individuals are encouraged to work collaboratively and to be less assertive about their own personal needs. Job satisfaction as well as work–family balance are both considered to be very important. Examples of countries that are considered to be more "feminine" are Sweden, Norway, and Thailand.

■ **Long-term vs. short-term** orientation refers to a culture's tendency to focus more on the future or the past, which includes economic success and values regarding savings and persistence. Long-term orientation implies a focus on the future, with trends towards delaying gratification, thriftiness (saving), and persistence. The top long-term countries are China, Hong Kong, Taiwan, Japan, and South Korea. These countries typically have higher savings rates and are more economically successful than countries with short-term orientation.

In countries where short-term orientation is found, there is a focus on values toward the past and present, with respect for traditions and fulfilling social obligations. These countries' values include the tendency to spend even if this means borrowing money. Countries with short-term orientation are Pakistan, the Philippines, Bangladesh, and all Western countries.

Strategies for Addressing Cross-Cultural Issues

The challenge for working effectively with others in an increasingly diverse workforce is upon us. By implementing the following strategies, you can improve your ability to work with others from cultures different from your own.

For Individuals

■ Live and work outside of your home country. Be willing to take an overseas assignment whenever the opportunity arises.

■ Travel outside of your home country extensively.

■ While away, adapt to the customs of the new country. Get to know the local residents, rather than spending your time with people of your own nationality.

■ Develop friendships with people from nationalities other than your own. Make it a point to learn from them about their customs, about the way business is conducted, about the differences and similarities between their country and yours.

■ Learn another language or languages.

■ Work at developing a non-home-country perspective on world events. Subscribe to newspapers and periodicals that broaden your understanding of key issues from multinational perspectives.

■ When traveling outside your home country on business, learn in advance about cultural differences and customs that will affect the way in which you conduct business outside your home country.[29]

For Companies and Organizations

■ Offer language training to your employees.

■ Encourage your employees to accept non-home-country work assignments.

■ Provide transition counseling to employees and their families both before and after a non-home-country assignment.

- Provide training to help employees learn about and be sensitive to cross-cultural differences.
- Examine your employment practices to ensure your company is not intentionally or unintentionally discriminating against anyone due to his or her religion or ethnicity. For example, requiring employees to work on Saturdays precludes members of certain religions from joining your organization.

Cross-cultural differences are natural. These differences will be welcomed rather than feared and will not become a source of embarrassment if individuals and organizations accept responsibility for learning about other cultures. Those managers and companies that are knowledgeable about and committed to accepting a diversity of backgrounds and perspectives will be more open to and able to manage cross-cultural differences than those who adopt a narrow, one-culture perspective.[30] This multiple perspective will be useful not only in business but also in life.

Affirmative Action and Diversity

We have looked at the definition of diversity, why it is important, and examined diversity from the perspective of gender and cross-cultural differences. While acceptance of diversity seems to be on the rise among individuals and in organizations, many organizations are managing representation rather than managing diversity. This means companies are focusing on hiring good people through affirmative action programs but are not creating an environment that allows diverse individuals to feel free to be themselves, to be accepted for who they are, and, most importantly, to be promoted through the ranks of an organization.[31] The problem is evidenced by the high number of women and minorities who leave corporate America to start their own businesses, citing as a primary motivation the lack of advancement opportunities and a lack of acceptance by their bosses and co-workers.[32]

Companies are beginning to view the concept of managing diversity more broadly than simply bringing in diverse people. It is now viewed as "a 'way of thinking' toward the objective of creating an environment that will enable all employees to reach their full potential in pursuit of organizational objectives."[33] This broader view challenges us to improve conditions for and relationships among both members of "majority" groups as well as those who are members of "underrepresented" groups. In the United States, underrepresented groups include women, people of color, and those who are physically disabled. Traditionally companies did not make concerted efforts to recruit members of these groups, resulting in a dearth of women, minorities, and the disabled at senior levels of management in many organizations today. Recent laws now govern certain hiring practices, and companies are encouraged to hire members of underrepresented groups over members of majority groups when all things are equal. This notion is called **affirmative action.** Some of the resistance to this notion on the part of some people is their concern about the way in which affirmative action was implemented in their companies, which simply leads to fulfilling quotas. Some believe that affirmative action resulted in a form of reverse discrimination, where individuals from majority groups were overlooked in favor of less qualified applicants from underrepresented groups.

In today's progressive times, the concept of affirmative action is being replaced by the concept mentioned earlier in this chapter, that of *managing diversity*. This notion challenges us to value the entire spectrum of individual experiences, abilities, and needs.[34] The more progressive companies have used the concept of managing diversity rather than affirmative action as a means to making their work environment more inclusive for all of their employees (including white males), not just those of a particular race or ethnic background.[35] The real innovators have gone beyond affirmative action to a focus on diversity that is voluntary, rather than government mandated, and is driven by an interest in enhancing productivity, rather than a concern for the law. Figure 8–5 details the differences between the essence of affirmative action and the more proactive approach to managing diversity.

**Figure 8–5
Differences between
Affirmative Action and
Managing Diversity**[36]

Affirmative Action	Managing Diversity
Government Mandated	Voluntary—Company Driven
Legally Driven	Productivity Driven
Quantitative	Qualitative
Problem Focused	Opportunity Focused
Assumes Assimilation	Assumes Integration
Internally Focuses	Internally and Externally Focused
Reactive	Proactive

"No culture can live if it attempts to be exclusive."

Mahatma Gandhi

The Imperative for Diversity

Accepting and managing diversity is essential for managers who wish to succeed and for organizations that wish to be competitive in today's marketplace. Four change factors that make managing diversity imperative include:[37]

1. The global economic paradigm shift—The competitive global economy increases our interdependence on foreign and domestic markets for sources of labor, manufacturing, and customers.

2. The "new worker" workforce—The numbers cited earlier indicate the increase in the number of women and minorities entering the workforce, the "graying" of the workforce not just in the United States but around the world, the lack of sufficient workforce entrants to staff the vast array of service and retail jobs that are available, the increased availability of technology that is enabling those with disabilities to enter the workforce, and the creation of new technologies that are affecting the way we work.[38]

3. The diversity of customers, clients and suppliers—Marketplaces are becoming more diverse, and with this change comes the expectation that diversity will be reflected in the organizations that provide the goods and services.

4. The shift to the empowerment model of management—This enables individuals to align their efforts with business objectives and gives employees greater involvement in decision making. "To empower all kinds of employees to perform at their best, organizational structure, systems, and policies must recognize and equally nurture the inputs of every group; integrate, rather than stifle, differences; and actively discourage both blatant and latent prejudice and discrimination."[39]

Benefits of Organizational Diversity

- Attracts and retains good people. Lack of diversity is stifling and causes good people to go elsewhere.

- Facilitates innovation. Anecdotal and empirical evidence clearly demonstrates that bringing together individuals with diverse talents and perspectives (and in a supportive atmosphere) results in greater innovation and creativity than that possible with a homogeneous group.[40]

- Increased ability to manage external diversity. The best companies develop strategies to manage both their employees and external forces,[41] such as their corporate image and social responsibility agenda.

- Increased customer service by promoting respect for and open interactions between employees and other employees as well as between employees and customers.

(continued)

- Improved organizational effectiveness. Teamwork, productivity, and work quality all increase when employees have or perceive they have the opportunity to contribute and have influence.
- Greater flexibility and readiness for change. Diverse organizations are better able to survive in changing environments.[42]

Tips for Managing Organizational Diversity

- Communicate diversity goals and expectations clearly to employees, spelling out the benefits for each of them as individuals as well as for the company and industry overall.[43]
- Communicate these goals through a wide variety of means such as in vision, mission, and value statements and written communications such as employee and shareholder newsletters, slogans, speeches, and vendor exhibits.
- Ensure that diversity is a top-down effort. Diversity must have visible support from the top to be viewed as real and credible by employees.
- The vital link between successful and unsuccessful diversity initiatives is supervisors: If a supervisor supports and "lives" diversity in the organization, it is more likely to be accepted by her or his employees.[44]
- Avoid the "melting pot" technique—don't try to make everyone the same; respect both differences and commonalities.[45] Some refer to this as the "salad bowl" approach.
- Create a management plan—including assessing the situation, setting objectives, and involving employees in generating solutions and initiatives. Some successful initiatives include:[46]
  - Aggressive hiring programs.
  - Early identification programs in the schools.
  - Partnerships with other businesses and community organizations.
  - Alliances with national advocate organizations.
  - Mentoring programs.
  - Minority employee networks.
  - Ongoing employee surveys.
  - Strict policies for dealing quickly and fairly with cases of prejudice, discrimination, and harassment.
  - Enhanced succession and promotion planning processes.
  - Tying manager pay increases to success in promoting diversity.
  - Accountability and reward programs.
  - Development of success measures.
  - Diversity awareness training programs.
  - Developing a comprehensive retention strategy.

Summary

We live and work in a diverse world. Diversity among our acquaintances, classmates, co-workers, neighbors, and friends is inevitable. How we interact with people who possess characteristics, values, and work styles that differ from ours plays a critical role in our ability to manage ourselves and help others achieve their goals. To work effectively with diverse others, we need to first understand and appreciate our own uniqueness. Use this information not to evaluate others' uniqueness, but as a starting point for building relationships. Seek opportunities to interact with diverse others. Share your insights, feelings, and values with them. Encourage them to do the same. The more you do this, the better you will accept and embrace diversity.

Key Terms and Concepts

Affirmative action	Long-term vs. short-term orientation
Backlash	Managing diversity
Blaming the victim	Masculinity vs. femininity
Discrimination	Power distance
Diversity	Prejudice
Ethnocentrism	Sexual harassment
Harassment	Stereotypes
Individualism vs. collectivism	Uncertainty avoidance

Endnotes

1. Case is based on JMU student Randa Chamma; case submitted in COB 202 Interpersonal Skills, Fall 1999.

2. Genevieve Capowski, "Managing Diversity," *Management Review,* June 1996, p. 12.

3. Marty Loden, *Implementing Diversity: Best Practices for Making Diversity Work in Your Organization* (New York: McGraw-Hill, 1995).

4. Taylor Cox and Ruby Beale, *Developing Competency to Manage Diversity* (San Francisco, CA: Berrett-Koehler, 1997).

5. Lee Gardenswartz and Anita Rowe, "Why Diversity Matters," *HR Focus,* July 1998, pp. 51–53.

6. Gardenswartz et al., 1998.

7. J. Orsburn, L. Moran, E. Musselwhite, and J. Zanger, *Self Directed Work Teams* (Homewood, IL: Business One Irwin, 1990).

8. Orsburn et al., 1990.

9. Jon Katzenbach and Douglas Smith, *The Wisdom of Work Teams* (Boston, MA: Harvard Business School, 1993).

10. Gail Robinson and Kathleen Dechant, "Building a Business Case for Diversity," *Academy of Management Executive,* Aug. 1997, p. 21.

11. Robinson et al., 1997.

12. Robinson et al., 1997.

13. R. M. Belbin, *Management Teams—Why They Succeed or Fail* (Woburn, MA: Butterworth-Heinemann, 1981).

14. U.S. Bureau of the Census, Statistical Abstract of the United States: 1990 (110th ed.), Washington D.C.

15. Capowski, 1996.

16. Capowski, 1996.

17. *Workforce, 2000: Work and Workers for the Twenty-First Century* (Indianapolis: Hudson Institute and U.S. Department of Labor, June 1987), p. xxi.

18. Robinson et al., 1997.

19. David W. Johnson, *Reaching Out: Interpersonal Effectiveness and Self-Actualization,* Sixth Ed. (Boston, MA: Allyn & Bacon, 1997), p. 342.

20. Portions of this are adapted from Johnson, 1997.

21. U.S. Department of Labor, *The Glass Ceiling Commission, New Release* (Washington, DC: Office of Public Affairs, USDL 95-483, 1995).

22. Deborah Tannen, *You Just Don't Understand: Women and Men in Conversation* (New York: Ballantine Books, 1991).

23. Judi Brownell, "Communicating with Credibility: The Gender Gap," *The Cornell H.R.A. Quarterly,* April 1993, pp. 52–61.

24. Sally Helgesen, *The Female Advantage: Women's Ways of Leading* (Garden City, NY: Doubleday, 1990).

25. Gary N. Powell, *Women and Men in Management* (Newbury Park, CA: Sage Publications, 1993), p. 261.

26. Portions from J. E. Williams and D. L. Best, "Cross-Cultural Views of Women and Men," in *Psychology and Culture* (Boston, MA: Allyn and Bacon, 1994), p. 193.

27. Deborah Tannen, "I'm Sorry I'm Not Apologizing," *Executive Female,* 1991, pp. 21–24.

28. Geert Hofstede, "Problems Remain, but Theories Will Change: The Universal and the Specific in 21st Century Global Management," *Organizational Dynamics,* July 1999, p. 34.

29. Barbara Pachter, "The Five Biggest Mistakes Americans Make When Doing Business Abroad," *Agency Sales Magazine,* Dec. 1997, p. 40.

30. Parshotam Dass and Barbara Parker, "Strategies for Managing Human Resource Diversity: From Resistance to Learning," *The Academy of Management Executive,* May 1999, p. 68.

31. Cheryl Comeau-Kirschner, "Beyond Fair Representation," *Management Review,* Dec. 1999, p. 8.

32. Dayle M. Smith, *Women at Work: Leadership for the Next Century* (Upper Saddle River, NJ: Prentice Hall, 2000), p. 18.

33. R. Roosevelt Thomas, Jr., "The Concept of Managing Diversity," *The Public Manager: The New Bureaucrat,* Winter 1996, p. 41.

34. Loret Carbone, "Different Strokes," *Restaurant Hospitality,* Oct. 1995, p. 38.

35. Dinesh D'Souza, "Beyond Affirmative Action: The Perils of Managing Diversity," *Chief Executive* (U.S.), Dec. 1996, p. 42.

36. Adapted from Marilyn Loden and Judy B. Rosener, *Workforce America! Managing Employee Diversity as a Vital Resource* (Burr Ridge, Ill: Irwin Professional Publishing, 1991).

37. Renee Bazile-Jones and Bernadette Lynn, "Diversity in the Workplace: Why We Should Care," *CMA—The Management Accounting Magazine,* June 1996, p. 9

38. Capowski, 1996.

39. T. Cox, "The Multicultural Organization," *Academy of Management Executive,* 1991, p. 34.

40. Susan G. Cohen and Diane E. Bailey, "What Makes Teams Work: Group Effectiveness Research from the Shop Floor to the Executive Suite," *Journal of Management,* 1997, p. 239.

41. Thomas, 1996.

42. Roger D. Wheeler, "Managing Workforce Diversity," *Tax Executive,* Nov.–Dec. 1997, pp. 493–495.

43. Charlene Marmer Solomon, "Communicating in a Global Environment," *Workforce,* Nov. 1999, p. 50.

44. Matti Dobbs and Oliver Brown, "A Vital Link: The Supervisor's Role in Managing Diversity," *The Public Manager: The New Bureaucrat,* Summer 1997, p. 53.

45. "Conversing in a Diverse World," *Association Management,* Feb. 2000, p. 31.

46. Katherine Giscombe and Adrienne D. Sims, "Breaking the Color Barrier," *HR Focus,* July 1998, p. S9.

Exercise 8–A
Assessing Yourself

Circle the response that most closely correlates with each item below.

	Agree	Neither	Disagree		
1. I recognize that diversity exists and I am learning to value differences.	(1)	2	3	4	5
2. I know what prejudices I have and am committed to reducing them.	1	(2)	3	4	5
3. I have developed plans for changing my biases.	1	2	(3)	4	5
4. I vocally dispel myths about diverse others when I am in groups of friends or colleagues.	1	(2)	3	4	5
5. I have broadened my experience base.	(1)	2	3	4	5
6. I am consciously practicing enhanced communication skills.	1	(2)	3	4	5
7. I use words that are inclusive rather than exclusive.	1	(2)	3	4	5
8. I avoid adjectives that spotlight certain groups.	1	2	(3)	4	5
9. I avoid terms that demean or devalue others.	(1)	2	3	4	5
10. I seek opportunities to interact with a wide variety of peers and associates.	1	(2)	3	4	5

	Agree	Neither		Disagree

11. I seek feedback from others in terms of how I communicate with them.   1 2 3 4 (5)

12. I try to incorporate the positive elements of both "female" and "male" types of communication.   (1) 2 3 4 5

13. I try to be well-read in subjects of interest to both women and men.   (1) 2 3 4 5

14. I avoid situations with co-workers that could be construed as intimate.   (1) 2 3 4 5

15. I encourage others to speak before I share my point of view.   (1) 2 3 4 5

16. I avoid using humor that could be viewed as insensitive to members of certain groups.   (1) 2 3 4 (5)

17. I know or am learning a language other than my primary language.   (1) 2 3 4 5

18. I have traveled, lived, or worked (or have plans to do so) in a country other than my own.   (1) 2 3 4 5

19. When I travel, I try to immerse myself in local life.   (1) 2 3 4 5

20. I have developed friendships with people from nationalities, ethnicities, or cultures other than my own.   (1) 2 3 4 5

21. I have developed nonsexual friendships with members of the opposite sex.   (1) 2 3 4 5

22. I do not impose my religious views on others and am accepting of people with religious views that differ from my own.   (1) 2 3 4 5

23. I learn about the business and social customs and practices of any new country before I visit it for the first time.   (1) 2 3 4 5

If your score is 69 or greater, it may be helpful to create a plan to improve your skills in working with diverse others.   47   36

**Exercise 8–B
Peanut Exercise**

1. Participants are to choose a peanut (still in the shell) from the bowl.

2. You now have one minute to get to know your peanut. Do not mark it, open it, or alter it in any way. You may sniff it, lick it, caress it, argue with it, confess to it—whatever will help you to get to know it better.

3. You are now to place your peanut (still in the shell) back in the collection of other peanuts.

4. After the peanuts have been emptied onto the floor or table, participants are to try to find their own peanut. If you are unable to find your own peanut, you may examine everyone else's peanut and you can negotiate ownership.

Questions

1. Were you able to recognize your peanut? How? What distinguishes it? How confident are you that this is your peanut?

2. Comparing your peanut to a neighbor's, how are the two peanuts similar? How are they different? Is one of the peanuts more identifiable than the other?

3. Does anyone want to trade his or her peanut?

4. If your peanut could talk, what might it say about you?

Source: This exercise is adapted from Christopher Taylor, "Nutty Buddy: An Exercise in Individual Differences," *Journal of Management Education,* 1999. Copyright © 1999 by Christopher Taylor. Reprinted by permission of Sage Publications Inc.

Exercise 8–C
Sentence Completion

Complete the following sentences:

1. As the construction worker surveyed the building site, _he was disappointed_

2. The nurse who works on the fifth floor is very helpful. In fact, yesterday _she organized the desk_

3. We're really excited about Michael's kindergarten teacher. Did you know that _he is good?_

4. My statistics professor makes us do tons of homework, and it's hard, too! I attend class every day, but I'm lost. Compared with other professors, _he is much harder_

5. The CEO was prominently featured in the *Wall Street Journal* for a program _that he created_

6. When someone wins the lottery, _she bis very excited_

7. After a judge instructs the jury, _the trial proceeds_

After completing the sentences, answer the following questions:

1. Did you have any difficulty adding a pronoun to each of these sentences? Which choices were easy? Explain.

2. Which were more difficult? Explain.

3. What about generic pronouns, such as "Everyone deserves his right to a fair trial," or "All men are created equal." Do you think our language is biased? Is this a problem? Explain.

4. What impact do our language biases and stereotypes about individuals have in the workplace?

Source: This exercise is adapted from W. B. Gudykunst, Stella Ting-Toomey, Sandra Subweeks, and Lea P. Stewart, *Building Bridges: Interpersonal Skills for a Changing World*, p. 211. Copyright © 1995 by Harcourt Brace and Company. Reproduced with permission of the publisher.

Exercise 8–D
Personal Stereotypes

Look at the words below. What stereotypes come to mind upon first seeing each word? Where did these stereotypes originate? What data or experience can be cited to dispel each of the stereotypes? From the list below, chose 5–10 groups for whom you can identify common stereotypes. In the first column write a few adjectives that describe the stereotype (e.g., arrogant, emotional). In the second column list the probable origin of these stereotypes for you (e.g., my parent's beliefs, the media). In the third column, cite a statistic, known fact, or example from your personal experience that dispels the stereotype. Share (depending on your comfort level) your stereotypes, their origins, and ways to dispel the inaccuracies with others in your class or small group.

Group	Stereotypes	Origins	Inaccuracies
Whites/Caucasians			
Native Americans			
African-Americans			
Asians			
Women			
Men			
Southerners			
Midwesterners			
Northerners			
Hispanics			
Jews			
Muslims			
Catholics			
Baptists			
Gays/Lesbians			
Elderly persons			
College students			
Teenagers			

Questions

1. What are some of the more common stereotypes?
2. From where do these stereotypes originate?
3. What facts can be cited to dispel the inaccuracies?
4. What, if any, stereotypes are you able to dispel as a result of this exercise?

Exercise 8–E
Personal Biases and Stereotypes in Employee Recruitment

Four volunteers serving as "candidates" will be given background profiles by the instructor to use while acting as potential employees. A fifth volunteer serving as "employer" reads a job description for a position to be filled. Individually, on a piece of paper, participants are to rank each of the four, from most likely to be hired (1) to least likely (4), citing reasons each candidate does or does not match the requirements for the job. Participants then vote for the person they think the employer is most likely to hire (out of the four candidates) for this position by going to that candidate. Participants should then explain to the candidate the reasons he or she was selected so candidates can compile a list. Participants are then to go to the candidate they believe would be the least favorable candidate and explain their reasoning for this decision. Candidates are to write on the board the characteristics or issues that made them appear more and less suited for the job.

Questions

1. What are some of the reasons certain candidates appear to be better suited for the position than the others?
2. What stereotypes emerged during the discussion of "fit" between the candidates and the position?
3. What are some of the legitimate factors used to differentiate among candidates, and what are some of the factors used to select one candidate over another that are less legitimate?

Source: This exercise is based on ideas from a JMU class presentation by Kim Aslen, June 1999.

Exercise 8–F
Cross-Cultural Communication Simulation

In this simulation, you will play the part of a manager employed by one of three firms—a commercial bank, a construction firm, and a hotel development company—which are planning a joint venture to build a new hotel and retail shopping complex in Perth, Australia. They come from three different cultures: Blue, Green, and Red. Each has specific cultural values, traits, customs, and practices.

You are a manager in the company to which you have been assigned. You will attend the kickoff get-together for the three-day meeting during which the three companies will negotiate the details of the partnership. Your management team consists of a vice president and a number of other managers. Consider the types of topics that would be discussed by the various corporations at an initial meeting.

Your instructor will provide you with information pertaining to your culture. You will be given about 15 minutes to meet with your fellow corporate members, during which you should:

1. Select a leader.
2. Discuss what your objectives and approaches will be at the opening get-together.
3. Using the description of your assigned culture, practice how you will talk and behave until you are reasonably familiar with your cultural orientation. Be sure to practice conversation distance, greeting rituals, and nonverbal behavior.

You will then return to the kick-off meeting where you will meet with the other firms. As the social proceeds, interact with the managers from the other companies. Maintain the role you have been assigned, but do not discuss it explicitly. Notice how other people react to you and how you react to them. We will discuss the experience after it is over.

Exercise 8–H
Diversity and
Perception

On a three-by-five card, write out some characteristics, abilities, dimensions, or information about you that are not readily apparent (e.g., you are a ballroom dance expert, your mother is a dentist, you are the oldest of six children). Include demographic and diversity information (e.g., you speak a foreign language, you have a disability). Only supply information that you feel comfortable sharing publicly. Give the card to the instructor.

The instructor will select five members from the class to stand in front. The audience (using the selection grid below) will attempt to match the pieces of information to the individuals. Place the number of the characteristic, ability, or fact with the letter of the individual.

Diversity and Perception Selection Grid

What belongs to whom?

Round 1

Person	A	B	C	D	E
Matching information					

Round 2

Person	A	B	C	D	E
Matching information					

Round 3

Person	A	B	C	D	E
Matching information					

Round 4

Person	A	B	C	D	E
Matching information					

Round 5

Person	A	B	C	D	E
Matching information					

Questions

1. Were any matches influenced by stereotypes, such as gender, race, or age? Why did you match certain characteristics with particular individuals?

2. What implications does your perception of an individual have on your treatment of that individual?

Source: Portions of this exercise are adapted from "What's My Line? An Exercise on First Impressions and Perceptual Shortcuts That Puts Students into the Picture," by Joan B. Rivera, *Journal of Management Education*, June 1999, p. 297. Copyright © by Joan Rivera. Reprinted by permission of Sage Publications.

3. In a managerial situation, what implications would perception and stereotypes have on working with or estimating an individual's abilities? What dimensions might you be overlooking?

After completing the above exercise and using the dimensions of diversity chart on page 147 as a guide:

1. Create a list of factors that makes you different from the person(s) sitting next to you in this group setting.

2. Create a list of factors that makes you different from anyone else in the room (including the instructor).

3. Create a list of factors that makes you different from anyone at your school or in your organization.

Compare your list with those of the other participants and discuss the amount and types of diversity that actually exist.

Exercise 8–I
Diversity Squares

Move about the room and try to find people who can answer yes to your questions. This is just like BINGO in that you are trying to complete a row. Once you have found someone to answer yes to the question, you can cross off the square, placing that person's name or initials in the box. Each person who answers yes to one of your questions can only be used once. Continue to find others until you are able to complete a row.

Have you ever worked with anyone who is 20 or more years older than you?	Have you ever worked on a farm?	Do you speak more than one language?	Have you ever worked with anyone with a physical disability?	Have you ever worked with anyone who is a non-Christian?
Have you ever had a female boss?	Are you of Hispanic or Latin American heritage?	Do you have a family member or friend on welfare?	Have you ever had an African-American boss?	Do you have a best friend of a different race?
Do you have a friend who is gay, lesbian, or bisexual?	Have you ever been discriminated against because of race or ethnicity?	Have you ever lived outside of your home country?	Have you ever known a convicted felon?	Did a single parent raise you?
Have you ever been sexually harassed at work?	Has either of your parents been in the military?	Are you of Asian heritage?	Are you a vegetarian?	Have you ever had a doctor whose race or ethnicity differs from yours?
Do you know someone with a chronic diseases such as Cancer or AIDS?	Have you ever dated someone who was less educated than you?	Have you ever been discriminated against because of gender?	Were your parents or grandparents immigrants?	Have you ever had a boss who was younger than you?

Source: This exercise is adapted from a presentation by Kari Calello, JMU student class presentation; and J. William Pfeiffer and Leonard D. Goodstein (Eds.), *The 1994 Annual: Developing Human Resources*, Pfeiffer & Company, 1994. Reprinted by permission of John Wiley and Sons Inc.

Questions

1. How did you feel asking individuals certain questions? What approach did you use to ask the questions?

2. Were some questions more difficult to ask than others (perceived to be potentially more sensitive or offensive)?

3. Why did you approach certain individuals for certain questions?

4. If you were approached by several people about the same question, how did it make you feel? Why did they select you for certain questions and neglect to ask you about others?

5. Would some of the questions be more difficult to ask or more likely to offend others if worded in the first person? For example, "Are you gay, lesbian, or bisexual?"

6. What did this exercise make you realize about stereotypes and prejudice?

Exercise 8–J
Gender Stereotypes

Part I

Your instructor will divide the group into smaller groups based on gender, resulting in male-only and female-only groups. Groups are to brainstorm a list in response to the following statements. It is not necessary for all members to agree with everything the group generates. Add all inputs to the list.

Female groups complete the following

■ All men are . . .

■ Men think all women are . . .

Male groups complete the following

■ All women are . . .

■ Women think all men are . . .

Part II

After generating your lists, your groups will present a role-play to the class based on the following scenarios by switching gender roles (females portray males, and males portray females):

Two friends (of the same gender) meeting each other back at school for the first time this year.

A person flirting with a member of the opposite sex at a party. (Females play a male flirting with a female; males play a female flirting with a male.)

Questions

1. What aspects of the role-plays were accurate, distorted, or inaccurate?

2. How did you feel portraying the opposite gender and how did it feel to see your gender portrayed?

3. On what stereotypes or experiences were these role-plays based?

Part III

Your group will now write its brainstorm lists on the board for discussion. Remember that these lists are a product of a group effort and are generally based on stereotypes and not necessarily the view of any one individual.

Analyze the lists for positive and negative results in both personal and professional settings. Generate a list of ways to dispel, reduce, or counter negative stereotypes.

Source: Portions of this exercise are adapted from concepts in Susan F. Fritz, William Brown, Joyce Lunde, and Elizabeth Banset, *Interpersonal Skills for Leadership* (New Jersey: Prentice Hall, 1999); and A. B. Shani and James B. Lau, *Behavior in Organizations: An Experiential Approach*, Sixth Ed. (Chicago: Irwin, 1996).

Questions

1. What similarities, patterns, or trends developed from the groups?

2. How do you feel about the thoughts presented about your gender?

3. What implications do these thoughts have on actions and situations in the work environment?

4. What can you do to reduce the negative affects of these stereotypes? What can you do to help dispel these stereotypes? (Brainstorm with your group or class.)

Exercise 8–K
Try This . . .

1. Subscribe to a magazine or newspaper that provides you with a perspective that differs from your own (e.g., if you're Caucasian, subscribe to *Black Enterprise;* if you're from the United States, subscribe to the *International Herald Tribune*).

2. Invite someone you know who is from a country other than yours to your next party.

3. Attend service in a church, synagogue, or mosque that is different from your own.

4. Volunteer to work for a cause that helps children from a country other than your own.

5. Volunteer to work at a nursing home or at a home for physically or mentally challenged children or adults.

6. Watch a movie that deals with diversity issues such as *Courage Under Fire, GI Jane, Glory, Soul Man, Revenge of the Nerds, Pleasantville, Tarzan, In and Out, Philadelphia, The Godfather, The Crying Game, Guess Who's Coming to Dinner, Boyz 'n the Hood, West Side Story, Romeo and Juliet, Schindler's List, Thelma and Louise, Matewan, Remember the Titans, Chocolat, The Color Purple, The King and I, Dances with Wolves, Stand and Deliver, The Joy Luck Club, He Said She Said, Regarding Henry, Driving Miss Daisy, La Bamba, Simon Birch, Yentl.* Write a paper addressing these questions: What types and sources of prejudice were in evidence? How did diversity, stereotyping, prejudice, or discrimination affect the characters? What effective and ineffective strategies were employed to handle prejudice? What strategies did you learn to either overcome prejudice or manage diversity?

**Exercise 8–L
Reflection/Action Plan**

This chapter discussed the skill of understanding and managing diversity—what it is, why it's important, and how to improve your skill in these areas. Complete the worksheet below upon completing all readings and experiential exercises for this chapter.

1. The one or two areas regarding understanding or managing diversity in which I am most strong are:

_____

_____

_____

_____

2. The one or two areas of understanding or managing diversity in which I need more improvement are:

_____

_____

_____

_____

3. If I did only one thing to improve in this area, it would be to:

_____

_____

_____

_____

4. Making this change would probably result in:

_____

_____

_____

_____

5. If I did not change or improve in this area, it would probably affect my personal and professional life in the following ways:

_____

_____

_____

_____

9 Persuading Individuals and Audiences

How do I:

✓ Persuade someone to do something they might not have considered?

✓ Persuade co-workers or team members even when I have no direct authority?

✓ Incorporate tactics and strategies in order to improve my persuasive skills?

✓ Influence others to change their behaviors, such as a roommate who . . . ?

✓ Use elements of persuasion to give an effective presentation?

Ed Garrett is a recently promoted senior-level manager in human resources at Titan Industries, a major industrial company in the Northeast. For years, Titan has been recruiting on college campuses for entry-level engineering and business hires. While the company has a good record, successfully hiring several students each year, it lacks a cohesive recruiting and retention strategy. As the marketplace for talent has heated up recently, the company is experiencing high turnover among its recent college hires. In addition, its image hasn't kept up-to-date with reality: it is a prestigious, global, high-tech organization, but is viewed on campuses as just one of many traditional, solid but unexciting companies trying to compete against the dot-coms and consulting firms for top talent. Lately, the company is experiencing even greater difficulty recruiting and retaining minority students from campuses across the country.

Ed has been given the specific charge of improving Titan's campus recruiting program in three areas: (1) recruiting effectiveness, (2) campus image, and (3) minority recruiting and retention. There's only one catch: Ed hasn't been given a staff to help him accomplish these goals. Instead, he's told to "work through others" to succeed. In other words, he has to get Titan's many major business units behind this change effort, including getting them to put up the necessary funding for Ed's new recruiting initiatives.

Ed is very bright and talented, and in previous positions has been able to effect significant change through efforts initiated by him and his staff. But this is different. He is full of ideas and energy, but without a staff to help him, he must rely on his own capabilities to motivate others to want to change. How does Ed do this? How does he get others who don't report to him to do the work that he knows needs to get done?

1. What is the nature of Ed's dilemma?

2. What resources does Ed have available to him to help him effect the changes that are necessary at Titan?

3. What strategies can Ed use to get people behind his change agenda? What about his boss?

4. If you were Ed, what steps would you take and why?

5. What barriers would you face in asking for time and financial resources? How would you overcome these barriers?

"Persuasion is a governing power. Those who have it use it to their advantage. Those who don't have it let it run their lives."[1]

Paul Messaris (Author)

The ways in which we conduct business are changing as fast as the business world itself. Organizations are becoming less hierarchical. Managerial levels have been flattened. Decision making is spread throughout all employee levels. What does this mean for you? As the power base has shifted to employees, and they make decisions which affect their work environment, they need to convince others of the soundness of their decisions, often without any direct authority. Such is the case in work teams where members make decisions previously made by managers about who does what, when, and how. This chapter is about persuasion—the ability to influence people through means other than issuing direct orders. We will provide a conceptual background on persuasion, discuss its importance in business today, provide several methods and tools of persuasion, address ethical issues involved in persuasion, discuss how elements of persuasion can be used in presentations, describe strategies for defending yourself against unfair usage of persuasion, and provide tips for effectively incorporating persuasion into your work and personal life.

What Is Persuasion?

Persuasion is a form of influence. It is a process of guiding people toward the adoption of some behavior, belief, or attitude preferred by the persuader.[2] It involves careful preparation and proper presentation of arguments and supporting evidence in an appropriate and compelling emotional climate. Unlike manipulation or coercion, persuasion does not rely on deceit or force, nor does it involve the direct giving of orders. Persuasion does not rob people of their ability to choose,[3] which is important when your goal is lasting, positive change of beliefs or actions. According to *Webster's, persuade* means "to urge; to cause [someone] to do something, especially by reasoning, urging, or convincing."[4] As Allied Signal CEO Lawrence Bossidy explains:

The day when you could yell and scream and beat people into good performance is over. Today you have to appeal to them by helping them see how they can get from here to there, by establishing some credibility, and by giving them some reason and help to get there. Do all those things, and they'll knock down doors.[5]

Persuasion is an essential component of doing business. Persuasion does not mean telling someone what to do; it means presenting information and interacting with a person in such a way that you both fully understand the situation and come to an agreement about how to approach the situation. In this view, persuasion is more of a problem-solving activity than it is a convincing activity. According to Jay Conger, a professor at the University of Southern California, persuasion is "a negotiating and learning process through which a persuader leads colleagues to a problem's shared solution."[6]

Effective persuasion ensures that the persuader is fully up to speed on the issues at hand. The persuader comes to the dialogue with an open mind, willing to change others' perspectives if the situation warrants. The persuader also works on developing an understanding of the situation as it is being experienced by the listener(s) prior to offering any proposals or solutions. Effective persuasion also means the listener is fully involved in a dialogue about the situation. The listeners are given the information necessary to make an informed decision; are consulted about their opinions, experience, and insights; are engaged in discussions that help to generate numerous options and solutions before a decision is offered; and are given time before a decision has to be made.

Good persuaders have strong interpersonal skills. They:

- Are good listeners.
- Solicit and give feedback.
- Read other people and sense what's appropriate in a given situation.
- Think creatively about what's best for the common good.
- Are prepared.
- Are empathetic.

Why Persuasion Is Important

To be an effective manager, you must be an able persuader. Gone are the days when managers could delegate to others and have their decisions implemented without question. Employees today show little tolerance for unquestioned authority.[7] Even the military, where unquestioned authority has been a core value, is making changes that include giving officers and nonofficers alike input into key decisions, into the way the organization should be run. More and more companies are adapting a participative work style where employees at all levels are involved in formulating strategy, discussing business needs, making bottom-line decisions, and implementing workplace changes. In this nonhierarchical environment, the skill of persuasion comes in handy.

Another trend that paves the way for persuasion to be a necessary skill in today's business world is the movement of work to teams and "virtual" work, or work done by employees who work off-site. In a team-based or team-supported workplace, seldom does a higher authority mandate decisions. More likely the work gets divvied up and is overseen by the members of a self-managing team rather than by a higher-level manager. In this new business world, persuasion is now the way to get your—and others'—tasks accomplished. Very often, especially in the early stages of a career, tasks will be achieved by convincing others of a particular point of view. Employees and teammates cooperate with you because they want to, not because they have to. More often than not, you'll be working with others who are your peers rather than your subordinates. In this situation the skill of persuasion is not simply the best alternative, it's the only one!

While the primary focus of this chapter is on persuasion as it is experienced in the business world, the concept of persuasion can also be applied in your personal life as well. Whether running for office, discussing a salary raise with your boss, convincing your parents to let you have a car at school, deciding with your spouse or partner what movie to see, or resolving a roommate or family conflict, the skill of persuasion can be an effective means for achieving your objective.

The Process of Persuasion

According to persuasion expert Kathleen Reardon, for persuasion's effects to be long lasting, you need to address the persuadee's motivation, get the person involved, and reward him or her for changing.[8] Let's say your best friend smokes. You not only dislike being around him when he smokes, but you also fear for his health. Saying that you don't like it may not provide enough motivation for him to stop, or at least not permanently. Given that your friend might want to change his behavior, what will it take to persuade him to change?

You must first start by exploring his mind—his values, attitudes, and beliefs—for clues on what to say or do to get him to do something he might not have done prior to your efforts. To persuade him to quit smoking, you need to understand his motivation, or why he smokes and the value that smoking has for him. To do this requires keen observation and investigative skills. Is there a pattern to his smoking, such as, after meals? Does he smoke more alone or with friends?

The next step to ensuring the effects of persuasion will be long-lasting is participation, or getting the person involved in the process. Remember, persuasion is not done *to* another, but rather *with* another—the problem-solving process we alluded to earlier. Think about it. Are you more inclined to change because someone tells you to or because you want to do it? Involve your friend in nonsmoking activities that he can do, such as hiking, working out, or spending time in places where smoking is prohibited. When your friend sees himself enjoying activities without smoking, this self-persuasion will go farther toward lasting change than that which is forced or ordered by someone else. Another option for participation is having him implement a part of the change rather than going for a cold-turkey cessation. Replacing the after-dinner cigarette with an after-dinner mint might be one way to do this.

Finally, reward your friend for his efforts—even if he slips a bit. Ensure and encourage him about his progress. Find out what makes him happy, such as words of encouragement, a good meal (on you, of course!), or a new widget to add to his collection. Most people dislike change because of the uncertainty and fear it brings. Show him that you recognize and appreciate his efforts. Eventually, he is likely to perceive his behavior change as rewarding in itself—fresher clothes and breath, increased stamina, and more disposable income.

We just discussed the role of persuadees in effective persuasion. They have to be motivated, involved, and rewarded in order to be persuaded. What about the persuader? According to Conger, persuaders are effective when they establish credibility, frame goals for common ground, reinforce their position, and connect emotionally with their audience.[9] These are described below.

1. *Establishing* **credibility.** To be persuasive, you must first be perceived as credible. You must be very knowledgeable about the subject matter and be able to present it in such a way that the listener(s) can be compelled to adopt a certain point of view. Credibility stems from four personal characteristics: expertise, trustworthiness, composure, and appearance.[10]

   - **Expertise**—acquired through developing an understanding or knowledge base about the subject matter or a track record of experience and prior success in the given area; demonstrated through passion or conviction, presenting reliable data, and giving nondefensive responses to questions or criticism.

   - **Trustworthiness**—acquired over time through personal and professional relationships in which others perceive you as consistent, reliable, and conscientious; demonstrated by showing empathy, humility, and solid emotional character; pursuit of common ground; and by looking out for the other's best interest.

   - **Composure**—acquired by practicing, having a plan and knowing what you're going to say and when; demonstrated by being confident and self-assured. When you are composed, you are solid and sure, even under pressure. "Never let them see you sweat" alludes to the contribution that composure makes to credibility.

   - **Positive Impression or Appearance**—acquired initially through one's appearance (attire, grooming), gestures (handshake, posture), and behaviors (etiquette), as well as through possession of credentials (title, reputation). Demonstrated over time through interactions with others, in particular taking a personal interest in the ideas and in the people involved in the interaction, being enthusiastic and engaged with the process. Others' historical impressions of you can work to your advantage or disadvantage. If you are perceived as a remarkable leader, everything you say (for better or worse) will be accepted at face value. Conversely, if your reputation is inconsistent, others are likely to question and search for faults in your reasoning, creating an uphill battle for your persuasion attempts.

2. **Framing** *for common ground.* Effective persuaders develop a framework, or a plan for how to proceed, that involves describing their position in ways that identify common ground. Framing sets a collaborative tone and attains three interrelated objectives:[11]

   - Provides a perspective we would like the other party to consider. Sometimes, it's all in the packaging of the message. For example, if you need to introduce a new computer system to your company, you could present the technology as something new and exciting versus something that can free up time to be spent on more important tasks. Chances are, the latter approach will be more effective. This relates to knowing what makes the persuadee tick.

   - Provides an open-minded way for alternatives and ideas to be compared and contrasted. For example, "We need a solution for this problem. I've jotted down some benefits these improvements will likely bring and a few ideas for consideration. How do you think we can arrive at a solution?"

   - Creates a logical structure by which decisions can be made. By planning and creating a framework ahead of time, you provide a manner in which you and others can collaborate in the problem-solving process.

3. *Reinforce with* **logic and reasoning.** Presenting compelling evidence is extremely effective as a persuasion technique. Passion and emotion are important, but facts and data can make the difference between your audience supporting your argument and not.[12] Know the sources for your data; others might ask. Any errors in your reasoning can give the listener reason to doubt you. This does not imply that you must say everything you know about the subject. You must judiciously select the information regarding the subject that will have the most impact on your audience.[13]

4. *Establish an* **emotional connection.** While logic is essential, so too is appealing to people's feelings, fears, values, dreams, frustrations, egos, vanities, or desires. Many charismatic leaders, such as John F. Kennedy, Martin Luther King, Jr., and Mother Teresa, inspired others to support or join their cause not only because of its importance, but also because of their contagious passion and conviction to the cause.

By engaging yourself and your audience in the subject matter, everyone is vested in working together to find solutions to the problem at hand. Inspire others to "join the crusade" by applying the above principles of persuasion and by combining elements of both emotion and reasoning.

Factors in Effective Persuasion

The ability to persuade or influence others has been a subject of study in numerous fields, including social psychology, communication, and business. This research has proposed and tested a number of theories that explain persuasion and the factors impacting its effectiveness. One of the earliest theories, advanced by Fritz Heider, is based on the notion of **balance.** He suggested that the success or failure of the persuasion attempt could be affected by whether the structure of the situation is balanced or unstable.[14] A balanced configuration is one in which the relationships among three elements—the person, another person, and an object or event—are all positive or contain one positive and two negatives. This relationship is illustrated in the triangle in Figure 9–1. P is the person, O is the other person, and X is the object or event. For example, if two people like each other and agree on an issue, the relationship is one that is in balance, and they are more likely to succeed at persuading one another. Heider also believed that we seek out balance, so in unbalanced situations (two positives and one negative) we attempt to change, avoid, or convince ourselves that the relationship between person, other, and thing is harmonious. So if you (P) like your instructor (O),

Figure 9–1
Balance Theory Diagram

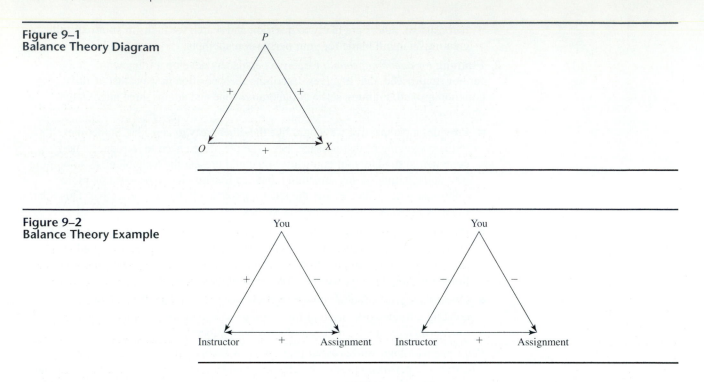

Figure 9–2
Balance Theory Example

and your instructor believes that a particular assignment is very important even if you don't (Figure 9–2), the instructor will have a better chance of persuading you of her view, in contrast to a situation in which you dislike your instructor. Imbalance exists when the three relationships are all negative or contain two positives and one negative. If two people dislike one another and disagree on a topic, there is an imbalance in the relationship. It will take more time for them first to find equal footing before they can begin the persuasion. Knowing where you and another stand on an issue, as well as your feelings toward one another, can help you determine a suitable strategy for effective persuasion.

Persuasion is also affected by the amount of dissonance, or tension, that is present in the relationship prior to the persuasion. Dissonance exists when the values or perceptions of the persuader and persuadee are different, or when conflict exists. For example, if the persuadee and persuader each come from a very different religious background, the chances of the persuader convincing the persuadee to change a religious belief are slim. This idea is an extension of Leon Festinger's **cognitive dissonance** theory.[15] He suggested that people are comfortable when their attitudes or beliefs are in concert with their behaviors. Let's say you believe that participation in a Greek organization is a waste of time. A good friend introduces you to other friends, and you all go out together and have a great time. It turns out that they are all in the same sorority, and your friend begins a campaign to persuade you to join. You like them, but can't get past your long-held beliefs that oppose the idea of joining this type of group. Do you join?

In this example, you are in a state of cognitive dissonance. To reduce the discomfort associated with this state, Festinger suggests that you are likely to increase the attractiveness of the chosen alternative ("It's more important to get good grades than socialize"), decrease the attractiveness of the unchosen alternative ("Sure, they're cool, but I bet they're the exception and not the rule"), create cognitive overlap ("Well, college has to be fun, and besides, extracurricular activities impress some employers"), or revoke the decision. If you were the friend in this situation, and armed with this information, her first step in persuading you to join should be to reduce the cognitive dissonance you feel.

Another technique that can be used to persuade others effectively is based on the **inoculation theory.** Borrowing from the medical field, McGuire suggested that in the same way individuals receive a small injection of a disease-producing substance to increase immunity against that disease, persuaders can be effective when they anticipate the objections of the persuadee and address those objections before they arise.[16] For example, if you were to ask your parents for a new car, you can easily guess one of the first objections: cost. By doing your homework and showing them how the costs of owning a new car are less than the cost of maintaining your 10-year-old, unreliable car—before they bring the cost issue up—you essentially take the steam out of their argument. It's hard for parents to argue with that logic, especially when you raise and address their objections before they communicate them. Another example of inoculation would be if a firm were to send out information showing lower-than-expected profits prior to announcing a decreased merit pool. Other strategies for countering include presenting all points (for and against) and demonstrating how what's being proposed is the right solution, and broaching controversial subjects gently and early, before your audience has the chance to raise an issue that could become contentious or divisive.

A more recent model of persuasion effectiveness is Reardon's **ACE Theory.** She suggests that people use three criteria to determine whether to respond to a persuader's arguments: *appropriateness, consistency, and effectiveness.*[17] This further reinforces the need for trust and trustworthiness in relationships to be able to implement persuasive communication. The most successful appeals are those judged to demonstrate:

- **Appropriateness**—the right thing to do, based on generally accepted standards or norms, or in some cases, rules of law or morality. Appropriateness appeals are geared to the persuadee's or audience's belief system and interests.

- **Consistency**—the degree to which the action or belief proposed compares to that of similar others or to their own past behaviors or espoused beliefs. Appeals to consistency demonstrate that the persuader understands the beliefs or past behaviors of similar others and presents arguments that make sense or track with these beliefs or behaviors.

- **Effectiveness**—the degree to which an action or idea leads to a desirable state or outcome. By knowing what the persuadee or audience wants or needs, a persuader can demonstrate how adoption of the proposed idea or action will help meet those needs.

Let's illustrate. You were recently hired into a marketing organization. During the interview, your prospective boss highlighted the company's commitment to the education and development of its employees. Six months into the job, you learn of a conference that could provide needed training to increase your ability to perform your current duties and marketing research, and could increase the skills you need to advance in the firm. Unfortunately, the conference comes just prior to the fiscal year end—a busy time. You could just give your boss a flyer describing the conference and ask if you could go. Or, you could apply the ACE theory. First, you make an appropriateness appeal and mention that other associates like you have been sent by their managers to conferences similar to this one. Next, you remind your boss that when you interviewed, she strongly emphasized the value of employee development. Your boss wouldn't want to be perceived as inconsistent, would she? Finally, if she hasn't yet agreed, you raise the issue of effectiveness and say: "You know, if I am able to take care of some of the more mundane marketing tasks you are responsible for, you will be able to spend more time on long-term planning and strategizing. This way, your talents—and mine—will be put to better use." Slam-dunk!

Tips for Effective Persuasion

Persuasion is not the simple task of talking to someone. It is a complex two-way communication process that is most effective when the persuader has taken into consideration several elements regarding him or herself, the audience, and the issue or object at hand.[18] Figure 9–3 summarizes and highlights key behaviors and tactics to remember when you want to persuade others.

**Figure 9–3
Persuasion Tips and Tactics**

■ *Believe in yourself.* Confidence, appearance, and attitude can help, especially if there is not enough time to solidify a relationship. When you believe you can accomplish something and it will benefit the organization, others sense this confidence and are more likely to back a "can-do" person than one who shows hesitation or reservation.

■ *Show your own commitment and passion about the ideas being discussed.* Sense where the audience is on a subject (ask them if you have to) and show that you understand and can relate to their position.

■ *Know your audience—start by examining their perspectives.* People are highly motivated by their own perceptions; arm yourself by using an overriding perception or belief of theirs that will be highly persuasive to them. When you understand what your audience believes and wants, you can better motivate them to work with you.[19]

  ■ Tailor your message to your audience. Don't talk above or below them. Adapt your style to your audience.[20] Make your message relevant and interesting to them. Use examples they can relate to.

  ■ Show the audience why it is in their best interest to do as you suggest. Even better, collaborate with them in such a way that they devise an idea that meets your objectives and theirs.

■ *Balance emotional appeals with solid reasoning and credibility.* According to Aristotle, the father of modern persuasive thought, all three cornerstones are necessary for winning others to your way of thinking.[21] All are important and complement one another.

■ *Use facts, data, and logic.* Question your logic or propositions before presenting them. If there are holes, fix them. Be careful not to make mistakes when presenting data. This can be damaging to your credibility with the audience.[22]

■ *Put your material in human terms rather than technical terms.* If you are trying to sell a computer, talk about the interesting things you can do and the ease with which you can do them as opposed to explaining the system configuration.

■ *Use assertive communication techniques:* be clear and specific; use appropriate behaviors; use straightforward, level tone and speech; maintain eye contact; acknowledge their feelings while expressing yours. This is especially important for women, who are more likely than men to use language that suggests uncertainty.[23] Social scientists Deborah Tannen and Kathleen Reardon both note that women tend to speak in ways that undermine and discount what they say. Such phrases as "I'm not sure you'll agree, but . . ." "I could be wrong, but . . ." "I hate to interrupt . . ." "If you don't mind, could you" could be damaging to anyone's credibility.

■ *Use appropriate nonverbal communication:* lean forward, smile, have an open posture, use good listening techniques. Display confidence in your ideas as well as openness to others' ideas.

■ *Maintain your composure;* show you are willing to discuss matters even if they are controversial. Appear reasonable; avoid yelling, insulting, belittling, or showing irritation. You can be passionate without throwing chairs!

■ *Use props to enhance your story, not steal the show.* Data (charts or graphs) or samples can be used and made available later (if your audience is poring over data, they're not listening to you).

■ *Provide reinforcement and follow through.* Once the interaction is over, offer praise and give the audience positive reinforcement to support their reasoning for being persuaded.[24]

Ethical and Cautionary Issues in Persuasion

By adhering to many of the principles we've discussed, persuasion efforts are likely to be effective, resulting in positive outcomes for both the persuader and persuadee. Used incorrectly or for the wrong reasons, persuasion has the potential to be used or viewed as **manipulation**—convincing people to believe or adhere to something that is neither in their best interest nor something they would believe or do without the presence of the persuader. For instance, some car salespeople have a knack for selling expensive cars to people who can't afford them. They make a good commission while the buyer is left wondering how to make the monthly payments. Another example is the cult leaders accused of brainwashing followers into believing they will be "cleansed" or "rewarded" if they give up all of their money and possessions to the cult.

Advertising and sales industries are tempted to use deception and even fear tactics to persuade consumers. Ever get a sweepstakes entry form that convinces you to purchase magazines for a chance to win millions? Ethical limits are constantly being examined to evaluate the rights of companies to use persuasive techniques versus the rights of the audience. The gambling and lottery industry has been highly scrutinized for luring gamblers to invest their funds for the hope of large returns. The time-share industry uses hard-pressure tactics, gift incentives, and confined time and situational factors to increase sales. Many advertisers use fear as a power base to convince consumers to purchase products or change behaviors, such as the car manufacturer or tire dealer that implies if you don't buy their brand you are putting your family in danger. There can be a fine line between effective persuasion and manipulation.

To determine whether a speaker is positively persuading or negatively manipulating, ask these questions:[25]

- Who is really benefiting as a result of this act?
- Is the information being presented accurately?
- Does this interaction feel like a test of wills—a competitive game—or is it a healthy and positive debate—a two-way interchange?

Warning signals of manipulation include the persuader having more to gain from the exchange than the persuadee, discrepancies in the facts being presented as part of the argument, and a war of words that heavily favors just one side. If any or all of these conditions are present in an interaction, it's best to disengage and either discontinue or agree to resume the interaction when you can gain a more equal footing. To defend yourself against manipulation:

- *Be clear on your convictions and why you hold them.* Avoid being a victim of unscrupulous manipulators by being smart when interacting with them. Ask plenty of questions to ensure you understand clearly all sides of an issue. Analyze their intent and evaluate their argument before accepting what's being said, especially if your opinion is based primarily on the person's likability or reputation.

- *Think substance, not appearance.* Base your acceptance of a persuader on the strength of his reasoning, not simply because he has connected with you or the audience emotionally. There can be a dark side to influence, according to social psychologist Robert Cialdini; witness the Jonestown Massacre of 1978.[26] For a less extreme example, consider the very powerful self-help guru making a pitch to an audience of about 600 for a new intensive seminar that was supposed to help people "get in touch with themselves" and discover their true purpose in life. Not surprisingly, the program was extremely expensive, costing several thousand dollars. The speaker wanted the payment on the spot—and the payment was nonrefundable! After an emotional pitch that seemed to win the admiration and sign-ups of many in the audience, one lone woman stood up and asked "What if it doesn't work?" It seemed a legitimate question, but the speaker reacted as though he had never heard the question before. Instead of giving a reasoned answer, he chided the young woman for expressing doubt about the veracity of what he was saying. How would you respond in such a situation?

- *Do doubt the truth about what's being said.* Do ask questions of speakers, before being convinced by the power of their words that they are right. Most of the time you will encounter presenters and persuaders who are truthful and honest. But it's a good strategy to be aware of the tactics that can be utilized by some whose self-interests override their interest in others. It's also helpful to keep these thoughts in mind when preparing your persuasive presentation. Brainstorm potential questions and criticisms and prepare a logical answer. You can't know all questions in advance, but you can prepare!

Making Effective Presentations

As persuaders, we often find ourselves making a formal presentation to others. Knowing how to create a persuasive presentation can increase sales, advance your career, enhance your reputation, and create professional opportunities along with personal satisfaction.[27] Being able to present, defend, and gain acceptance for your ideas is a critical skill in today's business environment. Persuasive presentations require the presenter not only to give information, but to get the audience to accept, believe, and act on the ideas presented.[28]

Many individuals spend great amounts of time and energy creating and developing their ideas, but forget to learn the techniques necessary to sell the ideas. The selling of the ideas is a critical component. A lack of "show and tell" ability can compromise a person's productivity, effectiveness, and opportunity to advance within an organization. Mastering these skills allows an audience to trust your expertise and your message, allowing you to sell your ideas and display your leadership ability.[29]

When creating persuasive presentations, it is crucial to determine your reason for giving the presentation and find the need behind your idea. This will provide the basis for your presentation. Once you have determined the information, shape the message to your audience. Your efforts will be more successful if you deliver the speech around the information needs of your audience. Imagine you need to make a presentation for a new product idea. You must first begin with the reason for the new product, the data and information necessary to show the projected demand for the new product. However, you

---

**Figure 9–4
Tips for Effective
Presentations**

Before the Presentation

- *Research your intended audience.*[30] What are their interests? Their beliefs? To what kind of presentation are they accustomed (i.e., length, format, and type of technology used)? Will they want to see your materials in advance? Will a handout or copy of the report being presented be expected?

- *Determine appropriate dress.* Many businesses are "business casual" every day of the week, while others reserve this for Fridays only or not at all. Find out what's appropriate in the environment in which you'll be speaking.

- *Prepare your remarks.* There are two kinds of presenters: those who are best when they have not prepared in advance, and those who are not. Those few who are blessed with the skill of relating to others extemporaneously, or "on the spot," can get away with minimal preparation. All the rest of us need to prepare, prepare, prepare!

- *Practice.* You don't have to write out the whole speech. Make a list of the key concepts you want to address and develop "talking points" that support each of these concepts. Practice saying these points in sequence, using a natural conversational tone.

- *Relax.* Just before the presentation, clear your head and focus on the task at hand.

During the Presentation

- *Begin with an anecdote or quote.* This ensures you begin with an attention-grabber that helps the audience focus on your presentation. Avoid the use of a joke—jokes can be offensive to members of a particular group. It's better to start with something of substance that relates to the subject matter or the audience.[31]

- *Give your audience an organizing framework.* Begin your presentation by telling your audience the key concepts you'll be addressing. You could also present an agenda as a visual aid and means to reinforce key points throughout your remarks.[32]

- *Present the core of your argument at the beginning.* This gives the audience a road map—they know where you're heading and why. "Tell them what you're going to tell them, then tell them." This also gives you a platform for demonstrating your enthusiasm about your subject, and for engaging them in that enthusiasm. Then build your case by presenting data or facts that support your argument.

- *Make your session interactive.* Take questions throughout. If there's no time for audience interaction, ask one or two rhetorical questions, or begin your presentation with a question[33] that can focus their thinking even if a response is not expected. The more engaged they are, the greater the likelihood that they'll buy in to your arguments.

- *Use technology, but sparingly.* You want to be up on the latest cutting-edge methods—as appropriate for the message and audience—but you don't want to lose the personal connection with the audience or give the impression that you're more style than substance.[34]

- *Be interesting but not necessarily entertaining.* It's important to engage your audience. Making people laugh can do this. Even more effective is making them think.

- *Close with a compelling thought or quote.* This helps focus the audience's attention on the essence of your presentation—the key take-aways or lessons of your message.

After the Presentation

- *Evaluate.* Ask yourself, and others who were present, what went well and what you can do differently in the future. It helps to debrief while your presentation is still fresh in your—and others'—minds. Debriefing is also helpful when recycling your presentation. If planned correctly, your presentation can serve as a "template" for your next one. The content will likely change but the format—opening, main concepts, key points that support your case, conclusion, close—can stay the same.

- *Follow up.* Prepare and send any materials or data you promised to the audience, and send a formal thanks to the organizer of the event at which you spoke.

will not get the rest of the team to buy into your product idea unless they have been shown the benefit it can provide to the organization. You must understand the group's concerns and its motivation for the new product development in order to create a persuasive pitch.

Elements of persuasion can be useful tactics when developing effective presentations. Figure 9–4 provides pointers for making persuasive business presentations successfully.

Strategies for Dealing with "Stage Fright"

Many people, when asked, would say they dislike giving presentations. It's been suggested that public speaking is at or near the top of lists of people's greatest fears, even higher than death.[35] Unless you're a natural salesperson or an expert on a topic, the prospect of giving a presentation can be a bit daunting. If you suffer from "stage fright," or find speaking in front of an audience difficult, consider the following pointers:

■ *Prepare.* Begin preparation as soon as you find out about your presentation. Set aside 10–15 minutes a day, outlining what you will cover so it feels natural. Determine and practice your opening story or remarks in order to get through the highest-anxiety time of your presentation—the very beginning.

■ *Visit the site.* Familiarize yourself with the speaking environment. Before the event, go to the place where you will be speaking so the setting won't surprise you and increase your anxiety. Find out who your audience is (their background, education, reason for attending) and how many will attend.

■ *Visualize success.* Picture yourself in front of your audience in the place you will be speaking. See yourself being totally confident, in control of the situation, and your audience enjoying your speech. Avoid all negative thoughts during the visualization. This helps to reduce damaging self-thinking and substitutes a positive image for a negative one.

■ *Maintain realistic expectations.* You don't have to be perfect. Just be the best you can be. Remember that you appear much more confident than you feel. You probably know as much or more about the topic than your audience does. They're there to learn from you, not to see you fail.

■ *Gain experience.* The more you rehearse your speech, the better you feel about it. Present your speech to a group of friends to become more comfortable and get feedback on what you did well and what you can do to improve. Noted public speaker Lilly Waters states that "rehearsal and preparation can reduce a speaker's fear by 75 percent."[36]

■ *Talk about something that interests you.* You will feel more positive delivering your message if it is something that you believe and is familiar to you.

■ *Develop a relaxation routine.* Relaxing the body can eliminate or reduce physical discomfort that can add to levels of anxiety. Relieve the built-up tensions in your body in advance by exercising, meditating, or doing deep breathing exercises.

■ Breathing deeply *before* a presentation relaxes the body and vents tension. Remembering to take breaths between sentences *during* a presentation can help you stay at a conversational level with the audience rather than quickening to a jittery "let's get this thing over" pace. Deep breathing can reduce stage fright by 15 percent.[37]

■ Tension restricts breathing and creates discomfort. Stand in a relaxed rather than a rigid position. Don't tense up your muscles or shoulders. Keep your shoulders low and relaxed, and your knees slightly bent. Before your presentation, stand in front of a mirror to get a visual and physical image of what a relaxed posture looks and feels like. Remember this image should tension creep in during your presentation.

■ *Use visual aids.* They divert attention away from you so you can feel more relaxed and less like the center of attention. It's best to use them at the beginning of your presentation when the level of your anxiety is probably the highest.

■ *Use gestures.* Don't be afraid to move. Be natural. When presenting, use the same gestures you would during a casual conversations. These movements will keep your body loose and relax your muscles. Smiles and other facial gestures convey confidence as well as engage the audience.

Summary

Persuasion is a skill that can benefit you in your personal and professional endeavors in many ways. Whether asking for an increase in salary, a higher grade, a promotion, or a warning (as opposed to a ticket) when caught speeding, your ability to get what you want is influenced by your knowledge and application of persuasion theory and techniques. Knowing what influences your persuasiveness—including characteristics of you, your message, those you hope to persuade—will enable you to effectively influence others to act or believe in something that benefits them as well as you. These principles can be applied to making persuasive presentations, something most if not all of us are called upon to do many times in our work and in our lives.

Key Terms and Concepts

ACE Theory	Expertise
Appropriateness	Framing
Balance theory	Inoculation theory
Cognitive dissonance	Logic and reasoning
Composure	Manipulation
Consistency	Persuasion
Credibility	Positive impression or appearance
Effectiveness	Trustworthiness
Emotional connection	

Endnotes

1. Paul Messaris, *Visual Persuasion: The Role of Images in Advertising* (Thousand Oaks, CA: Sage Publications, 1997).

2. Kathleen K. Reardon, *Persuasion in Practice* (Newbury Park, CA: Sage Publications, 1991), p. 2.

3. Reardon, p. 2.

4. *Webster's New World Dictionary and Thesaurus,* M. Agnes Ed. (New York: Simon and Schuster, 1996).

5. Jay A. Conger, "The Necessary Art of Persuasion," *Harvard Business Review,* May–June 1998, p. 84.

6. Conger, 1998.

7. Conger, 1998.

8. Reardon, 1991, pp. 9–11.

9. Conger, 1998.

10. Reardon, 1991.

11. Lyle Sussman, "How to Frame a Message: The Art of Persuasion and Negotiation," *Business Horizons,* July–August 1999, p. 2.

12. Deborah C. Andrew, *Technical Communication in the Global Community* (New Jersey: Prentice Hall, 1998).

13. James P. T. Fatt, "The Anatomy of Persuasion," *Communication World,* Dec. 1997, p. 21.

14. Fritz Heider, *The Psychology of Interpersonal Relations* (New York: John Wiley, 1958).

15. Leon Festinger, *A Theory of Cognitive Dissonance* (Stanford, CA: Stanford Univ. Press, 1957).

16. W. J. McGuire, "The Effectiveness of Supportive and Refutational Defenses in Immunizing and Restoring Beliefs against Persuasion," *Sociometry* 24 (1961), pp. 184–197.

17. Reardon, *Persuasion in Practice,* p. 70.

18. Fatt, 1997.

19. David Stiebel, "Getting Them to See Things Your Way," *Canadian Manager,* Winter 1997, p. 13.

20. Kimberly Paterson, "Making an Impact with Speeches and Presentations," *Rough Notes,* June 2000, p. 118.

21. Dianna Booher, "The Power of Persuasion: Emotion, Logic and Character," *Manage,* August 2000, p. 22.

22. Deborah Tannen, *You Just Don't Understand: Women and Men in Conversation* (New York: Ballentine Books, 1991).

23. R. T. Lakoff, *Language and a Woman's Place* (New York: Harper and Row, 1975).

24. Joseph D. O'Brian, "The Gentle Art of Persuasion," *Supervisory Management,* Feb. 1995, p. 14.

25. Perry Pascarella, "Persuasion Skills Required for Success," *Management Review,* Sept. 1998, p. 68.

26. R. B. Cialdini, *Influence: Science and Practice* (Chicago: Scott Foresman, 1985).

27. Bernard Rosenbaum, "Making Presentations: How to Persuade Others to Accept Your Ideas," *American Salesman,* Feb. 1992, p. 16.

28. Robert W. Rasberry and Laura Lemoine Lindsay, *Effective Managerial Communication,* Second Ed. (Belmont, CA: Wadsworth Publishing Company, 1994), p. 256.

29. Robert E. Kelley, *How to Be a Star at Work: Nine Breakthrough Strategies You Need to Succeed* (New York: Times Business, 1998), p. 225.

30. Paterson, 2000.

31. Beth Cole, "Connecting with the Audience," *Associate Management,* June 2000, p. 24.

32. Debra Hamilton, "Prepare and Practice," *Officepro,* March 2000, p. 14.

33. Cole, 2000.

34. Paterson, 2000.

35. David Wallechinsky and Irving Wallace, *The Book of Lists* (New York: William Morrow, 1977).

36. Hamilton, 2000.

37. Hamilton, 2000.

Exercise 9–A
Assessing Yourself

Circle the response that most closely correlates with each item below.

	Agree	Neither	Disagree

1. When trying to convince someone to do something, I engage my audience or listener in seeking solutions collaboratively rather than impose my own views. 1 2 ③ 4 5

2. I enter interactions with others with an open mind; I am open to changing my perceptions about what others say. ① 2 3 4 5

3. I give myself and others time before having to make decisions. ① 2 3 4 5

4. I prepare in advance so I am knowledgeable about my subject matter. 1 ② 3 4 5

5. I answer questions nondefensively. 1 2 ③ 4 5

6. Co-workers or classmates would describe me as consistent, reliable, and conscientious. 1 ② 3 4 5

7. I demonstrate interest in the concerns of others. ① 2 3 4 5

8. When engaged in discussions with others, I offer a plan or plans for how to proceed. 1 2 3 ④ 5

9. I support my arguments with facts and data. 1 ② 3 4 5

10. I establish an emotional connection with those I'm trying to persuade. ① 2 3 4 5

11. I demonstrate my own passion for the ideas being discussed. ① 2 3 4 5

12. I tailor my message to my audience. 1 ② 3 4 5

13. I offer positive reinforcement to others. ① 2 3 4 5

14. I encourage presentation of several options and discussion of what's proposed as the best solution. 1 2 ③ 4 5

15. I broach sensitive subjects early, before others raise a potentially divisive issue. 1 2 ③ 4 5

16. When trying to persuade someone, I aim to appeal to his or her sense of appropriateness, consistency, and effectiveness. 1 ② 3 4 5

17. I research my audience in advance. 1 2 ③ 4 5

18. I relax and focus on the matter at hand. ① 2 3 4 5

19. I start and end my presentations with a compelling quote or point. ① 2 3 4 5

20. I present the core of my argument at the beginning of my presentation. ① 2 3 4 5

21. I make presentations interactive. 1 ② 3 4 5

22. I use cutting-edge technology but don't let it take attention away from the substance of my remarks. ① 2 3 4 5

23. I evaluate, debrief, and follow up after presentations. ① 2 3 4 5

24. When I'm the subject of someone else's persuasion, I ask questions and listen carefully to all the facts being presented before making a decision. ① 2 3 4 5

Sum your circled responses. If your score was 72 or higher, you may want to develop a plan to improve your persuasion skills. 41   43

Exercise 9–B
Billy Goat's Gruff

This exercise is based on the children's fable, "Three Billy Goat's Gruff." The instructor or a facilitator plays the role of the troll. The troll is big, mean, ugly, and hungry (no reflection on your personal instructor) and has decided that it does not like the original story. In the original story, the three billy goats proceed to cross the bridge. The smallest billy goat tries to go across and convinces the troll not to eat him because his big brother is coming and would be a much bigger and better meal for the troll. The second billy goat attempts to cross and is also successful in convincing the troll that he should wait for the next brother who is even bigger and tastier than him. The biggest billy goat comes and is big enough to beat the troll so he can proceed across the bridge. The troll realizes that if it had not let the first billy goat across, it would not have been tricked and beaten up by the last goat. So the troll has decided it will just eat the first goat this time around.

You play the role of the first (baby) billy goat. In your triad or small group, you are to devise a persuasive argument that will convince the troll to let you across the bridge to the other side where the pasture is lush and green. One member from each team approaches the troll and tries to persuade it to not eat them. The troll will try to find holes in your argument; you should have a plan for overcoming any potential arguments. The class will vote on whether you have convinced the troll and whether you truly have created a persuasive argument. Determine whether the team was successful in having all the elements of a persuasive argument. The class will decide if you get to cross or if you get eaten. Repeat if desired.

Questions

1. How successful were you in devising and presenting a solid persuasive argument?
2. What areas of your argument were weak or lacking in support?
3. What could you have done differently to ensure greater success?
4. What objections were presented for which you were not prepared?

Exercise 9–C
Deserted Isle

Your group has been stranded on a deserted island with an active volcano. There is a limited food supply and the future is uncertain. It is unknown how long the island will be able to sustain human life. A raft is available, but it is capable of taking only one team to safety.

In triads or small groups, you are to develop a persuasive argument to present to the instructor to convince him or her that your team should be the one rescued from the deserted island. Make up any information that will help support your arguments.

Groups will take turns presenting their arguments to the instructor, who will decide which team will be taken to safety.

Questions

1. How successful were you in devising and presenting a solid persuasive argument?
2. What areas of your argument were weak or lacking in support?
3. What could you have done differently to ensure greater success?
4. What objections were presented for which you were not prepared?

Exercise 9–D
"I Deserve a Raise" Role-Play

"You have been employed in your first job after college for a little more than one year. When you were hired, you were promised a raise after the first year. However at your recent performance appraisal, there was no mention of a raise despite the fact you received above average ratings on most performance criteria. You are considering leaving your employer to go to graduate school if you don't get a raise."

In your triad or small group, devise a persuasive argument to present to your boss to convince her or him you should get a raise. In each round, two of you play the roles of employee and boss, while the third and other persons are observers. In round one, person A is the employee, B is the boss, and C is the observer. In round two, person A is the boss, B the observer, and C the employee, and so on. Each round should last about 10 minutes and should include first the persuasion role-play and then a round of feedback in which the observer(s) gives feedback to the employee about his or her persuasion skills.

Questions for the Observer(s)

1. How successful was the employee in devising and presenting a solid, persuasive argument?

2. What areas of the employee's argument were weak or lacking support? Which were positive and supportable?

3. What did the employee do that contributed to her or his success? What could the employee have done to ensure greater success?

4. What, if any, objections were presented by the boss that the employee was not prepared for?

Exercise 9–E
Back to the Future

Your parents own a small print shop, one that had been passed down from one of their parents during the B.C. (before computers) period. Inventory and sales records are kept in notebooks or on cards filed in shoeboxes. Customers' names and numbers are listed on a Rolodex file. The annual Christmas card is sent by having one of the employees hand-address about 350 envelopes. While technology has changed, things in the print shop have not.

You are home over winter break and wish to apply some of your technology-based knowledge and skill to improve things in the print shop. You know of several computer systems and software applications that can keep track of customers, sales, and inventory all at the touch of button. Send a letter to only those customers in a particular city? Piece of cake most anywhere else, but not at your parents' shop. You explain the value of computers to them, but they insist that all is well in the print shop. Besides, they tell you, "If it ain't broke, why fix it?"

To convince them to adopt (and use!) the kind of computer system you know will benefit them, you decide to apply Reardon's three-pronged approach. Use the worksheet below to develop a script for what you'll say and do to address each of these prongs:

Motivation: What do they want? How do I know this?

Supposedly nothing

could save money & time

Participation: How do I get them involved in the problem-solving process—get them to acknowledge how they would benefit from this change? How can I ease them into such a change?

demonstrate one change that could be made

Reward: How will the change benefit my parents?

time & money

**Exercise 9–F
Applying the ACE
Theory**

Scenario One

Your roommate will be spending a semester abroad. Just as you begin planning out a new and better arrangement of your room, you get a knock on your door from your RA. Standing beside him is someone who is, from the looks of it, likely not to be a lot of fun: the thick-rimmed glasses, the pocket protector, the skin color suggesting little if any time spent outdoors. You keep your stereotypes to yourself and hope for the best. Unfortunately, your expectations are met. Pat rarely talks, leaves the room, or spends time with anyone or anything besides the books and computer. You'd like to see Pat have a little bit of fun, but you're afraid that your offer will be declined, only adding to the tension in the room. Tomorrow night is movie night at your university, when a relatively recent film is shown for free in the main auditorium on campus. Perhaps, if your persuasion attempt follows the ACE Theory, you might be successful. Use the worksheet below to prepare a script for what you would say or do to convince Pat to take a break from the books and join you in a movie.

Appropriateness (What is typical, common, or accepted practice for similar others?)

Consistency (In what ways might going to the movies align with Pat's behaviors or beliefs?)

Is it an educational or technical film?

Effectiveness (How would going to the movie result in a positive outcome for Pat?)

meet people
see something new about campus

Scenario Two

You work at an insurance firm, consisting of approximately 150 employees, with most involved in desk work. You would like to convince the owner that an exercise/wellness program should be added to the workplace. The owner is a man in his mid 50s and is highly concerned with attendance and productivity. Use the worksheet to script out how the ACE Theory could help you in being successful in your persuasion attempt.

Appropriateness (What is typical, common, or accepted practice for similar others?)

Consistency (In what ways might developing an exercise/wellness program align with the owner's behaviors or beliefs?)

better health = better productivity, fewer sick days

Effectiveness (How would developing an exercise/wellness program result in a positive outcome for the owner?)

**Exercise 9–G
Try This . . .**

1. Watch a TV show or video movie (*Twelve Angry Men, Crimson Tide, Henry V, Braveheart, Miracle on 34th Street, Jakob the Liar, Harvey, A Civil Action, Norma Rae, The Pied Piper of Hamelin, Body Heat, The Verdict*) in which one person is trying to persuade one or more persons to do something. What tactics are used? What behaviors do both persuader and persuadee(s) display? What works? What doesn't?

2. Observe a persuasion interaction that occurs in your personal or professional life over the next few days—perhaps a conflict with a roommate, a group of friends discussing a movie to see, a group of colleagues discusses a team project plan. What persuasion tactics are used? What behaviors do both the persuader and persuadee(s) display? What works? What doesn't?

3. Prepare a script for a persuasion activity you're facing in the near future, such as asking for a raise or asking your parents if you can have a car at college. Apply one or more of the methods or techniques (e.g., ACE, inoculation, dissonance) discussed in the chapter, role-playing it with a friend or co-worker.

**Exercise 9–H
Reflection/Action Plan**

This chapter focused on persuasion—what it is, why it is important, and how to improve your skills in this area. Complete the worksheet below upon completing all reading and experiential activities for this chapter.

1. The one or two areas in which I am most strong are:

   _____

   _____

   _____

2. The one or two areas in which I need more improvement are:

   _____

   _____

   _____

3. If I did only one thing to improve in this area, it would be to:

   _____

   _____

   _____

4. Making this change would probably result in:

   _____

   _____

   _____

5. If I did not change or improve in this area, it would probably affect my personal and professional life in the following ways:

   _____

   _____

   _____

10 Networking and Politicking

How do I:

✓ "Work a room"—meet many different people in a short amount of time?

✓ Identify a job opening or arrange an interview through a friend or a friend of a friend?

✓ Reach out to and connect with others when I am a newcomer in an organization?

✓ Use my connections to successfully champion a cause within an organization?

✓ Identify those people whom others go to if they want to get something done in an organization or professional setting?

✓ Learn how to create a positive impression of myself and interpret the impressions that others want us to read?

Mr. Zaven Yaralian is a prime example of how networking can help individuals progress through their careers (see chart diagramming his career below). Yaralian was a professional football coach for the New Orleans Saints. Like most other professions, success in obtaining coaching jobs relies on both technical expertise and networking skills. Yaralian's career has benefited time after time from contacts he made at the beginning of and throughout his career. He acquired his former position directly as the result of networking.

Coach Yaralian played football for the University of Nebraska, a highly recognized program that produces outstanding players as well as coaches. He honed his game through one of the best college coaches, Tom Osborne. Yaralian played for Nebraska, and after graduation, he kept in close touch with Coach Osborne. Following his unsuccessful attempt at pursuing a career in the NFL, Yaralian contacted Osborne. Osborne, who knew Yaralian's heart belonged to football, suggested coaching. Coach Osborne gave Yaralian his first job in coaching, as a graduate assistant in his own program.

Yaralian then began moving up in his profession. He began his first full-time job in football at Washington State University. He got the job through a referral and recommendation from Coach Osborne. From there he progressed to other schools including the University of Colorado. While in Colorado, Yaralian's team made a bid for the national championship. His boss and well-respected head coach, Bill McCartney, helped Yaralian reach the next level of performance in his career. Through recommendations from him and Osborne, Yaralian was offered and accepted a position to join Mike Ditka of the Chicago Bears. Ditka then helped Yaralian receive an offer from Dan Reeves of the New York Giants. Yaralian then reunited with the Hall of Famer, Mike Ditka, five years later in New Orleans, where Yaralian became the defensive coordinator for the New Orleans Saints.

The once unknown defensive back coach was given the opportunity to coach with some of the best coaches and teams in the NFL because of a network of key relationships he had made and cultivated throughout his career.[1]

Mr. Zaven Yaralian's Career through Networking

Top: Career opportunity
Bottom: Connection used

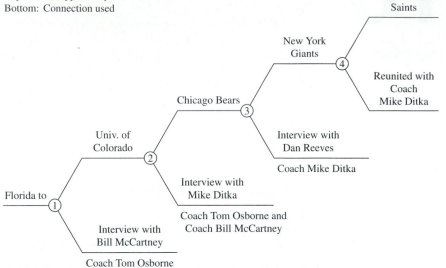

Source: B. Yaralian et al.

1. In business, neither technical skills nor networking abilities are sufficient by themselves. Do you agree with this statement? Why or why not?

2. When Yaralian proves he is an effective coach, why would others help him move up—and out—of their organization? Wouldn't you prefer keeping outstanding performers as opposed to helping them leave?

3. What are some benefits of networking?

4. What are some potential downsides of networking?

5. In what ways have you used networking to get a leg up on a job or other opportunity?

"It's not what you know, it's who you know."

The old adage about the valuable role others can play in opening doors for us has stuck because often it's true. As illustrated in the above case, moving up successfully can happen as the result of both acquiring knowledge and fostering important relationships with others who can be helpful to you as your career progresses. While we wouldn't say that credentials aren't important, the fact is that having the credentials to do a job is just the first step. Equally important is getting access—to information, people, and jobs—and other people are often the conduit through which this access is obtained. In this chapter, we discuss networking with people and politicking within organizations to get your ideas accepted and needs met. We discuss the definition and importance of networking and politicking, how they are used, and tips for becoming more effective when meeting others and advocating for organizational change.

What Is Networking?

Networking is the building and nurturing of personal and professional relationships to create a system or chain of information, contacts, and support. In the business world, the goal of networking is to establish an interconnected series of contacts with people who can be helpful to you, your employer, or your organization. Successful networking requires a certain mindset or philosophy: an attitude of giving advice, information, and help rather than expecting this from others.[2] Effective networking is most likely to occur between two or more people who build rapport by finding common interests through meaningful, balanced, two-way communication. A networker who appears too needy or self-centered might face resistance from others who might otherwise be able to help him or her.

Whether through face-to-face, phone, written, or electronic means, the networker attempts to connect with others who can provide needed information and opportunities. A person's network is evolving constantly. Studies estimate that over a lifetime, a person will have several thousand acquaintances. Moreover, as age and income increase, so too will the number of acquaintances. Some contacts are cultivated deliberately and others evolve naturally.[3] The largest portion of a person's network actually consists of secondary contacts—friends of friends who are close to the situation about which you need information.

Why Is Networking Important?

Creating a personal network and developing networking skills can provide numerous professional benefits for individuals and organizations. Networking is invaluable for both those who are seeking advancement within an existing organization as well as those who are seeking a new career opportunity. Building a network of contacts can keep you current with industry trends and expedite your career advancement from one position to another, either within an existing organization or in a move from one organization to the next.[4]

Networking is essential when taking on a new assignment or project. It is a good habit to get to know others, both inside and outside your department, and at all levels—peers, subordinates, and superiors. By networking with co-workers as well as with individuals at more junior and senior levels of the organization, you can learn about the broader business in which your organization is involved and about the challenges and opportunities that lie ahead.[5]

Networking while on the job increases your access to available resources and information.[6] Networking with others helps you to augment your thoughts and ideas with those of others, creating a concept that incorporates "best practice" thinking from the outset of its development. Networking helps you to increase your effectiveness when researching a new concept, starting a new project, or developing a new product idea.[7] By consulting with others who are experts in the topic in which you are involved, you incorporate the thoughts of others into your knowledge base in the given area. For example, when charged with developing or testing a new product, an important first step is to identify internal and external experts who can serve as sources of information on the relevant topic, preventing you from "reinventing the wheel" and building allies who can later advocate for the change you are proposing.

Staying in touch with people and trends in your company enables you to prepare for and adapt to organizational changes. Access to information and "connectedness" enables you to acquire a more strategic view of the business, one that is holistic rather than limited to your specific functional area. This helps you to position your department and organization to respond strategically to marketplace changes as they inevitably occur.[8]

This heightened understanding can increase your effectiveness as a businessperson and value to the organization as you learn to make decisions from multiple rather than one-dimensional business perspectives. For example, an aerospace firm during the early 1990s found defense budgets shrinking substantially. The CEO's directive—cut 30 per-cent across the board—could have spelled disaster if not for the willingness to network on the part of division and department managers. Some programs were nearly dead, while others—early in the life cycle though potentially a financial success—were struggling to make ends meet. Managers met and discussed the directive, deciding that cutting costs by one-third did not necessarily mean firing one-third of the employees, and cutting all programs or departments at the same rate did not make sense. They networked, shared information and resources, and found ways to meet the directive in a way that met the needs of the organization.

Organizations may be represented on charts as groups of self-contained work units, such as marketing, finance, research and development, purchasing, information systems, planning, logistics, communications, public relations, human resources, and legal counsel, but in fact, most departments rely heavily on outputs of other departments. Most decisions made by one segment of an organization affect other segments of an organization. What happens between the boxes on the organization chart—the "white spaces"[9]—could mean the difference between failure and success of the organization. Managing the white spaces through organizational networking not only facilitates organizational synergy but also helps you when you're promoted to positions elsewhere in the company or when you move to other companies and industries.

Networking can be instrumental in helping managers find key people to hire.[10] Firms in high growth areas, such as computer information systems and wireless or digital technologies, experience great difficulty in recruiting and retaining talented professionals. There is a growing competition for a shrinking pool of employees with this type of talent and expertise. Even with promises of signing bonuses and stock options, some firms come up empty handed. Often, the personal recommendation from a friend—alone or combined with a signing bonus—can help to entice a prospective employee to accept a job offer.

Where Are You on the Network Timeline?[11]

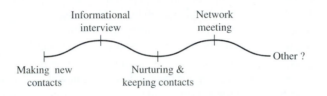

Networking can also help you to learn about new job opportunities. In today's fast-paced, global, high-tech environment, your attitude about and comfort with networking can significantly impact your ability to establish contacts, get interviews for jobs, and identify and cultivate mentors within organizations.[12] By improving your ability to sell yourself, you can benefit in terms of a new job as well as increased skill in selling and promoting—useful skills in any business today. Networking skills are crucial for career and personal success. Career specialists estimate that 70–80 percent of the best jobs come from effective and consistent personal networking with others rather than through executive search firms (commonly referred to as "headhunters"), sending in blind resumes, posting a resume on the web, or responding to job ads.[13]

Effective networking leads to a ripple effect. Like a stone thrown in the water, creating numerous waves and movements, one personal contact can lead to others that eventually result in knowledge about multiple career opportunities.[14] You might recall the commercial for Fabergé Organics shampoo ("I told two friends, and they told two friends, and so on"). Another way of explaining the value of networking is the premise of "six degrees of separation,"[15] the notion that most of us can find a connection to anyone else in the world through six levels of contacts. This is referred to as the **"secondary network"** and validates the importance of not relying solely on those you know when doing research, getting to know an organization, or when searching for a job.

Finally, networking is a great way to locate providers of goods and services. This can serve individuals and organizations by helping them to identify good deals or valuable savings to help reduce costs. Have you ever wanted to buy a car; needed to find office supplies at a discount; or relocated to a new area and needed a doctor, a dentist, or hairdresser? A network of friends, peers, and acquaintances can help you streamline your search.

Simply put, networking is an important skill for those who want to succeed within an organization or find a new employer. Networking enables us to break out of old patterns (it's always been done this way) and find new, more efficient solutions to fulfill our organizational and career-related needs.

Barriers to Networking

Networking may sound simple enough, but for some the prospect of networking can be intimidating. For many people, the skill of networking does not come naturally. Meeting others, making small talk, and especially marketing or promoting oneself are processes that require practice in order to be performed successfully. There are varying reasons why people fear or avoid networking.

- Lack of self-esteem or confidence in personal skills and abilities.
- Difficulty in asking others for help.
- Wanting to reach goals without any special help from others.
- Concern about being able to reciprocate the favor immediately.
- Concern about sharing sensitive or competitive information.

Whatever your personal barrier or discomfort with networking might be, it is important to resolve the issues that can prevent you from becoming an effective networker. Those who do not learn how to network will fall behind in today's competitive and global environment.[16] Luckily, these skills can be learned and applied in a variety of contexts. For those who are shy, networking can be achieved through means other than face-to-face meetings, such as an e-mail or letter. Once your confidence and competence increase, try combining these approaches with more direct, face-to-face methods, such as through meetings and conferences. Networking takes conscious effort. It is very much like working out: if you do not continue to work at it, you will lose what you have already gained.

Steps for Building a Network

The following steps will help get you started in developing and maintaining a beneficial network:

- *Organize your current network.* Identify people you already know and enter their names and contact information into a database. Consider friends; classmates; teachers and former teachers; guidance counselors; working parents; friends of parents; co-workers; bosses; former bosses and co-workers; members of organizations of which you are or have been a member such as a fraternity or sorority, church, student organization, or civic club; even the family dentist, doctor, or accountant!

- *Use the web.* An important element of networking is the use of technology.[17] The web offers unlimited potential. By sending e-mails and joining online lists, chat rooms, and web boards, you can get multiple responses to your questions with the click of a button. For example, if you've been charged with conducting a best-practice study on advertising agencies, join a chat room made up of ad account executives. (It's a good idea to read recent discussion threads before jumping right in with your question. It may have recently been asked and answered.)

- *Get involved* in civic, professional, or social organizations.

- *Let others know your goals and ambitions* and ask them for names of people you can contact. Some opportunities should not be ignored, such as the person sitting next to you on an airplane. Should you talk to each other, and it's hard not to in an airplane, you might be surprised to find out how much you have in common.

- *Ask how you can help.* End every conversation with people in your network by asking how you can help them.

- *Do something every day* to expand and improve your network. Fit this activity into your work plan.

- Court these people *one-on-one.*

- Always *exchange business cards,* even if your exchange is brief.

- *Keep in touch periodically* with your friends and associates to maintain your existing relationships.

What If I Don't Have Any Contacts? Everyone has contacts! A contact is simply a person who is willing and able to help you. Below are a few examples of who your contacts might be. If you're having trouble identifying names of potential contacts, you might be overlooking the obvious—friends, relatives, and neighbors. Remember, these people may not have the information you need but they may know others who do. Another strategy for meeting potential contacts is to get involved in organizations. These can be community service, career, professional, recreational, civic, fraternal, academic, religious—any group where you are likely to meet people who share an interest or commitment to a cause with you.

Who Are Contacts?[18]

Friends, Relatives, Neighbors, Sorority/Fraternity Members

Co-workers of Parents, Spouse or Significant Other, and Other Family Members

Current and Former Classmates

Priests, Ministers, Rabbis, and Fellow Church or Synagogue Members

Fellow Club Members

Personal Lawyer, Insurance Agent, Realtor, Accountant, Doctor, Dentist, Beautician

Teachers and Former Teachers

Employers and Former Employers

Co-workers and Former Co-workers

Members of Your Employer's Human Resources Department

Grade School, High School, College, and Graduate School Alumni and Alumni Associations

Business Associates and Members of Professional Organizations

Networking Tips

■ **Expand your network:** A common strategy is to begin by asking your own co-workers for names of people they know or have heard about in the field of interest. At the same time, check the Internet and other publications to identify other people and organizations to add to the list. Professional associations that are related to your field of expertise or interests are an excellent source of names of people with whom to network. You or someone you know might already be a member of one or more of these organizations. Using associations as sounding boards can help you to get the needed information, as well as help you assess the strengths and weaknesses of the information you receive.[19]

Review the list with anyone involved in the project to obtain additional names. Then contact each name on the list (via phone, e-mail, or memo), one at a time, introducing yourself, explaining the reason you're making the contact, and describing where you found the person's name. Explain to them why you need the information and offer a little background that helps them understand why you're contacting them. It helps to say something positive about why you're contacting them specifically—such as you know they're an expert, you heard good things about them, or you know they have the experience that could benefit your project.

■ **Expand your internal network of contacts:** After you've been in your new job for a period of time, make it a point (with your boss's knowledge) to meet other department heads and members. Ask them about their work, such as the key issues they face and the key services in which they're involved. Ask about their perspective on the company and the direction in which it's heading. Ask their advice on things you can do to improve your performance that can result in positive changes in their department.

An excellent source of networking information is a mentor. Mentors are people in an organization who are experienced and usually well respected who take an interest in helping a more junior person "learn the ropes"—learn what it takes to succeed in a particular organizational culture. A good mentor can help you build a network of contacts. He or she can direct you toward the "right" people and assignments (those that will enhance your success) and away from those who could harm your career. Mentors can be assigned to you through a formal program sponsored by the company, or can seek you out informally. Either way mentors are ideal for helping you meet people and find the resources you need to do well in your organization.

■ **Use networking when seeking a job:** Most advertised jobs are for entry-level positions. Typically, the more senior positions are made known only through word of mouth. When looking to change jobs, companies, or industries, you will likely benefit by contacting others within your network and identifying those who might know someone or know someone who knows someone in the targeted arena.

■ **Network for information:** A successful job-hunting technique is informational interviewing. This means interviewing people about their own careers and jobs. In **information interviews,** the goal is to learn from the person with whom you're speaking, not to obtain a job. This can be done by asking what they like and dislike about their job, getting advice from them about how you might embark on a similar career path or join a similar organization. A sample set of questions to ask during information interviews appears in the table below. When used early in the job search process, networking for information, rather than for specific jobs, can help you clarify your job goals and improve your interviewing skills. Wouldn't it be better to realize that you are not cut out to spend eight hours a day in front of a computer than to take a job and quit? This focused task will help you to achieve your short-term goal as well as clarify your interest or compatibility with a particular job or career field.

Networking for Information: Questions to Ask in Information Interviews

1. How did your interest in this career develop?
2. How did you prepare for this career?
3. What do you like and dislike about this career?
4. What are the current and future trends in this career?
5. What are the key issues with which you're working right now?
6. Describe a typical day in this job.
7. If you could change one thing about this career, what would it be?
8. What advice do you have for someone like me?
9. Would you have a few minutes to critique my resume?
10. Who else can I talk to about a career in _____?

This principle can be applied both as a student and as a manager. As a student, it is important to identify key resource people who can help you attain your goals. Through networking with your resident advisor, upper-class students, coaches, and teachers, you can learn the names of people you can consult or organizations that can be of benefit to you on school projects or when dealing with personal problems. Those students who are willing to reach out to others rather than trying to solve all of their own problems are better able to make changes and solve problems than are those who refuse assistance from others and try to fix or change things on their own. Students who utilize their contacts are more likely to get internships and jobs than those who do not.

Developing an Appropriate Mindset for Networking

There is more to networking than just understanding the tactics and techniques for developing and practicing the skill. Networking involves building and maintaining relationships.[20] Successful networking requires a positive, cooperative mindset. So far, we have discussed networking as a way to use your connections to get your needs met. This sounds rather one-sided. The most successful networkers have an attitude derived from viewing relationships as opportunities to give to, rather than take from, others.[21] There are two kinds of networkers: those who are self-oriented, and those who are focused on others.

■ The "self-oriented" networker approaches a room and surveys the room for potential customers or clients, thinking, Who can I sell? Who might be able to give me a job lead? What can I get them to buy? How do I convince them they need me or what I offer?

■ The "other-oriented" networker approaches a room and identifies people who need to be connected with others in the room, thinking, Who in this room could use my help? Who can I introduce to whom? How can I help you? I know someone who might be able to help you; can I have them contact you?

Networking in Action[22]

Met Mrs. Gonzales at Trade Fair June 7.
She suggested I contact Mr. Kerne at
Trim Tech.

June 11
Took Mr. Kerne to lunch.
Discovered we had much in
common. He made an
appointment to see a
John Grant at Jaco Co.

June 18
Mr. Grant, a vice president, took me to
their human resource director.
Two interviews followed.

June 30
Accepted position with Jaco.

Contact Record[23]

Here is a good format to use to keep up with your contacts. You can keep track of your contacts in an organizer, rolodex, notebook, or computer database. This will allow you to access all the pertinent data when you need to and to keep it current.

Name: _____

Contact: _____

Company/Organization: _____

Address: _____

_____

Phone: _____

E-mail Address: _____

How do I know this person? _____

_____

_____

Why are they a good first contact? _____

_____

Contact record. List date(s) of all contacts and brief subject/nature of contact. Keep track of items sent and "to do" items here. _____

_____

_____

Those who are approached by the self-interested networker might feel taken advantage of. A relationship was not formed; instead, pleasantries were exchanged as a way of getting some need met. Should this networker contact the person at a later date, there's a possibility that the person will be less willing to help.

To prepare mentally for a networking meeting, follow these three steps:

1. Analyze the *process*. Ask yourself with whom you'll need to network—the types of individuals you will be seeking, and for what purpose.[24] Be sure to identify what you hope to gain as well as ways in which you can contribute. Remember that networking is a two-way street. Others will be more apt to help you when you show your willingness to help them.

2. Identify the *place* where the networking might or will occur. Identify community organizations; professional associations; clubs; social, professional, or fraternal organizations; alumni associations; and chambers of commerce—any source that might be a good place to meet others interested in similar topics as you.

3. *Practice* networking. Focus on the specific steps and techniques of networking. Practice these steps and learn to be comfortable with networking. Success breeds success. The more you practice, the better you'll be at networking. You might begin practicing and build up your confidence by using a "safer" method to network, such as a letter or e-mail.

Before, during, and after Networking

We've discussed the importance of networking and ways for you to increase your network and networking skills. The following table is organized chronologically, highlighting key things to do or consider before, during, and after a networking meeting.

Before	During	After
■ Make networking a high priority; allot time in your weekly or monthly planner for networking activities. ■ Set specific networking goals (why, with whom, about what, when, where, how). ■ Start with a small circle of well-known associates and friends; small goals will lead to big goals. ■ Practice small talk—develop conversation starters before entering a room or attending a conference or meeting. ■ Know the organizational culture, the norms, customs, dress.	■ Focus completely on the others' needs initially when establishing professional relationships. ■ Get all vital information (name, title, address, company, phone number, e-mail address, etc). ■ Verify how to pronounce the person's name correctly. ■ Be visible, not pushy. Check nonverbal language for cues. ■ Respect the other's time—if you ask to chat for 10 minutes, don't exceed that. ■ Refrain from praising, fawning, self-deprecation, flirting, or cuteness. ■ Be sincere; give only genuine, specific compliments. Instead of "You were great" try "The lead you gave me on the consulting job was very helpful. I was able to . . . Thanks!"	■ As you walk away, jot down a few notes on the back of the person's business card to jog your memory when writing a follow-up note.[25] ■ Follow up with new contacts within 48 hours, and again when you achieve a goal they helped you attain. ■ Send thank-you notes (by mail, not e-mail). Be sure to maintain professionalism in all follow-up correspondence (phone messages, e-mail), including proper grammar, pronunciation, etiquette. ■ If you follow up by phone, consider writing a script or key ideas to mention. Be organized—sketch out in advance how you plan to approach the conversation. ■ Assess yourself; how did you do? What kind of impression do you think you made? ■ Follow through on your promises and be conscious of how you can help others in your network.

Politicking—What It Is and Why It's Important

Politicking is an internal form of networking, a means to build your network within the organizational structure. The word "politicking" may conjure up negative connotations, as the term can be used to define behavior that is motivated primarily or even exclusively by self-interest. Organizations, like people, do have a "dark side." It is not uncommon to find people willing to put their needs above those of others, to do whatever it takes to get what they want. In this chapter we prefer to focus on the positive view of politicking, where **politicking** is the use of power and information to move resources towards preferred objectives.[26] In this view, politicking is speaking up on behalf of our and our employees' or company's interests and is part of the process of rule making and decision making in organizational life. People use political behavior to affect decisions, get scarce resources, and earn the cooperation of people outside their direct authority.[27] Politicking, simply put, is advocating for your interests in a way that meets your and your company's objectives. One who is effective at politicking in business is fully engaged in the life of the organization, understands the key issues and drivers within the organization and the industry, and exercises sound judgment when making decisions that affect the people in and resources of the organization. One who is politic is cautious, not rash, and makes decisions carefully, not impulsively.

Politicking is important because of the complexities involved in being in business today. The global marketplace, the changing attitudes and growing diversity of employees, the intense competition for profits, the explosion of technology, the constant changes in business strategy, and the changing cast of characters who run companies are just a few of these intricacies. Politicking is a way to strengthen and expand your existing network of contacts within your organization. It can be used to learn about available resources and how to get them allocated to objectives that support your and your employees' interests.[28] Developing skills in politicking is what enables effective managers to understand the ways in which their business is constantly evolving and to seek ways to keep well informed so they can adapt as needed.

Politicking in Action

Politics exists at varying levels in many dimensions of both social and professional life. Just like networking, politicking requires forethought before being put into action. There are three basic dimensions involved in determining your political strategy:[29] analyzing yourself, reading others, and assessing the organization.

Analyzing Yourself

Politicking begins with a clear understanding of yourself and the politicking qualities you possess naturally. What are your personal strengths and limitations, and how do these help or hinder your ability to be political within an organization? What strengths can you bring to your interactions with others, and what limitations might make it difficult for you to influence others, particularly within an organizational context? Several personal characteristics, such as being confident, articulate, and sensitive, make it easier for a person to be an effective politicker (see list below for additional characteristics). Having an honest perception of your goals, and your capability for achieving them, will help in highlighting your positive aspects while diminishing or controlling your negative factors. For example, if you have a tendency to dominate conversations, focus on listening intently to others while they are speaking. If you are by nature an introvert, you might want to focus on seeking others out for their opinions before making decisions.

An important aspect of self-understanding with regard to politicking is the role of power. Understanding your personal power bases increases your capacity and ability to obtain information from and share information with others. Power is a necessary factor in getting others to move towards a desired goal. Leaders use power to achieve organizational goals. To influence someone to move towards a desired goal, hence be political, it is important to understand the power base from which you are working and which power base would be effective for a specific situation or person with whom you are interacting.

How Political Are You?[30]

Take a look at the list below. Circle the number that most describes the degree to which each word describes you.

	Agree		Neither		Disagree
Articulate	1	2	3	4	5
Sensitive	1	2	3	4	5
Competent	1	2	3	4	5
Extroverted	1	2	3	4	5
Self-confident	1	2	3	4	5
Assertive	1	2	3	4	5
Collaborative	1	2	3	4	5
Intelligent	1	2	3	4	5
Logical	1	2	3	4	5
Socially adept	1	2	3	4	5

Total the numbers circled. If your score is less than 30, you have what it takes to be naturally political in organizations.

Power bases can be formal or informal. A **formal power base** comes from authority: which position and managerial level do you hold within the organization and over whom do you have power by virtue of your position? An **informal power base** comes from respect and credibility. Informal power is based on how others perceive you and who is willing to be influenced by you by virtue of your reputation or knowledge base. For example, a long-time employee who has not progressed up the ladder but has influence and respect due to his or her vast accumulation of company "know-how" probably has a significant informal power base. An informal power base or connection can have just as much impact as a formal base.[31]

Your power base can provide you with credibility and provide others with a rationale for accepting your position on a matter of importance. For example, marketers may use their market intelligence, product knowledge, and experience to push a new product idea through R and D. Managers might use their formal positions and titles to get battling and incompatible employees to sit down and discuss their differences.

Power Bases[32]

Legitimate—a result of the organizational structure and denoted by title.

Reward—based on power to give rewards that are valued by the recipient or to withhold rewards.

Referent—based on possession of attractive traits or likeability; awarded to people who are similar to us in interests, lifestyle, or culture or who have charismatic qualities or serve as a point of reference for qualities to which we aspire.

Expert—based on possession of knowledge or superior skills in an area of expertise.

Coercive—a negative power base obtained through the use of threats or force.

Power, in and of itself, is not negative or bad. It is the abuse of power that can be perceived as negative. Each power base has its place and, when used appropriately and positively, can provide the necessary fuel to support your stance. Understanding your power bases and how and when to use them is an important component of politicking and self-awareness.

Reading Others

Effective managers who are good at politicking within their organizations know the importance of being able to "read" people,[33] or understand others' perceptions, reactions, and motivations. To be effective in politicking, it is important to understand others quickly: their power base; their perceptions regarding their position, the situation, and organization; and their stance on the issues at hand.

In some instances there is insufficient time to form impressions and check our understanding of these perceptions with the person or with a trusted colleague. In these cases, we have to rely on our instincts about the person—understanding where they're coming from and what they want to obtain from the situation. Let's say your star employee just left for an overseas assignment and you need to find a temporary replacement. There's no time for a formal search, especially given the temporary nature of the assignment, so you'll have to rely on your hopefully accurate impression of potential candidates in your network. You'll do this by identifying a potential applicant or pool of applicants, asking a few respected others for their opinions, making a few discreet inquiries about the availability of one or two applicants, talking with those you are considering, and offering the position to the person who you think best fits your profile.

Following Are Some Tips on Reading Others.[34]

- *Listen aggressively.* Listen for what is said and how it is said, not for what you think the person *should* be saying. Use pauses frequently; silence often encourages a person to say more.

- *Observe aggressively.* Interpret others' body language and check for consistency or lack of consistency between what's being said verbally and what's being displayed nonverbally.

- *Turn up your sensitivity.* Be aware of more than simply the conversation that is taking place. Use all your senses to pick up the nuances that are occurring within and between groups of people in the room.

- *Analyze first impressions.* Think about what the person is trying to present or hopes to gain before accepting what you see. If something seems inconsistent, ask.

- *Be discreet.* Don't always let others know what you have learned. Only share the information you have when it is to your best advantage. *Never* share information that has been shared with you in confidence.

Assess the Organization: Its Structure and Culture

People who use politicking strategies effectively are likely to be those who have a good handle on the way an organization is structured, how it operates, how things get done, and on its people and culture. They use their connections to people and information to obtain resources, get decisions made and implemented, navigate through complex bureaucracies, and generally facilitate processes in a way that meets organizational objectives.[35] Often, politicking behaviors are used by managers to influence people and processes when they lack formal direct authority. In your organizations—professional and personal—consider using some or all of the following tactics to politic appropriately and effectively.

- *Observe and listen.* Pay close attention to the organizational norms. Know what type of behavior is acceptable and what is frowned upon by individuals and by the organization. Pay attention to successful and unsuccessful practices and actions: Do employees speak up in meetings when their managers are present? What time do employees usually arrive and leave the organization? Do they work on Saturdays? One employee at Microsoft, a company known for its intense work culture, decided to come in early to get work done so he could leave early to pick up his children from school. Others paid little attention to the time he arrived, but were quick to point out his "early" departure. He earned an unfavorable perception, despite the fact that he worked as many hours as his co-workers, and eventually was asked to leave.[36] Although this employee eventually won a lawsuit against his employer, it's a good example of the role that politicking can play in organizations. Unfair? Perhaps, but we have to know and follow both the written and unwritten rules to succeed in an organization.

- *Evaluate the organization.* You may know who reports to whom on the organization's chart, but this may not represent how authority actually flows or the way in which certain practices are carried out. Know the formal roles individuals play in the organizations, as well as the informal roles. For example, don't overlook departmental clerical and administrative staff members. To the politically astute, these individuals can be a wealth of information. When treated with respect, they can help get you what you need, whether access, information, or "insider" tips.

■ *Pick your battles and strategies carefully.* Do you remember the children's story about the boy who cried wolf? After several trial calls—just to see if others would come—the townspeople ignored subsequent calls, figuring it was yet another trial or joke. When the call was real, no one came. Similarly, if you were to wield your power (or political influence) for each and every "cause," others may eventually reduce the attention they pay to subsequent causes. You'd be better off conserving your "political capital"— your reputation, influence, energy, and resources—for more important actions or causes.

Just as it is important to determine which situations warrant politicking, it is also crucial to decide how you will approach the situation. There are various politicking strategies (see chart) that can be utilized to achieve your goal. You should carefully select a strategy based on the organization, the situation, and the individuals involved, as well as weigh the potential consequences of your political action. Each strategy can have elements of effectiveness if used appropriately and negative repercussions when used in haste.

Politicking Strategies[37]

Assertiveness—being able to speak up for your and your employees' rights without interfering with the needs of others in your organization.

Upward Appeals—demonstrating that more senior and powerful people in your organization support the decision for which you are advocating.

Exchange or **Bargaining**—using the "give and take" or compromise approach; e.g., "I do this for you if you do this for me."

Reciprocation—offering something to someone else and then expecting them to support your stance on a topic.[38]

Coalition Building—gaining support for a position from others.

Ingratiation—putting the other in a friendly mood before approaching, or building a friendly rapport first before transacting business.

Rationality—using logic and reasoning to support your appeal.

Inspirational Appeals—using emotional appeals based on values and ideas to gain support.

Consultation—seeking participation and input in the process before making a decision about a position to support.

■ *Adopt a "win-win" attitude.* When making a request for organizational resources (e.g., staff, budget, time, project approval), it's best to frame your request in terms of the "greater good" and show that you've thought through the impact of your request on other areas and departments within your organization.

■ *Choose words you say in public carefully.* Never say anything in private that you can't defend in public. A good rule of thumb is to not say things behind a person's back.[39] People tend to confide things to others, sharing information or opinions they hope will be kept private. But in business, seldom can anything be kept private. Only share those items about yourself and others that you wouldn't mind hearing from someone else. Keep your private thoughts about someone to yourself. Only talk publicly about things that are job-related.

Impression Management

An important element in politicking is the perception others hold of you. You can attempt to increase positive perceptions by using the concept of impression management. You've heard the saying "You only have one chance to make a first impression." This saying stems from our human tendency to form opinions about others before we've actually gotten to know them. Whether this is fair or not, we form impressions about others—consciously or subconsciously—based on subtle factors such as their dress, speech, handshake, phone manner, writing style, prior reputation, and behavior and mannerisms. **Impression management** is a process by which we attempt to influence the reactions and images people have of us and our ideas.[40] We do this when we wear our best suit on a job interview or when we send a copy of a congratulatory e-mail or note to our boss. Through impression management, we become aware of all the ways in which we convey an initial impression of who we are to others and make a conscious choice about what parts of us we want to display to others.

Why is impression management important? In the same way networking can help others take notice of your resume and invite you to an interview, impression management can get you noticed—and keep you noticed once you've been hired.

Imagine a school principal who has unfortunately gained the reputation of being an ogre due to exaggerated comments from some of the children at the school. When parent night approaches, the self-aware principal will realize that she might need to display those aspects of her personality that emphasize that she is a caring, attentive person as well as a consistent and fair disciplinarian.

How Can You Manage Others' Impressions of You?

Here are some suggestions:

- Be Punctual—demonstrate self-control and respect for others' time.
- Dress Appropriately—inquire ahead whether business or business casual is the norm. Dress to impress—err on the conservative side—but don't overdress. It could make others feel uncomfortable.
- Flatter Legitimately—say positive things about the person based on fact or personal observation. Be genuine. Others can sense when you're not.
- Have a Good Sense of Humor—it helps put people at ease. Do try to use humor appropriately—as a lead-in to, not as a replacement for, substance. Beware of humor that can be construed as prejudiced against a certain group.
- Be Friendly and Approachable—talk about things you have in common with the other, such as experience, hobbies, or views on current events. One way to do this in a business setting is to stay current with business periodicals, e.g., *Wall Street Journal, Fortune, Business Week, International Herald Tribune,* and others.
- Make Friends—and value all contacts.

Information Management

"Information is power." This saying underscores how having knowledge can be a source of influence in organizations (see previous Power Bases table). Managers who are effective at politicking stay well informed about the organization and the industry and use information they gather to help them make better business decisions.[41] **Information management** involves obtaining useful information and managing the information received so that it is accessible and available as needed. As technology advances and we are bombarded "24/7," 24 hours a day seven days a week, by all kinds of information, the skill of information management is becoming even more critical. The most effective managers are those who understand the importance of information and know how to access, sift through, store, and use information to their advantage. In high-tech fields, innovations become old news by the time they are available to end users. Knowing what's coming, what's in the works, and who's involved in these efforts can make the difference between success and failure. Relying solely on the information easily accessible, or worse, ignoring such information, is a recipe for disaster.

Being able to effectively organize current and emerging information that relates to your work is important in many professions. In sales, for example, when your customer has indicated particular likes or needs, has asked you to contact them in six months, or has referred you to another potential customer, this information is critical to your success. Does your information management technique rely on numerous nondescript piles of paper on your desk? If so, you may want to come up with a different system. It doesn't have to be formal. For example, a series of Post-It Notes stuck to your bulletin board might work.

 You might consider the following tips for managing information:

- *Set up a simple, user-friendly file system* (both print and electronic).
    - The system should include both specific project folders as well as general "resource" folders that are topical rather than pertain to a specific assignment. Resource folders might include technology, reports, or current events that may affect your organization or career.
    - Cleanse these folders on a regular basis to ensure they are current.
    - File the folders from past projects in a separate place from your active files. Limit the clutter in your active pile.
- *Glance briefly at all information* that comes to you either electronically or in print.
    - Quickly make "importance" decisions: must handle, handle if time, or discard.
    - Discard items that are not relevant or can be obtained later. Process or file the remaining items immediately. One rule of time management is to handle each piece of paper only once.
- *Make printouts of sensitive e-mails* and file them in your personal files. Then, remove them from your electronic inbox.
- *Refer to your project and related resource files prior to attending a meeting about the topic.* These few minutes can help get you up to speed and reduce wasted time in meetings.
- *Keep written notes on all meetings attended.* Date the pages and jot down key issues discussed and decisions made. Bring these notes with you to subsequent meetings to prevent having to revisit topics that have already been addressed.
- *Keep a telephone log* to track phone messages received and follow up calls.
- *Manage your e-mail.* Respond to professional e-mail messages during the day, preferably during one or two blocks of time set aside for this task. Only respond to personal e-mail after hours, or better still, maintain a separate personal account. Many organizations offer this service for free.
- *Keep running "to do" and "tickler" lists.* Maintain all "to do" items on one master list, and a separate "tickler" list to remind you of upcoming deadlines and activities. Related folders can be kept in the current file until you work on a specific "to do" item.
- As you receive information from all sources (e.g., mail, e-mail, phone, reading, colleagues), decide who else should see this information and arrange for them to be copied or informed.

Ethical Issues in Politicking

When engaging in political behaviors, it is important to keep in mind any ethical implications of your actions. As physicists tell us, "For every action, there is an equal and opposite reaction." Before taking action, ask yourself whether the action you're considering might cause an imbalance in your or someone else's area of the organization. For example if you are advocating salary raises for your staff, what are the implications for the staffs of other managers? It's also important to consider whether you are achieving your objective at the expense of someone else's objectives. Always think through the implications of your objectives on the work of others. You don't want to "win the battle but lose the war," an old saying that reminds us to consider the long-term implications of a change effort as well as the short-term benefits or implications. While your staff might appreciate the raises you were able to obtain for them, the other staff with whom they work might perceive inequity and reduce their cooperation and effort to equalize the situation.

> To address the ethical implications of potential politicking efforts, ask yourself these questions:
>
> ■ Why am I considering doing this?
> ■ Who will be benefited by this action? Am I doing this for my own exclusive benefit?
> ■ Who (if anyone) might be harmed?
>   ■ How can I adjust my strategy to ensure others' needs will be taken into account?
>   ■ What alliances can I form that will make this action more likely to meet my own as well as others' needs?
> ■ Is this request in the best interest of my colleagues and organization?
> ■ Are the tactics I'll use and the outcomes that will result fair and equitable?
> ■ Would the tactics I use and words I convey be acceptable if known publicly?

When done correctly, politicking can be a powerful tool for achieving your objectives and being successful within an organization. Asking yourself the questions listed above should help you to reduce or prevent potential negative side effects from developing from your efforts. As a manager, it is your role to create an environment that supports a healthy level of politicking, one that helps others understand the power and appropriate use of politicking within the organization. Sometimes organizations experience unfair or negative politicking—devious, self-interested efforts to sway opinion or a decision toward one point of view, at the exclusion of all others. While politicking will always exist at some level in organizations, you can ensure your staff's use of fair, positive politicking and work to reduce the level of unfair, negative politicking. Some tips for doing this follow.

■ *Reduce Task Ambiguity*—Employees need to be clear on what they can and cannot do and how tasks are prescribed. There should be no misunderstanding about what's expected of employees, their role, the amount of authority they have, and the level of work in which they're expected to get involved. For example, make it clear if they will be doing routine things in addition to more creative work. This will reduce the inevitable "infighting" that develops when people feel they're being taken advantage of in the workplace.

■ *Increase Communication Channels*—Open up two-way communication. Ensure that all involved have input into key decisions and resource allocation requests before they're made. Be clear on where everyone stands, and ensure that all have the equivalent amount and quality of information needed to make informed decisions. This will prevent employees from feeling left out of important decisions and increase the degree to which they support or buy into your company's change efforts.

■ *Ensure a Clear and Consistent Reward and Promotion Structure*—Have a reward system that is well organized, fair, and clearly communicated. One of the best ways to reduce unfair politicking is to put careful thought into designing a compensation structure that is understood by all current and new employees, accessible and beneficial to employees at all levels within the organization, and motivating to current as well as to potential employees. This increases employee motivation, reduces concerns about potential inequities, and helps to focus attention on business objectives rather than on an individual employee's or department's perceived salary inequities.

■ *Provide Sufficient Resources*—A scarcity of resources leads to a high degree of politicking within organizations. It's not always possible, but managers should try to the best of their abilities to offer a work climate in which the staff has the resources necessary to do a job well. For example, as a hospital administrator, you would want to make sure that as the occupancy rate at your hospital increases, sufficient additional staff will be called in to accommodate the increased patient volume.

■ *Formalize the Structure*—The more formal the structure, the more reasoning and performance-based data will be used for politicking.[42] In informal work settings that are less established, such as in some high-tech and dot-com startups, reasoning and performance-based data are supplemented with personal contact, emotional appeals, and future-oriented thinking.

Summary

Networking and politicking are essential skills for developing relationships that will help you succeed personally and professionally. If you are skilled at networking and politicking, you'll be well positioned to advance your career, build relationships that are mutually beneficial, enhance your understanding of your company's culture and norms, and obtain the resources needed for you and your staff to be effective.

Key Terms and Concepts

Bargaining	Ingratiation
Consultation	Inspirational appeals
Formal power base	Networking
Impression management	Politicking
Informal power base	Reciprocation
Information interviews	Secondary network
Information management	

Endnotes

1. Blake Yaralian, "Networking," unpublished student paper, James Madison University, COB 202, Fall 1999.

2. Deb Haggerty, "Successful Networking," *The National Public Accountant,* Sept. 1999, p. 30.

3. Moshe Even-Shoshan and Tamar Gilad, "Network Your Way to Better Recruitment," *Workforce,* June 1999, p. 106.

4. Frank Sonnenberg, "The Professional (and Personal) Profits of Networking," *Training & Development Journal,* Sept. 1990, p. 55.

5. Marcia A. Reed, "Through the Grapevine," *Black Enterprise,* July 1999, p. 62.

6. Catherine M. Petrini, "Building a Chain of Contacts," *Training and Development Journal,* Jan. 1991, p. 27.

7. Dorothy Riddle, "Networking Successfully," *International Trade Forum,* July–Sept. 1998, p. 13.

8. Richard J. Henley, "Enhancing What You Know through Who You Know," *Healthcare Financial Management,* Dec. 1999, p. 14.

9. Geary A. Rummler and Alan P. Brache, "Managing the White Space," *Training,* Jan. 1991, pp. 55–67.

10. Even-Shoshan et al., 1999.

11. Ivillage, "How to Network," **www.ivillage.com/twn/print/0,2707,1548.htm.**

12. A. Andrew Olson, "Long-Term Networking: A Strategy for Career Success," *Management Review,* April 1994, p. 33.

13. Laura Koss-Feder, "It's Still Who You Know . . . In the Boom Economy, Job Hunting Is a Way of Life. Here's How to Do It," *Time,* March 22, 1999, p. 114F.

14. Brian Kreuger, "Job Hunter," **www.collegegrad.com,** May 2000.

15. David Berman and Sean Silcoff, "Have Rolodex, Will Go Far," *Canadian Business,* Nov. 13, 1998, p. 50.

16. Riddle, 1998.

17. Koss-Feder, 1999.

18. Andrea Nierenberg, "Masterful Networking," *Training and Development,* Feb. 1999, p. 51.

19. Henley, 1999.

20. Jeffrey Gitomer, "Building Good Relationships Puts the Work in Networking," *The Kansas City Business Journal,* Feb. 25, 2000, p. 24.

21. Haggerty, 1999.

22. Mike Godwin, Megan Fandrei, Josh Bare, Scott Longendyke, Cheryl Morgan, Brian Sweet, "Politicking and Networking," unpublished student paper, James Madison University, COB 202, Fall 1999.

23. M. Godwin et al., 1999, adopted from Tom Irish and Peter Grassl, "How to Build Your Network," **www.smartbiz.com/sbs/arts/irish5.htm.**

24. Jeffrey Gitomer, "Networking Not Working? Try Smart-Networking," *Birmingham Business Journal,* Jan. 7, 2000, p. 10.

25. Gitomer, Jan. 7, 2000.

26. D. Farrell and J. C. Petersen, "Patterns of Political Behavior in Organizations," *Academy of Management Review,* July 1982, p. 405; and D. J. Vredenburgh and J. G. Maurer, "A Process Framework of Organizational Politics," *Human Relations,* Jan. 1984, pp. 47–66.

27. Joseph E. Champoux, *Organizational Behavior: Using Film to Visualize Principles and Practices* (South-Western: Cincinnati, OH, 2000).

28. Runzheimer International, "Enhance Your Networking Skills," *Agency Sales Magazine,* March 1999, p. 52.

29. Stephen P. Robbins and Phillip L. Hunsaker, *Training in Interpersonal Skills: Tips for Managing People at Work* (Upper Saddle River, NJ: Prentice Hall, 1996), p. 128.

30. Allen, Madison, Porter, Renwick, and Mayes (1979).

31. David Krackhardt, "Assessing the Political Landscape: Structure, Cognition, and Power in an Organization," *Administrative Science Quarterly,* June 1990, p. 342.

32. Based on J. R. P. French and B. Raven, *The Bases of Social Power,* University of Michigan, Institute for Social Research, 1959, pp. 150–167.

33. Iris Randall, "The Key to Networking: Knowing How to 'Read' a Person Makes Networking Easier," *Black Enterprise,* March 1996, p. 56.

34. Sam Meadema et al., "Networking and Politicking," unpublished student paper, James Madison University, COB 202, Spring 2000.

35. Krackhardt, 1990.

36. Video case, "Joys and Risks of the Daddy Track," *Nightline,* August 14, 1991.

37. Reprinted from D. Kipnis, S. M. Schmidt, C. Swaffin-Smith, and I. Wilkinson, "Patterns of Managerial Influence: Shotgun Managers, Tacticians, and Bystanders," Organizational Dynamics, Winter 1984, pp. 58–67. Copyright 1984 with permission from Elsevier Science.

38. John Mariotti, "Understanding Influence and Persuasion," *Industry Week,* April 5, 1999, p. 126.

39. Reed, 1999.

40. Asha Rao, Stuart Schmidt, and Lynda Murray, "Upward Impression Management: Goals, Influence Strategies, and Consequences," *Human Relations* 48, no. 2 (1995), p. 147.

41. Thomas H. Davenport, Robert G. Eccles, and Laurence Prusak, "Information Politics," *Sloan Management Review,* Fall 1992, pp. 53–65.

42. Rao et al., 1995.

Exercise 10–A
Assessing Yourself

Circle the response that most closely correlates with each item below.

	Agree		Neither		Disagree

1. I am comfortable interacting with both small and large groups of people.   1 2 3 ④ 5

2. I know how to champion a cause within an organization successfully.   1 2 3 ④ 5

3. I actively network with existing and new contacts when I am researching a new concept, project, or product, and I keep track of these contacts through a database.   1 2 3 4 ⑤

4. I am a member of one or more professional organizations, and I consciously network with members of these organizations.   1 2 ③ 4 5

5. I network with people at a variety of levels: peers, subordinates, and superiors.   1 2 ③ 4 5

6. I make contact with people in other organizations as a way of keeping abreast of industry trends and developing relationships with people who can help me advance professionally.   1 2 3 4 ⑤

7. I have identified resource people in my school, company, or profession who can help me attain my professional goals, and I periodically ask them for names of other people who can support me in attaining my goals.   ① 2 3 4 5

8. I view networking as a way to give to, rather than take from, others, and I consciously ask others how I can be of assistance to them.   1 2 3 4 ⑤

9. I am conscious of the reason I am networking—I know what my networking goals are.   1 2 ③ 4 5

10. I practice before I actively engage in networking and develop "conversation starters" before entering a room or meeting.   1 2 ③ 4 5

11. I use the web to research additional names for my contact database.   1 2 3 4 ⑤

12. When politicking, I advocate for my or my employees' interests within the context of what's best for the organization overall.   1 2 3 4 ⑤

13. I am professional and sincere, and I refrain from inappropriate behaviors when networking.   ① 2 3 4 5

14. I focus completely on the other's needs when contacting someone initially and am respectful of their time.   1 ② 3 4 5

15. I am socially adept and effective at interacting with others.   1 ② 3 4 5

16. I make decisions cautiously and thoughtfully.   ① 2 3 4 5

17. I am aware of the impression I give to others and consciously manage this impression.   1 ② 3 4 5

18. Others would describe me as punctual.   1 2 ③ 4 5

19. I dress appropriately in business meetings and activities.   ① 2 3 4 5

20. I use humor appropriately in business situations.   1 ② 3 4 5

21. I am good at reading others and their intentions.   1 ② 3 4 5

22. I don't share confidences told me in private.   ① 2 3 4 5

23. I stay well informed and have a system for managing, storing, and processing the information I receive from all inputs (e.g., print, electronic, voice, face-to-face).   1 2 ③ 4 5

	Agree	Neither	Disagree

24. I am aware of the various means available for politicking within organizations, and am aware of what's appropriate in my organization.   1   2   3   ④   5

25. I assess my power base before I choose to use it and determine when best to use my authority to politick on behalf of a specific person or request.   1   2   ③   4   5

26. I take into account potential consequences before I politic and practice steps that can reduce unfair or negative politicking within my organization.   1   2   3   ④   5

Sum your circled responses. If your total is 78 or more, you might want to explore ways to improve your skill in the area of networking and politicking.   *82*

**Exercise 10–B
Your Personal Network**

1. Working on your own, write down all of your primary contacts—individuals you know personally who can support you in attaining your professional goals. Then begin to explore their secondary connections. Make assumptions about possible secondary connections that can be made for you by contacting your primary connections. For example, through one of your teachers (primary), you might be able to obtain some names of potential employers (secondary). (10–15 min.)

2. Then meet with your partner or small group to exchange information about your primary and secondary networks and to exchange advice and information on how to best use these connections, as well as how you could be helpful to them. (about 5 min. per person; 10–30 min. total, depending on group size).

3. Add names or types of names to your list based on ideas you get by talking with others in your group. (2–5 min.)

4. Discuss with large group or class, using discussion questions below. (10 min.)

**Primary and Secondary
Connections**

Questions

1. What were some of the best primary sources identified by your group?
2. What were some of the best sources for secondary contacts identified by your group?
3. What are some suggestions for approaching primary contacts?
4. What are some suggestions for approaching secondary contacts, and how is contacting secondary sources different from contacting primary contacts?
5. What did you learn about yourself and others from this exercise?

Exercise 10–C
Networking Scenarios

1. Working on your own, develop a networking strategy for the following three scenarios. (10 min.)

2. Working with your partner or small group, collaborate on identifying the best strategy for dealing with each of the three scenarios. Each group should develop one best strategy for each scenario. (20 min.)

3. Each group reports, sharing its best strategies for each of the three scenarios (or at least one if not enough time is available). (2–3 min. per group per strategy).

4. The large group or class engages in discussion, using the questions at the end. (10 min.)

Scenarios

I. You are running for Student Government President. What steps would you take to make your candidacy a success?

1. _____
2. _____
3. _____
4. _____
5. _____
6. _____

II. You are in an internship and are interested in becoming a permanent full-time employee at the organization. What people would you approach and what steps could you take to obtain an offer?

1. _____
2. _____
3. _____
4. _____
5. _____
6. _____

III. You just moved to a new community and your company's business growth relies heavily on referrals. How do you make contacts in a place where you don't know anyone? How can you build a client base?

1. _____
2. _____
3. _____
4. _____
5. _____
6. _____

Questions

1. What was difficult about this exercise?

2. What creative means were devised to build networks of contacts in these scenarios?

3. Which of these ideas would be easy to implement? Which would be difficult? What makes some strategies easier to do than others?

4. What personal qualities are needed to actually use these strategies?

5. How can someone who is shy about approaching new people use (some or all of) these strategies successfully?

6. What did you learn about yourself and others from this exercise?

Exercise 10–D
It's a Small World

1. Find someone in the room whom you barely know. Discuss people and connections you have to see if you can find common ground (e.g., shared personal interests or viewpoints, acquaintances you have in common). (2–3 min.)

2. Determine whether you have any acquaintances in common and determine how many levels or layers of connections it will take you to arrive at a commonality. Discuss organizations you belong to, classes you have been in, where you grew up, sports you play, and so on. (3–5 min.)

3. Mention a goal you would like to achieve, such as an internship connection you would like to make, a contact in a particular industry in which you are interested, or a person you would like to meet. Work with the other person to see if he or she might know someone who has a valuable connection for you. (5–7 min.)

4. Discuss this activity in a small group, sharing information and receiving additional information for your contact sheet. (10–15 min.)

5. Discuss the exercise with the class or large group, using the discussion questions below. (10 min.)

Questions

1. Was it difficult or easy to approach someone relatively new with whom to discuss this topic? Why?

2. Did the exchange get easier as it proceeded? Why and how?

3. Did you establish a connection to a person of interest to you such as a potential summer employer? If so, with whom, and how did you make this connection?

4. What is your plan for following up on the contacts you made through your discussion(s) with your teammate(s)?

5. What did you learn about yourself and others through this exercise?

Exercise 10–E
The 30-Second Introduction

listener
focused
detail-oriented
enjoy challenge

Imagine you are going to a career conference. Representatives from a few hundred firms known to recruit at your school will be there. Your job is to network—meet as many people as practical while attempting to find what would be the perfect job and organization for you. To do this it is crucial to be able to communicate quickly and neatly what contribution you can offer to a prospective employer. Each new person you meet will want a thumbnail sketch of who you are, what skills and experience you offer, and any other special information. They don't have time for your life story, nor will they want to ask 20 questions to get the information they need to decide whether to continue talking to you about possible opportunities.

1. To network effectively in this situation, you will need to create a "30-second introduction." Think about how you'd like to present yourself to this particular audience. Create a script—one that will take between 20 and 30 seconds to verbalize—that you can use in this setting. Focus on a short, *genuine* appraisal of your capabilities.

2. Now, practice your script. How long does it take? How does it sound—confident but not arrogant? What changes might you make?

3. Now pair up with someone in the class. Practice meeting each other (take turns playing student and potential employer) and using your introduction. Exchange feedback and advice to refine both "commercials."

Questions

1. How did it feel pitching yourself? Why?

2. How did it feel being pitched to? Explain.

3. Why is it important to have this commercial rehearsed and ready?

4. What are the benefits and downsides to using this commercial?

Exercise 10–F
It's Not What You Know . . . It's Who You Know: A Hands-on Networking Exercise

Participants will be given role assignments (available from your instructor). Consistent with the practice of networking, these role assignments (and potential combinations thereof) contain three possible outcomes as described below.

- "I help/need you, you help/need me." In this scenario, two people each have something the other wants.

- "I help you now, you help me later." In this scenario, two people can each help each other in the near future.

- "I can't help you directly, but I know someone who knows someone who can possibly help you." In this scenario, three or more people are involved.

1. Read the following role descriptions. Take a few minutes to think about how you would market yourself and your "needs." Think about creative, yet not necessarily obvious or "in-your-face," ways to make your needs and wants known. (3–5 min.)

2. You now have approximately 15–20 minutes to network. Take your time and make a positive impression—even if the person with whom you first connect is of no immediate use to you. You can politely ask the unuseful participants to direct you to others whom you may have met who may be able to provide what is being requested.

3. Continue until you find the person or persons who can help meet your needs. Along the way, make note of others' needs and direct those people to each other.

4. Discuss the exercise in a small group or with the group as a whole, using the discussion questions below. (20 min.)

Questions

1. How did you find who you were looking for? What interpersonal skills were helpful in enabling you to achieve your objective? Explain.

2. What were some of the lessons you learned about networking—what works well and not so well (e.g., role of eye contact, being persistent, being positive)?

3. How did it feel when you approached someone new with your need?

4. What was most difficult for you to do in this exercise?

5. In real life, what would be most difficult for you in approaching someone new about something you needed?

6. What did you learn about yourself and others from this exercise?

Source: Suzanne C. de Janasz and Stephen C. Davis, "It's Not What You Know . . . It's Who You Know: A Hands-on Networking Exercise," Presented at Organizational Behavioral Teaching Conference, Carrollton, GA, 2000.

Exercise 10–G
Politicking—Elevator Role-Play

1. Divide into pairs or small groups.

2. Role-play the following scenarios, each time playing a different role. Ad lib as appropriate. When you finish, discuss in your pair or small group the questions printed below the scenario.

Role-Play I: You find that you are on an elevator for a few minutes with an important superior, one who can potentially open doors for you in the organization. You decide to use this time to try to establish an important connection with the superior. What do you say to this person? How do you strike up a conversation, and about what? What topics do you raise to steer the conversation toward either making connections, obtaining recognition, or making an important point? (2–3 min.)

Roles

Person A—Employee

Person B—Superior

Persons C–F—Observers

Questions for your small group:

- What effective and ineffective behaviors were displayed?

- What strategies were successful getting the boss's attention?

- How did the employee feel and react (before and during the interaction with the superior)?
- How did the superior feel and react when approached by the employee?

Role-Play II: Switch roles, giving two others in your small group the opportunity to play a role. You are an employee and once again have a chance to ride an elevator for a few minutes. This time it's with a colleague with whom you have been having a disagreement but whose cooperation you need on a team project. Specifically, this person has some information you need to be successful on this project. How do you approach this person? What do you say? What topic(s) do you raise? How do you turn the conversation toward the information you need? (2–3 min.)

Roles

Person A—Employee

Person B—Colleague or Associate

Persons C–F—Observers

Questions for your small group:

- What effective and ineffective behaviors were displayed?
- What strategies were successful getting the attention of the colleague with whom you were having the conflict?
- How did the employee feel and react (before and during the interaction with the colleague)?
- How did the colleague feel and react when approached by the employee?
- 3. Now, discuss the exercise in your large group or class using the questions below. (10–15 min.)

Questions

1. How many of you got your point across (to the superior in Role-Play I or the colleague in Role-Play II)?
2. What happened to the observers on the elevator when the employee approached the superior/colleague?
3. How do these role-plays relate to politicking in organizations?
4. What did you learn about yourself and others from this exercise?

Exercise 10–H
Try This . . .

1. Draft a list of 10 questions you could ask in an information interview for your next summer job or a full-time job in an industry in which you lack experience.
2. Analyze the politics that exist at your job (present or past) within an organization you currently belong. Draft a set of guidelines you would issue to fellow members of your organization to inform them of appropriate ways for them to politick in your organization. Determine what you would do to regulate or reduce the need for politicking.
3. Observe a business meeting being held. Record the effective and ineffective networking and politicking behaviors you observe being performed by one or more members of the group. What makes the behaviors effective or ineffective? What role does someone's authority (or power in his or her position) play in his or her use and effectiveness of political behaviors?
4. Rent a movie or watch a TV show that depicts one or more of the characters in a networking or politicking situation. List the ineffective and effective networking or politicking behaviors that are depicted in the show. Some videos you might consider include *Wag the Dog, An American President, Working Girl, The Secret of My Success, Bonfire of the Vanities, Jerry Maguire, 9 to 5, Clueless, Primary Colors.*

**Exercise 10–I
Reflection/Action Plan**

This chapter focused on networking and politicking—what they are, why they are important, and how to improve your skills in these areas. Complete the following worksheet below upon completing all readings and experiential activities for this chapter.

1. The one or two areas in which I am most strong are:

_____

_____

_____

2. The one or two areas in which I need more improvement are:

_____

_____

_____

3. If I did only one thing to improve in each of these areas, it would be to:

_____

_____

_____

4. Making these changes would probably result in:

_____

_____

_____

5. If I did not change or improve in these areas, it would probably affect my personal and professional life in the following ways:

_____

_____

_____

Negotiation

11

being professional

focusing ob others' needs
list of contacts

create lists
focus on others' needs

better networking

...itate my ability to achieve this?

✓ Determine what I'm willing to accept if I don't get all that I want in a negotiation?

✓ Understand what the other party's wants and needs are in a negotiation?

✓ Involve the other person in a collaborative and interest-based negotiation?

✓ Know when to walk away from a negotiation if a resolution doesn't appear possible?

✓ Utilize framing, scripting, and other negotiation tactics to increase my effectiveness as a negotiator?

Last year, as a freshman at the University of Miami, John didn't have or need a car. The Metrorail provided ample opportunity to get around Miami. Now a sophomore living off campus, John would like to buy a used car. It should be dependable, economical, and must have air conditioning. He would like to spend no more than $4,000. He noticed in Sunday's newspaper that an area automobile dealer has numerous used cars for sale. He walks onto the lot with a classmate and zeroes in on a late model Corolla. It is in very good condition and has all the features he is looking for, including a killer stereo system. The car is priced at $4,995—about $1,000 more than he wanted to spend. A salesman approaches, asking John if he'd like a test drive.

1. At this point, what should John do? Is there anything he shouldn't do?

2. What kind of preparation should John have done prior to his visit?

3. Do you think the price—$4,995—is negotiable? How do you know?

4. Assuming John takes a test drive and likes the car, what should his next step be?

5. What are some specific arguments he could use to improve his chances of getting the car for a price nearer to that which he wanted to spend?

"You often get not what you deserve, but what you negotiate."[1]

John Marrioti

Everyone negotiates. Children negotiate to decide which games to play or which television show to watch. Friends negotiate to decide where to spend Saturday night or in whose car they'll ride. Students try to negotiate a higher grade from their professor. Employees negotiate for a certain salary, benefits, or perquisites. Couples negotiate to decide where to live, whether to rent or own, and for how long. Parents negotiate where to invest savings for their children's education and their own retirement. Corporations negotiate with other organizations on the sale or purchase of assets, materials, or operating units. Negotiations occur globally as in the case of the Mideast Peace Accord, NATO treaty, and NAFTA. Whether you're a diplomat or dignitary, spouse or sales-person, student or teacher, you negotiate almost daily. Sometimes the stakes are high, as in the case of a buyout of a firm; sometimes the stakes are low, as in the case of which movie you and your friends choose to see. In this chapter, we discuss the fundamentals of negotiation, benefits of doing it well, types and stages of negotiation, and principles and strategies for enhancing your skill in this arena. At the end of the chapter are several exercises to help you build your negotiating skills, as well as a list of references used and resources available to pursue this important topic further.

What Is Negotiation and Why Is It Important?

Negotiation involves two or more parties who each have something the other wants and who attempt to reach an agreement through a process of bargaining.[2] It occurs when all parties have both shared interests (meaning they're committed to a resolution) and opposed interests (meaning they don't agree on everything). This definition implies that both parties have an incentive for devoting energy to the negotiation, and that they are willing to collaborate on reaching a shared agreement.[3] Sometimes we use the terms bargaining and negotiating interchangeably, although most associate bargaining with the type of haggling that occurs over items in a yard sale and negotiating with a more formal process in which parties attempt to find a mutually agreeable solution to a conflict situation.

Why Do We Negotiate?

As in the case with John and the automobile dealership, we negotiate when what one party wants is not necessarily what the other party wants. The conflict of interests may be clear and simple. If the dealership lowers its price, John is likely to buy the car but the dealership will earn less on the sale. Should the dealership stand firm on its price, John may shop elsewhere and the dealership may wait days, weeks, or months until another qualified buyer expresses interest in buying the car. At other times, the conflict is more complex, consisting of multiple issues, competing interests, and unlimited potential solutions. Examples of this type include the merger or takeover of a company, a rift between a company's management and its unionized employees, or a divorce. While some conflicts wind up in court, most conflicts of this type, even those that appear to be quite complicated, are typically negotiated and settled before trial.

Complex negotiation is a fact of life for anyone in business. Managers ensure work gets done on time and within a budget. To do this successfully, managers negotiate for the necessary resources. As long as there is a scarcity of resources, negotiation will always be an essential skill for businesspeople. Another factor driving the need for negotiation skills in business is the increased use of teams in the workplace. As individuals from "competing" business units are brought together on projects, the ability to negotiate with others—both inside and outside the team—is critical for the ultimate success of the project team. Global diversity is another factor motivating the need for acquiring skills in negotiation. As employees from a variety of countries and cultures are brought together to work on projects and joint ventures, an inevitable clash of customs and business practices results in almost constant negotiating as relationships and expectations are developed and modified over time. A backlash against the litigious tendency of our modern society is another reason why it is important for managers to develop skill in negotiating. As the court dockets fill with numerous (and often frivolous) lawsuits, the negotiation of differences has become accepted and valued as a cost-effective alternative to litigation. Witness the growth of the number of organizations dedicated to helping individuals and companies improve their negotiating skills. The increasing number and availability of books, audio and videotapes, and Internet sites devoted to this topic provide further testimonial to the importance of effective negotiating in today's world. All of these factors build a compelling case for acquiring and enhancing your negotiating skills.

Benefits of Honing Negotiation Skills

Negotiating holds many benefits for individuals who strive to master this skill set. Studies show that those who have sound negotiating skills are able to maintain better control in business and personal situations.[4] In an effective negotiation, the parties focus on identifying each other's key interests and viewing the situation objectively, while placing emotions aside. Over time, those who practice negotiating find they are better able to resist responding emotionally to a potential conflict.

Negotiation is a much better way to reach a solution than either a lawsuit or arbitration.[5] In a lawsuit, the adversarial nature of the environment pits one set of interests against the other. The goal is a "win–lose" situation, where one of the parties is clearly victorious over the other. In arbitration, both parties agree to a settlement that is reached by a third party, which may or may not reflect the interests of the conflicting parties. Arbitration occurs outside of the courtroom; however, the parties involved are bound by the verdict—one which may or may not bring satisfaction. Verdicts resulting from arbitration often resemble "win–lose" or even "lose–lose" resolutions, where either one party is victorious or both parties must compromise so severely that the final agreement is perceived as losing by both parties. In contrast, negotiation, when handled properly, typically results in identifying the primary interests of both parties and generating an agreement that addresses key issues of both parties. This can result in a "win–win" solution where both parties feel their primary interests have been listened to if not addressed.

If a resolution can't be reached, arbitration or litigation may be necessary. However, these options tend to require more time and effort than negotiation. In a lawsuit, many hours are spent doing research and preparation by the attorneys. In arbitration, an outside third party (an arbitrator) spends numerous hours getting up to speed on a case before being able to rule on the case. In negotiation, both parties are involved from the outset. Each party serves as the chief spokesperson for her or his point of view. Naturally others are involved, principally the negotiator or negotiators. But they work in partnership with the two parties, not as surrogates. The principal work is performed by the two parties themselves, resulting in a saving of time and energy spent on the negotiation process.

Another benefit of negotiation is that when it works, it helps both parties not only to achieve a workable resolution, but also to help preserve and improve their relationship, reputations, and sense of professional achievement. Conversely, after an arbitration or lawsuit has concluded, the parties involved often experience lingering feelings of resentment and anger that preclude them from being able to continue working together.

Lastly, negotiation reduces stress and frustration, and often results in a reduction in the number of potential future conflicts. When a negotiation is conducted properly, most if not all of the major and minor issues that are involved get surfaced and addressed. They are not placed on the "back burner" in deference to a narrow set of key issues, as is often the case in a lawsuit or arbitration. Being able to clear the air and deal with all legitimate concerns results in a clean slate—a feeling that both parties have been fully listened to and understood. This reduces frustration and the chance that these issues will resurface and generate additional conflict.

Integrative and Distributive Bargaining Strategies

Once we decide to negotiate,[6] our approach to negotiation or bargaining will generally fall into one of two categories or strategies: integrative, or "win–win," and distributive, or "win–lose."[7] Both strategies have their benefits and disadvantages and can be used depending on the needs inherent in a specific situation.[8]

Negotiators use an **integrative bargaining strategy** when they believe that a win–win situation exists and can be reached. This means that there's a chance both parties can achieve their primary objectives, without either having to feel as though they lost in the negotiation. In integrative bargaining, the goal is to collaborate and generate one or more creative solutions that are acceptable to both parties. A simple example would be a couple trying to decide on a movie to rent. Taking an integrative approach, they would begin their discussion by drawing up a list of only those movies that were acceptable to both parties. They would discuss the available choices and choose a movie to see from that list, rather than arguing in favor of a movie that only one of the two parties wants to see.

A more complex example involves the creation of a "preferred supplier" agreement. Many firms seek to formalize the arrangements they may have with a particular supplier or vendor in order to reduce the uncertainty of changes in price and other market conditions. Should both organizations take an interactive approach to this solution, they would look beyond price—after all, the supplier's likely interest to maximize price is at odds with the organization's need to minimize it—to understand both the short- and long-term needs of both organizations. Issues of availability, reliability, quality, and prompt delivery and payment all enter into the equation in which price is but one factor. It's in both parties' best interests to find a workable solution, one that meets these multiple criteria. The supplier wins because it has a consistent customer for its product, ensuring a positive cash flow, steady employment, and predictable operations. The organization wins because it can rely on consistently receiving the supplier's product, when it's needed, at a fair price, and in the requested quantity. It doesn't need to search for additional options to save a few pennies; when all factors are considered, a preferred supplier arrangement benefits both parties.

Integrative bargaining only works when both parties are committed to preserving the relationship that exists between them. Integrative bargaining requires a great deal of creativity, problem-solving ability, and time, as well as a set of ultimate goals on which both parties can agree. Arriving at a truly integrative or collaborative solution requires that those involved gain the skills, knowledge, and attitude (including patience) necessary for this approach to resolving conflicts to work. Another requirement for integrative bargaining to work is a climate that supports and promotes open communication. Both parties need to be willing to change and to confront their conflict directly rather than run from it, resolve it through brute force, or pretend it will go away. The parties must be open to establishing longer-term goals on which they can both agree. For example, the couple choosing a movie must recognize that their relationship is more important than the choice of a movie and must be willing to collaborate or, if necessary, compromise for the sake of the overall relationship.

A **distributive bargaining strategy** is based on an attempt to divide up a fixed "pie" or amount of resources, resulting in a win–lose situation.[9] Negotiators taking a distributive approach typically take an adversarial or competitive posture to dividing a fixed amount of resources. One improves its lot at the expense of the other. This scarcity mentality implies that only one of the two parties can have the conflict resolved to its satisfaction. In distributive bargaining, the focus is on achieving immediate goals, with little or no regard for building future relationships. Little time or energy is expended in resolving the conflict in a distributive negotiation, resulting in the generation of few if any creative solutions. Generally, one or two fixed solutions are presented and a decision or choice is expected almost immediately, with possibly some consequence if a choice is not made soon. If distributive bargaining were used to resolve the movie decision mentioned earlier, the couple would likely not be very close, and one or both parties would not care whether the relationship was a good one or lasted much longer. In this example, one

**Figure 11–1
Comparing Bargaining
Approaches**

Considerations	Integrative Bargaining	Distributive Bargaining
Likely solution or end result	Win–win	Win–lose or lose–lose
Importance of continued relationship with bargaining partner	High	Low
Goal	Collaborate and generate multiple options or solutions; expand the pie	Winner takes all (scarcity mentality); distribute a fixed pie
Bargaining climate	Open, communicative, creative, willing to change	Determination to win, willingness to walk away, cards held close to the chest, ends justify the means
Amount of time needed	More	Less
Time horizon in consideration	Current and future	Immediate only

member of the couple would say something like "This is the movie I want to see. Take it or leave it." There would be no real discussion of the wants and interests of both parties. The "agreement" would be reached either by dictate or after some fierce arguing.

While win–lose is not a recommended strategy for resolving issues, it can be used in situations where achieving short-term goals is more important than maintaining or building longer-term relationships. Distributive bargaining is also appropriate to use in situations that are so contentious there is no possibility of a win–win solution, when there's a sense of urgency and time is short, and where the relationships involved are relatively unimportant compared to the issue at hand. Forcing children to wear protective gear when bicycling is an example of this. "Aw mom, do I have to wear my helmet? What if I promise to be really careful?" Allowing the child to negotiate on this issue is a waste of time, as his or her safety is paramount in this situation. Despite the intuitive appeal and apparent societal acceptance of the "winner take all" or "ends justify the means" approach to negotiation, distributive bargaining generally tends to be ineffective and counterproductive and should be used only in certain circumstances. Figure 11–1 above summarizes these two approaches.

Five Stages of Negotiating

We've discussed why people negotiate and the types of negotiation. Now we turn to the how, or the process of negotiating. Keep in mind that all negotiations are different. Simple negotiations, such as choosing which movie to rent, need not require an extensive negotiation process. However, when negotiations involve significant or complex issues, you should consider using the five-stage process model depicted in Figure 11–2. As illustrated, negotiating consists of five stages: (1) preparation and planning, (2) defining ground rules, (3) clarifying and justifying your case, (4) bargaining and problem solving, and (5) closure and implementation.[10] These stages are described below.

1. *Preparation and planning.* Without question, preparation and planning are the keys to successful deal making. While some may think they can negotiate effectively "on the fly," all negotiators benefit from thorough advance thought and preparation. Be clear about what you want and why. Gather data to support your position. Consider ways to present your arguments persuasively. Consider what the other party wants and why. What data or tactics might they use? How will you counter? Answer these questions when preparing your negotiation strategy. Understand your and the other party's strengths and weaknesses, and take these similarities and differences into account in your strategy. If negotiating is new to you, learn and practice the basics of negotiating well in advance of a planned negotiation. Build new skills that are appropriate to this particular situation.

Figure 11–2
The 5 Stages of Negotiation

1. Preparation & planning	2. Defining ground rules	3. Clarifying and justifying your case	4. Bargaining and problem solving	5. Closure and implementation
• Clarify what you want and why • Establish a BATNA • Develop a frame • Create a strategy/script	• Set an agenda • Agree on objective criteria • Agree on what to do if an agreement is not reached • Discuss what is, is not acceptable e.g., yelling	• Clarify your interests • Use a frame to make your case persuasive • Use questions to understand others' interests • Share relevant information that supports your case	• Focus on problems, not people • Focus on interests, not positions • Look forward, not backward • Create options for mutual gain; adapt win–win attitude • Select from options using principles, or objective criteria	• Verbally summarize what both parties agreed to • Review key points to ensure understanding • Draft agreement in writing • Have both parties sign agreement

Many of the strategies or tips discussed in the chapter that should be considered during each phase are listed under the corresponding stage.

Another important component in preparing for negotiations is determining your **bottom line;** identifying what you ideally want, what you'd be willing to accept, and the range between these two points gives you an indication of how much flexibility you have going into the negotiation. Lastly, prepare for a negotiation by learning as much as you can about the other party prior to the negotiation. In addition to the questions above, see what you can uncover about their negotiating style by talking with others with whom they've negotiated. If possible, try to become acquainted with the other party before the planned meeting. By establishing your willingness to get to know the other party, you will be better able to begin the negotiation with a positive, relationship-based tone rather than on an adversarial note.[11]

2. *Definition of ground rules.* Determining your own guidelines or rules for the negotiation helps you to plan a strategy that can be successful.[12] Establish who will or should be present and at what part of the negotiation. Decide where the meeting will be held and offer a possible agenda for how the time will be allocated and for which issues. The location has implications in terms of who's in charge. While there may be a benefit to having the negotiation at your office—the home court advantage—agreeing to have the negotiation at the other party's office might show flexibility and willingness to negotiate on your part. When the topic covered is potentially divisive or difficult, a neutral location might help level the playing field for both parties—an important consideration when an integrative solution is desired.

Set enough time in the negotiation to deal with the critical issues that are involved. Getting two opposing parties to agree, especially when multiple issues are being simultaneously considered, requires more time than you might imagine. Shortening the time available for the discussion serves as a conversation stopper and is counterproductive. Prior to the negotiation, establish a flexible, reasonable plan which outlines what you hope to accomplish, how you intend to talk about the topic, how you plan to introduce the topic, and how you will handle any responses from the other party. Set clear parameters for the discussion and the process such as no name calling, it's okay for either party to call a time out, additional issues may be set aside for a later discussion, and ensure you both agree. Finally, seek agreement on standards and criteria to use when discussing the various alternatives that are generated as part of the discussion.[13]

3. *Clarification and justification.* As the negotiation begins, state what you want and why. Being clear about your interests and expectations sets the stage for the other party to be similarly honest about their needs and hopes for the negotiation. Allowing the other party to state what they want and why they want or need it offers them a chance to become fully engaged in the process. Clarifying to one another your proposals and the rationale

Figure 11–3
Verbal Negotiation Tactics[14]

Tactic	Description	Example
Promise (conditional, positive)	I will do something if you will do something I want you to.	I will lower the price by $5 if you will order in bulk.
Threat (conditional, negative)	I will do something you do not want me to do, if you do something I don't want you to do.	If you don't give me a good price, I'll take my business elsewhere.
Recommendation	If you do something I want you to do, a third party will do something you want.	If you give me a good deal on this item, I will get my friend to buy one too.
Warning	If you do something I don't want you to, a third party will do something you do not want.	If you do not replace this item, the government will investigate your operation.
Reward (unconditional, positive)	I will give you something positive now, on the spot.	Let's make it easier on you tomorrow and meet closer to your office. I have appreciated your meeting at my building.
Punishment (unconditional, negative)	I will give you something negative now, on the spot.	I refuse to listen to your screaming. I am leaving.
Normative Appeal	I appeal to a societal norm.	Everybody else buys our product for $5 per unit.
Commitment	I will do something you want.	I will deliver 100 units by June 15.
Self-disclosure	I will tell you something about myself or important information.	We have had to lay off 100 employees this month. We really need to sign a major contract by the end of the year.
Question	I ask you something about yourself.	Can you tell me more about your foreign operations?
Command	I order you to do something.	Lower your price.

behind them enhances both your and the other party's understanding of the key issues that are involved. Clarifying and justifying require sound communication skills. Some of the verbal tactics that can be used in effective negotiations appear in Figure 11–3.

4. *Bargaining and problem solving.* In the fourth stage, both parties are actively and constructively engaged in working toward solutions. Once the interests and criteria are clearly communicated, it becomes time for a creative, idea-generating process. This requires skill in finding solutions that might address one or more of the parties' collective needs, as well as "expanding the pie" and generating even more creative solutions that may not be readily apparent. At this stage, it is best to remain open-minded, considering options without making value judgments about or critiquing the options. Judgment curtails creativity. By exploring all possibilities for solutions, rather than trying to focus too quickly on one fixed solution, interesting ideas and combinations of ideas may emerge.

Consider for example the aging patriarch who is looking for a potential suitor to buy his company. It would be easy to argue over dollars and cents—what the company is worth—and never arrive at a mutually agreeable solution. First, the assumptions or models both parties used to estimate the company's value are likely different. Second, there is a great deal of hidden "value." The business is not just a collection of assets, employees, customers, patented processes, and accounts receivable; it is, in the founder's mind, a child he nurtured for years and years. No amount of money can buy one's child. Putting yourself in the shoes of the founder, think about what he really might want, besides money. Recognition for his business acumen? A position as chairman emeritus and consultant? A monthly stipend and benefit package? An opportunity to share in the profits for the years he remains as a consultant to the new owner? When you look outside the box of the calculable solution, you might find something even better.

Once a number of alternatives have been put forth, analysis and discussion of each can begin. Take the time to assess carefully how well each alternative meets the interests of both parties, the benefits and disadvantages, and its relation to the key issues involved in the negotiation. At this stage, it is appropriate to begin narrowing the options to the one or few that appear to best solve the initial problem in a way that is satisfactory to both parties. Don't worry about "dotting all the i's and crossing all the t's" at this point. Details like the exact percentage of the profit-sharing plan described above can be worked out later. Structure a deal on which you can both agree by recording key terms of the agreement and the steps necessary to complete the details and maintain the agreement.

Sometimes, you don't have all the data available to finalize a decision. For example, you might agree to provide a benefits package to the founder of the company for a period no longer than three years and at a price no greater than 30 percent of his monthly draw. Determining which insurance company and whether they cover monthly chiropractic visits is more detail than is necessary at this point. Other times, you might have to end the discussion with some terms still up in the air. Perhaps a key piece of information will only be available at year-end. Record the terms to which you've reached agreement, and agree to postpone deciding on the remaining issues until a specified future date. This approach is generally preferable to one in which the last few details are quickly and perhaps forcibly pushed through. If the deal is likely to stipulate how two parties will work together over the next five, ten, or more years, isn't it worthwhile to invest a proportionately similar amount of time and energy to ensure that the partnership will be successful?

5. *Closure and implementation.* In this final stage, the terms of the agreement that has been reached are formalized. Unfortunately, many overlook or ignore this step, thinking that once an agreement is reached it will be implemented automatically. Leaving out this step can lead to future misunderstandings. No two people will leave a communication with the same perceptions. The only way to ensure both parties know what they're agreeing to is to:

- Document what you agreed on.
- Review the key points to avoid misunderstanding.
- Discuss issues that were hedged on, describing clearly all stipulations of the agreement.
- Get it in writing.
- Read the written agreement before signing to ensure clarity of and commitment to what was negotiated.[15]

Every negotiation is likely to present you with different challenges and opportunities. By following these five steps and the advice contained therein, you can increase the likelihood of arriving at an agreement that meets the needs of all parties involved in the negotiation.

Strategies for Negotiating Effectively

The process model we described provides a helpful template for preparing for and participating in a negotiation. Within these stages, and as depicted in Figure 11–2, there are a number of tips and techniques that can improve the likelihood of achieving success. Because of their importance in the negotiation process, three of these concepts—scripting, framing, and managing—are discussed in greater detail below.

**Figure 11–4
Negotiation Script**

Goals:

- Develop an interest-based strategy/approach prior to a face-to-face negotiation
- Identify potential options/plans that can be proposed

Topics to Consider:

1. The other person's probable strategy. What do they want (goals) and why (interests)?
2. My strategy. What do I want and why? What am I willing to accept (my BATNA—best alternative to a negotiated agreement)?
3. How I'll begin the negotiation. What can I say to positively position the negotiation, and to express my desire to arrive at a solution that is mutually rewarding and satisfactory?
4. The core issues, and any assumptions about those issues, include: (Remember to focus on the problem and not the person.)
5. The primary focus, or the real problem(s) to be resolved is:
6. What might get in the way of achieving the desired outcome? How can I overcome this?
7. How I'll react to . . . (list several potential proposals that may emerge during the negotiation and how you feel about those proposals):
   a)
   b)
   c)
8. Potential creative options or integrative, win/win solutions that I might suggest:
9. Components of a plan and/or objective criteria on which we can both agree:

Scripting

There is no substitute for adequate preparation in negotiation. Unlike other business interactions that can be handled simultaneously, negotiation is a serious enterprise that requires focus, attention, time, research, and planning. The more prepared you are, the greater the chances that you'll get what you deserve and bargain for.

One of the best ways to ensure adequate preparation time is to develop a **script** (see Figure 11–4). Take some time to think about the negotiation situation in which you find yourself. What are your interests—and those of the other party? What would you each ideally like to see come out of the negotiation? How would you each like things to end up? What are some ways in which that might be possible? What can you do to make this happen? By thinking through the issues, objectives, options, and solutions from both your and the other's perspective, you are better able to handle almost anything that develops during the negotiation. Preparing ahead doesn't prevent surprises. But it can certainly lessen the number of surprises and make it more likely you can handle the unexpected if and when it happens.

Framing

Another important element to consider when preparing for or managing a negotiation is a **frame**. A frame is a point of view or perspective we bring to an interaction such as a negotiation. How we view a situation can impact how willing we are to engage in a negotiation and even our goals. Negotiation experts Max Bazerman and Margaret Neale offer the following example.[16] You and a friend go to the beach. After a few hours, your throat becomes dry and you'd like a sparkling water—if the price was right. Your friend offers to investigate the options, and you consider your limits. In one scenario, you're about a mile from town and notice a small, run-down market about a block away. How much are you willing to pay for a bottle of water? In another scenario, you and your friend are lying on the beach owned by a four-star resort. The waiter is about to approach and ask if he can get you anything. Now, how much are you willing to pay for that sparkling water? Chances are, you'll pay more in the second scenario—for the same bottle of water.

When we use frames in negotiation, we provide a perspective that helps others understand where we are coming from and manages expectations. When proposing a plan for downsizing an organization to shareholders, one possibility is to frame this move as a means to minimize costs or losses. Another possibility is to frame this move as a means to maximize competitiveness. While both frames involve the use of downsizing, the frames—posed as either losses or gains—will likely have differing effects on the perceivers. Similar to framing a picture, the frame highlights the points you want to make in negotiation and provides a filter for the other party to assess your position and supporting evidence. This is done by selecting a perspective believed to be credible, compelling, and appropriate to your intent. Frames can also provide a rationale for the evidence presented and a sequential pattern for presenting the evidence. This is done by creating a structure for organizing and presenting the evidence.[17]

Framing has several benefits. It focuses attention on the priorities you want to emphasize—on data and premises within the frame. Framing establishes a "big picture" context for the listener to use in perceiving and sorting through various options. Extending the picture analogy, since a picture is worth a thousand words, a frame that paints a picture can not only enliven the goals you are pursuing, but it can also save time and words. Imagine two CEOs discussing a potential merger of their companies. One uses a metaphorical frame and alludes to a "melting pot of employees" in describing his hoped-for outcome for the merger. Not bad. The frame paints a picture that both parties understand. The second CEO is a bit more creative. She recasts the frame and refers to the "mixed salad of employees" her plan is designed to create. Both plans highlight employee diversity, but the second frame recognizes the individual talents and skills of employees who can collaborate and work together while the first plan may be interpreted as a homogenization of all employees.

As negotiators we can use frames to recast the other party's notion of what is desired in a negotiation. We do this by reframing the discussion—describing it differently to ourselves. By reframing we're able to see it in a new light and approach the negotiation in a different way. A frame can be used to sell a proposal and overcome objectives others might raise. To do this:

■ Develop a frame based on *both* your needs and those of the other party.

■ Construct a set of messages that influence the other party's perception of these needs.

■ Provide the other party with a filter to interpret your message—such as "half-empty or half-full," "good or bad," "profit or loss," "cost or benefit."

Managing

The last strategy to consider when preparing for and in the thick of the negotiation is *managing*. Every negotiation is an opportunity for you to manage: yourself, your expectations, the timing of the event, the way in which you approach the situation, your feelings toward the other person. The more you respond to a negotiation as a management challenge, the more proactive you can be in looking at it positively. A negotiation can be a learning experience, a chance to acquire some new skills, and maybe even a way to get what you want! Or it can be something you dread, fear, and avoid if possible.

The adage "practice makes perfect" really applies here. Negotiation doesn't come naturally to most people. Practicing negotiation greatly improves your ability to manage a negotiation situation successfully. Start small, with minor events day-to-day, such as negotiating an earlier lunchtime with co-workers. The more you negotiate—paying attention to your needs and speaking up for them—the better prepared you will be for significant negotiations in business and in life. Only negotiate when you're ready—when you have the time, have had the time to prepare, and are in an appropriate state of mind. Thorough negotiations can be exhausting; you have to be ready to endure. You can ensure you're ready by managing the circumstances under which you'll negotiate. Only agree to terms that are acceptable to you. For example, where, when, and with whom you'll negotiate are all things that make a difference and things over which you have some control. Assert that control so that you are at your best at the time of the negotiation.

Manage your emotions. Demonstrate exceptional listening and clarifying (communication) skills. This helps you to focus on the issues at hand, not on how you are responding emotionally. Plan to engage only in discussions or arguments that are constructive. Be prepared to walk away or take a "time-out" if necessary. Sometimes called a caucus, this time could be used alone (or with a negotiating partner in a team negotiation) to gather your thoughts, adjust your strategy, and discover new frames or solutions.

Agree to disagree. Sometimes issues are unsolvable at that moment. It's better to quit while you're ahead and set another time to continue discussing remaining issues. Don't put anyone on the defensive. When we're upset, we often blame or label others, causing them to strike back in kind. This kind of negotiation will go nowhere. Make statements that are factual and "I" based rather than "you" based. For example say, "I am upset about the amount of raise I got," rather than "You're unfair for giving me such a low increase."

Other techniques for managing negotiations include the use of agendas, questions, and summarizing techniques. A negotiation is a meeting and should be treated as such. If an agenda was not created in advance, and the negotiation is getting off-track, spend a few minutes establishing an agenda. Decide key issues to discuss, and allocate time accordingly. Post the agenda and refer back to it to keep the discussion on track. Periodically summarizing what's been discussed and agreed upon not only helps to keep the discussion focused, but can also help reduce redundancy (i.e., beating a dead horse). Sometimes, negotiators revisit issues that have already been resolved because they forget or are unsure whether a point was resolved or deferred for later discussion. By saying, "Okay, let's review. We agreed to points a, b, and d, but are still working out the details on points c and e. Does that track with how you see it?" you can manage time and stay focused on the negotiation.

Finally, questions can be useful in many ways. Aside from helping you understand others' viewpoints and needs, questions can help steer the discussion toward desirable issues in a more subtle way. Depending on the goals of the negotiation, consider using various types of questions as appropriate from the list shown in Figure 11–5.

Additional Tips for Effective Negotiating

What else can you do to ensure that you not only reach an agreement but also maintain or enhance your relationship with the other party? The following principles of successful negotiation should help ensure that negotiations are integrative, objective, and potentially relationship enhancing.

■ *Determine the importance of the outcome for you.* What do you want and why? Only negotiate when the matter is something you truly care about and when you have a chance of succeeding. Identify what you really need from the deal, not what you assume you need. Identify several items of interest to you and rank them in descending order of importance.[18] Do your homework. If the negotiation includes a financial outcome, consider several options or scenarios and the economic implications of each. This information will serve to eliminate the guesswork and strengthen the rationale of your proposal during the negotiation. Will you lease or buy the car? What if you put 10 percent, 20 percent, or nothing down? How does the financing rate change when the loan period changes or if you decide to buy a used instead of a new car? Calculating the implications in advance can also increase your confidence and strengthen your position in the negotiation.

■ *Look forward, not backward.* It's easy to get caught up in who did what and who is to blame. We sometimes do this to avoid having to resolve the problem or just out of habit. While it may be easy to get into long discussions about the past, it is clearly unproductive. Focus on where you want to be and not where you've been. There's no harm in brief discussions of the conditions that led to the current problem, but move on to what to do now and in the future.[19]

■ *Separate people from problems.* To negotiate effectively, separate the people involved in the discussion from the issues that are being addressed. Remain objective. Avoid personalizing issues, and don't allow yourself to be drawn into an emotional

Figure 11–5
Questioning[20]

Questioning is recommended in negotiation when it is necessary to clarify communication. **Manageable** questions start thinking, get information, and prepare the other person for additional questions. **Unmanageable** questions cause difficulty by bringing the discussion to a false conclusion. Manageable questions can produce dialogue and creative approaches, while unmanageable questions may produce defensiveness and/or anger.

Manageable Questions

Type of question	Example
Open-ended	Could you explain the reasons for your decision?
Open (to get the other person thinking)	What is your feeling on the matter?
Leading (point toward an answer to the question)	Do you feel our proposal is fair?
Cool (without emotion)	How much would be charged for the additional work?
Planned (follows an overall sequence of questions)	After the additional work is completed, may we begin our phase?
Treat (flatters the opponent while soliciting information)	You are an expert in this area; what is your opinion?
Window (assists in seeing what the other person is thinking)	What brought you to that conclusion?
Directive (focus on a specific point)	How long will it take to complete the job?
Gauging (assists in determining how the other person feels)	What do you think about our proposal?

Unmanageable Questions

Type of question	Example
Close-out (forces your opinion on the opponent)	You wouldn't want to make us look bad, would you?
Loaded (puts opponents on the spot regardless of answer)	So, you are not willing to negotiate further?
Heated (triggers an emotional response)	Haven't we spent enough time on this crazy idea?
Impulse (tends to get the conversation off track)	While we are on the subject, is there anyone else who might care about this?
Trick (appear straightforward, but are actually "loaded")	What are you going to do—agree to our position, or go to court?
Reflective "trick" questions (direct the opponent into agreeing with your point of view)	Here is the way I see it, don't you agree?

Source: Adapted from R. J. Lewicki and J. A. Litterer, *Negotiation* (Richard D. Irwin, Inc., Homewood, Illinois, 1985).

debate.[21] If the negotiation veers in this direction, request a time out. After you reconvene, remind the negotiators of the ultimate goal and the ground rules previously set. If emotions are still running high, consider deferring the remainder of the negotiation to another time. Focus on the problem, the issue at hand. Avoid personal attacks, criticism of style or personality traits, and placing blame. Negotiate in such a way that the person knows if he or she has to back down on something so he/she will not be losing face. For example, match the other's concession with one of your own. A good rule of thumb is to be hard on the problem, soft on the people. Throughout the negotiation constantly ask, "Am I dealing with the person or the problem?" Entangling people, issues, and relationships with the problem dooms the negotiation to failure.[22]

■ *Adopt a win–win attitude.* Negotiation is not war, it is a collaboration between parties with common interests and objectives. Think in terms of helping, not hindering; of listening, not ramming something down someone's throat; of a team and partnership, not a competitor. Take the perspective that both parties can win and that it's in your best interest to want the other side to thrive, as future cooperative ventures may be possible.[23]

■ *Know your Best Alternative To a Negotiated Agreement* (**BATNA**). Renowned negotiators and authors Roger Fisher and William Ury introduced this concept. They showed that results from a negotiation can be improved by identifying your best alternative for each of your goals. For example if you want to sell your house by June, what will you take if it hasn't sold by then? This is one way to determine a BATNA—the outcome you can accept that is better than never having negotiated at all.

Don't set your BATNA too low. When you go to a job interview with no other offers or prospects, you go in with a low BATNA—this job or nothing. Sometimes you have to do this. But whenever possible, it's better to have options in mind to avoid being or appearing desperate. For example, in the absence of job offers, you could consider living with family for a while rather than desperately taking a job you don't want. This alternative gives you flexibility and a sense that you don't have to take whatever is offered.[24]

■ *Focus on interests, not on fixed positions.* A **position** is a stance—typically a firm one—taken by a negotiator. "I'll give you $4,500 and that's my final offer." An **interest** is the explanation behind the position, the ultimate need or desire that expresses why a negotiator wants what he or she wants. Fisher and Ury argue that negotiators ought to be problem solvers who explore interests as opposed to refusing to change or compromising only slightly on their positions. When a negotiation is a test of wills, it is destined to fail. By locating compatible interests, you can build a bridge from your goals to the others.[25]

Returning to the opening scenario, John and the dealership may go back and forth on price: each goes up and down accordingly until they arrive at a number. This process can be painstakingly slow—especially when the salesperson has to make numerous visits to the invisible sales manager—and may result in both sides either not reaching agreement or feeling that each compromised too much. John should ask the dealership why the price is $4,995. The dealership should ask John why he's only willing to pay $4,000. This may sound simple; it may or may not be. By asking why, or the reasons behind the interests, you're likely to find at least one with which you can identify and agree. Interests from John and the dealership, respectively, might resemble: "I want a fair price for the car and am willing for the dealership to make a fair profit." "We stand behind our cars and want to ensure we don't lose money or you as a return customer." People listen better and are more likely to accept change if they know they've been understood and that their interests are being addressed.

■ *Go into the negotiation with objective criteria.* This leads to principled negotiation—negotiations based on **principles,** or objective criteria on which both parties agree. Bringing standards of efficiency, fairness, scientific merit, for example, can facilitate agreement and final satisfaction with an agreement. Rather than struggling for dominance, locate objective criteria both of you can agree to apply in determining goals and actions. For example, why is the car priced at $4,995? What features are included in this model? How does that compare to similar models? What kind of warranty will I get? Sometimes objective criteria are readily available, such as the standard "blue book" value, or what similar cars are selling for in the local paper. Other times, the negotiators will have to research, present, and jointly decide on these criteria.

Objective criteria should be independent of each side's will and should be legitimate and practical. For example, you can find published data on industry salaries, comparable house sales prices, and area bank or finance company mortgage rates. Once you have determined objective criteria, you can frame each issue as a joint search for the solution that best fits the criteria.[26]

■ *Respond, don't react.* When the other party throws their power around, don't react negatively or emotionally. When this happens, Fisher and Ury recommend that you invite feedback and input with regard to the problem. Ask them their opinion. You can also reframe or recast their objections as attacks on the problem, not on you—attacks that are

**Figure 11–6
Principles of the
"Power of Nice"**[27]

1. To get what you want, help the other side get what it wants.
2. Aim for win–win: a substantial win for your side, a satisfactory win for the other side.
3. Negotiation is a process, not an event.
4. Practice the three P's: Prepare, Probe, Propose.
5. Listen to the other side: They are trying to tell you how to make the deal.
6. Build relationships rather than make one-time deals.

understandable given the circumstances or pressure they might be experiencing. When the other party attacks, ask questions. Avoid getting bullied into battle.

■ *Use a* **third party**—someone who is objective and has no vested interest in the outcome of the discussions. When two parties can't arrive at a mutually agreeable resolution, it can be helpful to involve a third party. Consider using the one-text procedure. Let someone draw up a plan that considers your interests and those of the other party. Then each of you does some editing. The third party redrafts it and perhaps requests additional feedback from both of you. By involving everyone in the development of a single text and having the parties involved edit it several times, at the end there is a feeling on the parts of both parties that they have been included in the solution. At the end all that is left to do is make a simple yes–no decision, not enter into a long discussion or argument over details.[28]

Special Situations in Negotiations

Not all negotiations involve two individuals who meet face to face in an effort to reach a resolution or sign a contract. Some negotiations involve teams of individuals, are done virtually (using teleconferencing, telephones, e-mails, and faxes), include third parties, and involve global negotiating partners.

**Third-Party
Negotiations**

Often serious negotiations—such as high-stakes strike threats—require the use of a third party to gain an agreement. Other times, it is simply a wise idea to bring in an objective third party to help two opposing sides develop a shared agreement. Bringing in a third party has several advantages. A third party offers each party a chance to "vent" in a nonthreatening environment. By venting out of earshot of the other party, you have a chance to disclose your feelings about the situation. By sorting through your emotions with a third party, you can then begin to uncover what's really important and why, and address these issues in the negotiation.

Another advantage of bringing in a third party is that you and the other party can both benefit from the third party's expertise and experience. Assuming they have helped others negotiate before you, they have models and templates to offer—ways to structure the negotiation—that can help you arrive at an agreement faster than if you were starting from scratch on our own. They won't have had the exact same situation presented to them in the past. But their experience with other cases can help them advise you on a strategy for which there is probably a successful precedent.

Lastly, bringing in a third party helps the negotiating parties to organize their thoughts and develop options that may be acceptable to both parties. The negotiator won't take sides, but will offer wise counsel about the potential benefits and pitfalls of each of the alternatives being considered. Part of what enables third parties to do this successfully is that they are just that, a third party. Third parties are able to help the negotiating parties develop criteria and solutions from an untainted, and therefore unemotional, perspective. This can be invaluable when it comes time to develop an agreement that is satisfactory to both parties. There are several types of third-party negotiators.[29]

■ A **mediator** is a neutral third party who has no stake in the outcome of the agreement. Many private training programs are now available for ordinary citizens to become mediators. Mediation is a very popular, low-cost option that is being used more and more as an alternative to costly litigation.[30] In schools, mediators are used to help children (and faculty) resolve conflicts with each other, and in many businesses, employees are encouraged to work out conflicts (e.g., grievances) with a trained mediator when possible.

■ An **arbitrator** is a neutral third party who has the legal power to bind both parties to an agreement determined by the arbitrator. Both parties submit information to arbitration and then are subject to whatever decision is made. Arbitration is mandated frequently as a cost- and time-effective alternative to litigation. One disadvantage is that neither party is involved in generating the solution that is ultimately decided by the arbitrator.

■ A **conciliator** is a trusted third party whose role is to ensure a steady flow of accurate information exists between the negotiating parties. A conciliator does not rule on an agreement but merely counsels the parties about ways to approach the agreement and ways to view the information that is being presented as part of the negotiation.

■ A **consultant** is a neutral third party who teaches and advises the negotiating parties on skills and techniques of negotiation. The consultant hears out both parties, suggests an operating plan and strategy, assists both sides in identifying their chief concerns, aids the parties in arriving at a mutually satisfying resolution or agreement, and assists the parties in writing up this agreement.

Global Negotiations

Many companies today find that the products or services they offer are much more accepted by and demanded in nondomestic or foreign markets. This means negotiations between domestic and foreign firms (**global negotiations**) are on the rise. Those involved in global business need to have a solid understanding of the practices and customs of their foreign counterparts, in addition to basic negotiation skills.

To be effective when negotiating across borders, prepare carefully and be familiar with cultural differences and expectations.[31] The basics of negotiation still apply: you will still need to clarify what you want and why; you should still develop your BATNA. However, your strategy and the way in which you implement it will likely vary based on what you know about the practices and customs of your foreign negotiating partner. For example, an American firm sent a business proposal bound in pigskin to a country in which pigs were considered unclean. The proposal was never opened.[32]

Start by doing background research on the organization's culture, practices, and business. Some information can be found on the Internet by searching government pages from the State Department. Other information can be obtained by identifying other firms who've done business with this organization or individuals who were born or spent time in the country. Salacuse suggests knowing the eight **elements of international protocol** for any country with which you do business.[33] These eight elements are listed below. Note special gender-based differences may also apply.

1. name (how individuals prefer to be addressed).
2. rank/title (how these titles compare with those in your organization, the importance of using titles in interaction).
3. time (whether punctual or casual, preferred time of day to do business).
4. dress (formal or casual, whether special or sacred articles are worn).
5. behavior (greetings, rituals, how decisions are made).
6. communication (verbal or nonverbal differences, such as the meaning of the words "yes" and "no," proxemic differences).
7. gift giving (whether gifts are appropriate, size of gifts, public versus private opening, importance of reciprocation).
8. food and drink (which foods [e.g., pork] and drinks [e.g., alcohol] are forbidden).

For example, in certain countries (e.g., Japan) silence is very common, whereas that is not typical in the United States. Businesspeople in many parts of South America prefer establishing a relationship first and will take much time to build an emotional bond— through dinners and other social gatherings—before talking business. The French often negotiate multiple issues simultaneously, while Americans prefer a linear approach,

Figure 11–7
The Essential Rules of "Winning with Integrity"[34]

Align yourself with people who share your values.

Learn all you can about the other party.

Convince the other party that you have an option—even if you don't.

Set your limits before negotiating begins.

Establish a climate of cooperation, not conflict.

In the face of intimidation, show no fear.

Learn to listen.

Be comfortable with silence.

Avoid playing split-the-difference.

Emphasize your concessions; minimize the other party's.

Never push a losing argument to the end.

Develop relationships, not conquests.

discussing and agreeing upon one issue at a time.[35] The Chinese often engage in gift giving, but you would be wise not to present your Chinese counterpart with a clock—it symbolizes death.[36]

Global negotiations are admittedly complex and uncertain. Planning is crucial to the process. Gathering information about a country and its practices and customs is a necessary step to understanding how to approach your negotiating partner. Understanding differences (and similarities!) between your and your foreign counterpart's communication style, behaviors, and practices can help you manage the negotiations and increase the likelihood that both parties leave the global negotiating table with satisfactory outcomes and a desire to continue the business relationship.

Summary

In this chapter we discussed the definition, importance, and benefits of negotiating. We reviewed the different types of negotiation strategies and the stages of negotiating. In addition, we provided strategies for negotiating effectively and tips for negotiating successfully. Lastly, we covered special situations in negotiating. Negotiating is a fact of life for all of us—in personal as well as business situations. Following the suggestions in this chapter will help you to be effective in developing negotiation strategies that meet your and others' needs.

Key Terms and Concepts

Arbitrator	Interest
BATNA	Manageable questions
Bottom line	Mediator
Conciliator	Negotiation
Consultant	Position
Distributive bargaining strategy	Principles
Elements of international protocol	Script
Frame	Third party
Global negotiations	Unmanageable questions
Integrative bargaining strategy	

Endnotes

1. John Mariotti, "Are You an Effective Negotiator?" *Industry Week,* Sept. 7, 1998, p. 70.

2. Robert Heller and Tim Hindle, *Essential Manager's Manual* (New York: DK Publishing Inc., 1998), p. 561.

3. Roger Fisher, William Ury, and Bruce Patton, *Getting to Yes: Negotiating Agreements without Giving In,* Second Ed. (New York: Penguin Books, Dec. 1991).

4. Darl G. Williams, "Negotiating Skills—Part I," *Professional Builder,* Jan. 2000, p. 155.

5. Danny Ertel, "How to Design a Conflict Management Procedure That Fits Your Dispute," *Sloan Management Review,* Summer 1991, pp. 29–42.

6. It is important to note, however, that one or both parties may choose to avoid negotiations or defer them until a future date. Doing so may serve a number of purposes. For more information on this, see Roy Lewicki, David Saunders, and John Minton, *Negotiation: Readings, Exercises, and Cases,* Third Ed. (Burr Ridge: IL: Irwin McGraw-Hill, 1999), pp. 45–46.

7. R. E. Walton and R. B. McKersie, *A Behavioral Theory of Labor Negotiations: An Analysis of a Social Interaction System* (New York: McGraw-Hill, 1965).

8. Stephen Robbins, *Organizational Behavior,* Eighth Ed. (New Jersey: Prentice Hall, 1998).

9. Max Bazerman and Margaret Neale, *Negotiating Rationally* (New York: Free Press, 1992).

10. R. J. Lewicki, "Bargaining and Negotiation," *Exchange: The Organizational Behavior Teaching Journal* 6, no. 2 (1981); and Stephen Robbins, *Organizational Behavior,* Eighth Ed. (New Jersey: Prentice Hall, 1998).

11. Janine S. Pouliot, "Eight Steps to Success in Negotiating," *Nation's Business,* April 1999, p. 40.

12. Ertel, 1991.

13. Pouliot, 1999.

14. Nancy J. Adler, *International Dimensions of Organizational Behavior,* Third Ed. (Southwestern College Publishing, Cincinnati, OH, 1997), p. 214.

15. Mariotti, 1998.

16. Margaret A. Neale and Max H. Bazerman, "Negotiating Rationally: The Power and Impact of a Negotiator's Frame," *Academy of Management Executive* 6, no. 3, pp. 42–51.

17. Lyle Sussman, "How to Frame a Message: The Art of Persuasion and Negotiation," *Business Horizons,* July–August 1999, p. 2.

18. Ron Shapiro, Mark Jankowski, Leigh Steinberg, and Michael D'Orso, "Powers of Persuasion," *Fortune,* Oct. 12, 1998, p. 160.

19. Fisher et al., 1991.

20. Adopted from R. J. Lewicki and J. A. Litterer, *Negotiation* (Homewood, IL: Richard D. Irwin, Inc., 1985).

21. Terry Neese, "Negotiations Should Not Be a Contest of Wills," *LI Business News,* August 13, 1999, p. 30A.

22. Fisher et al., 1991.

23. Shapiro et al., 1998.

24. Danny Ertel, "Turning Negotiation into a Corporate Capability," *Harvard Business Review,* May 1999, p. 55.

25. Harvey Mackay, "Flexibility Is a Word for the Wise," *Providence Business News,* August 9, 1999, p. 30.

26. Fisher et al., 1991.

27. Ron Shapiro, Mark Jankowski, and James Dale, *The Power of Nice—How to Negotiate So Everyone Wins, Especially You!* (New York: John Wiley & Sons, Oct. 1998).

28. Fisher et al., 1991.

29. J. A. Wall, Jr., and M. W. Blum, "Negotiations," *Journal of Management,* June 1991, pp. 283–287.

30. Robert D. Benjamin, "Mediation: Taming of the Shrewd," *Commercial Law Bulletin,* Jan.–Feb. 2000, pp. 8–10.

31. Robert Rosen, Patricia Digh, Marshall Singer, and Carl Phillips, *Global Literacies: Lessons on Business Leadership and National Cultures: A Landmark Study of CEOs from 28 Countries* (New York: Simon and Schuster, 2000).

32. Rosen et al., 2000, p. 176.

33. Jerald W. Salacuse, *Making Global Deals: What Every Executive Should Know about Negotiating Abroad* (New York: Times Books, 1991).

34. Leigh Steinberg and Michael D'Orso, *Winning with Integrity—Getting What You're Worth without Selling Your Soul* (New York: Villard, Sept. 1998).

35. Dean Allen Foster, *Bargaining Across Borders: How to Negotiate Business Successfully Anywhere in the World* (Burr Ridge, IL: McGraw-Hill, 1995).

36. Foster, 1995.

Exercise 11–A
Assessing Yourself

Circle the response that most closely correlates with each item below.

	Agree	Neither	Disagree

1. I only negotiate when both parties are committed to a positive outcome.
   1 **(2)** 3 4 5

2. I am able to resist responding emotionally to a conflict situation.
   1 2 3 **(4)** 5

3. I only use "win–win" negotiation in instances where the relationship is important to me and I want to preserve it.
   1 2 **(3)** 4 5

4. When negotiating, I try to provide a climate that is open and supportive.
   (1) 2 3 4 5

5. I am flexible and willing to change.
   (1) 2 3 4 5

6. I am willing to compromise for the sake of a long-term relationship if necessary.
   (1) 2 3 4 5

7. When negotiating, I leave enough time to generate creative options.
   (1) 2 3 4 5

8. I avoid giving ultimatums or offering only fixed solutions.
   (1) 2 3 4 5

9. I approach negotiations thoughtfully and carefully rather than impulsively and without preparation.
   1 **(2)** 3 4 5

10. I understand my and the other party's strengths and weaknesses and take our similarities and differences into account when devising a negotiating strategy.
    1 **(2)** 3 4 5

11. I have learned and practiced the basics of negotiating.
    1 2 **(3)** 4 5

12. I know my "bottom line" before negotiating.
    1 **(2)** 3 4 5

13. I try to understand the other party's interests, needs, and motivations before negotiating.
    1 **(2)** 3 4 5

14. When possible, I try to get to know the other party before negotiating.
    1 **(2)** 3 4 5

15. I define ground rules before negotiating.
    1 2 **(3)** 4 5

16. I set aside enough time in a negotiation to deal with the critical issues that are involved.
    (1) 2 3 4 5

17. I keep an open mind and am willing to consider creative options without judgment or criticism.
    (1) 2 3 4 5

18. I weigh all alternatives carefully before making a decision and take the time I need to make a decision.
    (1) 2 3 4 5

19. I clarify my and the other party's understanding of our agreement.
    (1) 2 3 4 5

20. I avoid attacking people personally and putting them on the defensive.
    1 2 **(3)** 4 5

21. I take responsibility for my feelings and use "I" language rather than "you" language.
    (1) 2 3 4 5

22. I develop and use objective criteria in negotiations.
    (1) 2 3 4 5

23. When criticized, I ask questions rather than respond emotionally.
    1 2 **(3)** 4 5

24. I develop a point of view or frame through which I and the other party can view the negotiation.
    1 2 **(3)** 4 5

25. I prepare a script before important negotiations.
    1 2 **(3)** 4 5

26. I am open to using a third party in negotiations.
    1 **(2)** 3 4 5

27. If necessary, I can leave a negotiation without settling for less than I wanted or forcing a quick solution.
    1 2 **(3)** 4 5

28. During negotiations, I summarize discussions and agreements periodically.
    1 2 **(3)** 4 5

	Agree	Neither		Disagree
29. I use effective communication skills during negotiation, e.g., active listening, questioning, asserting.	① 2	3	4	5
30. I only negotiate over matters I truly care about.	1 ②	3	4	5
31. I avoid blaming others and dwelling on the past.	1 2	③	4	5
32. I approach negotiations collaboratively rather than competitively.	1 2	③	4	5

If your score is 96 or higher, you might want to consider creating a plan for increasing your negotiation skills.   65

Exercise 11–B
Negotiation Role-Play

Working in groups of four or five persons, choose one of the scenarios below and develop a script to prepare for a negotiation you are about to enter. Role-play the script with another member of your group and get feedback from the other members on your skill as a negotiator. When all in the small group have taken a turn as a negotiator, discuss the activity with the class or group as a whole, using the discussion questions below.

Negotiation Scenario 1

Your parents have told you that you cannot have a car at school. They are concerned about your safety (you have already been in one car accident that was your fault), your grades (you have a C+ average), and your ability to keep up with the payments financially (your part-time job earns you enough just to cover your expenses while at school). How do you prepare to negotiate with your parents?

Negotiation Scenario 2

This past summer you worked at a car dealership. Now that you're back to school, you need to cut back your hours. After looking over your class schedule, you tell your boss that you can work Fridays, Saturdays, and Sundays. He's glad you'll continue with the dealership—after all, you were the top salesperson in two of the four summer months—but he's concerned that the other salespeople will feel slighted by your schedule. All salespeople work on commission and are required to work at least 45 hours per week, including slow or nonpeak times. How do you prepare to negotiate with your boss?

Negotiation Scenario 3

You and two roommates moved off campus together in the fall. Since then one of the roommates has refused to help keep the apartment clean or to pay for the snacks and beverages you and your other roommate purchase for weekend parties. How do you prepare to negotiate with the offending roommate?

Negotiation Scenario 4

You have been working hard on the job for five years. Your wife recently gave birth to your first child. She has an opportunity for a promotion at work and has asked if you would be willing to work part-time for a time while she pursues her career. You support the idea and agree to switch to part-time status on your job, pending your boss's approval. How do you prepare to negotiate with your boss to get his approval on this request?

Negotiation Scenario 5

You have worked in your current assignment for two years. During that time, your company initiated a new bonus system. However, neither you nor other employees know very much about the new system. Your employer cautioned everyone to keep their salaries and bonuses confidential, so you have little information about how others in your company are compensated. At year-end, you received a bonus, but it's significantly smaller than you anticipated. You want to approach your boss to ask for a larger bonus, but without information on what everyone else got, you have little information on which to base your argument. How do you prepare to negotiate with your boss?

Questions

1. What was your strategy going into the negotiation? Was it effective? What worked? What didn't?

2. What ideas did you get from other group members about how you could improve your negotiating skill?

3. What was difficult about negotiating (other than having to role-play!)?

4. What did you learn about yourself as a negotiator from this exercise?

Exercise 11–C
Creating and Using Frames in Negotiation

Earlier in this chapter, we discussed frames—their use and advantages in negotiation. We provided an example of two metaphorical frames potentially used by CEOs discussing the potential merger of their companies. Now, it's your turn. Apply the concept of frames to one of the scenarios in the previous exercise (11–B). Select one scenario and come up with a creative frame that achieves many if not all of the goals discussed in the chapter. Write it below.

Scenario ____

Frame:

_____

_____

_____

1. How and when would you use this frame?

2. How would you interpret this frame?

3. How could others interpret your frame, and could they potentially use it against you or your arguments?

4. What are some other frames that might work for this scenario?

Exercise 11–D
Negotiation Scripts: Looking Backward and Forward

1. Think of a situation you've been involved in recently where you wish you had negotiated. Using the script outline in this chapter, develop a script for how you would approach the situation if you had a second chance. Comparing this script to what actually happened, what aspects of your actual negotiation were positive? In need of improvement? What impact would the changes alluded to in your script have had on the actual outcome? Explain. Discuss this situation with a partner.

2. Use the script outline to prepare for an upcoming negotiation—with a friend, relative, significant other, current or prospective boss, or co-worker. Role-play with a partner who will play the person with whom you'll negotiate. Request your partner's feedback on what worked well and what you could do differently in the future. Make adjustments to your script outline.

Exercise 11–E
Negotiating a Home Purchase

The Situation

You and your family have been renting a house for the last eight months. During a recent visit from your landlord, he mentioned his desire to sell some of his properties. "Not this one," he tells you, "but I have another house a few miles away." Hmmmm. You love the area, the school district is great, and you've been thinking about buying, although there have been few if any properties available in your price range. Your landlord, who lives in another state, gives you the address and his phone number. "Call me if you're interested and we'll talk," he says. You and your spouse drive by the house the next day. Not your dream home, but it is a possibility—if the price is right.

The Players

The landlord (additional information available from your instructor)

The renter (additional information available from your instructor)

An observer

The Process

Decide who will play which role in your triad. Read the situation and additional information, create a plan, and then negotiate. The observer should take notes on effective and less-than-effective negotiating behaviors. The observer will then lead a feedback discussion after the negotiation is complete.

Exercise 11–F
Negotiating a Raise

The Situation

You have worked hard at your job for three years. During that time, you also went to school at night and completed your MBA degree. You have discovered that your company is bringing in newly minted MBAs at a salary that is 25 percent higher than yours. You want to ask your boss for a raise. How do you prepare to negotiate with your boss?

The Players

The boss (additional information available from your instructor)

The subordinate (additional information available from your instructor)

An observer

The Process

Decide who will play which role in your triad. Read the situation and additional information, create a plan, and then negotiate. The observer should take notes on effective and less-than-effective negotiating behaviors. The observer will then lead a feedback discussion after the negotiation is complete.

**Exercise 11–G
Team-Based
Negotiations:
Newtown School
Dispute**

In this simulation, you will play a member of either a school board or teachers' association bargaining team. You and the other members of your team, and the members of the other team, are negotiators representing constituencies. You will deal with a complex mix of bargaining issues; these issues have differing preference functions for each side. Finally, you will be subject to a variety of pressures during the negotiation.

Your instructor will be giving you additional information prior to the negotiation. You will meet with members of your bargaining team, determine your objectives and strategy, and prepare your initial offer.

After the negotiation, you will be given a list of discussion questions to consider individually and then discuss in your negotiating team.

Source: This exercise, originally developed by Frank W. Masters, appears in *Negotiations: Readings, Exercises, and Cases,* edited by Lewicki, Saunders, and Minton, 1999, pp. 503–509. Reproduced with permission from the McGraw-Hill Companies.

**Exercise 11–H
Try This . . .**

1. Watch a movie or TV show in which a negative or positive negotiation is depicted. What are the attitudes and behaviors displayed by both parties in the negotiation? What behaviors are effective? Ineffective? Why? Examples are *Gung Ho, Air Force One, Greed, Wall Street, The Negotiator, Ransom, Cadillac Man, A Civil Action, Jerry Maguire, The Associate.*

2. Observe a conversation between two family members, co-workers, or roommates where one person wants to do something one way and the other a different way. What strategies does each use? What is successful and why? What other strategies can be used effectively for the situation? Why?

**Exercise 11–I
Reflection/Action Plan**

This chapter focused on negotiation—what it is, why it is important, and how to improve your skills in this area. Complete the worksheet below upon completing all reading and experiential activities for this chapter.

1. The one or two areas in which I am strongest:

_____

_____

_____

_____

2. The one or two areas in which I need to improve:

_____

_____

_____

_____

3. If I did only one thing to improve in this area, it would be to:

_____

_____

_____

_____

4. Making these changes would probably result in:

_____

_____

_____

_____

5. If I did not change or improve in these areas, it would probably affect my personal and professional life in the following ways:

_____

_____

_____

12

Conflict: Sources and Solutions

How do I:

✓ Deal with unresolved anger in a constructive way?

✓ Identify the source of conflict as it's occurring?

✓ Understand what my natural conflict style is and know which strategy to adopt in a conflict situation?

✓ Change my attitude toward conflict and treat it as a normal and potentially beneficial part of relationships?

✓ Prevent conflict when appropriate?

✓ Learn how to manage conflict personally and professionally?

I am so angry with my boss I can't even speak to him. We had always been pretty close. Only a few years older than me, he was a member of my fraternity when he was in college. We met at a chapter career networking event. He said I would fit right in at the investment bank where he worked and that hired me as I graduated from college. For the first few years he was always there for me. I was placed in another department, but he stayed in touch, providing me informally with information and tips. People knew that we were close, and I have to admit I didn't mind being affiliated with him in people's heads. As his stature and reputation at the bank grew, I felt lucky and proud to have been taken under his wing. Don't get me wrong. I worked hard and earned my promotions on merit. But it didn't hurt to be associated with him and to get useful advice from him. At least, not until now.

Last year he was placed in charge of all campus recruiting for the bank. He was the senior person in charge, and people in all departments who recruited for the bank, like me, had a dotted line reporting relationship to him for our recruiting results. That's where things began to go wrong.

As soon as he was put in charge, he made me his lieutenant. I worked closely with him to ensure his strategic recruiting objectives would be implemented. I began to travel extensively with him and with the other recruiters, line people like myself who had been "lent" to the function for just one season. It was an honor to be selected. The opportunity to recruit at top-tier campuses is only offered to people who are "up and comers" at the bank. I was proud of his belief that I could contribute to the effort and do a good job. Plus the added visibility couldn't hurt when it came time for my next bonus and promotion. Or could it?

One night after our firm's presentation at a top-tier school, he and I ended up the only recruiters left at the bar from our team of eight. Everyone else had retired for the evening. We were the diehards, left with a group of students who didn't seem to want to leave. I noticed my boss, Bob, over in a corner of the bar with one of the students. A female student. Uh-oh. I was worried how this might look and thought I'd better saunter over and join in. I got there just in time to hear the student, who sounded like she had already had enough to drink, order a drink whose name I hadn't heard since back in college on spring break in Florida. Bob told the waiter to charge it to his room. He also politely told me to scram. I left, slightly worried about what might be happening but figuring he knew how to handle himself.

To make a very long story short, a few weeks later, I found out that Bob had propositioned this student and that she had filed a complaint against him, and by association, against me and our firm's entire recruiting team. Apparently she thinks it was wrong of us to have sent the wrong signal to the students by staying out so late with them. She says she stayed because she thought we were interested in her as a potential hire. And that one of the reasons she didn't get invited back (for an interview the next day) is she refused to sleep with Bob.

Now both Bob's job and mine are on the line. Since he's the senior person in charge of recruiting and the one who made the pass, he's almost certain to lose his job. And since I'm his lieutenant, I'm vulnerable too. The rest of the team will probably get reassigned.

I am so angry I can't even talk to anyone about this. Not him. Not his boss. Not my fiancee. Not human resources. It's humiliating, childish, and shouldn't be involving me. All my hard work at the bank is about to go down the tubes. I'm so angry. I thought we were friends. I thought he would look out for me, not get me in trouble. I don't know what to do. I just want this all to go away.

1. Is this a solvable conflict? Why or why not?

2. By choosing not to speak to his boss or boss's boss, what impact does this have on the parties involved?

3. What options are available, assuming a resolution is desired?

4. While the bar scenario might not have been predicted or avoided, in what ways could the boss–subordinate conflict have been ameliorated before it progressed to this point?

5. What role do personal style and comfort with conflict play in our response (and resolution) to situations like these?

We're told that conflict is inevitable, that it's part of human nature to have conflicts with others. Yet seldom do we as human beings get comfortable with conflict. Many of us would prefer to avoid it at all costs. As we can see from the opening case, avoiding it doesn't make it go away. It bothers us emotionally whether we confront the source of the conflict or not. Managing conflict is one of the toughest yet most rewarding skills to acquire. Foremost, it is a skill that does not come naturally; it is learned. In this chapter we discuss conflict, what it is, and why learning to manage it is important. We discuss common sources of conflict and present a model for approaching conflict. We also include strategies and tips for dealing with conflict as well as suggestions for preventing conflict when possible and for being selective about which conflicts you choose to tackle. Exercises to help you process and build skills in managing conflict are at the end of the chapter, as is a list of references for further exploration.

"Speaking without thinking is like shooting without aiming."

Ancient Proverb

What Is Conflict?

Conflict is any situation in which there are incompatible goals, cognitions, or emotions within or between individuals or groups that lead to opposition or antagonistic interaction.

It is the struggle between incompatible and opposing needs, wishes, ideas, interests, or people. Conflict is a form of interaction among parties who differ in interests, perceptions, goals, values, or approaches to problems. Conflict arises when we begin to feel that the other person is interfering with our ability to attain a certain objective. It begins when we believe the other party is interfering or standing in the way of an action we want to take, an idea we want to pursue, or a belief we hold. Conflicts may involve individual or group disagreements, struggles, disputes, quarrels, or even physical fighting and wars. Because human beings are unique—possessing a variety of physical, intellectual, emotional, economic, and social difference—conflict is inevitable.

Conflict is also a fact of life in all types of organizations. Each organization is composed of people, and each person has a set of goals that is likely to be distinct from the goals of others in the organization. When individuals with different interests compete for the same resource pool, dissension is sure to follow.[1] That tension can be dealt with constructively, in a way that stimulates creativity and positive change. In fact, lack of creative tension sometimes reflects an "I don't care" attitude that can lead to stagnation on the job. Effective managers are not afraid of conflict. They have been trained to deal with conflict and have trained their employees to deal with conflict constructively. They accept that conflicts must be faced and strive to find constructive means to manage them. Effective managers are those who are selective as to which conflicts they choose to pursue. Sometimes the best course of action in a difficult situation is to take "the path with least resistance"—to be silent!

Is Conflict Normal?

Society's view of conflict and conflict management has evolved substantially over the last century. These views can be summarized in three perspectives on managing conflict:[2]

1. **Traditional View**—This view was predominant in the early 20th century when it was believed that conflict was always bad and should be avoided at all costs. This perspective posited that conflict was a result of dysfunctional managerial behavior and therefore should and could be stopped at the source. Presumably, if the dysfunctional behavior was stopped (i.e., the manager is fired), the conflict would cease to exist.

2. **Human Relations View**—This was the overriding perspective for the three decades spanning 1940 through 1970. In this view, conflict was viewed as a natural and inevitable part of human existence and was accepted as a normal part of group interaction and relationships. Sometimes the conflict was functional, other times dysfunctional, but it was always present.

3. **Interactionist View**—The contemporary view holds that not only is conflict inevitable, but maintaining a degree of tension can actually be helpful in keeping a group energized and creative. In this view, conflict is seen as a positive force for change within organizations, groups, and relationships. The challenge is finding constructive means for man-aging conflict while still maintaining some differences that energize a group toward continued discussion and innovation.

Although managerial mistakes do sometimes cause unnecessary and even unhealthy conflict, it is important to discard the traditional notion that conflict automatically means one performs ineffectively. Conflict is a certainty for any manager, or any person, for that matter. The best managers recognize this and learn how to manage conflict in such a way that it has positive and fair outcomes for all involved.[3]

Why Is Conflict Management Important?

Conflict is a normal part of organizational life. In every organization, family, relationship, and community, there are conflicts of ideas, values, thought, and actions. Conflict is a given. What isn't given is how we choose to react to conflict. As Marcus Aurelius says in *Meditations:*

> *If you are distressed by anything external, the pain is not due to the thing itself, but to your own estimate of it; and this you have the power to revoke at any moment.*

We can successfully face and resolve conflicts if we take a few steps: recognize conflicts are normal and inevitable,[4] train ourselves not to overreact when conflicts arise, and have a strategy to use when conflicts—some of which are predictable—arise.

Conflict can be either positive or negative. The outcomes of conflict depend on how the conflict is managed or resolved. **Positive conflict** is functional and supports or benefits the organization or person's main objectives.[5] Conflict is constructive when it leads to better decisions, creativity, and innovative solutions to long-standing problems. Conflict is viewed as positive when it results in:

- *Increased Involvement*—Organizational members have the opportunity to develop goals, share ideas, and voice opinions, gaining greater insight into others and situations.

- *Increased Cohesion*—Members build strong bonds from learning how to resolve differences; "if we can survive this, we must have a true relationship" embodies this benefit of conflict.[6] In some cases conflict initially reduces cohesion that can in turn reduce the likelihood of "group think" occurring. In this case conflict is positive.

- *Increased Innovation and Creativity*—Members are encouraged to "put their ideas on the table";[7] this can lead to more discoveries, improvements, and creative solutions. "Two heads are truly better than one" when conflict brings about synergy instead of chaos.

- *Positive Personal Growth and Change*—Individuals learn their strengths and weaknesses; conflict of ideas challenges individuals to learn and grow by expressing their ideas and thoughts through self-disclosure and sharing of important concepts with others.

- *Clarification of Key Issues*—Through discussion, members reduce ambiguity and focus energy on the real sources of conflict, then work together to target remaining issues that need to be addressed.

- *Values Clarification*—Members clarify who they are and what they stand for, understand who the other party is and what his or her values are, and learn when to sublimate personal interests to the larger needs of the group or organization.

Negative conflict is dysfunctional and hinders the organization's or the person's performance or ability to attain goals or objectives. Conflict is destructive when it leads to stress and anxiety, inability to take action, and loss of esteem or purpose.[8] Conflict is viewed as negative when it results in:

- *Unresolved Anger*—Members leave the interaction believing they have legitimate concerns that have not been addressed appropriately or goals that cannot be achieved; companies can be slowly poisoned by anger and hostility.[9]

- *Personality Clashes*—Members lack understanding of their style differences and how to work cooperatively and are more tied to their own interests than those of others.

- *Low Self-esteem or Self-confidence*—Members have a diminished sense of self-worth or identity as a result of the conflict. Often this results from impulsive things said or done in the heat of the conflict.

- *Unclear or Opposing Views on Who Is or Should Be Responsible for What*—Members have different expectations of each other and their roles; the conflict was unresolved, unproductive, or ended too soon, leaving ambiguity in its wake.

- *Problems of Efficiency*—Members decide they are unwilling or unable to work together, resulting in redundancies and poor use of existing resources.

- *"Unfinished Business"*—Members are still unclear about the issue or have remaining concerns that will get in the way of being able to move forward.

The benefits of positive conflict far outweigh the time it takes to manage conflict well. As managers, it is our responsibility to learn how to manage conflict effectively and how to help others manage conflict. This is done by creating a climate and culture at work that support constructive conflict—encouraging the clash of ideas (not personalities) and developing processes, training, and tools that help people work through their inevitable differences with each other. This requires a collaborative approach and a commitment to eliminating or at least reducing the occurrence of destructive conflicts.

Sources of Interpersonal Conflict

Not everyone within a group or organization will have the same goals and objectives. By definition, different groups, business units, functions, operating companies, or locations within one organization will each have a set of expectations and operating principles that differs from the others. Each specific entity within an organization may have a unique customer set, employee profile, product orientation, management style, business niche, set of tasks and procedures, and culture or work environment. Business units in the same organization differ significantly in such areas as primary role, task assignments, workloads, vacation scheduling, pay or promotion policies, chain of command, work flow process, and others. For example, within General Motors are very different entities—separate organizations whose primary business is financing (cars and homes), production (building or assembling cars), sales and service (dealership and warranty organizations), and research and development (making continuous improvement on existing car lines as well as developing new ones such as GM's electric vehicle). Employees in these different units likely work together, sharing expertise as well as information. A variety of situational or organizational factors lead to conflict.[10]

Limited Resources

Despite clear differences between units within an organization, one commonality remains. In general, all are vying for the same resource pool. This pool is usually limited, causing the various units within an organization to compete against each other for finite resources. No matter how prosperous an organization might appear from its facilities, salary levels, or private jets and limousines, few if any organizations have infinite resources. This usually results in competition among business units for the restricted resources available through the parent organization. People in organizations compete for what they consider to be their fair share of resources such as money, time, senior management attention, technology, supplies, equipment, and human talent. This inevitably results in conflict.

Differences in Goals/Objectives

A common source of conflict within organizations is differences in personal and/or professional goals and objectives. If we are working on a project with someone whose objective is different from ours, tension or conflict is likely to occur. For example, perhaps one team member wants to "coast" or do as little work as possible toward the team's expected output or deliverable. If this person is on a team of individuals who are committed to a high-quality output, there will be differences between them on a host of items, such as approach to the work, ways to get the work done, and standards of work quality and quantity. This tension can be from **intragroup conflict,** differences between members of one group, or from **intergroup conflict,** differences between competing subgroups of an organization. For example, the marketing department might have a different goal than the finance department. Marketing folks might push to increase spending on advertising and promotion in order to improve sales, while finance folks push for increased cost-cutting efforts.

Miscommunication

Many times, personal and professional conflicts arise due to poor communication. Seldom is miscommunication intentional. More often than not, it's the result of our not taking time to clarify our understanding of something, or gender or cultural differences, or errors in semantics. Often we say one thing and mean another. Or in our haste, we will speak quickly and cryptically in hopes that others know what we want. Or perhaps we speak clearly but our nonverbal communication contradicts the verbal message. In any case, misunderstanding is likely to occur. These communication issues are further compounded by the jargon shared by and understood within specific groups of people, such as engineers and military personnel. The processes and principles of communication may also differ between work groups. For example, one group might have a division newsletter, through which employees are kept informed of important organizational changes, while another group might rely on word of mouth to spread key bits of information. This results in each group having a very different understanding of what's going on in the organization. Interaction between these groups could lead to numerous miscommunications, each one a potential source of conflict.

Differing Attitudes, Values, and Perceptions

Many conflicts are the result of differ-ences in attitudes, values, and perceptions. Sometimes, without even realizing it, we bring feelings or concerns into an interaction that predisposes us to react in a certain way. For example, if you are afraid of dogs and encounter a neighbor with a dog while out walking one morning, you may react with fear or even hostility. Upon reflection, you realize this fear is due to a fear of animals you've had since you were a child. But the neighbor, without knowing this background, might misinterpret your strong reaction and conclude you dislike the neighbor rather than fear the dog. Without a chance to communicate—for the neighbor to share his or her perception with you and for you to explain the background behind your reaction—it is likely that you will each emerge from the interaction with a vastly different understanding of what just occurred, and with different, possibly negative, opinions of each other.

Conflicting values are a common and difficult-to-resolve source of conflict between people. Differences in religious beliefs, attitudes towards diverse others, clashes in family values, or in work ethic might result in interpersonal differences that surface in the work environment. For example, a young consultant who must leave work by Friday afternoon is viewed by her colleagues as a slacker when they are left to work late on a client deliv-erable. The fact is she is an Orthodox Jew. Her manager knows this but her colleagues do not. In this case it would be preferable for her colleagues to be aware of her beliefs. This way the team could make accommodations for her early departure on Fridays, and she could perhaps offer to work late on Thursdays. Fear, confusion, anxiety, and hostility are common attitudes and perceptions and a frequent source of conflict between individuals and groups, and these feelings are often magnified when the individuals are demographi-cally different. As can be seen from the above example, these attitudes toward and perceptions about others can be long lasting and self-fulfilling. When such feelings are allowed to develop, conflict is bound to occur.

Personality Clashes

Another common source of conflict is differences in personal style or personality. An obvious example of this is the predictable tension between two roommates who are on different "body clocks." The early riser who gets up at dawn and the night owl who sleeps until noon are almost certain to get into conflict with each other. Conflicts likely occur between the "slob" and the "neat freak." The manager who is task-oriented and the employee who is a perpetual socializer are likely to encounter much tension and conflict in their boss–subordinate relationship. Personality conflicts can result in unproductive behaviors at work including gossip, jealousy, insults, taking sides or playing favorites, slowing of work speed, forming of cliques, and even looking for another job!

Conflict Management Strategies

Knowing what causes conflicts is half the battle. Knowing what to do when conflicts arise, as they inevitably do, composes the other half. In this section we are focused on conflict management, as opposed to resolution. Conflict management recognizes that sources of conflict will probably always be present (for example resource limitation) and seeks ways to live with it, minimize its effect, and manage it. Conflict resolution (e.g., in arbitration or alternative dispute resolution) seeks to eliminate the cause of the conflict, thus eliminating the conflict itself. This is not always possible. When deciding on a strategy for dealing with a specific conflict, keep two factors in mind: your goals, or what you hope to accomplish through the interaction, and the importance of the relationship to you.[11] The first consideration when selecting a strategy is assessing your goals: What personal or organizational goals are to be accomplished, and how important is it to achieve those exact goals? Remember that conflicts often exist because of opposing goals. The nature and importance of a particular set of goals for you will determine which strategy is most appropriate for the situation.

The second consideration when choosing a conflict resolution strategy is the depth, quality, and duration of the relationship.

Before selecting a strategy, work through answers to the following questions:

- Is this relationship long term or passing?
- Is the relationship substantive (goes beyond business issues to more personal matters) or narrow?
- Is the relationship more important to me than the matter under discussion?
- How important is it to maintain a working or friendly relationship with those with whom I am in conflict?
- What possible ramifications will surface after the dust settles?

How you answer these questions will impact the conflict strategy you ultimately select.

Research on conflict management proposes five strategies that are available based on the intersection between relationship and goal importance.[12]

The figure below helps illustrate how each conflict management strategy maps with the assessed importance of the goal and the relationship. Each option has advantages and disadvantages. The appropriate option depends on your preferences and on the context of the specific situation.

Conflict-Handling Orientation

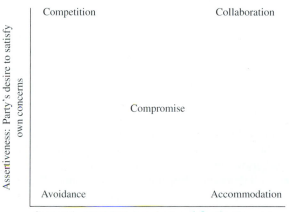

Avoiding—in an avoidance or withdrawing strategy, you choose not to deal with the issues or the people involved. You retreat from the situation, hoping it either goes away or resolves itself. This strategy is suitable for situations in which the issues are trivial or of only minor importance to you, when emotions are high, you feel you have no chance of satisfying your concerns, or when others could resolve the conflict more effectively. Avoiding is dangerous if the matter under discussion requires your attention. It may resurface if not dealt with effectively. What's worse, conflicts that are set aside or ignored can fester due to lack of communication and clarification, making it more difficult—and necessary—to address at a later time. If the conflict is one that must be addressed, save time and emotional energy by speaking up soon after the conflict is recognized. Avoidance can lead to a "lose–lose" scenario; goals may not be addressed or achieved and the relationship may not be able to progress beyond its current state.

■ **Accommodating** (Smoothing)—when you use an accommodation strategy to resolve a conflict, you are more concerned with maintaining the relationship than in accomplishing a specific goal through the interaction. This strategy is appropriate when the issue is not that important to you or when harmony is of greater importance to you than "winning" on the issue. For example, if your children challenge your decision to take them to Burger King for lunch (McDonald's has the better toy this week), it's okay to give in to their wishes if both choices are equally suitable. It saves time and emotional energy, and it can be used in a later conflict negotiation ("I did what you wanted; now I want you to do . . . for me"). If you are always accommodating, as in "you win and I lose," it might signal that you are possibly sacrificing some important goals for the sake of the relationship. You might wonder why others never seem to do the same for you. Sometimes we do this because we want to be "nice" and have others like us. However, over-reliance on accommodating in conflict situations could be harmful to you and the relationship in the long term as you are likely to build up resentment over your unmet needs.

■ **Compromising**—when you compromise or "split the difference" in a conflict, you agree to give up part of your goal and part of the relationship in order to reach an agreement. This strategy is effective for achieving temporary solutions, when both parties are at a comparable level, when there are time pressures, or as a backup when collaboration or competing is neither possible nor successful. This strategy is the political equivalent of "win some, lose some." In other words, you consciously agree to accept that sometimes in the relationship you'll get your way and other times you won't. This is possible in a long-term relationship where there's time for give-and-take exchange. However, many people and groups jump to this strategy too quickly without pursuing synergy or collaboration. Perhaps it's our feelings about risk: I'm better off getting half of what I want than risking it and getting nothing. Whether this is true or appropriate depends on the situation.

■ **Competing** (Forcing)—in a competing strategy, you work to achieve your goals at all costs, even if it means sacrificing the relationship. This is an "I win, you lose" strategy. Forcing may be appropriate when you have severe time restrictions, are in a crisis situation, need to issue an unpopular decision, or have to take an action that is vital to an organization's welfare. Some salespeople are guilty of forcing sales. They care about the commission they earn if they sell you a car—today—and use techniques (this is the last one [or day]; if you leave now, the deal expires) that make buyers feel pressured into the sale. More successful salespeople realize that future sales from this person and others in his or her network are likely if agreements are reached collaboratively as opposed to with a forcing approach. However, forcing children out on a specific path when the fire alarm rings is not only appropriate but is safer than discussing or arguing over other options.

■ **Collaborating** (Integrating)—the ultimate "win–win" strategy. It involves energy, commitment, and excellent skills in communication, problem solving, and negotiation. Collaboration is appropriate when there is plenty of time, when all want a solution that satisfies all parties' objectives and maintains the relationship, and when the issue is very important to all parties involved. It is also critical when the conflicting parties are responsible for implementing the solution. If you feel a solution was only partly effective or was forced on you, you will be less likely to put your heart and soul into its implementation. Coming to a consensus or finding an integrative solution takes considerable problem-solving effort and time. In collaboration, both parties don't necessarily agree, but both feel comfortable enough to express their disagreement and opinions and can work towards an optimal solution.[13]

Figure 12–1
Gains and Losses Associated
with Conflict Styles[14]

		Competition	Avoidance	Accommodation	Compromise	Collaboration
Gains		Chance to win everything	No energy or time expenditure	Little muss or fuss, no feathers ruffled	No one returns home empty-handed	Both sides win
		Exciting, games-manship	Conserve for fights that are "more important"	Others may veiw you as supportive	"Keeps the peace"	Better chance for long-term solutions
		Exercise own sense of power		Energy free for other pursuits	May or may not encourage creativity	Creativity in problem solving
						Maintains relationship
						New level of understanding of situation
						Improves quality of solution and commitment
Losses		Chance to lose everything	Less stimulation	Lowered self-assertion and possibly self-esteem	Since neither side is totally satisfied, conflicts are likely to recur later	Time, in the short run
		Alienates others	Less creative problem solving	Loss of power		Loss of sense of autonomy
		Discourages others from working with you	Little under-standing of the needs of others	Absence of your unique contribution to the situation	Neither side realizes self-determination fully	
		Potentially larger scale conflicts in the future (or more avoidance of conflict)	Incomplete comprehen-sion of work environment	Others depen-dent on you may not feel you "go to bat" for them		

Although collaborating or the win–win option appears to be the ideal strategy, it is not appropriate in all cases. Each of the strategies has strong and weak points. No one solution is best suited for all situations. The best managers are those who can move fluidly from one style to the next depending on the situation and circumstances. As a manager, you will find yourself using all of these strategies. The choice of one over the other depends on the situation and persons involved as well as your own personality. Each of us has a style with which we're naturally most comfortable. (You'll have an opportunity to identify yours using one of the chapter exercises.) Be aware of your natural tendency and develop proficiency in using other, less comfortable styles, depending on what a situation dictates.

Tips for Managing Conflict Following are some tips for making these strategies work.

■ *Control your temper and emotional response.* Demonstrate your respect for the other party's feelings. Validate that the conflict is real to them no matter how trivial it may seem to you.[15] Embracing conflict builds honest relationships. By validating both parties' feelings about a situation you can then move into a problem-solving mode.

(continued)

■ *Understand the issues.* Don't react impulsively when faced with a conflict situation. Take the time needed to fully assess the scope of the situation: the key players, the source of the conflict, the issues involved, the goals, and the dynamics of the relationship(s) involved.[16] Accept the faults of the parties involved and be willing to admit to them. Focus on changing behaviors, not people. Then select a conflict strategy from the above choices and apply it to the situation as appropriate.

■ *Pick your battles.* Not all conflicts are manageable. Get all the facts before making any judgments. Choose the time and place carefully. A good manager will carefully choose the battles worth handling and select an appropriate strategy for handling them. In the same way small children bring their conflicts to grown-ups to solve, employees frequently do the same with their manager. Sometimes, in the interest of developing the skills of and relationships between employees who report to you, it's wise to determine if a particular conflict is best ignored by you and addressed by the individuals responsible for the conflict.

■ *Search for a common goal or ground.* Know your options, and select your best option. Attempt to work for win–win solutions that will be acceptable to both parties.[17] Do this by asking open-ended questions and demonstrating you've heard and understood others' goals or objectives. When this is not possible or time is short, try to accommodate as many of the others' interests and then make the decision that is ultimately the most fair and helpful for the organization. Sometimes a compromise solution will have to suffice.

Conflict Prevention Techniques

While conflict can be healthy in an organization or relationship, it still makes sense to eliminate some sources of friction before they even begin. By effectively managing conflict, managers can gain the benefit of conflict without the costs.[18] Following are some techniques that can be used to minimize or deflect conflict.

Team building. As organizations have gotten flatter and less hierarchical, indivi-duals are working in teams dedicated to specific project goals. Providing training and coaching on team-building skills can reduce the amount of conflict that occurs in the team setting. Some of these skills include:

- Setting clear objectives.
- Developing shared goals.[19]
- Establishing team norms.
- Understanding the stages through which teams progress.
- Clarifying expectations.
- Planning projects and meeting deadlines.

Diversity training. As organizations have become more diverse, individuals find themselves working more and more with people who vary in terms of background, physical ability, culture, ethnicity, gender, religious beliefs, education, economic status, sexual orientation, political view, values, goals, ideas, and knowledge base.[20] Diversity training is now offered by many large companies as a way of ensuring that employees understand the importance of differences among individuals and how to manage them effectively.[21] This training often includes components such as:

- Self-awareness of personal prejudices and stereotypes.
- Individual differences and how they develop.
- Valuing differences.
- Maximizing each person's strengths and capabilities to the advantage of the organization.
- Understanding and reducing discrimination.

- Legal guidelines for dealing with issues such as sexual harassment.
- Cross-training and cross-functional team training.[22]

Open communication. Companies are beginning to adopt more informal and personalized ways of connecting with their employees. By exchanging information freely and keeping people informed, companies find they are able to reduce some of the conflicts that arise from lack of information. Companies with open communication systems encourage:

- Regular staff meetings.
- Internal newsletters.
- Employee attitude surveys.
- 360-degree feedback (programs in which employees and managers receive performance feedback from subordinates, peers, and superiors).

Conflict management training. Many companies have discovered the benefits of providing their employees with training in dealing effectively with conflict. These programs teach participants to:

- Handle conflict constructively.
- Respect the legitimacy of others' points of view, feelings, and perceptions.
- Listen actively.
- Communicate assertively.
- Problem-solve collaboratively.
- Support conflict constructively.
- Help others avert unnecessary strife.
- Use communication skills to influence the way in which conflict is handled.[23]
- Anticipate and act accordingly.
- Be aware of potential problems and deal with them while they are still minor.[24]

Resource allocation. As long as resources need to be shared among various departments within an organization, conflict will be a part of organizational life. While some conflict can be healthy and constructive, conflict also has negative side effects. Unresolved and continuous conflict can lower productivity and morale and lead to high turnover. One technique effective managers use to reduce the possible effects of negative conflict is to seek new ways in which resources can be obtained and allocated. If internal resources can be increased or reallocated, the number of win–lose situations is likely to drop. Of course, it still might not be possible to increase resources sufficiently to allow all parties to become winners. Related to this issue is the process by which resources are allocated. The more secretive this process, the greater the likelihood that organizational members will perceive inequity and take steps to reduce this. To the degree possible, organizations should establish rewards at the highest level—to encourage collaboration across departments and unit—and involve key players in resource allocation decision processes to increase the fairness and effectiveness of these decisions.

The techniques just described focus primarily on what managers can do in their organizations to reduce sources and consequences of conflict. Following are a few additional techniques that individuals can use when interacting with others in a personal or professional setting.

Communication. Two communication techniques helpful for avoiding conflicts are using "I" language and paying attention to nonverbal cues. When we say things like "you just don't understand," or "your idea will never work," we put others on the defensive. They feel attacked and strike back, causing conflict to escalate. Take responsibility for your communication—"I'm not sure I've clearly stated my objection," or "I have a concern about the marketing part of this plan. Can we discuss this?"—and conflicts are less likely to occur.

On the other hand, there are times when we add to conflict by communicating. We flame the fires by paying too much attention to issues that would be better dealt with via the reinforcement technique of "extinction," providing no reinforcement at all by simply ignoring the event. Much as we would prefer this to be the case, things don't always get better by communicating openly. Sometimes it's best simply to express your opinion, "agree to disagree," and table the matter.

Managing others' expectations. Two techniques worth mentioning are setting limits and communicating consequences. Imagine your boss provides you with yet another project. You can do it, for sure, but not today, or this week for that matter. At least not with everything else on your plate. Most managers can't read minds. If you won't be able to complete the project when and how it is expected, let your boss know now instead of waiting until a critical deadline has passed. Setting limits—"I'm happy to do this project, but I need to let you know that the other project you wanted me to do will have to be placed on hold"—can help manage your boss's expectations and avoid a future conflict. Similar to setting limits, sometimes we need to communicate consequences. Returning to the lazy teammate scenario, realize that saying nothing is akin to approving this behavior. If you've tried reasoning, clarifying the issue, and asserting the team's needs but nothing has changed, it may be time to use consequences. "We've tried several times to get you to do what we've asked. If your part of the project is not up to the standards we've agreed to by Friday, we're going to ask the team leader to have you reassigned off the team."

Focusing on others first. Often when we disagree with another person, we rush to explain why our ideas are superior. Like "you" language, this tendency can motivate others to defend themselves. One effective technique for preventing conflict involves anticipating another's disagreement or objection and explaining how your proposal takes this issue into account. "I know you're concerned about x, so let me tell you how I think this can be overcome." Even helpful advice could be taken the wrong way, implying that the listener is performing ineffectively. When you are looking to change or improve organizational processes, consider first how others might benefit from the change. Since most people dislike change, you can increase their willingness to listen to your idea if they feel doing so can benefit them and their organization. You can avoid conflicts by appealing to another's self-interest; for example, "I know that the current reimbursement process works. However, if we can reduce the number of approval signatures needed, you'll reduce time spent on your inbox and show us that you trust us to act appropriately."

Summary

Conflict is inevitable. People are unique and have different interests, goals, perspectives, values, and needs. For this reason, conflict can and does occur. Not all conflict is dysfunctional; some conflict can actually increase innovation, creativity, and the bond between conflicting parties. Practicing conflict prevention techniques can help you eliminate or diffuse conflicts before they surface. By knowing likely sources of conflict and appropriate strategies for dealing with different types of conflict, you can manage your response to conflict and improve your interactions with others.

Key Terms and Concepts

Accommodating

Avoiding

Collaborating

Competing

Compromising

Conflict

Interactionist view (of conflict)

Intergroup conflict

Intragroup conflict

Negative conflict

Positive conflict

Endnotes

1. James H. Keil, "Coaching through Conflict," *Dispute Resolution Journal,* May–June 2000, pp. 65–69.

2. Stephen Robbins, *Organizational Behavior,* Eighth Ed. (Upper Saddle NJ: Prentice Hall, 1998), pp. 435–36.

3. Kathleen M. Eisenhardt, Jean L. Kahwajy, and L. F. Bourgeois III, "How Management Teams Can Have a Good Fight," *Harvard Business Review,* July–August 1997, p. 77.

4. Alfred Fleishman, "Going Back a Little Bit," *St. Louis Business Journal,* Jan. 3, 2000, p. 29.

5. Shari Caudron, "Keeping Team Conflict Alive," *Training and Development,* Sept. 1998, p. 48.

6. Jeri Darling and Diane Russ, "Relationship Capital," *Executive Excellence,* May 2000, p. 14.

7. Shari Caudron, "Productive Conflict Has Value," *Workforce,* Feb. 1999, p. 25.

8. Personnel Decisions International, "Five Steps to Mediating Conflict," *Workforce,* Oct. 1999, p. 30.

9. Michael Barrier, "Putting a Lid on Conflicts," *Nation's Business,* April 1998, p. 34.

10. John S. Morgan, revised by Beth Z. Schneider, *Interpersonal Skills for the Manager,* Fifth Ed. (Institute of Certified Professional Managers, 2000), pp. 139–145.

11. David Johnson, *Reaching Out,* Sixth Ed. (Allyn and Bacon, 1997), p. 240.

12. Kenneth Thomas, "Conflict and Conflict Management," in *Handbook of Industrial and Organizational Psychology* (Chicago: Rand McNally, 1976), pp. 889–935.

13. Caudron, Feb. 1999.

14. Adopted from work of Ronald Fry, Jared Florian, and Jacquie McLemore, Department of Organizational Behavior, Weatherhead School of Management, Case Western Reserve University, Cleveland, Ohio, 1984.

15. Ted Pollock, "When Conflict Rears Its Head: A Personal File of Stimulating Ideas, Little Known Facts and Daily Problem Solvers," *Supervision,* Oct. 1999, p. 24.

16. Ed Rigsbee, "Conflict Management and Resolution," *Business Forms, Labels and Systems,* Feb. 20, 2000, p. 62.

17. Robert F. Pearce, "Developing Your Career Skills," *Compensation and Benefits Management,* Winter 2000, p. 15.

18. Allen C. Amason, "Distinguishing the Effects of Functional and Dysfunctional Conflict on Strategic Decision Making: Resolving a Paradox for Top Management Teams," *Academy of Management Journal* 39, no. 1, pp. 123–148.

19. Eisenhardt et al., 1997.

20. Scott Sedam, "Why Muddle through Conflict?" *Builder,* June 1999, p. 148.

21. Caudron, Sept. 1998.

22. Sedam, 1999.

23. Joseph Eby Ruin, "Six Factors in Conflict Management," *The New Press Times,* June 14, 1997, p. 1-EX.

24. Pollock, 1999.

Exercise 12–A
Assessing Yourself

Circle the response that most closely correlates with each item below.

	Agree	Neither	Disagree

1. I confront conflict rather than avoid it.   1 2 3 4 5
2. I am not afraid of conflict.   1 2 3 4 5
3. I understand the difference between positive and negative conflict.   1 2 3 4 5
4. I know how to deal with conflict constructively.   1 2 3 4 5
5. In a group or work situation, I create a climate that supports constructive conflict and encourages differing ideas.   1 2 3 4 5
6. I don't overreact when conflict develops and have a strategy to use when conflict does occur.   1 2 3 4 5
7. I accommodate others when the relationship is more important to me than the issue.   1 2 3 4 5
8. I use compromise as a back-up conflict strategy when appropriate.   1 2 3 4 5
9. I use collaboration as a conflict strategy when the issue is important and both parties have the time necessary to deal with the conflict.   1 2 3 4 5
10. I view conflict as a positive force for change.   1 2 3 4 5
11. I use a collaborative approach when dealing with conflict.   1 2 3 4 5
12. I consider the source of the conflict as well as my goals and the type of relationship I have with the person before developing a strategy for dealing with the conflict.   1 2 3 4 5
13. I avoid conflict if the situation is minor or emotions are high.   1 2 3 4 5
14. I am able to control my temper in a conflict situation.   1 2 3 4 5
15. I focus on learning about the issues involved before attempting to resolve a conflict.   1 2 3 4 5
16. I understand the types of strategies available to deal with conflicts and know how to select a strategy that is appropriate for the situation.   1 2 3 4 5
17. I focus on changing behaviors, not people.   1 2 3 4 5
18. I pick my battles.   1 2 3 4 5
19. I search for common ground in conflict situations.   1 2 3 4 5
20. I work toward win–win solutions whenever possible.   1 2 3 4 5
21. I have acquired skills and training to help me know how to manage conflict. 1 2 3 4 5
22. I understand the role of team building in reducing conflict.   1 2 3 4 5
23. I appreciate diversity and don't let differences with others lead to unnecessary conflict.   1 2 3 4 5
24. I respect the legitimacy of others' views.   1 2 3 4 5
25. I help others avoid unnecessary strife.   1 2 3 4 5
26. I use communication techniques that can keep conflict from occurring or manage conflict once it does occur.   1 2 3 4 5
27. I use techniques geared toward others—focusing on their needs or objections or appealing to their interests—to reduce the occurrence of conflict.   1 2 3 4 5
28. I use limit setting and consequences (when appropriate) to manage others' expectations and reduce the chances that conflict will occur.   1 2 3 4 5

Sum your circled responses. If your total is 54 or higher, you might want to explore ways to improve your skill in the area of conflict management.

**Exercise 12–B
Conflict Case Studies**

Case Study #1

As freshman year came to a close, I looked forward to moving onto the main campus and to living with five other girls whom I thought of as my friends. At that time I had no idea as to what I was getting myself into. We all had been friends freshman year, but I guess I did not know them well enough to suspect that there might be some problems. My biggest concern is their disrespectfulness. They not only disrespect our shared living room, but they also disrespect my personal belongings. They are very inconsiderate of my feelings. Three of them are probably the dirtiest people I have ever met. I am not saying that I am super clean, but I am not dirty. I may make a mess or two and clean it up, but I am not dirty. These girls, my suitemates, leave their garbage all over the suite room: soda cans, potato chip bags, and half-eaten melted ice cream cartons. It is absolutely disgusting and it makes me very angry. No one ever takes out the garbage or the recycling except me. I know that I should not accept this dirty habit, but I have a difficult time of standing up for myself and being assertive.

The other way that they are disrespectful is that they go through my personal items when I am not around and often take things, especially my food. I usually do not mind when people use my things, but a little courtesy to ask permission goes a long way. It has gotten to the point where I have to hide my food and other personal items that I don't want them to touch.

1. What is your immediate reaction to the scenario? How would you feel if you were the person writing about this situation?
2. How could this situation have been avoided?
3. What approaches to resolving this conflict are appropriate?
4. What are some things that, if done, would make this approach successful?
5. What are some things to avoid when attempting to resolve this conflict? Why?

Case Study #2

My boss and I are having some interpersonal problems. There are several things that he does that I find really annoying. To start, he is not considerate of my employees or me. I often find myself thinking that I would be reluctant to do the things he does around me that annoy me. Yet he's my boss so what can I do? He comes in late to the office, after my co-workers and I have been working for a while and have our day planned. Inevitably he'll come in, interrupt, and lay on us a whole new set of priorities for the day. To be fair, he does stay late (we have flextime in our office) and he has a good reason to be late—he has child care responsibilities to fulfill on school mornings. But his habit of coming in and interrupting the schedule for our day is really off-putting. By the time I've listened to his concerns, reprioritized my and my staff's work, and gotten back on track, it's almost lunchtime and I feel I've wasted almost a half day trying to respond to his concerns. I'm afraid to confront him—he's a good guy and it would only put him on the defensive. And wouldn't really change anything. But I'm also tired of not feeling productive. I just wish he would be a little more sensitive to our situation and be better organized and more aware of our time constraints. Is that asking too much?

1. What is your immediate reaction to the scenario? How would you feel if you were the person writing about this situation?
2. How could this situation have been avoided?
3. What approaches to resolving this conflict are appropriate?
4. What are some things that, if done, would make this approach successful?
5. What are some things to avoid when attempting to resolve this conflict? Why?

Exercise 12–C
Who Gets the Money?

You are members of a board whose goal is to decide on the distribution of funds. A total of $200 million is available for medical research. You represent a special interest group interested in receiving a portion of the funds. You need to fully support your position and to verbalize your reasoning for getting the funds distributed to your interest group.

Special Interests: (information on the roles will be provided by instructor)

- AIDS
- Breast cancer
- Alzheimer's
- Diabetes
- Birth defects

Questions

1. What process did you use to advocate for your interest over the interests of others?
2. How did each individual in the group feel about the group discussion?
3. Was participation between each member balanced? Did all have a chance to advocate for their special interest?
4. What process did the group use to arrive at a decision on how the funds should be allocated?
5. Why was the exercise difficult?
6. What feelings surfaced during the exercise? Would you have preferred staying out of the group process? Explain.
7. Let's say you were asked to lead the group in a process used to complete this task. What would you do before, during, and after the process to ensure it was efficient and effective?

Exercise 12–D
Conflict Role-Plays

In small groups, role-play one or more of the following scenarios. Perform them in the small group or in front of the large group or class. For each scenario acted out, analyze and discuss:

- What strategies were used?
- What attitudes were depicted?
- What worked and why?
- What didn't and why?

Scenarios

1. You and your roommate are in disagreement over how clean to keep the apartment.
2. You and your parents disagree on whether you should have a car at school.
3. You think one of your employees is harassing another employee sexually.
4. Two of your employees are unable to agree on anything in staff meetings.
5. One of your co-workers is accepting gifts from a supplier; this is forbidden by your company's policy.
6. You think a fellow swimmer is cheating in competitions.

Exercise 12–E
Conflict Assessment

1. Briefly describe one conflict situation in which you found yourself recently (in the past couple of years). What were the reasons for and outcomes of this conflict? _____

_____

_____

_____

2. Using the five conflict styles discussed in this chapter, describe the style you used in resolving the conflict discussed in number 1, pointing to specific behaviors and communication patterns that are evidence of this style. In what ways was this style effective and/or ineffective in this situation? _____

_____

_____

_____

3. What style did the person with whom you were in conflict use? Evidence? In what ways was s/he effective and/or ineffective in this situation? _____

_____

_____

_____

4. If you could replay this scenario, what things would you do the same, and why; what things would you have done differently, and why? _____

_____

_____

_____

_____

5. What conflict style are you most comfortable using? Why? _____

_____

_____

_____

_____

**Exercise 12–F
Humpty Dumpty's
Spaceship Challenge**

In teams of three to six, create a spaceship for Humpty Dumpty (an egg) that will withstand the gravitational forces that occur during a three-foot drop. The spaceship that withstands the highest drop will be the winner. If there is a tie, then the winner will be the spaceship fabricated out of the greatest number of materials. Each spaceship must be fabricated out of at least three materials. Each team only has possession of one material, so you will need to negotiate with other teams to acquire new materials.

Your team will be given 10 minutes to plan your spaceship design. You are to decide what material your spaceship will be made from and determine which teams you will need to negotiate with for materials.

Your team will be given 20 minutes to negotiate material and construct the spaceship. Negotiate as effectively as you possibly can; use any strategies or tactics.

Questions

1. Before approaching your opponents, how did you prepare for the negotiation process?

2. Did you use the same conflict-handling styles for all opponents that you negotiated with? Explain.

3. In this situation, which conflict-handling styles were most successful? Why?

4. Did every negotiation work out exactly as you planned and hoped? Why or why not?

5. What factors helped you in the negotiation process? What could you have done differently to make your negotiations more successful?

6. In performing this exercise, what lessons did you learn about negotiation? How does this exercise relate to negotiations in the "real world"?

Source: Used with permission of the author, Kim Eddleston, doctoral student, University of Connecticut, Storrs, CT. This exercise was presented at the 2000 Eastern Academy of Management/Experiential Learning Association Conference.

**Exercise 12–G
Try This . . .**

1. Observe an argument at work or school. Afterwards, analyze the situation: What is the source of the conflict? What is the level of relationship involved? What strategies are the parties using? What's working? What's not?

2. Analyze a recent news event that involved the use of force or violence (e.g., a school shooting). How could this situation have been handled differently?

3. Observe a TV show or movie. How do the main characters handle conflict effectively and ineffectively? What strategies are used? What strategies could be used? Some potential movies include *The Outsiders, Red Dawn, Easy Rider, Red October, Braveheart, The Little Mermaid, Antz, West Side Story, 12 Angry Men, You've Got Mail, Network, Guess Who's Coming to Dinner, The Color Purple, Iron Giant, Hercules, Pocahontas, Mutiny on the Bounty, Glory.*

Exercise 12–H
Reflection/Action Plan

This chapter focused on conflict management—what it is, why it is important, and how to improve your skills in this area. Complete the worksheet below upon completing all reading and experiential activities for this chapter.

1. The one or two areas in which I am most strong are:

    _____

    _____

    _____

    _____

2. The one or two areas in which I need more improvement are:

    _____

    _____

    _____

    _____

3. If I did only one thing to improve in this area, it would be to:

    _____

    _____

    _____

    _____

4. Making this change would probably result in:

    _____

    _____

    _____

    _____

5. If I did not change or improve in this area, it would probably affect my personal and professional life in the following ways:

    _____

    _____

    _____

    _____

13 Coaching and Mentoring for Improved Performance

How do I:

✓ Identify characteristics of effective coaches and mentors?

✓ Utilize these characteristics to improve my skill as a coach or mentor?

✓ Help others set and achieve goals?

✓ Identify and develop relationships with mentors who can help me in my job and career?

✓ Utilize techniques and strategies to coach or mentor others with whom I work?

Maggie McNair, a bright engineer in her late twenties, realized she needed some guidance in furthering her career. Since she graduated college, she'd been working as a mechanical engineer for a prominent aerospace firm on the West Coast. When she was first hired, she was assigned to several exciting defense-related projects and served as team leader on one of them. She had quickly gained a reputation as a talented, competent engineer; her leadership abilities, along with her technical skills, were being noticed by management. One of her managers, Sam Thompson, mentioned to her that he believed she would be an excellent candidate for the firm's high-potential program.

Recently, however, her work environment lacked motivation and inspiration. Maggie was working with a team of designers and engineers where she felt that her contributions to the projects and the experience she received were invaluable. With defense funds shrinking and firms merging, Maggie also feared being a victim of industry downsizing and wondered if she should be looking elsewhere.

Last week while chatting over an espresso with a former college roommate, Maggie started thinking about a possible career change. Min, a web designer at a young dot-com firm, bubbled over with enthusiasm as she described her job, her co-workers, and her organization. Being part of the start-up team, Min was able to take part in decision making that guided crucial market decisions for the firm. She felt special, like part of a big family. Aside from the good feelings, Min was well compensated—almost 50 percent more than Maggie. And on top of that, Min stood to reap even more substantial rewards once the company went public.

Maggie thought to herself, I could do that. She had several programming classes in college, and more recently, she had taken two computer information systems courses while working part time toward an MBA. Maggie felt confident that she could make the shift if she decided to change careers. Besides, wouldn't it be better to be in an industry that's growing than one that has seen a precipitous decline? However, she had built a reputation and foundation in the aerospace industry. Were there other opportunities she

261

had not examined associated with her current career? If only she knew how to proceed or if she could find someone to provide her with greater insight.

1. What would you do if you were Maggie?
2. What are some steps Maggie could take to help her decide whether a career switch was right for her?
3. What role might Min play in helping her? What role could Sam Thompson play in being a coach or mentor?
4. What role might one of Maggie's professors play in helping her?
5. What benefits might Maggie obtain by getting help? She's been successful thus far; isn't this trend likely to continue?

"Good management consists of showing average people how to do the work of superior people."

Ron Zemke[1]

Good managers are in business to help their business succeed—and they know that the way to do this is to help those around them succeed. Good managers and team leaders take regular employees and team members and give them the confidence, guidance, and information necessary to become exemplars in their work—people who are superior workers. Long reserved for athletes or top performers in business, coaching and mentoring are two techniques recently adapted and formalized by organizations as ways to motivate employees to superior performance. Coaching involves guiding, instructing, and training,[2] with a focus on teaching individuals, groups, or teams specific skills needed to improve their performance. A mentor is a friend or advisor, working one on one. Mentors are typically individuals who have expertise, knowledge, or experience—someone who knows the ropes—within an organization or field and are willing to sponsor and advise the protégé. They gently guide an individual through an organization, giving a person perspective on what it takes to succeed in an organization. Many times coaching or mentoring helps the person being coached or mentored to rise to greater heights than his or her advisor. In this chapter we look at both coaching and mentoring—what they are, why they are important to individuals and organizations, and ways you can develop your skills in both coaching and mentoring others.

"Coaching is unlocking a person's potential to maximize their own performance. It is helping them to learn rather than teaching them."

Harvard Educator Timothy Gallwey

What Is Coaching?

Coaching is a means for managers to provide guidance, insight, and encouragement to their employees for improved work performance through frequent interactions. It is designed to strengthen and enhance learning through a continual day-to-day process going beyond the once-a-year appraisal system.[3] Coaching conveys a set of beliefs, values, and vision and enables goal setting and action steps for the realization of extraordinary results.[4] Because of the interdevelopmental nature of the coaching process, both coaches and the individuals whom they coach benefit by building skills and developing as people. Traditionally, coaching is recognized as a term and process used in sports. In athletics, coaches demonstrate or encourage the effective use of skills, reinforce positive behaviors, and identify and correct negative behaviors. The term "coaching" is now seen as a useful concept in other walks of life, such as business.

In response to merger mania, the proliferation of dot-coms; ever-changing technology, and calls for downsizing and cost cutting, organizations are expecting their employees to do more with less. With fewer employees and frequent changes in job roles, managers cannot watch over every aspect of the job (and employees don't want them to!). Instead, managers need to use their sideline vantage point to empower their employees to perform at high levels when the "coach" is off the field.[5] This notion that managers act as coaches—instead of traditionally top-down oriented supervisors—is especially important given the demands that the globally competitive, technologically complex environment places on organizations' educated and adaptable employees.[6] By acting as a coach (like a facilitator or enabler), rather than a supervisor (like a director or superior), employees' abilities and creativity can be unleashed instead of controlled, resulting in increased morale, productivity, and enhanced interpersonal working relationships.

The Importance and Benefits of Coaching

Traditionally employees looked to their supervisors for direction, decision making, and control. Today's more fluid, less hierarchical working environment calls for a different philosophy or mindset. To remain competitive, organizations need to harness the creative and synergistic capacity of all their employees, not just the ones in leadership positions. The very capabilities that led an organization to success a few years ago could cause its undoing if it refuses to engage in continual learning and renewal. By adapting and creating a new environment where there are leader–employee partnerships—where leaders are more like coaches and less like bosses—individuals thrive and organizations remain competitive and survive.[7] A coaching philosophy and process benefits both individuals and the organization. Specific benefits for individuals and teams include:[8]

■ Coaching reduces employees' fears related to their (and others') status in the organization. By emphasizing collaboration, partnership, and mutual growth, the perception of "manager versus worker" is replaced with a more team-oriented view of "Together we can . . ."

■ Coaching enables workers to feel they are part of the organization rather than used by it. They take ownership in and contribute to organizational performance and success. Employees enjoy working in a healthy environment, one where relationships are rooted in mutual respect and rapport, and constructive and respectful language is encouraged. While some employees are used to and respond to fear and threats, the outcome of this "motivational" approach is compliance, not commitment.

■ Effective coaching endorses rather than diminishes people's skills and abilities. Imagine the little league coach who publicly scolds or belittles a child upon making an error. Now imagine another coach who encourages children to play to their potential, scolds parents for their unhealthy and belittling remarks, and utilizes not only the best players but those who have yet to develop their full potential. For which coach would you rather play? When managers coach effectively, they "accentuate the positive and eliminate the negative," to quote a popular 1940s song. They see more possibilities than limitations in the individual and the organization and take personal responsibility for overcoming those limitations.

■ Coaching helps people to overcome personal obstacles to their success. Good coaches use goal setting and constructive feedback.[9] When good coaches help employees set and achieve goals, they feel a sense of accomplishment. World class athletes Tiger Woods and the Williams sisters (Venus and Serena) didn't fit the traditional mold for American golf and tennis stars. As racial minorities, they sometimes faced prejudice from competitors and detractors. They could have accepted a lesser fate, but the sense of self-worth and self-esteem facilitated by their coaches, their fathers, helped them put concerns about acceptance aside and achieve phenomenal success.

■ When used in team settings, coaching improves team communications and provides a structure for managing conflict. Coaching helps to reinforce team goals and commitments by providing them with external support and insight to effective team processes.

■ Coaching behaviors encourage others to coach. In essence, coaching behaviors beget coaching behaviors. With greater trust and support, employees are more likely to take risks and suggest creative solutions to organizational problems. As employees feel supported and trusted, they become more supportive of other employees and more trusting of management.

Beyond individual and team benefits, coaching provides many benefits for the organization as well.[10] Coaching helps to improve workforce recruitment and retention. People want to join and stay in an organization where they will be respected, trusted, listened to, and valued. It also reduces misunderstanding and mistakes by resulting in a more positive and supportive climate at work through the use of a common language to which everyone can relate. Coaching emphasizes the unique potential of individuals to evoke hidden talents, thereby increasing their ability to contribute to the organization's success.

Effective coaching can help enhance organizational communication with internal and external customers. As employees are more involved in decisions and communications, they play a more active role in relationships with customers both inside and outside of the organization. This will lead to improved performance management, positively affecting external customer service while internally promoting focused performance discussions, the development of new skills, and planning for personal career advancement.

Another important result of coaching is seen in the expansion of entrepreneurial thinking within organizations. Coaching fosters creativity and a building of shared vision. Building on the benefit of trust and support of individuals, coaching creates an atmosphere in which individual creativity is not only supported but also deeply encouraged. Coaching provides organizational members with the opportunity to start new projects or initiate partnerships with suppliers or customers.

Skills and Characteristics of Effective Coaches

Effective coaches acquire a mindset, skills, and values that will help build employee commitment to the organization. Coaching skills or techniques are not seen as genuine when accompanied by an attitude or behaviors that run counter to the goals of coaching. Merely possessing a coaching philosophy is not enough; it is also necessary to have good skills in communication, feedback, and goal setting. Effective coaches have all of the following characteristics or abilities:

■ *A desire to bring out the best in others' performance.* Effective coaches support employees' needs, create choices, seek commitment, and provide means for self-expression.[11]

■ *Ability to give negative (constructive) and positive feedback.* Coaching enables employees to understand their mistakes and how to improve or develop their skills. Effective coaches are able to talk face-to-face with others about performance problems, and they also affirm and acknowledge others' contributions to the organization.

■ *Honesty and trustworthiness.* Effective coaches have a high level of awareness of themselves and how they impact others. Through their actions, they demonstrate their trustworthiness, high personal standards, ability to develop mutual relationships, and willingness to share their wisdom.[12]

■ *Willingness to NOT assign blame.* "Blame the process, not the person." Good coaches are process- and problem-oriented; they focus on how to solve problems rather than focusing on the personality of the people. To do this, they get involved and collaborate to find solutions.

■ *Good communication skills.* Good coaches create an environment in which communication is open and two-way, encouraging employees to bring forth problems as well as opportunities without fear of blame or retribution. Such dialogue builds mutual trust and commitment.

■ *A parallel style of thinking and acting helps managers to balance and attend to both human and business needs.*[13] Good coaches realize that in order to accomplish the organizational goals, they must balance the need for learning with the need for results.

■ *Responsibility and accountability.* Good coaches accept full responsibility for their actions and for what occurs in their environment and encourage others to do the same.[14]

■ *Constructive conflict management.* Effective coaches encourage the clashing of ideas for creativity and innovation and discourage personal conflicts. They stress the team approach and facilitate mutual understanding among all parties involved.

Effective Coaching Behaviors

Now that you know the benefits of coaching and what makes coaches effective, you might be wondering exactly what to do when planning to call an employee (or teammate or team) in for coaching. All situations are different and call for different strategies. The following represents findings of a study of a major service organization in which Stowell examined the behavior of effective and ineffective coaches and their coaching sessions.[15]

■ Coaching sessions require managers to use face-to-face discussions of performance problems. For many managers, this is considered an unpleasant task and is therefore avoided. The best sessions last between 35 and 45 minutes.

■ Effective coaches don't legislate quality; they model it. "Do as I say, not as I do" does not work in this environment. For the leader–employee partnership to work, there has to be mutual respect and trust.

■ Effective coaches and their sessions contain high levels of **supportive behaviors** (words or actions that denote concern or acceptance), low levels or minimal usage of non-supportive behaviors (words or actions that express aggression or power), and moderate levels of **initiating** *or problem-solving* **behaviors** (words or actions that encourage problem solving/resolutions), as shown in Figures 13–1 and 13–2. The leader establishes a framework for the coaching discussion, which might look something like: "We have a situation that deserves some attention. What can we do to solve it? I'm confident in your ability. I'll support you. What do you think would help in this situation?"

Figure 13–1

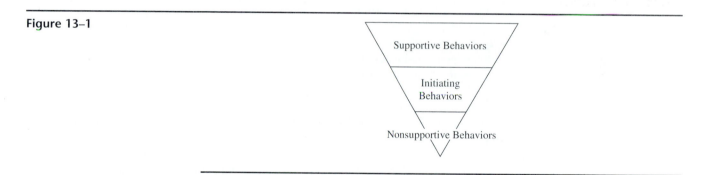

Figure 13–2
Key Leadership Behaviors for Successful Coaching and Coaching Sessions[16]

Supportive Behaviors—A leader's words and actions showing concern and acceptance of employees.

■ Collaboration regarding solutions to problems.
■ Providing help and assistance through training and resources.
■ Concern over the employee's needs and objectives.
■ Empathy for the employee and attention to obstacles and problems.
■ Expression about the value of the employee and his or her contribution to the work.
■ Acceptance of responsibility in situations.
■ Interaction that provides time for the employee to air his or her feelings.

Initiating Behaviors—Initiating and structuring actions and discussions.

■ Feedback and analysis of issues and concerns.
■ Clarification of leader expectations and requirements.
■ Exploration of impact and effects of employee's actions.
■ Action planning around solutions and desired changes.
■ Seeking commitment to the action plan.
■ Clarification of positive and negative consequences connected to future action and plans.

■ Successful coaches use supportive behaviors far more frequently than unsuccessful coaches. These behaviors fall into three categories: verbal (statements which indicate the coach's commitment to and backing of the employee), tangible (statements which offer help, resources, links to other people and information), and active (behaviors and actions that indicate complete and empathic listening, including asking questions, acknowledging and appropriate body language, showing genuine interest). This last category might be most important; it demonstrates the coach's willingness to understand before trying to be understood.

■ The best coaches ask questions that enable the employee to discover how to improve. They collaborate with the employee to analyze situations and performance and jointly find solutions.

■ Successful coaches challenge employees and stimulate resolutions. This is done through initiating action-oriented problem analysis discussions. These problem-solving discussions are best when focusing on one or maximum two issues. Any more would be overwhelming.

■ The best sessions were those in which the coach planned, prepared, and rehearsed prior to the coaching session. Because many find such sessions difficult to do, this preparation can be key to reducing the coach's discomfort with the process, enabling him or her to do the same for their employee.

Counseling

Coaching should not be mistaken for counseling. Some situations call for counseling rather than coaching. It is important for managers to understand the difference between the two. (See Figure 13–3.) **Counseling** is used to address personal or attitudinal problems rather than those related to an individual's ability (or lack thereof). Counseling is a complex task and is best reserved for professionals. It involves listening skills, feedback skills, trustworthiness, and a good deal of patience.

Two methods facilitate the counseling process. The choice of method will be determined by the manager's comfort and ability with counseling and the severity of the problem being addressed in the session. **Directive methods** include probing, questioning, and discussing specific problems and possible solutions. In addition, a manager may have the person discuss her behavior, beliefs, and perceptions in order to help the manager put the individual's emotions and attitudes into perspective.

Another method, the **nondirective approach,** involves being a good listener and sounding board. Listening may be the most valuable and helpful means for identifying the source and solution for counseling-related problems. Sometimes people just need to disclose the way they are feeling to relieve stress and gain a new perspective on a situation. In so doing, they often find solutions to their own problems.

Seldom should a manager get involved in counseling an employee. Good managers recognize their limitations in helping others and refer employees with personal or

**Figure 13–3
A Comparison between
Coaching and Counseling**

	Coaching	Counseling
Objective:	To reinforce positive behaviors and correct negative behaviors, to gain positive work outcomes and enhance relationships.	To facilitate understanding of behaviors and to obtain a willingness to change.
Means:	Pass information, set standards, provide insight, encouragement, direction, and guidance.	Two methods: Directive—assuring, probing, and questioning. Nondirective—listening and supporting.
Problems Stem from:	Lack of ability, information, or understanding and incompetence.	Attitudes, defensiveness, personality clashes, and other emotional problems.

emotional problems to other professionals or resources, such as the organization's employee assistance program. Many organizations have employee assistance and wellness programs to assist with personal and health problems ranging from mental illness, substance abuse, day care, and family issues as well as physical health issues and financial planning.

Helping Others Set Goals

A major component of coaching is helping others to set goals. Receiving performance feedback through coaching can be difficult for employees. By incorporating goal setting into the coaching activity, a manager can motivate an employee to set a new course or direction.

Managers and organizations can have a dramatic impact on subordinate goal attainment.[17] To increase employees' chances for attaining goals, the organization's environment must be conducive to individual growth and development in the context of organizational goals. Underscoring this philosophy with managerial support via coaching—both in setting the example and supporting others to do the same—will also facilitate the goal-setting process. Managers need to be aware of behaviors that can positively impact others in the setting and achievement of personal and organizational goals.

Goals you set for yourself are more likely to be achieved when they are SMART (specific, measurable, achievable and attainable, realistic, and time bound). This is also true of goals set by your teammates or employees. Coach others to ensure their goals conform to and contain SMART elements. Work with them to ensure that the desired outcome is clear and that they have the necessary skills and resources to accomplish their goals. Good managers help others set "stretch" goals—those that require total effort but are not so unrealistic that subordinates avoid committing to what is perceived to be impossible. Studies demonstrate that performance increases with the level of goal difficulty, providing that the individual is committed to achieving it and has the ability to do so.[18] Goals should be challenging yet realistic.

Once SMART goals are set, your work isn't done. As a coach, you might need to provide periodic feedback and encouragement, especially if the goal is particularly complex and long-term. Encourage others to break up large, complex goals into smaller objectives, and set checkpoints and processes to follow up. Some employees may prefer feedback initiated by the manager, while others prefer to provide periodic updates. There may even be employees who are accustomed to the "no news is good news" approach. Use your judgment and assessment of their capabilities and past performance to determine how often and by what mechanism interim performance is checked and modified, if necessary. In addition, goal setting is an ongoing process. Your work helping others set goals is likely never done, though your level of involvement may change over time. Encourage employees to establish and update goals periodically, annually at the minimum.

Goals that are SMART are more likely to be achieved. The same can be said for goals that are personally meaningful or externally rewarding. When employees set goals that advance personal needs and desires for growth and development, their intrinsic motivation to achieve those goals will be high. Employee commitment can be increased further when they stand to gain recognition, perquisites, or other financial rewards when goals are achieved. Managers or coaches can clarify the existence of such organizational rewards or create new ones. A perfect example of this is in sales organizations. Top sellers within a specified period of time are likely to be awarded bonuses, priority parking spaces, minivacations, or other special treatment, like access to desirable training opportunities. These rewards can encourage individual commitment to (and healthy competition between co-workers in obtaining) rewards in such organizations. When such rewards are not available, managers can increase goal commitment and achievement by using an informal chat or note to express their satisfaction and appreciation for the employee's positive efforts and improvements.

Finally, commitment to goals will vary directly with the amount of participation and input from the employee in setting the goals. You cannot set someone else's goals and expect to have high commitment and motivation. In addition, some researchers have

**Figure 13–4
Five Steps for
Helping Others
Set Goals**[19]

PREPARE—Be informed on the organization's goals and direction to ensure a match between these and the goals of the individual. Also be sure to review the individual's past performance and accomplishments to ensure goals are attainable and challenging.

CLARIFY—Provide an overall picture on how the individual's goals and objectives fit with the organizational objectives. Ensure that they know their part in the whole.

DECIDE—Work together to decide what would be attainable, desirable, and challenging goals. Put the goals in writing and make them public.

COMMIT—Determine how you can commit to support, assist, and facilitate others in achieving their goals. Such support might include making phone calls, arranging for training, coordinating with the efforts of other individuals or departments, and obtaining needed equipment.

PARTICIPATE—Schedule regularly planned meetings to discuss progress, revise goals if necessary, and set higher or additional goals. Make goal setting a part of the process, continue the cycle on a regular basis.

hypothesized that allowing participation in the goal-setting process increases a person's perception of control and fairness.[20] Have you ever been asked by someone else to get high grades, quit smoking, or lose weight? Were you successful? Chances are, unless and until the goal is yours, you're likely not to give it your all. Depending on the employees' understanding of organizational goals and their role in achieving those goals, managers can trust employees to set their own goals or managers can solicit employee input and set goals participatively. Extend the notion of participative goal setting to include goal checking. In other words, jointly develop a system that will enable individuals to gauge their performance to jointly established goals and know whether (and why) they have successfully completed them.[21]

Effectively helping others to set goals is a key element in managerial coaching. Figure 13–4 summarizes and highlights steps and behaviors necessary for helping others set and achieve goals.

What Is Mentoring?

"Mentoring is an enduring phenomenon that has survived several major, historical paradigm shifts. The fact that it has endured, documented, for millennia . . . suggests that mentoring fulfills some deep, important yearnings for connection between the generations."

James Clawson[22]

Mentoring has been traditionally defined as a unique interpersonal relationship between two individuals, a *mentor* and a *protégé*. The **mentor** is generally a higher-ranking employee who has advanced organizational (or industry) experience and knowledge and who is committed to providing guidance and support to the **protégé's** career development.[23] Recently, mentoring has been described in more reciprocal terms, indicating the belief that benefits of such relationships accrue to mentors as well as to protégés.[24] For example, at General Electric, CEO Jack Welch and his management team found that more senior employees were benefiting from their partnerships with their protégés—the younger protégés were teaching their mentors about how to better utilize their computers!

The popularity of formalizing mentoring within organizations has grown in the last decade. More and more companies are attempting to reap the rewards of implementing mentoring programs. In fact, in one of *Fortune* magazine's issues on the 100 best companies in the United States, 60 of 100 companies had implemented formal mentoring programs. Similar examples are shown in Figure 13–5. Mentoring relationships were even the theme of a half-hour episode of the enormously popular 1990s television situation comedy *Seinfeld,* yet another example that mentoring is perceived to be of high societal interest.[25]

**Figure 13–5
Formal Mentoring in
Action**[26]

IBM—(1999) Executive Resource Program which has been particularly helpful to retain women—it helped to increase the number of women in executive positions by 27% from 1998–1999.

Arthur Andersen—(1998) Initiated a mentoring program for the growth and retention of women (GROW).

Digital Consulting Software and Service (Houston)—formalized mentoring has helped them to achieve an 80% retention rate for female employees.

Coca Cola Co.—developed mentoring programs to help with diversity training for all employees

Hewlett Packard—(1992) developed an Accelerated Development program to combine mentoring, planning and leadership workshops, helping them to save on the cost of hiring new employees.

Lucent Technologies—actively recruit employees to participate in mentoring programs to help attract and retain talented employees.

Hewlett-Packard, Intel, and National Semiconductor—developed mentoring programs for high schools, colleges, and grade school students and teachers to encourage interest in IT careers.

We all know that teaching through experience can be one of the most effective methods of transferring knowledge. Which would you prefer, being handed a company's five-inch-thick manual, or having someone "show you the ropes"? In addition to teachers, mentors play many roles, including role model, confidant, coach, suggester, advisor, counselor, encourager, and friend. These roles fall into two broad categories of mentor functions, career and psychosocial:[27]

Career functions: Aspects of the relationship that enhance career advancement such as sponsorship, exposure, visibility, coaching, protection, challenging assignments, and career strategizing.

Psychosocial functions: Aspects of the relationship that enhance a sense of competency, identity, and effectiveness in a professional role, including role modeling, acceptance and confirmation, counseling, friendship, support, and personal feedback.

When done well, mentors can help protégés gain needed job information and experience, as well as support and encouragement (or psychosocial support[28]) to advance in their job and career.

The Importance of Mentoring

Why are we interested? First, because of trends in the business environment that make mentoring not only desirable but also essential for the success of both organizations and employees. Second, because of the indisputable benefits available to those involved in a mentoring relationship. We'll begin with the business trends.

One trend responsible for the increasing reliance on mentoring is the fact that more organizations are viewing their people—as opposed to their products, services, or assets—as the chief source of sustainable competitive advantage.[29] Peter Drucker asserts that knowledge is the only meaningful resource in today's economy; knowledge and the people within which knowledge resides have become the primary assets and sources of competitive advantage. As the competition for highly skilled and dedicated professionals heats up, firms are focusing more attention on developing their current employees. If sharing knowledge provides added value in the knowledge economy, then involvement in productive mentoring relationships should benefit both individual participants and the organization.[30] Already companies are finding that mentoring programs are very attractive to candidates in the recruiting marketplace. Companies with mentoring in place are viewed by candidates as more people-oriented than those that don't have these programs.

Another trend is the dramatic changes in the nature of individual career development. Bidding farewell to the days when employees climbed the same corporate ladder over the course of 30 years, we now see new career patterns described as "Protean" or "boundaryless," meaning that individual careers can change shape or form at any time.[31] Part of what is driving these changes is organizational downsizing and rapid technological change that can cause previously valuable skills to suddenly become obsolete, necessitating changes in an individual's career path. Mentors can assist protégés to navigate the less secure waters of today's careers, helping them to learn specific skills and establish connections with influential decision makers.

Benefits of Mentoring

One reason for the popularity of mentoring is that it can provide benefits to both protégé and mentor. Anecdotal evidence suggests that protégés may be assisted in many ways, both professionally and personally. Figure 13–6 explains many of the benefits that can be derived from obtaining a mentor.

Recent research on mentoring's effects confirms much of what has been expected. Studies which empirically examined the impact of mentoring compare protégés and nonprotégés, and confirm that protégés receive more promotions, have higher incomes, have higher career satisfaction, have higher job satisfaction, and are less likely to express an interest to leave than their nonmentored counterparts.[32]

Effective mentoring programs can bring about benefits for the mentor as well, some of which are listed in Figure 13–7. Mentoring has been found to be a reciprocal process, "in learning you teach and in teaching you learn." Through their relationship with a protégé, mentors have been able to hone their interpersonal skills, gain insight into their ideas and perceptions, and increase their awareness through diverse experiences.[33]

Another reason mentoring is being offered by more and more corporations is its applicability to company diversity programs. Mentoring programs, which have been proven to bolster a person's chances for advancement, are now being offered by many corporations to all employees, with an emphasis on minorities and women, who have long been underrepresented in many industries and organizations. Companies are finding that offering mentoring programs is an excellent way to boost the performance and advancement rates of minorities and women, as well as build confidence and boost morale.

Given the tangible benefits available to both individuals and organizations, it is easy to see why mentoring has been integrated into the structure and processes of numerous and diverse types of organizations, including higher education, law firms, police departments, and large corporations such as Douglas Aircraft, Motorola, and Coca Cola.

Qualities of an Effective Mentor

What makes for effective mentors? What characteristics or qualities facilitate their ability to help others—inside and outside their firm or industry—reach their full potential? Mentoring expert Kathy Kram compiled a list (see Figure 13–8) of qualities—ranging from willingness and desire to be a mentor to possessing highly developed interpersonal skills—that aid in a mentor's effectiveness.

**Figure 13–6
Mentoring Benefits
for Protégés**

- Career and leadership development—career preparation and leadership training.
- Increased self-confidence, self-awareness, and growth.
- Mutual sharing and enhancement of relationship.
- Development of friendships that can provide valuable contacts and expand associations in related networks.[34]
- Development of interpersonal skills—by working with a more experienced individual, protégés learn by observation[35] and practice.
- Protection for individual and organization against potentially damaging experiences.
- Gaining valuable inside information into the workings of the organization for movement in the organization, insight into informal workings.
- Saving time. By allowing the protégé to learn from others' experience, they don't have to reinvent the wheel; they can speed up the advancement process and get a jump on the learning curve.[36]

**Figure 13–7
Mentoring Benefits
for Mentors**

- Experiences shared learning and positive results.
- Gains personal satisfaction from helping another.
- Develops patience, insight, and understanding.
- Is exposed to cultural, social, or economic characteristics different from their own.
- Improves their leadership and communication skills.
- Gains personal experience for future career options, including training, teaching, or counseling.
- Trains employees in ways which will meet future needs for their organization, thereby ensuring its future competitiveness.

**Figure 13–8
Characteristics of
Effective Mentors**[37]

- Expertise and experience in their profession, successful in their professional endeavors.
- Enthusiasm and genuine interest for the profession.
- Desire and energy to help others.
- Available time to help others.
- Ability to relate to others in all types of settings.
- Good interpersonal skills; good listening skills, a high level of emotional intelligence or ability to read others and situations and act appropriately.
- Skilled in giving honest and detailed constructive feedback.
- Supportive in their work for others.
- Ability to work well with a diverse group of people.
- High yet achievable standard of performance for themselves and others.
- Worthy of emulation.
- Willingness to expose their protégé to a broad-based network of professionals and to share information about organizational norms.
- Ability to separate personal needs and concerns from professional demeanor when interacting with a protégé.

Types of Mentoring Relationships

Many of us have functioned as mentors at one time or another, perhaps without the formal designation. We might have a kid brother of sister whom we taught how to ride a bicycle, or perhaps we helped a new classmate or employee learn the rules of the game. Mentoring, and mentoring relationships, can be formal or informal. **Formal mentors** (also called *organizational* or *managerial mentors*) are relationships officially designated by the institution through a formalized mentoring program. Mentors' relationships with protégés are arranged through a formal matching process and with the assistance of an external organizing force (for example, human resources). Formal mentoring relationships usually have a specific time frame, a method for termination, and one or more checkpoints for goal setting and meetings.

Most of us have been involved in the other type of relationship, known as an **informal or peer relationship.**[38] These relationships often develop spontaneously and without a specific plan. They occur when a mentor and protégé find each other (either when a potential protégé seeks another's advice or a potential mentor notices another's potential and offers to take the protégé under his or her wing) and negotiate terms of their relationship. Many informal or peer relationships develop over time and are very effective and rewarding if there is a consistency with needs, goals, and resources. Based on the level of commitment, intensity, types of issues, and needs addressed by those involved in a peer relationship, three types of relationships can be identified and represented on a continuum:[39]

- **Informational peers** benefit most by exchanging information about their work or organization. The relationship is characterized by low levels of self-disclosure and trust and demands little in terms of time and support.

- **Collegial peers** tend to trust more and share more, delving somewhat into issues beyond work, including family and personal. Peers request and receive direct and honest feedback.

- **Special peers** exhibit high levels of trust, self-disclosure, and self-expression; they share ideas and advice on a multitude of issues and allow for the exchange of dilemmas, fears, and concerns.

As a peer mentoring relationship deepens toward the "special" category, we find a greater number and depth of mentoring functions being served. In addition to the formal and informal types of relationships, we see the development of a new form: co-mentoring.[40] In this type of relationship, each person is both mentor and protégé. The newer or less experienced members share their technology skills or what's considered the latest thinking in a field, while the more experienced members share their expertise and experience in the organization and industry.

Four Stages of Mentoring Relationships

Most mentoring relationships evolve through four stages. They are described below:[41]

1. Orientation and initiation. In this phase, the mentor and protégé are assigned or select one another, disclose information, and begin to build trust. This phase usually lasts between 6 and 12 months, during which time initial wishes become realized (e.g., coaching is provided) and the relationship takes on significance for both parties. Traditional relationships begin face to face and within a single organization; however, technology has enabled such relationships to occur virtually, using e-mail and other methods (e.g., phone, and videoconference) to connect geographically distant partners. (See Online Mentoring, Exercise 13–H.)

2. Cultivation. During this phase, which may last between one and five years, the relationship becomes more rewarding for both parties. There is continued growth and development in career and psychosocial support functions, mutual trust, sharing and challenging of ideas, and learning—for both protégés (gain knowledge and insight) and their mentors (gain loyalty, a sense of helping another).

3. Separation. Most mentoring relationships typically fade after a few years. At this point, the protégé is ready to assert more independence and work more autonomously, or perhaps the mentor experiences a significant change in his or her career (for example, retirement). Or, one or both may change jobs, creating geographical and psychological distance to the relationship. When opportunities to interact are constrained, mentor and protégé may step back from the formal relationship, or they may continue, depending on their commitment to the relationship.

4. Redefinition. Depending on the nature of the separation, the mentor and protégé will often redefine their mentoring relationship. Typically, the mentor's job is "done" and peer status is achieved. Protégés express appreciation for their mentors, who now see their protégés as equals, similar to peer colleagues or friends.

How to Find a Mentor

If your company does not have a formal mentoring program, you can find a potential mentor or mentors through informal channels.

- Clarify your career goals and coaching needs. Ask yourself why you're seeking a mentor, what your objectives are, and how someone more senior in the organization (who's not your boss) can be helpful to you.

- Identify potential candidates. Have you served on a committee or task force with someone who's a few levels above you and whose ideas you respect? Did you have a chance to develop a rapport with that person? If so, approach the person directly, indicating your interest in succeeding at the organization and ask whether he or she would be willing to meet with you from time to time to offer career advice and insights into the company and industry.

- Involve your boss. Often your boss will be supportive of your interest in being mentored, especially if your boss is people-oriented and understands the importance of developing staff.

- Network with others. If you're relatively new and haven't had the chance to develop your own network, your associates and co-workers might have some contacts that could be helpful to you.

Limitations of Mentoring

It's hard to deny the value of mentoring, especially in this environment of continuous, complex, and transformational change. However, mentoring may not always have the positive impact it is designed to have. Mentoring partners and organizations should be aware of the limitations or possible roadblocks associated with the building and maintaining of mentoring relationships. As much as we would like to believe otherwise, mentoring relationships don't always work. Just as relationships with friends and loved ones can become dysfunctional, so too can those with a mentor. When dysfunctions arise (e.g., codependence, abuse of power, inappropriate intimacy), it is important for organizations and individuals to take steps to redefine or dissolve the relationship when it is not working for one or both of the parties involved.[42]

Another issue in mentoring is that mentors, despite their desire to help, may not have adequate time to devote to a protégé. Formal programs typically take the time commitment into account when designing and implementing mentoring. However, mentors may be promoted or become involved in projects which require additional time. This forces the mentor to choose between job-related needs and those of the protégé. When the former is chosen, mentors might feel guilty, and without the benefit of an explanation, protégés might wonder why their support system is suddenly unavailable. By contrast, a protégé might become promoted or be given greater responsibility or visibility. Some mentors, feeling threatened by the protégé's success and seeing the protégé as a competitor or rival who could threaten their professional or personal image, might subtly (or not so subtly) attempt to sabotage their protégé's career. This is more likely to occur when a mentor is in the same function and organization as the protégé and is compounded when the mentor lacks personal or organizational assurance of his or her role in the organization.

Mentoring may result in a mismatch of resources or a mismatch between the mentor and protégé in goals, perceptions, and personality. For example, a mentor may be selected on the basis of his or her position in the organization, yet may lack the specific skills or resources desired by the protégé. Similarly, a protégé may feel that the mentor has delivered less time or attention than what was expected or promised. Finally, despite their strengths, mentors may inadvertently display weaknesses, such as a negative work style and bad habits, which are then emulated by the protégé.

Mentoring relationships can also suffer when protégés become overly submissive to the mentor. This is especially likely when both parties are in the same chain of command. A protégé may become submissive to the mentor, unwilling to disagree with the mentor's viewpoints or share pertinent information that might be damaging (e.g., concerns about performance), when a protégé fears power inherent in the mentor's position. In such a situation, the benefits of mentoring are not realized because of the protégé's concerns about how their true views or beliefs could impact performance appraisals or desire for retribution.[43] What starts out well may not remain so. A mentoring relationship can be destructive, and the dynamics change if interests of the parties change. This may be especially problematic in a formal mentoring program where there is inertia supporting the status quo and possibly fear of loss of prestige or reputation should either party request the dissolution of the relationship.

These limitations can exist in any type of mentoring relationship or in any context. Other limitations might be specific to the organization as a whole. Even in organizations that formally support and implement mentoring, such support may be more lip service or marketing hype than reality. This could happen for several reasons. First, should an organization suddenly face a severe market threat, it is likely to respond in a reactionary mode. That is, short-term thinking and shortcuts take precedence over planning and long-term fixes. While mentoring may be seen as valuable, the current "fire" may need immediate attention, whereas the long-term building of human capability is relegated to the back burner. Another possibility is the potential disconnect between the leaders' espoused philosophy about mentoring and a reward system which runs counter to it. Related to this are fears or mismanaged expectations that reduce managers' willingness to carry out the mentoring policy or philosophy. Mentoring will fail if the environment does not support it.

A limitation for mentoring facing many organizations is a lack of sufficient female and minority role models.[44] The glass ceiling effect, argued by Kanter and others, explains why so few women have positions at the most senior organizational level. For female and minority employees hoping to partner with someone who understands them and their challenges, finding a high-ranking female or minority—especially one who is willing to devote the time and attention necessary—might be difficult. Discouraged, they may ignore their desire for a mentor or look outside the organization or industry for a mentor. It is suggested that gender of the parties involved may impact the functionality of a mentoring relationship. Sexual harassment or improper behaviors have been reported in cross-gender partnerships. There is also the potential for improper behaviors, such as abuse of power and discrimination, in cross-racial relationships.[45]

Consequently, since some organizations do not have formal mentoring programs, they remain unconvinced that mentoring brings about measurable outcomes. Despite the touted benefits of mentoring, some may question whether the outcomes are a result of the relationship or would have evolved naturally.

Means for Protégés to Make Mentoring Work

- Respect the mentor's time constraints. Focus on just a few quality meetings rather than numerous surface discussions.

- Act professionally at all times. Only meet in public places during standard business hours.

- Be realistic. Having a mentor doesn't guarantee you'll receive promotions and advancement opportunities. Mentoring does offer you insights into how an organization operates and helps you understand decisions that are made—both about the company overall and about you and your career.

- Be selective. Choose a mentor who is respected in the organization and understands the organizational processes, one who knows the ropes.

- Make mentoring a two-way street. After awhile you should be contributing to the mentor's knowledge of the business you're in, just as that person is contributing to your understanding.

- Demonstrate your trustworthiness. Always treat as confidential any sensitive company information the mentor shares with you.

- Be willing to accept gracefully all feedback the mentor is willing to provide you. Encourage feedback by requesting it from the mentor.

- Use your mentor to discuss professional interests, not personal problems.

- You might want to seek out two types of mentors: One would be a senior person in the organization regardless of gender or race who can offer you solid information about the company; the other would be the same gender or race as you who can offer you insights into success strategies that are particularly effective for someone of your gender or race at the organization.

Misperceptions of Mentoring

The key to effective mentoring relationships is to fit the mentor with the protégé, in terms of goals, commitment, and needs. The matching process should go beyond personality—they need to be able to work together, trust and respect one another; the relationship may develop and enhance the situation at a later time.[46] Mentoring needs to be kept in perspective with its benefits, limitations, and variations. Research has shown that the importance of mentoring may have been overestimated; by presenting it as the answer to all developmental problems, its meaning may have become oversimplified. Some of the major misperceptions about mentoring are:[47]

- The primary beneficiary in the mentor relationship is the junior person. In truth, an effective mentoring relationship provides reciprocal benefits.

- A mentor relationship is always a positive experience for both individuals. As discussed, there can be negative effects of dysfunctional mentoring relationships.

- Mentoring relationships look the same in all work settings. Actually, each mentoring relationship takes on unique characteristics, even those that exist within the same company or industry.

- Mentor relationships are readily available to those who want them. In reality, not all organizations subscribe to mentoring so informal relationships need to be cultivated. Identifying mentoring opportunities and building relationships is left to individual effort.

■ Finding a mentor is the key to individual growth and career advancement. We must remember that mentoring is not the magic solution to success; it is a tool to aid in achieving success. Everyone must take responsibility for all aspects of their growth and development.

Summary

Coaching and mentoring do not guarantee that our careers will advance. We still need to take our careers into our own hands. But they are extremely effective tools for companies interested in developing their people. In this chapter we have seen how coaching and mentoring can be of benefit to individuals and organizations, and discussed strategies for effective coaching and mentoring. The best managers are those who actively seek out coaching and mentoring relationships for their own benefit, as well as for the benefit of their employees and their organizations. Following are some exercises designed to help you assess your skills and improve in both areas.

Key Terms and Concepts

Career functions	Mentoring
Coaching	Mentor
Collegial peers	Nondirective approach
Counseling	Orientation and initiation stage
Cultivation	Protégé
Directive methods	Psychosocial functions
Formal mentors	Redefinition stage
Informal or peer relationships	Separation stage
Informational peers	Special peers
Initiating behaviors	Supportive behaviors

Endnotes

1. Ron Zemke, *Coaching Knock Your Socks off Service* (Amacom: New York, 1997).

2. Brian Walker, "Debunking the Five Myths of Coaching," *Training and Development,* March 2000, p. 2.

3. Gary S. Bielous, "Effective Coaching: Improving Marginal Performers," *Supervision,* July 1998, p. 15.

4. Corporate Coach University International, **www.ccui.com,** May 2000.

5. Jeremy Lebediker, "The Supervisor as a Coach: Four Essential Models for Setting Performance Expectations," *Supervision,* Dec. 1995, p. 14.

6. Bruce Hodes, "A New Foundation in Business Culture: Managerial Coaching" *Industrial Management,* Sept.–Oct. 1992, p. 27.

7. Hodes, 1992.

8. Corporate Coach University International, **www.ccui.com,** May 2000.

9. Robert W. Lucas, "Effective Feedback Skills for Trainers and Coaches," *HR Focus,* July 1994, p. 7.

10. Corporate Coach University International, **www.ccui.com,** May 2000.

11. Steven J. Stowell, "Coaching: A Commitment to Leadership," *Training and Development Journal,* June 1988, pp. 34–38.

12. Ibid.

13. Ibid.

14. Corporate Coach University International, **www.ccui.com,** May 2000.

15. Stowell, 1988.

16. Ibid.

17. Gary P. Latham and Edwin A. Locke, "Goal Setting—A Motivational Technique That Works," *Organizational Dynamics,* Autumn 1979, pp. 68–80.

18. Shawn K. Yearta, Sally Maitlis, and Rob B. Briner, "An Exploratory Study of Goal Setting Theory and Practice: A Motivational Technique That Works?" *Journal of Occupational and Organizational Psychology,* Sept. 1995, p. 237.

19. Cynthia A. Mulhearn, "Seeking New Heights: How and Why Goal-Setting Works," *Managers Magazine,* June 1994, p. 13.

20. M. Erez and F. H. Kanfer, "The Role of Goal Acceptance in Goal Setting and Task Performance," *Academy of Management Review,* 1983, pp. 45–46.

21. Yearta et al., 1995.

22. Quote by James Clawson, Professor at University of Virginia Darden School, 1996.

23. Ellen A. Fagenson, "The Mentor Advantage: Perceived Career/Job Experiences of Protégés versus Nonprotégés," *Journal of Organizational Behavior,* 1989, pp. 309–320; Kathy E. Kram, *Mentoring at Work* (Glenview, IL: Scott Foresman and Co., 1985); Raymond A. Noe, "An Investigation of the Determinants of Successful Assigned Mentoring Relationships," *Personnel Psychology,* 1988, pp. 457–479; and Terri A. Scandura, "Mentorship and Career Mobility: An Empirical Investigation," *Journal of Organizational Behavior,* 1988, pp. 169–179.

24. Kathy E. Kram, "A Relational Approach to Career Development." In D. T. Hall (ed.), *The Career Is Dead—Long Live the Career,* pp. 132–157 (San Francisco: Jossey Bass, 1996); B. R. Ragins, "Diversified Mentoring Relationships in Organizations: A Power Perspective," *Academy of Management Review,* 1997, pp. 482–521.

25. Troy R. Nielsen, "The Developmental Journey of Mentoring Research and Practice," paper presented at the annual Academy of Management meeting, Chicago, 1999.

26. Jade Boyd, "Firms Work to Keep Women—Flextime, Mentoring Programs Interest Retention Efforts in IT," *Internetweek,* Nov. 27, 2000, p. 90; and Talila Baron, "IT Talent Shortage Renews Interest in Mentoring," *Information Week,* April 24, 2000.

27. Terri A. Scandura, "Dysfunctional Mentoring Relationships and Outcomes," *Journal of Management,* May 1, 1998, p. 449.

28. Kathy E. Kram, *Mentoring At Work: Developmental Relationships in Organizational Life,* Scott Foresman, 1985. Reprinted by permission of Addison-Wesley Educational Publishers, Inc., p. 23.

29. Peter F. Drucker, *Managing for the Future: The 1990s and Beyond* (New York: Dutton, 1992); J. Pfeffer, T. Hatano, and T. Santalainen, "Producing Sustainable Competitive Advantage through the Effective Management of People," *Academy of Management Executive,* 1995, pp. 55–72.

30. Nielsen, 1999.

31. M. B. Arthur and D. M. Rousseau, "The Boundaryless Career as a New Employment Principle." In M. B. Arthur and D. M. Rousseau (eds.), *The Boundaryless Career* (New York: Oxford University Press, 1996), pp. 3–20; D. T. Hall, "Protean Careers of the 21st Century," *Academy of Management Executive* 10 (1996), pp. 8–16.

32. List of benefits confirmed in the following studies: Dreher and Ash, 1990; Scandura, 1992; Whitely, Dougherty, and Dreher, 1991; Turban and Dougherty, 1994; Chao, Walz, and Gardner, 1992; Fagenson, 1989; Scandura and Viator, 1994.

33. Patricia M. Buhler, "A New Role for Managers: The Move from Directing to Coaching," *Supervision,* Oct. 1, 1998, p. 16.

34. Buhler, 1998.

35. A. Bandura, *A Social Learning Theory* (Englewood Cliffs, N.J.: Prentice Hall, 1977).

36. Buhler, 1998.

37. Kram, 1985.

38. Kram, 1985, pp. 134–139.

39. Kram, 1985.

40. Andy Hargraves and Michael Fullan, "Mentoring in the New Millennium," *Theory into Practice* 39 (2000), p. 50.

41. Kathy E. Kram, "Phases of the Mentoring Relationship," *Academy of Management Journal* 26, (1983), pp. 608–625.

42. Scandura, 1998.

43. Ibid.

44. Gary N. Powell, *Women and Men in Management,* Second Ed. (Newbury, CA: Sage Publications, 1993), p. 207.

45. Scandura, 1998.

46. Buhler, 1998.

47. Kram, 1995, pp. 194–200.

Exercise 13–A
Assessing Yourself

Circle the response that most closely correlates with each item below.

	Agree		Neither		Disagree

1. When I work with others, I serve as a facilitator or enabler, empowering those with whom I work (classmates, team members, employees).   1 2 3 4 5

2. I find ways to draw out the creativity and synergy inherent in those with whom I work.   1 2 3 4 5

3. When working with others I emphasize collaboration and partnership rather than a superior/subordinate mindset.   1 2 3 4 5

4. I try to make employees and team members feel they are part of the organization or team rather than powerless to effect change.   1 2 3 4 5

5. I develop relationships that are based on mutual respect.   1 2 3 4 5

6. I use (and encourage others to use) constructive and respectful language when working with others.   1 2 3 4 5

7. I use goal setting and constructive feedback rather than fear or threats to motivate others to action.   1 2 3 4 5

8. I try to acknowledge rather than minimize others' skills and abilities.   1 2 3 4 5

9. I look for the positive in all with whom I work.   1 2 3 4 5

10. I take risks and suggest creative solutions in work settings and encourage others to do so.   1 2 3 4 5

11. When working with others, I acknowledge the unique potential each person has to offer.   1 2 3 4 5

12. I am committed to bringing out the best in others.   1 2 3 4 5

13. I am able to give both negative (constructive) and positive feedback to others.   1 2 3 4 5

14. I help others learn from their mistakes rather than criticize them.   1 2 3 4 5

15. I am aware of myself and how I impact others.   1 2 3 4 5

16. I have high personal standards and am willing to share these with others.   1 2 3 4 5

17. I focus on problem solving rather than on blaming individuals when problems arise.   1 2 3 4 5

18. I encourage others to offer input.   1 2 3 4 5

19. I accept full responsibility for my actions.   1 2 3 4 5

		Agree		Neither		Disagree
20.	I encourage the clashing of ideas for the purpose of fostering creativity.	1	2	3	4	5
21.	My actions are consistent with my words.	1	2	3	4	5
22.	I ask questions that enable others to improve their performance.	1	2	3	4	5
23.	I initiate action-oriented problem-solving discussions.	1	2	3	4	5
24.	I refer someone with personal or emotional problems elsewhere for help.	1	2	3	4	5
25.	I set (and help others to set) goals that are specific, measurable, achievable, realistic, and time specific.	1	2	3	4	5
26.	I set "stretch" goals for myself and others.	1	2	3	4	5
27.	I provide ongoing encouragement and feedback to others.	1	2	3	4	5
28.	I let others set their goals, rather than imposing my own.	1	2	3	4	5
29.	I serve as a mentor or protégé to others or am willing to do so.	1	2	3	4	5
30.	I am willing to share my experience and expertise with others.	1	2	3	4	5
31.	I have the desire and energy to help others.	1	2	3	4	5
32.	I am able to relate to others in all types of settings.	1	2	3	4	5
33.	I maintain a professional demeanor when interacting with others.	1	2	3	4	5

If your total score was 99 or higher, you may want to develop a plan to improve your skills in coaching and mentoring.

Exercise 13–B
Is a Winning Coach an Effective One?

Below is a list of several well-known coaches and the teams or individuals whom they've coached (presently or formerly). Most of these individuals are considered successful by their teams, peers, and fans. Evaluate what you know about the behaviors, mannerisms, and techniques they use in their coaching.

Bela Karolyi (coached several gold-medal winning women gymnasts and teams)

Pat Riley (LA Lakers, NY Knicks, Miami Heat)

Bobby Knight (Indiana University)

Jimmy Johnson (University of Miami, Dallas Cowboys, Miami Dolphins)

Vince Lombardi (Green Bay Packers)

Debbie Ryan (University of Virginia, women's basketball)

Tom Landry (Dallas Cowboys)

Rick Pittino (University of Kentucky, Boston Celtics)

Phil Jackson (Chicago Bulls, LA Lakers)

Pat Summit (Tennessee Lady Volunteers)

Lou Holtz (Notre Dame, University of South Carolina)

Bobby Bowden (Florida State University)

John Thompson (former coach of Georgetown basketball)

John Chaney (St. Johns University)

Dennis Green (Minnesota Vikings)

Questions

1. Why are they successful? _____

_____

_____

_____

2. What characteristics do they possess that facilitate the building of world-class athletes and teams?

_____

_____

_____

_____

3. Even though they and their athletes win, is it possible their coaching style and methods leave something to be desired?

_____

_____

_____

_____

4. Based on your observation and evaluation, what might you do differently and why? ___

_____

_____

_____

_____

**Exercise 13–C
Coaching Clinic**

Think of a coach you have had in the past. It can be from sports, school, debate club, and so on. From your experiences with this coach, answer the following questions.

What about their coaching style made them effective (characteristics, behaviors, attitudes)?

_____

_____

_____

_____

_____

What about their coaching style made them less than effective? _____

_____

_____

_____

_____

From your observations, and using the grid that follows, make a list of characteristics that you believe are necessary for effective coaching. Compare and supplement your list with characteristics provided in the chapter. Now evaluate yourself as to your level of competency with the skill, trait, or characteristic. Then determine an action plan on how you can improve this characteristic, trait, or behavior.

Necessary Characteristic	Your Level of Competency (Low, Medium, High)	Action Plan for Improvement
1.		
2.		
3.		
4.		
5.		
6.		
7.		
8.		
9.		
10.		

**Exercise 13–D
I Need a Coach**

In groups of three you will conduct a coaching session. One person will serve as the observer, one as the coach, and the third will be coached with regards to an ability issue.

1. One participant is to explain a trait, skill, or ability in which they would like to become more proficient.

2. The coach is to devise a coaching session and use various coaching techniques to help the other person.

3. The observer should note characteristics of the coach and techniques used to help the other person. Discuss with the pair tactics used, what might have been attempted, and what areas need to be improved upon. It is a means for all members to give feedback.

Questions

1. What coaching techniques were utilized? _____

_____

_____

_____

2. In what ways were they effective? _____

_____

_____

_____

3. What aspects of coaching or of being coached were most difficult and why? _____

_____

_____

_____

**Exercise 13–E
Everyone's a Coach**

We're all coaches and mentors, whether we realize it or not. Anyone who's younger or less experienced than us looks to us for guidance, information, and ideas about how to do things better. Reflect on your role as a coach or mentor in others' lives. With a partner, share a current relationship in which you're involved, formally or informally, in a coaching or mentoring situation, and answer these questions:

1. Describe the situation and the key players.

2. In what ways are others relying on you to be a role model or advice giver or teacher?

3. In your capacity as informal coach or mentor, what things are you doing well?

4. In what areas could you improve? Explain, citing examples.

**Exercise 13–F
Team Goal Setting**

1. In your work or project teams, identify specific goals and objectives for your team. Write out your goals, both short-term and long-term.

2. Begin with your team's long-term goals and discuss what your team goal is regarding the final deliverable(s), such as the quality standard, time frame, deadlines, and so on.

3. Now write the team's short-term goals and objectives that are needed to ensure the end result. Short-term goals may encompass meeting management skills, commitment levels, and means for resolving conflicts and associated behaviors (e.g., we will all be on time to meetings, or we will all have our work completed by . . .).

4. Work together to help each team member set individual goals that are necessary to clarify their contribution to the project (commitment levels, deadlines).

5. As a team, evaluate the goals for the team and for individual members. Analyze them to ensure they are "SMART" goals, identify resources needed for successful completion, and provide feedback on means for supporting the team and individuals throughout the project.

**Exercise 13–G
Helping Others Set
Goals—Modeling
Exercise**

In groups of three or four, you will be role-playing the following scenarios. For each role-play, there will be two participants and at least one observer. After each role-play, the observer should provide feedback and lead the group in a discussion based on the following questions.

Observer Questions

1. What techniques were used in helping others to set goals? Which ones were effective and why? Which ones were ineffective and why?

2. What could have been done differently? What impact would that have had on the outcome?

3. Evaluate the goals that were set. Are they "SMART" goals? How can they be improved upon?

4. How will completion be ensured? What type of control or check-up system has been put in place?

5. In what ways have the goals been tied to rewards? How clear is the goal measurement system?

Scenario One

The roles include:

Mother and/or father (Mom and Dad)

College-level son or daughter (Terry)

A silent observer

Using the following scenario, help Terry set "SMART" goals:

Terry is about to leave for his/her sophomore year at college, where he/she is majoring in marketing in the College of Business.

Mom and Dad have talked with each other and have concluded that Terry was unfocused in virtually every area of life during his or her freshman year. They would like for

Terry to become more serious and goal-directed this year. So, before Terry leaves for college, they want to talk with Terry and get him/her to set some goals for sophomore year.

Scenario Two

The roles include:

Jamie Harper—the supervisor

Pat Phillips—the subordinate

A silent observer

Using the following scenario, help Pat set "SMART" goals:

Pat is a researcher for a marketing firm and is assigned to do background research on various projects. At any given time, Pat may be assigned as many as three projects.

Jamie is having a feedback session (in Jamie's office) with Pat regarding her inability to meet project deadlines. In the past six months, Pat has been unable to meet any of the eight deadlines. Pat is consistently two to three days behind schedule, and works extra hours (in a panic) just before every deadline. Pat always seems to be busy and very disorganized; he/she is constantly taking on side projects from various people in the organization who need a little extra help or favor. Jamie would like to help Pat set some goals to help him/her start creating realistic deadlines and work schedules.

Exercise 13–H
Online Mentoring

You will identify and develop an online business mentor relationship with a current business manager, with whom you will correspond periodically on course-related topics.

Start thinking about who might be an appropriate mentor for you. Consider professional and personal acquaintances of your family and friends—lawyers, accountants, doctors, owners of small businesses, executives. It is not necessary that the mentor you select is in the field in which you are majoring; however, such "matching" may be helpful in establishing rapport with your mentor and providing you with insight into your chosen field. For example, those students with an interest in international business may want to select an online mentor who currently works overseas or who is employed by a domestic branch of an international corporation.

Getting Started

1. Select a mentor. Your instructor will provide you with criteria for mentor selection. In addition to professional and personal acquaintances of your family and friends, consider former bosses, fraternity/sorority colleagues (preferably those who have graduated several years ago), and neighbors.

2. Contact the potential mentor, discuss the assignment, their potential role, and an estimate of the time commitment (about 15 minutes for each of three e-mail exchanges during the semester). Explain why you have selected the mentor or believe he or she would make a good mentor; for example, you have similar career interests, you are aware of his or her success/expertise, etc. Ascertain the mentor's ability to commit to providing you valuable feedback in a timely fashion.

3. Develop your first set of questions. Please give your questions careful thought. A few things to consider about your questions:

(a) You are making an impression, so ask intelligent questions, and ask them in an appropriate format. The question: "Do you use empowerment in your workplace?" is a closed question which is likely answered with a simple yes or no. Rewording the question, "In what ways do you empower your employees?" is likely to result in a more thoughtful and complete response. You might want to go a step further and establish a context for your question, such as "In class, we discussed some of the benefits and pitfalls of empowerment, which is a way to give employees greater discretion over their work environment. To what extent do you empower your employees and what impact has that had on their productivity and satisfaction?" Typically, if the answers your mentor gives you are less than satisfactory, the question was too vague, ambiguous, or closed-ended.

(b) Try to ask questions that help clarify topics currently under discussion. You are welcome to ask questions that relate to topics not yet covered, but you may find it more difficult to compose such questions.

(c) Ask questions that are personally meaningful to you. If you chose a mentor who has experience in a field you would like to enter, fashion questions that are industry specific, such as "Given the rapid rate of change in the computer industry, how do you keep abreast of both technology and management issues?" or "In what ways does managing technical professionals differ from managing nontechnical or administrative employees?"

(d) Don't assume that your mentor understands all the terms you discuss in class. If you are interested in interpersonal style differences and would like to know your mentor's style, do not ask "Are you a Theory X or Theory Y manager?" (from a personality profile exercise) without some context or explanation of these styles. Even more commonly used terms like empowerment may not mean the same thing to people at different levels in the organization or in different types of organizations. Instead try a question like: "In class, we learned that individuals have different preferences in the way they handle conflict. The five styles we discussed are (briefly describe each). Which style is most (least) comfortable for you and why? Share an example where your style did (or did not) accomplish your intended goal."

(e) Feel free to build on previous questions, especially if you feel your mentor's answer was incomplete or you would just like to delve deeper. The goal is that you find value in the exchanges with your mentor.

Source: Victoria R. Whiting and Suzanne C. de Janasz, "On-Line Mentoring: Erasing the Border between the Classroom and Business. Presented at the Organizational Behavior Teaching Conference, Las Cruces, NM, 1999.

Exercise 13–I
I Need a Mentor

You have just been assigned the task of finding an online mentor. You have no idea where to start. You are the first person in your family to attend college. Your network of friends and associates won't yield many possibilities for a mentor in your chosen field of human resources. Working with your small group, tell them your career experience, interests, and/or goals. Brainstorm with them the names of several potential mentors for you. Names can be gotten through members of your small group or of other small groups in the class. (Rotate so every person in the small group has a chance to obtain potential contact names.)

Exercise 13–J
Build Your Own
Support System

We all need positive people in our lives—people who believe in us and can support us as we move toward our goals. At all times we need a variety of people in our lives to play one or more of the following roles. Working on your own, identify people in your life who are playing or could play the following roles for you. With a partner or small group, discuss your observations, reactions to the exercise, and lessons learned.

Supporter—to encourage you to persist in attaining your goals.

Challenger—to stretch you to achieve even more.

Friend—to have fun with and to confide in.

Source of Unconditional Love—to accept you no matter what.

Mentor/Advisor—to show us the ropes at school or at work.

Coach/Instructor—to teach you skills needed to achieve success.

Role Model—someone (real or fictional) to whom we can aspire personally and/or professionally.

Note

■ No one person can be all of this for us. Too many people make the mistake of overrelying on just one person such as a significant other to be all of this for us.

■ Just as important—don't try to go it alone. Seek out positive people who can help you achieve your goals.

Exercise 13–K
Try This . . .

1. Become involved as either a coach or mentor. There are multiple opportunities to do this, including:

   ■ Junior Achievement.

   ■ Big Brothers, Big Sisters.

   ■ Literacy program.

   ■ Coaching for a neighborhood sports program (soccer, swimming, baseball).

   ■ Community organizations—contact information available through local campus service learning office.

   ■ Working as a counselor for a day camp.

   Prior to beginning your work as a paid or volunteer coach or mentor, decide which skills you want to concentrate on most.

   At the conclusion of the first month or 20 hours of service, evaluate your coaching abilities—what's working well and what could be improved. If you developed a trusting relationship with another coach, ask him or her for feedback on your strengths and opportunities for improvement. You might even ask the people whom you coach two simple questions: In my role as your coach (Big Brother, teacher, counselor), what are some things I'm doing that are helpful for you? What are some things that I don't do or should stop doing? In other words, how best can I help you achieve what you want to achieve?

2. Watch a video that depicts a coaching or mentoring relationship, such as *My Fair Lady, Remember the Titans, Hercules, Mighty Ducks, Trading Places, Dead Poet's Society, Karate Kid, Wall Street, The Mask of Zorro, A League of Their Own, Star Wars* (the original episode or Episode One), *Working Girl, Glory, Independence Day, Mulan, The Color of Money, Hoosiers, Rocky*. Evaluate both the coach and/or mentor (what do they do effectively, what could they do better) and the trainee or protégé (ditto). If you were the coach in these situations, what specific things would you do differently and why?

**Exercise 13–L
Reflection/Action Plan**

This chapter focused on coaching and mentoring—what it is, why it's important, and how to improve your skills in this area. Complete the worksheet below upon completing all reading and experiential activities for this chapter.

1. The one or two areas in which I am most strong are:

   _____

   _____

   _____

   _____

2. The one or two areas in which I need more improvement are:

   _____

   _____

   _____

   _____

3. If I did only one thing to improve in each of these areas (coaching and mentoring), it would be to:

   _____

   _____

   _____

   _____

4. Making these changes would probably result in:

   _____

   _____

   _____

   _____

5. If I did not change or improve in these areas, it would probably affect my personal and professional life in the following ways:

   _____

   _____

   _____

   _____

14

Empowerment and Effective Delegation

How do I:

✓ Adopt a mindset that allows employees to take responsibility for their work, as opposed to controlling their every move?

✓ Provide information about the organization to help employees understand where they fit in?

✓ Increase employees' knowledge and training to better equip them to contribute to organizational performance?

✓ Reduce any fears I have about my mistakes made by my empowered subordinates?

✓ Empower myself when an organization or manager does not provide it?

✓ Motivate others to take risks and do what they think is best?

✓ Give responsibility of doing a task to another while ensuring quality of work?

You drive up to your hotel, exhausted after a long, protracted plane ride and subsequent taxi ride. After a full day of traveling, you are looking forward to settling into a comfortable night's sleep at the residence hotel your assistant booked for you. Tomorrow is a big day. You will be making an important presentation to a potential client—one potentially worth millions of revenue to your consulting organization.

One of the hotel's desk clerks, Derek, happily greets you and gets you checked in. One small problem, Derek informs you, the nonsmoking room you requested is unavailable. "Will this be a problem?" Derek asks. You are visibly upset. "I don't understand what the problem is. My assistant made the arrangements and he confirmed that the room is nonsmoking. I have terrible allergies and must be in a smoke-free room. You must have another room available! Please do something! It's 1 A.M., I'm tired, and I want to go to bed." Derek apologizes, "I can't help you, but perhaps my manager can. I'll page her for you. She should be here in a few minutes."

While you wait, your anger and resentment deepen. You think to yourself, how hard could it be to scrounge up a nonsmoking room? Where else could I go? By the time I find another place and take a taxi there, it'll be at least 2 A.M.! This is ridiculous . . . I'll never stay at this hotel again!

Derek is also feeling very uncomfortable while waiting for the manager to appear. He knows that they keep a few rooms in reserve at all times for emergencies. However, he does not know what qualifies as an emergency. An error resulting in overbooking, a VIP showing up unannounced, or this person who demands a nonsmoking room? What is taking the manager so long to come to the desk? He can feel the heat from the glare of the customer's gaze.

1. Why was Derek unable to fix the problem?

2. What impact did his inability to deal with the issue have on you?

3. Why do you think he had to get the manager?

4. Are you confident that the manager will rectify the situation? Why or why not?

5. Has something like this ever happened to you before? How did you react?

6. Have you ever been in a position similar to Derek's—one in which you wanted to help a customer but were neither trusted nor trained to make decisions like these? If so, how did it feel?

"Great leaders often inspire their followers to high levels of achievement by showing them how their work contributes to worthwhile ends."

Warren Bennis and Burt Nanus,
Leaders

A recent survey suggests that the majority of "hits" received by job search websites occur on Mondays. Why are some employees happy to come to work, while others start looking forward to Friday as soon as the work week begins each Monday? One reason is that many of the more satisfied employees play a meaningful role in the business of the organization, while many of the dissatisfied ones are not involved in the life of the organization; they only go through their assigned roles and collect a paycheck. Empowerment and delegation are two tools managers and team members can use to keep themselves—and their employees and teammates—motivated and involved in their work. This chapter discusses what empowerment and delegation are, why they're important, benefits and roadblocks to empowerment and delegation, and offers specific ways to empower and delegate to employees.

What Is Empowerment?

In simple terms, **empowerment** is the process by which a leader or manager shares his or her power with subordinates.[1] This definition provides a starting point for understanding empowerment, yet you might be asking yourself: Power to do what? In the traditional workplace, which was centered on manufacturing, all you needed was obedience to get work done.[2] Workers' tasks were preplanned and simplified; managers observed employees closely to ensure adherence to prescribed ways of completing tasks.

In today's environment of hyperturbulence, complexity, speed, competition, and constant change, the old command-and-control system no longer works. Shortened product life cycles and constant focus on change create today's need for the "**knowledge worker**."[3] Knowledge workers are those workers who need and use information to perform their work. This category can include everyone from product developers or producers to programmers to consultants to clerks who deal with customers. Knowledge-focused companies recognize people are their greatest assets and keep their workforces involved and informed.[4] The best workers today are those who are adaptable and self-managing, flexible and autonomous, and enabled and motivated to accomplish what they choose.

Why Is Empowerment Important?

One of the key reasons for empowerment is in its ability to provide motivation. Managers realize that employee motivation is necessary to achieve directed organizational goals. According to Maslow and his **hierarchy of needs theory**,[5] people are intrinsically motivated in direct relationship to their needs. (See Figure 14–1.) His theory states that

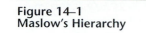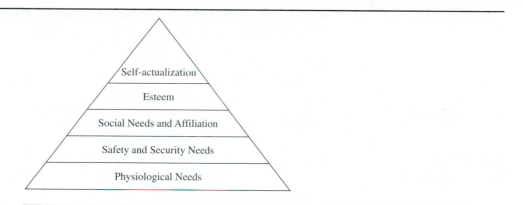

Figure 14–1
Maslow's Hierarchy

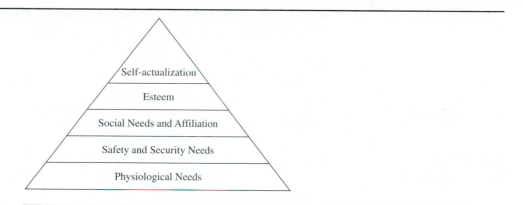

people begin trying to satisfy their lower-level needs first. Physiological needs are related to the sustaining of life (e.g., food, shelter, oxygen) and safety needs are related to security, stability, and freedom of the fear of loss of the physiological needs. Once these needs are satisfied (which is usually provided by money and obtaining a job), they tend to lose their motivating potential. Individuals then move up the pyramid, striving to satisfy the needs on the next higher level. For example, once an employee has taken care of his physiological and safety needs, he will crave to have the social, esteem and self-actualization needs fulfilled. This is indicative of today's workforce; they are no longer simply motivated to just work; they want to be satisfied with their accomplishments and contribution to personal and organizational goals.

The implication of this theory supports the need for empowerment. Through empowerment, organizations are able to continue the motivational process of satisfying the higher-level needs. The fulfillment of the higher-level needs will come in the form of autonomy, respect, power to make decisions, status, and freedom to grow and develop within the organization.

Maslow's theory is one of many theories that attempt to explain motivation and human behavior. One theme that is consistent with almost all motivational theories is that at some point in a person's life, some part of each individual has a need for personal satisfaction or self-actualization. Empowerment provides the intrinsic rewards that motivate many individuals.

Now return to the opening case scenario to extrapolate the benefits of empowerment. If you were the owner of the hotel chain, would you be satisfied knowing that your client's needs were unmet at first? If you were the clerk, would you feel you did everything in your power to ensure customer satisfaction? Chances are, you answered no to both questions. Thanks to the information revolution, aided by the Internet, many of us have become quite proficient at identifying the best value for purchasing products and services. We can "name our own price" for anything from groceries to airline tickets. One might think that, as a result, the need for good customer service has declined. In fact, it has increased. Once price and ease of obtaining a good or service no longer matters, how do successful firms differentiate themselves in the eyes of their customers? How do organizations build customer loyalty to current and future products and services? Through their human assets or their employees.

When employees feel aligned with an organization's mission and goals, supported to target such outcomes, and rewarded when they and the organization achieve desired performance and outcomes, they do whatever it takes to produce a deliverable or satisfy a customer. Contrast that philosophy with one in which employees are closely monitored, given information on a need-to-know basis, and rewarded on a random basis. When workers are empowered, they are involved in decision making, asked to suggest new services and processes, and encouraged to solve problems creatively and effectively. Derek, our hotel clerk, is not empowered. He is not able to problem-solve or suggest potential solutions to the weary traveler. Such decisions are better left to someone in charge, right? Wrong!

Had Derek been given the power to satisfy his customer, a different, more positive outcome would have emerged for the customer, Derek, and, ultimately, the organization.

However, giving employees power, or empowering them, may not be as easy as it seems. Many managers view the sharing of power and authority as risky and question the notion that empowerment is actually beneficial. We'll discuss why shortly. We'll also help you understand why today's leaders need to recognize that empowering their workforce is an opportunity, rather than a threat.[6] In addition, given the tight labor market, an organization that empowers its employees may be better suited to attract and retain its highly skilled and trained professionals, thus maintaining its competitive edge.

Benefits of Empowerment

There are numerous benefits to empowerment. After reading the list of benefits below, you might wonder whether you or the organization for which you work can afford *not* to empower its employees!

■ Empowerment reinforces member participation and growth, commitment to quality, and a more open, honest environment. This results in greater job satisfaction, motivation, and commitment—a sense of achievement.[7]

■ With empowerment, people have a greater sense of achievement, confidence, self-esteem, and a sense of belonging.[8] Mary Kay cosmetics exemplifies empowerment in how its representatives do business. They are provided support and training through conventions and other educational materials, they are able to control their schedule and amount of effort they wish to exert, and they are able to receive recognition and rewards for their efforts. Because they are treated as owners of their businesses, Mary Kay employees feel confident and have a sense of belonging and control over their work. This empowerment helps to release their energies toward even greater achievements.

■ Empowerment speeds up reaction time and decision making and provides speed and flexibility, allowing quicker response to customers. Empowered employees who deal directly with customers will be able to better meet their needs and demands, leading to more satisfied customers.[9] Imagine you are boarding a plane when you realize you have been ticketed for a seat that is already "rightfully" occupied. Some airlines would have you deplane and wait until all passengers are seated and then consult a supervisor about fixing the problem. In an empowered airline organization, the agent, who is likely part owner in the airline, immediately takes the problem into his or her hands and finds a solution. Perhaps you are bumped to first class, or perhaps you are given another option or compensation. Either way, the problem is solved quickly and without management intervention, and the customer is satisfied. Empowerment is often cited as a key reason for the phenomenal success of Herb Kelleher's SouthWest Airlines.

■ Empowered employees are more likely to offer ideas, exercise creativity, and develop more innovative processes and products than those who are not.[10] In an empowered organization, employees are encouraged to take risks and are not afraid of failure. They look for opportunities to improve products, processes, and services that seem to work well, in addition to reacting to problems that need immediate attention. Because they have the authority to act in the best interests of their work unit and organization, empowered individuals positively affect their environment through proactive behaviors.[11] An example of an empowering organization is 3M. When the scientist created the failed glue that eventually became the key ingredient in Post-It Notes, he was not "punished" by his management. Instead, he was encouraged to see if he could come up with a use for his "failure." Wouldn't you want to get a percentage of Post-It Notes' revenues?

■ With empowerment, employees are more responsible, which leads to greater loyalty, trust, and quality. By transferring power and authority to employees, they become accountable and responsible for their decisions and actions. Since they solve their own problems and find their own solutions, empowered employees will be more committed to a quality outcome and to stay long enough to see the fruits of their labor. This kind of loyalty is invaluable to an organization's ability to attract and retain talented personnel.

■ Empowerment reduces operational costs by eliminating unnecessary layers of management, staff, quality control, and checking operations. The traditional hierarchical design assumes that employees cannot be trusted to make sound organizational decisions. Each successive layer of management has a role in ensuring that employees representing the previous layer follow the stated rules and procedures and, if not, they are to be corrected by their management. For example, at one large aerospace company, the process of ordering a $2 package of pencils could cost as much as $75 when accounting for the seven layers of management and approval all orders had to go through before being placed. However, by defining parameters, the ordering process was streamlined to a single individual ordering products within certain reasonable limits, without the need for management consent. In terms of quality control, empowered workers take responsibility and receive rewards for the quality of their product and are therefore committed to producing products and services of the highest quality possible. In many empowered organizations, employees not only take responsibility for their operations, but they also engage in activities designed to streamline and improve processes—building in quality from the start. This eliminates the need for surveillance or inspection by a "big brother" or quality assurance engineer.

■ Empowerment reduces turnover and aids in retention—In this booming economy, employee turnover is near a 20-year high. Schellenbarger reports that due to the costs of replacing an employee—about 1.5 times a year's pay—companies are pouring millions of dollars into efforts designed to increase employee loyalty.[12] By tending to such issues as fair pay, involvement in decision making, and trust in leadership—all elements associated with an empowered workforce—employees remain more committed and loyal to organizations.

Disadvantages or Costs of Empowerment

At this point, you might be thinking to yourself, if empowerment is all this and more, then why don't we see more organizations doing it? Many managers and organizations want to empower their workforce but are not sure how to do it without jeopardizing the achievement of the jobs and organizational goals. Truth is, many managers and organizations resist empowerment for a number of reasons.[13] For one, empowerment results in greater costs in selection and hiring. When hiring employees to do a simple, controlled task, little difficulty is likely to be encountered finding individuals capable of performing at this level. When employees are to be empowered—trusted with organizational information and the means to improve it—selectivity in hiring is increased.

Empowerment can also result in lower and inconsistent delivery. In the control model, employees follow a specific script and set of instructions, eliminating any inconsistency (and creativity, for that matter). Employees in an empowered environment have a different experience. In their efforts to satisfy the customer, empowered employees may take more time and personalize the service for the customer's needs. Depending on the business and strategy, this could be good or bad. A recent article suggests that fast-food franchises do significantly more business in their drive-through windows than through their walk-up counters. Reducing the service delivery time by a small increment can have a substantial positive impact on profits.[14] There is also the possibility for giveaways and bad decisions. What if Derek was empowered to satisfy the weary traveler and, to compensate for the hotel's error, gave the traveler an upgraded room for the same price? Would this be a bad or a good decision? One such decision is likely not to impact an organization's profits; however, empowered employees may go too far in satisfying customers, to the point that profits are affected. Giving away products and services—while it increases customer satisfaction—reduces revenues. Empowered employees may also make changes in their environment that improve their work unit yet negatively impact another work unit. Hopefully, this is not likely to happen when employees have information about how all the pieces fit together. However, such freedom could result in a costly error.

Empowerment typically comes with boundaries. While an organization gives empowered employees the authority to make decisions, these decisions must generally be made within certain broad operating principles. However, what if employees were to stray beyond those boundaries? What if employees abuse their power? For example an overzealous or disgruntled employee, acting like a "loose cannon" on his own, without regard for company guidelines, might satisfy one customer in the short term but damage relationships with the home office in the long term. An example of this would be Derek the desk clerk. He could overcompensate, not only offering the guest a room upgrade but also coupons for free stays at the hotel chain for the next three months. Organizations that empower employees must give their employees authority, but also responsibility and structure.

An important dimension that hinders empowerment is the fact that some individuals cannot handle or do not want the responsibility. Despite the intrinsic and extrinsic benefits of empowerment, some employees prefer to show up, be told what to do, get their paycheck, and go home. Empowerment may be perceived as freedom by some but as ambiguity by others. Some prefer keeping things simple and known. They fear the responsibility inherent in thinking about and making decisions that could change, and possibly improve, the way things have always been done. It's important to remember that just because you value empowerment, others may not.

Finally, one reason some managers avoid empowerment—even when their organization embraces it—is fear of change and the unknown. "It's working now, so why should I change? What if my empowered employees mess up; will I be fired? What if they do so well—become self-managing—that I'm no longer needed? How can they know better than me; I've been here longer and have more experience than they do." It takes a certain mindset or philosophy to empower successfully. What makes some leaders more willing and able to empower their subordinates than others? Some individuals possess a leadership style or proclivity towards empowering (or disempowering) behaviors while others understand that empowerment can actually expand their power base, that more might be gained than lost.

To Empower or Not to Empower?

It seems clear that empowerment is an important and necessary element, at least in some form, in today's global environment. Only the fittest and most innovative companies will survive; empowerment increases the energy level of the workforce and channels it into good use.[15] Is empowerment a one-size-fits-all proposition? Luckily, no. There are multiple approaches to empowerment, and there are several criteria worth considering when determining the degree to which empowerment should be implemented in your workplace.

There are different levels of empowerment that can be used in empowering your workforce; deciding which level will be appropriate for your situation or workforce can facilitate successful implementation.[16] These approaches differ in terms of the degree with which ingredients of empowerment are present.

■ In **suggestion involvement,** the organization makes a small shift from the production line or control model. Employees are encouraged to contribute ideas, possibly via an anonymous suggestion box. In general, day-to-day activities remain unchanged, unless a manager decides to implement a suggestion. This step is helpful in that employees are encouraged to be creative and think about ways to improve products and processes; however, employees may not know whether their ideas are acknowledged or be asked to get involved in implementation.

■ In the **job involvement** approach to empowerment, employees are given greater freedom in their job and tasks. Their responsibilities become more open or fluid, such as a team in which all employees are cross-trained to perform a variety of tasks. Their jobs become enlarged and enriched,[17] and they receive feedback on their performance. This can aid in increasing employee satisfaction and productivity. Managers' roles in this approach are more like advisors; they give some choices to employees but must be kept apprised, especially if problems surface.

■ Employees in a **high involvement** organization have much greater voice and discretion over their work environment. Managers provide the necessary resources, information, and rewards to employees while acting as coaches or facilitators of employees and teams. Because they understand their role in the organization and its success, empowered employees are in the best position to redesign their work, solve problems (or find new ones!), and share in the profits realized by their innovative and productive efforts. Employees take ownership in their work unit and the organization, and often manage themselves.

Figure 14–2[18]
Empowerment
Considerations

Contingency	Production Line vs. Empowerment Approach
Basic business strategy	efficient high volume vs. customized differentiated
Tie to the customer	transaction vs. relationship
Technology	routine vs. nonroutine
Business environment	predictable vs. dynamic
Type of people	McGregor's Theory X managers vs. Theory Y managers

Is empowerment an appropriate strategy for your organization? Certain considerations or contingencies (see Figure 14–2) should be evaluated in making this decision. These considerations determine whether a lower level of empowerment, or production-line approval, is more appropriate than a higher-level empowerment approval.

The production line approach works effectively when the primary business value is speed and efficiency. Empowerment takes time. The production line approach breaks tasks out into predetermined components, whereas in empowerment employees are given more time for processing situations and generating solutions.

The production line approach works well when customer ties are secondary to the product or service being delivered. Organizations that value longer term customer relationships will find empowerment a more useful strategy than organizations with a "one-off," transactional approach to service delivery.

The production line approach works in environments where technology enables workers to perform many of the most important tasks routinely. In organizations with a lot of variety and complexity, where employees perform tasks that are primarily nonroutine, empowerment will be required.

The production line approach works well in business environments that are predictable, where most of the problems that may arise can be anticipated and prepared for. Empowerment is preferred in those environments that are ever-changing, where manuals are out of date before they're even printed.

Lastly, the production line approach is best when an organization's managers are primarily hierarchical, "top-down" **Theory X**[19] **managers.** An X manager believes subordinates dislike work and shrug responsibility, leading them to be more directive with the tendency to dictate work efforts. An organization predominated by participative, open **Theory Y managers**—holding the belief that people enjoy work, crave responsibility, and strive for excellence—is the perfect environment for an empowerment approach to problem solving. These managers, and the employees, are more comfortable with higher levels of employee involvement.

Leadership style and behaviors play a key role in the success of empowerment. For empowerment to be implemented successfully, managers must adopt an appropriate style of leadership that will lend itself to empowerment. Where do you see yourself along the following continuum of leadership styles?[20]

Autocratic   Participatory   Coaching

An **autocratic or controlling leader** shares little power with his or her employees and decides which tasks must be accomplished. These leaders might delegate small tasks to employees, but they maintain control over coordination.

A **participative leader** allows and encourages input from subordinates but still maintains the last say. They ask for employee recommendations, and perhaps jointly create a workable solution, but proceed with employee implementation with caution and control.

A **coaching leader** delegates tasks to employees and responds to their questions or concerns about the task. They trust their employees to make decisions as they see fit and are available for advice if needed.

Figure 14–3[21]

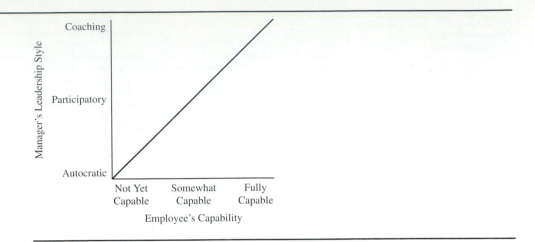

Where does your style fit? Does this match the kind of organization you plan to or currently work for? The appropriate leadership style will be one that fits the situation as well as the type and capabilities of the employees.[22] As illustrated in Figure 14–3, managers may need to adjust their managerial style in accordance with the type of employee. The managerial style and the level of empowerment will therefore become dependent on the capability or maturity level of the employees and the development of the manager–employee relationship.

This is not to say that the leadership style cannot change over the implementation of empowerment. As more organizations empower individuals and teams, leaders will see changes in the capabilities and skills of the employees and a need to redefine their roles and style. They will need to use more support and guidance, negotiation and conflict tactics, two-way communication, problem solving, and facilitation. Therein lies another reason to improve your interpersonal skills!

Guidelines for Implementing and Improving Empowerment[23]

1. Walk the talk—managers need to "practice what they preach."

2. Set high performance standards—set standards that force others to excel, and show that you have confidence in their ability to reach them.

3. Empowerment must be recognized (in the structure of the organization)—empowerment must be reflected in attitudes and in processes within the organization.

4. Change old habits—managers must be ready to relinquish power, and subordinates must be ready and able to accept new responsibilities.

5. Start small—changes need to be made little by little; empowerment does not happen overnight.

6. Build trust—managers must emit confidence and be open and honest with their co-workers.

Implementing Empowerment

So, exactly how does an organization empower its workforce? According to Bowen and Lawler, there are four ingredients of empowerment. These basic ingredients need to be present in an environment for effective employee involvement. They include:[24]

■ Information about the organization and its performance. Unlike the old model, wherein only top management is interested in and can understand an organization's financials, operating costs, and competitive position, empowered employees are given this information and the training to understand what this information means to their work unit and how their actions can and do impact the bottom line. If you don't know where you are, how will you know if you're improving?

■ Rewards based on the organization's performance. Many organizations still reward employees for nonperformance-related criteria such as tenure. While there are some benefits to employee loyalty, what message does an organization send when it rewards employees who are less productive but more senior than those who actively and productively contribute to the organization's bottom line? In an empowered organization, employees engage in collaborative efforts—for the collective good—and share in the organization's success through profit sharing and stock ownership. Recall the slogan for Avis: "We're the employee owners of Avis . . . we work harder!"

■ Knowledge that enables employees to understand and contribute to organizational performance. Along with the training to understand organizational performance, empowered employees are given training and access to resources to fix problems and improve processes. This knowledge may come in the form of education (problem-solving and quality classes) or resources (bulletins for charting progress, meeting times, outside experts).

■ Power to make decisions that influence organizational direction and performance. This ingredient brings us back to our original definition of empowerment. Training, knowledge, and rewards are great, but if all employees can do is recommend—rather than implement—solutions, commitment to the outcome will be constrained. Empowered employees are given the authority, usually within defined parameters, to make decisions and implement changes that improve the performance of individuals, teams, work units, and the organization.

Through these ingredients, we can see that empowerment is more than just a sharing of power. Empowered employees are enabled. They are provided with the freedom to successfully do what they want to do, rather than getting them to do what you want. Whetton and Cameron refer to this as a pull strategy, rather than a push strategy; this means that employees accomplish tasks because they are internally meaningful or motivating, and not because someone or something external to them deems it important.[25] In order to make empowerment work, managers have to believe in and want empowerment, and employees must feel empowered—perceive that there is a liberating rather than constraining environment. It is their perception of the environment that shapes the empowerment.[26] Spreitzer discusses four psychological attributes of empowerment: meaning, self-determination, competence, and impact.[27] This view holds that it is essential for organizations to be empowering. Organizations need to provide the right climate, tools, training, and support for empowerment to exist. However, for empowerment to actually exist, it must be felt or experienced by employees. In other words, only through acts of empowerment, as carried out by employees, can empowerment come alive and be more than just words on a page in a company brochure. It is the manager's role to engender the four psychological attributes in those they intend to empower.[28] However, individuals can still refuse to accept empowerment or feel empowered.

Six Social Structural Characteristics That Create an Environment That Facilitates Empowerment[29]

Low role ambiguity—a clear set of responsibilities and duties, defined guidelines, and standards for accountability.

Wide span of control—decentralization to allow for greater contribution to overall operation; to avoid micromanagement.

Sociopolitical support—the existence of relevant support networks of bosses, peers, subordinates, and members of the work group.

(continued)

Access to information—Availability of information on operations and procedures to determine strategy and frameworks for the accomplishment of organizational goals; freely sharing information across levels and functions.

Access to resources—ability to marshal resources essential to tasks to eliminate dependency and powerlessness.

Participative unit climate—a climate and culture that emphasizes and encourages individual contribution and initiative rather than top-down command and control.

There are five stages to implementing empowerment.[30]

   1. **Investigation**—analyzing whether empowerment should be implemented and in what form. In this phase, the organization evaluates its current business processes and strategies for success, and weighs the current situation against preferred goals. Using the chart in Figure 14–2, the company first identifies its core business strategy, its customer links, the prevalence of technology throughout the organization, the business and environment in which the business is operating, and the type of people currently working for the organization. Then it considers data such as employee morale, customer satisfaction, and industry best practices. After this analysis the organization can determine whether empowerment will bring the desired changes and outcomes needed to achieve greater success.

   2. **Preparation**—setting the stage for generating and demonstrating organizational support. This is a crucial step. Changing from a production-line approach to decision-making and problem-solving approach that is more empowering requires a significant culture shift. The way people act and are rewarded will change dramatically. In this phase managers and employees all receive information about the desired shift, why it's occurring, the changes that will result, the training and tools that will be available to help them through the change, the benefits of the change, and information on how and when the changes will take place.[31]

   3. **Implementation**—assessing all current systems and adjusting to support an environment based on empowerment. In this phase job descriptions are redesigned, reporting relationships are examined, and reward systems are aligned with the changes. For example, an employee who was formerly paid on an hourly basis might be placed in a bonus pool and receive periodic recognition for "best practice" examples of excellent customer service. Operating procedures and policy manuals are updated, ongoing training is developed and offered, and information and communication systems are realigned to support the ongoing changes that will result from the empowerment initiative.

   4. **Transition**—moving from the former system to the new one. This phase marks the end of the introduction or "roll out" of the new system and starts the permanent implementation of the new system. This phase involves receiving feedback on how the new system is working and making modifications as required. Numerous adjustments are made as employees and managers gain experience with the new guidelines and techniques. In this phase employees are also mobilized—allowed to have an impact, given the freedom to take action, supported in their decisions, and encouraged to take risks.

   5. **Maturation**—the new system is firmly rooted. This phase involves maintaining the new system and continuously improving it. There is a constant need for reexamination of current processes to determine how changes or new adaptations need to be implemented to remain vital.

Specific Techniques That Can Be Used to Empower a Workforce[32]

Job enlargement: adding more tasks or elements to a job; horizontal expansion—helps to reduce boredom.

(continued)

Job enrichment: adding managerial functions to a job; vertical expansion—increases job satisfaction and skill development.

Job rotation: shifting of people's jobs and responsibilities; employees learn a succession of tasks or related tasks—reduces monotony and boredom.

Self-managed teams: creating teams, reorganizing to have team orientation rather than individual effort—results in high levels of productivity while satisfying the group's and individual's work needs.

Job redesign: allowing employees to design their own jobs with corresponding responsibilities and processes—gains employee buy-in, greater insight and efficiency, and long-term effectiveness.

Flextime: allowing for varying work schedules to fit the needs of the employees—increases employee morale and productivity.

Self-empowerment

So far, we've discussed what empowerment is, why it's used, and its benefits and disadvantages. We've also discussed that in order for empowerment to result in increases in productivity, innovation, satisfaction, and commitment, organizations and their managers have to be empowering and individuals have to accept empowerment. Employees must demonstrate and prove that they have the ability and desire to handle the responsibility that empowerment brings. What if empowerment does not exist in your organization or your work group? Do you give up and wait for others to tell you what to do? Here's where self-empowerment comes in; follow these steps:

■ Create a vision of preferred achievements for yourself and your group. Set high standards for performance and establish goals and deliverables needed to achieve that standard.

■ Understand your need for dependency—and let go of your need. We all start out that way. As children, we look to our parents for rules and norms of accepted behavior. When we succeed—or fail—we look to others for recognition or acceptance. When you empower yourself, you set the goals and the rules and you evaluate your performance. No one will tell you what to do or whether you were successful. Believe in yourself and your capabilities to succeed. When you do, you can have pride in your accomplishments and the knowledge that you made it happen.

■ Identify and manage your allies and adversaries, and network and politic where appropriate. Even the best-laid plans are subject to roadblocks. After setting a vision and goals, determine what and who can help—and hinder—your ability to achieve those goals. Find ways to reduce obstacles or enlist the support of others, including your peers and managers, to remove or reduce those obstacles. Who might champion your efforts? Maybe your boss is uncomfortable with empowerment, but her boss is not. This is not to say that you should skip the chain of command; rather, you do what you need to get the job done. Inform your boss of your plans and where they fit in. If your boss chooses not to get involved, don't let that stop you. Get others involved, and keep your boss informed of your progress. Find others who will and persuade them to support you. Most people will offer help or resources to individuals and projects that have the potential to make a positive difference in the organization.

■ Develop risk-taking strategies; find the courage and confidence to live out your vision. The old saying, "nothing ventured, nothing gained" holds true. Why be an average performer when you are capable of so much more? Why do only what others expect of you when your expectations and aspirations are higher? By accepting self-empowerment and daring to go where others may not have gone, you have to accept that failure is a possibility. Then again, so too is success. Evaluate the costs and benefits of taking on a self-empowered "adventure"; if the net result is positive, what have you got to lose? Former Chicago Bulls superstar Michael Jordan was cut from his high school varsity basketball team as an underclassman. What would have happened if he lacked the courage to persist when others told him he didn't make the cut? Luckily for his fans, he pursued his vision.

One final note about empowerment. Research suggests that empowered managers are more likely to empower their subordinates than managers who are not empowered.[33] Referred to as the falling dominos effect, this phenomenon suggests that beyond the benefits already mentioned, empowerment can be downwardly contagious. When you feel empowered, you are likely to take steps to do the same for those reporting to you, and so on. Because of this cascading effect, when empowerment starts at the top of the organization, the benefits are likely to be exponential!

Empowerment through Effective Delegation

As you progress in your career, you're likely to find that no matter how skilled and experienced you are, you can neither do everything nor make all necessary decisions. Even if you could—and that would probably make you superhuman—you would be preventing your subordinates from developing and reaching their full potential. One means of empowering others is through the technique of **delegation.** Delegation involves assigning work—and the authority and responsibility for the work—to others. Healthy environments are characterized by delegation; if done properly it can be one of the most effective management tools for getting things done, and it is considered a critical part of being a good leader.[34]

Delegation is not as simple as it sounds. In fact, many managers avoid delegation or do it poorly. Delegation involves the transferring of authority, responsibility, and accountability to others, typically subordinates. It is not abdication or "dumping"; rather, it can help create a positive, team-oriented environment. In this section, we discuss why delegation is important and how to do it effectively.

Benefits of Delegation

Benefits of delegation accrue to both the delegatee and the delegator. Some of these benefits are listed below.

- Delegation enables development of staff to handle specific tasks that are routine. This enables others to deal with tasks that are more complex.
- Transferring responsibility to staff aids in their development and increases staff readiness for promotions.[35]
- Delegation increases the delegatees' level of job satisfaction through greater autonomy and the feeling that they are making a contribution to organizational success.
- Delegation can lead to better decision making because people closer to the issue have input on decisions. This pushes organizational decision making downward, leading to better ways to do things and a more democratic or inclusive process.[36]
- Delegation allows for growth and development of the manager who's delegating. By giving responsibility for tasks to others, the manager's time is available for other tasks, for conceiving of new ideas, or for innovation.
- Delegation demonstrates a manager's trust in his or her employees. It shows the manager's ability to manage and develop other individuals, to effectively communicate and work through others.

Despite these benefits, many of us choose not to delegate or do it poorly. Delegating responsibility is easy to understand yet hard to do; yet not delegating can be disastrous.[37] Some reasons people fail to delegate include:

Lack of time: Perhaps you feel you can do it yourself more quickly. True, there is a learning curve to doing tasks, and training will be needed, but next time it needs to be done, you will be doing the task. The biblical adage, "You can give a man a fish or teach him how" reminds us that delegation is important.

Perfectionism: Perhaps you feel you can do it better, which may be true, but by letting others perform a task you help them learn, grow, and develop. Let go of the idea that asking a less-qualified person to do a task seems illogical.[38]

Fear of surrendering authority: Perhaps you fear a loss of power. If, for example, you believe that you are the only one who can do something, that belief reinforces your perception that you maintain control or power in a situation.

Lack of confidence in staff: Perhaps you don't trust in the abilities of your staff or you fear they might purposely fail in order to make you look bad.

Dual accountability: Perhaps you feel that this task is your responsibility and that it's not right to share that responsibility with someone else.

Activities Included in Delegation

To be effective, delegation requires three activities: assignment of responsibility, transferring of authority, and establishing of accountability.[39] All three elements are needed and should occur simultaneously. These activities are described below.

1. The assignment of responsibility. When assigning the responsibility to accomplish a task, the delegatee must understand exactly what is to be accomplished and accept the responsibility for doing so. This requires two-way communication to ensure both parties clearly understand the task and the expectations that go along with it. Manager and subordinate might discuss and clarify all potential contingencies and ascertain whether the subordinate has the necessary skills and sufficient general and specific knowledge to perform the assigned task.[40]

2. The transferring of authority. The delegatee must have the proper authority to obtain the necessary resources to complete the task. This includes the formal granting of control over necessary resources, clarification of parameters or guidelines, and an understanding of the authority given and the limits therein.[41] As appropriate, others should also be apprised of the transfer of the authority. For example, suppose a manager is traveling for two weeks and he delegates the collection and processing of time cards to a subordinate. Before he leaves, he needs to make subordinates aware of this temporary change and make arrangements with the payroll office to ensure the acceptability of the subordinate's signature on the time cards.

3. Establishing accountability. Delegation is not complete without holding delegatees accountable for the completion of the assignments. They need to be aware of the rewards and consequences of their actions and must realize that they will have to justify decisions for the tasks for which they are responsible. If the delegatee forgets to turn in the time cards and her co-workers don't get paid, co-workers are likely to become unhappy. When delegating tasks, it is important that consequences—both good and bad—be clearly understood.

A Process for Effective Delegation

Effective delegation begins with an open, supportive environment. Create a work environment that has mutual support, mutual trust, and clear lines of communication.[42] Communication and delegation go hand in hand—most problems associated with delegation such as lack of motivation, dissatisfaction, and inferior work can be traced back to a lack of understanding.[43] Two-way communication—aided by effective speaking, listening, and feedback skills—is necessary throughout the entire delegation process.

Next, decide what to delegate. Examine tasks that can and should be delegated; determine why (i.e., what is the goal of the delegation) and how (the process) you will do this. Determine what will be required with the delegation, such as training, information, resources, and experience. Just because an employee lacks experience is no reason to avoid delegating or to only delegate mundane tasks to him or her.[44]

Assess and select capable individuals. To do this, you will need to match the person to the task, design a training program if necessary, make sure the person will be able to complete the task and goal, and work with him to anticipate any potential problems and ways to overcome them. Employees need to feel confident and competent to succeed.

Delegate over stages, allowing employees to work more and more on their own without constant supervision. In other words, start small. Show your support of and trust in them by allowing them to prove themselves and their ability to work with little or no supervision on simple tasks or on an initial task related to a larger project. For example, you can start with low levels of delegation where you ask someone to get baseline information. Then you can move the person to a medium level by asking him or her to get information, analyze it, and suggest options. This way you are able to assess the person's skills and decision-making abilities and determine whether they are capable of handling the next level or an entire assignment on their own.[45] This process allows you to maintain an appropriate level of control and responsibility over the task.

Next, you'll want to establish controls. While you are ultimately responsible for the task, delegation does not mean that you no longer are accountable or responsible for the end results. Make it clear at the time of delegation how and when checks will be held, and develop feedback mechanisms to ensure the task is on target and being performed properly.[46]

As needed and requested, provide help and coaching. Encourage a delegatee to complete the task by demonstrating your confidence in their abilities. Accept only finished work—do not allow for reverse delegation—and make others understand that their success depends on their contribution. Try not to give in to the fears associated with delegation or let others give you the work the delegatee took responsibility for. You can be a support factor—ask questions and give guidance, and teach employees to be problem solvers and decision makers.[47]

Finally, provide feedback. Give rewards and credit for jobs completed successfully, and provide constructive feedback for insufficient work. If you accept unacceptable work and fix or finish it, you deprive the delegatee of the opportunity to learn from mistakes.

Summary

Empowerment is a powerful tool in motivating your workforce. In today's dynamic business environment, managers must find means to increase employee participation and creativity in order to remain viable and competitive. By understanding the benefits and tactics for empowerment, along with being aware of the potential consequences of improper empowerment and delegation, managers will be able to increase employees' job satisfaction while effectively achieving organizational goals.

Key Terms and Concepts

Accountability

Assignment of responsibility

Authority

Autocratic leader

Coaching leader

Delegation

Empowerment

Hierarchy of needs theory

High involvement

Implementation stage

Investigation stage

Job involvement

Knowledge worker

Maturation stage

Participative leader

Preparation stage

Suggestion involvement

Theory X manager

Theory Y manager

Transition stage

Endnotes

1. Jay A. Conger and Rabindra N. Kanungo, "The Empowerment Process: Integrating Theory and Practice," *Academy of Management Review* 13 (1988), p. 473.

2. Joanne Cole, "Building Heart and Soul," *HR Focus,* October 1998, pp. 9–10, quoting Hornstein, author of *Brutal Bosses.*

3. Peter Crush, "New Product Development: Letting Staff Be Creative," *Marketing,* July 13, 2000.

4. Larry English, "Information Quality Management: The Next Frontier," *DM Review,* April 2000, p. 38.

5. Abraham H. Maslow, *Motivation and Personality,* Second Ed. (New York: Harper and Row, 1970).

6. Gretchen M. Spreitzer, "Social Structural Characteristics of Psychological Empowerment," *Academy of Management Journal,* April 1996, pp. 483–504.

7. Rob MacLachian, "Regeneration X," *People Management,* April 2, 1998, p. 34.

8. Wong Pang Long, "Managing Problems: To Empower or Not, Is the Question," *The New Press Times,* Dec. 22, 1996, p. 32.

9. Ibid.

10. Ibid.

11. Spreitzer, 1996.

12. Sue Schellenbarger, "To Win the Loyalty of Your Employees, Try a Softer Touch," *Wall Street Journal,* January 26, 2000, p. B1.

13. David E. Bowen and Edward Lawler III, "The Empowerment of Service Workers: What, Why, How and When," *Sloan Management Review,* Spring 1992, pp. 31–39.

14. Jennifer Ordonez, "Next! An Efficiency Drive: Fast Food Lanes Are Getting Even Faster," *Wall Street Journal,* May 18, 2000, p. A1.

15. Long, 1996.

16. Reprinted from "The Empowerment of Service Workers: What, Why, How, and When," by David E. Bowen and Edward Lawler, III, Sloan Management Review, Spring 1992, pp. 31–39, by permission of the publisher. Copyright © 1992 by Sloan Management Review Association. All rights reserved.

17. See, for example, Greg R. Oldham and J. Richard Hackman, "Relationships between Organizational Structure and Employee Reactions: Comparing Alternative Frameworks," *Administrative Science Quarterly,* March 1981, p. 66.

18. Bowen et al., 1992.

19. Douglas McGregor, *The Human Side of Enterprise* (New York: McGraw-Hill, 1964), pp. 68–78.

20. Brent Ward, "How to Empower," *Canadian Manager,* Winter 1996.

21. Ibid.

22. Daniel Goleman, "Leadership That Gets Results," *Harvard Business Review,* March–April 2000, pp. 78–90.

23. Leaders Direct, **www.leadersdirect.com/empower.html.**

24. Bowen et al., 1992.

25. David A. Whetton and Kim S. Cameron, *Developing Management Skills,* Fourth Ed. (Reading, MA: Addison-Wesley, 1998), p. 377.

26. Republished with permission from the Academy of Management from Gretchen M. Spreitzer, "Social Structural Characteristics of Psychological Empowerment," *Academy of Management Journal,* April 1996, Vol. 39, No. 2, pp. 483–504; Permission conveyed through the Copyright Clearance Center, Inc.

27. Ibid.

28. K. S. Cameron, D. A. Whetton, and M. U. Kim, "Organizational Dysfunctions of Decline," *Academy of Management Journal,* 1987, 30, pp. 12–138.

29. Spreitzer, 1996.

30. Carol Yeh-Yen Lin, "The Essence of Empowerment: A Conceptual Model and a Case Illustration," *Journal of Applied Management Studies,* Dec. 1998, p. 223.

31. Carole Schweitzer, "Empowerment by Example," *Associate Management,* May 1998, p. 50.

32. John S. Morgan, revised by Beth Z. Schneider, *Interpersonal Skills for the Manager* (Institute of Certified Professional Managers, 2000), pp. 68–69.

33. Bernard M. Bass, David A. Waldman, Bruce J. Avolio, and Michael Bebb, "Transformational Leadership and the Falling Dominoes Effect," *Group & Organization Management,* 1987.

34. Carl Holmes, "Fighting the Urge to Fight Fires," *Harvard Business Review,* Nov.–Dec. 1999, p. 30.

35. Joseph H. Foegen, "Are Managers Losing Control?" *Business Horizons,* March–April 1998, p. 2.

36. Ibid.

37. Holmes, 1999.

38. Foegen, 1998.

39. S. C. Bushardt, D. L. Duhon, and A. R. Fowler Jr., "Management Delegation Myths and the Paradox of Task Assignment," *Business Horizons,* March–April 1991, pp. 34–43.

40. William W. Hull, "Passing the Buck vs. Making an Assignment," *Supervision,* March 1999, p. 6.

41. Ibid.

42. Holmes, 1999.

43. Robert Rohrer, "Does the Buck Ever Really Stop?" *Supervision,* April 1999, p. 11.

44. Monique R. Brown, "Management by Delegation: Don't Be a Micro Manager: Share the Responsibility," *Black Enterprise,* Feb. 1998, p. 76.

45. M. E. Haynes, "Delegation: There's More to It Than Letting Someone Else Do It," *Supervisory Management,* January 1980, p. 9.

46. Hull, 1999.

47. Pat Weisner, "Delegating Up," *Colorado Business Magazine,* Dec. 1997, p. 9.

Exercise 14–A
Assessing Yourself

Circle the response that most closely correlates with each item below.

	Agree	Neither		Disagree

1. I am willing to give up some of my control over projects to other team members or employees. 1 2 3 4 5

2. I do whatever it takes to produce a high-quality deliverable in my work. 1 2 3 4 5

3. I encourage those with whom I work or serve on a team to be involved in decision making, suggest new procedures, and solve problems creatively. 1 2 3 4 5

4. I delegate tasks to employees or teammates, respond to their questions, and trust them to make decisions as they see fit. 1 2 3 4 5

5. I accept responsibility for my work and for those for whom I am responsible. 1 2 3 4 5

6. On class projects or team assignments I create a vision of preferred achievements. 1 2 3 4 5

7. On class projects or team assignments I set high standards for performance and establish goals and deliverables needed to achieve that standard. 1 2 3 4 5

8. I look to myself for recognition and acceptance rather than wait to receive it externally. 1 2 3 4 5

9. I believe in myself and my capabilities to succeed. 1 2 3 4 5

10. I have a mechanism through which I can evaluate my performance. 1 2 3 4 5

11. I identify my allies and adversaries, and network and politic where appropriate. 1 2 3 4 5

12. After setting goals, I determine what and who can help or hinder my progress. 1 2 3 4 5

13. I identify potential obstacles and enlist the support of others in reducing those obstacles. 1 2 3 4 5

14. I take risks appropriately. 1 2 3 4 5

15. I consciously spend time helping those with whom I work to feel empowered. 1 2 3 4 5

16. I am comfortable assigning work to others. 1 2 3 4 5

17. I don't avoid delegating to others when it's appropriate. 1 2 3 4 5

18. I take the time to train others so they can take on added responsibilities. 1 2 3 4 5

19. I have let go of the notion that if I want a job done right, I have to do it myself. 1 2 3 4 5

	Agree	Neither		Disagree

20. I am willing to share responsibility for tasks with someone else.   1 2 3 4 5

21. When delegating I ensure the delegatee has the authority to obtain the necessary resources to complete the task.   1 2 3 4 5

22. When delegating I hold the delegatee accountable for the completion of the assignment.   1 2 3 4 5

23. When working on a class or team project I make an effort to establish an open, supportive environment.   1 2 3 4 5

24. When possible I delegate tasks that are correlated with the strengths and interests of the persons involved.   1 2 3 4 5

25. When working with a new team member or co-worker I delegate in small steps initially.   1 2 3 4 5

26. I set up regular checkpoints for the delegatee and obtain feedback regularly to ensure a project is on target and is being performed properly.   1 2 3 4 5

27. I provide delegatees with help, coaching, and feedback as appropriate.   1 2 3 4 5

28. When delegating, I ensure that the delegatee understands the task being assigned.   1 2 3 4 5

If your score was 84 or higher, you may want to develop a plan to improve your empowerment and delegation skills.

Exercise 14–B
It's Plane to Me

Each group will consist of five production employees and one supervisor. You will be instructed to create a paper airplane. The instructor will supply the supervisors with their instructions for their production process. Production workers are to follow the instructions provided by their supervisor. Any questions or suggestions should be discussed with your supervisor.

Questions

1. How did you feel while doing your job?
2. How do you feel about your supervisor?
3. How did you respond or react to your supervisor's instructions?
4. Would you enjoy working for this company? Why or why not?
5. What was your productivity level? What was the quality?

Exercise 14–C
Case Study: "Am I the Manager?"

Gail was hired at the apparel manufacturing company to be the office and production manager. She was very excited about her new position; the job responsibilities seemed to be a perfect fit with her skills and strengths. Her responsibilities included running the office and the ordering department and coordinating the production facilities. Larry was the owner of the company and he handled all the financial aspects of the business. L.J. was the plant manager and was Gail's direct supervisor.

On the first day of work, Larry instructed Gail to make the order and production department more efficient. Gail soon began to realize that there were a few employees in the ordering department who were very inefficient and lacking in motivation. One employee in particular, Kathy, would come in 10–20 minutes late, have several personal calls that lasted anywhere from 5–25 minutes, and refused to answer the phones when anyone else seemed to be free. She would simply say to the other order people, "I need you to get that call; I'm busy doing my account summaries." Larry had already warned her of Kathy's unacceptable behavior and informed her that Kathy had several documented violations and notations in her personnel file. Larry felt that Gail should try to work with her, but if she was not able to change her behavior, he wanted Gail to document one final complaint and terminate her.

Gail decided to have a feedback session with Kathy, during which Kathy was very defensive yet said she would try to change her behavior. Kathy insinuated that even though she did these things, Larry liked her and he was not really bothered by them. Over the next two weeks Kathy did not change her behavior, so, with the documented results of the feedback session and the other citations in her file, Gail decided she would terminate Kathy. Kathy caused a scene in the office and ran into Larry's office. After a considerable time period, Gail was called into Larry's office and he told Gail that Kathy was not fired and that "Gail just needed to help Kathy improve upon her behaviors." Gail left the meeting feeling like she had just been undermined in front of the entire staff.

Another situation that had been developing dealt with Gail's reorganization of the production department. In order to gain efficiency between the ordering staff and the production department, there needed to be an order and prioritization schedule. After developing a new system, Gail proceeded to explain the new system to both the ordering department and to Maggie, the production supervisor, and her staff. Not much was said and Gail felt confident her new system would work out. Soon she discovered that nothing had changed. Maggie was making her own determinations regarding production regardless of the orders put in and prioritized by the order department. Gail went to discuss it with Maggie and the reply she got from Maggie was, "This is my department, I have been here much longer than you and I'll have them produce what I want them to. Go cry to Larry if you don't like it. Until I hear it from Larry I will do as I please." This dream job was starting to seem more like a nightmare.

The final straw came regarding the ordering of materials. Gail quickly realized that they did not have the necessary materials to make the high demand products. She worked on an inventory count with L.J. and between the two of them they were able to come up with an accurate count and an order plan to get production back on schedule. Gail then proceeded to place an order for the necessary supplies. At least she had control over something around here. Two days later, Larry called her into the office furious about the orders. "How dare you order supplies," Larry stormed. "You do not have the right to requisition materials; I handle the finances and this just put me in a bad spot with a supplier I owe money to. I make the decision on when we purchase materials. Understand?" Gail was beginning to understand all too well. She was mad, frustrated, hurt, and disillusioned all at the same time. "What have I gotten myself into with this organization?" she thought.

Questions

1. What guidelines of empowerment were violated by Larry or Gail?

2. What guidelines of delegation were violated by Larry or Gail?

3. What should Gail plan to discuss with Larry? What issues need to be raised?

4. What does Gail need to do in order to obtain the necessary elements of empowerment and delegation? What does Larry need to do to facilitate Gail's success?

5. What advice would you give to Larry and Gail regarding their working situation?

**Exercise 14–D
Case Study: "Make It
or Break It"**

Rob was faced with a big decision. He had four weeks to complete the research and present a recommendation and action plan for tackling the new demographic market. Rob was the marketing manager for the Mid-Atlantic region for Sportster Athletic Wear's footwear division. Sportster was now wanting to add footwear to its stores in the Southeast, where they traditionally have been supplying only apparel and sporting equipment.

Rob started to consider the steps for developing his research and recommendations. Within his department he had several employees at his disposal. Sue had previous experience working for a national footwear producer. Ken had transferred in from the apparel division for the Southeast market. Ryan, Amy, and Sandy have worked for Sportster for five, three, and two years (respectively) but had limited experience beyond their work with this organization. Rob himself had several years of footwear experience, yet had very little experience with the Southeastern market.

Questions

1. Should Rob make this decision on his own? Why or why not?

2. If he should involve others in this decision process, whom should he include and what level of empowerment or involvement should he utilize? Why?

3. What are the most important factors in deciding whom to involve?

4. What will he have to provide and what ingredients will need to be given for effective empowerment?

**Exercise 14–E
Delegating Tasks**

From a past or present job, group project, or organizational task (from a fraternity, fundraiser, committee activity), think of a task you would like to or could delegate to another person.

The task to be delegated including all contingencies and related activities: _____

_____

_____

The goal and benefits (to me, to the delegatee) of delegating the task: _____

_____

_____

The person or persons who will be chosen (What skills, abilities, and competencies do they possess?): _____

_____

_____

The assignment of the responsibilities (How will I clearly communicate all the requirements for this task? How can I motivate them to do this task?): _____

_____

_____

The transferring of authority (What power must they have? Who else will need to be informed? What parameters will be set for limitations?): _____

_____

_____

The establishing of accountability (What are the rewards and consequences? How will completion be measured? What are the standards for completion?): _____

_____

The establishing of responsibility (What degree of responsibility will I give? What level of delegation will I use and why?): _____

_____

_____

The establishing of controls (What control mechanisms will I need to develop? When and how will I evaluate progress?): _____

_____

_____

Questions

1. What will be the most difficult aspect of this delegation for you?

2. What potential problems, barriers, or consequences can you foresee for this delegation?

3. What other steps or aspects must be taken into consideration in order to make this an effective delegation?

Exercise 14–F
Try This . . .

1. Interview a manager about the way in which she or he empowers employees. (You might need to define the term for them.) Ask them questions such as:

   ■ How many direct reports do you have?

   ■ Do you consider them to be effective performers? Why or why not?

   ■ Do you consider them to be trustworthy? Why or why not?

   ■ In what ways do you empower your employees?

   ■ Is this process successful? Why or why not?

   ■ If you were called out on a two-week assignment, is there an employee you would feel comfortable putting in charge of your unit? Why or why not?

   ■ What concerns would you have in doing so?

   ■ In what ways does an empowering management philosophy help or hinder your success as a manager?

   Based on his or her answers, would you say this manager used empowerment successfully? Defend your answer with examples shared in your interview.

2. Several of the following videos present varying views of how employees or groups of individuals are empowered or not, including *A Christmas Carol, Scrooged, Mr. Holland's Opus, Office Space, 9 to 5, The Color Purple, Norma Rae, Working Girl, Ghandi, Zulu, Antz.* Using principles discussed in this chapter, write a brief essay (2–4 pages) discussing the implementation and outcomes of empowerment (or lack thereof) as depicted in the video you watched. Support your answers with references to specific behaviors or actions of key characters.

**Exercise 14–G
Reflection/Action
Plan**

This chapter focused on empowerment and delegation—what it is, why it's important, and how to improve your skills in this area. Complete the worksheet below upon completing all reading and experiential activities for this chapter.

1. The one or two areas in which I am most strong are:

_____

_____

_____

_____

2. The one or two areas in which I need more improvement are:

_____

_____

_____

_____

3. If I did only one thing to improve in this area, it would be to:

_____

_____

_____

_____

4. Making this change would probably result in:

_____

_____

_____

_____

5. If I did not change or improve in this area, it would probably affect my personal and professional life in the following ways:

_____

_____

_____

_____

15 Teams in the Workplace

How do I:

✓ Form a team and help it progress through developmental stages?

✓ Form or join a high-performance work team?

✓ Ensure that all members of a team contribute equally?

✓ Handle differences in values and work styles in a team setting?

✓ Allocate team roles and responsibilities?

✓ Motivate a team to achieve its objectives?

Jeremy was perplexed. He had been looking forward to what was the first class team project of his college experience. He had heard from his father how prevalent teams were in the workplace. As a student, he hadn't encountered teams in the classroom, just in sports. He had done virtually all of his schoolwork on his own, such as doing research, writing papers, and studying for exams. This class was going to be different.

At the outset of the class, everyone was put into small groups. Each group was given a project on which to work. Over the course of the semester, the group was supposed to evolve into what the instructor called a high-performance work team. But now, at the project's midpoint, Jeremy felt his group was anything but high performance. Things had started out great. Right away, Jeremy hit it off with his fellow teammates. While the team was diverse in terms of gender, ethnicity, and major, most members had similar interests and got along well with each other. They had even gotten together socially a couple of times during the semester. At the beginning, the group was very task-oriented. They seemed to communicate well and were able to clarify their objective, determine their topic and research priorities, allocate roles and responsibilities, and set up a planning schedule working backwards from their end of the semester project due date.

After a few initial organizing meetings, the group members were left to work on their own. That's where the problems started occurring. In preparation for an interim project due date, Jeremy and his team had planned a team meeting the night before to combine everyone's work and produce the deliverable that the instructor expected the next day. To his horror, Jeremy discovered that only he and one other team member were ready. The others had procrastinated and thought they could "wing it." He was contemplating pulling an all-nighter to make up the others' work. "This project is going nowhere," he thought. "Why didn't I just do everything on my own? I could have done better working on my own. This team stuff isn't all it's cracked up to be."

1. What is the situation faced by Jeremy? What are the core issues here?

2. How did this situation develop? What could have been done to achieve a different outcome?

3. How would you feel if you were Jeremy? Has a similar situation happened to you?

4. What would you do if you were Jeremy?

5. What should Jeremy do?

"We are a pack animal. From earliest times we have used the strength of the group to overcome the weakness of the individual. And that applies as much to business as to sport."[1]

> Tracey Edwards (Skippered
> the First Women's Crew to
> Circumnavigate the Globe)

From the popular CBS television show *Survivor* (premiered Summer 2000) to most of the *Fortune* 500 and many high-tech startup firms to competitive sports, teams are an everyday occurrence in our personal and work lives. As the nature of work progresses from individually based work to group settings, understanding teams and how to work in team settings has become a crucial interpersonal skill. Not everyone is convinced that teams are more effective than individuals working on their own. But the reality is that many companies are attempting to set up a team-based structure when tackling particular issues or processes, and the ability to work as a team is one of the most commonly required skills in the work environment.[2] While teams may not provide the best structure for all work tasks, teams are so common now that they warrant a complete chapter in this book.

This chapter covers the basics of teamwork. We define teams and detail their importance in business today. We discuss strategies for forming teams and tips for making teams effective and successful. We also include several exercises at the end of the chapter for you to assess and further enhance your team skills, as well as resources available for further exploration.

What Is Teamwork?

A team is a formal work group consisting of people who work together intensely to achieve a common group goal. The essence of teamwork is to create a product through a collective effort that exceeds the quality of any individual endeavor or the collective efforts of several individuals.[3] The word *team* is not synonymous with *group*. A **group** is a collection of people who may or may not be working collectively toward the same goal. A **team** is composed of three or more interdependent individuals who are consciously striving to work together to achieve a common objective, which in business tends to encompass improvements in products, services, or processes. A group becomes a team when members demonstrate a commitment to each other and to the end goal toward which they are working. In a team, there is a higher degree of cohesiveness and accomplishment than in a group.[4]

From earliest times, human beings have used teams or groups to overcome the weaknesses of individuals. Collections of nomads in search of food and land, kingdoms composed of villagers and their leaders, native settlements, wagon trains and pioneers, the crews of ships—all were formed with the idea that more could be accomplished together than by an individual.[5] Even Adam and Eve decided to band together, as did the quasi-"alliance" on the CBS television show *Survivor*. Aside from gains in sheer horsepower, as in the case of a ship's crew, teams exist because few individuals possess all the knowledge, skills, and abilities needed to accomplish all tasks. Simply put, two heads are often better than one.

Within many professional sports teams, we can find shining examples of teamwork. Michael Jordan, one of the world's greatest basketball players and author of the book, "I Can't Accept Not Trying," writes, "One thing I believe to the fullest is that if you think and achieve as a team, the individual accolades will take care of themselves. Talent wins games, but teamwork and intelligence win championships." He says he never forgot that he was only one-fifth of the effort at any time.[6] Staying with sports for a moment, consider the differences between a gymnastics team and a football team. In gymnastics, the members of a team may work together, but the ultimate achievement of a team is based on the collective efforts of the individual gymnasts. A winning team has the highest combined score. In football, by contrast, a great quarterback is nothing without a great wide receiver, tight end, or offensive line that can keep him from getting sacked. A football team wins when all members work interdependently toward the same goal— passing and rushing their way toward touchdowns.

Returning to the workplace, it is estimated that between 70 and 82 percent of U.S. companies use the team concept, making teamwork skills one of the most commonly required skills in the work environment.[7] Many businesses are adopting a collaborative management approach that encourages the sharing of ideas and strategies throughout the organization. This collaboration provides many benefits to the organization as well as to the individuals who make up the teams.[8]

Why Teams?

Teaming is more than a phase or a buzzword. If it didn't work, organizations would abandon this strategy or mechanism for getting work done. There is much evidence that teams can be effective, especially when tasks are complex and task interdependence is high. It is not always appropriate, of course, for work to be done in teams. But when a team structure is employed, and those teams work effectively, many benefits accrue to the organization and to the team members themselves.

Benefits of Teams

- Increased creativity, problem solving, and innovation.
- Higher quality decisions.
- Improved processes.
- Global competitiveness.
- Increased quality.
- Improved communication.
- Reduced turnover and absenteeism and increased employee morale.

■ Increased creativity, problem solving, and innovation: Bringing together a group of individuals who possess a wealth of ideas, perspectives, knowledge, and skills can result in a synergy through which new ideas can be entertained. We each have a unique set of skills. Working with others allows us to combine our skills and talents with those of others to create new approaches to solving problems.[9] An example is a team of marketers where each person applies his or her strengths to the issue at hand. One person who is very creative can lead the process of coming up with ideas; another who is detail-oriented can do the initial research; a third person who is skilled in graphic applications can put together a great sales presentation.

■ Higher quality decisions: Teamwork enhances the quality of the outcomes. Teamwork involves the collective effort of a group of people who represent diverse backgrounds and experiences. As more ideas are produced and alternatives are considered, the team gets closer to optimal decisions—decisions that are stronger because they have been made with various perspectives and interests in mind.

■ Improved processes: Teamwork results in a systematic approach to problem solving. Because of the necessary coordination between and transfer of learning among team members, teamwork results in organized approaches to the situation at hand. For example, a team is more likely than an individual to set up project checkpoints and planning systems to enable all team members to contribute to the project as it unfolds. Teamwork also permits for distribution of workloads for faster and more efficient handling of large tasks or problems.[10] When members representing different organizations work together to improve a process that cuts across multiple organizational functions, more glitches and interdependencies will be uncovered and addressed than would be if individuals working independently were to tackle this project.

■ Global competitiveness: Teamwork enables companies to compete globally. Firms in the United States are relying increasingly on diverse teams to compete in the global economy.[11] Diverse teams have skill sets and perspectives that are superior to what a single individual can bring to the table. For example, back in the 1980s when Clairol marketed its popular Mist Stick in parts of Germany, it flopped. Had the Clairol marketing team included someone of German origin, they could have informed the group that mist was a slang word for "manure." As we continue developing and marketing our products in a global marketplace, combining diverse perspectives is essential.

■ Increased quality: Studies show that those large, complex, global companies that have moved to teams show increases in productivity, employee ownership of and accountability for their work, timeliness, efficiency, and customer service.[12] This results in higher quality standards than are possible when individuals or groups of individuals, who lack a common goal, are doing the work.

■ Improved communication: The use of teams in the workplace enhances employee communication. In a traditional, hierarchical organization, communication tends to flow primarily in one direction—downward. In a team-based organization, communication flows laterally, upward, downward, and even outside the organization's boundaries (e.g., customers and suppliers). Teamwork requires collective action that is grounded in words and actions. It's not sufficient for one person to determine how he or she wants to work. Each person must get others on board before proceeding. In effective teams, there is rich sharing of information and ideas that improves communication within the team and between the team and the organization.[13]

■ Reduced turnover and absenteeism and increased employee morale: Teamwork results in changes in employee behaviors and attitudes. Teamwork fosters a camaraderie that helps many employees to feel more a part of the organization than when working independently. They feel ownership to the problems on which they work, get immediate feedback from teammates, see the fruits of their labors, and feel they have an impact on their job and the organization. Compared with the alienation often experienced by employees in traditional firms, employees in team-based organizations are happier, more committed, and more loyal to their organization.

The chart below contains examples of the positive outcomes that resulted when organizations embraced and encouraged team-based work:

Examples of Successes by Self-managed Teams[14]

Organization	Reported Successes
Harley-Davidson	Returned to profitability in six years.
Hallmark	Two hundred percent reduction in design time. Introducing 23,000 new card lines each year.
Liberty Mutual	Fifty percent reduction in contract process time. Saving of more than $50 million per year.
Johns Hopkins Hospital	Patient volume increased by 21 percent. Turnover reduced, absenteeism reduced by 20 percent.
Monsanto	Quality and productivity improved by 47 percent in 4 years.
Saab and Volvo	Four percent increase in production output. Inventory turnover increased from 9 to 21 times a year.

Potential Limitations of Teams

While this chapter focuses primarily on the effectiveness of teams and how-tos for being a productive team member, there are some concerns about teams and their ability to make the most effective decisions. Some of these concerns are expressed briefly below.

Limitations of Teams

- **Group think. Group think**—or individuals agreeing reluctantly with a group's decision—is a potential problem for teams. Group think can happen when a decision is made in a hurry, when one or a few members are extremely dominant in a group setting, or when one or more members present believe they haven't had a chance to air their concerns before an action is taken.
- **Social loafing.** By definition a team is a collection of three or more people. Invariably, a team will be composed of members with different work ethics and work styles, and this can result in some individuals doing more work than others.
- **Quality concerns.** Ironically, although there is much evidence that teams produce quality outcomes, the fact is that some individuals have the expert knowledge necessary to be able to make decisions independently without the benefit of a team.
- **Timeliness.** Individuals can make decisions more quickly than teams, especially if gaining buy-in from others is not an essential component of the action under consideration.
- **Diversity.** In general, diversity of background and thought process is a good way to ensure that multiple perspectives will be incorporated into a particular decision. Sometimes, especially when expedience is desired or when management has a clear preference for a particular course of action, a homogenous group can make decisions more quickly and easily than can a more diverse group.

Organizing work into teams is the wave of the future. But like any new phenomenon, it is important to understand that teams have both upsides and downsides. Teams may not be optimal for every business situation. But when you are placed in a team, be aware of the potential problems and develop strategies early on that can overcome these concerns.

Types of Teams

In the same way sports teams differ in function, makeup, and ultimate goal or purpose, so do teams in the workplace. Based on the purpose or goal of the team, organizations may choose among several options by which to structure teams: cross-functional, self-managed, task force, process improvement.

The more commonly used team types are:

Cross-functional teams: These include members from various departments or business specialties such as marketing, information systems, communications, public relations, operations, human resources, accounting, finance, planning, research and development, and legal. Cross-functional teams are usually charged with developing new products or investigating and improving a companywide problem such as the need to increase speed and efficiency across departmental lines or the need to adopt a new companywide computer system. Cross-functional teams derive their strength from diversity. By including representatives from all or most of an organization's primary functional areas, the team can diagnose a problem from multiple perspectives simultaneously, ensuring that all relevant points of view are taken into account. This can speed up the problem-solving process and result in an outcome that is more readily accepted by the various departments that are affected by the change.

Case in point: Prior to producing their LH line of cars, Chrysler followed what most would call a serial design process. Engineering would design a car and throw it over the wall to manufacturing. "We can't build this," manufacturing replied, and sent it back over the wall to engineering. This would continue for months or years until marketing was charged with marketing a car that no one wanted. From product inception to market, this process could take as long as six years or more. By that time, technologies were obsolete and other companies easily stole market share. Realizing this, Chrysler moved to a simultaneous, cross-functional team-based design process. Everyone who had a stake in or was affected by the design of a new product was on a team that hashed it out— together. This included people from marketing, sales, engineering, design, and many others. These meetings had conflict, but the conflict was actually helpful. Chrysler was able to reduce the cycle time from over six years to less than 18 months!

Another example of a cross-functional team is a top management team. In many large organizations, the CEO typically makes strategic decisions in collaboration with the leaders of the major functional areas. Even at this level in the organization, top management recognizes their individual strengths and weaknesses and the value that diverse perspectives can add when making key organizational decisions.

Self-managed teams: These are "groups of employees who are responsible for a complete, self-contained package of responsibilities that relate either to a final product or an ongoing process."[15] Also known as self-directed, self-maintained, or self-regulating, self-managed teams are typically given a charge by senior management and then are given virtually complete discretion over how, when, and what to do to attain their objective. Self-managed teams are expected to coordinate their work without ongoing direction from a supervisor or manager. Self-managed teams set their own norms, make their own planning schedules, set up ways to keep relevant members and others informed of their progress, determine how the work is going to be accomplished, and are held accountable for their end product or "deliverable." Many of these teams are responsible for hiring, training, and firing team members. The flattening of organizational structures, resulting in less hierarchy and fewer managers, makes self-directed teams a popular concept in business today. Of course, it's not as if management flips a switch and a team becomes self-managing. It's a long process of team building and teamwork combined with sufficiently greater responsibility and accountability gained through the team's demonstrated capabilities and performance.

Task force: This is an ad hoc, temporary project team assembled to develop a product, service, or system or to solve a specific problem or set of problems. Companies are always faced with the challenge of getting ongoing, day-to-day work done while utilizing available resources to work on various change processes or product innovations. For example, a technology company might designate a group to study the next wave in software development while others are maintaining and servicing existing software programs. Often task force members are individuals who have demonstrated interest or skill in the area being examined by the task force, so the members are enthusiastic about the project and its potential. The task force process is very common in business today. It is lower in cost than hiring an outside consultant or group of contract workers and allows for management to allocate resources at will to various projects as the needs of the company and the interests of its employees change.

Process improvement teams: These teams focus on specific methods, operations, or procedures and are assembled with the specific goal of enhancing the particular component being studied. Process improvement teams are typically composed of individuals with expertise and experience in the process being reviewed. They are assigned the tasks of eliminating redundant steps, looking for ways to reduce costs, identifying ways to improve quality, or finding means for providing quicker, better customer service.[16] Process improvement teams are often given training on problem-solving tools and techniques to help them map processes, identify root causes of problems, and prioritize potential solutions.

To analyze a system and make recommendations for changes, process improvement team members diagnose the current state of a process and chart how it occurs step by step. They review customer or internal data and collect data from other sources such as managers, competitors, and others as needed. They identify ways the process can be enhanced, make their recommendations, and sometimes assist the operating units involved in implementing the changes. Process improvement teams are usually temporary and disband once the process being studied has been changed to the satisfaction of management.

Team Developmental Stages

Groups typically pass through a series of stages as they grow and evolve into teams. Theorists postulate that a team goes through five stages in its life cycle:[17] forming, storming, norming, performing, adjourning. Each phase has distinguishing characteristics and presents particular challenges to team members and their managers.

Stage One—Forming

In this stage, a team is established to accomplish a particular task. Typically the group members will not know each other, and even if they do, there is a feeling of uncertainty and tentativeness because people haven't had a chance yet to get to know one another and set group objectives.[18] In the **forming** stage, members will engage in behaviors such as defining the initial assignment, discussing how to divvy up the necessary tasks, understanding the broad scope and objectives of the project, and learning about the resources (time, equipment, personnel) available to the team as it works to complete the project. In this stage, there is some testing by members of leadership roles, some discovery of personality similarities and differences, some initial disclosure, and usually relatively little progress on the task.

As a team member or team leader, your role in stage one is to encourage the group to establish its mission and purpose, set up a work schedule, get to know one another, and establish some initial norms for working together.

Stage Two—Storming

In this stage, a group experiences differences over factors such as direction, leadership, work style and approach, and perceptions about the expected quality and state of the end product or deliverable. As is true of any relationship, conflict is inevitable. Many couples feel bad when they experience their first fight, and teams are no exception. When the first conflict among group members emerges, some or all of the members begin to feel less enthusiastic about the group and might even doubt the group can come together and achieve its objective. There may be struggles over leadership ("my way is best"), power ("if you don't agree we'll leave you behind") and roles ("who appointed you chief?"). In the **storming** stage, feelings emerge such as resistance to the task or approach being taken by the group, resentment about differences in workload, anger about roles and responsibilities, and changes in attitude about the group or toward individual group members and concerns. Typically in the storming stage, the group is in conflict and chaos, as the group has not yet established ways to communicate about these differences. During this stage, few if any processes and procedures are in place, as the need for them wasn't anticipated due to the lack of prior conflict. All of this can result in arguing among members, emergence of subgroups, and disunity. If and when a group on which you are serving enters this stage, what can you do?

In the storming stage, your role as a group member or leader is to refrain from taking sides. Encourage the group to develop communication channels. Help your group members to focus on the task and not on personal differences. Promote an environment of open communication to ensure that the inevitable conflict is healthy and results in improved communication and commitment to the group's task. Remember that an appropriate level of tension motivates a team, but too much or too little can affect productivity.[19] If your group cannot resolve or work effectively with conflict, request the assistance of a trained process consultant or facilitator. A group that can't resolve this conflict may never achieve its deliverable.

Stage Three—Norming

In this stage, the group faces its issues, conflicts, and power and leadership struggles openly and directly. The members establish and adhere to patterns of acceptable behavior and learn to incorporate new methods and procedures into their working together. In the **norming** stage, members feel a new ability to express constructive criticism; they feel part of a working team and a sense of relief that everything will work out.[20] In this stage, members attempt to achieve harmony by avoiding unnecessary conflict, acting more friendly toward and trusting of each other, and developing a sense of team unity ("together, we can solve this").

As a team member or leader, your role is to encourage team members to take on more responsibility, work together to create means acceptable for solving problems, set challenging goals, and take personal responsibility for team success. As a leader, you set the tone. Don't expect others to "do as you say, but not as you do." If you are seen bickering with colleagues and secretly plotting political moves, team members are less likely to emulate the helpful norming behaviors and may regress to the storming stage.

Stage Four—Performing

In the **performing** stage, teams have worked through their differences. Their membership is stable, the task is clear, and eyes are on the prize. Team members are highly motivated to accomplish their task and focused on team objectives rather than individual interests. Through working closely together, team members have developed insights into each other's strengths and weaknesses (many even finish each other's sentences), feel satisfied with the team's progress, and believe the team will successfully reach or even exceed its goals. In this stage, members engage in constructive self-change for the good of the group; experience greatly enhanced ability to communicate with and give feedback to each other; are able to anticipate, prevent, or work through group problems; and, as a result, develop a close attachment to the team.[21]

As a team member or leader, your role at this stage is to encourage members to provide support to and serve as resources for each other. Make sure the team continues with its progress and maintains its cohesion and morale, and guide it toward success. Do remain vigilant, however. It's easy to kick back and relax, believing that once a team gets to this phase of development, it stays there. That may or may not be true. Changes in membership, scope of the task, or broader organizational changes can cause a team to regress developmentally. In addition, the close attachments members have to a team could possibly blind them to other developing problems.

Stage Five—Adjourning

After successfully completing the task or objective, teams may disband permanently or take a temporary break. Some may get new members or receive a new objective. This stage is usually brought on by an imminent deadline. At the **adjourning** stage, members are likely to feel disappointment—if the experience was positive—or gratitude—if the experience was negative! The task at this stage is to tie up loose ends and complete final follow-up on projects.

As a team member or leader, your role at this end stage is to encourage the team members to debrief the project, discussing the lessons learned that members can take with them to new projects and convey to new teams tackling similar issues. It is also helpful at this stage to recognize the team for its efforts. This could take the form of public recognition (a blurb on the team's accomplishments in the monthly newsletter), a reward (some organizations reward teams with a percentage of the savings or revenues realized as a result of the team's work), or other benefit (use company funds to take the team out for lunch). By providing encouragement and recognizing accomplishments, hard work, and efforts, you help to continue momentum and build motivation.[22] Of course, ongoing work project teams may not physically adjourn. They may remain intact, continuing with a new set of objectives once a particular project is complete. In this case, rather than adjourning, the team members may choose to debrief at certain checkpoints along the way, evaluating their processes and communication efforts to ensure they're keeping current and are as productive as they can be.

It is healthy for groups to move through each of these stages as they evolve into a team. Not all groups go through all the stages, and some go through them at different paces. For example, if a group's members knew each other previously and had similar values and goals—as well as a tight deadline—they might be able to move almost immediately to the norming stage. In another case, where the group members don't know each other well and they have some time before the deliverable is due, they might take longer to reach the norming phase and coalesce as a real team just before the deliverable is due. Some may get stuck in one of the stages and disband before progressing to the next stage or perform at a lower level than what might have been possible. A group stuck in the storming stage but facing an imminent deadline has to continue performing. In this case, it is likely that its performance will suffer due to the inability to function cohesively. In some extreme cases, a group will be dysfunctional and will require outside intervention in order to complete their task. As is true with relationships, teams have developmental cycles. Understanding this ahead of time can help you to develop strategies for helping your group evolve into a team and to increase its effectiveness every step of the way.

Characteristics of High-Performance Teams

As former Notre Dame coach Lou Holtz said, "Winning is never accidental. To win consistently you must have a clear plan and intense motivation." As we have said, not all teams are alike. As a team member or leader, your primary goal is to encourage your group to evolve into a motivated, goal-oriented, successful team; we refer to these types of teams as high-performance teams. In **high-performance teams,** there is a commitment to quality and a dedication to producing the best outcome possible. Research shows that most high-performance work teams possess the following characteristics:[23]

■ Common purpose and goals: High-performing teams have a clearly defined mission, purpose, and goals. Individual team members understand why the team has been formed and what is expected from the team.[24]

■ Clear roles: High-performing teams have clarity about roles and responsibilities. Team members understand their roles and assignments and how they impact the group, have clear and stable boundaries, awareness of task interdependence and how their work affects other members, and the direction that is needed to get there.[25]

■ Communication processes: High-performing teams have extensive communication mechanisms. They communicate regularly with each other either in person, via telephone, or through e-mail and keep those unable to attend meetings informed of the group's progress. They constantly update their planning calendar and communicate about adjustments, as they are needed.[26]

■ Accepting and supportive leadership: Studies have found that team leaders, who function more as coaches than managers, facilitate the development of participative, motivated teams.[27] These leaders were proactive, committed to the team, and provided encouraging, positive influence over the team and its members. Whereas a manager pulls a group along, a coach gently pushes it from behind; a manager works to maintain control, and a coach works to give up control.[28]

■ Small size: The size of the team can be essential to a team's success. The optimal size is between 6 and 10. This is large enough to accomplish the work and provide enough human resources and ideas, and small enough for a team to coalesce and reach consensus on major issues.[29]

■ High levels of technical and interpersonal skills: High-performing teams are composed of members who have a breadth of both specialty and people skills. Understanding how to work with and through others, problem solving, managing project work flow, giving and receiving feedback, goal setting, time management, and conflict management are some of the most valuable skills in team settings.[30]

■ Open relationships and trust: In high-performing teams, the members develop cooperative behaviors including understanding what is needed from one another; defining the interrelated activities necessary to complete the project; volunteering to assist each other in doing what's needed; and completing assigned tasks competently, on time, accurately, and with quality. Trust is built through behaviors such as being dependable, doing what is agreed upon, being kept informed and informing others of necessary facts and information, keeping confidential information private, and allowing others to use their specialized knowledge and abilities.[31]

■ Accountability: High-performance team members understand for what (and to what degree) they and others are held accountable. The team receives the message from the organization that performance matters—that it makes a difference whether goals are achieved or not. Expectations are clarified, and members are held responsible as individuals (quality standards) as well as mutually responsible as members of the team (team's performance on the deliverable or task).[32]

■ Reward structures: High-performing teams are rewarded for team accomplishments in addition to individual recognition. Organizations that support the team concept organize their recruiting, training, development, sales, business development, strategic planning, compensation, performance appraisal, and promotion strategies so that teamwork is supported and rewarded.[33] When these strategies don't match with or undermine team processes or philosophies, the organization sends a mixed message and members find ways to game the system—often at the expense of their team. If an individual team member who "saves the day" for the department is rewarded for individual behavior, it sends the message that collaboration is not as valued as individual contributions or heroics, even if management's rhetoric suggests teams are truly valued.

Tips for Effective Teams

As a member of a team, it is important to be self-directed and work for the betterment of your team. You and your team members will be working with minimal supervision, and it is everyone's responsibility to make the team work. As athletes have learned, if one team member doesn't come through, this affects the quality and performance of the entire team. Teamwork requires full dedication and participation by all members of the team.

The following tips can help make your next team experience more positive and successful.

■ Be focused. Cooperate with your team members in concentrating on the current issues being faced by the team. Cooperation builds trust and mutual respect. Be willing and dedicated to working towards the common purpose.

■ Handle conflict directly and be willing to compromise. Be willing to explore conflict in a constructive, win–win fashion. Stand up for things that are important to you, but don't insist on getting your way in every discussion. When working together, put personalities aside and confront issues that arise. Resolve conflicts and walk away from sessions with regard, respect, and esteem for yourself and your team members.[34]

■ Focus on both process and content. Pay attention to the *process* of becoming and working together as a team as well as the *result* or end goal that is expected from the team. Teamwork is more than producing a deliverable. It also entails the approach or process used when people are working together.[35] The ends don't necessarily justify the means if team members despise and lack respect for team members because of the way decisions and outcomes were rammed through as opposed to using a consensus approach. At team meetings, review both the processes being used as well as the status of the project.

■ Actively participate, and encourage others to do the same. At the beginning of a project, talk about roles and responsibilities. Also talk frankly about team members' schedules and their availability to participate fully in the project. Set up checkpoints to ensure that all are contributing equally.

■ Keep sensitive issues private. At the beginning of a project, discuss the importance of confidentiality. All teams engage in discussions that could be hurtful if made public. Have a pact that private information and views shared will be just that—not relayed to others outside of the group. "What's said in the room, stays in the room."

■ Communicate openly and positively. In order to have full team participation, and for the team to learn and develop, it is essential that team members do not embarrass, reject, mock, or punish someone for speaking up and sharing ideas and perceptions. Foster a climate of psychological safety in order to motivate members to participate, admit errors, and share ideas and beliefs openly and comfortably.[36]

■ Take time to establish operating guidelines and clarify expectations. Make sure everyone is present for initial discussions of roles, responsibilities, and operating guidelines. For these guidelines to work, it is best that everyone participate in establishing and agreeing to uphold these guidelines. Put them in writing and have everyone sign them.

■ Monitor what's going on with the team. Watch for reactions, nonverbal cues, level of participation (or lack thereof), and general changes in the group's dynamics. Develop observational skills to help the team reach its full potential. A side benefit of doing this is that you increase your own interpersonal skills as you try to set a tone that is conducive to all members enjoying and participating in the team experience.[37]

■ Practice giving (and receiving) effective feedback. Express support and acceptance by praising and seeking other members' ideas and conclusions. If you disagree with others' viewpoints, criticize ideas but not the people. Be specific about the ideas that concern you and accept others' concerns about your ideas.

■ Work with underperformers to keep them in the flow of the project and prevent them from becoming excluded from the group.[38] If slackers are an issue in your team, talk with them immediately, preferably one on one. Find out if there is a personal problem preventing the member from being more engaged. Offer to be supportive but don't carry the workload. Give that team member specific, manageable tasks and hold him or her accountable. If the underperformance continues, talk with your manager or instructor. The person may need to be removed from the group or reassigned to a different team.

■ Energize the team when motivation is low by suggesting new ideas, through humor or use of enthusiasm. Encourage a time-out, if one is needed, or suggest a work or coffee break.

■ Be reliable and conscientious. Respect other members by honoring deadlines, commitments, and project milestones.[39] If you are having difficulty making a deadline, don't wait until the last minute—discuss this immediately with a team member or with the team. There might be a different way of approaching the problem. It's easier for a team to be flexible when there is adequate time to review the situation and come up with a different plan.

■ When needed, give direction to the team's work by stating and restating the purpose of assignments, setting or calling attention to time limits, and offering procedures on how to most effectively complete the assignment.

■ Be supportive of your team members. Always ask how you can help. It's a great way to remind everyone you're a team with collective objectives, not a group of individual contributors competing against each other.

Why Teams Fail

A note of caution: for teams and teamwork to succeed, there must be ample time in which to complete an assignment. Also needed are adequate resources to achieve the stated objectives and full management support of the team's effort. While the concept of teamwork is prevalent in both work and nonwork settings, not all situations warrant or are conducive to teams. Teams may be faced with tight deadlines; merging of processes and responsibilities; technological challenges; mismatched skills and abilities; unresolvable personality clashes, styles, and behaviors; limited work or teaming experience; or power struggles. In these situations, or in cases where there is no interdependence or need for collaboration, teamwork is going to be difficult if not impossible. These issues should be addressed early so that modifications can be made if necessary.

For example, if a team lacks the proper skill sets, additional members or training sessions can be added. If a power struggle is unfolding, a facilitator can be appointed. Inexperienced team members can be assigned informal mentors or coaches. Sometimes, if it's in the best interests of an organization, a team can be disbanded altogether. Perhaps the mission wasn't clearly defined at the outset of a project and the team members find they are unable to devote the time necessary to do the job. Or perhaps management requested individuals to work on a team project but made no allowances for mandatory day-to-day tasks. In situations such as these, it's appropriate for the team to be reconfigured (or disbanded) so that the original objective can be attained through either a different team or a different approach. Oftentimes, teams ignore early problems—perhaps believing such problems can be overcome—and become dysfunctional.[40] Intervening early, in a proactive way, can turn a team around or cause the organization to consider other, non-team-based approaches to solving a problem.

How can you deal with team members who aren't performing? Following are some tips.

Dealing with Problem Team Members

■ **Absentee member:** A member can become distracted by a work or personal problem that prevents him or her from following through on commitments made to the team. In this case, the best strategy is to be direct immediately. Discuss the situation with the team member in a way in which the person does not feel he or she is being put on the defensive. Explain the problem and find out the team member's perception of the situation. Ask specifically if the team member still has the time necessary for the team. If not, part ways if possible. If this is not possible, determine a way for the team member to make contributions outside of the normal meeting times and make the person accountable for a specific segment of the work that limits reliance on the team.

■ **Social loafer:** As mentioned earlier, it is not uncommon for one or more persons on a team to be able to "hide" the fact they're not contributing. This typically happens when the team members' work ethics differ and one or more team members "step up to the plate" and take on additional responsibility to ensure the work gets done, effectively covering for the less productive team members. Work standards will always vary from person to person. A strategy for dealing with this is to raise the issue at the onset of the project. Divide the responsibilities and set up checkpoints to ensure each member is contributing roughly equally. If a discrepancy appears, try to quantify it and reallocate the workload so all members are contributing roughly equally.

■ **Procrastinator:** We're all human, and a seemingly human tendency is to "put off until tomorrow what we should be working on today." This is particularly problematic for work teams. Teams are composed of individuals with different work schedules and work styles. Some people thrive on the pressure of imminent deadlines while others find waiting until the last minute to be overly stressful. In this situation it is best to do two things: (a) set up interim checkpoints, or minideadlines, to ensure the work progresses at a reasonable pace, and (b) be realistic when work schedules are drawn up and deadlines determined. Prior to establishing deadlines, ask all team members to check personal and work calendars to catch any problems before they occur. At each meeting reclarify the commitments that might affect a person's inability to adhere to a deadline set earlier. And build in some slack: Set the final deadline for a few days before the *actual* deadline—just in case!

Teams may not be a cure for all that ails an organization. But, teams can be very effective if the team structure makes sense and members practice the suggestions outlined in the chapter. Other steps team members and their managers can take to improve the likelihood of team success are summarized in the chart below:

Tips for Managing for Outstanding Results

■ Care about the people you work with—understand them, know what's important to them, and be able to motivate them.

■ Don't worry about who gets the credit—emphasize team effort and rewards; use the "whatever is best for the team" approach.

■ Respect individual differences—accept individuals and work to emphasize strengths and minimize weaknesses.

■ Subordinate yourself to a higher purpose—keep the common goal in the forefront.

■ Know yourself—be aware of your strengths and admit your weaknesses; surround yourself with people who can compensate for your weaknesses.

■ Don't be afraid to follow—some of the best teams are those where the leader doesn't call all the shots.

Source: Stephen Covey, "Team Up for a Superstar Office," *USA Weekend,* Sept. 4–6, 1998, p. 10.

Summary

Workplaces in the United States and abroad have embraced teaming. This is no accident. Organizations that implemented work teams as a way to improve products, services, and processes have witnessed tremendous measurable benefits. Some of these benefits accrue because of synergies—the notion that teams produce more and better solutions than individuals—gained from the combining of various skill sets, perspectives, abilities, and workstyles on a single team. Not all teams produce phenomenal outcomes. By understanding the normal phases of group development and ways to gain and maintain group productivity and motivation, you can help your teams reach their full potential.

Key Terms and Concepts

Adjourning

Cross-functional teams

Forming

Group

Group think

High-performance team

Norming

Performing

Process improvement team

Self-managed team

Social loafing

Storming

Task force

Team

Endnotes

1. Quote by Tracey Edwards in "Teaming with Talent," by Jim White, *Management Today,* Sept. 1999, p. 56.

2. Lillian Chaney and Julie Lyden, "Making U.S. Teams Work," *Supervision,* Jan. 2000, p. 6.

3. Karl L. Smart and Carol Barnum, "Communication in Cross-Functional Teams: An Introduction to This Special Issue," *Technical Communication,* Feb. 2000, p. 19.

4. Kevin McManus, "Do You Have Teams?" *IIE Solutions,* April 2000, p. 21.

5. Jim White, "Teaming with Talent," *Management Today,* Sept. 1999, p. 56.

6. Harvey Mackay, "Get on the Team and Be a Winner," *Providence Business News,* August 16, 1999, p. 38.

7. Chaney, Jan. 2000.

8. McManus, April 2000.

9. Ibid.

10. Smart, Feb. 2000.

11. Chaney, Jan. 2000.

12. Mohsen Attaran and Tai T. Nguyen, "Succeeding with Self-managed Work Teams," *Industrial Management,* July–August 1999, p. 24.

13. Larry Cole and Michael Scott Cole, "Teamwork is Spelled Incorrectly: Teamwork = Communication," *Communication World,* April 2000, p. 56.

14. Attaran, 1999. Reprinted by permission of the Institute of Industrial Engineers, 25 Technology Park, Norcross, GA 30092, 770–449–0461. Copyright © 1999.

15. Ibid.

16. David Rohlander, "Building High-Performance Teams," *Credit Union Executive,* March 2000, p. 36.

17. Bruce W. Tuckerman, "Developmental Sequences in Small Groups," *Psychological Bulletin* 63 (1965), pp. 384–99.

18. Peter R. Scholtes, *The Team Handbook* (Madison, WI: Joiner and Associates, 1988).

19. John R. Myers, "What It Takes to Make a Team," *Purchasing,* Sept. 2, 1999, p. 91.

20. Scholtes, 1988.

21. Ibid.

22. Rona Leach, "Supervision: from Me to We," *Supervision,* Feb. 2000, p. 8.

23. Ruth Wageman, "Critical Success Factors for Creating Superb Self-Managing Teams," *Organizational Dynamics,* Summer 1997, p. 49.

24. Rohlander, 2000.

25. American Management Association, "HR Update: Creating Real Teamwork at the Top," *HR Focus,* Jan. 2000, p. 2.

26. Smart, 2000.

27. Paulo Vieira Cunha and Maria Joao Louro, "Building Teams That Learn," *The Academy of Management Executive,* Feb. 2000, p. 152.

28. Renee Evenson, "Team Effort: Beyond Employees to Team, beyond Manager to Coach," *Supervision,* Feb. 2000, p. 11.

29. Chaney, 2000.

30. Avan R. Jassawalla and Hemant C. Sashittal, "Building Collaborative Cross-Functional New Product Teams," *The Academy of Management Executive,* August 1999, p. 50.

31. Cole, 2000.

32. Russ Forrester and Allan B. Drexler, "A Model for Team-Based Organizational Performance," *The Academy of Management Executive,* August 1999, p. 36.

33. Becky L. Nichol, "Top Ten Reasons Teams Become Dysfunctional," *The National Public Accountant,* Feb. 2000, p. 12.

34. Jassawalla, 1999.

35. Cole, 2000.

36. Cunha, 2000.

37. Myers, 1999.

38. Ted Gautschi, "Strengthen Your Team," *Design News,* Oct. 18, 1999, p. 158.

39. Myers, 1999.

40. Smart, 2000.

Exercise 15–A
Assessing Yourself

Circle the response that most closely correlates with each item below.

	Agree	Neither		Disagree	
1. When working on a team project, I first attempt to define the objective and scope of the project.	1	② 3	4	5	
2. I encourage my team to clarify its mission and purpose and assess the resources that will be necessary to complete the task.	1	2 ③	4	5	
3. I try not to take sides in conflicts between team members.	1	2 3	④	5	
4. I encourage team members who are in conflict with each other to communicate openly and directly.	① 2	3	4	5	
5. I help team members to focus on the task at hand and not on personal differences.	1 ②	3	4	5	
6. I encourage team members to take personal responsibility for the team's success.	1	2 ③	4	5	
7. I encourage team members to debrief a project once it's completed.	1	2 ③	4	5	
8. I encourage team members to provide support to and serve as resources for each other.	① 2	3	4	5	
9. I consciously make an effort to become aware of my own and my team members' strengths and weaknesses.	① 2	3	4	5	
10. I encourage groups of which I'm a part to evolve into high-performance teams.	① 2	3	4	5	

	Agree	Neither		Disagree

11. I am committed to the best, highest quality product possible in any team effort of which I'm a part. — (1) 2 3 4 5

12. When I'm in a position to lead a team, I assume the role of coach or facilitator rather than director. — (1) 2 3 4 5

13. I encourage open communication and trust building when I am in team situations. — (1) 2 3 4 5

14. I regularly provide support, recognition, and positive feedback to team members. — (1) 2 3 4 5

15. I consciously do things to build team morale. — (1) 2 3 4 5

16. I cooperate with team members and concentrate with them on the current issues being faced by the team. — 1 (2) 3 4 5

17. In teams, I stand up for things that are important to me but don't insist on getting my way in every discussion. — 1 (2) 3 4 5

18. In teams, I pay attention to both the process of working as a team and the content or end goal that's expected from the team. — 1 (2) 3 4 5

19. I actively participate in the work of the team and encourage others to do so. — (1) 2 3 4 5

20. I encourage the team to talk frankly about team members' schedules and set up checkpoints to ensure that all are contributing equally. — 1 (2) 3 4 5

21. I keep sensitive information and information shared in confidence private. — 1 2 3 (4) 5

22. I foster a climate where team members are supported for sharing their ideas. — 1 2 (3) 4 5

23. I encourage the team to establish and adhere to group operating and communication guidelines. — 1 2 (3) 4 5

24. I try to use observational skills to monitor what's going on with the team. — 1 (2) 3 4 5

25. I express support and acceptance of my team members by praising and seeking their ideas and conclusions. — (1) 2 3 4 5

26. I willingly accept others' feedback about my ideas. — (1) 2 (3) 4 5

27. I work with underperformers to keep them in the flow of the project and to prevent them from being excluded from the group. — 1 (2) 3 4 5

28. As a team member, I am reliable and conscientious. — (1) 2 3 4 5

29. As a team member, I participate willingly. — (1) 2 3 4 5

Sum your circled responses. If your total is 87 or higher, you might want to explore ways to improve your skill in the area of working in teams.

55

**Exercise 15–B
Bridge Building**

Teams will be given four paper cups, four paper plates, and three sheets of heavy freezer paper and tape. Their task is to build a bridge that is 8 inches high and 16 inches long and can withstand rolling a light ball across it.

Groups of four–six are tasked with creating a bridge out of the materials provided. You have 30 minutes in which to complete this task. When the project is complete, or time is called—whichever comes first—your instructor will roll a ball across your bridge to ensure it meets the project specifications. Following this activity, discuss these questions in your group.

Questions

1. How did your group decide how to build the bridge? Did it make a plan or did it just start building?
2. Did anyone play a leadership role in the task? Explain.
3. What made building the bridge as a group, rather than as an individual, more difficult?
4. In what ways did the group make the project easier? Explain.
5. Was your group a group or team? Explain.

**Exercise 15–C
The Story: A Team
Exercise**

1. Read the story below and answer the corresponding questions. You will have between 5–10 minutes to complete this task.
2. You will then be assigned to a group of five or six. Each group will be given a "clean" answer sheet and 10–15 minutes in which to complete the task, as a group. You should not change any of your individual answers to the questions.
3. After time has elapsed, your instructor will help your group score the exercise.
4. Answer the questions which follow the activity, first as an individual and then discuss in your small group.

What Does the Story Tell?

Instructions

Read the following story and take for granted that everything it says is true. Read carefully because, in spots, the story is deliberately vague. Don't try to memorize it since you can look back at it at any time.

Then read the numbered statements about the story and decide whether you consider each one true, false, or questionable. Circling the "T" means that you feel sure that the statement is definitely true. Circling the "F" means that you feel sure that the statement is definitely false. Circling the "?" means that you cannot tell whether it is true or false. If you feel doubtful about any part of a statement, circle the question mark.

Take the statements in turn and do not go back later to change any of your answers. Do not reread any of the statements after you have answered them.

Story

The owner of the Adams Manufacturing Company entered the office of one of his foremen where he found three employees playing cards. One of them was Carl Young, brother-in-law of foreman Henry Dilson. Dilson, incidentally, often worked late. Company rules did not specifically forbid gambling on the premises, but the president had expressed himself forcibly on the subject.

Statements about the Story

1. In brief, the story is about a company owner who found three men playing cards.	T	F	?
2. The president walked into the office of one of his foremen.	T	F	?
3. Company rules forbade playing cards on the premises after hours.	T	F	?
4. While the card playing took place in Henry Dilson's office, the story does not state whether Dilson was present.	T	F	?
5. Dilson never worked late.	T	F	?

6. Gambling on the premises of the Adams Manufacturing Company was not punished. T F ?
7. Carl Young was not playing cards when the president walked in. T F ?
8. Three employees were gambling in a foreman's office. T F ?
9. While the card players were surprised when the owner walked in, it is not clear whether they will be punished. T F ?
10. Henry Dilson is Carl Young's brother-in-law. T F ?
11. The president is opposed to gambling on company premises. T F ?
12. Carl Young did not take part in the card game in Henry Dilson's office. T F ?

Questions

1. What process did you use to come up with the group answers?
2. Did anyone act as a leader or facilitator in the exercise? Explain.
3. In what ways was it difficult to achieve a group decision?
4. What behaviors blocked the group's process?
5. What behaviors helped the group's process?
6. What are the advantages or disadvantages of working in a group compared to working as an individual?

Exercise 15–D
Team Self-assessment

1. Working on your own, complete the following self-assessment.
2. Meet with your team. Appoint a facilitator, recorder, and spokesperson.
3. Engage in discussion about each member's results, strengths and weaknesses, and the meaning of the results for everyone's participation in the project at hand.
4. Discuss potential pitfalls faced by the team and ways you can work together for the success of the project.
5. Using the form below, summarize the combined strengths and weaknesses of the team and the pitfalls and ways to improve and share with the large group or class.
6. Report your results to the large group or class.
7. Discuss with the large group or class ways to improve participation in teams—lessons learned from past team experiences (negative and positive) and ways to make the current experience better.

Team Self-assessment

	Agree		Neither		Disagree
1. I participate willingly in team activities.	1	2	3	4	5
2. I stay with tasks I have taken on or been assigned.	1	2	3	4	5
3. I try to encourage the group to get back on track when needed.	1	2	3	4	5
4. I use team experiences as a potential learning activity.	1	2	3	4	5
5. I try consciously to be aware of my own behavior style and that of others.	1	2	3	4	5
6. I try to engage in active listening during team projects.	1	2	3	4	5
7. I help the team by keeping track of time, facilitating, recording our discussions, summarizing results, taking notes, and being a team spokesperson as needed.	1	2	3	4	5
8. I practice disclosure of feelings and perceptions of the team process.	1	2	3	4	5
9. I practice giving constructive, honest feedback.	1	2	3	4	5
10. I do what I can to make the team experience a positive one for all involved.	1	2	3	4	5

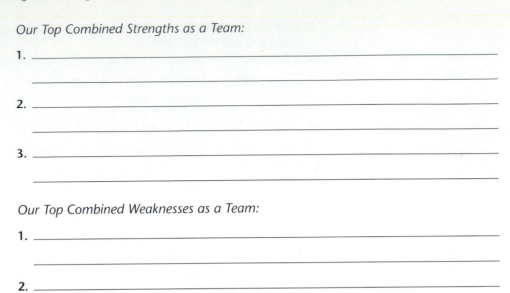

Our Top Combined Strengths as a Team:

1. _____

   _____

2. _____

   _____

3. _____

   _____

Our Top Combined Weaknesses as a Team:

1. _____

   _____

2. _____

   _____

3. _____

   _____

Potential Pitfalls We Face (e.g., conflicting schedules, lack of specific skills) and How We Can Overcome These:

Ways We Can Contribute to the Success of This Project:

**Exercise 15–E
Case Study on Forming Teams**

Due to reorganization and downsizing, a manager was told to develop teams to work on issues that were important to his department, division, and business unit. He sat down with several of his colleagues and developed a vision and mission statement for his people. They then identified four major areas of concern to the department and division.

In a subsequent meeting, the manager presented the mission statement, and the four identified areas of concern to all of the employees in the department. He then established four teams—one per major area of concern—by assigning 8–10 members to each team.

Questions

1. Given this scenario:
   - What do you think the outcome will be?

   - What did the manager do wrong?

2. As a team, develop an effective managerial approach to forming teams. (Use the first sentence of this case study as a starting point.)

**Exercise 15–F
Case Study on Gaining
Appropriate
Membership on Teams**

This is the team's third meeting. The team's task, deliverables, and membership have been dictated by a steering committee which oversees the teaming efforts of a division. Members represent different labs and management levels within the division. A new team member, one who missed the first two meetings, enters the room. The discussion goes something like this:

SCRIBE: "Okay. Here's our agenda. Does this sound okay to everyone?"

NEW TEAM MEMBER: "Well, not exactly. I have a question regarding the team's task. I know I missed the first two meetings, but I'm unclear about our purpose. I mean, without a well-understood purpose, are we ready to talk about membership? I'm not even sure if I should be here!"

SCRIBE: "Well, I suppose we can add "team purpose" to the agenda. How much time should we allot?"

TEAM LEADER: (Feeling strained by all the necessary structure.) "Could we hold off with the agenda for a few minutes . . . I know we need the agenda, but I think we should talk about purpose for a few minutes at least; then we can get back to the regular agenda. She (the new team member) brings up a good point."

Some discussion ensues. It becomes clear that the team's purpose *is* unclear. Other additional information is revealed, such as the fact that there had been three other team members who, shortly after being appointed by the steering committee, decided to excuse themselves from the team. Also, the team leader brought a new person in (call her Possible New Member), who is not really a full-fledged member until the steering committee okays it.

SCRIBE: "Back to the agenda. Were there any corrections to the minutes? (No response.) Okay, now for today's meeting roles . . . oh, our time keeper isn't here today."

NEW TEAM MEMBER: (Looking at Possible New Member) "Would you like to keep time?"

TEAM LEADER: "Well, we're not sure if she is an official team member yet. Remember, the steering committee hasn't okayed her yet. Should she keep time if she's not?"

NEW TEAM MEMBER: "What's the difference? And why do we have to have the steering committee's blessing? Let's just do it."

TEAM LEADER: "Actually, there are some other names, in addition to Possible Team Member, that we've submitted to the steering committee. After all, we've lost three people since the team began."

NEW TEAM MEMBER: "Do we need additional people? Why? Again, doesn't it depend on what we're trying to accomplish?"

Questions

1. Why is it important to clarify a team's purpose? Once the task is given, why is clarification necessary?

2. What role does this purpose play in defining team membership? Why do you suppose others have "excused themselves" from the team?

3. How effective is the team leader? Explain.

4. Meeting management techniques—using agendas, having a scribe and timekeeper—are intended to make meetings more effective. In what ways could these techniques have the opposite effect?

5. If you were asked to participate in this meeting, what would you do to get the process back on track? Explain.

**Exercise 15–G
The Case of the Take-
Charge Team Leader**

You are a member of a team that is meeting for the third time. Your goal is to reduce the number and dollar amount of workers compensation claims. The team consists of members from safety, human resources, legal, and medical (e.g., staff nurses and doctors). The team leader—a senior level manager—demonstrates a "take-charge" approach in that he/she believes he/she knows more about the task and assignment than anyone on the team. Early in the team's existence, the leader shared a project milestone chart that the team accepted. While the group has kept up with its assignments and is working rather effectively, the team leader seems impatient with the team's progress. In fact, the leader would like to exert greater control over the team's activities because he/she already has supporting data from outside groups and departments about the task and wants to complete the project in record time. However, you and other team members are concerned that (1) there may be other issues that have not yet surfaced, and (2) if his/her ideas are accepted, one of the team members may lose his/her position in the firm.

Questions

1. What issues are at play?

2. How would you feel in this situation?

3. If the leader is so capable, why do you suppose management created a team to address this particular (and highly visible) problem?

4. At this point, what would you do and why?

5. If no changes were made, what do you think the final outcome would be?

**Exercise 15–H
Try This . . .**

1. Watch a sports team in action—either at your school, in your community, or via a televised game. What effective teaming behaviors are displayed? What ineffective teaming behaviors are displayed? Explain and discuss the impact of how members interact on the outcome and how members seem to feel about the outcome.

2. Watch a video or movie that has a primary focus on a group or team, such as one listed below. Write an essay in which you compare this group with elements contained in this chapter. As appropriate, include a discussion of the following:

■ Is this a group or a team? Explain, and discuss the process by which the team develops.

■ What is the team's goal? How do you know?

■ Does the team achieve its goal? If so, to what do you attribute the team's success? If not, to what do you attribute the team's failure?

■ What barriers did the team face? How did it overcome those barriers?

■ What roles did individual participants play in the functioning of the team? Was there a leader? A facilitator or mediator? A devil's advocate? A follower?

■ If you were asked to be a consultant for this team, what improvements would you recommend and why?

Some videos to consider for this activity include: *A League of Their Own, Twelve Angry Men, The Mighty Ducks, Bull Durham, Sneakers, Dirty Dozen, Memphis Belle, Three Musketeers, Red Dawn, Stripes, Lord of the Flies, Galaxy Quest, Remember the Titans.*

**Exercise 15–I
Reflection/Action Plan**

This chapter focused on teams in the workplace—what they are, why they are important, and how to improve your skill in this area. Complete the worksheet below upon completing all the reading and experiential activities for this chapter.

1. The one or two areas in which I am most strong are:

   _____

   _____

   _____

   _____

2. The one or two areas in which I need more improvement are:

   _____

   _____

   _____

   _____

3. If I did only one thing to improve in this area, it would be to:

   _____

   _____

   _____

   _____

4. Making this change would probably result in:

   _____

   _____

   _____

   _____

5. If I did not change or improve in this area, it would probably affect my personal and professional life in the following ways:

   _____

   _____

   _____

   _____

16

Planning and Running Effective Meetings

How do I:

✓ Decide whether a meeting is necessary?

✓ Invite the appropriate people to a meeting?

✓ Get everyone prepared for the meeting?

✓ Keep meetings from exceeding the agreed-upon time allocation?

✓ Keep the meeting running smoothly?

✓ Keep team members on task during meetings?

✓ Ensure the next meeting will be effective?

Paul Atkins sold luxury new and preowned vehicles at a dealership on the East Coast. The money was pretty good, but there were some aspects of the job that always left him wondering what else he should do with his time and talents. One thing he hated was the hours—salespeople were typically scheduled for a minimum of 50 hours per week. This was especially bothersome since many hours, if not days, would go by with not a single customer walking in the showroom. Added to the boredom was another problem—the Monday morning all-hands sales meeting.

Going to a meeting wouldn't be so bad if it was useful. But this was rarely, if ever, the case. Ted, the general sales manager, would seemingly decide what he would do for the half-hour meeting on his way in. Some weeks he couldn't decide on an objective for the meeting (or chose instead to play golf), and the meeting was canceled—without notice to anyone. Other weeks, most participants left feeling their time was wasted. Paul, who sold only Mercedes and other European imports, would sit through videos on the Toyota Corolla—a car sold by the dealership next door yet owned by the same person. Still other times, the meetings were focused on selling techniques, some of which were about as archaic as you can imagine. Yet everyone was required to be there, even salespeople who were off or not scheduled to begin their day until noon (the dealership was open 9 A.M. to 9 P.M. Monday through Friday and until 6 P.M. on Saturdays).

When the European import dealership got its own sales manager (who reported to the general sales manager), the salespeople were relieved, believing that they would no longer have to waste their time at the Monday morning meetings. Unfortunately, that was not the case. In fact, the sales manager and the general sales manager frequently butt heads on this issue. After two successive weeks of last-minute meeting cancellations, the European import car staff decided enough was enough. They boycotted the meetings.

331

Eventually, the general sales manager put pressure on the sales manager and made them attend.

1. Many organizations have standing meetings. What benefits could be obtained from these meetings?

2. What are some potential downsides of a standing meeting?

3. Who should be required to come to the "all-hands meeting"? If you answer "it depends," on what should this depend?

4. Assuming the general sales manager is unwilling to change this requirement, what would you recommend he do to improve the meetings?

5. When you rate a meeting you've attended as "useless" or just "bad," what characteristics of the meeting caused this rating?

6. When caught up in a "bad" meeting, what are some things you can do to improve the situation?

Meetings are an important part of the business world. Meetings occur within organizations and between members of different organizations, for example, customers and suppliers. Managers use meetings to share necessary information and to train and coordinate efforts of their employees. Project teams, either school- or work-based, use meetings to set objectives, allocate resources, make decisions, schedule individual components of complex projects, discuss project progress, share needed information and status reports to ensure all are "on the same page," and solve problems. Many firms and campuses even have the capability for **virtual meetings,** where members are not physically in the same place but are connected via video conferencing technology or e-mail. In this chapter we discuss the importance of meetings, the how-tos of running effective meetings, and tips and suggestions for making the most of meetings. At the end of the chapter is a series of exercises and activities to help you assess and enhance your skill in running meetings.

Types of "Virtual" Meetings

- Meetings via e-mail
- Project intranets and extranets
- Video conferences
- Chat groups
- Conference phone calls

The Importance and Benefits of Meetings

Meetings serve an important function. In this increasingly complex and competitive environment, members of a team or organization need to be kept abreast of critical functional, political, technological, and legal issues facing the firm. This becomes especially important in an empowered and team-based environment. When more work and decision making is being spread to team members and employees at all levels of the organization, meetings are used to ensure good decisions are made and others are kept apprised of progress and problems.[1] The need for meetings typically increases as the number of teams and team-based projects increases.

Problems with Meetings

"A committee is twelve men doing the work of one man"

John F. Kennedy

This quote underscores a common question contemplated by students and employees alike, namely, "Wouldn't it be easier to fly solo?" A recent study found that in the average eight-person committee, each individual member wished that three of the other seven weren't there.[2] And according to a *Harvard Business Review* study, the average executive spends three and a half hours weekly in formal committee meetings and at least a day each week in informal meetings and consultations.[3] Some suggest this figure is understated—that meetings take up more than half of executives' working hours.[4] As you climb higher on the corporate ladder, meetings become more frequent and lengthier.[5] A survey of middle managers showed the top three reasons for failed meetings are: they get off subject, they lack agendas or goals, and they last too long.[6]

A big cause of ineffective or useless meetings is the lack of preparation and planning. How many times have you walked into a meeting having no idea what the meeting was about or why it was called? Perhaps it's a standing meeting, as in the case of the all-hands meeting chronicled in the opening scenario. Perhaps you have a general idea of what to expect; after all, it's always been done this way. For example, the weekly status report, pep talk, or communication of the sales objective. In either case, meetings are doomed to fail when participants (and the person calling the meeting) neither know what to expect nor what to prepare for a meeting.

Have you ever come to a meeting only to find it's been canceled, rescheduled, or moved to another room? What if the goal of the meeting is to discuss complicated technical information, yet no one received any reports or documentation ahead of time? Valuable time is wasted getting individuals up to speed. More time still is wasted when the goal of the meeting—plus any previous decisions made—is not or has not been clearly communicated. If you walk into a meeting and can't answer the question "Why am I here?" within the first few minutes, you can bet this meeting will not be optimal. If you meet because you've always met, that may not be a sufficient reason to have a meeting. What is the point of meeting? What do you want attendees to think, do, or feel as a result of the meeting?[7] If there is simple information to transmit to a group of employees, a meeting may not be the best use of everyone's time. For example, if human resources decides to add another provider to the list of HMOs currently available through employees' health benefits plan, this information could be easily transmitted via a paper memo. If, however, human resources is leading a charge to modify the current performance appraisal and merit pay system toward one that accounts for not only individual performance but also individuals' contributions in the many teams in which they work, a memo would likely be insufficient.

One lesson in this example is that despite what may seem as standard operating procedure, as in the case of Paul and the car dealership, meetings may be unnecessary and even costly, in terms of employees' time and productivity taken away from other tasks and objectives.

Work becomes more complicated when you have to interact with others. You're probably not alone if you've felt that you could do the work assigned to your group more easily than being one of five or six people working together on a project.

There are probably several explanations for this.

■ First, there's the issue of interpersonal dynamics. When we work with others, our uniquenesses—work style, personality, preferences, values, and attitudes—often clash with those of others. Sure, others may have important information to offer, but they're combative, overly analytical, or just plain critical. Couldn't they just send the needed information via interoffice mail?

■ Second, in general, the more people involved in making a decision, especially a consensus decision, the more time it takes. Despite the benefit of others' input, and the existence of **synergy**—the belief that two heads are better than one[8]—some wonder whether the costs (individuals' time and energy) overshadow the benefits.

■ Third, there may well be redundancies—of people and effort. Someone might wonder, "If other members of my group are represented, why must I be here too?"

These three reasons may underlie why meetings are the source of frustration (and water cooler humor!) over the loss of work time[9]—an increasingly valuable resource. In one study, 70 percent of American executives surveyed considered many of the meetings

**Figure 16–1
Strategies for
Effective Meetings**

The Four P's of Effective Meetings[10]	
Purpose	Determine if a meeting must be held Decide what the objective or outcomes of the meeting should be
Participants	Determine the appropriate size and the composition of the participants Consider the skills, knowledge base, and background of the participants Have a balance of task and process oriented members
Plan	Make logistical arrangements: time, place, equipment needs, visual aids, space Prepare and circulate an agenda Consult with participants before the meeting Decide on decision-making process
Process	Begin with review of past progress and clarify purpose of the meeting Establish ground rules Use visuals (flipchart or board) and denote progress and ideas Summarize meeting's accomplishments and review assignments

they attend as a waste of time.[11] Given the preponderance of poorly planned and executed meetings, it is easy to see why many view meetings as a necessary evil. Not surprisingly, the lack of a clear objective or purpose is a main reason for failed meetings, as evidenced by 89 percent of American executives who blame meeting failure on lack of proper planning and organization.[12]

If done effectively, however, meetings can be useful for dispensing or gathering information, morale building, decision making, creative brainstorming, and encouraging group action.[13] As much as we might want to be left alone to do our work, many of us appreciate being in the fold—knowing what's going on and being involved in decisions and problem-solving efforts. Meetings don't have to be a waste of time or necessarily evil. By learning a few principles and practicing several techniques, meetings can be more efficient, productive, and possibly even enjoyable!

Strategies for Effective Meetings

**Clarify the Purpose
of the Meeting**

The first principle in running effective meetings is clarifying the purpose. Whether or not a meeting should be held is completely dependent on the goal to be achieved. Employee input should be sought, and discussions—at multiple levels and parts of the organizations—need to occur.

Before the Meeting

Legitimate purposes for calling a meeting include generating ideas for a project, discussing the pros and cons of potential solutions to a problem, gaining employee input and buy-in for a program or company point of view, or deciding on a strategy or course of action.[14] By clarifying the purpose or goal of a potential meeting, you will be able to determine whether the objective could be accomplished just as easily in a memo, e-mail, or article in the weekly newsletter. Consider whether the potential benefits of getting members together outweigh the costs.[15]

Evaluate whether a meeting should be held based on its stated purpose. Even if this evaluation is made, don't assume that invitees know this unless it has been clearly articulated before (and clarified during) a meeting. To say, "to have our all-staff sales meeting," is not clear enough, especially when this is a standing meeting. Without a clear understanding of why there's a meeting and how they can contribute, employees waste time contemplating the purpose and reason for being at a meeting instead of doing their normal work. Worse still, when a meeting is held without a clear, stated purpose, discussions meander about endlessly and with minimal if any closure. To ensure a successful meeting, decide on a clear achievable task[16] and communicate this before the meeting begins. This task should support a project or task team's overall objective, which could come from management, the team members, or a combination thereof.

Four General Types of Meetings

- **Information Sharing**—several or all members share gathered information or report status on group or individual progress. For example, a team designing a new minivan may include members from engineering, manufacturing, marketing, quality assurance, and legal. Subcommittees tasked with specific goals (e.g., gather data on consumer satisfaction, quality tests) may be asked to update the rest of the team on their findings to ensure the group that the subcommittees are on track as well as furnish the entire group with information needed for group decisions. These meetings tend to be relatively short, in that the purpose is to share information, and not solve problems or make decisions.

- **Information Dissemination**—used when critical information must be conveyed and shared with members. Typically, such information is too important for a memo and may require more in-depth explanation or discussion, as in the case of introducing a new reward system. Information dissemination meetings focus primarily on the relaying of information to the members or employees, with some time allocated to address the audience's questions and ensure they have a full and clear understanding of the information.

- **Problem Solving/Decision Making**—employees or members are assembled to solve a problem or make a decision. In contrast with the information dissemination meeting, a problem-solving meeting typically requires full participation of all members present, particularly if the outcome or disposition of the problem affects them. You might also include subject matter experts—those who have specific knowledge in a related area but may not be a member of the group that is meeting. Because of the time needed to make well informed, consensus decisions, it's important to carve out sufficient time for this type of meeting. Decision-making meetings require more time than information-sharing meetings.

- **Symbolic/Social**—used to celebrate a special event or share recognition for a job well done. When long-time or key employees retire, for example, it would be appropriate to invite those people with whom they have worked to recognize the retiree's contributions publicly. Or perhaps one of the customer service teams just completed one year of complaint-free service. A meeting or social event may be just the thing to recognize this accomplishment. Finally, meetings could be valuable when social interactions are needed and encouraged. One example is the holiday meeting or party. Another example is the case when two firms merge. It would be easy for each firm to continue operating autonomously (while gossiping about "the other guys" behind closed doors). However, if one of the reasons behind the merger is to gain synergy, it behooves the merged firm to encourage the kind of interaction that will increase trust and lead to cooperation among employees of the previously separate firms.

Decide Who Should Participate in the Meeting

The second principle for running effective meetings is to spend time considering who needs to be at a meeting. Whom do we invite? The answer: those who can best contribute to the objective.[17] Returning to our opening case, if all you are planning to do is show a video and hand out updated brochures, perhaps all 40 salespeople should come. But if the purpose of the meeting is to get employees to generate creative ideas, 40 may be too many people. For this type of activity, the optimal size would be between 5 and 7, and no more than 10.[18] Breaking up the group into four or five smaller groups, or having several smaller meetings, may better serve your purpose.

What if your top salesperson can't attend the meeting? Should you have the meeting anyway? If part of the meeting is being used to share and discuss sales tips and techniques, it might be best to postpone the meeting or, if deemed necessary and cost-effective, use videoconferencing to include a key person if he or she is in a different location.

What about support staff and people from a business function such as finance? Again, this depends on the purpose and intended benefit for those who attend. If the receptionist is interested and feels he can contribute based on his experience with call-in customers, perhaps support staff should come. (They might even appreciate being asked!) What can the functional folks offer? Depends on their position and perspective relative to the purpose of the meeting. Multiple perspectives can help; they can also lead to communication challenges. Other considerations in answering the "whom to invite" question are organizational politics, need for objectivity, and potential for problems.[19] Sometimes individuals are invited to meetings for political reasons, for instance, because they hold a particular title or have access to other important individuals in the organization. However, their presence could stifle lower-level employees' creativity. Evaluate the trade-off, and consider whether a one-on-one meeting with this individual would do the trick.

Another consideration is the need for objectivity. Sometimes it is effective, depending on the meeting's purpose, to have outsiders come to the meeting. While they might not be directly affected by the meeting's outcome, they may be able to offer valuable, unbiased, and novel perspectives to the group. Finally, consider potential problems that may result from or during the meeting. For example, consider the company "troublemakers." These are the individuals who have a knack for stirring up the pot needlessly or turning every issue into a power struggle. Perhaps their perspective is valuable, but the way in which they share it is not. If possible, you might want to exclude these persons from the meeting but schedule a time for you to meet with them one-on-one.

Inviting the right people—those who have a stake in the outcome or who own the problem, those affected by the outcome, subject matter experts, problem solvers, and idea people[20]—helps ensure that the purpose is served and time-wasting diversions are minimized. For example if you suspect that the meeting's objective and discussion centers on financial impacts, you might invite representatives from accounting or finance and meet them in advance to gain insight into their attitudes, opinions, or hidden agendas.[21] In addition, it is a good idea to know the participants ahead of time. If you know that Mary in accounting has experience in a particular industry and that her insights would be valuable if shared, you can plan when and how you solicit that input should she not share without prodding.

Develop a Plan for the Meeting

Next, develop plans that will ensure the success of the meeting. First, create and distribute an **agenda** or specific plan for the meeting. The meeting agenda (see Figure 16–2 for a guide) clarifies the goal and lists the points of discussion and their priority for the meeting. A well-defined agenda spells out the tasks, estimated time allocated to each task, the decisions to be made, and expected outcomes or deliverables.[22] It also includes logistical information, such as where and when the meeting will be held and the roles individuals will play.

Circulating a specific agenda to invitees prior to the meeting is important, but it's also important to be flexible about potential changes. By soliciting their input on potential additions or modifications to the agenda, you can increase participants' ownership in the meeting and its purpose.

In planning the meeting and preparing the agenda, decide on a time and place that is likely to suit the schedules and needs of the invited participants. If manufacturing is typically busy with month-end inventory, it might be best to wait a week, if possible, to ensure manufacturing can and will participate in a meeting in which their input is necessary. If you are planning a lengthy planning or team-building meeting, for example a half-day or full-day session, you might want to consider having the meeting at another location to minimize distraction and interruptions. Based on the purpose of the meeting, select a site that has adequate space, visual tools, and resources (e.g., copy machine, clerical staff). Select a temperature (a little cooler is better than too warm), seating arrangement (discussions are best when all participants can see one another), and schedule (i.e., include breaks and coffee) that will facilitate lively participation.[23] Include specific directions and a phone number to ensure everyone makes the meeting—and on time.

**Figure 16–2
Sample Agenda**

Start and End Time:_____
Place:_____

*Stage one (# of minutes):*_____

- Clarify objective
- Agenda overview, vision and goal clarification
- Introduction of members

*Stage two (# of minutes):*_____

- Review of last meeting's minutes
- Review of roles for today's meeting
    - Facilitator—
    - Time keeper—
    - Scribe—
    - Other—
  - Set ground rules or operating guidelines
  - Continuing business
    - Progress reports from committees, etc.
  - New business
    - Information to be shared
    - Decisions to be made

*Stage three (# of minutes):*_____

- Review accomplishments
- Summarize

*Stage four (# of minutes):*_____

- Process check
- Preparation for the next meeting
  - Action items
  - Roles, next agenda
  - Time and place verification
- Future meeting

"Be sincere . . . be brief . . . be seated."

Theodore Roosevelt

Pay Attention to Process during and after the Meeting

During the Meeting

When you preside over a meeting, your role is to make the discussion lively, proactive, creative, and focused.[24] To make this happen, think of the meeting as a collection of tasks or services—communicating, facilitating, documenting[25]—and consider who can assist you in performing those services. The more you do to control the meeting, the more other participants will look to you for this control. Instead, encourage the participants to take an active part in contributing to and controlling the meeting. There are many ways you can do this during the meeting. To simplify matters, we'll divide the meeting into four stages.[26]

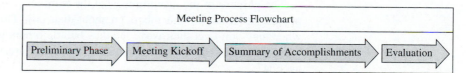

Meeting Process Flowchart

Preliminary Phase → Meeting Kickoff → Summary of Accomplishments → Evaluation

**Figure 16–3
Ground Rules**

- We will use an agenda, time keeper, and meeting leader for each meeting.
- Meetings will start on time (with a review of the agenda) and end on time (with a process check), unless there is team consensus to extend it.
- Team members who have been absent or tardy must take measures to "get up to speed."
- Team members will practice active listening.
- It is OK to talk about/address the inappropriate use of power by team members.
- A time-out can be called if the meeting is off track or otherwise ineffective.
- Items identified as sensitive will be kept confidential.
- Silence by team members indicates a need for further inquiry.
- The meeting's facilitator should remain neutral but may formally step out of the role to contribute to the discussion.

1. The **preliminary phase.** In the first few minutes of the meeting, clearly articulate the meeting purpose and objectives. Then proceed with a general overview of the agenda to set the tone and give members a feel for how the meeting will be conducted. Next, explain why the participants were selected and invited to the meeting. These three steps help establish clear expectations for what will occur.[27] If members do not know one another, briefly allow members to introduce themselves and the department for which they work.

2. **Meeting kickoff** or the heart of the meeting. If a group of individuals will be meeting on a regular basis, it is important that they establish operating guidelines, or the standard or set of norms to which they will be held, collectively. Operating guidelines are the rules of engagement for meetings.

These guidelines establish how meetings should be run, how members will interact, and what kind of behavior is acceptable.[28] A sample set of operating guidelines appears in Figure 16–3. While some of the guidelines may sound like common sense or common courtesy, the fact that the group collectively believes in and articulates the importance of starting and ending meetings on time, and not interrupting others, makes the implied explicit. It also gives members the ability to "call each other" on behaviors that violate the operating guidelines and therefore undermine the group's ability to effectively operate and achieve its goals. After the guidelines are created, post them where members can see them. By helping the group establish operating guidelines, you help create common expectations among members, encourage desirable behavior, and enhance the group's ability to be self-managing.[29] Good managers not only plan and run effective meetings, they also teach and encourage their employees to do the same.

Encouraging individuals to perform meeting roles also facilitates self-management. Early in the meeting (or in the previous meeting), establish who will play which role—scribe, timekeeper, facilitator, or meeting leader. Typically, groups rotate these roles so that all members develop each of these skills. The recorder or scribe publicly takes notes—using a flip chart or white board—on issues discussed, key decisions made, and action items assigned. The timekeeper keeps track of the time as it relates to the agenda, and reminds the group when it is about to exceed the agreed-upon time allotment for a particular topic or discussion. The group should then decide whether the time should be extended (and for how long) or the discussion should be tabled for a future meeting. The meeting leader is tasked with keeping the discussion task oriented and in line with the agenda. The facilitator helps ensure that participation is balanced, communication is effective, and the process is smooth. Many problems are avoided when members take responsibility for using these meeting roles.[30]

The purpose of the meeting is what the team is attempting to accomplish. The process describes how members go about their task. Do members yell and scream when they don't get their way? Do they belittle others who offer opposing views? Does the group go off on tangents, discussing items that are neither important nor on the agenda?

Some Meeting Process Suggestions Include:

■ Encourage the clash of ideas, not personalities. One way to do this is alternate pros and cons. After hearing a proponent's views on a subject, ask for any other or opposing views.[31]

■ Maintain focus and stick to time frames. When appropriate, stick to the agenda—it's the plan to which all members agreed. While there are times when unforeseeable issues arise between meetings and must be addressed at the meeting, it is important to bring the potentially divergent discussion to the attention of the group and check whether adjustments should be made. If the group decides that an issue is important but does not require immediate discussion, make use of a "parking lot" or a visual bin (such as a piece of newsprint on a blackboard) where issues are collected and stored for future use. Alternatively, you can ask the scribe to record the issue under "next meeting." By taking one of these steps, as opposed to just noting an issue's irrelevance, you demonstrate to the person who suggested that idea that it was heard, noted, is important to the group, and will be discussed in the next meeting or handled outside of the meeting.[32]

3. The **summary of accomplishments** or wrap-up stage. In this stage, the team leader—with the help of the scribe's notes—will review decisions made and summarize the key points discussed. This can be done during the meeting, as you move through and complete agenda items, as well as near the end of the meeting. By summarizing each point before moving to the next item, you help ensure that everyone is in agreement, that members remain focused, and the scribe takes clear meeting notes.[33] By summarizing at the end, you allow another opportunity for clarification or agreement and help bring closure to the meeting as well as clarify the group's accomplishments. Knowing you've completed all or most of the agenda items often gives group members a sense of satisfaction.

4. Evaluation and closing remarks. This step is often missed in meetings and could negatively impact future meetings. First, determine whether the meeting objective has been met. One way to do this is by having members do a **process check.** Each person might share a comment or two on how she or he felt about what was accomplished and how it was accomplished. What did the team do well? For example, "We got through all our items, we kept focused, and we came to agreement on a tough issue." What can the team do better next time? One person may note that despite all that was accomplished, he felt his input wasn't valued when he was frequently interrupted. Another may note that the meeting lasted longer than the agreed-upon hour. By having an opportunity to air concerns like these, issues are more likely to be nipped in the bud before they escalate into full-blown conflicts. If the person who didn't feel valued didn't say so, and if no one else noticed and addressed the interrupting behavior, this person is likely to dislike the group, find ways to avoid coming to the meeting, or give the appearance that they are on track while secretly planning to sabotage the team's efforts. Process checks also tend to minimize the need for the meeting after the meeting. These are the impromptu, out-in-the-hallway, or in-the-bathroom exchanges in which real feelings and issues are discussed. Again, these processes may undermine the team's objective by weakening the trust and confidence members have in each other's ability and desire to achieve the objective.

After the process check, plan the next meeting. While the discussion and decisions are fresh, decide what should be covered in the next meeting, as well as the logistics of when, where, and meeting roles. If parking lot items neither made it to the current or next meeting, capture its contents in a section known as "future meetings" or "future action outside of these meetings." At this point, review the action items. Will there be sufficient time to complete them? Should resources be made available to the actionee? Bring closure to these items to ensure that members are sufficiently prepared and ready for the next meeting.

After the Meeting and between Meetings

So far, by following the tips and techniques we've shared, you're likely to plan and run meetings that are effective in accomplishing the objectives you've set. This is great, but don't stop there. There is a tendency to slack off at this point, yet the follow-up after the meeting and before the next meeting is essential in maintaining effective meetings and active progress toward the group's goals.[34]

To maximize the group's effectiveness, consider implementing the following after- or between-meeting strategies:

■ Immediately after the meeting, have the minutes (summary of key points and decisions) and next meeting agenda typed up and distributed in advance of the next meeting. Request that members review these immediately to ensure accuracy and again just before the next meeting to be prepared for and ready to contribute to the next meeting.

■ As appropriate, send out checkpoint memos or e-mails, especially if external team issues may impact the team's objective or ability to achieve it. Offer support resources for actionees, such as whom they might contact or where they might get certain information.

■ Make sure members have phone, fax, and e-mail lists of all members. When things come up that may preclude someone's attendance, contacting other members of the team should be easy. Also, by having the list, members are able to contact others for clarification or assistance with action items.

■ If appropriate, use the time between meetings to meet with individual members to ensure they are clear about and committed to the goals of the team. Depending on the work or communication styles of some group members, it may be hard to gauge whether or not this is the case from their meeting behavior. Off-line you may get a different response. Depending on the experience level and track record of members, it may be necessary to ensure that action items are carried out. If not, offer assistance. Tread carefully however. It is important to show members that you trust them and have confidence in their abilities. Saying you do is not the same as showing it. If the individual comes to the next meeting without a completed action item, the lack of progress—for whatever reason—may deter the progress of the group. Talk to the person about this and ensure he or she understands the need to follow through on commitments made to the group so that this doesn't happen again.

■ Minutes may not always be the best way to disperse important information about a meeting. Perhaps the team can design a meeting summary form that meets its particular needs. It might include places in which to capture what tasks were decided on, who is going to do the tasks, the deadlines for these tasks, as well as a running record of key points made throughout the meeting. If the form is simple to use, it may be possible to complete the form during the meeting and make copies members can take with them upon departing the meeting. Doing this helps confirm everyone's responsibilities, clarifies assignments, and establishes accountability.

■ Be sure to send meeting notes to those members who could not be present and let them know of any action items they may have been assigned in their absence. Taking this important step helps ensure that those who missed the meeting can get up to speed, and have a record of what was done, and lets everyone have equal access to the process.

■ Have subcommittee meetings if necessary. Remember, not all work needs to be done by every member of the team. In fact, this is rarely the case in effective teams given time and expertise constraints. Typically, a subcommittee may go off to develop a draft—a suggested process, a working set of objectives—as a starting point for other members' input and ideas. Using subcommittees can be a highly effective use of time and energy.

■ Track progress against a milestone chart. The process checks can help you determine how the team is doing relative to its task. It can also uncover potential problems or deficiencies. By examining the trend of evaluations, you can strategize and plan for corrective action, if necessary, before the group gets irrevocably off course.

■ Keep key stakeholders informed of team progress and setbacks. Perceptions of a team's effectiveness (or lack thereof) are not only impacted by what and how they accomplish their objectives; they are also a function of how well informed those external to the process are kept.[35] In an environment where teaming and empowerment are the norm, it is easy to take the ball and run with it—and never inform others who may have a need to know. This may include other departments, top management, customers, or suppliers. By ensuring communication flows freely within the team, as well as beyond the team's boundaries, perceptions and support of the team are likely to remain positive.

Other Helpful Meeting Hints

Following are some additional tips and hints to help you in future meetings. Try implementing some of these ideas in future meetings.

■ Write down the cost per minute of the meeting (total all salaries of those present and divide by the number of participants) on the flipchart. This can have a focusing effect; it is an effective way to illustrate that time is money, so let's not waste either!

■ Announce the adjournment time right when the meeting starts. This clearly informs participants how long they will need to focus and will help them adjust their comments to fit the schedule.[36]

■ Set rules for debating if one is likely to ensue. For example, "No one can speak for more than five minutes," or "No one can speak twice until everyone who wants to speak has had a turn."[37] It's easy for a meeting to denigrate into a one-person show or a case where "those who talk the longest and loudest win." By establishing these rules up front and encouraging all members to adhere to them, this problem is less likely to surface.

■ Try to schedule all internal meetings for 30 minutes or less, unless a key decision must be made. This relatively short meeting period forces members to be prepared if they plan to accomplish anything and puts pressure on members to focus.[38]

■ Have a meeting standing up. Researchers at the University of Missouri's College of Business and Public Administration found that meetings involving creativity and judgment held with members standing up were 34 percent shorter than those in which members were seated. This, and their finding that the shorter, stand-up meeting resulted in the same quality of and satisfaction with decisions made,[39] suggests that shorter meetings may be more efficient and effective.

■ Preestablished timetables should be followed unless the situation warrants change. Start and end the meeting on time, but be open to change if needed. If you run a tight ship but it runs aground, you have not achieved your objective. Be firm but flexible and get member input on proposed time changes.

■ If possible, complete the meeting summary and send it out the same day while it is fresh in everyone's mind.[40] This aids closure and ensures action items are completed and members are prepared for subsequent meetings.

■ Demonstrate management support and commitment to the team and its tasks. Ask if you can come to team meetings periodically. Remove or reduce impediments (policies, individuals, insufficient resources) to show your commitment to a team's success. Provide the team with adequate time and logistical arrangements to have effective meetings.

■ Have fun. When the goal of a meeting is for people to be creative and innovative, they need to loosen up to think in different ways to gain better perspectives.[41] To do this, encourage an off-site meeting and casual dress, have food, and intersperse activities (appropriate physical or experiential exercises) to lighten up the mood and reenergize the members.

Summary

So many people find meetings to be a waste of time. It's not surprising. If you've ever been in workplace meetings, or perhaps have had meetings for a class project assignment, you're likely to agree. When done well, meetings can fulfill multiple, important purposes. When poorly planned and executed, meetings become the source of wasted time, humorous water cooler talk, and plain old misery. With so much to do in such little time, wasting time in useless meetings is not an option. Today's manager must be skillful not only at running meetings, but also in deciding whether a meeting is necessary. Planning is essential and can prevent many problems from occurring. If they do occur, you'll be better equipped to resolve these problems and help groups have and run their own effective meetings.

Key Terms and Concepts

Agenda

Evaluation (meeting stage)

Information-dissemination meeting

Information-sharing meeting

Meeting kickoff (meeting stage)

Preliminary (meeting stage) phase

Problem-solving/decision-making meeting

Process check

Summary of accomplishments (meeting stage)

Symbolic/social meeting

Synergy

Virtual meeting

Endnotes

1. Frank Basil, "Advance Planning Is Key to Successful Meetings," *Indianapolis Business Journal,* March 13, 2000, p. 21.

2. Winston Fletcher, "The Meeting Game and How to Win," *Management Today,* Dec. 1999, p. 32.

3. Fletcher, 1999.

4. Charlie Hawkins, "First Aid for Meetings," *Public Relations Quarterly,* Fall 1997, p. 33–36.

5. Fletcher, 1999.

6. Basil, 2000.

7. Anonymous, "Making Your Short Meetings More Productive," *Agency Sales,* Oct. 1992, p. 15.

8. Jan Smith, "If Meeting Is Necessary, at Least Keep It Controlled," *Sacramento Business Journal,* Nov. 5, 1999, p. 42.

9. Becky Jones, Midge Wilier, and Judy Stoner, " A Meeting Primer: Tips on Running a Successful Meeting," *Management Review,* Jan. 1995, p. 30.

10. David A. Whetten and Kim S. Cameron, *Developing Management Skills,* Fourth Ed. (Reading, MA: Addison Wesley, 1998), pp. 522–527. Reprinted by permission of Addison-Wesley Educational Publishers, Inc.

11. Basil, 2000.

12. Ibid.

13. Ibid.

14. Hawkins, 1997.

15. Roy Woodard, "Meeting, Bloody Meetings," *Credit Control,* 1993, p. 14.

16. David Dunning, "Steer Clear of Pitfalls That Can Doom Meetings," *Puget Sound Business Journal,* Jan. 21, 2000, p. 29.

17. Hawkins, 1997.

18. Ibid.

19. Ibid.

20. Ibid.

21. Jones et al., 1995.

22. Luis G. Flores and Janyce Fadden, "How to Have a Successful Strategic Planning Meeting," *Training and Development,* Jan. 2000, p. 31.

23. Jones et al., 1995.

24. John F. Schlegel, "Making Meetings Effective," *Association Management,* Jan. 2000, p. 121.

25. Stacey R. Closser, "Creating Memorable Meetings Is Key," *Triangle Business Journal,* Feb. 18, 2000, p. 37.

26. Mark J. Friedman, "How to Run a Problem-Solving Meeting," *Training and Development,* Oct. 1996, p. 11.

27. Schlegel, 2000.

28. Peter R. Scholtes, *The Team Handbook* (Madison, WI: Joiner and Associates, 1988).

29. Ibid.

30. Charlie Hawkins, "First Aid for Meetings," *Book Partners,* 1998, ISBN 1–885221–61–4. Reprinted by permission of Seahawk Associates Inc., Sedona, AZ.

31. Jim Slaughter, "How to Keep Discussions Short," *Association Management,* Jan. 2000, p. 123.

32. Hawkins, 1997.

33. Smith, 1999.

34. **www.sna.com/switp/between.html**

35. D. G. Ancona, "Outward Bound: Strategies for Team Survival in an Organization," *Academy of Management Journal* 33 (1990), pp. 334–365.

36. Slaughter, 2000.

37. Ibid.

38. John R. Brandt, "Time's Up (Limiting Business Meetings)," *Industry Week,* Jan. 10, 2000, p. 2.

39. Tricia Campbell, "Speed Up Your Meetings," *Sales and Marketing Management,* Nov. 1999, p. 11.

40. Jones et al., 1995.

41. Hawkins, 1997.

Exercise 16–A
Assessing Yourself

Circle the response that most closely correlates with each item below.

	Agree	Neither		Disagree	
1. When deciding whether to hold a meeting, I first clarify its purpose and determine whether my objective can best be met by holding a meeting or by some other means such as writing a memo.	(1)	2	3	4	5
2. I vary the type of meeting I hold based on the purpose and audience.	1	2	(3)	4	5
3. I give careful thought to who should be invited and invite those who can contribute to the objective directly, those who have special expertise, those who have useful contacts and experience, or those who offer a fresh perspective.	1	2	(3)	4	5
4. I limit the size of the group invited to a meeting to a manageable number or divide a large group into small groups to facilitate participation and discussion.	(1)	2	3	4	5
5. I assess potential problems that might develop between personalities in group meetings and develop a strategy for ensuring a smooth, successful meeting.	1	2	3	4	(5)
6. I plan and distribute an agenda in advance of meetings I am leading.	1	2	(3)	4	5
7. I prepare in advance for meetings and ensure relevant materials are sent ahead of time to participants.	1	2	(3)	4	5
8. I let participants know in advance if a meeting has been cancelled, rescheduled, or moved to a different location.	(1)	2	3	4	5
9. I clearly communicate the purpose of meetings and the ways participants can contribute to the meeting.	(1)	2	3	4	5
10. I schedule meetings at times and in places that are convenient for participants' schedules.	(1)	2	3	4	5
11. I encourage participants to rotate the roles of leader, facilitator, scribe, and timekeeper.	1	2	3	(4)	5

		Agree	Neither	Disagree

12. I encourage participants to establish operating guidelines and norms to which all are held collectively.   1 2 ③ 4 5

13. I conduct meetings that are lively, proactive, creative, and focused.   1 2 ③ 4 5

14. I encourage the clash of ideas, not personalities.   1 2 ③ 4 5

15. I maintain focus and stick to time plans.   1 ② 3 4 5

16. I wrap up and summarize key points and decisions toward the end of a meeting.   ① 2 3 4 5

17. I allow time at the end of a meeting for participants to evaluate and debrief the meeting and make plans for the next meeting.   1 2 3 ④ 5

18. After meetings I send out checkpoint notices and offer support resources for participants and meet with participants to make sure they're clear about and committed to the goals of the group.   1 2 ③ 4 5

19. I don't monopolize meetings.   1 2 3 ④ 5

20. I collect and disseminate contact information on meeting participants.   1 ② 3 4 5

21. I ensure the group has a system set up to deal with participants who have to miss meetings for whatever reason.   1 ② 3 4 5

22. I encourage a large group to divide into subcommittees.   1 ② 3 4 5

23. I announce the meeting adjournment time at the outset of the meeting.   1 2 3 4 ⑤

24. I keep key stakeholders informed of team progress and setbacks.   1 2 ③ 4 5

25. I track group progress against a milestone chart and share this with participants.   1 2 3 ④ 5

26. I set rules for debating if one is likely to occur.   1 2 3 4 ⑤

27. I try to schedule internal meetings for 30 minutes or less.   1 2 3 ④ 5

28. I demonstrate management support and commitment to a team and its task.   1 2 ③ 4 5

Sum your circled responses. If your total is 84 or more you might want to explore ways to improve your skill in the area of working in teams.

Exercise 16–B
Committee Meeting

You are the chairperson of the social event committee for your school or community-based organization. Much is riding on you and your committee, as you begin making preparations for the annual dance/celebration. This annual event is one of the biggest in your town and typically brings in between $1,000 and $2,000 that can be spent on resources, travel, and outreach efforts. It's very important that the dance go smoothly. It has for the last 15 years.

You are about to call a meeting of the social event committee to discuss arrangements for the dance. In this meeting, which is about six weeks away, you'll have to decide on location, food, music/entertainment, tables and chairs, decorations, and admission fee. You might even look for corporate sponsors to help fund the event.

1. What needs to be handled in your meeting? _____

location
food   decs
music/ent   admin fee
tables/chairs

2. Who should be invited? all in the social event committee

_____
_____
_____
_____

3. What preparation work should be done? _____

_____
_____
_____
_____

4. What could you do before the meeting to ensure everyone will come with ideas and enthusiasm? _____

_____
_____
_____
_____

5. What should you do during the meeting to ensure that you get closure on the key issues? _____

_____
_____
_____
_____

6. After the meeting, what can you do to ensure that other committee members follow up on their promises to complete certain tasks? _____

_____
_____
_____
_____

**Exercise 16–C
Prepare an Agenda for
a Team Meeting**

Prepare an agenda for your next project group meeting.

**Exercise 16–D
Plan and Have a
Meeting**

Working in groups of four to six, you will be given a topic and a block of time in which to plan and have a meeting. Consider the meeting's topic (see list below) and:

1. Prepare an agenda. Be sure to include:
   - Issues to be discussed.
   - The amount of time allocated to each issue.
   - Role assignments (e.g., scribe, timekeeper, leader, facilitator).
   - Time for a process review.

2. Have the meeting. Record key points and decisions on a flip chart or other "public" device. Plan to have one or more members present the findings of your group.

3. Do a process review. Discuss what worked well and could be improved in this meeting.

4. Report out on your group's outcomes (what recommendation or conclusions your group offers) and processes (how your group got to that point).

Topics

- Feedback on this course: What elements are effective in terms of your ability to learn and apply what's being taught, as well as suggestions for strengthening elements that could be improved.
- The role of technology in your team's next presentation. What options are available? What are the strengths and weaknesses of the options? What recommendations would you make for future team-based presentations?
- Add your own.

**Exercise 16–E
Try This . . .**

1. Observe a meeting in your workplace or school (group project, school organization meeting). Overall, how well was this meeting executed? Take notes on what happened (and didn't happen) during and immediately after the meeting so that you can answer the following questions.
   - What was the purpose of the meeting? How do you know this?
   - Was the purpose or objective met? How do you know this?
   - What were some specific things that were effective? Explain and cite examples.
   - What made the meeting ineffective? Explain, citing specific examples.
   - If you were to lead the meeting, what would you have done differently and why?

2. Watch a meeting that occurs in a sitcom, video/movie (e.g., *Tucker, Barbarians at the Gate, Working Girl, Wall Street, The Firm*), or news program (e.g., *Crossfire, The Lehrer Report,* or *Politically Incorrect with Bill Maher*). Take notes on what you observed during and immediately after the "meeting" and answer the following questions.
   - What was the purpose of the meeting? How do you know this?
   - Was the purpose or objective met? How do you know this?
   - What were some specific things that were effective? Explain and cite examples.
   - What made the meeting ineffective? Explain, citing specific examples.
   - If you were to lead the meeting, what would you do differently and why?

**Exercise 16–F
Reflection/Action Plan**

This chapter focused on meetings—why they're important and strategies for planning and running effective meetings. Complete the worksheet below upon completing all reading and experiential activities for this chapter.

1. The one or two areas in which I am most strong are:

_____

_____

_____

_____

2. The one or two areas in which I need more improvement are:

_____

_____

_____

_____

3. If I did only one thing to improve in this area, it would be to:

_____

_____

_____

_____

4. Making this change would probably result in:

_____

_____

_____

_____

5. If I did not change or improve in this area, it would probably affect my personal and professional life in the following ways:

_____

_____

_____

_____

17

Project Management

How do I:

✓ Keep projects on track?

✓ Help my team to meet deadlines?

✓ Know if a project is maintaining the necessary standards or quality?

✓ Handle multiple projects simultaneously?

✓ Incorporate my personal project time lines into my professional project time lines?

✓ Keep long-term objectives in mind while working on day-to-day objectives?

✓ Improve communication with my team members or employees?

✓ Handle unexpected events that interfere with my pre-planned schedule?

Carol Marshall is a bright young engineer in a large manufacturing facility. Although she's been out of college for three years, she's been promoted twice and is now in a supervisory position. She is very comfortable with projects in which she is the key contributor. She has high work standards and always goes the extra mile to bring projects in on time and budget. Working autonomously, she has developed good systems that allowed her to accumulate an enviable success record. Her managers, noticing her leadership potential, have given her a very important task force to oversee. A lot depends on the results of the task force. Carol is eager to show her bosses she can be just as effective working with others as she is working on her own. She has devoted a lot of energy to the task force. She has helped them build confidence in and rapport with each other. She has involved the group in several social gatherings to strengthen their comfort level in working with each other. She has good communication with the group as a whole and with each of the five other group members. They've been together for four months, and the deadline for their task force deliverable is drawing near. Carol is eager to see the results of her task force's efforts. She heard two weeks ago that they were on schedule and today she's expecting to see the final report.

In looking over the project report, Carol is shocked to discover the development subcommittee is behind schedule and needs more time to complete the report. Carol is worried. She has a presentation to senior management scheduled for the end of the week. There's no way she's going to be ready by then. She wonders, "What happened? What could I have done differently? How come this always happens?" She concludes she's not cut out for supervision and thinks she needs to go to her managers and request a reassignment. "From now on," she mutters, "I'll just do important things like this on my own. I'm not going to depend on anyone else but me."

1. Why was Carol left in this situation?

2. Why do you think Carol's team let her down?

3. Do you think Carol should give up supervision? Why or why not?

4. What could Carol have done over the four months to ensure timely completion of the project?

5. Has something like this ever happened to you before? How did you react?

6. Have you ever been in a position similar to Carol's—one in which you depended on others to get work done and were disappointed with the outcome? If so, what did you learn from this experience?

"Plan the work. Work the plan."

This old saying is the cornerstone of management today. If you don't plan, you will be reacting to situations constantly and will not have time to take advantage of new opportunities.[1] It's easy for most people to develop plans. What separates successful plans from unsuccessful ones is the implementation. For a plan to become reality, it needs to be operationalized—brought to life. This chapter introduces the concept of project management and discusses how this concept can be used to organize projects and assignments that are managed by teams. The definition and importance of project management are discussed, as are steps involved in managing projects, and strategies and tips for honing your project management skills. We also include information on tools available to help you manage projects. The chapter ends with exercises to help you assess and improve your project management skills.

What Is Project Management?

Have you ever been involved in a team project where team members had different definitions of quality? Or different perceptions of the meaning of the phrase "on time"? Or where everyone procrastinated until the last minute? When used effectively, project management can help prevent (or reduce the likelihood of) these problems from occurring. **Project management** is the coordination of your work and that of others such that organizational objectives can be achieved while meeting time, budget, and quality standards or expectations.[2]

Project management is a systematic process through which almost all of the steps involved in starting and completing a project are anticipated and outlined in advance.[3] We use the word "almost" because no one can predict everything that will happen between the present and the project deadline. In project management, the known steps are anticipated and accounted for; in addition, the schedule includes some "slack" to account for unforeseen difficulties or events that invariably arise. Project management involves tracking a project from its inception to completion. This includes scheduling steps, allocating tasks to various team members, creating and overseeing time budgets for projects, and monitoring progress made toward goals.

Why Project Management?

In today's rapidly changing and highly competitive workplace, managers are being asked to reduce costs while increasing productivity. This imperative forces managers to develop new models of operating for every aspect of the organization.[4] One way to "do more with less" is to encourage employees to be efficient in plotting their work flow—for projects that are worked on independently and for those that are implemented by teams. As employees work increasingly in teams, it is essential to have a system to help team members work collectively on a project that has multiple milestones or deadlines. This is especially true when individuals are involved in multiple projects. They, and their managers, must juggle many balls simultaneously. Being involved in multiple individual and team-based projects, project managers and project team members have a lot—perhaps too much—on their plates today. Project planning and management becomes essential as project managers attempt to adapt to changing technology, coordinate with multiple people and departments, meet financial goals, and manage business strategy while simultaneously monitoring multiple projects with day-, week-, or year-long or more time spans. And all of this must get done while getting the day-to-day work done![5]

Projects that encompass many tasks and run over several weeks or months require planning and coordination with other projects and activities, both personal and professional. As a manager or employee, your ongoing job priorities and commitments have to be factored in when planning new projects. The same is true for students. Coursework and extra assignments need to be incorporated into your plans, as well as personal commitments. Vacations, medical appointments, sports competitions, community involvement, carpooling the children, child care, and elder care are examples of personal commitments that should be taken into account when planning project schedules either independently or with others.

Benefits of Project Management

Applying a project management approach to your work has numerous benefits for the organization and for individuals. We've mentioned the need to "do more with less" or perhaps "work smart, not hard." Project management helps organizations do this and ensures that:

■ Resources such as time, money, and personnel are appropriately allocated to the organization's numerous priorities and objectives.[6] Through advance planning, individual project calendars can be adjusted to be in sync with other organization commitments. For example, in planning a major new product rollout, a company can ensure that it occurs at a time when other projects aren't absorbing needed time and energy of the managers and employees involved in the rollout effort.[7]

■ Long-term objectives can be kept in mind while short-term objectives are being implemented. Through thinking strategically about an organization's long-term objectives, short-term activities that help move the organization toward the longer-term goal can be planned and implemented. Using project management, a company can ensure that weekly or monthly tasks and objectives—in addition to those responsible for them—are included in plans that support a new marketing strategy. If a company strives to expand sales by 20 percent by adding an online business to compliment its brick and mortar business within two years, they could set up multiple milestones that track this progress. Within 3 months, content for the website is researched; within 6 months, the website is up and running; within one year, sales should increase by 5 percent; within 18 months, sales should increase by 15 percent, and so on.

■ Contingencies can be anticipated. By articulating in advance the known steps to complete a project and building in some slack in the schedule, each unanticipated event that occurs during the project time line does not have to be treated as a crisis that affects the ultimate deadline or deliverable. Let's say a company is implementing a new integrated computer system that tracks inventory, sales, costs, and so on. The consultants who are installing the package estimate that complete installation and implementation will take eight months. This includes installation of software, training all employees, testing and debugging the system, and making modifications. For project planning purposes, it's best to add 10 to 20 percent additional time to each phase. This will ensure that slack is built into the schedule to accommodate the unexpected, such as incompatibility with previous hardware, heavier than usual sales, or vacations or even holidays. By allocating extra time to projects at the outset, you have a better chance of getting ahead of your workload and staying there.[8] Sarah Gavit, an experienced project manager at NASA's Jet Propulsion Laboratory, notes, "Manage the risk. There always will be certain parts more susceptible to going wrong. Before we ever lay out a schedule, we look at four or five areas with high risk. We develop contingency plans and watch extra closely. Other project managers sometimes don't look until they're up against the wall."[9]

■ Project output is made more consistent. By developing quality standards in advance, team members, managers, and employees have the opportunity to discuss and clarify their perceptions of the project objectives and their expectations for the end product, or project deliverable(s). For example, when developing a new interviewer training program, a company can outline the legal requirements, research industry benchmarks or best practices, and develop a set of specifications for the project that are agreed to in advance by all members of the planning team. By getting all involved on board before any project output is generated, the quality of the components comprising the end product is going to be higher and more harmonious than if everyone established his or her own quality standards independently.

Project management has numerous benefits for the individuals involved as well as the organization. In addition to enabling individuals to be more efficient and organized, through project planning and management:

■ Collegiality is enhanced. Through meeting with other team members and organizational employees who have a stake in the success of a project, you have the opportunity to build relationships that contribute to a sense of belonging in the organization.[10] Let's say you are part of a group tasked with implementing a new budget tracking system for the company. By meeting regularly as a team and with department heads and other stakeholders, you are able to form relationships that contribute to the success of the project at hand and last beyond the duration of the project. These relationships facilitate your knowledge and understanding of where you and your work fit with that of others in the organization. This enhances your perspective and enables you to think more "globally" in how you do your work. In addition, by being connected or networked with others in the organization, trust and helping behaviors—part of collegiality—are increased.

■ Morale is enhanced. No one likes feeling that they're all alone in overcoming a mountain of work at the office. Planning work in advance and achieving the desired outcome successfully boosts your morale and the morale of others involved in the effort. For example, tackling a thorny problem such as designing a new budget monitoring system can be a tedious task. When the various components of the task are articulated, planned for, and carried out systematically and in increments, what might be an overwhelming task appears more manageable. And when you are able to make progress on this task—even one small component at a time—your self-efficacy increases along with your morale. "Projects that succeed are just about the most satisfying work experience you can have. It's as much fun as you can have and still get paid," notes Steve McMenamin, Vice President of Customer Service at Southern California Edison Co.[11]

■ Job satisfaction is increased. Once we have mastered the basics of any job, most of us want more. Once we prove our capabilities, most people want to be involved in greater levels of responsibility, more variety of work, more complex work.[12] Being involved in multiple projects or tasks affords you this opportunity to stretch and grow further and, as a result, become more satisfied in your job. Let's say that in recognition for your outstanding capabilities as a waiter, the owner of a busy restaurant asks you to participate in a task force that is evaluating ways to improve customer service. Project management gives you the tools needed to juggle both roles simultaneously, facilitating your ability to take on both roles and, in so doing, increase your ability to multitask and to contribute to the organization beyond your daily job.

■ Learning is enhanced. Project management results in learning about others' jobs and work styles, not just your own. Working with others on projects increases your understanding of how your and others' roles and responsibilities fit into the whole. This increases your knowledge of the complexities and interdependencies in the organization, enabling you to make more substantive and appropriate contributions to the organization's success. For example, you might be involved in a group project at school where the ultimate deliverable is a presentation on a cutting-edge business topic. By planning the project in advance with other team members, you exchange ideas about preferred ways to approach the project, manage time, communicate with each other, make decisions, and solve problems. This collaboration increases everyone's skills and knowledge base.

■ Creativity and synergy are enhanced. Through planning a project in advance with your manager and team members, you are more likely to envision a new way to approach the situation than if you simply dove in and got the work done in the same way it's always been done. Imagine you are part of a team charged with implementing a membership expansion campaign for a fraternity. By planning the project in advance, you can ask big picture questions such as, "What do we want to accomplish?" "How can we do things better than before?" "What worked and what didn't work previously?" "Ideally what would we like the new program to look like?" "What do we want to accomplish?" By brainstorming with other team members to answer these questions, you're likely to tap into the synergistic potential that resides in most diverse groups. This process energizes and synergizes a group toward identifying more creative, innovative, and better solutions than could have been produced by any one team member working on their own.

Let's face it. Despite, or perhaps because of, all the technology that is now available, working today is harder and more pressure filled than ever. The average workday for today's white-collar worker is longer today than it was in the 1960s.[13] With the availability of e-mail, fax machines, and voice mail, our expectations for quick turnaround have changed from a week or so to an hour or two! Customers want service now. Managers want deliverables yesterday. With all this pressure, it's a wonder that any projects with a time line of more than a few days get done. Managing projects can be tedious and time-consuming work. The time that an organization or individual invests in planning will yield paybacks and returns through reduced implementation time and costs.[14] A project management mindset can serve as a way to spread the work around, making working on projects more effective and, just as important, fun!

Eight Steps to Managing Projects

Knowing what you are managing is as important, if not more so, as how you manage it. To gain clarity on the task or project, follow the eight steps for managing projects (Figure 17–1).

Step One—Define Project Objectives and Scope

First, as a group, assess the goals of the project. What deliverables and outcomes are expected? What would you ideally like to accomplish? The answers to these questions may be different. If so, focus first on the essentials or must haves, and then, if there is room in the schedule, incorporate the optionals or nice to haves. For example an essential element would be to meet the deadline imposed by the instructor or manager. An optional element would be to have deliverables prepared a week ahead of time. After going

Figure 17–1
Steps to Managing Projects

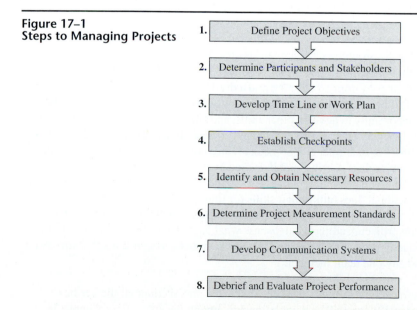

1. Define Project Objectives
2. Determine Participants and Stakeholders
3. Develop Time Line or Work Plan
4. Establish Checkpoints
5. Identify and Obtain Necessary Resources
6. Determine Project Measurement Standards
7. Develop Communication Systems
8. Debrief and Evaluate Project Performance

through all the steps of project management, you'll then be able to assess whether getting done a week early is possible.

■ Relate the project goals to overall organizational goals and strategy. For example, if your team's goal is to produce a set of recommendations for consideration by senior management, determine your boss's objectives—as well as those of his or her boss—to ensure your project goals support the organization's broader goals. Without taking this step, you risk "doing things right" instead of "doing the right things."

■ Once you've determined the project objectives, clarify these with the project manager or instructor to ensure everyone's on the same page about the expected outcome. This might surprise you, but the phrase zero defects means different things to different people. Quality of 99.9 percent is impressive, unless you consider that a .1 percent error rate equates, for example, to Americans consuming over 14,000 cans of "bad" soda in a single year. The clarification of objectives can be one of the most critical steps in the process of project management.

Step Two—Determine Project Participants and Stakeholders

Now that you are clear about what to do, it makes sense to consider who should be included in the project. Even though some people may not seem necessary at first, the fact that their work or organization is affected by the outcomes of the project, thereby making them **stakeholders,** may suggest that their inclusion is more important than you might think. Key considerations for this stage include:

■ Make sure that vital employees and teammates are made and kept a part of the project and that key stakeholders—those who have a stake in the outcome such as your manager or instructor—are either involved or kept apprised of the group's efforts throughout the project.[15] For example, a functional organization charged with procuring materials for projects became frustrated with a system that took anywhere from four weeks to 18 months to obtain even simple, low cost items. The group worked together and devised a new system designed to save countless hours and, hence, costs. But they weren't done. The proposed system required extensive changes in the way accounts payable did its work. The group presented their plan to their management as well as members of accounts payable, and then asked representatives from the latter to join their group to flesh out the details and then implement the new system. Had they not included this step, the group might have faced an uphill battle—even though their proposed new system could save valuable resources.

■ Once the project group has been assembled, begin a master calendar on which members' availability (and lack thereof) is noted. Indicate specific dates in which one or more of the team members will not be available to work on the project. Holidays, vacation days, anticipated personal days, travel days, meeting days, or commitments to other projects should be noted and accounted for when designating project steps and entering "to do" items on the project calendar. Some dates may have to be skipped completely if key group members are unavailable, while others may be okay to include as long as tasks performed by others are unaffected by individual absences.

■ Discuss what the group members' interests are—their strengths and desired contributions to the project. For example, one might volunteer they would like to contribute by doing research, another by doing data entry, and a third by doing analysis, and so on. Two considerations: (1) if possible, allow members not only to do what they do best but also afford them the opportunity to develop other skills, and (2) if individuals don't volunteer, or if all members lack needed skills, roles will have to be assigned regardless of personal interest or strengths. For example, give someone with a computer background the chance to take on a marketing role if possible and if desired by the person. While they may be better equipped to prepare the final report or presentation, allowing members to stretch and possibly cross functional lines builds their skills for future projects as well.

■ Consider the team members' planning and organizing skills. Discuss expectations regarding meeting project deadlines and discuss what each person can contribute to the task. When allocating project steps to specific team members, assign tasks that stretch but don't overextend any one team member.

Step Three—Develop a Time Line or Work Plan

The next step is to create a specific plan, one that takes into account all the various steps—large and small—as well as the relationship among the steps. For example, in

Figure 17–2
Sample Work Plan

Project: Team presentation on business topic of current interest

Due Date: End of quarter

Team Members Names and Initials: James Smith (JS), Mary Conover (MC), Jesse Baron (JB), Nomi Hussein (NH), Maria Santanella (MS)

Step	Date	Initials
1. Meet with team; decide topic	Week one	All
2. Research topic	Week one	All
3. Re-group to share results	Week two	All
4. Further research and develop outline	Week two	JS, MC
5. E-mail to group and solicit and incorporate feedback	Week three	JS, MC
6. Develop presentation and share draft with others, edit	Week four	JB, NH
7. Plan presentation, prepare slides, and share with group	Week five	MS
8. Rehearse	Week five	All
9. Prepare copies for distribution	Week six	JS, JB
10. Present	Week six	All
11. Prepare and pass out evaluation	Week six	NH
12. Debrief	Week six	All

building a car, you would never install the headrests before installing the seats. Figure 17–2 shows a work plan for a five-member team project and presentation. It includes all the steps necessary to complete the project, a time frame to allow for completion of the project, and assignment of responsibilities for individual team members. Following are some tactics for developing a time line or work plan.

■ Working with a large blackboard, whiteboard, easel and newsprint, or computer program (something that can be seen by all involved), begin brainstorming all of the steps that will be needed to complete the project. Ideally, start with the end goal and work backwards from there. This process is called **backscheduling** and involves looking backward from a target date, beginning with your goal or objective and then plotting out the means to achieve it. This is done by[16]

1. Identifying the individual tasks necessary to achieve the objective.

2. Estimating how long it will take you to complete each task and determining the best time to do it.

3. Listing each task on a calendar, appropriately backdating each task from the project due date.

Let's take you away from business to share an example of backscheduling. If you were preparing a meal, the Spanish *paella* to be exact, you wouldn't put all the ingredients in at the same time. This complex dish includes meats (sausage, chicken), seafood (fish, shrimp, mussels), and vegetables (carrots, peppers), each of which has an optimal cooking time. If you were planning to serve the dish in 40 minutes, you would put the meats in first, as they would take the longest to cook. Then you'd add the vegetables, and finally the seafood. Shrimp that has cooked for 40 minutes tastes mushy, and the fish would fall apart and taste dried out. If you put the meats in last, say with only 10 minutes to go, you may subject your guests to undercooked meats (and the problems that brings). When you backschedule, you determine what happens last, next to last, next to next to last, and so on. For the example in Figure 17–2, the team would need to start with the presentation date and work backwards to determine when they would need to begin the project to ensure quality and timely completion. By doing so, they would determine that they will need six weeks to allow for creating this particular presentation.

If the project is complex and it's easier to start at the beginning, do so. List each step and allocate all steps to specific dates on the calendar. Realize that some tasks are serial (one must precede another) while others are parallel (two noninterrelated tasks can occur simultaneously).

■ Determine and specify the dependencies that exist between all the tasks, participants, and activities in a project plan. Each step relates to others in the plan. Understanding these interrelationships can help the group know where potential problems could arise or where a delay or lag in one could change the process.[17] If employees at the manufacturer supplying the upholstery material for the car seats are on strike, this impacts not only car seat readiness, but also the installation of the headrests.

■ As a group, clarify the objectives when specific tasks are assigned. Clearly communicate the expected deliverables and the desired results. Monitor tasks delegated and record to whom specific tasks are allotted. Set precise and realistic deadlines for short-term deliverables, adjusting the time line as necessary throughout the project.

■ Build in time for the unexpected. Planning and communication with teammates are essential here. Watch for the tendency to try and make up losses late in the project cycle. It's not atypical for a project to stay on schedule for the first 80 percent of the time and then fall apart due to overconfidence ("We're practically done"), reduced attention to the schedule ("We know what we have to do . . . who needs to see the schedule"), or just procrastination. Once group members recognize this slippage, they stress and rush to completion, resulting in lower quality output than would have been the case had the original time line been adhered to. Many people and teams grossly underestimate the time needed toward the end to complete details that bring a final deliverable up to quality standards. Let's say your team is assembling a report based on a survey conducted over a six-month time period. Who's going to check the accuracy of the data? Who will proofread? Edit? Check for content? Run the report by the research and legal departments? Share a preview copy with a few stakeholders to ensure buy-in? Copy and prepare presentation materials, or ensure they're available online? All these minute details take much more time than most people imagine. It's wise to build them into the schedule from the outset of the project.

Talking through these kinds of details with a project group has several benefits. It helps the group become realistic about what can and cannot be accomplished. It helps individuals think of additional steps that might otherwise have been omitted from the planning phase. And it helps team members to begin defining in real terms quality standards for the project.

■ Avoid the tendency to wait until late in the project to buy time for these important details. Budget for them up front. Stay vigilant and look at the whole project to determine where time can be bought earlier on in the process. Taking time for this discussion will pay off in a higher quality outcome, and with less stress than "winging it!"[18]

■ Some final advice from a veteran project manager. "Be very flexible. In this day where we're on these faster, better, cheaper programs, with very high turnaround and very high-risk technologies, you can come up with a great master plan, but things never go according to plan. You have to be flexible when changes come in to rapidly replan and not be discouraged by it."[19] The goal of your project is set, but the action plan or means of getting to your end result must constantly be adapted to address deviations from the original path. Effective project managers recognize when and how to change directions and ask for help when extra resources are needed.[20]

Step Four—Establish Checkpoints and Control Mechanisms

Step four involves setting up a series of checkpoints, or points at which progress on the project will be checked, and entering these onto the project calendar. Even after your group lists all the tasks, identifies interdependencies, and assigns specific due dates, it is wise to establish periodic checkpoints. These may be progress meetings that entail status checks, expectation clarification, or raising issues. If unanticipated problems arise, these checkpoint meetings can be used to problem-solve and make necessary adjustments to the schedule.

■ Evaluate your project for important steps or tasks to be completed and insert interim deadlines or checkpoints in the project plan. In the previous step, we broke the project into smaller tasks or objectives. In this step, break these down further into milestones or incremental steps in order to determine when checks and tests should be completed. For example, break a 30-day project into three 10-day subsections, and check after each one. This will help to shorten the time between when an error or misunderstanding occurs and when it can be discovered and corrected.[21] It will also help to prevent or reduce the possibility of time line slippage.

■ Review and update the project plan regularly. Monitor other projects and events that might interfere with your project schedule and adjust accordingly. One suggestion is to post the project plan in an area visible to all group members. Don't confine the schedule to the conference room in which you meet only monthly. Instead put it in a hallway that all members pass through, such as the hallway to the bathroom or break-room. By keeping the plan highly visible, potential interferences and problems can be raised and dealt with before they impact the expected outcomes.

Step Five—Identify and Obtain Necessary Resources

Project managers and their teams need to identify and obtain the resources that are needed to complete the project within the specified time frame, cost parameters, or budget in order to meet quality standards. It is therefore necessary to:

■ Look through the tasks and objects and discuss what will be required to carry out the assignment. Be realistic about what can be accomplished given the resources that are available and the time constraints that are inherent in the project. If your group anticipates a shortfall of personnel, budget, time, computer support, administrative support, or supplies, now is the time—before you roll up your sleeves and begin the project—to discuss these needs with your manager. If the resources can be provided, great. If not, it's important to "push back" on management and negotiate which elements of the deliverable can be achieved, given the resources available. Don't assume you can get these resources later. Get what you need before you start or, if the resources are not forthcoming, manage stakeholders' expectations about the group's ability to achieve a desired outcome.

■ Know when to let a project go or when to start over. Sometimes a project team discovers early on that the project expectation is unrealistic or the scope of the project is more complex than originally envisioned. Perhaps the team thought its job was to make recommendations when their manager saw the task as ending with implementation of the recommendations. These perceptions differ substantially. Or perhaps a pilot project is expanded to include the entire organization. The project team might need to reconsider its objectives and change course. If this happens to you, consult with your manager or instructor. Possibly the task can be reconceived. Don't let politics, pride, or the thought of failure keep you from asking for help or from scrapping a project that is not going to contribute to the organization. Use active decision making throughout to help you make these determinations.[22] Maintain constant and clear communication about these determinations with appropriate stakeholders.

Step Six—Determine How Project Results Will Be Measured

This is important to consider before the project starts. Understand how the project will be evaluated and who will assess it. This will ensure that steps are built into the process to obtain the data needed to evaluate the success of the project. If your group's task is to improve customer satisfaction, how will you know whether you've done it? Are they happier? Do they file fewer complaints? Is the wait time for help shorter? Especially in a case like this, your group might first have to measure and establish a baseline. How do you know if the wait time is shorter after your recommendations are implemented if you don't assess the wait time before you begin?

Step Seven—Set Up an Ongoing Communication System

There is no substitute for effective communication in project management. Typically, projects get in trouble when people are confused. Avoiding confusion requires seeing over the horizon and conveying to others your ideas, your perceptions, and the objective with clarity and confidence. It also requires listening skills.

■ Communicate with team members and stakeholders. The ability to deal with people—using your interpersonal skills—can be the primary factor in success of a project.[23] Important skills to use throughout the process are listening, giving and receiving feedback, persuasion, delegation, seeing things from another's perspective, and getting people to respond to you.[24]

Figure 17–3
Project Management
Tips from Bill Gates[30]

1. Choose carefully. Projects should be large enough to be worthwhile and should suit your skills and qualifications.
2. Establish a realistic time line.
3. Let employees know how important the project is.
4. Keep employees informed and involved so they understand the constraints under which they're operating.
5. Meet across boundaries—involve people from various parts of the organization if possible.
6. Keep in touch with the progress and morale of the crew.
7. Share bad news and information when things aren't going well—don't keep employees in the dark.
8. Make trade-off decisions crisply to minimize big changes, but be flexible to adjust to marketplace developments and changes.
9. Know when to give up.
10. Breed healthy competition.

■ Start the project with face-to-face or telephone contact if possible. E-mail contact can occur once the group is formed and people are clear on their roles and responsibilities. Misunderstanding is less likely to occur when members are able to meet and fully discuss project expectations and concerns in real time, with the benefit of nonverbal language.

■ Meet regularly (in person or virtually) to check on project status and progress. Meetings are usually a necessary element that can keep a project on task. Meetings are a good place to check and recheck all members' understanding of dates and deliverables. To be effective, meetings should be primarily decision oriented. In addition to sharing status, meetings can be used to maintain agreed-upon deadlines, discuss changes that might be necessary in the plan or work schedule, address questions and issues, and clarify roles and expectations.

■ Revisit initial decisions made by the group if they are not working. An important aspect of project management is continuously reviewing the initial prioritizing of steps. Perform continuous "triage" or cross-checking of all interrelated project components to make sure that the critical aspects and requirements are getting implemented. Constantly review and modify where necessary, ensuring your ability to deliver what is promised by your deadlines.[25]

■ Keep people informed by issuing progress reports. This can be done face to face, but written methods (e.g., an e-mail sent to the team) may provide an easier means for keeping track of individual and collective progress. Err on the side of going overboard on updating people on how your objectives or tasks are measuring up to the goals of the project.[26]

■ Ensure a positive, open atmosphere. Provide encouragement throughout the project. If the project occurs over an extended period of time, plan some fun get-togethers to build camaraderie, trust, and rapport among team members.

■ Monitor performance and catch problems early on. If this is not done, you risk marginalization, wherein the poor performers bring down the group's standards rather than the other way around. Since a change to a single step can have a ripple effect on the whole project and system, communicating instantly is critical in keeping projects on time and on budget.[27] Providing constructive feedback as soon as possible can do this. A good project manager will be able to question others and give feedback without alienating the members.[28]

■ Give less experienced team members more initial attention and direction. As they acquire experience and confidence, you can be less involved in overseeing their work.

■ Be clear on accountability and clarify where overall responsibility for the ultimate quality of the deliverable lies. Make sure everyone understands and is held accountable for the responsibilities they assume.

■ Develop records that document the group's progress on the project. This will help the group stay on track without having to replicate earlier discussions. This also aids future groups working on similar projects. The records can be print or electronic and

**Figure 17–4
A Gantt Chart on the Development of a Team Presentation**

		Week	1	2	3	4	5	6	7	8	9
A	Decide Topic	Plan	▓								
		Actual	▓								
B	Research Topic	Plan	▓								
		Actual	░	░							
C	Meet to Share Results	Plan		▓							
		Actual		░	░						
D	Further Research and Develop Outline	Plan			▓						
		Actual			░	░					
E	Get Team Feedback and Incorporate Ideas	Plan			▓						
		Actual			░	░					
F	Develop Presentation and Discuss Draft	Plan				▓					
		Actual									
G	Plan Presentation, Develop Slides	Plan					▓				
		Actual									
H	Rehearse Presentation	Plan					▓				
		Actual									
I	Prepare Audience Handouts	Plan						▓			
		Actual									
J	Present	Plan						▓			
		Actual									
K	Prepare and Pass Out Evaluation	Plan						▓			
		Actual									
L	Debrief	Plan						▓			
		Actual									

should include the original project plan and changes that are made, meeting schedules and minutes, team to-do lists, memos and e-mail correspondence, and samples of interim and final deliverables.

Step Eight—Debrief and Evaluate the Process and Results at Project End

Remember that all processes and efforts can be improved. Keep notes of lessons learned throughout the process and share them with group members at the end of the project. Discuss what worked well and what didn't. Discuss what everyone learned from the group's mistakes and how similar mistakes can be prevented when engaged in future team projects. This allows for all involved to offer feedback and to share ideas for improving group behaviors and processes in the future.

Project Management Tools

Several tools are available to help you track progress on projects. One of the more common and simple tools is the **Gantt chart.** Named after its developer, Henry Gantt, this chart describes the temporal relationships of events of tasks that unfold over time.[29] It can also show projected and actual schedules. Figure 17–4 shows how the earlier presentation project (illustrated in Figure 17–2) has been made into a Gantt chart. From this chart the team can track the planned activities, control individual activities, and identify delays or deviations from the original plan. The team can see where they have lost time and can plan and make adjustments to complete the project on time. The Gantt chart will also be helpful when debriefing the project and team process for future improvements on their next assignment.

To make a Gantt chart,

1. Brainstorm all the tasks necessary to complete the final project.
2. Reorganize this list in order from beginning to ending tasks.
3. Create a grid (or use graph paper) wherein the columns represent weeks (or days if the project is very short) and the rows represent specific tasks. Plan to post this where all group project members can see it.
4. List each task in order and estimate the time needed to complete each task. Traditionally, this would be represented by a rectangle whose endpoints show the start and finish time of the task; the longer the rectangle, the longer it would take to complete this task.
5. You could also include two rows for each task—one that shows the projected or planned time (using an opaque rectangle) and one that shows the actual time (using a shaded rectangle).

While it may not be critical to have the planned and actual schedules on a Gantt chart, adding the actual schedule helps in at least two ways. First, you will be able to make real-time adjustments to the schedule, especially when a preceding, interdependent task was delayed in starting or finishing. Second, the comparisons will help in the overall project debrief and provide feedback and lessons learned for future projects and planning.

Another common tool used in project management is the **PERT (Program Evaluation and Review Technique)** chart. A PERT chart diagrams all of the steps involved in completing a project and estimates the length of time needed in each phase of the project. By mapping out tasks in a flowchart pattern, the PERT helps identify sequences of dependent activities (see sample below).[31] It answers the questions of what are the most optimistic estimates of the time to complete the project under the best conditions, what's the most pessimistic under the worst conditions, and what is the most likely under normal conditions.[32] The PERT process can also determine the longest anticipated single line of activity from start to finish,[33] which is known as **critical path method (CPM)**.

The procedures for PERT and CPM are:[34]

1. Define the project and all of its significant activities and tasks.
2. Develop the relationships among the activities. Decide which activities must precede and follow others.
3. Draw the network connecting all of the activities.
4. Assign time and/or cost estimates to each activity.
5. Compute the longest time path through the network; this is called the critical path.
6. Use the network to help plan, schedule, monitor, and control the project.

The critical path represents tasks and activities that, if delayed, will cause the entire project to be delayed. This information can be used by teams to identify noncritical tasks for replanning, rescheduling, and relocating resources to gain flexibility and allow for alterations. Therefore, PERT and CPM can play a major part in controlling a project. Figure 17–5 illustrates the team presentation project (from Figure 17–2) showing the relationship between the activities and the estimated time needed to complete the presentation. The critical path shows that they will need a minimum of 33 days to complete all the steps as well as identifying which steps are critical for keeping on schedule and which activities have some slack time.

Figure 17-5
PERT Chart for Development of Team Presentation

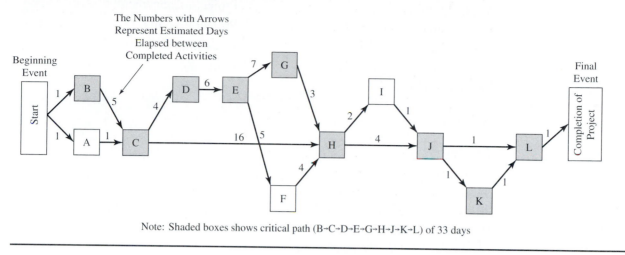

Note: Shaded boxes shows critical path (B→C→D→E→G→H→J→K→L) of 33 days

Both of these methods are immensely helpful in planning out a project. By creating either chart, most groups discover missing steps, clarify whether the anticipated time line is realistic (or not), and identify critical dependencies and resources. One recommendation for creating a first draft Gantt or PERT chart is to use Post-Its or other easily movable notes. Since so many hidden tasks or issues arise in the building of these charts, the use of Post-Its can reduce group members' frustration in the process. Software programs can also be used to create PERT charts; the team identifies the tasks and time estimates, and the programs prepare the charts.

Numerous Web-oriented software programs are available. These programs enable group members to enter tasks, estimate time lines and other dependencies, and create the project management chart.[35] One benefit of these programs is that changes—added tasks, modified time lines—create instant adjustments to the overall schedule, enabling members to see the immediate impact of a midterm slippage. Another benefit is that many of these programs can be "connected" to company systems, enabling stakeholders such as department heads and customers to access information on how a project that concerns them is progressing, while the project team maintains control over the project.[36] This allows for others, besides the team members, to participate and have easy access to project information. Of course, as is true of any computer program, their availability does not replace the need for human interaction. Keeping people informed through personal contact is an important complement to electronic communication about project status.[37]

Summary

In today's environment, company and individual success comes more readily to those who can do more with less while working smarter, not harder. One way to do this is to make effective use of project management skills and tools. This becomes especially important when you are involved in one or more complex projects. Taking time to clarify project expectations, determine contributors and stakeholders, establish specific objectives or milestones, create contingency plans, and communicate regularly with stakeholders are among the steps needed to make all your projects a success. In the final analysis, others expect project outcomes or deliverables—on time and on budget—not excuses or explanations!

Key Terms and Concepts

Backscheduling	Project management
Critical path method (CPM)	Project time line
Gantt chart	Stakeholders
Program Evaluation and Review Technique (PERT)	Work plan

Endnotes

1. David L. Coles, "Step Back to Get Ahead; The Key to Completing Projects on Time Is Working Backward from Your Deadlines," *Coles and Associates,* March–April 1988, p. 14.

2. Joe E. Beck, Worley Johnson, and R. Steve Konkel, "Project Management Insights," *Occupational Health and Safety,* June 2000, p. 22.

3. Alexander Laufer, "Project Planning: Timing Issues and Path of Progress," *Project Management Journal,* June 1991, p. 39.

4. Robert D. Landel and J. Robb Dixon, "Assessing the Potential for Office-Productivity Improvement," *Operations Management Review,* Fall 1983, pp. 3–8.

5. Kathleen Melymuka, "Born to Lead Projects: Some People Have Innate Talents for Managing Projects," *Computerworld,* March 27, 2000, p. 62.

6. Howard Millman, "On Track and in Touch," *Computerworld,* June 26, 2000, p. 88.

7. Sonia Tellez, "Think Globally When Designing a PM Solution," *Computing Canada,* Dec. 10, 1999, p. 28.

8. Coles, 1988.

9. Quoted in article by Kathleen Melymuka, "Project Management Top Guns," *Computerworld,* Oct. 20, 1997, pp. 108–109.

10. Lawrence Todryk, "The Project Manager as Team Builder: Creating an Effective Team," *Project Management Journal,* Dec. 1990, p. 17.

11. Melymuka, 1997.

12. See J. Richard Hackman, "Motivation through the Design of Work—Test a Theory," *Organizational Behavior and Human Performance,* Aug. 1976, p. 250; J. R. Hackman, "Is Job-Enrichment Just a Fad," *Harvard Business Review,* Sept.–Oct. 1975, p. 129.

13. See Frank Swoboda, "Workers Generally Worse Off Than a Decade Ago, Study Finds," *The Washington Post,* Sept. 7, 1992, p. 25; and Susan Cartwright, "Taking the Pulse of Executive Health in the U.K.," *The Academy of Management Executive,* May 2000, p. 16.

14. Lloyd A. Rogers, "Project Team Training: A Proven Key to Organizational Teamwork and Breakthrough in Planning Performance," *Project Management Journal,* June 1990, p. 9.

15. Robert Thompson, "More Heads Better Than One in Project Management," *Computing Canada,* Dec. 10, 1999, p. 27.

16. Coles, 1988.

17. Paul S. Adler, "Never-Ending Mission to Find Magic Solution," *Computing Canada,* Oct. 1, 1999, p. 17.

18. Don Reinertsen, "The Best-Laid Plans Become the Enemy of Vigilance," *Electronic Design,* March 20, 2000, p. 57.

19. Quote attributed to Uwe Weissflog, manager of strategic planning Structural Dynamics Research Corp., as captured by Kathleen Melymuka, 1997.

20. Rogers, 1990.

21. Don Reinertsen, "Projects Can Slip by More Than One Day at a Time," *Electronic Design,* March 6, 2000, p. 56.

22. Daphne Main and Carolyn L. Lousteau, "Don't Get Trapped," *Strategic Finance,* Nov. 1999, p. 74.

23. Melymuka, 1997.

24. Melymuka, 2000.

25. Yourdon, Ed, "The Value of Triage," *Computerworld*, March 20, 2000.

26. "Ask Bill Gates (Project Management Tips)," *Management Today*, Feb. 2000, p. 38.

27. Tellez, 1999.

28. Melymuka, 2000.

29. Peter R. Scholtes, *The Leader's Handbook* (Washington, DC: McGraw-Hill, 1998), p. 205.

30. Haymarket Publishing, 2000.

31. Scholtes, pp. 99 and 205.

32. Haidee E. Allerton, "How To," *Training and Development*, Nov. 1999, p. 15.

33. Scholtes, 1998, p. 205.

34. Barry Render and Ralph M. Stair, Jr., *Introduction to Management Science* (Boston, MA: Allyn & Bacon, 1992), p. 368.

35. "Get a Grip," *Fortune*, Summer 2000, Supplement, pp. 74–90.

36. Matthew J. Liberatore, "A Decision Support System Linking Research and Development Project Selection with Business Strategy," *Project Management Journal*, Nov. 1988, p. 14.

37. Thompson, 1999.

Exercise 17–A
Assessing Yourself

Circle the response that most closely correlates with each item below.

	Agree	Neither	Disagree
1. I am in the habit of planning my daily, weekly, monthly, and annual priorities and commitments.	1 2	3	4 5
2. I maintain a day planner and incorporate personal, academic, family, and professional responsibilities into it.	1 2	3	4 5
3. I outline all the steps that are likely to be involved in a project and enter these steps into my personal day planner.	1 2	3	4 5
4. I constantly monitor my planner and make adjustments to the time line as necessary.	1 2	3	4 5
5. I develop project quality standards and discuss these with my team, manager and/or instructor prior to beginning a project.	1 2	3	4 5
6. I allow slack in my schedule to allow for contingencies or the unexpected.	1 2	3	4 5
7. I assess the ultimate goals of a project and relate these to my overall goals or those of the organization.	1 2	3	4 5
8. I focus first on completing essentials or must-haves.	1 2	3	4 5
9. I identify and gain input from key stakeholders.	1 2	3	4 5
10. I volunteer to take on assignments that give me exposure to functions outside my known area of expertise.	1 2	3	4 5
11. When possible, I take on assignments related to my interests and assign tasks to others based on their interests.	1 2	3	4 5
12. I backschedule, listing all project steps starting with the final deadline and working backwards to the present.	1 2	3	4 5
13. I identify the dependencies that exist in a plan.	1 2	3	4 5
14. I monitor tasks that I have taken on or delegated and keep record of who was assigned each task and when.	1 2	3	4 5
15. I set specific and realistic deadlines for each step involved in a project.	1 2	3	4 5
16. I don't procrastinate.	1 2	3	4 5
17. I include in my planning all details such as clerical steps.	1 2	3	4 5
18. I set up specific times throughout a project when I monitor progress and check for understanding.	1 2	3	4 5
19. I break projects into small, manageable components.	1 2	3	4 5

	Agree	Neither	Disagree
	1 2	3	4 5

20. I determine in advance how results will be measured. 1 2 3 4 5

21. I evaluate projects midstream and am willing to make changes if necessary. 1 2 3 4 5

22. I estimate in advance the resources that will be required to do a job and adjust my expectations so they are in line with the available resources. 1 2 3 4 5

23. I ensure that project-planning meetings I attend or lead are decision oriented and that notes are kept about the issues and outcomes discussed. 1 2 3 4 5

24. I keep people informed by issuing regular progress reports. 1 2 3 4 5

25. I communicate regularly with team members, my manager, and key stakeholders. 1 2 3 4 5

26. I encourage a positive, open atmosphere for all with whom I work on group projects. 1 2 3 4 5

27. On projects, I give my all and help others to do the same. I resist the tendency to let myself or others marginalize the quality of the group's ultimate deliverable. 1 2 3 4 5

28. I give less experienced team members more attention and direction at the outset of a project. 1 2 3 4 5

29. I clarify roles, responsibilities, and accountabilities with my team members and manager or instructor. 1 2 3 4 5

30. I maintain records that document my and my team's progress on a project and share these with future project managers as appropriate. 1 2 3 4 5

31. I debrief with myself and/or my team and manager at the end of each project. 1 2 3 4 5

If your score was 93 or less, you may want to create a plan to further your project management skills.

**Exercise 17–B
Individual Day Planner
Update**

Each person should bring two sharpened pencils and his or her own personal day planner to this session. Have extra pencils on hand, as well as copies of blank calendars (8 ½" x 11"—one-sheet per month for 9 to 12 months) for those who don't have personal calendars.

1. Make a list of all activities and projects, personal and professional, in which you're currently involved. This can include work activities or classes in which you're enrolled, children's commitments such as carpooling or after-school activities, family, church or community obligations, exercise, planned travel (trip, vacation, holidays), and medical appointments.

2. Working through the list, enter all known dates for all commitments, activities, and appointments into your personal day planner, using a pencil. Be as thorough as possible. For example, if you are a student, enter all class sessions, exams, paper and project due dates, and vacation schedules. If you are unsure of a specific date, write the activity in the expected week, month, quarter, or semester in which it is likely to occur.

3. Make adjustments as you discover conflicts.

4. Keep this list up to date. As your schedule changes or as additional activities and deadlines are made known, add these into your day planner on a regular basis.

**Exercise 17–C
Personal Project
Time Line**

You will need your up-to-date individual day planner and project sheet or computer project management program.

1. Working on your own, consider a project in which you're currently involved or in which you anticipate being involved soon.* The project can be personal, such as planning a trip; academic, such as preparing to give a class presentation; or professional, such as conducting an analysis of available products that compete against those of your company.

2. Develop a work plan for the project, following the steps outlined in this chapter. Starting backwards from the project deadline, list every step needed to complete the project. Use a pencil if working on paper. Be as thorough as possible. Assign initials to each step and projected dates for each step.

3. Now transfer each of these dates (in pencil if using paper) to your personal day planner. If there are conflicts between this project and other classes, projects, or activities that are already in your planner, adjust the dates accordingly on both the project work plan and in your personal day planner.

4. Share your project work plan with a partner and obtain feedback on how realistic your plan is, how detailed it is, and on any suggested steps for adding or deleting. Modify your plan accordingly.

*If you can't think of a project, imagine it is the start of the fall semester and you are asked to prepare a 20-page term paper and presentation on a cutting-edge business topic by the end of the semester. You have twelve weeks in which to plan and complete this project. Other ideas: Building a new house, opening a retail store, producing a TV documentary, manufacturing and marketing a new product.

**Exercise 17–D
Team Project
Worksheet**

1. As a team, use the following sheet to develop a work plan for your team project. Use the guidelines outlined in this chapter.

2. Transfer the dates that affect you into your individual day planner (in pencil). Apprise the group of any potential conflicts. As a team, discuss how to adjust the project calendar to ensure that personal, academic, and professional commitments of all team members are incorporated into the overall project planning process.

3. Present your team's work plan to the class or group. Obtain feedback from them about steps that might have been overlooked or time lines that may be unrealistic. Adjust accordingly. Remember to make adjustments both on the team work plan and in your own day planner.

Team Project Work Plan

Project:

Due Date:

Names and Initials of Team Members:

Project Step: **Date:** **Initials:**
 1.
 2.
 3.
 4.
 5.
 6.
 7.
 8.
 9.
10.
11.
12.
13.
14.

(continue with additional steps on reverse or on blank sheet of paper)

Exercise 17–E
Product Recall

The Scenario

You are part of the Yum Yum Bubblegum's management team. Yum Yum Bubblegum manufactures and sells bubble gum in the United States and Canada.
You have three manufacturing plants:

- Chewing, Mississippi
- Bubbleton, Alabama
- Poppingsburg, South Dakota

The same products are manufactured at all plants and then sent to Yum Yum's distribution center in Shipit, Arkansas, where they are then shipped to customers via distribution trucks. Assume that the company has no contingency or preventive product recall plans.

The Problem

- The company has just been notified that six people have been hospitalized for toxic poisoning related to substances found in Yum Yum Bubblegum.
- Three of the hospitalized individuals purchased gum in Dallas, Texas; one in San Antonio; one in San Diego, California; and one is believed to have purchased the gum in an airport in Utah.

Questions and Task

Using the tips and techniques provided in the chapter, work as a team to manage the clean-up project.

1. How should you as managers attack this problem? What's your plan? Create a list of key steps and time frame for each.
2. Next, choose your project team. Who should be on this team? What is each team member's role? Who should be the leader?
3. Determine a contingent plan of attack. How to approach the problem? How to control the process?
4. Finally, determine a preventive plan for the future, assuming that this fiasco does not *blow* the company's ability to continue to do business.

Source: Permission provided by creator Sherry Ghodes, JMU MBA Student, presented Fall 2000.

Exercise 17–F
Try This . . .

1. Get on the Internet and research existing project management tools and resources. New products are becoming available all the time. Bring an example of a new product that you think looks particularly effective to your class or group.
2. Contact your computer department and ask them for recommendations of new software programs that can be used easily for tracking projects. Try one out and report to your group on its effectiveness and potential applicability to your group's project.
3. Visit a local office supply or stationery store and investigate the current day planner systems that are available. Make a note of the particular strengths and limitations of each. Report to the class or group on the top one or two that you believe are the best available for your group's purposes.
4. Interview someone you know or work with who is a project manager. Ask that person about the job—the highs, the lows, the lessons learned, tips, and so on. What advice would they give you for applying principles of project management to school projects? To workplace projects?

**Exercise 17–G
Reflection/Action Plan**

This chapter focused on project management—what it is, why it's important, and how to improve your skills in this area. Complete the worksheet below upon completing all reading and experiential activities for this chapter.

1. The one or two areas in which I am most strong are:

_____

_____

_____

_____

2. The one or two areas in which I need more improvement are:

_____

_____

_____

_____

3. If I did only one thing to improve in this area, it would be to:

_____

_____

_____

_____

4. Making this change would probably result in:

_____

_____

_____

_____

5. If I did not change or improve in this area, it would probably affect my personal and professional life in the following ways:

_____

_____

_____

_____

18 Making Effective and Ethical Decisions

How do I:

✓ Decide between competing options and interests?

✓ Make a decision before having all of the necessary information?

✓ Make a decision that I can stick with?

✓ Decide whether I should make the decision by myself or involve my team?

✓ Know if I am making an ethical decision?

✓ Know that I'm making the right decision?

✓ Help my employees make sound decisions?

Ashley was torn. She looked down at her registration card. She had gotten the courses she wanted. Or had she? Approaching her junior year in college, Ashley was contemplating changing her major. She just didn't know what to do. Ashley is very intelligent and capable. Like many other students, she thought she would major in business—a practical major for any field, her parents and advisors assured her. She took the right courses and got the necessary grades, even excelling in some areas. She had also worked summers and as an intern for a consulting firm. Everyone told her she would be good in business.

Despite all these positive signs, something was holding her back. In her sophomore year she had discovered a love of literature. Nothing could be more different than business. Yet she found it more interesting and satisfying than the business courses she was taking. Ashley didn't know what to do. She was fearful of approaching her parents. They had made it clear they were willing to pay for her college if she majored in something practical. Then again, her parents wouldn't know what classes she was taking. Ashley tried contacting her advisor, but he didn't have time to see her. Her friends had their own registration hassles. Her teachers wouldn't be supportive, she thought. Why would they encourage her to drop out of their classes in favor of someone else's? She didn't know what to do.

1. Why is Ashley in this situation?

2. What issues is she facing?

3. What options does she have available to her?

4. What should she do?

(Alice standing at the crossroads), "Cheshire-Puss," she began . . . "Would you tell me please which way I ought to go from here?"[1]

Alice in *Alice in Wonderland*

Making decisions—and being able to live with them rather than second-guessing them—is one of the most difficult tasks we face in life and in business. Deciding what major to choose can be just as difficult for a college student as deciding which company to acquire for an ambitious CEO. In this chapter we discuss what decision making is and why it is important, and we also examine ethical decision making. We describe the steps involved and the strategies that can help you make decisions clearly and easily, or at least in an organized way that gives you the confidence that you've made the right decision. At the end of the chapter, we've included some exercises to help you assess and improve your skills in decision making.

What Is Decision Making?

Decision making is a process by which several possibilities are considered and prioritized, resulting in a clear choice of one option over others. Decision making is a fact of life personally and in business. We make dozens of decisions each day. Some decisions are simple, while others are complex. Some are made for us while others require a great deal of analysis and thought. From what to wear to work to what computer system to choose to how to reward top performers to what movie to see, we use a variety of complex thought processes to make decisions from an array of options. Our ability to make decisions helps us to navigate through life, avoiding potential problems and expanding our horizons. Decision making plays a similar role in business. Decision making aids managers in identifying and selecting among potential opportunities, helping them solve immediate problems and make future problems more manageable.[2] Good decision makers are those who are effective at processing information, assessing risks, and making choices that will have positive outcomes for their organization.[3] While at times intuitive or "gut" decision making is appropriate, in this chapter we focus our attention primarily on the rational decision-making process, as it is most relevant to working in organizations and as part of a group.

Why Is Decision Making Important?

Effective decision making is essential for both organizations and individuals. Changes in organizational structures, processes, technology, and the availability of data have increased the need for members at all levels of organization to make decisions, and make them effectively.

■ With the change from hierarchical to flatter, more participative organizational structures, it is crucial for employees at all levels of the organization to have the information and authority they need to react quickly to customer concerns, business issues, and changing market trends. Having a decision-making frame of reference enables employees to react quickly and make decisions that are in the best interest of the organization.

■ Today more business decisions are being made in team environments. Group decision making is even more complex than decisions made by one or two individuals. Employees in team environments need to understand how to gain buy-in for their positions and how to work with others to arrive at a consensus about a preferred course of action. A decision-making framework can provide the basis for identifying mutual interests. This can serve as the foundation for healthy discussion and eventual selection of one option over others.

■ Technology is literally speeding up the pace of business. Quick decision making is not only desired, it is expected.[4] Poor or slow decision making can result in failure or a lack of competitiveness. In our fast-paced business environment, the ability to identify potential problems and opportunities, collect the data needed to analyze their limitations and merits, and make expedient determinations based on the information available has become one of the most important managerial skills. Companies that train their employees to be good decision makers and encourage smart decision making can increase efficiency and boost profits. By eliminating unnecessary steps, combining knowledge, and simplifying processes to help speed up decisions, managers with honed decision-making skills can have a tremendous impact on a company's bottom line.[5]

■ The vast amount of information available today through the media, Internet, and other outlets makes decision making an essential—rather than a "nice to have"—skill. The most effective managers are those who are able to quickly scan a wide variety of data from numerous sources and determine which information is relevant for their needs. Through decision-making processes, managers learn to translate, assimilate, and activate the information they receive.[6] Decision-making skills play a vital role in managerial success.

The Decision-Making Process

Figure 18–1 represents a straightforward process for making almost any type of decision. This framework can be used for decisions you face in your personal life, at school, and in the workplace.

Step One—Identify the Core Issues

What is the concern you are addressing? What is it you're trying to change or react to? In the first step of decision making, you need to determine your objective, stating clearly and specifically what you want the end result to be.[7] You want to select a movie everyone can agree on. You want to choose a major that makes you happy. You want to acquire a business that will increase your share of the market. By specifying the end goal or desired state, you have a logical foundation for making a good decision—for sorting through options and determining which one or ones best meet your overall objective.[8]

One of the most common errors in decision making is solving the wrong problem. There is a tendency to define the problem too narrowly, resulting in fewer alternatives from which to select to implement a satisfactory outcome. This is a condition known as **satisficing**.[9] It is important early in the decision process to step back and analyze the situation from a broader perspective to ensure you are focusing on the real issues.[10] This takes discipline. Returning to our opening case, if Ashley were to rush to make a decision about a major before she's ready because of the school's registration schedule, the resolution of the problem might be temporary. Without the time to address the real issues that are involved—deciding what is best for her long term, not just this semester—she might find herself faced with the same dilemma next term. It's best to define a problem clearly before taking action.[11]

**Figure 18–1
The Decision-Making Process**

- Identify the core issues
- Determine a decision-making approach
- Generate options
- Research options
- Evaluate options
- Reach a decision
- Implement and monitor the decision

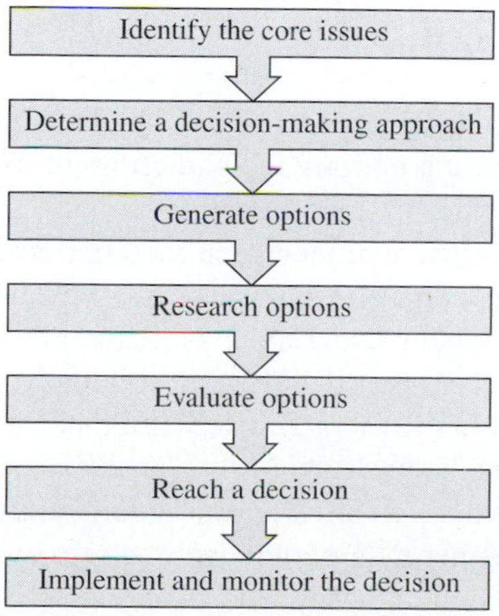

Step Two—Determine a Decision-Making Approach

How will you (and your group) make the decision? What options are available to you? What are the possible ways in which you can respond to a situation? What are the different steps that can be taken? In the case of selecting a movie with a group of friends, you can flip a coin, you can each vote on your top choice, you can defer to the person paying for the tickets, or you can take turns selecting a favorite to see. In our case example, Ashley could agree to talk with her parents, make an appointment to meet with an advisor, or even defer her decision and take a career planning course, all of which could help her eventually make the real decision on which major to select.

Establish a course of action before attempting to make the decision. This sounds simple. But often people rush to make a decision before agreeing on how the decision will be made. The very act of discussing a potential process paves the way for consideration of options that might not otherwise have surfaced.

Step Three—Generate Options

By definition, making decisions implies that more than one option is available to you. It is very rare and unusual for any problem or situation to have only one solution or possibility. People who only consider one alternative or solution are setting themselves up for failure or marginal success. Often the initial solution presented is not the best one. Sometimes, we are unable to generate additional options because of our mistaken beliefs or assumptions about a situation, such as there is only one right answer or one course of action that meets our needs. It's a good idea to test such assumptions by asking questions such as, "What if there's a cheaper way to fix the problem?" or "What if I could get my parents to see that there are other practical fields in which to major?"

The best decisions are those made after consideration of varied or multiple options. Be creative and brainstorm as many potential alternatives or solutions as possible. In cases where more than one person is involved, examine alternatives from all perspectives to get a near optimal or creative solution.[12] In Ashley's case, she might find—after taking time to explore her situation and discussing it with others—that she can double major in business and literature, or major in literature now and study business in graduate school. Generating options is often a liberating step in decision making. Where initially you might feel overwhelmed and pessimistic about the chances of solving your dilemma, by generating alternatives you free yourself to consider things you might not have thought about before.

Step Four—Research Options

Well, if your decision is which movie to see, and you and your group are standing in front of the theatre, you're probably not going to take the time to research the options, unless you count reading movie reviews ahead of time as research! For most other decisions, and for virtually all decisions in teams and in organizations, this is a crucial step. Often one of the reasons we're unable to move forward and make a decision is we simply don't have the information needed to make a good decision. In Ashley's case, she lacks information about how her parents would react, about suggestions her advisor might have for her, or about how to make a double major or a combination of a major and a minor work. By taking the time to gather data, you are able to increase your confidence that once the decision is made it will be the right one, as it is based on the information available at the time.

Step Five—Evaluate Alternatives

At this point, a little healthy pessimism is needed. Once you've been creative and nonjudgmental in generating options and gathering information about them, you can assess the pros and cons of each option.[13] Assess the gains that would be derived from each and any limitations that are inherent in each option. Also consider other factors that are important to you when making the decision and evaluate the degree to which each option relates to the factors of importance. For example, factors that might be important to Ashley are choosing the major that's right for her, pleasing her parents, and choosing a course of action that allows her to graduate within the next two years. The one option that best meets these goals is the one Ashley should likely select. Majoring in business would meet her need to please her parents. Majoring in literature is the option that would make her happy. But changing her major at this point might result in her having to stay in college for a fifth year, something she doesn't want to do. Overall, majoring in business and adopting a literature minor might be the option that best meets a combination of all of

Ashley's needs. She can please her parents, take courses in an area in which she's truly interested, and graduate in four years.

Many times we work with incomplete or imperfect information in the decision-making process. We can reduce the risk factors by hypothesizing potential scenarios. For each option, ask questions such as, What would happen if I decided to do option *X*? How would I feel if I were to implement option *X*? How would option *X* affect other areas of my life or the business? At this stage, it's also appropriate to narrow the alternatives. Only consider the options that are truly realistic and fulfill the goal or desired end state you defined in step one.

Seldom do we have a chance, like Ashley, to choose an option that meets most of our primary needs. In real life we are faced with decision trade-offs—accepting options that don't meet all of our needs in order to meet our most important or highest-order needs. A systematic way to do this is to make a list of all of the factors that are important to you in a decision, prioritize those factors, and then weigh each option against the factors to determine the one that best meets your most important needs (see Figure 18–2). This option may not meet all of your priorities, but it should meet your top two or three.

Figure 18–2
Priority Grid

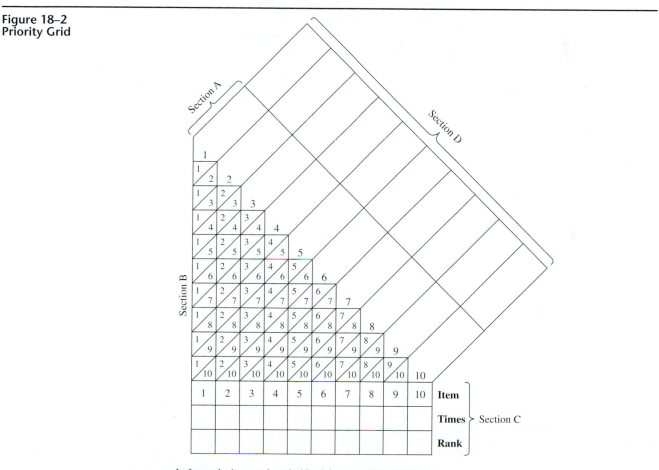

1. Insert the items to be prioritized, in any order, in Section A.

2. Compare two items at a time, circling the one you prefer—among the two—in Section B.

3. Count the number of times each item was circled. Enter total in "Times" box.

4. "Times" total determines item's ranking. Most circled = #1, next most circled = #2, etc. If two items are circled the same number of times, look back in Section B to see when those two were compared and which one you preferred. Give that one an extra half point. Complete the rank order in "Rank" line of Section C.

5. List items in Rank order in Section D.

Figure 18–3
Seven Helpful Techniques for Generating and Evaluating Alternatives[14]

Look for analogies—make comparisons to other situations, projects within and outside of your company.

Let data and impressions flow—manipulate data in various ways, allow for a variety of outcomes.

Build alternative hypotheses—develop lists of possible strategies.

Take a break and let the subconscious work—allow for the experiential and instinctual parts of decision making to evolve.

Do an outcome analysis and measure the downside—check the comparisons, weigh and understand probabilities.

Check for spurious precision—reexamine data and information to determine if specifics and vital information were created and incorporated in the gathered data.

Do a reality shakedown—examine the alternative for the quality of execution by asking questions such as, Do I have the resources needed for implementation? Do I have the time and people to make this work?

With the availability of so much information in today's technology age, it is possible to get caught up in having too many alternatives, too many ideas, and too much work. This can lead to a lack of focus and momentum, which can lead to indecisiveness and a loss of power.[15] We may become overwhelmed by the options and never proceed to selecting one, a condition known as **analysis paralysis.**[16] Prioritizing the factors that are important to you and evaluating your options against these priorities can help you to narrow the options to those that are the most viable given the circumstances and your goals in a specific situation.

Step Six—Reach a Decision

Once all the information is in and you've had a chance to consult with others as necessary and weigh the alternatives, it's time to make a decision. Determine which option best meets your overall needs and resolve to act on that option. But before taking the plunge, envision taking the plunge first. Do a self-visualization to make sure the decision you're making is one you can live with. One way to do this is to make a decision, but take 24 hours to think about it. Let your subconscious act as though you've made the decision, but don't let anyone know and don't act on the decision yet. The next morning, before you even rise, ask yourself how you feel about the decision you made yesterday. Listen to what your heart tells you. Do you feel positive? Calm? Like it was the right choice? Or do you feel negative? Panicked? Like it would be the wrong choice? If you feel fine about the choice you've made, it's an intuitive sign you've made the best decision given the information available and you can probably act on it. If you still have serious reservations about your decision, then you're not ready to act and you should defer action until you've had a chance to resolve the conflict you're experiencing.

Step Seven—Implement and Monitor

Once you've reached a decision, it's time to act on your decision and monitor it to make sure it's resulting in the outcome you expected. Develop a plan that specifies the steps you'll take, a time frame, and the key players. In Ashley's case, she would make plans to go home and talk with her parents, make an appointment to see her advisor, meet with those of her instructors who might be affected by her decision, and plan a visit to her college's Career Center to learn about career options for the major(s) she's considering. Then, monitor the plan to see if it is following the direction you wanted. Also observe whether external factors have changed or if you're receiving information that might affect your decision, and adapt your plan accordingly. For example, Ashley might find a book that lists internship options for literature students, giving her hope she could look for a job the following summer that utilizes her literature background. Taking the time to plan and to monitor the decision after making a decision ensures that you'll do the follow-through necessary for the decision to be successful.

Group Decision Making

Organizational decision making is more complex than individual decision making because of the number of people involved in making the decision and the volume of people affected by the decision. Several different types of decision-making processes can be used when making organizational decisions.[17] The process chosen depends on the type of leadership, on the people involved, and on the time available for a decision to be made.

- **Autocratic decision making:** This approach involves making decisions on your own or independently. This approach is fast and timely and can be effective in matters that are minor or trivial or where there would be more to lose than to gain by getting others to participate. This approach can also be appropriate in times of crisis, when it is critical for one strong person to be in charge. Potential problems that could stem from an autocratic decision approach are lack of commitment by individuals to decisions imposed on them, an increased likelihood that decisions made are wrong, lack of creative expansion or development of ideas, and that decisions are made that reflect a single perspective. For this approach to work, collect the data needed to make a decision and communicate to others your rationale for taking a certain route immediately, pointing out the benefits of that route to those who will be affected by the decision.

- **Expert member soliciting:** This approach involves obtaining input from and relying on the advice offered by a person with particular skill or knowledge in the area of concern. This approach is effective when those involved in the decision lack expertise in the area being addressed and when there is time to bring in outside opinions for consideration by the decision-making body. A limitation of this approach is that it is difficult for an outsider, no matter how competent, to understand fully the dynamics involved inside any organization. The expert's opinion about the subject might be viable in other organizations but not in yours. To make this approach work, seek outside counsel, and involve internal group members when making the final decision.[18]

- **Consultative decision making:** This approach involves obtaining input from those responsible for and affected by the decision and then making a decision independently (rather than by consensus by the whole group, as outlined below). This approach has the advantage of allowing for some suggestion and involvement by others (limited empowerment). In this way, you can obtain others' perspectives and help others to feel included and to feel their insights and thoughts are taken into account before a decision is made. The disadvantage of this approach is that it is more time-consuming to get others involved before making a decision. Asking for others' opinions without making your own perspective known sometimes makes a manager appear to be indecisive. This approach can also backfire if it appears that decisions are made without ever taking into account others' perspectives, leading others to believe their opinions were neither desired nor included. For this approach to work, let the group know you have a strong opinion but don't want to make a decision until they've had a chance to give input. Incorporate at least part of their suggestions into the decision. If this can't be done, explain clearly the rationale so the group members feel they were heard, and assure them they will be included in future decisions.

- **Minority control:** This approach involves allowing a small portion of a larger group to make a decision. This approach is effective when time constraints or logistics make it impossible to get a large group together and the decision makers act on behalf of the large group. It is also appropriate when only a small part of the group has the expertise or interest in the issue. The disadvantage of this approach is that it is risky; the chances of the majority of the group not being satisfied with the outcome are greatly increased. For this approach to work, offer those who won't or can't be present for the decision the chance for input and keep them informed of the issues under discussion and the rationale for the decision ultimately made.

- **Majority control:** This approach involves making the decision that is favored by the largest number of people in the group. The advantage of this approach is that it allows for the largest percentage of those involved to make and control the decision. It is a practical means for large groups to bring closure to discussions to which many have had input. A disadvantage of this approach is that it is often very time consuming to get a majority on an issue. Another limitation is that sometimes in a "majority rules" context, a few members can dominate the discussion, making it less possible for other perspectives to surface and be considered. By definition, in a majority-rule situation, it is likely that not all group members will be satisfied with the outcome. As the saying goes, "You can please some people some of the time, but can't please all of the people all of the time." Unfortunately this approach often results in an either/or proposition with one side appearing to "win" and the other to "lose." In fact, the solution reached might not actually be the best solution, but the one to which the fewest objected. To make this approach work, lengthen the time during which creative options can be entertained, increasing the likelihood of an option surfacing that can be acceptable to the vast majority of the group and not just a small majority. In addition, consider imposing a two-thirds rule, where at least two-thirds of the group has to support the decision, rather than a simple 51 percent majority.

■ **Consensus:** This approach involves finding a proposal acceptable enough that virtually all members can support it.[19] This is the "win–win" scenario. To be clear, consensus does not necessarily mean 100 percent agreement. Instead, because all members were involved in an open and complete decision process and had input into the decision, virtually all of the members of a group are satisfied with the outcome, and confident in the viability of the solution reached. The chief advantage of this approach is that the quality of the decision will be greatly enhanced because of the attention paid to all interests in the group and the creativity involved in generating potential options. The limitations of this approach are that it is very time-consuming and involves a great deal of skill in dealing with people and helping the group to deal creatively with the situation. It also means the manager cannot impose his or her will on the group and must be open to others' perspectives on how the situation should be addressed. To make this approach work, provide the group with the information they need to take all important factors into account, provide an atmosphere and resources that support creativity, and develop a timetable that allows the creative process to work and the group to find a viable, creative solution.

Group Decision-Making Considerations

Each of the decision-making approaches we've discussed can be appropriate given the situation you're facing as a manager. **Group decision making considerations** that determine the approach that's best to use in a specific situation include time, member competence, level of autonomy, amount of information available, and group size.

■ *Time:* Each approach has a different time requirement. The autocratic approach generally takes the least amount of time while the consensus approach takes the most. For any approaches other than autocratic to work, provide the time available to make a good decision. When time is short, choose an approach by making trade-offs based on the time available.

■ *Member competence:* Each approach implies a different level of group member competence. The autocratic approach assumes the least competence; the consensus approach, the most. Consider the skills and abilities of others in determining whether they should be a part of the decision-making process. For any but the autocratic approach to work, train the staff in how to interpret data and make comparisons between opposing alternatives. Group decision making requires that each member has an understanding of the issues involved and has the evidence needed to support the final decision.[20]

■ *Autonomy and self-direction:* Each approach assumes members have a specific level of freedom and motivation. The autocratic approach assumes the group members have the least amount of authority or desire for change; the consensus approach, the most. The type of people involved, the amount of authority they have, and the extent to which they are self-directed will influence the decision-making approach selected. For any but the autocratic approach to work, increase the ability of the group to not just make but implement the decisions made by the group. The more ownership they have over the outcome, the more involved they will be in the process of sorting through alternatives and selecting one to implement. And the more committed they will be to the outcome.

■ *Availability of necessary information:* Each approach assumes a different level of information is available to group members. The least amount of information is available in the autocratic approach; the most in the consensus approach. For any but the autocratic approach to work, the group's members need access to essential information. Provide information that is relevant to the topic at hand and that is easy to access and interpret.

■ *Group size:* Each approach assumes a different group size. The larger the group, the more difficult it is to gain a consensus decision and the more likely it is for a manager to revert to an autocratic approach. While group size is an important variable, it should not be used as an excuse for making decisions autocratically. Technology now makes it possible for large groups of employees to be informed about and have input into important matters before a decision gets made. For example, in universities it is now common practice for faculty committees to post their deliberations online so other faculty who were not present at the meetings can learn about and react to the discussion before the committee makes their final decision. In businesses, the communications departments, which previously focused on company newsletters, now play a vital role in devising creative means for employees to be involved in decision making on important topics. This is done through techniques such as virtual meetings between the company chair and officers and employees, round-table discussions with committee members and heads, online submission of ideas for improvement, and regular meetings and communications about the status of important activities. For any but the autocratic approach to work, think about ways employees can be incorporated into the decision-making process before decisions that affect them are made.

Victor Vroom, Phillip Yetton, and Arthur Jago have created a normative model (see Figure 18–4 below) that managers can use in deciding whether and in what capacity to involve others in making a decision. The **Vroom-Yetton-Jago model,** which takes into account many of the considerations discussed above as "problem attributes," assumes that with any managerial decision, five processes are possible:[21]

1. The manager solves the problem, using the information available at the time (AI style).

2. The manager obtains the necessary information from employees and then makes the decision (AII style).

**Figure 18–4
The Vroom–Yetton–Jago
Decision Model**

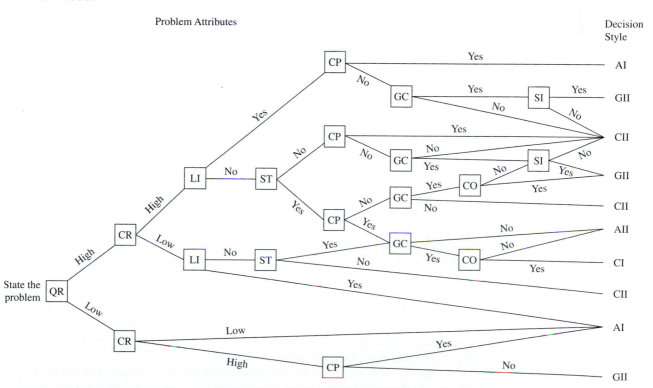

Source: Victor H. Vroom and Arthur G. Jago, *The New Leadership,* Prentice-Hall, 1988, p. 184. Reprinted by permission of Pearson Education Inc. Upper Saddle River, NJ.

3. The manager consults with subordinates individually, getting their ideas and suggestions, and then makes a decision (CI style).

4. The manager consults with subordinates as a group, again getting their ideas and suggestions, and then makes a decision (CII style).

5. The manager explains the problem to the employees as a group, and the group makes the decision (GII style).

Based on answering one at a time the eight questions listed below, a manager can arrive at the most appropriate decision style. To use the model, you begin with the decision under consideration. Starting at the QR node (see Figure 18–4), you would ask, "How important is the quality of the decision?" If your answer is "high," you'd take the upper path; if "low," you'd take the lower path. Then, at the CR node, you would ask the second question: "How important is employee commitment to the decision?" Again, based on your determination of the answer, you would move to the third mode via the second node's upper or lower path. The eight questions,[22] in order, are:

1. *Quality requirement (QR).* How important is the technical quality of the decision?

2. *Commitment requirement (CR).* How important is employee commitment to the decision?

3. *Leader's information (LI).* Does the leader have sufficient information to make a high-quality decision?

4. *Problem structure (ST).* Is the problem well structured?

5. *Commitment probability (CP).* If the leader makes the decision alone, will subordinates be committed to the decision?

6. *Goal congruence (GC).* Do employees share the organizational goals to be attained in solving this problem?

7. *Subordinate conflict (CO).* Is conflict among employees over preferred solutions likely?

8. *Subordinate information (SI).* Do employees have enough information to make a high-quality decision?

Advantages of Group Decision Making

Whenever possible, it is best to involve as many members of a group as possible in making decisions about matters that affect them. There are many benefits to involving employees in group decision making.

■ Group decision making results in more alternatives. In group decision making, more resources, creative ideas, and perceptions are applied to the process, strengthening the quality of the ultimate decision.[23]

■ Involvement by group members in the decision leads to greater buy-in to the decision. In group decision making, those involved understand the broader context and the considerations that went into the decision, along with the importance and need for implementation of the decision. They will feel that they have a vested interest in the project and are more likely to support you in resolving the situation.[24]

■ Group decision making helps team members to develop new skills. In group decision making, team members enhance their knowledge base through exposure to a broader array of issues and perspectives than typically found in their job alone. An employee will learn more by being involved in thinking through a situation than by being told what to do in a situation. Again, the adage "teach them how to fish rather than give them fish" applies here. For example, if an employee comes to you with a question, rather than answering right away, look at this as a training opportunity and ask, "What do you recommend?" Teaching people to make responsible decisions prepares them to move ahead faster and more effectively in their careers.[25]

■ Group decision making is a means for enhancing empowerment. Those with good decision-making skills are able to make important judgments and determinations in a number of key areas of responsibility, doing so quickly and accurately. This results in enhanced productivity and efficiency.[26]

Potential Problems of Joining Group Decision Making

Despite the many advantages, group decision making has some limitations. You may have experienced situations in which one or more of these phenomena occurred:

- **Group think:** Businesses are full of examples where "group think," or a collective mentality, has replaced individual judgment, resulting in negative consequences for the organization. In group think, employees succumb to the will of the group for fear of being perceived as uncooperative or incorrect.[27] It is widely thought, for example, that peer and competitive pressure caused individual engineers who were involved in the launch of the "Challenger" spaceshuttle in 1986 to support decisions that were being made by the group even though they as individuals had reservations about the safety of the ship. As a manager, it is your role to ensure everyone feels safe and free to disclose to you and the rest of the group any concerns they might have about a project before a final decision is made.

- **Dominant members:** In group decision making, there is a tendency for a few individuals to be highly verbal or strong willed. This can cause others who are more quiet to defer to what they think is the majority, when in fact it might be just a vocal minority. The danger in group decision making is that individual views might not become known through the standard group process of discussing factors before making a decision. As a manager, ensure that all have spoken and shared their views with the others, either orally or in writing, prior to a decision being made.[28]

- **Social loafing or free riding:** In group decision making, it is easy for one or more members of the group to choose not to contribute, or to contribute much less than other members. If the group is large, such noninvolvement might not even be noticed. Even if it is, if a deadline is looming, the tendency will be for a few to pick up the slack and ensure the necessary actions are taken or steps are completed, leaving the "free riders" seemingly off the hook. As a manager, take time to ensure each member of the team has a clear role and responsibility and contributes equally to the outcome. When indications of social loafing or free riding appear, it's best to deal with the situation early rather than give the appearance that such behavior is acceptable.

- **Risky behavior:** The adage "safety in numbers" might apply here. Groups often make riskier decisions than do individuals working alone because of the perception that vulnerability and accountability are shared between team members. This phenomenon is known as **risky shift.** As a manager, put necessary checkpoints and safeguards in place. These include specifying who's accountable prior to a decision being made. Also, ask hypothetical questions to ensure all factors have been considered and contingencies have been anticipated. You might even discuss the decisions with one or two members in private to get a clearer assessment without the impact of risky shift.

- **Self-censorship:** Some members of a group ignore realistic appraisals of alternatives in order not to make waves.[29] In group decision making, it is difficult to go against

---

Figure 18–5
10 Reasons People Err When Making Decisions[30]

Plunging in—gathering information but not taking the time to think through possibilities.

Frame blindness—setting out to solve the wrong problem and not being open to other scenarios; creating a mental framework that presupposes the decision.

Lack of control—failing to define the problem in a variety of ways; need to control it rather than allow it to control you.

Overconfidence in judgment—failure to seek out key information, believing that our assumptions and opinions are correct.

Shortsighted shortcuts—relying on "rule of thumb," trusting in readily available solutions and convenient facts.

Shooting from the hip—believing we can wing it rather than follow a systematic procedure to cover all bases through the entire process.

Group failure—failing to manage and ensure an effective group decision-making process.

Fooling ourselves about feedback—failing to analyze and interpret evidence from past experiences; not learning from hindsight.

Not keeping track—failing to keep systematic records and track results.

Failing to audit our decision process—failing to create an organized approach to decision making; failing to control the direction and outcomes of the project.

the tide. If the majority feel one way, it's not easy to speak up with a different point of view that contradicts the group's sentiment. This leads individuals to censor themselves and choose not to share important information. As a manager, don't let the team's enthusiasm get in the way of sound decision making, which includes gathering data and asking the tough questions before a decision is made.

Effective Decision-Making Checklist[31]

- Make small everyday decisions without delay.
- Base important decisions on the real issues, not just those that on the surface appear to be the key factors involved.
- Have several solutions or alternatives and examine each for potential negative consequences before solving a problem.
- Be firm in your selection of alternatives.
- Once you have made a decision and have thought about it for up to 24 hours, carry it out immediately.
- Make sure those involved are given an opportunity to play at least a minor role in helping you make the decision.
- Once your decision is made, communicate in detail how it will involve those who are affected by the decision.
- Explain the rationale for the decisions you made—the "method to your madness" if the decision is contrary to what most thought it would be.

Ethical Decisions

Have you ever witnessed someone cheating on a test? Have you ever called in sick when you actually went skiing or to the beach? Have you ever been given too much change and kept it? Every day we face situations where we have to make decisions where there are no apparent, clear-cut rules. For example, concerns about Internet security fraud are on the rise. Securities firms are constantly on the lookout for employees who are involved in insider training. Recent surveys suggest that increasing numbers of applicants lie about their backgrounds in employment interviews. Employees are creating "intellectual capital" during their day jobs and selling their expertise as consultants after hours. And ordinary employees are being entrusted with valuable financial and strategic information to help them make on-the-spot judgments about how to handle difficult situations. Managers and employees are constantly faced with challenges such as these. An ethical framework for decision making is needed.[32]

Ethical decision making involves applying principles or standards to moral dilemmas. Asking what is right or wrong, good or bad in business transactions is a basic business ethic.[33] Ethics guide people in making decisions that are not completely based on factors that have already been specified. Ethics can present a different perspective and give a new dimension to decision making. For example, it might be obvious—on paper—that opening a new manufacturing center in the remote areas of the Florida wetlands would be profitable due to low cost factors. Yet the detrimental environmental effects on the wetlands would be significant. Should the company open a wetlands plant? It's legal, but is it "right"? Who should make this decision? The company? Or the people in the area who are advocates for the wetlands? How should this decision be made? Is profitability the only criterion that should be used in making this decision? What should the decision be? Who will be affected by the decision? Who pulls the plug if it's the wrong decision? These are all ethical considerations that make the decision much more complex than it originally appeared on paper. Your own character, and that of the organization for which you work, are revealed by the types of decisions you make, how you make them, and to what end. Ethical decision making guides you in making decisions that are right not just for you but for those who are affected by the decisions.[34]

What are Ethics?

The word **ethics** comes from the Greek word *ethos,* which means a notion of character permeated with values that determine the identity and good or bad of an individual or group.[35] "Ethics [is] not so much a matter of right or wrong as it is a process by which an organization evaluates its decisions."[36] The difficulty with ethics is that the situations we face as managers are seldom black and white, with a clear understanding of which answer is the best for all concerned. Each person has a different world view (based on life experiences, education, family background, religious and political affiliations, perceptions, and values) that they bring into the decision-making process. Each person possesses a different **"ethical barometer"**[37] that stems from his or her experience and background. This diversity affects the ethical decision-making process, outcomes, and the ramifications of the decision.

Ethics and character reflect on our true inner self; they determine how we respond to managerial dilemmas. Many choices appear to be minor, but in reality these actions build up over time and set a foundation for more challenging decisions.[38] It is important to be aware of the guidelines we use for making small decisions. These guidelines can affect the way we approach larger, more significant decisions in other areas of life and work.

Ethical Dilemmas

Ethics play a part in our decision making whether we are acting as an individual, a group, an organization, or a member within an organization. **Ethical dilemmas** are situations where we are faced with making a decision that will be based largely on judgments and determinations rather than on indisputable facts. Ethical dilemmas can be the result of gross misunderstanding, values conflicts, cultural differences, conflict of interest, differences based on gender, economic level, religion, age, sexual orientation, upbringing, race or ethnicity, or greed. Examples of ethical dilemmas are exchange of inappropriate gifts, making unwanted sexual advances, discovery of unauthorized payments or overpayments, and hiring an untrained person from a "name" family over a more qualified individual.

An ethical dilemma arises when a manager must choose between his or her own interests and the interests of someone else or some other group. Those with an interest in the outcome of the decision are referred to as **stakeholders.** As a manager in an organization, it is up to you to take into consideration the needs and interests of all key stakeholders—the employees, customers, suppliers, and shareholders who are affected by the decision—in addition to yourself. Decisions you make reflect not only your values but also the values of the organization you represent. Decisions you make on behalf of your organization carry consequences for the company's reputation and success in the community.

Benefits of Ethical Decision Making

Many companies today are providing ethical guidelines or codes of conduct for their employees to use when faced with a situation that is not covered by standard policies and procedures. This practice has several benefits listed as follows.

Figure 18–6
Eight Rules of Ethical Thinking[39]

1. Consider others' well-being and avoid actions that will hurt others. Before taking action, ask yourself if anyone stands to be hurt by the action, financially, emotionally, and other ways.

2. Think of yourself as a member of a community, not as an isolated individual. Before taking action, reflect on who will be affected by the decision, positively and negatively.

3. Obey—but don't depend only on—the law. An action may be legal yet unethical.

4. Think of yourself and your organization as part of society. What you do and how you think affect a larger entity beyond you and your immediate circle.

5. Obey moral guidelines by which you have agreed to live. Consider them "categorical imperatives" with no exceptions.

6. Think objectively. Be sure your action is truly ethical and not rationalized self-interest.

7. Ask, "What sort of person would do such a thing?" Or, "Will I be able to look at myself in the morning after doing X?"

8. Respect others' customs—but not at the expense of your own ethics.

■ *Customer relations:* Employees in companies with ethical guidelines are better prepared to treat customers fairly if a conflict arises. This helps customers to feel they are respected and understood by the employees, resulting in higher levels of customer satisfaction.

■ *Goodwill:* By doing the "right thing" consistently, consumers, suppliers and others in the community at large see your organization as a desirable one with which to do business. The ethical reputation of a firm can actually increase its opportunities and sales, as shown by Anita Roddick's company, The Body Shop.[40] Her decision to buy ingredients that might have gone to waste (good for the environment) from countries that are economically depressed (good for society) is praised by many. Employees and customers have noted decisions like these positively impact their continued association with and patronization of The Body Shop. A company's goodwill also enhances its attractiveness and value to potential acquiring businesses.

■ *Employee satisfaction:* Employees in companies with ethical guidelines experience high comfort levels—they are pleased and relieved when they see their organization acting in an ethical way and actively promoting ethical behavior.[41]

■ *Employee empowerment:* Employees in companies with ethical guidelines feel empowered to think clearly about dilemmas at hand, to make decisions clearly, to articulate the rationale for their decisions, and to be supported by senior management if their judgment is questioned.[42]

Ethics-Enhancing Tools

Unfortunately, it is a fact that workers often accept unethical actions as the consequence of doing business today. Lapses in ethics are viewed as standard—expected in today's diverse, complex, and fast-paced world. In one survey, it was reported that 48 percent of workers surveyed said they respond to job pressures by performing unethical or illegal activities.[43] The most common unethical behaviors cited were:

■ Cutting corners on quality control (16 percent).

■ Covering up incidents (14 percent).

■ Abusing or lying about sick leave (11 percent).

■ Lying to or deceiving customers (9 percent).

It is not easy to raise the ethical consciousness of an organization. Organizations are made up of individuals who may behave in an unethical manner for what they believe are justified reasons. When people are faced with pressures at work and need to make fast decisions, they are not very likely to consult rules, regulations, and policies that often don't apply to the specific situation with which the employee is dealing.[44] This leads to many of the ethical lapses that occur in business today. In addition, organizations themselves might have policies that encourage employees to make unethical decisions. For example, a company might set unrealistically high sales targets, possibly leading some employees to engage in questionable tactics to increase sales to customers.

Making ethical decisions is more a matter of having the right values than a set of rules. To help employees cope with the need to make ethical decisions, organizations must raise the employees' level of ethical consciousness. This starts by first declaring the organization's values and expectations, and then laying out guidelines and a decision framework that employees can use when faced with decisions that require use of judgment in addition to adherence to company guidelines. The following are some tools that companies can use to educate employees about ethical decision making.

■ **Code of ethics:** A written statement of values and guidelines for how to treat employees and customers. Codes of ethics provide a tangible description of what the company stands for, what they want to achieve, and the means for achieving their goals. Codes are a good first step in raising ethical issues, although on their own they are insufficient to ensure that organizational ethical standards are followed.[45]

■ **Ethics test:** A series of questions that aids employees in making well-considered judgments about a situation before making a decision. Using this test will not provide one "correct" answer. The test provides criteria to be considered when determining a course of action that is ethical.[46] The test has four components:

- ■ The test of *common sense:* "Does this action I am about to take make sense?"

- ■ The test of *one's best self:* "Is this action or decision I'm getting ready to take compatible with my concept of myself at my best?"

- ■ The "*light of day*" approach or making something public: "How would I feel if others knew I was doing this? Would I be willing to stand in front of my family, friends, peers and be proud to tell them what I had decided to do?"[47]

- ■ The test of the *purified idea:* "Am I thinking this action or decision is right just because someone with appropriate authority or knowledge says it is right?" For example, if an accountant told you it was okay to claim certain entertainment and travel expenses as business expenses, although there is doubt in your mind about the fairness of this determination, do you abdicate responsibility for this decision since the accountant said it was acceptable?

■ **Ethical audit:** A broad-based, agreed-upon system that lets an organization consistently focus and refocus on its values and whether its performance is meeting the standards it professes. In an ethical audit, the situational and environmental factors that have significant impact on ethical behaviors and internal policies are analyzed. These audits encourage self-reflection across all levels of an organization and raise ethical consciousness, leading to less unethical or corruptive behavior.[48]

■ **Decision-making model:** Frameworks that can be used to help employees by giving them a short, step-by-step list of rules they can use to make decisions by taking an ethical course of action.[49] Models in ethical guidelines, such as those shown in Figure 18–7, aren't a guarantee that employees will always act ethically. They are a means to get employees to think through their actions and consider the ethical standards involved when making decisions that affect them and those around them.

■ **Ethics training:** For any of the above ideas to work in organizations, companies can offer their employees training about a company's policies and values and how to incorporate an ethical component into their decisions on an everyday basis. This training can be provided via a manual, a workshop, a Web-based self-directed program, or through one-on-one mentoring and coaching sessions.

Figure 18–7
A Sample of an Ethical
Decision-Making Model[50]

Step 1: Identify the facts and issues
- a. Who will be affected by my decision?
- b. What will be the short- and long-term consequences of possible courses of actions?

Step 2: Identify applicable values
- a. How will possible courses of action impact potential stakeholders?
- b. What consideration should I have with regard to:
  The rights of stakeholders?
  Justice among stakeholders?
  The short- and long-term balance of good among stakeholders?
  My gut feeling about what is the "right thing"?
  What I think those whom I respect for their virtue would judge to be "the right thing?"

Step 3: Seek help if needed
- a. Which course of action might keep me awake at night?
- b. Can my supervisor or human resources department provide guidance?

Step 4: Reach the best decision based on the available information
- a. Is my decision legal and within organizational policy?
- b. Do organizational values and my personal values support my decision?

Summary

We face decisions every day. Some of these are tough—mired in ambiguity, complexity, and ethical considerations—while others are easy. The process by which you make decisions can significantly impact whether the decision is right—effective, ethical, and successful in the long term—for you and those affected by the decision. We provided a process for you to follow when making decisions, as well as approaches and considerations when making decisions as a member of a group. While simple decisions, such as whether to wear a blue or red shirt, may not require a multistep decision process, more complex and consequential decisions do. Your effectiveness as a manager can be greatly enhanced by your ability to make effective and ethical decisions.

Key Terms and Concepts

Analysis paralysis

Autocratic decision making

Code of ethics

Consensus

Consultative decision making

Decision making

Decision-making model

Dominant members

Ethical audit

Ethical barometer

Ethical decision making

Ethical dilemmas

Ethics

Ethics test

Ethics training

Expert member soliciting

Group decision-making considerations (five)

Group think

Majority control

Minority control

Risky shift

Satisficing

Self-censorship

Social loafing or free riding

Stakeholders

Vroom-Yetton-Jago model

Endnotes

1. Lewis Carroll, *Alice in Wonderland* (NJ: Castle Books, 1978).

2. Raymond Suutari, "Tale of Two Strategies: How Does Your Company Make Its Strategic Business Decisions," *CMA Management,* July–August 1999, p. 12.

3. Rosemary Kane Carlough, "From the Publisher (The Importance of Communicating Decisions)," *HR Focus,* July 1999, p. 1.

4. Sal Marino, "Rely on Science, Not Your Gut," *Industry Week,* Jan. 24, 2000, p. 18.

5. D. Keith Denton and Peter Richardson, "Making Speedy Decisions," *Industrial Management,* Sept. 1999, p. 6.

6. A. Read, "Managers Making Dicey Decisions," *Internal Auditor,* Dec. 1999, p. 14.

7. Winston Fletcher, "It's Make Your Mind Up Time," *Management Today,* Sept. 1998, p. 31.

8. Ralph L. Keeney, "Foundations for Making Smart Decisions," *IIE Solutions,* May 1999, p. 24.

9. Herbert A. Simon, *Models of Bounded Rationality* (Cambridge, MA: MIT Press, 1982). It is important to note that satisficing may actually be preferred in certain situations where the decision maker lacks time, money, or access to sufficient data to make a "best" decision. When all information is not available, as in the case of forecasting, satisficing is appropriate and warranted.

10. Interview with Howard Raiffa, John S. Hammond, and Ralph L. Keeney, "Ready, Fire, Aim," *Inc.,* Oct. 1998.

11. Manufacturers' Agents National Association, "A Guide to Practical Decision Making," *Agency Sales Magazine,* March 1999, p. 39.

12. Ibid.

13. Fletchen, 1998.

14. John Rau, "Two Stages of Decision Making," *Management Review,* Dec. 1999, p. 10. Reprinted from *Management Review,* December 1999. Copyright © 1999 American Management Association International, New York, NY. All rights reserved. http://www.amanet.org

15. Jennifer White, "Maintaining Focus: The Best Way to Overcome the 'Too Much Syndrome,'" *The Business Journal,* March 10, 2000, p. 39.

16. Joel Barker, *Paradigms: The Business of Discovering the Future* (New York: Harper Business, 1993).

17. David W. Johnson and Frank P. Johnson, *Joining Together: Group Theory and Group Skills,* Sixth Ed. (Needham Heights, MA: Allyn and Bacon, 1997), p. 245.

18. Carlough, 1999.

19. Peter R. Scholtes, *The Team Handbook (*Madison, WI: Joiner Associates Inc., 1988).

20. Read, 1999.

21. V. H. Vroom and P. W. Yetton, *Leadership and Decision Making* (Pittsburgh, PA: University of Pittsburgh Press, 1972), p. 13, as cited in Shani and Lau, *Behavior in Organizations,* 6e, 1996, 7ed., 2000. Burr Ridge, IL: McGraw-Hill/Irwin.

22. V. H. Vroom and A. C. Jago, *The New Leadership* (Englewood Cliffs, NJ: Prentice Hall, 1988), p. 184, as cited in Shani and Lau, *Behavior in Organizations,* 6e, 1996, 7ed., 2000. Burr Ridge, IL: McGraw-Hill/Irwin.

23. Larry K. Michaelsen, Warren E. Watson, and Robert H. Black, "A Realistic Test of Individual versus Group Consensus Decision Making," *Journal of Applied Psychology* 74 (1989), pp. 834–839.

24. Copyright © 1999, Manufacturer's Agents National Association, 23016 Mill Creek Road, P.O. Box 3467, Laguna Hills, CA 92654-3467. Phone (949) 859–4040; toll-free: (877) 626–2776; fax (949) 855–2973; Email: mana@manaonline.org; website: www.manaonline.org. All rights reserved. Reproduction without permission is strictly prohibited.

25. Tom McCarthy, "Encouraging Decision Making," *Lodging Hospitality,* August 1999, p. 16.

26. Ibid.

27. Janis L. Irving, *Groupthink,* Second Ed. (Boston: Houghton Mifflin, 1982).

28. George P. Huber, *Managerial Decision Making* (Glenview, IL: Scott, Foresman, 1980).

29. P. M. Mulvey, J. F. Veiga, and P. Elsass, "When Teammates Raise a White Flag, *Academy of Management Executive* 10 (1996), pp. 39–49.

30. Marino, 2000; referring to the book *Decision Traps,* by J. Edward Russo and Paul J. H. Shoemaker (Doubleday/Currency, 1989).

31. Manufacturers' Agents National Association, 1999.

32. Ronald R. Sims, "The Challenge of Ethical Behavior in Organizations," *Journal of Business Ethics.*

33. J. W. Weiss, *Business Ethics, A Stakeholder and Issues Management Approach,* Second Ed. (Philadelphia: The Dryden Press, 1998).

34. Tom Maddix, "The Essence of Ethics," *CMA Management,* Nov. 1999, p. 20.

35. Ibid.

36. Arthur Gross Schaefer and Anthony J. Zaller, "Why Ethics Tools Don't Work," *Nonprofit World,* March 1, 1999, p. 42.

37. Maddix, 1999.

38. Curtis C. Verschoor, "What's Ethical? Here's a Simple Test," *Strategic Finance,* March 2000, p. 24.

39. Schaefer et al., adaptation from Robert C. Solomon and Kristine Hanson, *It's Good Business* (New York: Atheneum, 1985).

40. Joanne Martin, *Cultures in Organizations: Three perspectives* (New York: Oxford University Press, 1992).

41. Schaefer et al., 1999.

42. Curtis C. Verschoor, Lawrence A. Ponemon, and Christopher Michaelson, "Values Added: Rules and Values in Ethical Decision Making," *Strategic Finance,* Feb. 2000, p. 24.

43. Elaine McShulskis, "Job Stress Can Prompt Unethical Behavior," *HR Magazine,* July 1997, p. 22.

44. Verschoor, 2000.

45. Schaefer, 1999.

46. Verschoor, 2000.

47. Ibid.

48. Schaefer, 1999.

49. Verschoor, 2000.

50. Ibid.

Exercise 18–A
Assessing Yourself

Circle the response that most closely correlates with each item below.

	Agree	Neither		Disagree

1. I am able to make decisions and stick to them.
   ① 2 3 4 5

2. I am able to make simple decisions quickly.
   1 2 3 4 5

3. I am able to scan a wide array of information and distill the information I need when making a complex decision.
   1 2 3 4 5

4. I clarify my purpose before making a decision.
   1 2 3 4 5

5. I clarify what process I will be using before making a decision.
   1 2 3 4 5

6. I take the time necessary when making complex decisions.
   1 2 3 4 5

7. I consider several options before making a decision.
   1 2 3 4 5

8. I invite multiple perspectives before making a decision.
   1 2 3 4 5

9. I gather the information necessary before making a decision.
   1 2 3 4 5

10. I consider the advantages and limitations of each option before choosing a course of action.
    1 2 3 4 5

11. I weigh the possible ramifications of each choice before making a decision.
    1 2 3 4 5

12. I list and prioritize the factors that are important to me and use these factors when making a decision.
    1 2 3 4 5

13. I take time to reflect on how a decision feels to me intuitively before acting on the decision.
    1 2 3 4 5

14. I communicate the rationale for my decisions to those who are affected by them.
    1 2 3 4 5

15. When I seek outside counsel, I involve internal group members when making the final decision.
    1 2 3 4 5

16. I seek input from those involved in a decision.
    1 2 3 4 5

17. Those with whom I work feel safe in raising ideas that contradict my own.
    1 2 3 4 5

18. I don't dominate meetings and ensure that all present have a chance to speak before decisions are made.
    1 2 3 4 5

19. I establish checkpoints and specify who's accountable for decisions made by my group.
    1 2 3 4 5

20. I have a set of guidelines I use when faced with an ethical dilemma.
    1 2 3 4 5

21. I take into account the needs of all relevant stakeholders before making a decision.
    1 2 3 4 5

22. I make decisions that make sense and are consistent with my "best" self-concept.
    1 2 3 4 5

23. I take responsibility for my actions.
    1 2 3 4 5

If your score is 69 or higher, you might consider creating a plan for increasing your skills in making effective and ethical decisions.

47   45

**Exercise 18–B
"Forced Choice"
Decision Making**

One way to make a decision is to weigh several alternatives and determine which option best meets each of several decision criteria. Working on your own, think of a decision you need to make in the present or will face in the future, such as choosing among multiple job offers, buying a new (or used) car, staying in a steady but unsatisfying relationship.

1. In the left column below, list all factors that are important to you. These are criteria you will be using to compare and contrast multiple options.

2. Across the top of the page list each option you are considering.

3. Then, working across the first row, put an X in the column of the option that best meets each importance factor. Do the same for each successive row, one at a time.

4. Total up the number of Xs under each option. The option with the most Xs is the one that meets more of your needs than the others.

Factor	Option A	Option B	Option C	Option D
1. Study Abroad	✓			
2. Cost		✓		
3. Resources		✓	✓	
4. Communication	✓			
5. Language	✓			
6. Size	✓			
7. Location			✓	
8. Resume				
9.				
TOTALS	4	2	2	N/A

Exercise 18–C
Weighted Average
Decision Making

Sometimes it's difficult to make a decision in which many variables are involved, all important to you. But since it's unlikely you'll be able to make a decision that satisfies all of your needs, weighted averaging gives you a way to differentiate those factors that are more important to you than others and to weigh these differences when analyzing the factors. Working on your own, think of a decision that you need to make now or that you will face in the near future.

1. On a separate sheet of paper, list all of the variables or factors (up to 10) that are important to you in making a specific decision. Identify these factors is to determine what you want to achieve from the decision's outcome.

2. In the left column below, list these factors in priority order, #1=most important.

3. Across the top of the page, list each alternative you are considering (up to four alternatives).

4. Start with the first factor. Working across this row, determine which option best meets this factor and assign the number 1 to that option. Then determine the option that next best meets the factor, assigning it the number 2. Continue with this determination using the numbers 3 and 4.

5. Move to the second (and subsequent factors) and repeat step 4.

6. Multiply each cell (#1–4) by the priority number in the corresponding row (#1–10). Note these numbers in each cell.

7. Sum each column. The column with the *lowest* sum below is the option that *best* meets your higher-priority needs (your top priority is #1).

Factor/Priority	Option A	Option B	Option C	Option D
1.				
2.				
3.				
4.				
5.				
6.				
7.				
8.				
9.				
10.				
Sum				

Exercise 18–D
Ethical Stance

Are the following ethical or unethical in your opinion? Why or why not? Consider individually and discuss in small groups.

- Calling in sick when you really are not. *Unethical, unless for family*
- Taking office supplies home for personal use. *Unethical, unless ask for permission*
- Cheating on a test. *Unethical all the time*
- Turning someone in for cheating on a test or paper. *Not on curve is unethical*
- Overcharging on your company expense report. *Unethical*
- Trying to flirt your way out of a speeding ticket. *Unethical*
- Splicing cable from your neighbor. *Unethical*
- Surfing the net on company time. *Unethical—break time*
- Cheating on income tax. *Unethical*
- Lying (exaggerating) about yourself to influence someone of the opposite sex. *Unethical*
- Looking at pornographic sites on the Web through the company network. *Unethical*
- Lying about your education on a job application. *Unethical*
- Lying about experience in a job interview. *Unethical*
- Making a copy of rental video cassette before returning it to the store. *Unethical*

Exercise 18–E
The Gold Watch

The Situation

John is a thirty-five-year-old salesman with Anderson and Sons, Inc., an established wholesaler of office equipment. He lives near Anderson's headquarters in Chicago with his wife and two adopted children.

On a recent sales tour abroad, John met J.R., an office-equipment supplier who was interested in a line of photocopiers worth $500,000. J.R. told John that he would give John an order for the photocopiers in return for a gold Rolex watch worth $13,000. J.R. showed John the watch he wanted in a catalog, and John said that he would see what he could do.

On returning to Chicago, John told Charles, his boss, about the proposition, asking if he could go ahead and buy the Rolex in order to obtain the order. Charles was outraged and said, "This is immoral! It's not decent business practice to offer bribes. We're living in a civilized society. If I find out that you've been bribing customers to get orders, I'll fire you on the spot! Have I made myself clear?"

After the confrontation with Charles, John left the office and drove to the home of Terry, his friend and colleague. He explained his plight and then said, "What can I do, Terry? It's an important order, and there's a chance of repeat business; J.R. is interested in office furniture and typewriters as well as more photocopiers in the future."

Terry thought for a moment and then said, "John, why don't you finance the deal yourself? Buy the stupid watch and land the contract. With your commission and any future business, you'll get a decent return on your investment. Don't even tell Charles; he's so ridiculously old-fashioned—he has no idea how to do business in this day and age."

John left Terry's home, went to his car, thought for a few minutes, and then drove to his bank. Mr. Gray, the bank manager and a close friend of John's father, listened to John's reasons for wanting the $13,000 loan. Despite the fact that John's checking account was overdrawn, he agreed to give John the loan immediately.

The next day John went to a jewelry store near his office and asked a clerk for the specific Rolex watch requested by J.R. While he was waiting for the clerk to bring him the watch, Jane, Charles' secretary, came into the store to buy a birthday present for her mother. Unobserved by John, she watched as the clerk gave the watch to John in exchange for the $13,000 cash. In her astonishment she forgot about finding a present for her mother, hurried back to Anderson and Sons, burst into Charles' office, and asked, "How can a salesman who earns $30,000 a year afford a $13,000 watch?"

Charles was furious. He rushed out of his office and found John just returning from the jewelry store. "You're fired!" he shouted.

"Let me explain . . .," muttered John.

"No excuses! I warned you!"

At that moment a Telex came through; it read as follows: "NO LONGER INTERESTED IN THE PHOTOCOPIER DEAL. FOUND ALTERNATIVE SUPPLIER. J.R."

Instructions

Rank order the following characters from 1 (least objectionable) to 6 (most objectionable):

_____ John

_____ J.R.

_____ Charles

_____ Terry

_____ Mr. Gray

_____ Jane

Source: Adapted from J. William Pfeiffer, *Handbook of Structured Experiences Kit*, University Associates, 1983, #GTB PS/A-17. Reprinted by permission of John Wiley and Sons, Inc.

Exercise 18–F
Ethical Dilemmas . . .
What Would You Do?

Individual dilemmas

- The cashier at the store gives you change for a $20 bill when you only gave her a $10. N
- You find a camera in the seat at a movie theater. ⋁
- You will lose your sick leave if you do not use it soon. However you are not sick. Y
- You have software available from work that you could copy onto your home PC. N
- You see your close friend's significant other in a compromising situation with another person. Do you tell your friend? Y

Organizational dilemmas

- You are offered a gift or bribe to close a big sale for a firm. N
- You are making a product that has government safety standards. Should you merely meet the standards or exceed them? Y
- You could set high production goals for your subordinates, knowing that in order to meet these goals they will cut corners on quality. N

Exercise 18–G
Try This . . .

1. Watch a TV show or a movie such as *Wall Street, Working Girl, Norma Rae, Silkwood, The China Syndrome, Saving Private Ryan, Nick of Time, Fail Safe, The Great Gatsby, The Hunt for Red October, Airforce One, Crouching Tiger, Hidden Dragon, Chocolat, Remember the Titans, The Negotiator*. What ethical dilemmas do the protagonist and antagonist face? How does each deal with the situation? What decision factors are used to make decisions? How is the situation resolved to take into consideration the needs of all involved (or is it)?

2. The next time you're in a group situation and an ethical dilemma arises, watch the group to see how the decision is made. What factors are considered? Is an ethics test applied? How is the decision made? Is it the right one? How do you know?

**Exercise 18–H
Reflection/Action Plan**

This chapter focused on ethical decision making—what that is, why it's important, and how to improve your skill in this area. Complete the worksheet below upon completing all reading and experiential activities for this chapter.

1. The one or two areas in which I am most strong are:

_____

_____

_____

2. The one or two areas in which I need more improvement are:

_____

_____

_____

3. If I did only one thing to improve in decision making, it would be to:

_____

_____

_____

4. If I did only one thing to improve in ethical decision making, it would be to:

_____

_____

_____

5. Making these changes would probably result in:

_____

_____

_____

6. If I did not change or improve in these areas, it would probably affect my personal and professional life in the following ways:

_____

_____

_____

_____

19 Problem Solving: Using Tools, Processes, and Creative Approaches

How do I:

✓ Define problems within an organizational context?

✓ Analyze the problem to determine its cause?

✓ Work with others to generate potential solutions to organizational problems?

✓ Evaluate potential solutions?

✓ Prioritize and select the best solution?

✓ Create an action plan for implementing the solution?

After searching the website for your favorite retailer, Abercrombie & Fitch, you find a T-shirt and a cap you want. Concerned about keying in your credit card online, you decide to call in your order. A few days later, when the order comes, you realize that the shirt is the wrong color and the cap looks different from the picture. Does this sound familiar? Perhaps it's no big deal. You make a phone call and after you send back the wrong shirt (taking it to the post office to insure it), you get the one you wanted a few days later.

Now, what if this were not an isolated case? If you were the director of operations for A&F, would it concern you that some customers are not satisfied with their telephone and online purchases? Research suggests that a satisfied customer tells another person (potential customer), whereas a dissatisfied customer tells 10 other potential customers. Can you afford to have problems in your operation? How would you solve problems such as these?

"If anything can go wrong, it will"

Murphy's Law

Murphy's Law is often quoted in life as well as in business. It implies the truism that seldom does everything turn out perfectly. All the planning in the world can't prevent the unexpected from happening. We can't control the unexpected. But we can control our attitude toward it. We can view a situation such as that presented in the case above negatively, as a problem that gets in the way of our business, or positively, as a chance to look at a situation and solve it creatively.

In the Chinese language, the symbol for the word *problem* translates into the word *opportunity*. In the view of many successful leaders, we have no problems, just opportunities for change. While we might quarrel with this outlook, the point is that as managers we can approach most "problems" with a positive mindset and view them as challenges to be dealt with proactively. Identifying problems and solving them are important skills for managers who are faced with dilemmas that require judgments every day. In this chapter we discuss problem solving, why it's important, strategies that can be used to solve problems, and tips to make your problem solving efforts more productive. At the end of the chapter are some exercises to help you enhance your skills in rational and creative problem solving as well as suggestions for further resources.

What Is Problem Solving?

Organizational problems come in many forms—whether in processes (how managers lead, how employees communicate, how work flows, how conflicts are solved, how employees deal with customers or suppliers) or outcomes (inadequate or unsatisfactory products or services, excessive employee absenteeism or turnover, insufficient profit margins). Problems such as these can significantly hamper an organization's ability to operate and succeed long term. To solve organizational problems effectively requires an appropriate mindset—viewing problems as opportunities or challenges and looking for solutions as opposed to placing blame, as well as developing skills in problem solving—a disciplined approach to defining the problem and identifying and implementing appropriate solutions.[1]

Returning to our opening scenario, when customers don't get what they want, this is a problem! What might be some of the reasons this problem occurred?

- The customer gave the wrong item number.
- The operator typed in the wrong number.
- There was an error in the integrated computer system.
- The picker picked the wrong item.
- The packer left out an item.
- The shipper was late or lost the package.
- The supplier sent items of a different color or quality than represented in the catalog.

The cause of such dissatisfaction could be any one or a number of these; it might also be unknown. For starters, it's best to stay away from finger-pointing. Effective managers and team members put their energies into solving problems, not placing blame on individuals who may (or may not) be responsible for them.[2] With that in mind, and your boss expecting solutions, you set out to figure out what caused the errors that have been serving to dissatisfy your customers.

Dr. Walter A. Shewhart suggests that **problem solving** is a cyclical process composed of four steps: Plan, Do, Check, Act (**PDCA**).[3] This process was introduced to Japan by W. Edwards Deming, one of the most highly recognized gurus of quality management techniques. As you can see from Figure 19–1, the most important step in the process is the plan. It is in this stage that we define and identify potential solutions for problems. This is easier said than done. What looks like the problem might actually be a symptom. Correctly defining the problem can be a challenge; with the remaining elements in this step we validate whether we identified the real problem and create a plan for fixing it. Once the plan is complete, the next stage is to "do"—or implement—the plan. Next, we "check" to see if the changes made resulted in lasting, measurable improvements. If not, we may need to take a step back. Did we solve the right problem? Did we unknowingly create a new one? Did we implement a short-term fix that will need modifications in the future? Based on our check, we then "act" by taking appropriate steps to adjust or ensure the problem is solved. The act step in the cycle may include:

- *Doing nothing.* The change resulted in its intended effect; it may be best to leave it alone and monitor progress periodically.

Figure 19–1
PDCA Cycle

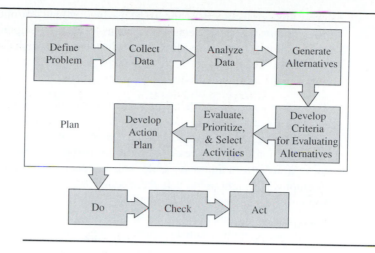

Figure 19–1
PDCA Cycle

■ *Making minor adjustments.* Perhaps the improvements are not as well suited as expected. Proceed to the planning stage and revisit the alternatives brainstormed previously. Perhaps the prioritization matrix should have been weighted differently, resulting in the selection of a different alternative. Create a plan for implementing this alternative and implement a new or modified solution.

■ *Making major adjustments.* In this situation, the group may have found a solution to the wrong problem. Perhaps the data collection process was flawed in that certain people or data were missing from the process. Perhaps the group arrived at a problem definition prematurely. Whatever the reason, the group needs to reconvene and discuss the next steps—which generally means a return to the planning stage. This situation happens frequently in business and illustrates the importance of planning before doing. It also illustrates the importance of the continual feedback and learning characterized by the PDCA cycle.

Why Is Problem Solving Important?

Problems such as those chronicled in the opening scenario are potentially very costly to organizations. How long can a business remain viable if problems like these persist? How many customers can a business afford to lose? A humorous example of this is illustrated in a 2000 television commercial for estamps.com. In it, veteran actor Bob Newhart plays a CEO of a bumbling firm that produces faulty products. He explains that estamps.com has been invaluable in enabling the firm to send out apology letters and replacement (but still faulty) products quickly. The ability to solve problems—and even apply problem-solving techniques to improve processes that work—can significantly and positively impact an organization's bottom line, as well as its long-term viability.

In the next section, we discuss problem-solving tools and techniques that can be used during the planning stage, which, as can be seen from Figure 19–1, is arguably the most important stage in the problem-solving process. It is in this stage that we actually define the problem. All too often, managers and employees rush to fix what they do not completely understand, in effect relieving symptoms temporarily using the proverbial Band-Aid. Then the problem resurfaces, possibly with greater intensity and impact than during its initial appearance.[4]

Problem-Solving Steps

Lacking a disciplined approach to problem solving—like the dog chasing its tail—can be costly in terms of time and financial and human resources. What follows is a series of steps that can be followed sequentially—especially when tackling complex problems.

These steps or techniques can also be used individually or in combination depending on the nature of the problem and resources available. As appropriate, we note the relationship between the technique and the elements which comprise the planning stage of the PDCA cycle.

Step One—Defining the Problem and Collecting Data

There are many ways to define a problem. For instance, we could observe or interview those who are involved in the process, analyze available data (e.g., defect rates or customer satisfaction), or hire consultants. Who gets involved in the process is another consideration. Whether we do it alone or as part of a problem-solving group will impact the options or techniques available. This section focuses on processes a group of students or employees might use to help them define and analyze a problem, generate potential solutions, and create a plan for implementing a solution. It is also important to note that many of these problem-solving processes can be performed virtually or through the use of available computer-aided problem-solving tools.[5]

Brainstorming

Brainstorming is a tool used to stimulate and capture creative thoughts and ideas. It involves the creative generation of many ideas to solve a problem. There are several variations of brainstorming, yet they all have in common the following ground rules:

Brainstorming Guidelines

- Articulate the theme or the question (e.g., Why are sales down? How can we cut costs in the manufacturing area?).
- Set a time limit (usually 5 or 10 minutes, depending on the size of the group and the complexity of the theme or question).
- Record the ideas for everyone to see (using a flipchart or whiteboard).
- Quantity is important (generate as many ideas as possible).
- Everyone should actively participate (no benchwarmers!).
- All ideas are good ideas (positive or negative critiquing is *not* permitted).
- Piggyback or build on ideas of others.

If the pace begins to slow, or participants seem stifled by constraints, the leader or facilitator of the brainstorming session may ask a hypothetical question such as "What if money were no object?" or "What if you could wave a magic wand to get rid of these problems . . . which ones would disappear?" During the process, it is important to enforce the ground rules should they be broken. Many people can't seem to resist evaluating others' ideas—it's human nature. However, such evaluation can stifle creativity or cause participants to censor their ideas before sharing them with the group.

After the flow of ideas slows, and all useful hypothetical questions have been used, it is time to ask questions and clarify and consolidate ideas. Evaluation should still be kept to a minimum, as the craziest of ideas may spawn other creative but useful ideas or solutions. Be careful not to remove or downplay ideas prematurely. Other steps in the problem-solving process will aid in future prioritization of ideas.

A normal or open[6] brainstorming session tends to result in the most ideas, the most creative ideas, and the most synergy among group participants and their ideas.[7] However, those who are introverted or feel inhibited by senior members of the organization may be overshadowed by those who are more verbal or dominant. To ensure that all members present fully participate in the idea-generating process, consider using variations on brainstorming, such as round robin, nominal group technique, and Post-It Note brainstorming.

- In **round robin** brainstorming, group members participate in a structured order, for instance, starting with the person at the head of the table and moving clockwise. Using this technique helps equalize the verbal and less verbal participants, but may inhibit some of the creative disagreement that comes when participants can shout out ideas as they come.

■ The **nominal group technique,** or NGT, is another variation on open brainstorming that ameliorates the negative impact that status differences may have on a problem-solving group. The technique "nominalizes" or equalizes hierarchical or status differences among members of a group, enabling individuals to speak out without concern for such differences or fears of being ridiculed.[8] To brainstorm NGT style, all team members are given index cards or pads on which to write their ideas. After the theme or question is posed, each person in the group must write down as many answers to the question as they can. After the silent writing of ideas slows, you ask each member in sequence to share one written idea, recording all ideas on the flip chart for everyone to see. Keep going around the group, asking for and recording one unique idea from each person until all written ideas are recorded. If individuals note that their idea was already listed, underline or put a check next to the idea.

■ When using the **Post-It Note brainstorming** variation,[9] participants' brainstormed ideas are scribed on Post-It Notes—one idea per note—instead of on a flip chart. For the open method, this variation requires one scribe to record each idea on a Post-It Note and then stick it to a wall or whiteboard. Post-It Notes can also be used in the nominal group technique; all participants are given a pad of Post-It Notes (instead of cards or slips of paper) on which to scribe their ideas. Scribing ideas on Post-It Notes may take a bit longer than using the traditional method, but one benefit is the ability to easily manipulate the idea in subsequent problem-solving steps or techniques such as affinitizing, which is described next.

Step Two— Analyzing Data

Once you have collected data, the next step is to analyze them. What are some trends? What are some interesting cases? The goal of this step is to systematically evaluate the data collected in order to categorize data into trends and differentiate major problems from minor problems or symptoms. Several options for doing this are described below.

Using Affinitizing to Synthesize Brainstormed Ideas

Brainstorming is a great way to generate an abundance of creative ideas. Now, what do you do with all those wonderful ideas? How can you efficiently and effectively analyze them? The **affinitizing** method provides a useful means to organize and produce agreement on categories of ideas; doing so facilitates a group's ability to address organizational problems.

The process is fairly simple. After brainstorming ideas on Post-It Notes (or cards), group members:

Affinitizing Steps

1. Stick the notes on a wall or whiteboard so that each note can be seen (or spread out cards on a large desk).
2. Silently (no talking allowed!), group related ideas by moving notes into groups of related ideas.
3. Discuss, clarify, and modify groups as necessary once the movement slows.
4. Brainstorm a title that encapsulates or expresses the theme for each group of notes. When all agree on the titles for each grouping, they are written on Post-It Notes (one per grouping) and placed at the top of each grouping.

At this point, instead of working with 20 or 30 unmanageable ideas, the group has now pared down the ideas into 3–8 manageable groups of ideas. As an added bonus, the highly participative nature of brainstorming and affinitizing helps build consensus among team members on identifying problems.

Building Consensus through Multivoting

Now, say your group was really successful in its brainstorm and affinitizing processes. With about 40 ideas in seven categories, solving this problem has been made easier, but we're not done yet. How do you build consensus on where to begin when there are multiple sets of issues and multiple members deciding where to start? One simple yet elegant method is **multivoting.** It can be used with a brainstormed list of topics or a pared down list of affinitized categories. The process is as follows:

Multivoting Steps

1. Begin with the brainstormed list. As appropriate, combine overlapping items. Another option is to use the categories that emerged from the affinitizing process.

2. Number each idea or category.

3. Divide the total number of ideas or categories by 3; this is the number of votes each member gets. If there are 13 ideas, each member picks his or her top 4; if there are 8 categories, each member picks 3. (Individuals may only give one vote per idea or category.) It might be useful to discuss selection criteria before members make their selections. For example, instruct members to consider those with the greatest potential impact or least time to implement when making their choices.

4. After members have had time to select and jot down their top choices, have a recorder tabulate the results. An easy method is to jot down the numbers and, for each number, ask which members had this as one of their top choices. Another method is to go around the room and ask each member their choices, placing hatch marks adjacent to the appropriate number.

5. The idea or category with the highest number of votes wins. In the event of a tie, utilize the multivoting process once more to arrive at a winner.

Because participants each pick their top choices, the winning idea or category tends to be on most everyone's list. While multivoting does not by itself produce consensus, it gets the group closer, quickly.

Step Three—Evaluating and Selecting Potential Solutions

Once the group has focused on one idea or problem, there should be some discussion of this problem. Is it a symptom or a cause? How do we know? Perhaps some data can be collected to confirm this. When there is agreement on the problem, the next step is to determine possible solutions. Brainstorming might be used again to generate a long list of potential, creative solutions. As appropriate, ideas are discussed, combined, and possibly affinitized. But which solution do we implement first?

Prioritization Matrix

The **prioritization matrix** is a useful tool for helping a group select the best alternative or solution when considering from among several and against multiple criteria. Let's return to the Abercrombie & Fitch example. Suppose that a problem-solving group narrowed down the issue to problems in the shipping facility. Suppose further that the following is a sample from the list of alternatives:

- Implement a bar code system.
- Generate a daily report.
- Flag unlabeled packages.
- Hire an additional person to double-check all outgoing packages for accuracy.
- Conduct problem-solving training.

Which will the group select? Will management accept its recommendation? Will the recommendation be implemented or will it be shelved? How can the group make the best decision?

First, there are multiple criteria to consider. Consider a student who is accepted by three or four different universities. One may be less expensive, another might have a better reputation, another might be located in a more temperate climate, while still another has a disproportionate number of males or females. Multiple alternatives and multiple criteria do not lend themselves to a simple listing of pros and cons. The criteria in this case would be cost, reputation, climate, and chances of meeting Mr. or Ms. Right. Still other criteria might include proximity to family, cost of living, availability of financial aid, chances of getting a scholarship, and probability of finishing in four years. To make this decision using the prioritization matrix, you would:

Prioritizing Solutions Steps

1. Brainstorm the criteria to be used in evaluating the multiple solutions. For the A&F example, these might include cost to implement solution, time it takes to implement solution, ease of implementation, management receptivity to the solution, employee receptivity to the solution, and likelihood of permanently fixing the problem.

2. Next, create a grid, placing the alternatives or solutions along the vertical axis and the criteria against which the alternatives will be evaluated along the horizontal axis (see Figure 19–2).

3. Decide on the scales for the criteria, ensuring consistency. Using a 1–5 scale, with higher numbers being more favorable, a group might determine that a high cost to implement would be valued at 1 while a low cost to implement would be a 5; conversely (though maintaining consistency), high management receptivity to a solution would get a value of 5, while low receptivity would correlate with a 1. Determine scales for each criterion.

4. As a group, evaluate every alternative (one at a time) against each of the criteria. Strive for consensus in the evaluation; however, compromise may be required at times. Alternatively, there may be a need to get further information. In this situation, leave the item blank and come back to it after assigning an action item to get cost or other data to make an informed evaluation.

5. Total the score horizontally in a final sum column. The highest-ranking alternative may "win," but discussion among the group is necessary in order to achieve consensus.

Another variation on this method is to *weight criteria* according to their importance. Of all the criteria, perhaps cost is the most critical. In this case, a group might want to weight this column 1.5 or 2 when all others are weighted a 1. To arrive at final sums for each alternative, multiply each score the group gives an alternative for a criterion by its weight and then sum across the row.

Figure 19–2
A Prioritization Matrix

Possible Solutions	Cost to Implement (high to low)	Time to Implement Solution (long to short)	Ease of Implementation (difficult to easy)	Management Receptivity (low to high)	Likelihood of Fixing Main Problem (unlikely to likely)
Implement bar code system					
Generate daily report					
Flag unlabeled packages					
Hire additional person					
Conduct problem-solving training					

Step Four—Developing an Action Plan for Implementation

Once a particular alternative or solution is chosen, it is time to create a plan for its implementation. Depending on the solution/s that will be implemented, an implementation plan may range from simple (a checklist of steps) to complex (a complete project plan which outlines dates of deliverables, contingent plans if schedules are not met, and individual responsibilities).

Tree Diagram

One tool helpful for stating goals and defining specific tasks necessary to reach that goal is a **tree diagram** (see Figure 19–3).

Let's say that of all the alternatives generated to improve the shipping facilities, the highest-ranking one selected involved implementing a bar code system. Sound easy? Possibly, but only after all the steps are detailed. The steps are:

Constructing a Tree Diagram

1. Start at the left of the diagram, writing the main objective inside a rectangle. In our example, we would write, "Implement bar code system."

2. On a branch extending from the rectangle, draw several more rectangles. In each one, write one answer at which the group arrives in response to the question: "What must we accomplish before we can accomplish the main objective?" Sample answers might include, "Sample other companies' bar code systems" and "Contact consulting firm specializing in inventory control."

3. For each rectangle in the second column, ask the same question asked previously, "What must we accomplish before we can accomplish this objective?" Draw as many branches and rectangles as answers.

4. Repeat this process until no further subtasks can be identified. What remains in the right-most column is a set of action items that can be easily assigned to team members.

Figure 19–3
A Tree Diagram

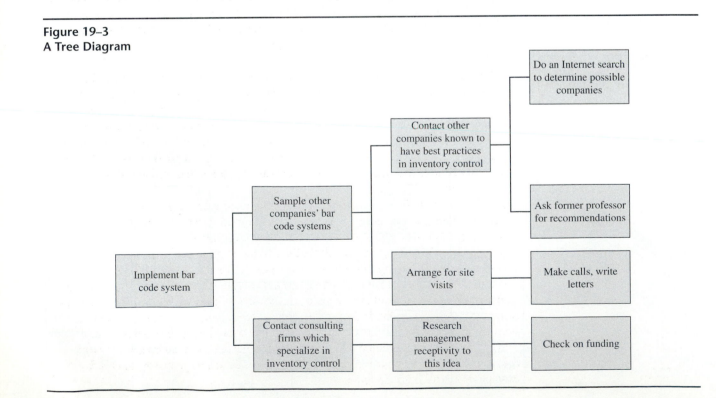

**Figure 19–4
Problem Solving: Summary
of Steps and Techniques**

PLAN	1. Defining the problem and collecting data
	Brainstorming variations:
	  ■ Round robin
	  ■ Nominal group technique (NGT)
	  ■ Post-It Note™
	2. Analyzing data
	  ■ Affinitizing
	  ■ Multivoting
	3. Evaluating and selecting potential solutions
	  ■ Prioritization matrix
	4. Developing an action plan for implementation
	  ■ Tree diagram

DO	5. Implement solution
CHECK	6. Evaluate outcomes, determine if problem is solved
ACT	7. Make adjustments as needed

Issues—and Ways to Overcome Them—in Problem Solving

As logical as the above approaches or techniques sound, problem solving doesn't always work, nor is it always successful. There are several reasons why this may be the case. After explaining each issue, we offer strategies or tips for overcoming the issue.

■ *Lack of time to move through all the necessary steps sequentially.* As is true of all good solutions, it takes time and effort to do problem solving well. Problem solving is best when time permits a group or team to assemble, develop operating guidelines, clarify their objective, and engage in the creative, consensus-building activities[10] outlined above. The problem-solving process results in the best solutions when members have time to share with and learn from each other, creating something that is far better than would have been true if only one or two individuals had been approaching the problem to be solved.

When faced with a significant problem that needs to be solved, try to ensure that those involved in solving it have the time needed to generate thoughtful and innovative approaches. If this is not possible, try to condense the process, moving quickly through the steps outlined above, rather than being tempted to skip some of the steps out of a sense of urgency. Deal with this issue up front if possible. Negotiate additional time, or manage the expectations of those requesting a solution (e.g., "If we only have one week, we may not be able to isolate the true problem, as opposed to the solution. If we had two weeks, we could . . .").

■ *Resistance on the part of some team members to a group approach to problem solving.* Problem solving, especially when done in groups by consensus, does not appeal to everyone. Managers who are accustomed to being in charge or to making decisions quickly without consulting others will find it difficult to make the transition from an individual problem-solving mode to a group mode. Some managers fear that they will appear to be weak for not having the magic solution at their fingertips. Still others simply get frustrated having to wait for the team to complete its process. While team outcomes tend to be superior to individual ones, the process of meeting and making consensus decisions may take longer. This is compounded when incompatible schedules cause delays in holding team problem-solving meetings. For the above approaches to work, most if not all members have to be on board—able and willing to use the approach being proposed by or to the group.

To overcome this issue, don't assume that everyone in the group or team will accept with open arms any of the techniques described above. To avoid a battle of wills over proposing one of these approaches, first engage in open discussion with the group about how they view their mission and the approaches they can see being used by the group to fulfill their charge. In essence, you're facilitating a creative problem-solving session—without calling it that—at the outset. After hearing some ideas about how to proceed, including introducing one or more of the above approaches as possibilities, the group can choose an approach to use that will work given its specific circumstances.

■ *Differences in work style.* The problem-solving approaches described above appeal to both "left brained" or logical types as well as "right brained" or creative types.[11] For these techniques to be successful, those involved must be able to stay focused on the task at hand, as well as be open to looking at things in new ways. Some managers are frustrated by problem solving, especially in group situations, because they are naturally too analytical or too intuitive. Those who are by nature very organized and structured may lose patience quickly and may not enjoy the process of bringing others up to speed. They may feel uncomfortable with the freewheeling atmosphere that can sometimes prevail at open brainstorm discussions. At the other extreme, managers who are by nature very discerning or insightful will be able to generate solutions quickly without benefit of discussion with others. These managers also may lose patience with the time-consuming process of engaging others in consensus-building activities. They may identify a solution quickly and be unwilling to wait for others to catch up with other good ideas.

To overcome this issue, develop ways to identify managers' strengths and use these to the group's advantage. For example, you might enlist the analytical manager described above as a timekeeper—giving this person a role that acknowledges an ability to stay on track. In the case of intuitive managers, let them know ahead of time that you value their opinion and respect their ability to discern quickly and perceptively creative options for solving a problem. Ask them to hold off on giving suggestions until the end of the session, when you can ask a question to get them engaged, such as "What else?" "What has been overlooked?" "What other ideas should we consider?" Or you can ask them to share a few ideas at the outset to get the group started.

■ *Lack of support from management.* Some managers are bottom-line oriented and resist group approaches to problem solving, believing they are not cost efficient.[12] They may believe that all it takes is one smart person to do the job, not realizing that few individuals have the perspective, expertise, and experience to adequately define and solve organizational problems. Time is money, and they want results yesterday.

If you find yourself in this type of organization, attempt to engage in the problem-solving approaches above in ways that are in sync with your organization's mission and in ways that are efficient as well as effective. For example, if your company is in a cost-cutting mode, you might decide to not hold a daylong off-site retreat complete with team-building activities, a gourmet lunch, and massages for everyone! You might decide instead to hold a "virtual" creativity session, soliciting ideas before the meeting and collating and presenting them at the meeting.

> *"The important thing is not to stop questioning. Curiosity has its own reason for existing."*
>
> Albert Einstein

At this point, you should be familiar with an assortment of tools and techniques you can use when attempting to solve a problem. While you may think that all organizations use a logical, rational approach similar to the problem-solving process we've outlined, this is not necessarily the case. Other approaches are available, and depending on the problem at hand and the people involved, other approaches to solving problems may be warranted. In the next section, we describe several intuitive or creative approaches that can be used to complement or substitute stages in the problem-solving process.

What Is Creativity?

Carol Goman, well-known creativity author and consultant, defines **creativity** as "bringing into existence an idea that is new to you."[13] She cites research done in the late 1940s by a group of psychologists attempting to prove that by age 45, few individuals could think creatively. By testing subjects at various ages, they found that 90 percent of five-year-olds were highly creative; by age 17, that number dropped to 10 percent; and by 20, the figure dropped and stayed at about 5 percent.[14] Why is this so?

There are several potential explanations. First, most children start school at age five, and by then they learn "the rules": you must color in the lines; you must conform to the rules (of dress, speech, etc.); and children with anomalous behavior must be controlled and even, perhaps, medicated. As we age, we learn to solve math problems in which *the* right answer is in the back of the book. Most are warned about being different and the failures associated with such behavior. In essence, while we are born to be creative, we quickly learn to temper those tendencies. Of course, we're not advocating anarchy or chaos. Instead, we're suggesting the need to balance conformity with creativity by shaping the will without breaking the spirit of creativity.[15]

Why Is Creativity Important?

What makes individuals and businesses ultimately successful is creativity and innovation.[16] Consider this: a plain iron bar is worth $5. If you take that iron bar and forge horseshoes from it, the value increases to $11. If it is made into needles, the price rises to $3,285. And if you make watch springs from it, it is then worth $250,000. The difference between $5 and $250,000 is creativity.[17] When we see things differently, we break with tradition and find solutions and often new problems. Creative problem solving helps us to view a situation from a new perspective and increases the likelihood that we will generate innovative, cost-effective ways to do business. Imagine coming to work one day and pretending you were a customer or competitor. What are your reactions? How could you use those observations to find new ways of solving old problems? How do our assumptions about how things have always operated constrain us from changing and finding more innovative ways to operate?

Strategies for Increasing Creativity in Problem Solving

Creative problem solving requires the use of both convergent and divergent thinking. **Convergent thinking** is starting with a problem and working to move towards a solution. Most of us take this approach. If you walk into your apartment and notice a foul odor, you're likely to first check to see if the trash needs to be taken out. Then you'll look in the refrigerator, and so on. Eventually, you may find (and eradicate) the problem. Another approach to solving problems is **divergent thinking.** This involves generating new ways to view a problem and seeking out novel alternatives to the problem.

Let's say your manager informs you that the incidence of shoplifting has been increasing at the apparel store in which you work as a salesperson. The convergent approach involves the usual—install video cameras, post warning signs, install antitheft tags on the clothing. Taking a divergent approach, you might first create **analogies** for the problem statement: how do we keep people from stealing? Trying to keep people from shoplifting *is like:*[18]

- Trying to keep kids from sneaking cookies out of the cookie jar.
- Trying to prevent people from jaywalking.
- Trying to keep flies away from cow manure.

Next, you solve the analogy. How do you keep kids from sneaking cookies out of the cookie jar? Hide the jar, put a lock on the jar, or give the kids cookies. How do you prevent people from jaywalking? Post warning signs, increase police presence, increase the number of tickets issued, or create physical barriers along the street. How do you keep flies away from cow manure? Cover the manure, move the animals to another site, or create a fly-friendly haven.

Finally, transfer the analogy solutions to the problem. To keep people from stealing, we could hide the expensive clothing or put it in a special room, give out free samples of apparel (something very cheap), give out free clothes for those who turn in shoplifters, or move the store to another area (or venue, such as catalog or Internet sales).

Four Stages of Creative Problem Solving[19]

There are four steps involved in generating creative solutions to problems:

- Preparation—gather info, define the problem, generate alternatives, examine all available info.
- Incubation—involves mostly subconscious mental activity in which the mind combines unrelated thoughts in pursuit of a solution.
- Illumination—occurs when insight is recognized and a creative solution is articulated. This is sometimes called the AHA! stage.
- Verification—involves evaluating the creative solution relative to some standard of acceptability. In this phase, you test to see if the idea can work. You might do a reality check (pulling the creativity down to fit within constraints and boundaries), ask for feedback from others (is this feasible or how can we make it feasible?), or try a pilot project.

Some Methods for Generating Novel Ideas

Not everyone gets to the illumination phase in the same way or time. Some people are naturally creative—they are tinkerers. Others either haven't developed this skill, have had it "beaten out of them," or could benefit from some techniques. We've included several methods and examples for generating novel ideas below.[20]

- Part Changing—involves listing parts or attributes that can be changed. Think about the first laptop computer. It did everything a desktop PC could do, only it was lighter and portable. How about the popular fruit smoothies? Before that, if you wanted something cold and thick, you'd get a milkshake. If you want to improve a product or service, list the parts or attributes. Brainstorm possible changes—even ones you think could never work. How about online banking and loans, online brokerage services, virtual real estate or vacation tours, or online doctors?

- Checkerboard—make a grid with parts or attributes listed on the vertical and horizontal axes to find new interactions or combinations. By considering "forced" combinations, new ideas could emerge—if you let them. How about the all-in-one office machine (printer, scanner, fax, copier)?

- Checklist—make lists to make sure nothing is left out or forgotten. Using questions such as those below can serve as a checklist for ensuring all possibilities are considered:

  - What else can this be used for?
  - What could be used instead? What else is like this?
  - How could it be adopted or modified for a new use?
  - What if it were larger, thicker, heavier, or stronger?
  - What if it were smaller, thinner, lighter, or shorter?
  - How might it be rearranged or reversed?

- Analogy Method—fix a problem or create something new by thinking of other products, people, animals, or social units that perform similar acts to make analogies. The shoplifting example we discussed is one application of the similarity method; another example is waiting for you to try at the end of the chapter. What follows is an actual situation in which this method was successfully used to solve a business problem.

  A cosmetics manufacturer watched as sales of its lipsticks continued to decline. They weren't sure why this was occurring, so they decided to investigate. Using customer information cards filled out at various cosmetics counters, they contacted customers and asked if they would be willing to participate in a focus group. It turns out that the customers liked the lipsticks—the colors, the texture, the staying power, the options (sheer, frosted, and matte), and the price were all judged satisfactory. What customers didn't like was the metal tube into which the lipstick was placed when not in use. Within weeks of purchase, the tubes looked old and tarnished. This made customers think that the lipsticks were perhaps old. After buying the product the first time, few customers made repeat purchases.

The manufacturer undertook several experiments to respond to this problem, but was unable to find a material that wouldn't tarnish. Employees were challenged to solve this problem. One employee, a hunting enthusiast, noticed that ammunition was always bright and shiny—even cases that had been in his closet for years. He contacted the ammunition manufacturer, explaining his dilemma, and requested a visit. While there, the employee learned what materials were used for the ammunition casings. These materials were then used for the lipstick cases. It worked! Within a short period of time, the trend toward declining sales was reversed. The moral of this story is to be willing to challenge assumptions about where to look for clues to solving problems.

Management's Role in Supporting and Stimulating Creativity

Many of the ideas we've discussed seem simple enough. With practice, we can all use analogies, checkerboards, or other approaches to find creative solutions to enduring problems. What happens when employees are creative but the rest of the organization is not? Unfortunately, this is often the case. How many of the following statements have you heard before in your organizations?

Idea Killers

- We tried it before.
- It would cost too much.
- That's not my job.
- That's not how we do things here.
- You may be right, but . . .

- That'll never work.
- You can't do that here.
- Our customers would never go for that.
- It's good enough.
- If it ain't broke, don't fix it.

Goman calls these and similar statements **idea killers.**[21] When creative suggestions or ideas are met with these responses, creativity is killed. Not just now, but in the future as well. Statements such as these send the message that any idea that "breaks the rules" will not be accepted, let alone listened to. If you are on the receiving end of one of these statements, chances are you'll learn to keep your mouth shut. Who wants to be ridiculed? Even when employees are told to be creative and innovative, any encouragement coupled with idea killers is likely to be canceled out.

Instead, as a colleague and manager of other employees, you can play a role in creating an environment that truly encourages and stimulates creativity. How you respond to others' creative ideas sends a strong message to future attempts. Statements such as the following show that you are listening to another's idea and are open to continued discussion.

Idea Growers

- How could we improve . . . ?
- How can (that suggestion) build on (a previous idea)?
- What have we missed?
- Who else would be affected?
- What would happen if . . . ?

- Who else has a suggestion?
- I don't know much about that. How about you?
- How many ways could we . . . ?
- May I ask a question?

Idea growers, as Goman calls statements like these,[22] really help continue conversations focused on creative problem solving and stimulate further creative ideas. Saying you value creativity isn't the same as demonstrating it! Think about it. If an employee were to come to you with an idea you believe is ill-conceived, how would you respond? We're not suggesting you should lie and treat employees like the two-year-old who managed to eat her food without plastering the walls with it. At the same time, you can give feedback in a way that encourages the employee to keep working at the idea while addressing concerns you may have.

One technique that you could use is called the **P-P-C,** which stands for *Positives, Possibilities, and Concerns.*[23] It works like this. Imagine you manage the women's wear section of a major department store. You have solicited the input of your employees on ways to improve customer service. One employee, Nancy, suggests clearing enough space to place comfortable chairs, a table, and reading material to increase the spouses' and boyfriends' willingness to wait while their partners try on clothes. She further suggests serving coffee or wine. You have some reservations, but there are some strengths in the idea. Using the P-P-C approach, you respond:

■ Positives: "I like your concern regarding the spouses."

■ Possibilities: "We could even include merchandise catalogues (e.g., automotive, tools, stereo) for them to read while they wait."

■ Concerns: "I'm not sure we could take down the display area to make enough room to implement the idea. How do you think it could be handled?"

You might take this idea a step further. Since most thinking in organizations is logical and rational, set aside a room (or part of another room or basement) and call it the **innovation chamber.**[24] Even if creativity is not totally valued in other parts of the organization, this is one place where it is not only valued but also desired. This chamber will become a safe haven for generating innovative, creative ideas. You might even decorate it in a way that stimulates creative thinking (i.e., neither white walls nor a linoleum floor). For example, paint the walls with abstract designs, use colored lights (pink, purple), play soft music, use floor pillows instead of a table and chairs, and have plenty of space for writing (or use flip chart paper taped to the walls). Put a sign on the door and send an official memo to employees about the purpose and use of this room. Post rules in the room, such as:

■ The innovation chamber is a criticism-free space.

■ All ideas—even crazy ones—are welcomed, discussed, and credited to the individual and the group.

■ All who enter must participate.

■ If no really deviant ideas emerge, then the session is less than successful.

Strategies for Increasing Individual Creativity

We mentioned earlier that as we age, we lose our capacity to be creative. There are many reasons why this occurs, but more importantly, how can you get this lost creativity back? Here are a few suggestions:

■ Do creative exercises: Challenge your mind. Resist the temptation to opt for quick, tried and true solutions. Experiment, play, and search out new solutions. Like any other muscle in the body, the mind becomes weak and rigid in the absence of exercise.[25]

■ Break some rules. Write in your books, order off the menu, question the validity (and objectivity) of news reports, challenge your religious beliefs, vote differently from your parents or how you might have voted 10 years ago.

■ Learn your language (or a new one). Commit to learning one new word a day. Ensure you pronounce it correctly.

■ Keep an open mind. When you meet someone new, take in all aspects of that person's personality and don't label them as a ditz, bum, and so on.

- Keep a journal. Writing down your thoughts helps you remember key discoveries, such as feelings, emotions, and beliefs. One of your most creative moments is right when you wake up. This is one of the best times to jot down your thoughts, especially if you can remember key aspects of a dream you had that night.

- Develop confidence in your senses.[26] Don't wear a watch; guess the time given available clues. Guess the temperature before looking at the sign above the bank. Guess your friends' heights and weights using your own as a comparison, and if you're brave enough, ask for confirmation. Cook something without a recipe or measuring devices. Use your sense of smell and taste to make needed modifications.

- Expose yourself to new perspectives. Take an elevator to the top of a tall building; what do you see that you couldn't see before? Read a novel or see a movie that you would ordinarily never read or see. Eat a type of food that you've never eaten before. Travel outside your comfort zone—this may be different for different people. For some, it's outside the town; for others, it's outside the continent. An excellent illustration of this is the scene in the film *Dead Poet's Society* in which Robin Williams' character has his students stand up on their desks to get a different perspective of the world. A bit unusual for a conservative school, but that was the point![27]

Being creative is not just a workplace skill; it's a life skill as well. How we approach situations is a function of how many possibilities we can see. Have you ever tried to buy a car and found out that your credit was less than perfect? Did you give up or begin looking for a creative way to finance this purchase? How about when you and your significant other are planning a date. Do you stop after suggesting movies or dinner? What about a picnic in the mountains? A lesson in ballroom dancing? Bungee jumping? When you exercise your creative potential, you can benefit both professionally and personally.

Summary

Organizations face problems (or opportunities) on a daily basis. Those firms that take a disciplined approach to problem solving—clearly defining the problem, identifying potential and creative solutions, selecting solutions based on appropriate criteria, and creating a detailed plan to implement the solution—are likely to succeed and prosper. Those that don't solve problems, or engage in finger-pointing and blaming, are likely to lose customers, alienate employees, and reduce their ability to compete in this increasingly complex, dynamic, and global marketplace. The bottom line is that if you want creative problem solving, there needs to be an environment that stimulates, encourages, and rewards creativity. "Do as I say, not as I do" will not work. Finding solutions—especially creative ones—to problems or inventing new products and processes requires creative employees and the right environment. Each is necessary but insufficient on its own—especially in the current environment!

Key Terms and Concepts

Affinitizing

Analogies (in problem solving)

Brainstorming

Convergent thinking

Creativity

Divergent thinking

Idea growers

Idea killers

Innovation chamber

Multivoting

Nominal group technique

PDCA cycle

Post-It Note brainstorming

P-P-C technique

Prioritization matrix

Problem solving

Round robin

Tree diagram

Endnotes

1. Carolyn B. Thompson, "Problem Solving Tools to Improve Productivity," *Journal of Property Management,* Sept. 1999, p. 14.

2. Peter Scholtes, *The Team Handbook* (Madison, WI: Joiner Publishing Co., 1988).

3. Paul Kiesow, "PDCA Cyle: An Approach to Problem Solving," *Ceramic Industry,* Oct. 1994, p. 20.

4. Quinn Spitzer and Ron Evans, "New Problems in Problem Solving," *Across the Board,* April 1997, p. 36.

5. For more information on computer-aided problem-solving tools and other resources, refer to the text's website.

6. R. Glenn Ray, *The Facilitative Leader: Behaviors That Enable Success* (Upper Saddle River, NJ: Prentice Hall, 1999).

7. Ibid., p. 103.

8. Larry Hirschhorn, *Managing in the New Team Environment: Skills, Tools, and Methods* (Reading, MA: Addison Wesley, 1991).

9. Ethan M. Rasiel, "Some Brainstorming Exercises," *Across the Board,* June 2000, p. 10.

10. Daisy A. Hickman, "How to Access All of Your Problem-Solving Abilities," *Manage,* July 1995, pp. 22–24.

11. Carol Kinsey Goman, *Creativity in Business: A Practical Guide for Creative Thinking* (Menlo Park, CA: Crisp Publications, 2000), p. 46.

12. Oren Harari, "Turn Your Organization into a Hotbed of Ideas," *Management Review,* Dec. 1995, pp. 37–40.

13. Goman, 2000, p. 3.

14. Ibid., p. 11.

15. The authors thank Roger A. Dean of Washington and Lee University for making this suggestion.

16. Harari, 1995.

17. Goman, 2000, citing a "Ripley's Believe It or Not" column.

18. This example is adapted from Goman, 2000, pp. 62–63.

19. J. W. Haefele, *Creativity and Innovation* (New York: Reinhold, 1962); Max H. Bazerman, *Judgment in Managerial Decision Making* (New York: Wiley, 1986), pp. 89–91.

20. G. David and S. Houtman, "Thinking Creatively: A Guide to Training Imagination," Madison WI: Wisconsin Research and Development Center for Cognitive Learning, 1968; and Goman, 2000.

21. Goman, 2000, p. 76.

22. Ibid., p. 77.

23. Example adapted from Goman, 2000, p. 82.

24. Floyd Hurt, "Creativity: A Hole in Your Head," *Agency Sales Magazine,* June 1998, pp. 58–60.

25. Tom Wujec, *Pumping Ions: Games and Exercises to Flex Your Mind* (New York: Doubleday, 1988).

26. Marilyn vos Savant and Leonore Fleischer, *Brain Building in Just 12 Weeks* (New York: Bantam Books, 1991).

27. The authors thank Robert A. Herring of Winston-Salem State University for making this suggestion.

Exercise 19–A
Assessing Yourself

Circle the response that most closely correlates with each item below.

	Agree		Neither		Disagree

1. When approaching problems, I follow a sequence of steps that includes planning, implementing, checking, and acting.   1 2 3 4 5

2. When initial improvements (from implementing a solution) are not as effective as expected, I return to the plan and make necessary adjustments.   1 2 3 4 5

3. When faced with a situation where an implemented improvement did not work as planned, I reconvene my group and suggest making major adjustments as needed.   1 2 3 4 5

4. I spend time on my own or with my group defining a problem before attempting to solve it.   1 2 3 4 5

5. I generate several ideas and options before making a decision as to how to solve a problem.   1 2 3 4 5

6. When brainstorming, I encourage a supportive atmosphere, set time limits, and record everyone's ideas for the group to see before choosing an approach.   1 2 3 4 5

7. I encourage all group members to participate in brainstorming.   1 2 3 4 5

8. I view all initial ideas favorably, without criticism.   1 2 3 4 5

9. I ask hypothetical questions to stimulate the flow of ideas and reduce the perception that the group is facing numerous constraints.   1 2 3 4 5

10. In brainstorming, I make sure everyone understands the ground rules and I enforce them as needed.   1 2 3 4 5

11. I ask questions and clarify ideas to ensure the group fully understands the suggestions being made by group members.   1 2 3 4 5

12. I don't remove or downplay ideas prematurely.   1 2 3 4 5

13. I educate my group members about the various techniques that are available for generating and synthesizing ideas.   1 2 3 4 5

14. I work with my group to achieve consensus on and to prioritize potential options before solving a problem.   1 2 3 4 5

15. I work with my group to create an implementation plan, state goals, and define specific tasks necessary to reach the goal.   1 2 3 4 5

16. I ensure my group has adequate time in which to proceed through all of the creative problem-solving steps before choosing a solution.   1 2 3 4 5

17. I ensure all group members are on board before a specific problem-solving approach is selected.   1 2 3 4 5

18. I make a conscious effort to reach out to group members whose personal work style might make them less prone to accepting a group problem-solving technique.   1 2 3 4 5

19. I ensure that group problem-solving processes of which I'm a part are in sync with my organization's mission, cost-efficient, and effective.   1 2 3 4 5

20. I am working consciously on enhancing my ability to think creatively.   1 2 3 4 5

21. When thinking creatively I prepare, allow ideas to incubate, strive for new insights, and evaluate potential solutions relative to some standards of acceptability.   1 2 3 4 5

22. I encourage my group to adopt new ways of generating novel ideas.   1 2 3 4 5

23. I resist using "idea killers" when interacting with group members.   1 2 3 4 5

	Agree	Neither		Disagree
24. I attempt to create a group environment that supports creativity.	1	2	3	4 5
25. I demonstrate to others through actions and words that I am listening to their ideas and am open to continued discussion.	1	2	3	4 5
26. I use "idea growers" to keep conversations focused on creative problem solving and stimulate further creative ideas.	1	2	3	4 5

If your score is 78 points or higher, you might consider creating a plan to increase your rational and creative problem-solving skills.

Exercise 19–B Brainstorming—A Warmup

How creative are you? Using the space below, brainstorm as many ideas as you can in five minutes on the *alternative uses of a paper clip.* Write down all ideas, even outlandish ones. If you get stuck, switch your point of view—what if you were lost at sea, in a desert, in a snowstorm, or on the moon? Challenge your assumptions about the paper clip—how can it be changed to produce different purposes?

Questions

1. How did you do?
2. Did you use the entire time? Could you have continued writing after time was up?
3. How could this technique be applied in the workplace?

Exercise 19–C Binge Drinking Problem Solving

The following questions pertain to the problem-solving exercise you were led through in class.

1. Did your problem-solving group arrive at a workable plan for implementing a solution? If yes, to what do you attribute the group's success? If not, what precluded you from generating a workable solution to the problem presented?

_____

_____

_____

2. In what ways did solving the problem as a group instead of individually improve the process and outcome?

_____

_____

_____

3. In what ways did solving the problem as a group instead of individually hinder or undermine the process and outcome?

_____

_____

_____

4. How did you overcome these hindrances?

_____

_____

_____

**Exercise 19–D
The Lawn: A Problem-
Solving Exercise**

1. Groups of five members are formed. Each group's goal is to sort through given data and define the problem from the data given.

2. Each group will receive 25 statements of data concerning a situation. Each member of a group gets *five* of that group's statements. (Your instructor has these.)

3. Your instructor explains the rules for the activity:

   a. The members are not permitted to exchange cards or to show their cards to other members of their group.

   b. All data must be communicated orally to the other members of the group; these statements may be repeated as often as the group feels is necessary.

   c. If all members of the group feel that a statement (data) is not relevant to arriving at the definition of the problem, the statement is to be placed face down and not repeated.

   d. Group members may *not* take notes during the process.

   e. Only one problem definition may be presented from each group.

4. Your group will have 30 minutes in which to define the problem. At the end of the allotted time, your group must write a definition of the problem on a sheet of blank paper and submit it to the instructor.

5. The instructor will collect the groups' problem definitions and posts them. The large group is reassembled, and a spokesperson from each group will report on how the group arrived at the problem definition.

7. The instructor will post the "correct" definition of the problem and ask groups to discuss:

   a. Their reactions to the experience.

   b. Any difficulties they had in separating irrelevant from relevant data.

   c. How the groups decided which data were relevant.

   d. Whether any groups reached total agreement on the definition of the problem.

   e. How the use of only verbal communication affected the difficulty of the task.

Source: J. William Pfeifffer, Handbook of Structured Experiences Kit, University Associates, 1983, #GTB PS/A-17. Reprinted by permission of John Wiley and Sons. Inc.

**Exercise 19–E
Problem-Solving
Analogies**

Use the shoplifting analogy example discussed in the chapter as a guide for completing this exercise.

STEP ONE: State the problem (what is the situation?). See potential problems below or use one of your own.

STEP TWO: Create analogies.

1.

2.

3.

4.

STEP THREE: Solve the analogy (pick one or two of your favorites from STEP TWO).

STEP FOUR: Transfer solution to the problem.

Potential problems to solve

(at school)

- Parking at your school is too expensive and difficult to find a space.
- Incidence of cheating is on the rise.
- Belief by some that grade inflation is occurring.

(in the workplace)

- Decreasing the chance of an Internet service attack.
- Too many cell phones and not enough towers to support.
- Too many phone numbers and increasing need to add area codes.
- When replacing old computers (or phones, copy machines, furniture) with new ones, how to discard?
- How to overcome the shortage of skilled high-tech employees.
- Due to changes in economic and labor conditions, organizations face salary compression (new employees are being hired at higher salaries than existing, more experienced employees). How to address?
- Takes too long to get security clearance for employees working on secret or government projects.
- More off-site employees but no way to monitor them.

Source: Goman, 2000.

**Exercise 19–F
Developing a New
Team Sport**

You are part of a team charged with creating a new team sport that will increase the use of some of the sporting equipment that your company produces. Your new sport must use at least two items from your company's product list (you may use other equipment or props if necessary):

Baseball bat	Soccer ball
Football	Tennis ball
Frisbee	Tennis racquet
Horse shoes	Swimming goggles
Volleyball net	Boxing gloves
Pogo stick	Hula-hoop
Jump rope	Bike helmets

Your team must provide the following criteria in developing the sport:

- The equipment that will be necessary.
- The playing surface or field dimensions and type.
- The number and type of team players, any specialized positions.
- The time frame for the sporting activity (innings, periods, etc.).
- The point systems and means for measurement; how to determine a winner; how to obtain a score; differentials in scoring, penalties, and so on.
- All rules that are required in playing the sport.
- The process for playing the game—sequence, format, instructions, or training.
- Name of the game.

Questions

1. Did your team go through the four stages of creative problem solving? Explain.
2. What method or techniques did you use to generate novel and creative ideas?
3. What was difficult about this exercise? Explain.
4. What was easy about this exercise?
5. Based on your experience, how would you express a team's ability to be creative as compared with an individual?

**Exercise 19–G
Creative Groups**

In groups of three:
Without lifting your pencil, draw no more than four straight lines to connect all nine dots to one another.

```
•    •    •

•    •    •

•    •    •
```

Now try to find other ways to connect the dots with three lines, two lines, and even one line. Compare your answers with others sitting near you.

Now join with another team. Your task is to pass an object (e.g., a ball, hat, notebook) so that every team member's hands have touched the object. Do an initial run, and then discuss and try process improvements that will shorten the time needed to complete a single process (passing through all members' hands once).

Questions

1. Discuss the creative process. How does it happen for you, as an individual? Compare your answer with your teammates.
2. Discuss the creative process in a group setting. What behaviors or actions helped and hindered your group when it tried to find new or better solutions?
3. What did you learn about yourself and others from this exercise?
4. How can you apply this to work groups at school? In the workplace?

Source: Based on J. L. Adams, *Conceptual Blockbusting: A Guide to Better Ideas,* 2nd edition, New York: Norton, pp. 25–30.

**Exercise 19–H
Try This . . .**

Activity A:

1. Select a problematic operation or process in your school or organization, perhaps one about which students or employees complain (e.g., too cumbersome, too time consuming, inaccurate).
2. Brainstorm (alone or with a group) potential causes for this problem. Why does this problem exist or what has caused this to be problematic?

3. Select a key cause by using affinitizing and or multivoting (see chapter for explanation if needed).

4. Focusing on this key cause, brainstorm as many potential creative solutions as you can in five minutes. Write them in the space below.

5. Which of these ideas, if implemented, is likely to result in a lasting improvement? Why? Support your answer with logic and possibly the results of a prioritization matrix.

6. What barriers are you likely to face if you were given the green light to implement this improvement? What are your plans for overcoming these barriers?

Activity B:

1. Watch one of the following videos for evidence of problem-solving behaviors: *The Magnificent Seven, Foul Play, Poltergeist, 48 Hours, All the President's Men, Apollo 13, October Sky, The Fugitive, Sneakers.*

2. What behaviors are effective? Explain. What behaviors are ineffective? Explain.

3. If you were part of the problem-solving process depicted in one of these films, what specific suggestions would you make and why? If these suggestions were implemented, what impact would they have on the outcome?

**Exercise 19–I
Reflection/Action Plan**

1. The one or two problem-solving or creativity areas in which I am most strong are:

_____

_____

_____

_____

2. The one or two problem-solving or creativity areas in which I need more improvement are:

_____

_____

_____

_____

3. If I did only one thing to improve in this area, it would be to:

_____

_____

_____

_____

4. Making this change would probably result in:

_____

_____

_____

_____

5. If I did not change or improve in this area, it would probably affect my personal and professional life in the following ways:

_____

_____

_____

_____

20 Team Facilitation[1]

How do I:

✓ Recognize when a team's process is ineffective?

✓ Help team members to work cohesively and effectively with one another?

✓ Teach and guide teams in utilizing effective process skills?

✓ Use interventions at the appropriate time and in the appropriate manner?

✓ Deter the eruption of dysfunctional behaviors of team members?

✓ Create an environment that allows teams to achieve goals effectively?

■ *You have been working with your project group for the last few weeks. During this time, you've had three meetings, and at each one, Anthony has either come late or left early. Even when he is at the meeting, it seems that his mind is elsewhere. Everyone's input on the project is needed, and you're concerned that his lack of participation and preparation is affecting the group outcome. What would you do?*

■ *You are on a team that is putting together an advertising campaign for a neighborhood pet store as part of your Marketing class. One member, Jennifer, has had several years' experience working in a pet store—and she lets you know it frequently during your planning meetings. In fact, she often volunteers to do more than her share in putting together both the campaign and the class presentation of the campaign. While you appreciate her efforts, you feel that it's hard to get your voice heard in these meetings since Jennifer always seems to "have the floor." What would you do?*

■ *You've been meeting on a team for the past couple of weeks, and while you really get along well with your teammates, it is clear that very little "work" is getting done at these meetings. The other members enjoy spending time with one another, but with the deadline only three weeks away, you're concerned that the team will have to pull an "all-nighter" to get the project done, and even then, it may not be as good as it could be. What would you do?*

■ *You are a member of a new product development team in a Fortune 500 firm. Management has put a lot of pressure on the team to be innovative, but all that ever seems to happen at the team meetings is a lot of yelling, name-calling, fighting, put-downs, and the like. The marketing folks believe the engineers don't truly understand what the customer wants. The manufacturing folks are upset that they're never asked—until after the product is designed and accepted by management—whether the product is relatively easy to manufacture and maintain. Then, there are the finance folks; all they ever seem to care about is the bottom line. Can't we all get along?*

"Our chief want in life is somebody who will make us do what we can."

Ralph Waldo Emerson

Teams have become an important vehicle for organizations to develop and improve products, services, and processes. However, "simply bringing together a group of professionals does not ensure that this group will function effectively as a team or make appropriate decisions."[2] Team members' varying beliefs, backgrounds, personalities, and work styles can hinder a team's ability to get work done. With such diversity comes the likelihood that individuals will misunderstand or undervalue the contributions of their team members. Some teams find it hard to reach agreements and solve problems. Just sprinkling pixie dust over a group of individuals does not necessarily result in the kind of team outcomes expected by organizations. Therein lies the need for team facilitation.

In this chapter we define facilitation and why it's important. We describe key facilitative behaviors and strategies, and provide tips for facilitating teams. At the end of the chapter are exercises that help you to assess and enhance your facilitating skills and a list of resources for further exploration.

What Is Facilitation?

Facilitation is a process in which a team is assisted in improving internal processes, such as how members communicate, make decisions, or resolve conflict, that are essential for achieving team goals. Effective processes (the means) are critical to achieving successful outcomes (the ends).[3] The diversity present on team challenges team members to actively and objectively listen to and search for agreement among their diverse counterparts. The team's ability to listen effectively or to communicate with one another represents a critical process or means by which desired outcomes can be achieved.

What Facilitators Do

A **facilitator,** or **process consultant,**[4] is a person who is either given a role formally or takes on a role informally of monitoring a team's process for effectiveness. The facilitator focuses more on how a team is working than on what the team is doing. The responsibilities of a facilitator vary from team to team, depending on the goals, technical requirements, duration, and employee makeup of that team. Employees or students who have worked on teams before, or who have been working with one team for a long time, may require less facilitation than would members of a newly formed team. In general, facilitators attend to such team processes as communication, meeting management, decision making, problem solving, and conflict resolution.[5]

To *facilitate* means "to make easier,"[6] and through their actions, facilitators work with teams to help them more effectively achieve their stated goals. Aside from "teaching the group how to collect data," a facilitator "may intercede if the team tries to solve a problem before defining what it is or if someone's ideas aren't being heard."[7] The facilitator's role may not be confined to what happens during meetings; many work outside meetings to further group cohesion or help gain sponsorship or support from key groups or individuals external to the team.[8] While facilitators' responsibilities may vary with respect to teams' expected outcomes, technical requirements, and employee makeup, they often do whatever it takes to help the team improve its processes and outcomes. This might start with helping a team clarify and buy into its goals and objectives, and progress through coaching a team to present its recommendations to management and eventually implement these recommendations.

Finally, facilitators model and educate team members in the use of facilitative skills. It would be very easy for a facilitator to provide continual assistance in improving team processes and outcomes. However, team members would likely become dependent on that help, rendering themselves unable to function effectively without the aid of a facilitator. When a facilitator not only helps the team use meeting management techniques, for example, but also teaches the team why and how to use them, the team will eventually become self-facilitating.[9] In other words, good facilitators often work themselves out of a job.

In summary, facilitators do whatever it takes to help the team improve its processes (and outcomes). Facilitators may do many things, from helping to create a safe and receptive environment in which to effectively communicate and make decisions to coaching a team to present its findings and recommendations to management or other stakeholders.

Facilitation Skills and Behaviors

Facilitation skills can be learned.[10] Even if you're not a natural at reading situations or mediating conflicts, there are several skills that can improve your ability to facilitate or use facilitative techniques. One of the most important characteristics of an effective facilitator is a keen awareness of strengths, weaknesses, and biases. Without this self-awareness, a facilitator's ability to set aside personal needs (e.g., power, being liked by group members) or goals for the good of the group and organization may be limited.[11] Though the following material is aimed at formal facilitators, anyone in a team situation can use facilitative behaviors. In team situations, it's important for individuals to take responsibility for productive processes as well as successful outcomes. To do this requires awareness of the process (and whether it is working), initiative, and a desire to help a team remain positive and proceed toward its goal.

A key facet of facilitator expertise is communication. Skilled in both verbal and nonverbal communication, effective facilitators are able to decode important cues that team members often miss. They listen to what is being said or what is not being said. They tap into the mindset of the group with distinct awareness and vigilance.[12] They recognize subtle indications that are likely to be ignored or overlooked by fellow team members, such as one member's not understanding or wanting to understand another's diverse point of view, or feeling threatened by other members, or not being committed to the team and its goals. Such signals may be deemed unimportant or unrelated to the task at hand by the other participants.

The adept facilitator has keen observation skills and can highlight and focus the group's attention on such cues and their implications. For example, you might be concerned about a team member who rarely participates or isolates him or herself geographically (e.g., sits on a chair against the wall instead of at the meeting table) at team meetings, but you choose to overlook this, assuming that as long as the team is making progress, you'll "let sleeping dogs lie." By contrast, an experienced facilitator knows that such behavior might indicate that team member's lack of ownership to the team or its goals. Unchecked, this behavior can resurface later—often in the implementation phase— in the form of uncooperativeness or sabotage and possibly lead to the downfall of a team.

Another important facilitation skill is to give behavioral feedback to team members in a way that gets them to recognize and modify unproductive behaviors. Apprise team members of their behaviors in a manner that addresses the issues while being reflective enough to avoid disempowering the participants. Use "I" language that will allow the team to improve its process and remain encouraged to participate fully.

Facilitators must also be knowledgeable about decision-making and problem-solving tools. On complex projects, members might lock on to one or more symptoms of an underlying problem and shift the team's resources toward solving the wrong problem. Help a team identify problems, symptoms, causes, and solutions[13] through the use of one or more problem-solving tools. Leading teams through the problem-solving process will help them in effectively achieving their goals and make them more self-sufficient in future endeavors.

Managing group dynamics[14]—relative to the team's current stage of growth—is another skill facilitators should possess. Be an avid observer of the way team members interact with one another, particularly when such interaction becomes strained or suppressed. Team members often lament, "These group projects wouldn't be so bad if I could do the work myself." Students and employees often complain about their teammates and the team process. Members' varying commitment levels to the project, unusual or incompatible work styles and personal or emotional issues, along with spending time in unproductive meetings are what members invariably oppose.[15] As indicated by the term, group "dynamics" tend to be unpredictable. An effective meeting can immediately precede an absolutely horrible one. Changes in membership, unexpected schedule or budget problems, and shifts in team goals can potentially cause team conflict, if not complete disbandment. Trained facilitators know what behaviors and emotions to expect from members during each of the stages of teaming and adjust their techniques accordingly.[16] For example, a facilitator may notice growing conflict among team members but may decide not to intercede. After all, such conflict is not only expected but also necessary over the life of a team.

Three specific types of role behaviors are typically exhibited in team meetings. A skilled facilitator will be equipped to recognize all three.[17]

- **Task-related behaviors** focus on the *content* of the meeting—the actions necessary to complete a task or goal. These task-related behaviors include contributing to, asking for, summarizing, and clarifying information. The facilitator will monitor these behaviors and intervene if the team's attention to task precludes them from paying attention to process or group dynamic issues. For example, a team might be so focused on their deadline that they will overlook the fact that one member has resigned from the group and is not attending meetings. In this case, a member or the facilitator can ask clarifying questions and help the team to acknowledge and deal with this problem, rather than ignore it.

- **Maintenance-related behaviors** relate to the *process* of how the group works together. Some quiet or shy members may need encouragement to participate. Tensions arising from conflicts need to be reduced. Other issues, particularly those that may not be obvious to some, must be diagnosed and resolved. Members of an effective team are likely to exhibit both task- and maintenance-related behaviors during meetings. If conflict surfaces, members may use these behaviors to resolve it. If unsuccessful, the facilitator can raise the issue and provide a model for team members to later emulate should another conflict emerge.

- **Dysfunctional behaviors** are actions taken by members that may hinder or even undermine the team's progress. When members intentionally block the team's progress by refusing to budge on their position on an issue, the facilitator can try to address the issue by using an intervention, such as asking justifying questions.

Figure 20–1 lists some examples of each type of role behavior, as well as their potential advantages and disadvantages.

Team facilitators, as opposed to team leaders, should focus primarily on group **process** (how the team is going about achieving its formal tasks, including who talks to whom, how decisions are made), with much less focus on team **content** or outcomes (reasons for the team's existence, what the team is talking about). Facilitators assist the team with its process (as opposed to the content) by intervening when necessary, such as refocusing a divergent discussion, ensuring balanced participation, or clarifying whether all options have been objectively evaluated.

In addition to process expertise, some facilitators may possess specific content or technical knowledge such as, an engineering background, which might potentially benefit a team. However, since a facilitator's primary responsibility is to ensure the open and objective discussion of diverse perspectives, facilitators will typically downplay content knowledge for fear of being perceived as nonobjective or vested in a particular outcome.[18]

Key Facilitative Preventions

Inevitably, problems will occur in teams. This is natural. There are many things a facilitator can do behind the scenes or before meetings begin that might help prevent problems from occurring or diminish their impact on the team should such problems surface. The list of **preventions,** shown in Figure 20–2, ranges from premeeting planning

Figure 20–1
Role Behaviors

	Behavior	Explanation	Examples	Pros (Cons)
Task Related	Initiating	Proposes a task	"Why don't we start by . . ."	Gets the "ball" rolling
	Giving/seeking information	Offers/asks facts, ideas	"In our department, we were able to cut costs by . . ."	Improves decision making
	Clarifying and elaborating	Clears up confusion	"So you're saying . . . "	Ensures members understand each other
	Summarizing	Restates, offers conclusion	"We've covered all but the last item on the agenda"	Can reduce time spent rehashing discussions
	Consensus testing	Checks on group position	"It sounds like we agree on points 1 and 2, but not 3 . . . "	Saves time, ensures decision buy-in
Maintenance-Related	Harmonizing and compromising	Reduces tension, looks for middle ground	"It doesn't have to be either x or y . . . why don't we use the best elements of both?"	Reduces tension in group (can reduce risk-taking)
	Gatekeeping	Facilitates balanced participation	(To silent member) "What's your opinion?"	Ensures members participate
	Diagnosing	Shares observations of group process	"It seems a few of us are unhappy with the decision . . . shall we revisit . . .?"	Ensures hidden problems are surfaced and dealt with
	Standard setting	Helps set norms, test limits	"Let's agree to brainstorm, then evaluate"	Facilitates team self-management
Dysfunctional	Blocking	Prevents consensus	"I'm not going to agree to a solution which . . ."	Could slow down a hasty decision process (and bog down an effective process)
	Dominating	Talks more than his/her share	Often talks the longest and loudest, overshadowing others' potential contributions	(Can stifle others' participation)
	Withdrawing	Silent, distracted	(Check body language)	Decision making may be quicker (if his or her concerns aren't aired, he or she might sabotage the outcome later)
	Self-seeking	Oppresses with personal needs	"The only way I'll agree to this is if you'll do . . . for me"	(Others might emulate this behavior or be biased against future inputs from him or her)

(e.g., working on agenda with team leader, ensuring quality of meeting logistics), to start-of-meeting process clarification (e.g., establishing ground rules), to things you could say or do during a meeting (e.g., suggesting or getting agreement on the process, educating the group) to ensure all members of the team are on the same page and working towards a common goal.

Figure 20–2
Facilitative Preventions[19]

General Approach	Specific Things You Can Say or Do
Establish ground rules—define roles (make your social contract)	Up front (and ongoing) discussion of your role and the ground rules of your involvement with the team leader and later the team members. "OK, before we get started, I would like to make sure we all agree on general procedures. While I'm facilitator we're going to operate by consensus. Consensus means . . . if we need to take a formal vote, I will turn the meeting over to your chairperson." "Mr. Smith is here as an observer. That is why he is sitting at the back of the room. He has agreed not to participate."
Get agreement on process	"Before we begin to evaluate the alternatives, are we agreed that we'll begin by saying what we like about each alternative, and then go on to our concerns about each one?" "Just a moment, before you begin your report. Do you want to entertain questions? . . . During your presentation or afterwards?" "To make sure we are clear, Joe is going to present his idea without interruption, then we'll ask clarifying questions, and then we'll go on to Bill's solution." "If there are no objections, we'll brainstorm different possible definitions of the problem, stating them as 'how to' questions. Any questions about how we are going to proceed?"
Get agreement on content/outcome	"Which issue are you going to discuss first?" "What's the purpose of this meeting? To design the agenda for the full commission next Wednesday? Does anybody have a different conception of this meeting?" "Today, we're just dealing with the issue of vacation policy—not benefits in general. That's right?" "What's success going to look like today?"
Stay neutral/stay out of content	Refrain from sharing your own ideas or opinions. (See *Boomerang*, page 424.) Remind the group of your role . . . "As your facilitator, I'm supposed to be neutral. This is your meeting. What do you want to do?" "I won't be able to help you work through this issue if I start taking sides." "I'll share with you my personal opinions after the meeting." "Actually, I don't have a personal opinion about the issue yet."
Be positive (win/win attitude)	If you really believe a win/win solution can be found, you will increase the chances of it happening. "I know this issue is quite emotionally charged for some of you, but if we take our time and work our way through the problem, I'm sure we can find a solution you can all live with."
Suggest a process	"Why don't we try brainstorming?" "I would suggest looking at criteria before trying to evaluate the options." "How about working backwards from the deadline?"
Educate the group	By offering short comments about why you are doing what you are doing and about the nature of the problem-solving process, you can help the team work through difficult situations and become better at facilitating itself. In addition, you educate when you illustrate how the team can use different problem solving or scientific tools. "There's no one right way to solve a problem. Which way do you want to try first?" "You can't solve two problems at once." "If we don't agree on the problem, we'll never agree on a solution." "Sounds like we might need a data-gathering tool. Are any of you familiar with control charts?"

**Figure 20–2
(continued)**

General Approach	Specific Things You Can Say or Do
Get permission to enforce the process agreements	"If you want to get through all these reports by 11:00, I'm going to have to hold you to your five-minute time limit. Is that OK? Any objections?" "Is it all right with you if I push a little harder to get finished on time?" "You've agreed not to bring up old history. Do I have your permission to cut you off if you do?"
Get the group to take responsibility for its actions	"This is your meeting, not mine. What do you want to do?" "It's up to you to decide if you want to change the agenda." "I can't make you reach an agreement. You have to really want to find a win/win solution."
Build an agenda	By working with the team leader to plan an agenda for your meetings, you can anticipate and prevent many potential meeting problems from occurring.
Get ownership of the agenda	Even though an agenda has been prepared in advance, don't assume that everyone in the meeting has seen it or agreed to it. Either you or the team leader needs to check for additions, revisions, and reordering of agenda items. "OK, that's the agenda. Any additions or revisions?" Once people have had a chance to revise or approve the agenda, then it becomes their agenda, not yours, and they are less likely to feel they have been manipulated.
Ensure quality of team logistics	Review with the team leader and members what materials will be necessary for the upcoming meeting. Ensure that the location, availability, and setup of meeting rooms are conducive to the team's success. "This is the second time we have been bumped from this room. Is there an alternative meeting place we can use for future meetings?"

Key Facilitative Interventions

Even the most skilled facilitator cannot prevent all problems from surfacing on a team. Sooner or later, one or more group members may decide to take a stand on an issue that is opposed to the position supported by other group members. Or, management may decide to change the scope of a team's goals and objectives, add or delete team members, or shorten the time for which completion is expected. Or, a team member may decide that his or her time is too valuable to be "wasted" at these "frivolous" team meetings. Any of these situations, combined with the diversity challenges outlined earlier in the chapter, provides ample opportunity for you to intervene in an effort to aid the team.

Some of the **interventions,** or things a facilitator can say or do to help a team assess and deal with what is going on in the present moment (see Figure 20–3), are fairly simple, straightforward, and innocuous. For example, the use of "say what's going on" is perfect for the team that is experiencing the formation of factions with respect to a particular issue. By sharing your observations with the team, you clarify what is happening while (hopefully) motivating them to reach a resolution. This intervention might sound like, "It seems we have two perspectives on this decision; John's approach would be to . . . while Mary's approach would involve. . . . Half of you seem to agree with John while the other half prefer Mary's approach. . . . Am I correct?" A similar intervention, which is simple yet powerful if not overdone, is the "play dumb" intervention. When a team has lost its focus or has become sidetracked on another topic, a facilitator might say something like, "I'm confused. What were we supposed to be discussing now?" This technique can help get the group to focus on its own process and how to improve it. Both of these interventions are fairly easy to do while having the dual benefit of regaining the team's focus and simultaneously improving their ability to be self-facilitating.

Figure 20–3
Facilitative Interventions[20]

General Approach	Specific Things You Can Say or Do
Boomerang	Don't get backed into answering questions the group should be answering for themselves. Boomerang the question back to the group.
	Group member: "Facilitator, which problem should we deal with first?"
	Facilitator: "That's up to the group. Which do you think we should discuss first?"
	Group member addressing the facilitator: "What was the inflation rate for last year?"
	Facilitator: "Who can answer that question?"
	Group member: "I don't like the direction we're taking here."
	Facilitator: "What do you think we should do?"
	(See *Don't be defensive,* page 425.)
Maintain/regain focus	"Wait a second. Let's keep a common focus here."
	"Just a moment, one person at a time. Joe, you were first and then Don."
	"I can't facilitate if we have two conversations going at once. Pleased try to stay focused."
	"Excuse me, Elizabeth. Are you addressing the issue of . . .?"
	"Let's work on one thing at a time."
Play dumb	When the group has gotten off track or the meeting has broken down in some way, playing dumb is a way of getting the group to focus on its own process by having to explain to you. It's a form of boomeranging and is easy to do when you're really confused.
	"Can someone tell me what's going on now?"
	"I'm confused. What are we doing now?"
	"Where are we?"
	"I'm lost. I thought we were . . . "
Say what's going on	Sometimes, simply identifying and describing a destructive behavior to the group is enough to change that behavior. Be sure to "check for agreement" after your process observation.
	"You are not letting John finish his presentation."
	"I think you're trying to force a decision before you're ready."
	"It seems to me that . . ."
	"My sense is . . ."
Check for agreement	Almost any time you make a statement or propose a process, give the group an opportunity to respond. Don't assume they are with you.
	"Do you agree?"
	"All right?"
	"OK?"
	A powerful way of checking is to look for the negative. Make silence a sign of confirmation. Rather than saying, "Do you all agree?" ask:
	"Are there any objections?"
	"If there are no objections (pause) . . . we'll move on to . . ."
	"Is there anyone who can't live with that decision?"
Avoid process battles	Don't let the group become locked into arguments about which is the "right" way to proceed. Point out that you can try a number of things, deal with more than one issue. The issue is which one to try first. (See Figure 20–2; *Educate the group.*)
	"We can try both approaches. Which one do you want to try first?"
	"Can we agree to cover both issues in the remaining time? OK, which do you want to start with?"

Figure 20–3
(continued)

General Approach	Specific Things You Can Say or Do
Enforce process agreements	Once the group has agreed to a procedure, your credibility and neutrality may be at stake if you don't enforce their agreement. "Wait a second, you agreed to brainstorm. Don't evaluate ideas . . ." "Harry, let John finish." "Sorry Beth, I'm afraid your time is up."
Encourage	"Could you say more about that?" "Why don't you try." "Keep going. I think this is useful."
Accept/legitimize/deal with, or defer	This is a general method of intervening that works well for dealing with problem people and emotional outbreaks of all kinds. "You're not convinced we're getting anywhere? That's OK, maybe you're right." "Are you willing to hang on for 10 more minutes and see what happens?"
Don't be defensive	If you are challenged, don't argue or become defensive. Accept the criticism, thank the individual for the comment, and boomerang the issue back to the individual or group. "I cut you off? You weren't finished? I'm sorry. Please continue." "You think I'm pushing too hard? (lots of nods) Thank you for telling me. How should we proceed from here?"
Use your body language	Many of these interventions and preventions can be reinforced, and sometimes even made, by the movement of your body or hands. For example: regaining focus by standing up and moving into the middle of the group. Enforcing a process agreement by holding up your hand to keep someone from interrupting. Encouraging someone by gesturing with your hands. Stopping a monopolizer's talking by walking over to him or her and standing next to or behind them.
Use justifying questions	When team members disagree on an issue, a facilitator can use justifying questions to help bring out discussions by uncovering facts and reasons behind team members' opinions Group member: "Well we tried it before and it didn't work then." Facilitator: "What could you share about that experience . . . lessons learned . . . , so we don't make the same mistake twice?"
Use leading questions	Use when the team has too narrow a focus and you want to gently guide them into another direction or if the team needs a "jump-start." "Have you ever thought about using . . .?" "Are you sure that is your only option?" "What precludes you from trying . . .?"
Use the group memory	The group memory (i.e., the easel/notepad on which minutes or key points are being recorded) can also be used to reinforce many of the interventions and preventions. For example: Walking up to the group memory can facilitate regaining focus by pointing to the agenda item the group should be dealing with. Getting agreement on content can be greatly supported by writing down or circling the subject to be discussed.

(continued)

Figure 20–3 (concluded)

General Approach	Specific Things You Can Say or Do
Don't talk too much	The better facilitator you become, the fewer words you will have to use. When you have really done a good job, the group may leave thinking that the meeting went so well it could do without you next time. Use your hands, eye contact, and partial sentences to communicate economically . . . "I'm sorry. You were saying that . . ." "Could you say that again?" "The point you were making was . . ."
Use hypothetical questions	When a team appears to be stagnant or more interested in maintaining the status quo, the facilitator could use hypothetical questions to spur creativity, innovation, etc. Group member: "I can't come up with any more ideas for change. We've already improved as much as we can." Facilitator: "What if money were no object . . .?" or "If you could change any one thing about your work or environment . . ."
Use a reality check	Use when a team needs to reexamine or modify its direction, progress, process agreements. "Time out for a reality check: are we doing what we said we would do? *OR* should we be discussing this now? *OR* do we need to change our milestone chart? *OR* is this something we should talk to our sponsor about?"
Use the "round robin" method	If a team member is monopolizing the conversations while others are nearly silent, you might make the suggestion: "Why don't we go once around the table? What do you think might be a way to improve . . .?" Call on members in a clockwise direction, ensuring that no member is skipped and the direction is maintained.
"Talk to your neighbor"	Sometimes you'll ask a question and get NO response. Either no one understood it, cares about it, or has had enough coffee. Rephrase the question and ask team members to discuss their responses with the person sitting next to him or her. A lively discussion is sure to ensue.
Use a time-out	When team members are fighting, losing sight of the big picture, or are uncooperative for some reason, try calling for a time-out. Ask that members take a five-minute break, after which the meeting will resume.
Trust the process	A novice facilitator panics easily. When an intervention doesn't appear to work, he or she may conclude that the sky is falling and rush in with an alternative intervention, only to get caught in a vicious circle. Instead, practice patience and trust the process (and the team!). Presume that the situation is "still cooking" and wait until things fall in place and the activity flows smoothly. Sooner or later, the good things will swamp the bad things.
Call a team member's bluff	Use when a team member threatens to do something unless or until the team changes direction. (This intervention is risky; you must be willing to accept a team member's decision.) Team member: "Well, since my opinion isn't valued, I guess I'll leave." Facilitator: "I'm not asking you to leave. You can do what you want—you'll have to live with that decision."

Another set of interventions involves the use of well-timed questions to help uncover important reasons behind a position (e.g., justifying questions), move the team into a different direction (e.g., leading questions), or get the team to take a leap outside the proverbial box (e.g., hypothetical questions). In the latter case, questions that cause the group to move beyond the "That'll never work here" or "We've tried that before and it didn't work then" types of responses can be really effective. For example, if a team member were to say something like "That's a great idea but management would never go for it," a facilitator might ask a justifying question, such as "Why do you think that is the case?" to clarify underlying reasons. If the team member responds with "Well, when the team in the finance department tried to . . . , management apparently shelved their recommendations," the facilitator might respond with the following hypothetical question: "If you had some assurance the management is going to listen and take action this time, what specific recommendations should we make about implementing . . .?"

Another set of interventions has the facilitator taking an active and perhaps directive role. Doing so is necessary in certain situations. It is important to remember that the more directive the facilitator is, the more the team members come to expect such behaviors from the facilitator as opposed to developing their own facilitative skills. One example is the use of time-out. If members are fighting or unusually uncooperative, continuing the meeting might prove unproductive if not harmful. In such a situation, the facilitator might end the meeting early or call a time-out—a five- or ten-minute break— after which the meeting resumes. A more risky intervention might be necessary when a team member threatens to leave the meeting or to do something that might sabotage the team's progress should the member not get his or her way. This team member may be waiting for others to cajole him or her back into the meeting or change their way of thinking. In such a situation, it might be appropriate for a facilitator to call the person's bluff, for example, "No one can make you stay . . . you can leave if you want to, just as long as you realize . . ." This intervention is risky in that the facilitator must be willing to accept the outcome (e.g., a team member's departure) and its impact on the team.

Using any of these interventions requires skill and practice. The exercises at the end of this chapter provide you with an opportunity to practice using facilitative interventions.

Deciding Whether and How to Intervene

Facilitators need to keep an open mind about what they think needs facilitating. Their perceptions may or may not match those of the team, leaving open the possibility that the facilitator could do more harm than good. The following five steps, in order, capture a helpful process in addressing the question "Should I intervene now?"

1. Know the group's primary task.
2. Determine what is going on.
3. Share observations.
4. Check for understanding.
5. Suggest options and alternatives.

Let's say that after discussing the pros and cons of two possible solutions to a quality problem, team members appear to have formed two factions: one supporting option one; the other supporting option two. Disagreement turns into conflict, and team members have lost sight of the underlying problem as they dig their heels more deeply into their respective "sides." In deciding whether to intervene at this moment, a facilitator should first clarify in his or her mind the team's goal or task, which is to solve a quality problem. Second, the facilitator should evaluate what's happening at the moment in the context of the team's overall situation. Is this conflict "healthy" and consistent with the storming phase of team growth? Is the conflict promoting the creation of multiple, synergistic viewpoints or possible solutions? If so, perhaps it's best to wait and see if team members can resolve their own conflict. Remember that the more a facilitator takes an active role in facilitating a group's process, the more likely the team is to become dependent on the facilitator doing so now and in the future. If this discussion is essentially a continuation

Figure 20–4

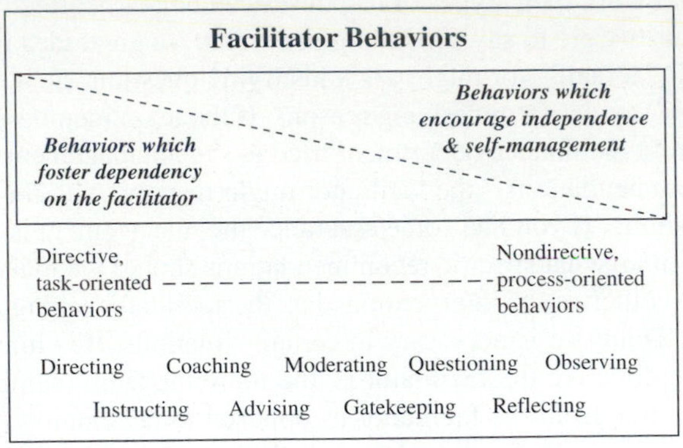

Facilitator Behaviors

Behaviors which encourage independence & self-management

Behaviors which foster dependency on the facilitator

Directive, task-oriented behaviors – – – – – – – – – – – – – – – Nondirective, process-oriented behaviors

Directing   Coaching   Moderating   Questioning   Observing

Instructing   Advising   Gatekeeping   Reflecting

or recapitulation of one that remained unresolved after the previous meeting, intervening may be appropriate.

At this point, as a facilitator, share your observations in order to check with team members whether your observations are correct (i.e., check for understanding). If you were to skip this step and actively promote a certain path to resolve the situation, you may cause more problems than you start. If your observations are correct, evaluate which approach would work best in this situation and then suggest these options to the team. By taking this step, and taking the team's input into account, the facilitator can be assured that the team is committed to this course of action and will try to make it work.

Facilitators or process consultants should focus primarily on the process or how the team goes about achieving its goals. However, early in the team's existence, it might be appropriate for you to be somewhat directive or task-oriented; it might help give direction when the team's start seems slow. If you remain directive in your approach, team members likely learn very little about managing and facilitating their own process. Further, if you play an active role in directing or advising on the task, others may reduce their participation and rely more on you, especially if they see you as an expert.[21] As teams move through their developmental stages and members learn and use effective process skills, facilitators should move towards being more nondirective, using questioning and reflecting behaviors to help the team help itself. By doing so, members adopt a balanced focus on team processes and outcomes: managing their own group dynamics while still attending to task and achieving their goals. This concept is illustrated in Figure 20–4 above.

Identifying and Dealing with "Problem People"

Now that you feel pretty comfortable with facilitative preventions and interventions, it is time to up the ante. You may think that most people working on a team have the team's best interests at heart, but this isn't always the case. Some people, with or without ill intent, can single-handedly hinder even the best teams. We call these **problem people.** Figure 20–5 summarizes some of the more common behavioral descriptors, clarifies the problem, and suggests possible solutions for handling these people or situations. You may encounter a team member who always complains and turns the conversation to an unrelated topic that is irritating them, leading the team astray. For example, the team may be working on a new computer system for the human resource department and every time the company or budget is discussed, a member begins to complain how the company should be spending funds on giving raises and benefits instead of upgrading the computer system. How would you deal with this individual? What preventive techniques might you use? What interventions might you use?

**Figure 20–5
Dealing with
Problem People[22]**

Problem Person	Problem	Effect	Solution
The Silent One	Withdrawn. May be bored, indifferent, timid, or insecure.	You lose a portion of the group's power. May have a negative effect on others in the group.	Ask for her opinions. Draw out the person sitting next to her, then ask the quiet one what she thinks of the view just expressed. If you are near her, ask her view so she will feel she is talking to you, not the whole group. Compliment the silent one when she does speak. Give positive verbal and nonverbal reinforcement.
The Advice Seeker	Wants you to solve his problems or those of others. May try to put you on the spot, trying to have you support one viewpoint.	Can put you in position of decision maker, rather than the group.	Avoid solving other people's problems for them. Never take sides. Point out your view is relatively unimportant compared to that of the group. Say, "Let me get some other opinions . . . Joe, what do you think of Sam's question?"
The Heckler	Combative individual who wants to play devil's advocate *or* may be normally good-natured but is upset by personal or job problems.	Can trap you into a one-on-one fight. Can stimulate group in-fighting.	Stay calm. Don't lose your temper. Keep the group from getting excited. Try to find merit on ONE of his points . . . then move on. Toss his statements out to the group; let them handle it. Talk to him privately . . . try to find out what's bothering him. Appeal to him or her for cooperation.
The Fighters	Two or more persons clash at the personality level.	Can divide the group into competitive factions.	Interrupt politely but firmly. Stress points of agreement, minimize points of disagreement. Ask direct questions on the topic. Request that personalities be set aside.
The Drifter	Talks about things not related to subject. Uses far-fetched examples. Gets lost.	Can cause confusion to self and the group.	1) Interrupt politely. Thank her. Refocus her attention by restating main points being discussed. 2) Smile. Indicate that you are having a problem relating her interesting comments to the subject at hand, or ask her directly to make this connection for the group.
The "Stand Pat"	Won't budge. Refuses to accept the group's decisions. Often prejudiced. Unable or unwilling to see your point or those of others.	Can turn group into competitive camps. Delays decision making.	Toss his view to the group: "Does anyone else feel as Pat does about this?" Tell him that time is short and ask him to accept the group's position for the moment. Offer to discuss the point with him later.
The Sidetracker	No drifting, just off the subject or agenda.	Can cause confusion and waste group time.	Take the blame for sidetracking her: "Something I said must have led you off the subject. This is what we should be discussing . . . (restate point)."
The Verbal Stumbler	Lacks ability to clearly express himself. Has the ideas but finds it difficult to put into words.	Frustration, both to the person and to the group.	Help the person out. Rephrase his statements: "Let me see if I understand . . . (paraphrase his point)." Don't say "What you mean is . . ." Keep the idea(s) intact and check for understanding.

(continued)

Figure 20–5 (continued)

Problem Person	Problem	Effect	Solution
The Griper	Has some pet gripe. Has a legitimate complaint.	Can turn the meeting into a grievance session.	Point out: "We can't change policies, but we can do the best we can under the system." Indicate you'll bring the complaint (if legitimate) to the proper person's attention. Indicate time constraints. Offer to discuss the problem after the meeting or at a future point.
The Whisperer	Engages nearby people in side conversations while someone else has floor. May or may not be related to the subject.	Distracts you and other group members.	Don't embarrass them. Interrupt politely and ask if they could share their information with the group. Ask one of them his or her opinion of a remark (restate it for the person). Explain you are having trouble hearing (or talking) when others are speaking at the same time.
The Eager Beaver	Overly talkative. Monopolizes the conversation. May be a showoff or just very well informed and anxious to show it.	Can shut out less aggressive members.	Don't be embarrassing or sarcastic. Interrupt politely with "That's an interesting point. What do the rest of you think about it?" (Look around group.) Might also use body language: walk over to and stand behind the Eager Beaver and/or use your hands (like a traffic cop) to diminish their talking while encouraging others. Let the group take care of him as much as possible.
The Overachiever	Although she is really trying to help, it makes it difficult to maintain control.	Shuts others out. May monopolize in genuine effort to be helpful.	Recognize the valuable traits of this person. Thank her. Suggest that "we put others to work . . ." Cut across tactfully by questioning others. Use this individual for summarizing.
The Mistaken	Member is obviously incorrect. Definitely in the wrong ballpark.	Can cause inaccurate information to spread. Causes confusion in the group.	Handle with care. Say "I can see how you feel . . ." or "That's another way of looking at it . . ." To bring out correction tactfully, say "I see your point, but how can we reconcile that with . . . (state correct point)?"
The Know-It-All	Can dominate group with comments like "I have worked on this project more than anyone else here . . ." or "I have a Ph.D. in economics and . . ."	May inhibit creativity causing others to feel inadequate or that their opinions are not valued.	Avoid theory or speculation by focusing the group on a review of the facts. Might suggest another opinion, e.g., "Another noted authority on this subject (state name) has said . . ."
The Latecomer	Comes late and interrupts meeting.	Slows down group's progress, particularly if latecomer insists on being brought up to speed.	Announce an odd time (8:46 AM) for the meeting to emphasize the necessity for promptness. Make it inconvenient for latecomers to find a seat, and stop talking until they do. Establish a "latecomer's kitty" for refreshments.
The Early Leaver	Announces, with regret, that they must leave for another important activity.	Interrupts meeting flow and can halt progress if the Early Leaver is critical to an upcoming discussion that now must be deferred.	Before the meeting begins, announce/confirm the ending time and ask if anyone has a scheduling conflict. If this is a standing conflict, ask group if they would like to change the meeting time.

Some Barriers or Limitations to Facilitation

Not all organizations or teams use or recognize the value of facilitators. The costs may be prohibitive, preventing work teams from having the luxury of adding (even temporarily) an outside member to facilitate them. If there are no employees with facilitation skills available in the organization, the organization may not want to pay for services of an outside facilitator. Even if internal employees with the necessary skills can be identified, there are costs associated with pulling them out of their normal duties and reassigning them—even temporarily—to work with one or more teams. In the absence of a trained facilitator, individual team members will be called upon to use facilitative skills as appropriate. In this case, **objectivity**—the ability to view a situation without personal bias and one of the benefits perceptually bestowed upon an "outside" facilitator—is not present. When such is the case, some of the problems inherent in culturally and functionally diverse teams (e.g., misunderstanding or devaluing others' opinions, fighting over scarce resources) are not likely to be overcome by an "inside" facilitator.

Even when outside facilitators or process consultants are offered to a team, other problems may exist. First, teams can see the job of process facilitation resting squarely and solely upon the facilitator. Such dependence precludes team development toward self-management. Second, at the other extreme, team members may not trust the outsider or "allow" him or her to intervene. This is especially likely when a team has existed for a period of time and resists the presence and questions the value of this appointed outsider. This problem can be exacerbated if management appoints a facilitator to a team without communicating the reasons or objectives for this step. Team members might become suspicious and choose to be less forthcoming in team meetings and discussions. Facilitators can only facilitate what they see and hear; if the team's work goes "underground," there is not much a facilitator can do to help, should help be needed.

As a facilitator you can reduce these effects by introducing yourself at the first meeting and discussing with the group how they see your role. Check out the team's expectation of the facilitator and discuss the importance of everyone's role in the process.[23] The members' perceptions and expectations will depend on their previous experiences. This role can then be negotiated over time. Example: "Hi, I'm Jan Smith. Your manager asked me to come to help you map your manufacturing process to find ways to decrease defects and cycle time. My background is in . . . and I see myself doing (list role or responsibilities) for you." Listen and honor their opinions and perspectives, further reinforcing that each person has an important role to play in the process.

Another problem facilitators may face is resistance due to a lack of familiarity with or credibility in a part of the organization,[24] despite the fact that such unfamiliarity may underlie valuable objectivity. Since facilitators often work between a team and its management, a facilitator who is seen as ineffective or incredible (or a deterrent to some "master plan") might be "blocked" from helping the team achieve its goals by other organizational stakeholders.

While team facilitation is not a panacea for all organizational challenges, benefits can be gained through the use of a trained process facilitator.[25] Facilitative skills can be learned and should be used either formally as a trained facilitator or informally whenever you are part of a team. Whether a facilitator is utilized or not, having all team members trained and skilled in facilitation techniques will greatly enhance the teaming experience and output.

Summary

Facilitation helps team members work cohesively and cooperatively to effectively achieve organizational and individual goals. Through the use of facilitation, teams will function more effectively, members will be more satisfied with the team experience and learn new skills, and output will be enhanced. However, facilitation is a rigorous task. It requires a facilitator to have self-awareness, awareness of others, and good interpersonal skills (listening, feedback, conflict management, problem solving, coaching, negotiation, assertiveness) in order to be effective. Facilitation is a skill that can increase the effectiveness of all members of teams and organizations. Even if your team does not have the benefit of a process facilitator, having knowledge and skills in facilitation will make you a valuable contributor to your team and organization.[26]

Key Terms and Concepts

Content	Objectivity
Dysfunctional behaviors	Prevention
Facilitation	Problem people
Facilitator	Process
Intervention	Process consultant
Maintenance-related behaviors	Task-related behaviors

Endnotes

1. Much of what is presented in this chapter also appears in S. de Janasz, "Teaching Facilitation: A Play in Three Acts," *Journal of Management Education,* forthcoming.

2. E. Cooley, "Training an Interdisciplinary Team in Communication and Decision-Making Skills," *Small Group Research* 25 (1994), p. 6.

3. Ibid.

4. E. Schein, *Process Consultation* (Menlo Park, CA: Addison-Wesley Publishing Co., 1988).

5. R. Sisco, "What to Train Team Leaders," *Training,* February 1993, pp. 62–63.

6. Michael Ayres, editor, *Webster's New World Dictionary and Thesaurus* (New York, NY: Simon & Schuster MacMillan, 1996).

7. Sisco, 1993, p. 63.

8. Ibid.; and D. G. Ancona, "Outward Bound: Strategies for Team Survival in an Organization," *Academy of Management Journal* 33 (1990), pp. 334–365.

9. The idea that effective modeling leads to mastery is consistent with A. Bandura, "Self Efficacy: Toward a Unifying Theory of Behavioral Change," *Psychological Review* 84 (1997), pp.191–215.

10. T. G. Cummings and C. G. Worley, *Organization Development and Change,* 7th Ed. (Los Angeles: Southwestern College Publishing, 2000).

11. David W. Johnson and Frank P. Johnson, *Joining Together: Group Theory and Group Skills,* 6th Ed. (Boston, MA: Allyn and Bacon, 1997).

12. American Business Women's Association, "The Art of Facilitation," *Women in Business,* Jan.–Feb. 1999, p. 38.

13. Kent D. Fairfield, "Facilitators: When Do We Need Them?" *Business and Economic Review,* July–Sept. 2000, pp. 16–20.

14. Patricia Faiello, "Employee Power," *CA Magazine,* March 2000, p. 45.

15. Kathryn Tyler, "The Gang's All Here . . . ," *HRMagazine,* May 2000, pp. 104–113.

16. Fairfield, 2000.

17. Johnson and Johnson, 1997.

18. Sisco, 1993.

19. This chart is adapted from S. de Janasz, L. Johnson, M. McQuaid, A. Paulson, D. Roccia, S. Stubblefield, P. Wahl, and C. Wojick, *Fundamentals of Facilitation,* Training manual created for Hughes Aircraft Company, 1992, pp. 6-38 to 6-40.

20. This chart is adapted from and expands on de Janasz et al., 1992, pp. 6-42 to 6-46.

21. P. M. Mulvey, J. F. Veiga, and P. Elsass, "When Teammates Raise a White Flag," *Academy of Management Executive* 10 (1996), pp. 39–49.

22. This chart is adapted and compiled from two sources (1) de Janasz et al., 1992, pp. 13-4 to 13-10; and (2) Peoples, *Presentations Plus*, 1988 (New York: John Wiley & Sons), pp. 147–155.

23. American Business Women's Association, 1999.

24. Sisco, 1993.

25. Tom Terez, "Can We Talk?" *Workforce*, July 2000, pp. 46–55.

26. Tyler, 2000.

Exercise 20–A	Circle the response that most closely correlates with each item below.
Assessing Yourself	

	Agree	Neither	Disagree

1. I am aware of the strengths and limitations I bring to meetings.
   1 2 3 4 5

2. I set aside personal needs or goals for the good of the group.
   1 2 3 4 5

3. Even when I am not formally a team leader or facilitator, I take initiative, monitor how my team's process is working, help my team remain positive, and help team members work toward our goal.
   1 2 3 4 5

4. I pay attention to and decipher important cues sent verbally or nonverbally by team members.
   1 2 3 4 5

5. I give behavioral feedback to members that helps them to recognize and modify problematic behaviors.
   1 2 3 4 5

6. I apprise team members of their behavior in a manner that addresses the issues while being reflective enough to avoid disempowering the participants.
   1 2 3 4 5

7. I use "I" language that allows the team to improve its process and remain encouraged to participate fully.
   1 2 3 4 5

8. I am knowledgeable about problem-solving and decision-making tools and use them in group settings as appropriate.
   1 2 3 4 5

9. I understand and am able to manage group dynamics in meetings.
   1 2 3 4 5

10. I know what behaviors and emotions are common to teams during each of the four stages of teaming and adjust my techniques accordingly.
    1 2 3 4 5

11. I am aware of the various interventions that are available for use in meetings.
    1 2 3 4 5

12. I call a time-out or end a meeting early if members are fighting or unusually uncooperative and continuing the meeting might be unproductive.
    1 2 3 4 5

13. I keep an open mind about what I think needs to be facilitated.
    1 2 3 4 5

14. I share my observations in order to check with team members if my observations are correct.
    1 2 3 4 5

15. Early in a team's existence I am somewhat directive or task oriented.
    1 2 3 4 5

16. I am aware of strategies to use to deal with "problem" people in teams.
    1 2 3 4 5

17. I am objective when I am facilitating a discussion.
    1 2 3 4 5

18. I discuss my and others' roles when first meeting with a team.
    1 2 3 4 5

If you scored 54 or higher, you might consider creating an action plan for improving your facilitation skills.

**Exercise 20–B
Intervention
Presentation**

Pick one of the interventions listed on Figure 20–3. For this intervention, prepare a two- to three-minute presentation in which you discuss the intervention, why or when it would be used, and how it is used—perhaps role-playing an example of what you would say or do in a situation requiring such intervention.

The Intervention	Description	Why/When Used	How Used
Example: Playing dumb	Helps the team realize when they're off track without being directive	When the group or an individual (e.g., expert, monopolizer) has gotten off track	"I'm confused. Can someone tell me where we're headed with this discussion?"

You will be asked to present and demonstrate this intervention to some or all members of your class. After several interventions are presented, discuss how these and other interventions can be used (separately or combined) with behaviors or situations that impede group progress.

Questions

1. Which interventions do you feel comfortable using?

2. With which interventions do you need more practice?

3. How can you increase your skills in facilitation? Create a plan and discuss with a classmate.

**Exercise 20–C
Case Study: Dealing
with Team Conflict**

You've been asked to facilitate a team that has not been doing too well lately. This cross-functional team is composed of eight members from various disciplines, including materiel, engineering, program management, operations, and finance and has been working together for about six weeks. Its task: to reduce the time necessary to procure materials for use on a particular program/line of business. Things were going well in the beginning, as everybody's job can be simplified if there weren't so many delays in the process. However, in the last meeting, the group identified three key causes that, in essence, suggest that one or more of the represented disciplines are to blame for the delays. These causes included:

1. Undependable suppliers (if it wouldn't take "them" so long to get the needed materials and deliver them on time, things would be fine).

2. Lengthy and cumbersome signature cycle (members of finance and program management are among those who must sign each request).

3. Too many engineering changes (when engineering makes design changes, new materials have to be ordered and "old" materials have to be returned).

Most members of the team, including managers and technical personnel, are hesitant to expose their organization's part (if any) in the delays.

Questions

1. Do you think it's possible to help this team achieve its goal? Explain.

2. As a facilitator, what specific things would you do and say to ensure an effective process? Why?

3. What impact would this likely have on the outcome?

4. What if anything can be done "behind the scenes" to improve the team's chances for success?

Exercise 20–D
Video Case: *Twelve Angry Men**

Your instructor will be showing a clip from the classic *Twelve Angry Men.* In this movie, members of a jury are about to decide the fate of a young boy charged with murdering his father. The following questions should be answered after viewing this clip.

1. In the beginning of this clip, we see the foreman suggesting a process (e.g., why don't we take a straw vote) and clarifying instructions related to this process. Using Schein's role behaviors as a guide (see Figure 20–1), which behaviors did the foreman use and what effect did they have?

2. During this initial or straw vote, we see hesitation on the part of some members when casting their votes. What explains this hesitation, in your opinion, and if you were the foreperson, what might you have done differently?

3. After this vote, some members can be seen pressuring the single dissenting member. If this were to happen in a team you were facilitating, what intervention would you use and why?

4. Midway through the clip, the foreman suggests one process ("Let's all go around the table and convince this man why he's wrong"), and immediately thereafter, another jury member suggests a different process ("It seems to me that he—the dissenter—should be the one who tries to convince us"). Both processes have value. How would you help the group choose between the processes? What, specifically, would you say or do?

5. Periodically, throughout the clip, we see jury members treat one another harshly (e.g., remarks that are ethnically or age discriminatory). If you were to facilitate this group, would you intervene during these moments? Why or why not? If you would intervene, what would you say or do and why?

6. The foreman is actually one of the 12 jury members. At times, he plays a leader-like role; other times, he is facilitative. Cite examples of each. Should he play both leader and facilitator? Why or why not?

7. Different jury members have different personality styles. Such is also the case on most teams. What are some ways to point out these differences in a way that enables members to benefit from instead of being aggravated by these differences?

8. The jury member played by Jack Klugman, who admits that he "grew up in a slum" and identifies with the defendant, speaks infrequently and only when requested by others to do so. Even then, he seems to lack confidence in sharing his ideas and concerns. If you were to facilitate this "team," what techniques might you use to help this character contribute? Identify at least one "prevention" and one "intervention," and describe how you would use them.

9. Another jury member, played by E. G. Marshall, is intelligent, articulate, and very confident in his opinions. You could see this when he tries to point out the defendant's guilt on the basis of the boy's inability to recall the name of the movie he saw. These qualities can both benefit and hinder a team's process. What impact did his behavior have on you? If you were to facilitate the meeting, what might you have said or done to facilitate this member and why?

10. Which of the four stages of teaming did this "team" go through? Identify the stages and cite evidence to support your answer.

*Distributed by MGM Home Videos, 1957 (Sidney Lumet, director; Henry Fonda, star).

**Exercise 20–E
Facilitation Assessment**

The following questions relate to the facilitation activity you did in your class. Please answer them completely yet concisely.

1. What interpersonal skills covered in our class (e.g., listening, problem solving) did you find yourself using when you played the role of facilitator during this activity? Name at least two skills and share an example for each.

2. When you facilitated, what do you believe to be the things you did particularly well? Please describe at least two instances when you felt your facilitation was effective.

3. When you facilitated, what do you believe to be the things you did not do particularly well or resulted in an outcome different from what you had anticipated? Please describe at least two instances when you felt your facilitation could have been improved.

4. What lessons did you learn about yourself and about the challenges of doing work in teams from this activity? What steps can you take to improve your skills as a facilitator and as a team member?

**Exercise 20–F
Try This . . .**

A critical step to developing facilitative skills is knowing when and why to intervene. Knowing when takes practice, and one way to get this practice is to start by observing other teams and meetings in process. To do this assignment, you will need to observe a team or work group meeting from start to finish. It is preferred that you are not a member of this particular team or work group, as it would be difficult to pay careful attention to the process while being expected to actively participate in the meeting. Answer the following questions completely yet concisely.

1. From what you observed, how clear are the goals for the team in general, and for this meeting in particular? What evidence is there that members clearly understand what they're supposed to do? Explain.

2. Did the meeting start on time? End on time? Did people arrive late or leave early? What impact, if any, did this have on the meeting process?

3. Did the team use an agenda for the meeting? If yes, in what ways did it facilitate or hinder the meeting's goals? If not, in what ways would an agenda have been helpful? Explain.

4. Did team members play defined roles for the meeting, such as timekeeper, scribe, facilitator, leader? Were these roles explicitly or implicitly determined?

5. What could you discern from communication patterns? Were there one or two members who monopolized the conversation, and what impact did that have on the meeting process? Were there any individuals who were mostly quiet, only speaking when spoken to? Were there any side conversations or overtalking? If so, did anyone attempt to stop this? If not, what impact did this have on the process?

6. Were any decisions made during this particular meeting? How was the decision made: What process was followed (e.g., the leader makes a suggestion and a debate ensued) and what decision rule (e.g., majority, consensus) was used? Did members appear to be satisfied with the outcome of the decision? Why or why not?

7. Did any of the members use facilitative behaviors in the meeting? Cite an example.

8. Were there any occasions in which you would like to have intervened? Describe the situation, what you would have done or said, and what you expect the outcome would have been had you been the facilitator.

**Exercise 20–G
Reflection/Action Plan**

This chapter focused on facilitation—what it is, why it is important, and how to improve your skill in this area. Complete the following questions upon completing all readings and experiential activities for this chapter.

1. The one or two areas in which I am most strong are:

_____

_____

_____

_____

2. The one or two areas in which I need more improvement are:

_____

_____

_____

_____

3. If I did only one thing to improve in this area, it would be to:

_____

_____

_____

_____

4. Making this change would probably result in:

_____

_____

_____

_____

5. If I did not change or improve in this area, it would probably affect my personal and professional life in the following ways:

_____

_____

_____

Index